POLITICAL SCIENCE—THE DISCIPLINE AND ITS DIMENSIONS

An Introduction

POLITICAL SCIENCE—
THE DISCIPLINE AND
ITS DIMENSIONS

An Introduction

112962

by **STEPHEN L. WASBY**

Southern Illinois University

with chapters by

William C. Baum / **John Houston** /

Joann Poparad Paine / **David M. Wood**

New York / **CHARLES SCRIBNER'S SONS**

ACKNOWLEDGEMENTS

To Allyn and Bacon, Inc., for permission to quote from Albert Somit and Joseph
Tanenhaus, *The Development of American Political Science: From Burgess to Behavioralism*, pp. 3, 43, 45, 61, 70, 87, 176, and 188. Copyright © 1967 by Allyn
and Bacon, Inc., Boston. Reprinted by permission of the publisher.

To The Brookings Institution, for permission to quote from Stephen K. Bailey, "Research Frontiers of Interest to Legislators and Administrators," *Research Frontiers
in Politics and Government*, ed. Stephen K. Bailey (Washington, D.C.: The Brookings Institution, 1955).

To Professors James Fesler and Walter H. C. Laves and the American Political Science Association, for permission to quote from "Goals for Political Science: A Discussion," *American Political Science Review*, XLV (1951).

To The Free Press of Glencoe and The Macmillan Company, for permission to
quote from Richard C. Snyder, *et al.*, "Decision-Making as an Approach to the
Study of International Politics," *Foreign Policy Decision-Making*, ed. Richard C.
Snyder, *et al.* (New York: Free Press, 1962), Copyright © 1962 by the Free Press of

Glencoe, A Division of The Macmillan Company; from Robert Lane, *Political Ideology: Why the American Common Man Believes What He Does* (New York: Free Press, 1962), Copyright © 1962 by the Free Press of Glencoe, A Division of The Macmillan Company; and from Heinz Eulau, Samuel Eldersveld, and Morris Janowitz, eds., *Political Behavior: A Reader in Theory and Research* (Glencoe: Free Press, 1956), © by the Free Press, a corporation, 1956.

To Harvard University Press, for permission to quote from V. O. Key, Jr., *The Responsible Electorate: Rationality in Presidential Voting, 1936–1960* (Cambridge, Mass.: The Belknap Press of Harvard University Press, 1966).

To *The Journal of Conflict Resolution*, for permission to quote from Charles McClelland, "The Function of Theory in International Relations," *Journal of Conflict Resolution*, IV (1960).

To Dr. Joseph Klapper and *The Public Opinion Quarterly*, for permission to quote from "What We Know About the Effects of Mass Communication: The Brink of Hope," *Public Opinion Quarterly*, XXI (1957–1958).

To Oxford University Press, for permission to quote from Henry Mayo, *An Introduction to Democratic Theory* (New York: Oxford University Press, 1960).

To Frederick A. Praeger, Inc., and George Allen & Unwin Ltd., for permission to quote from Maurice Duverger, *Introduction to the Social Sciences, With Special Reference to Their Methods*, trans. Malcolm Anderson (London: George Allen & Unwin, 1961, and New York: Frederick A. Praeger, 1964).

To Princeton University Press, for permission to quote from Sidney Verba, *Small Groups and Political Behavior: A Study of Leadership* (Princeton: Princeton University Press, 1961), pp. 4, 166. Copyright © 1961 by Princeton University Press.

To University of California Press, for permission to quote from Bernard Crick, *The American Science of Politics: Its Origins and Conditions* (Berkeley: University of California Press, 1959).

To University of Chicago Press, for permission to quote from Herbert Hyman, *Interviewing in Social Research* (Chicago: University of Chicago Press, 1954). Reprinted by permission of The University of Chicago Press. © 1954 by The University of Chicago Press.

To University of Illinois Press, for permission to quote from Charles Hyneman, *The Study of Politics: The Present State of American Political Science* (Urbana: University of Illinois Press, 1959); and from Evron Kirkpatrick, "The Impact of the Behavioral Approach on Traditional Political Science," and Austin Ranney, "The Utility and Limitations of Aggregate Data in the Study of Electoral Behavior," both in *Essays on the Behavioral Study of Politics*, ed. Austin Ranney (Urbana: University of Illinois Press, 1962).

To John Wiley & Sons, Inc., for permission to quote from Angus Campbell, *et al.*, *The American Voter* (New York: John Wiley & Sons, 1960); David Easton, *A Systems Analysis of Political Life* (New York: John Wiley & Sons, 1965); and Morton Kaplan, *System and Process in International Politics* (New York: John Wiley & Sons, 1957).

To the memory of

the late EGBERT S. WENGERT

—a teacher of highest standards,
who shared the excitement of the
intellectual endeavor with his students.

FOREWORD

From the first moment I started teaching undergraduates (shortly after World War II) to this day, I have heard college and university administrators galore chide us "working blokes" about the fact that, even though by every objective measure our students come to us brighter and more knowledgeable than in days of yore, we continue to pitch our courses and grade our students on the basis of old norms. This is said to be true of even the young among us. In the welter of grievances, real and imagined, voiced by our students, one of the most persistent is the lack of quality and relevance of our courses. In the conviction that these complaints are valid as to the so-called introductory courses, we at Scribners determined that we should seek out a young, able, creative, imaginative political scientist with a reputation for being an outstanding classroom teacher, to do an Introduction to Political Science text designed to have relevance for the students presently in our classes. We approached Professor Stephen Wasby who amply fitted the criteria we had established and we were gratified to find that the challenge of the proposal appealed to him. From that point on, the book was his to construct and this is the end product. Scribners is most proud of the result, an Introduction to Political Science which is different, imaginative and sophisticated, yet constructed in such a way that a student unlearned in the discipline is deftly brought quickly to a high level of understanding in a way which he or she will see as interesting and relevant. Toward that end, Professor Wasby has selected a talented array of collaborators, Joann Paine, William C. Baum, David Wood, and John Houston. Each has written a chapter where their special expertise enables them to make an unusual and creative contribution. In addition, Professor Wasby has woven into his text outstanding articles which illustrate or buttress an explanation or an approach, but done in such a way and in such a context as to combine the best features of both a text and a reader.

As we see it, this book will make an admirable text for an Introduction to Political Science course at any stage of undergraduate education. It requires only that the student be inquisitive. The book will be a challenge for most students but a challenge which they can master because it presupposes no specific previous coursework. However abstract the ideas become, they are developed step by step from the beginning. At the conclusion of a course based on this text, a student should not only have a good beginning to an understanding of what the discipline is all about, but will be aware of the hard problems and controversies in the field and will see its relevance to the modern world as well as its relevance to other disciplines. And isn't that par for the introductory course?

HAROLD W. CHASE

Minneapolis, 1969

PREFACE

While my debts, both general and specific, are many in an undertaking of this sort, I accept the responsibility for any misstatements and other errors. In matters of interpretation and emphasis, I ask the indulgence of my readers.

Three men—John Sparks, Richard "Mickey" McCleery, and Heinz Eulau, all then at Antioch College—were responsible for inducting me into the study of politics. The faculty at the University of Oregon made immeasurable contributions to my quest; William Mitchell, the late Egbert S. Wengert, to whom this book is dedicated, and sociologist Robert Dubin opened the largest vistas for me. I was privileged to have been exposed to the "real world" of politics under the direction of Representative John E. Moss and Senator Ralph Yarborough, during a year in Washington under the auspices of the American Political Science Association.

My greatest debt is to my friend Harold Chase, University of Minnesota, who helped spawn this project and provided constant support. My colleagues on the Carbondale campus of Southern Illinois University and friends teaching elsewhere who provided, through conversations and correspondence, idea upon idea as well as general intellectual stimulation, and the others who both added substance and helped untangle awkward phrases, type, and read proof, have my deepest appreciation for their efforts.

The four political scientists who have contributed major original chapters to this volume deserve separate mention. They are experts in fields which the principal author, by virtue of his own continuing specialization, was ill-equipped to discuss in detail. Although their authorship is noted elsewhere, I wish to acknowledge my vast debt to them here. They are:

William C. Baum of Grand Valley (Michigan) State College; John Houston, Knox College; Joann Poparad Paine, Southern Illinois University, Carbondale; and David M. Wood, University of Missouri, Columbia.

STEPHEN L. WASBY

Carbondale, Illinois, 1969

CONTENTS

Part III / THE FIELDS OF POLITICAL SCIENCE

INTRODUCTION

Because, as a wise professor once told me, work is judged on the basis of how well the author covers what he says he has set out to cover, some words are in order concerning the reasons for this book and its contents and exclusions. When the suggestion was first made that this volume be written, the author remembered that nowhere in his undergraduate political science study had he found any systematic examination and discussion of political science as a discipline or field of study. Comments by graduate school friends and teaching colleagues reinforced the realization that the absence of such an examination often left the impression that political science was simply a collection of courses, no more than an academic department where people interested in the study of politics were located, and not a field like physics or economics or history, with clear standing in the intellectual community, precise boundaries, and votaries possessed of a definite and secure self-conception. To be sure, graduate schools offered courses in "Scope and Methods of Political Science," but they came too late. They did not help the undergraduate "government" or "politics" or "political science" major, who had to piece together for himself, as best he could, a view of what political science was all about. The student also had little or no guidance in trying to divine the meaning of oblique references to intra-disciplinary arguments, such as that, for example, between "traditionalists" and "behavioralists."

This book was written because the author believes (1) that the study of politics does have "clear title" to a definite position as an acknowledged field of learning, and (2) that a knowledge of what is happening in the discipline will provide the student with a better basis for the study of specific substantive areas of politics. The author's purpose is to provide undergraduate students of political science with an examination of the discipline he is studying, its history, organization, and current issues, as well as its scope.

Differences of opinion exist concerning the need for a student to have been exposed to factual data about politics before he begins to study the theory and methodology of political science. The author has attempted to focus the text so that it can be used either in a student's first course in political science or in a second-level course once the student has been exposed to basic materials. The present volume is not designed to provide the full range of data to which a student should be exposed in his sole college course in political science; in fact, its purpose is not to provide data about politics except in connection with a portrayal of the development and status of the discipline and its subfields.

An attempt is also made here to remedy the lack of an "overview" of the field. Students often leave college with only a faint awareness of areas of their major in which they have not taken courses. They seldom have time to take all the courses they should to provide a broad look at politics, or they have chosen to specialize in one portion of their major at the expense of obtaining breadth. By providing an elemental idea of what has transpired within the generally recognized sub-fields of the discipline, this volume may give the student a map of the field, and help bring about a greater integration of political science than now exists for most undergraduates. (At another level, perhaps this volume can help answer a question asked by hundreds of parents of college students: "Political science—what is that?" While parents are not the author's principal intended audience, they, too, perhaps may benefit from the "look at the field" taken here.)

In view of the rapid speed with which new materials are being produced in the field of political science, no claim can be made here that the present volume is "up-to-date." Even if it were, the student would still have to adapt himself to materials still in the womb of time. Because of this situation, the material presented is meant to serve as background from which the student can comfortably move to deal with later developments. The materials covered are almost entirely American, because, until quite recently, political science has been an American endeavor, but the American materials provide a more than adequate base for the beginning student.

The book is divided into three major parts. In the first, the author has attempted to provide some basic definitions of the field of political science and of politics. Various approaches which have been used in studying politics are next examined. The meaning of theory in political science and various frames of reference used to explain the phenomena of politics are discussed. This is followed by material on methodology and techniques, where the emphasis is on general questions concerning research and on basic methods now in use. Throughout the volume, definitions of important terms are provided, set apart from the text in bold-face type.

In the second part of the volume, we take a look at political science as an institutionalized discipline, at its history and relations with the social sciences, and at the people who labor in its vineyard. The third part of the volume is an exposition, area by area, of the scope of and developments in the fields within political science. While the entirety of political science could be divided in several different ways, eight areas (or subfields) have been identified: political theory, voting behavior and public opinion, parties and interest groups, legislative process, public administration, public law, comparative government and politics, and international relations. Considerable overlap exists between these fields and, where it does, interrelatedness rather than separateness will be stressed. An annotated bibliography of basic works in each field is provided so that the student can start to explore those.

fields for himself. Material cited in footnotes will provide additional leads.

Material written by other political scientists has been incorporated into this book in two ways. Several subfields of political science are discussed by experts in those fields. In addition, several items are reprinted from other sources, and two papers are published for the first time; they are presented to illustrate some of the more general points made in the text and to provide, through the language of other political scientists, a difference in perspective.

The true value of this volume will become most clear to the student when he ventures on to more specialized courses. If what the author has attempted is successful, knowledge acquired in each course will fit together better and references made by teachers and in the literature will be more intelligible. It goes almost without saying that the author fervently hopes that some of the excitement which pervades not only politics but the study of politics, and which both attracted him to the discipline and has kept him there, will "rub off" on the student who reads the pages which follow. Whether or not the student decides to cast his lot with the fraternity of political scientists, the author hopes he leaves this book with a better understanding of what that band of individuals is studying.

Part I / THE STUDY OF POLITICAL SCIENCE

1 / WHAT IS POLITICAL SCIENCE?

Elements of a Definition / What Is Politics? / An Excursion
Into "Science" / Fact and Value

ELEMENTS OF A DEFINITION

Introduction.   Before beginning a study of the content of political science, its methods, or the approaches people use to study politics, we must
answer the question, "What Is Political Science?" We must at least *try* to
answer the question, perhaps by providing a number of different answers in
terms of the field's scope and content. Several answers are necessary because
no "twenty-five words or less" definition—or even one of several hundred
words—is available. Confusion and disagreement about political science, as
well as its changing nature and uncertain boundaries, make a single, fixed
definition inaccurate. This confusion and fluidity require us to delineate the
scope of our study so we do not find ourselves studying an unlimited universe
of material.

Taking the position that definitions, or formulations of the boundaries of
political science, are only more or less *useful,* not correct or incorrect, we will
limit ourselves to a working definition of political science. More flexible than
a formal definition (the sort you might expect to memorize), a working definition allows us to spell out various elements which writers have suggested
should be included within the study of politics and leaves the door open for
the future.

Two definitions of political science which have been offered more than
their usefulness would warrant are that it is (1) the study of politics and (2)
what political scientists do from 9:00–5:00. The first definition is of little help
until we define politics, and the second doesn't tell us what political scientists are. They study politics—and so we are back where we started. The
second definition is used to suggest the absence of agreement on a definition
of the field as well as to show the wide range of activities which some would
like to have called political science.

This lack of agreement has been a source of ridicule and dissatisfaction,
bringing comments that "political scientists are riding off in many directions,
evidently on the assumption that if you don't know where you are going, any
road will take you there," [1] and references to the "polyglot army that

---

[1] Heinz Eulau, "Political Science," *A Reader's Guide to the Social Sciences,* ed. Bert
F. Hoselitz (New York, 1959), p. 91.

3

marches under the banner of 'political science'." [2] However, others think that the resultant ambiguity is a preferred state of affairs.

Both those who opt for freedom for a multiplicity of activities and approaches for political science and those who adopt a more firm definition feel that an excessive amount of time is spent debating the proper confines of political science. They think that this effort could be better put to producing relevant studies. There is no denying that, particularly since World War II, a great deal of effort has been spent (for example, in the annual addresses of the presidents of the American Political Science Association) in attempting to define political science, although it is not clear whether the more recent discussion has raised new matters instead of repeating old arguments in different language. Most of this effort is indicative of the fact that there is something we can call political science. Had practitioners of political science not felt they were engaged in *some* sort of common endeavor—even if their endeavors in common were limited—they would not have devoted this attention to what political science means.

Academic Field.   Because there are Departments of Political Science (or Government), we can say that political science is an academic field. Or can we? Because there is no exact congruence between the borders of a field of study and the borders of a department in an institution of higher education, some political science is perhaps to be found outside the Department of Political Science, and some of what is found inside may not be political science. Making a separate university department for political science does not, unfortunately, automatically bestow a unity upon the field. (Some go so far as to say that not only is political science not now unified, but that it is not systematizeable.)

As an academic field, political science includes the study of politics or government or matters which governments consider relevant, and the teaching of the material produced by this study. Most political science research is carried on in universities, but some is carried on outside the groves of academe. However, not all those who carry out research using the data of politics—such as journalists, party workers, and interest group officials—are political scientists. Although—to add to our confusion—politics as well as political science involves scholarship and research, not all research about political phenomena is automatically political science, because not all research is carried out by means of processes which might be called scientific. No one stands at the gate, determining what shall be admitted as political science. However, material developed to achieve a certain goal, such as that produced by political organizations for external consumption (for example, party literature on candidates), is generally considered not to be political science, although it is clearly of interest to political scientists.

Profession.   Those who are now or who have been political scientists have had special training, through which special knowledge has been trans-

[2] Charles B. Hagan, "The Group in a Political Science," *Approaches to the Study of Politics,* ed. Roland Young (Evanston, 1958), p. 39.

mitted, and share a feeling that, despite differences in approach and interest, they are in some sense united in the same endeavor. These characteristics of special training and a feeling of community help identify political science as a profession. Graduate departments carry on the special training; the existence of a formal professional organization and scholarly journals reinforces the feeling of community, or "common state of mind." There are some who argue that political science has no "special" knowledge, because each citizen insists on being his own political scientist. However, the fact that many people show an interest in politics and discuss it often does not give them the type of information—more specific, more accurate, and more esoteric—to which one trained in political science has access.

Not all those trained in the profession are now practicing political scientists; this is particularly clear with respect to many of those working for the government, holding high appointive or elective office or simply helping run the bureaucracy. Some Congressmen and Senators, for example, Representatives Brademas (D–Indiana) and Hechler (D–West Virginia) and Senator Tower (R–Texas) were political scientists teaching in colleges before moving on to elective office. However, unless we are going to make the mistake of equating politics and political science, we cannot say that they are political scientists now; they are politicians, although they may later return to endeavors in the field of political science.

A listing of the ingredients of a discipline or profession may serve as a check-list by which the reader can determine whether political science is a profession or something less. Here is one such listing: [3]

- "Disciplinary self-consciousness, reflected in the emphasis placed on critical analysis of the growth and development of the field of study."
- A body of classic works.
- Specialization of personnel by subfield.
- Easily differentiated subject matter.
- "A body of generalizations or abstractions, part of which are added, deleted, or modified over time as deemed necessary and appropriate."
- Concepts peculiar to the field.
- Relatively standardized methods of analysis.
- A body of data and reports about the data.

Goals. Like those who argue that "art is for art's sake," some would have political science produce "knowledge for knowledge's sake." Although they do not reject the eventual application of political science knowledge, they say that we need to know a great deal more about the workings of politics before we can begin to suggest how certain goals can be achieved. Research should be performed solely for the sake of adding to our storehouse of information, they say. Another argument is that, because we are equipped at the

[3] Cyril Roseman, Charles G. Mayo, and F.B. Collinge, *Dimensions of Political Analysis: An Introduction to the Contemporary Study of Politics* (Englewood Cliffs, 1966), pp. 4–6.

present time to deal with only symptoms of social ills, we should wait to apply the knowledge until we can eliminate the causes of these ills. The response of reform-proposers has been stated well by Charles Hyneman:

> To counsel political scientists to propose no changes is to counsel society to make changes proposed by people whose guesses are less adequately supported by evidence than those which political scientists now make. . . . We should not terminate our reform literature or refrain from giving advice until that far-distant day when we can meet the demands imposed by a rigorous scientific method.[4]

At almost the other extreme from the "knowledge-collectors" are those who argue that our task should be "citizenship education." (If you think that arriving at a definition of political science is difficult, consider the difficulties in arriving at a consensus about "good citizenship.")

At a minimum, they would have political scientists teach students how to find their way around in the world of everyday politics, and some would have political scientists indoctrinate. While not denying that students use knowledge they acquire from their teachers, many political scientists feel that purposeful instruction in political participation should not be a part of their work.

A half-way house between the extremes of "political study for political study's sake" and "citizenship education" is the idea of political science as a policy science. What political science does is relevant for political activity, either directly or indirectly. One view is that the subject-matter of political science should therefore be determined by existing or future policy problems or issues. Information collected would be directly applicable or usable by policy-makers, who cannot wait several generations for us to develop a more complete description and analysis of politics. To say that political science should be a policy science is not necessarily to say that political officials should define what should be studied by political scientists. The policy science idea simply helps provide criteria for what is significant to study. However, we should not forget that material derived from action-oriented research can provide the basis for theoretical knowledge, as has happened with our information about attitude change (which came from marketing research), just as findings which derive from scholarly study are put to use in the "real world" of politics.

Science. Whether (or to what degree) political science is a science is perhaps most crucial and controversial part of the present "great debate" about the meaning of the study of politics. And it is here that there is least consensus. Very few political scientists who argue that their subject is a sci-

Consensus. Agreement by a substantial proportion of people affected by an issue or responding to a question. Consensus exists when, e.g., 75% or more of a group indicate agreement; 50% + 1, however necessary in win-

---

[4] Charles S. Hyneman, *The Study of Politics: The Present State of American Political Science* (Urbana, 1959), p. 173.

ning elections, is insufficient for consensus. In fact, the closer one approaches 50%, the greater the *dissensus*.

ence mean that it is so in the same sense as the "hard" sciences of physics, chemistry, or geology. However, although political science is considered a "soft" science along with the behavioral or social sciences, some political sci-

Behavioral Sciences. Those fields of knowledge concentrating on human behavior, in both its individual and collective forms. In one sense, it is a broader term than "social science," which would seem to imply a concentration on only the collective (i.e., social) forms of behavior. Psychology, economics, sociology, anthropology, and political science are considered behavioral sciences, but behavioral science is not co-extensive with the totality of those fields; they only qualify to the extent they emphasize the study of behavior.

entists use models from the "hard" disciplines and would like to pattern political science along the lines of physics even if the latter's precision can never be attained. To most political scientists, talk about a scientific study of politics means only that the study will be systematic and orderly, and that students will attempt to find what actually exists; in short, they will use the general mode of examining and treating phenomena known as scientific method. They will also use the information they gather to form generalizations and theories about political life, even if in the foreseeable future one over-arching theory of politics cannot be found. In trying to develop these generalizations, the political scientist will be interested more in the common characteristics of his data than in the uniqueness of political events or political actors, a focus different from that of historians, who generally concentrate on the unique or outstanding.

Methods. In developing their findings, political scientists use the methods of the historian, the sociologist, the economist, the psychologist and the anthropologist, although methods borrowed from sister social sciences are usually adapted to fit better the specific problems of data collection and interpretation faced in political science. As a result of this borrowing, political science seems to some like history or sociology or economics applied to political data. Political science *is* different from these other fields, even when members of these several disciplines study the same objects, but political science can *not* be defined in terms of special or unique methods.

Terminology. The terminology used by political scientists might be a better identifying characteristic than its methods, but much of the terminology, at least in recent years, has also been borrowed. The concept of the "State," which once identified the study of politics, is now generally con-

State. A collection of people in a certain territory having organized government and possessing autonomy with respect to other such units.

sidered obsolete. Words like "democracy" and "coalition," which may seem to be particular to political science, really belong to the language of everyday politics and share the ambiguity of such language. Some attempts have been made to develop new words with stipulated definitions, resulting in charges that a science of politics is built on jargon, but not enough has been done to

> *Jargon.* The technical language of a field, usually meant to imply that it is not understandable to those outside the field. "Outsiders" and critics claim the "difficult" language is developed solely to inflate the importance of those within the field and to confuse and confound outsiders.

warrant identifying political science through its terminology.

Recapitulation. Where has all the foregoing taken us? Perhaps we can now put together some elements of a definition. Political science is an identifiable field of study, with oft-disputed scope and content, whose practitioners are found most frequently in institutions of higher education, where they teach and conduct research, or in the government. These practitioners are *not* the same as politicians. The study of politics carried on within political science is relevant for the country's political life, although political scientists differ as to whether it should be applied immediately or after more thorough development, with some suggesting that pressing policy issues be the prime subject of study by political scientists. Political science is not a science in the same sense as physics, but politics can be studied systematically with the scientific method. However, political science can be identified precisely neither by methods special to it nor by a particular terminology. The length of time needed to discuss even a tentative definition of political science should make clear that "political science has been unable to evolve a central model that could serve as a reasonably stable point of departure into political inquiry. . . . Modern political science resembles a Gothic cathedral, built over many centuries, with its turrets, spires, balconies, nooks, and crannies." [5]

Having developed a "working" definition of political science, or at least specified some elements which might be included in one, we shift our attention to a number of important subjects which bear on the definition we are developing. First will be a discussion of definitions of politics and the political. We need to know not only the content of the political, but if and how we can distinguish the political from other aspects of life. Extended discussion of the question of "science" in political science will follow.

WHAT IS POLITICS?

Art or Science? Politics is generally agreed to be an art, the art of the possible, while the study of politics is thought to be a science, although we must be careful not to overemphasize this distinction. Some of the skills in politics can be learned, and to that extent it has its scientific aspects, while much of the process of collecting data (or deciding where and how to collect it) is "creative," and therefore partakes of the qualities of art. To be sure, the techniques for analyzing that data have far less of this quality, although

[5] Eulau, p. 92.

knowing which techniques to apply in order to extract the most from what is available also involves creative talent. We think of politics as an art because a politician is judged primarily in terms of his results, although the means he uses are not unimportant. A political scientist, by comparison, is judged at least as much in terms of the methods he has used in his work as in terms of results, because the methods affect the validity of his results. However, to agree, even for the purposes of argument, that politics is an art tells us little if anything about the content of politics. We need a more systematic and complete definition.

Power. To some, politics involves *power* and *influence.* One formulation of these ideas is that politics gives an answer to the question, "Who Gets What, When, and How?" Another is that politics involves "influence and the influential." The concepts "power" and "influence" are central to the study of politics, as well as among the most difficult concepts to define. One might think a field of study would have achieved consensus on at least its central concepts, but in political science that is not the case. Power is generally thought to involve the bringing about of an action by someone against the will or desire of another. (See further discussion at pp. 81–82.) Some qualify this definition by the addition of the idea that the power must be used to implement the "public good." Others suggest the addition of the possibility of the use of force. Force need not be used all the time—paradoxically, it may be that one who always resorts to force is not powerful—but its availability contributes to a person's ability to achieve his ends over the opposition of others. Influence is often thought to involve persuasion, and thus to be different from power, but there is often little practical difference between the two concepts, which we tend to use interchangeably. In any case, the problems involved in operationalizing the terms, of determining whether a person has power and,

> *Operationalizing.* **Defining concepts in terms of the operations necessary to give them concreteness. There can be more than one way of operationalizing a given concept.**

if so, how much, are great. Despite the claim that the struggle over power is the political scientist's central subject-matter, and while the earliest political philosophers talked of man as inherently a political animal, we definitely have not developed a theory of Political Man, seeking out power, that compares with the work of the economists in developing Economic Man, motivated by the search for profit.

If politics does involve power, the exercise of control by some over others for particular purposes, how far afield do we go to find that power? Do we accept the charge that political science involves "a study of the organization of society in its widest sense, including all organizations, the family, the trade union and the State, with special reference to one aspect of human behavior, the exercise of control and the rendering of obedience"?[6] Is the power, for example, of parents, labor unions, and corporations *political?* Again, as in the

[6] Angadipuram Appadorai, "Political Science in India," *Contemporary Political Science: A Survey of Methods, Research and Teaching* (Paris, 1950), p. 39.

case of political science, we come to the problem of definitions. Until recently, most political scientists would probably have agreed that power exerted *on* the government or *by* the government was political power, but that power exerted within "private" organizations (such as unions and businesses) was not political, and that power within the family, because apolitical or pre-political, was clearly not part of the study of politics. Groups like unions were useful to study only because their internal processes were analogous to those of politics. Recently, these limits on what is considered political power have been altered and expanded. Quite a number of political scientists now feel that power within unions, other interest groups and private associations, within business, or even within the family, is clearly part of politics because of its relevance for the pressures which are brought to bear or not brought to bear on government. If political values are transmitted within the family from parents to children, the distribution of power within the family is relevant to politics outside the family, as is a decrease in parents' power because adolescents spend more time than previously with their peers. The effect of the distribution of power within an interest group is also clear, because the policies demanded of government may vary depending on the individuals or factions which hold power in the group at a particular time.

However, if the family, labor union, and business corporation fall within the ambit of political science, not all their aspects are necessarily to be studied. Besides, as a practical matter, everything cannot be studied simultaneously, and political scientists must limit what they study to what they can handle; they have decided to study the politically relevant actions of social institutions.

Allocation of Values.   It has been suggested that politics involves the authoritative allocation of values within a society, for the society as a whole, backed by the ultimate use of a monopoly of physical force.[7] When we say that something has a certain "value" to someone, we mean that he desires it to some extent relative to other items available to him. The extent of the desire may be measureable in terms of the amount of money he is willing to pay to obtain it, or the amount of effort he will expend in its pursuit, and an individual's preferences can be ranked in these terms as well, so that we can talk about a "hierarchy of values" which citizens have. What becomes difficult in politics is to determine accurately which policies are preferred to which others. For the economist's calculus to work, it must be possible to place a dollars-and-cents value on an object. Many of the desired states of affairs (values) in politics cannot be so measured. In addition, agreement on abstract values is not always followed by equal agreement on policies thought

---

[7] David Easton, "An Approach to the Analysis of Political Systems," *World Politics,* IX (1957), 383–400. An alternative construction of part of this definition is that politics is "more or less incomplete control of human behavior through voluntary habits of *compliance* in combination with threats of probable *enforcement.*" Karl Deutsch, "On the Concepts of Politics and Power," *Journal of International Affairs,* XXI (1967), 232.

by some to embody those abstractions. Moreover, political values (or goals) which do not necessarily conflict in the abstract, such as "freedom" and "order," are likely to do so when applied to specific instances, as when someone's freedom to demonstrate or march disrupts the order a businessman or politician has come to value highly. It is this type of situation which leads to the definition of politics as "the pursuit of incompatible goals." When people try to obtain one goal, it may decrease their chances of getting others. They also find that they often cannot get what they want without impinging on the goal-seeking activity of others, so that, when others get something, they get less, as when someone's "right to a job" conflicts with someone else's "right of association," or a newspaper's "freedom of the press" conflicts with an accused's "right to a fair trial."

To some, the "authoritative allocation of values" does not distinguish politics adequately from other means of social control. Values are "authoritatively allocated" within the family, church, and business corporation, as well as within government, political parties, and interest groups. The argument runs that we must be able to distinguish between informal means of social control and those means more forcefully backed. Perhaps a prime problem is the lack of a test. A policeman sometimes uses force in making an arrest. Physical force is clearly used in that situation to enforce a value. The use of a monopoly of force is also clear when the National Guard is called out to control civil disorders, and in imprisonment or the carrying out of the death penalty. However, there are many other situations when the use of force is not visible, and it is hard to tell who is allocating values. For example, after two companies begin discussing a merger, they sometimes discontinue the discussions. Is this because they decided it was not economically feasible to merge? Or was it because they feared forceful action by the Anti-Trust Division of the United States Department of Justice? How do we judge who allocates in this situation without clearer evidence? Or several companies set prices for their products. Assume that company representatives have not sat down together and agreed upon these prices, but that a great similarity in prices results from the companies' separate decisions. The government, for lack of evidence of a conspiracy, for lack of manpower to investigate the case for possible action, or for a host of other reasons, ignores the pricing action taken by the companies. Have not the companies "allocated values authoritatively" for the society, even if these values are "economic" and not directly "political"? If so, this illustrates the possible decentralization of political power within the system, so that not all is in the hands of the formal government, even though, in most cases, the monopoly of *ultimate* physical force remains there.

Other examples may be taken from the field of public law, where controversy over the "state action" doctrine in the field of civil rights has existed for many years. The Fourteenth Amendment to the United States Constitution prohibits the states from depriving people of their rights. The question then becomes: "When is the state acting?" A state-passed law declaring that a

Negro may not buy land is unacceptable under the Amendment, according to the Supreme Court.[8] But is the government acting if it allows individuals to keep Negroes from buying or renting through the use of racial restrictive covenants attached to property, only allowing them to use the courts to enforce the covenants? In 1948, the Supreme Court said yes, because court enforcement quite clearly involved the state government.[9] Attempts by the states to abandon regulation of primary elections were likewise struck down,[10] thus destroying the states' hope that the primaries would be considered to be privately run (by political parties).[11]

In the early 1960's, the Court was faced with many "sit-in" cases in which Negroes entered restaurants in which they were not served. If a policeman arrested a Negro as a result of Police Department policy, the state was considered to be involved just as if the legislature had passed a law requiring segregation.[12] If there were no law or executive policy, and the proprietor, fearing the loss of business, called the police to arrest the Negro for trespass, is the government involved? The Supreme Court never clearly ruled on the matter, and so the question is still open.[13] Perhaps the examples involving the civil rights of Negroes are clearer than those involving business price-setting, but the general point which evolves from all this is that it is often extremely difficult to pinpoint where the *effective* policy-making ability exists. To say that the ultimate monopoly of the physical force in society is located somewhere is not to say who will use force, or power short of force.

The key word in the phrase "authoritative allocation of values" may be "authoritative;" while many politically important decisions are made outside the government structure, only those made within that structure can be considered authoritative. The word suggests an air of finality and conveys the idea that once decisions are made, they will stick. In other words, they are binding. In a monarchy or dictatorship, locating the source of policies considered legitimate within that political system might be relatively easy. However, where power is diffused, as it is in America, and where economic decisions with their considerable impact are made largely in the private sector of the economy, location of the source of "authoritative" allocation is often a search for a will-o'-the-wisp. The idea of legitimacy or correctness

[8] *Buchanan* v. *Warley*, 245 U.S. 60 (1917). The citation means that a report of the case, and the Supreme Court's opinions, may be found starting at page 60 of Volume 245 of the *United States Reports*, and that the Court handed down the decision in 1917.

[9] *Shelley* v. *Kraemer*, 334 U.S. 1 (1948).

[10] *Rice* v. *Elmore*, 165 F2nd (1947), that is, Volume 165 of the *Federal Reporter*, Second Series, starting at page 387. The Supreme Court refused to hear the case, leaving the lower court (Court of Appeals) decision standing.

[11] See *Smith* v. *Allwright*, 321 U.S. 649 (1944), and *Terry* v. *Adams*, 345 U.S. 461 (1953).

[12] Concerning city ordinances, see *Peterson* v. *City of Greenville*, 373 U.S. 244 (1963), and concerning administrative action, *Lombard* v. *Louisiana*, 373 U.S. 267 (1963).

[13] The public accommodations section of the Civil Rights Act of 1964 resolved the practical question of Negroes' obtaining service in restaurants, although the legal question of "state action" remains unanswered.

also seems to be suggested by "authoritative." While many people, including some of those operating in violation of the law, have political power, only policies coming from a certain source or sources or which have been determined in a certain way, e.g., through "due process," are accepted as proper.

Public v. Private. In defining politics, we often distinguish between "public" and "private." Sometimes we talk about "public" officials (elected office-holders, bureaucrats, civil servants) or the "public" life of an individual, while some organizations, like Kiwanis, Rotary, and Lions Clubs, are usually considered "private," even though they often become engaged in community activities. Fraternities and sororities are also generally put in this class, giving rise to considerable controversy when attempts are made to regulate alleged racial discrimination by those groups at public colleges and universities. The terms "public" and "private" are also occasionally used to denote preferences. What is labelled "private" is supposed to be beyond the touch of government; what is labelled "public," as in the phrase "business affected with a 'public interest'," is supposed to be subject to government regulation and control.

The American philosopher John Dewey said that actions were public when they had indirect consequences, that is, consequences which spread beyond the individuals or groups immediately or directly involved in the actions. Dewey's distinction appears to be useful, although oftentimes people do not recognize the indirect consequences of someone else's action or may not know the action has occurred. If a labor union (often considered "private") does not admit Negroes to membership or to its apprenticeship programs, and at the same time has the power, through picketing and the strike, to prevent non-union men from working on desirable jobs, such action will have consequences extending outside the union. For example, the per capita income of Negroes and their unemployment rate may be affected.

The British have, over the last two decades, been moving toward a position in which sexual acts involving minors or the use of force or fraud will be considered criminal and therefore "public," while sexual acts committed by consenting adults will not be considered to be criminal acts, that is, they will be considered "private." In addition, the activity must take place out of the eye of the populace, leading to the arrest of "streetwalkers" but not to the stopping of prostitution *per se.* One could argue that this embodiment of the distinction between public and private ignores the repercussions of those acts which take place "out of view" and with consent, both on the institutions of marriage and the family which governments have historically regulated (if adultery is involved), and on the welfare rolls, if illegitimate children result. Regardless of the difficulty of drawing lines, Dewey's distinction between public and private does help us to determine what is within the realm of politics (public) and what is not (private).

In a related definition, Christian Bay limits "politics" by requiring that activity "aimed at improving or protecting conditions for the satisfaction of human needs and demands" be based on a "universalistic scheme of priorities" to be called political. Activity for private ends or not motivated by universalistic concerns, "exclusively concerned with either the alleviation of personal neuroses or with promoting private or private interest-group advantage," would be called pseudopolitical.[14] The difficulty with this distinction is that it requires the specification of motive in the study of politics, and also ignores the substantial effect of pseudopolitical activity on the making of policy and the allocation of values.

Controversy. Another element in a definition of politics is controversy. Where there is politics, it is said, there is controversy; where there are issues, there is politics. Where no controversy exists, where no issues are being debated, politics does not exist. This controversy, it should be noted, is not limited to the activities of contending political parties, but includes other groupings and individuals, whether explicitly political or not. Thus, to take a government activity "out of politics" by putting it under non-partisan control perhaps removes it only from political party politics, but not from political controversy. One reason for controversy is that "values" are scarce. For example, several companies may apply for a license to run a television station in a city, but the Federal Communications Commission (FCC) may rule that only one new station can be built in that city until 1975. If the FCC permitted as many stations as companies that applied for licenses, each and all could be satisfied, and conflict would be reduced. (However, the person awarded the station will undoubtedly defend his position of advantage against demands for more stations.)

The late Peter Odegard argued that conflict *per se* was not political unless it was directed at something, particularly the control of matters external to those in conflict. In addition, he felt that, if political activity is to occur, there must be agreement that adherence to certain rules will bring people to their goal.[15] If what we define as politics is controversial, then much routine work within the government is not political, although the impact for the life of the people of actions of lower-level clerks in carrying out assigned tasks is clear and undoubted. The non-controversial, however, remains *politically relevant* even if not directly and immediately political.

Consensus. While debate and conflict, cleavage and dissensus, are frequently associated with politics, concentration on them to the exclusion of agreement or consensus would leave an incomplete picture of the political world. Cleavage and consensus are frequently considered to be at opposite ends of a range of activity, that is, at opposite ends of a continuum. Viewed in this fashion, what is located toward the cleavage end of the continuum is po-

> *Continuum.* **A device for representing a range of possible behavior or events, or for categorizing items relative to each other. It is represented by a straight line. The concepts or items at either end are frequently "pure,"**

[14] Christian Bay, "Politics and Pseudopolitics: A Critical Evaluation of Some Behavioral Literature," *American Political Science Review*, LIX (1965), 40.

[15] Peter H. Odegard, "Research in Politics," *The Research Function of University Bureaus and Institutions for Government-Related Research*, ed. Dwight Waldo (Berkeley, 1960), p. 152.

in the sense that no event will be found which exactly matches the concept or item. Specific items are then located at points along the line. For example,

	Break in diplo-			World
War	matic relations	Neutrality	Alliance	government

CLEAVAGE —————————————————————————————— CONSENSUS

If instead of indicating a continuous range of behavior, one wants to show that items fall into mutually exclusive categories, one uses a *dichotomy*, e.g., Cleavage/Consensus.

litical, while what is located at the consensus end is non-political. This view, facilitated by the negative attitude many people have toward politics and politicians, is now recognized to be too simplistic. Consensus is necessary for conflict to occur; agreement on a number of values usually undergirds conflict about other values. Sometimes basics are agreed on and only specifics are the subject of argument, but there are other times when even basics become the area of clash. If we stop and ask ourselves what would happen if controversy existed about *everything*, perhaps we can see more clearly how much we actually do agree upon. We also see that if we did not agree on some things, we could not disagree on others. To take an extreme case, two nations at war have implicitly agreed to fight each other. War has been characterized by many generally agreed-upon norms, such as those involving the exchange of prisoners and agreements not to fight on religious holidays, showing the pervasiveness of consensus in the midst of conflict. Consensus may also affect the amount of cleavage, as when pressure to end a conflict is stimulated by recognition that a certain level of conflict may endanger a community or nation.

State and Boundaries. The foregoing discussion has not included mention of more traditional definitions of politics. Political science for many years concentrated on what we now consider to be only a limited aspect of politics, that relating to government, to formal institutions, and particularly to the State. Difficulties arose in connection with implications of the State concept that political activity took place only within well-defined boundaries and that politics could not exist in the absence of a set of formal institutions. The boundaries in which political activity take place change, in some cases with great rapidity. Concentration by earlier students of politics on the nations of the Western world, particularly those of Western Europe, led to the idea that a political system had clear, well-defined boundaries. Perhaps the many wars of the last several centuries in Europe over such boundaries, and the concern over who would govern people located in such places as Alsace-Lorraine, contributed to this overemphasis. The anthropologists, however, brought to our attention two kinds of communities which did not fit the State concept. One such grouping was the nomadic people, who appeared to have government officials but obviously did not stay in one place. Their ability to move their government with them, leaving a previously inhabited territory vacant, led to questioning the insistence on the inclusion of fixed geographical boundaries in defining politics, although the impact of geography on the structure of governments or the political behavior of the governed could not be ignored.

The second type of people noted by the anthropologists were those, such as African or aboriginal tribes, living in "stateless societies." They possessed no apparent formal government, but it became clear that the same tasks which our governments performed were being performed, regardless of the degree of formal structure or differentiation of personnel. Just as too much attention had been paid to Western European countries with clear boundaries, so had too much attention been paid to what we call modern or developed forms of government, which have clearly differentiated institutions of government with full-time occupants. This recognition led to increasing attention to key tasks or functions as elements of politics, regardless of where and by whom performed, although formal structure was not to be ignored. Many political scientists agree that the concept of the State is no longer useful because it is too formal. However, the emphasis the term produced on the central functions of the formal government has pervaded much of American political science.

Another emphasis of an older political science, which perhaps subsumed the State, was that on the "political order," a term which indicated concentration on constitutions, whether written or not, and on "constitutionalism," or principles of order for governments. (We find this interest revived in different guise in the concern of current theorists about "regime.") Emphasis on constitutions also brought an emphasis on law, which has remained in the discipline ever since.

What we as political scientists are willing to include within our studies has moved from the State, the constitutional order, and law, to "politics" in the current everyday sense of the word and to minute examination of the individuals participating in politics, although there has been a recent revival of interest in "macro" phenomena. Perhaps this change has come about simply because of new ways of looking at social phenomena. Without doubt that accounts for a larger part of our increased scope. But the vast expansion in government itself has played a substantial role and will continue to do so: political science will change as politics and government themselves change. A true science would not be caught with a rigid definition when its object of study is dynamic.

The increased tasks of government mean that proportionately more of what government does is to be included in, or relevant to, the political. Perhaps politics is meant to be instrumental, to be aimed primarily at creating and controlling government and its agencies, an idea reinforced by the distinction between government and politics; somehow one gets the impression that politics only impinges on government, never taking place within government. There is, however, no longer any question that government officials "politic" in much the same way as individuals not in the government, even if the idea of intra-governmental politics conflicts with personal notions of a preferred neutrality on the part of government. Government officials often feel that they must protect and attempt to expand their agencies and the interests which the agencies represent.

Politics in Society. A theme implicit in much of the foregoing is that politics is one aspect of the society in which people live. Even if special institutions are developed to perform political functions, politics is never separate from the larger society. In a sense, it is simply a facet of the social system, which is separated analytically in order to be examined more closely, just as economic functions are separated for examination by the economist. Any action may have both political and economic components; it may allocate goods and services as well as allocate power. It is one action, but it can be analytically divided. To study politics is to take the social whole in order to examine one part—an important and even crucial part, but a part—of its structure and operation. When we do this, we need to know what the political aspect of society—the political subsystem, or polity—does for the entire society.

The chief function the polity performs for the society is that of goal-attainment; goals are selected and attempts are made to attain them for the collectivity. That we have looked at politics in this manner only recently is clear; that we do not pay sufficient attention to this perspective is still more clear. There is a "tendency on the part of political scientists to overemphasize the distribution of values and either to ignore or to minimize the goal attainment function of the polity." [16] Our attention to value-allocation has probably come through our acceptance of power as the central focus of the discipline. However, if one takes the position that power is only one aspect of politics, and government helps to steer society, then goal-attainment becomes more crucial. Increased attention to the goal-attainment function, the one most likely to involve controversy, should not blind us to the other functions with which the polity is concerned, such as integration of the system, which relates to binding the system together and increasing consensus. Because the functions performed by the individual subsystems are closely related, we find political science closely related to the other social sciences.

AN EXCURSION INTO "SCIENCE"

Introduction. Earlier we talked about whether or not political science can be considered a science. Students of politics, struggling to make their field one of greater precision, have tended to wonder whether they could ever achieve the status of a science. In order to understand more clearly in what ways political science is a science, we need to know more about science, although it is possible for someone to be a good scientist without his being completely clear as to the validity of the basic endeavor in which he is involved.

Perhaps the first thing to be said is that science does not possess perfec-

[16] William C. Mitchell, "Politics as the Allocation of Values: A Critique," *Ethics,* LXXI (1961), 85.

tion or unity. Nor is it solely a body of fixed data, drawn particularly from the fields of chemistry and physics and dressed up in mathematical formulae. Because people tend to deify what they do not fully understand and, in such circumstances, to attribute perfection where perfection does not exist, the impression has grown that science is almost fully developed and that its findings have ultimate precision. What people tend to see of science (as made manifest in the physical sciences) is either a final and applied result, such as a launching of a moon rocket, or a description of what is considered the ideal way to go about achieving "scientific" explanations. What they see is neither an accurate description of the hard, difficult, and even awkward way in which findings and theories in science have been achieved, nor the many failures of scientific work, nor the way in which findings have changed over time, because the picture of science they see usually is presented by philosophers of science rather than by scientists and has evolved over a period of time, certainly many times longer than the period in which contemporary social science has developed. By contrast, much of the writing about methodology and principles in social science has been done by practicing social scientists, who have seen science "warts and all" and have therefore tended to exaggerate differences (such as degree of complexity) which seem to exist between fields such as physics and chemistry and their own disciplines.

Basically, science involves a method, some assumptions, and certain goals.

> The scientific attitude consists of a syndrome of belief, method, and value. The *belief* is that there is an underlying continuity between man's natural and human environments to which he can gradually penetrate through his creative powers of imagination . . . logical reasoning, and observation . . . The *method* requires that ordering concepts and propositions, procedures of selecting and analyzing evidence, and modes of interpretation be public, communicable, and ultimately connectible with the experience of others. The *values* lie in the enjoyment of the common motivation and heritage known to men who seek the truth.[17]

Science does not require a fixed or absolute subject matter. As Meehan notes, "the logic of explanation is independent of the subject matter."[18] For this reason, we often talk about the sciences, rather than of a single science. We are referring to method when we talk about science generically. The method has been referred to as the Scientific Method, leaving the impression that there is only one true way to achieve findings which can be considered scientific. The method of science can be more accurately looked at as a general way of doing things, the specifics of which vary in practice from situation to situation. It is an outlook, a means of study which involves precision, rigor, and a systematic way of proceeding. It involves a heightened consciousness

[17] Avery Leiserson, "The Behavioral Approach," *Teaching Political Science: A Challenge to Higher Education*, ed. Robert H. Connery (Durham, N.C., 1965), p. 52.
[18] Eugene J. Meehan, *The Theory and Method of Political Analysis* (Homewood, Ill., 1965), p. 88.

of what one is doing in one's work. (See Chapter 6 for the steps generally followed.)

Patterns. Among the principal assumptions of science is that phenomena occur in patterns, and that it is the task of science to ascertain what these patterns are. This does not necessarily mean that the specific pattern described by the scientist is embedded in nature to be discovered. Nor can one prove or disprove that the world is regular; however, if we thought of the world as totally irregular, we could not study it through science, nor survive in it. As Churchman quotes Kant: "The world is regular in its behavior, and we must expect it to behave tomorrow as it did today, simply because without such a presupposition all questions that science can raise (other than the trivial immediacies) become meaningless." [19] The scientist uses patterns he has determined to best explain the set of occurrences which he is examining; in a sense, he creates the best explanatory device. However, the phenomena under study do not act randomly; patterning of some sort is assumed to be there, although it is claimed that entropy, or randomness, is increasing as the world "runs down." Because the scientist imposes order on what he studies, the question often arises whether he has forced his data into a given pattern, or whether some other pattern might better serve to explain that at which he is looking. Regardless of the patterns the scientist indicates explain his data, the important point is that he presumes that each event does not have to be treated idiosyncratically, that is, as a separate, unique item basically not comparable with any other item.

Many, many pages have been consumed in disquisitions about the nature of reality and whether it can be experienced by humans. Without being involved in these great and important philosophical arguments, the scientist feels he is examining something which, if not reality, very closely approximates reality. The verb "feels" indicates that faith or belief—quite nonscientific commodities—play a large role in establishing this foundation of science, and that it, too, contains elements of an "art," something true of both social science and physical science. However, that science is based on a nonscientific assumption does not undercut or destroy science. What is important is that the scientist assumes that the observable world *is* the real world for him. Another assumption is that if something is to be subject to scientific study, it must be subject to study in the same way by more than one person. It must be "inter-subjectively communicable." The ways of detecting and of measuring a phenomenon must be "public," so that different individuals can investigate independently and possibly arrive at the same conclusions. This assumption depends on another, and crucial, assumption, that the same "object" can be received through the senses in like ways by more than one person.

The question of whether matters not directly observable can be part of science is an issue of considerable importance for those aspects of political

[19] C. West Churchman, *The Theory of Experimental Inference* (New York, 1948), p. 128.

science related to psychology. Some psychologists rebelled at earlier "non-sense" about what went on inside the human body, and decided they would deal only with stimuli which were detectable and measurable and the re-sponses the human organism made. What went on inside "the Black Box" was no concern of theirs. This "stimulus-response" (S-R) psychology, called "Behaviorism," and associated with the names of Watson and Skinner (and not to be confused with "behavioralism," an approach to the study of politics discussed in Chapter 2), generally has been rejected. While attitudes and ideas cannot be verified by an outsider in the same sense that other scientific data can be, valid measures for these internal "happenings" can be devel-oped, without reducing them to physiological impulses. Essentially what is at issue is the type of empiricism one is to adopt. There is an empiricism which admits only "public" data and another which permits the use of subjective knowledge. The earliest students of voting behavior, who used only voting statistics, used a different (and one might argue, stricter) empiricism from that utilized by more recent analysts of voting, who have tried to explain voting in terms of socio-economic status, various attitudes, and perceptions.

Explanation and Prediction.   There is disagreement as to the goal of sci-ence. Some claim that science constructs a symbolic world which reflects the everyday one we know. Others assert that the goal is explanation. For some, science *is* explanation, of a particular type. Still others postulate prediction as science's goal. The elements of a good prediction may be necessary for an adequate explanation, and scientific explanation may entail a version of pre-diction. On the other hand, some scientists feel that prediction cannot exist without explanation, and thoroughness of explanation can often increase our predictive ability; however, prediction of an accurate sort will not always fol-low directly from an explanation, particularly if that explanation is only par-tial.

Scientific prediction indicates what will happen if certain conditions are met. The predictions can be cast in either deterministic or probabilistic form, with the present state of the art generally allowing only the latter. However, the prediction does not tell us what we might do to control events: to be able to do that, explanation is necessary.[20] When we talk about scientific predic-tion, we are interested in much more than the one-shot "prediction" of who will win the Presidency, based on early returns from selected precincts, in the manner of the television networks. With the aid of computers, the net-works are simply speeding up what journalists, using "bellwether" precincts, have been doing for years. The statements of "expected victory" are largely extrapolations from early vote to total, based on the implicit assumption that other precincts, of which selected precincts are supposed to be representa-tive, will vote in the same fashion, rather than predictions from one factor to another. The interest of the television networks, however elaborate the theory on the basis of which precincts are chosen, is in being able to declare a win-

[20] See the argument of Eugene Meehan, *Explanation in Social Science: A System Par-adigm* (Homewood, Ill., 1968), p. 21.

ner quickly rather than developing a predictive model which would help us predict elections in the future. For this reason, the Gallup Poll type of prediction, prior to voting and based on statements of voting intent, is of greater usefulness to political scientists, because from it they can determine something about the relationship between intention and vote.

Accepting explanation as the goal of science brings us face to face with the question of the basis on which we accept science or particularly scientific explanations as valid. It has been argued that the scientific approach to viewing phenomena cannot be accepted on scientific grounds, and therefore is equivalent to a religion. While some scientists live their work as if they were in the service of an orthodox type of religion, the above claim does not mean that we have no stronger basis for accepting science than that it is only one of a number of equally valid ways of explaining phenomena. Scientific findings can be checked independently of the original finder, whereas other sorts of explanations cannot be checked in this way. Two or more people can agree that God created the Earth or made two cars collide, but there is no way to prove this explanation directly. Similarly, there is no way to prove God did *not* create the Earth or make the cars collide. Such matters are simply beyond proof: they are questions of metaphysics—literally, beyond physics.

Even when it is agreed that scientific findings can be checked for their validity, the problem of how to determine which explanations to accept remains. Here, we come down to essentially non-scientific (not *un*-scientific) answers. The explanation which is considered the most acceptable in science is usually the one which will explain the greatest number of phenomena the *most simply*. A classic example in the history of science concerns the solar system. The old Ptolemaic system explained the travels of the planets, but required the device of a considerable number of epicycles to account for deviations from basic circular orbits. The Copernican system had the virtue of explaining planetary paths more simply, through the use of elliptical orbits. The acceptance of one explanation over another on the basis of simplicity essentially involves the use of aesthetic considerations rather than purely scientific ones. But we are not substituting aesthetics for science: we would not accept a simple explanation which explained little over a more complicated one which explained many more phenomena. Aesthetics is brought in to aid, not displace, scientific considerations. Another criterion for determining which of two valid explanations of a phenomenon should be accepted is that of extendability of theory. Will an explanation help us to fit a phenomenon into a pattern we already know about with regard to other phenomena? Does it take us toward a multiplicity of separate sets of explanations or toward a single, more general one? Certainly experience in political science should warn us that we can stretch too far toward one grand theory, thus forcing our explanations unnecessarily. However, keeping this warning in mind, we can still accept explanations which help unify science rather than divide it.

Intuition as well as aesthetics may be involved in determining acceptable explanations within political science. While the most "scientific" of political scientists tend to reject intuition and *Verstehen* (understanding) out of hand, others argue that they have their proper place. One philosopher of science has even argued that "if we should demand of an adequate [scientific] method that it employ no intuitions in any form, then science could never make any progress in its search for truth." [21] While intuition and *Verstehen* should not be used as substitutes for empirical work in data collection, they can, particularly if "educated" or "informed" on the basis of long exposure to a particular research problem, provide a "grasp" of a problem not available from tests of hypotheses alone. Both assist science without being either scientific or anti-scientific, primarily by helping generate hypotheses and by telling us when a satisfactory explanation has been obtained—something which is said to occur when one's mind has come to rest. If *Verstehen* leads us to believe an explanation is inadequate, it does not provide us with new data: the scientific method must do that.

Theory.   Scientists are looking not simply for isolated, discrete explanations, but ultimately for related sets of explanations which can be called theory. In connection with the development of theory, arguments have raged as to whether science is inductive, moving from data to generalizations, or deductive, moving from generalizations to data. To some extent this is a false argument, as both induction and deduction are used in science. The scientist dealing with the empirical world does not simply collect "raw" facts and put them together into generalizations, nor do "facts" arrange themselves. A scientist often knows what "facts" he is looking for, before he looks; he has begun to work from pre-existing theories or generalizations, or at least with categories or concepts. Because some process of fact selection generally exists in scientific work, even basic data-collection, which we often tend to think of as the basis for induction, involves deduction. And deduction from tentative generalizations called hypotheses to data-collection will often proceed from generalizations established in part by inductive means. Thus, "theorizing is an integral part of empirical investigation, just as empirical analysis has meaning only by reference to a theory from which it is generated." [22] It is this orientation toward theory which, according to some, distinguishes the social science researcher from the mere observer, who only answers isolated questions. Asking questions is important but it is only a first step; relating those questions to some larger theory is also necessary in the scientific endeavor.

Mathematics.   A word about the relationship between mathematics and science ought to be injected into our discussion of theory. Some of the more "elegant" (again a word from aesthetics) scientific theories have been cast into mathematical form. From this and the heavy use of mathematics by physicists has developed the idea that science necessarily involves mathematical formulae, with the corollary that theories are not acceptable if not expressed in mathematical language. Mathematical language is most helpful in preserv-

[21] Churchman, p. 73.
[22] Robert Dubin, *Theory Building* (New York, 1969), p. 7.

ing the sharpness of our reasoning. Translation of verbal statements into mathematical statements can often help to resolve the ambiguity of the former, and they fit in well with our desire for theories simply expressed, particularly when we consider the difficulties which "normal" language can create because of its ambiguity. As Snyder has noted, "there is nothing like a cold shower of mathematical symbolization to sober up the imprecise words and phrases that stagger from one meaning to another."[23] In some instances, we can move from regular words to mathematical symbols, we can reason using the symbols, and we can re-translate to words more precisely than if we had used the words throughout. But mathematical statements by themselves are formal: they tell us nothing about content or substance. And they are not to be taken as substitutes for examination of data, which they do not produce. Because some scholars tend to over-mathematize their work, it should be pointed out that the amount of generalization and the degree of quantification in the field must be evaluated in terms of the amount and type of data available; they are not absolute measures of scientific progress, although quantification is important in developing scientific data, allowing us to make clear statements about large quantities of data or about relationships between groups of data quite simply.

Experimentation. Experimentation for many has come to represent the true test of science. One cannot establish true scientific facts, it is said, unless one can experiment; otherwise, one cannot control the impact of extraneous factors, and relationships found may well be spurious or meaningless. Lest we over-rate the importance of experimentation in science, we must remember that parts of the physical sciences, for example, geology and particularly astronomy, cannot proceed on the basis of controlled experiment, yet are clearly considered central parts of science. In effect, experiments are conducted for the astronomer and geologist by "Providence," and, even absent experimentation, these fields rely on observation as the basis for the findings which are reported by their practitioners. In other situations, controlled experiments may assist in the production of basic generalizations, but so many extraneous factors which occur in the "real world" may have to be removed for the purposes of the experiment that the latter gives us only a rough guide to what actually happens naturally. This is particularly true with respect to laboratory experiments in the social sciences, for example, with small groups.

While experimentation is an extremely important part of science, study can remain scientific even in the absence of experimentation. While it would be desirable to be able to test our tentative conclusions about the operation of the world of politics, we must recognize that, at least in democratic societies, we are not going to be able to try certain practices unless they are accepted for other than scientific considerations, that is, because they are politically acceptable. As Kingsley Davis notes, "social science gets tangled up

[23] Richard C. Snyder, "Game Theory and the Analysis of Political Behavior," *Research Frontiers in Politics and Government*, ed. Stephen K. Bailey (Washington, D.C., 1955), p. 88.

with the control mechanisms of a society." [24] The results of the experiments which might be allowed could be confused by people who attempt to have them come out the way they want to see the results. While we can adopt the position of John Dewey and view as experiments policies which are adopted,[25] we must recognize that this method is the reverse of having our experimental approaches adopted as policies so that we may watch how they work.

What Is Significant?   While one might use the criterion of experimentability as a basis for determining what to study, we need to examine other criteria by which it may be determined what is significant for science to deal with. That we need some criteria if we wish to develop political science to its fullest capacity is clear, and scientific method alone cannot provide us with the answers. Political science does not have a paradigm, "a common set of beliefs, constituting a kind of open-ended model that more or less explicitly defines the legitimate problems and methods of a research field," [26] which can provide the answer. Other sources, including genius and luck, must be used. The age of a problem may be an indication of its significance, but it may also indicate that the question has been considered to be so trivial by so many that it has been ignored. Each field also will tend to have problems considered "insoluble" at a given point in time; a number of these will be considered significant ones on which to work.

The consensus existing among scholars at a particular time as to the relative importance of general areas of study also provides guidelines. At the present time, many consider the building of theory more significant than adding discrete, unrelated generalizations to our storehouse of information. Exploring previously unexamined fields is considered a worthwhile endeavor, although initial findings are often limited and apparently unrelated to extant materials. Matters of popular concern are often considered significant for study, as in the "policy science" view of political science. Thus, what is useful for practice (or what is in principle subject to control) as well as what is worth knowing intellectually may be criteria of what should be studied. In some areas, of which political science may possibly be one, they will be closely related, but the distinction is nonetheless important. Moreover, "what is useful for practice" brings us to technology, which is clearly not the same thing as science, even though science frequently leads to it. Another important criterion for judging the areas with which political scientists should concern themselves is the staying power of the work we do. In short, will our writings be of interest only to the historian of political science or will they excite working political scientists of a future day? It is difficult, of course, for someone to judge in advance what will be acceptable to those who follow after him, but

[24] Testimony, June 2, 1967, "National Foundation for Social Sciences," *Hearings*, Subcommittee on Government Research, Committee on Government Operations, United States Senate (Washington, D.C., 1967), p. 267.

[25] John Dewey, *The Public and Its Problems* (New York, 1927).

[26] David B. Truman, "Disillusion and Regeneration: The Quest for a Discipline," *American Political Science Review*, LIX (1965), 865.

he can attempt to select problems which seem to have more than passing interest, or at least to cast his work in such a form that momentary concerns are made secondary.

Physical and Social Sciences. A discussion of the "science" in political science would be incomplete without mention of the differences between the physical sciences and the social sciences, although the differences are often overdrawn and the two areas tend to blur at their boundaries. Even if it is recognized that the precision, completeness, and fixed nature of the physical sciences have been over-estimated, there is still no question that they are more precise, complete, and fixed than the "soft" or behavioral sciences. A major reason the latter are "soft" is that human beings, the subject-matter of the latter, have the ability to think, to calculate, and to prefer. The human can act in a manner directly contrary to the findings made by social scientists if he wants to or if he is feeling perverse ("They can't tell *me* how I'm supposed to act!"). He can attempt to influence the generalizations made by social scientists, by behaving in a certain way when studied or by giving interviewers answers he wants them to have (or which he thinks they want). Even if he is not acting perversely, the results of our studies, fed into the stream of everyday knowledge, have their effect on behavior, and thus, in turn, on the findings of new studies. And, if an experiment is involved, the subject may know it is such and behave differently from the way he would in a "normal" situation.

Man also can readily adapt himself to changing situations. As there is a vast multitude of situations in which the human may find himself, to generalize his behavior becomes difficult. As society becomes increasingly complex, human beings combine and recombine in endless ways. The difficulty of explaining and predicting the behavior of individuals is increased many-fold because the interaction of the researcher with those studied may easily affect the latter's behavior. Rocks are much more obliging to those who study them in the constancy of their behavior, even when we recognize that physical substances can be affected and changed by the very process of being studied, and that the measuring instruments, even in physics, are themselves subject to the laws of physics. And rocks cannot object to being studied, as people can, or pass laws limiting access to certain types of data. Isolating individuals for study is usually extremely difficult, and, even if one could isolate them, the resultant studies would help explain only a portion of their behavior. While man in isolation may be difficult to study, he is still more difficult to describe and explain accurately in large aggregates, particularly those with which the political scientist is often concerned, and humans, either individually or in groups, are not easily subject to experimentation.

There are those who argue that political science, like the social sciences generally, differs from the natural sciences in the quality of the statements which it can produce. They say that unless we accept some statements as scientific which would not be accepted in the physical sciences, we will have to discard much of our study as non- or even un-scientific. In this connection, some assert that social science is basically internal, in that it can result ultimately only from the researcher's understanding of what the human being does because of a thought-process in some respect shared by the studied and the student, while physical science is external. But this distinction, like others drawn between the physical and social sciences, can easily be overworked; the differences tend to be differences in degree. Evidence in the social sciences may not be "available in near-identical form to all observers" because humans have collected it, e.g., through interviews, and therefore it cannot be reported with total precision. However, there is an "ample opportunity to judge whether [our] evidence supports [our] findings," and to "test . . . findings by further studies as nearly identical . . . as may be possible," if we have given empirical evidence the highest weight possible,[27] increasing the external character of the social sciences.

Perhaps the largest single area of controversy concerning the scientific status of the social sciences, and their differences from the physical sciences, revolves around values. Argument exists as to whether values can be studied, although there are entire "sciences" which study nothing but norms and values, e.g., ethics and jurisprudence. Argument also exists as to whether their presence does not invalidate possible generalizations about human behavior. And argument further exists as to whether the scientist can ever study society or politics or economics, in all of which he himself participates, without his values interfering so much that his findings cease to have scientific validity in even a loose sense of the term. Many political scientists now feel that values, like ideas and attitudes which derive from them, are subject to study as data of a scientific study of society or politics, but, at the same time, they make that study more difficult, because they are a part of the scientist's intellectual and emotional apparatus. Because values are crucial to politics, and are its motivating and lubricating force, they are crucial to a study of politics. Without them, politics might be simpler to study but would not exist as we know it.

FACT AND VALUE

Introduction. Discussions of science, particularly with respect to the social sciences, require an examination of the distinction between fact and value. This examination is particularly necessary because of the centrality of values in politics and because of the frequent confusion between statements of fact and statements of value by those who write about politics. Those who argue that these types of statements are different and should be kept separate say that the former are scientific, the latter, non- or un-scientific. Science, it is claimed, is value-free. Metaphysicians may deal with values, but scientists may not, unless they treat the values as facts. However, to treat values as facts is not to suggest that no difference exists between factual statements

[27] Hyneman, pp. 76–79.

and statements of preference. (A third type of statement, the logical statement, which depends upon form only, should also be recognized.)

Types of Statements. Statements which allege to describe what is actually happening (*empirical* statements) are not always true, but they are verifiable and their accuracy can be tested. This is not possible with statements of preference (*normative* statements). The most that can be done with normative statements is to ascertain whether someone has actually made such a statement—a factual matter—or to determine how many people agree with the preference. A student should learn to distinguish between statements which describe and those which state a preference, because in common discourse people frequently treat what they wish to be true as if it existed, while others act as if what is, should be. Sometimes normative statements can be easily recognized because of the word "should" or "ought," such as "People should vote in every election." Or, "You ought to know the program for which the candidate stands." However, not every "ought" or "should" statement is a normative one. If put in conditional terms, the statement may be empirical (although it is sometimes called "prescriptive" or "tactical"). For example, "If democracy is to survive, people should vote in every election." Or, "For the people to hold their officials responsible for their actions, they ought to know the program for which the candidate stands." Both of these statements contain "should" or "ought," but the truth of both can be examined; they are verifiable statements. That both contain premises which are implied value-judgments ("democracy should survive" in the first, and "people should hold their officials responsible" in the second) does not change their status.

Prescriptive or tactical statements involve the idea that once someone has said where he wants to go, the scientist can tell him how he can get there. Here the scientist is not dealing directly with goals and values, but only with the (technical) means to assure complete performance or satisfaction of a certain goal. However, in Western culture, some means are themselves considered to involve values, thus complicating our neat distinction. To the extent a value-judgment rests on a factual base, science can assist by strengthening that base. The meaning of value proposals can also be clarified, and practical implications of the proposal can be analyzed. Demonstration might also be made that certain purposes are impossible to attain.

To adopt the current position that we should restrict our work to the empirical is not to say that political scientists have not written normative works. Political philosophers as far back as Plato undertook the task of indicating what the Good Society ought to be, both in broad outline and in detailed particulars, although emphasis on the empirical can also be found in ancient Greece in some of Aristotle's work. In fact, political philosophy in earlier times in effect was political science. Sometimes this philosophical writing took the form of utopias, which have provided a standard by which to judge existing situations; more frequently in modern times it has involved criticism of the existing order from the point of view of an implicit ideal system. Such idealist criticism is valuable in reminding us that even though we are under-taking the study of what is, we should not become so preoccupied wth real-ity that we forget that there are many differing conceptions of what should be. There are some who feel that behavioral research can produce values, based on what most people in fact do, but this position is definitely not widely accepted.

Values and the Study of Politics.   A balanced view of the proper place for values in political science requires recognition that they affect the study of politics. Although we can never completely succeed, our concern is to at-tempt to keep values to one side, rather than to eliminate them completely. The researcher must be aware of the various values held by those he is study-ing, and of the possible impact of those values on their behavior. Thus what we are interested in is not value rejection but value neutralization, a sensitiv-ity to, rather than ignoring of, values. This means that we must confront the values. Most social scientists would agree the value problem has to be faced, although not all would agree to state their own "value premises" or biases. They do agree that an effort must be made, during research, to keep values from interfering with the collection of data and its interpretation. Even if in-terpretation of findings is affected by one's own values, the presentation of findings to one's colleagues, an accepted part of the research process, makes them available to scrutiny and criticism and open to different interpretation by others.

Even if these efforts are successful, political scientists will find their values guiding them in the choice of what they study. For example, a child-hood in lower-class economic surroundings may have produced a concern about the community's elite which had what the lower class did not and which seemed to keep the "have-nots" from getting it. This concern might very well draw a social scientist to the study of what we now refer to as "com-munity power structure." [28] Because there is no single agreed-upon criterion of what is significant as an object of study, the political scientist is frequently thrown back upon his own interests in his choice of topics, and his choice of significant variables to examine within the topics. He is not completely on his own, because training will have exposed him to certain problems and he will have come to consider a number of subjects as extraneous or irrelevant to his work. But within those minimal boundaries, he relies on his own interests. (The availability of money from various foundations or government agencies for research on certain subjects may, however, pull some away from their closest interests.)

In arguing that personal interests, when they guide choice of topics for study, contaminate our research, critics ignore both the impact of profes-sional training and an important aspect of "human nature." They seem to

---

[28] An interesting account of personal reasons for involvement in research is Maurice R. Stein, "The Eclipse of Community: Some Glances at the Education of a Sociologist," *Reflections on Community Studies*, ed. Arthur Vidich, Joseph Bensman, and Maurice R. Stein (New York, 1964), pp. 207–208.

expect scholars to do their best work on subjects in which they have little interest. Students will have no trouble recognizing they are more likely to do a better job with something in which they are interested. Professional political scientists can and do perform well even tasks they do not enjoy, and they may generate interest by thinking that what they are doing is important. However, if a wide range of topics remains unexplored, political scientists would object to being forced to ignore topics of personal interest to them. (This is particularly true because of the extremely unregimented character of the discipline.)

That we cannot put our preferences completely to one side in choosing what to study leads to the criticism that the distinction between fact and value is completely contrary to our personal experience. Undoubtedly many people have not tried to separate the two or see no useful purpose in doing so, nor in developing theories not immediately directed to the attainment of some set of values. While keeping "professional man" and "personal man" separate is harder than writing about the fact/value distinction, this criticism ignores the possibility that an individual can differentiate between the various roles he is expected to perform; in the role of political scientist-scholar, he may be expected to be neutral, while in the role of the citizen, the expectation may be one of active participation and the adoption of preferences. However, the researcher will have to be quite conscious of his own values in order to be able to put them to one side.

Values and Teaching. Teaching is the area in which political scientists have been most concerned about what to do with their values. Political science has been viewed as a "recognized profession of secular preaching," [29] and students often come to courses expecting (although not necessarily wanting) to hear preaching. However, there has been a reaction in most quarters, but particularly among more recent generations of political scientists, against such behavior as open campaigning at election time.

There is no question that a professor, however he defines his role, will have some impact. If he decides in advance to remain completely neutral with regard to values, this neutrality may promote indifference toward those values on the part of his students. If students ask questions demanding value-laden answers, and the professor puts them off, the students may draw conclusions of their own about the professor's position, so that refusal to deal with the questions does not eliminate the teacher's impact on values. An impact of another sort is caused by the professor who teaches well. He will undoubtedly interest his students in his subject-matter, and thus bring them to examine politics more closely, regardless of his intention. His selection of certain problems or issues for study, even if they are studied objectively, is also likely to reveal some of the professor's preferences.

The professor, knowing that he will have some impact, may try as hard as he can to achieve one. Although some students do grow and change politi-

[29] Leiserson, p. 69.

cally during college, the professor may find indoctrination futile in most cases. By the time students reach college their political party preference is generally established and orientations toward business and politics are becoming firm. Specific opinions on current issues undoubtedly are more open to influence, but the amount which could be accomplished in this direction in the few hours a professor comes in contact with a student in class, particularly in a large lecture situation, leaves little chance to bring about major change.

There are studies, most notably Newcomb's Bennington study, which indicate a general movement from conservative to liberal in a student's political views during college.[30] These results are all too frequently attributed to "liberal" (or worse) college professors, particularly those in political science (who are, in fact, Democrats by a large margin, and usually liberal). These results are more likely to stem from the student's independence of his parents and related factors than from explicit political indoctrination. Particularly where students' rights are being fought for by students, the "student atmosphere" is likely to have a greater impact on the students' values, political and others, than is the teaching they receive in the classroom.

Values in Facts?   Those who find the distinction between factual statements and value statements hardest to accept are those who see a valuation inside every fact. What is a fact to one person is, or indicates, a recommendation to someone else. Segregation is an example. A social scientist not previously knowing anything about the subject might observe that those with light ("white") skin color and those with dark ("black") skin color do not eat together and otherwise mingle socially; that in some areas of the country, they attend school together only when men in black robes (judges) order them to, if not prevented by men in white sheets (the KKK); and that in most areas of the country, they live in separate parts of the same community. This objective description, when given the label "segregation," often indicates to many citizens a desired state of affairs, the "separation of the races," to be reinforced through force if not law, and to others it indicates "racial discrimination," implying suppression of those of dark skin, a situation to be eliminated through law and such other methods as economic boycott. Neither program of action is inherent in the description; the need for preserving the arrangement or changing it is in the eyes of the beholder. At another level, the explanations developed by political scientists may appear to contain implications for certain value positions. For example, those who indicate that

[30] Theodore Newcomb, *Personality and Social Change* (New York, 1943). Newcomb's study was done at a small, private liberal arts college with high tuition charges. The students at the beginning of their college years were almost all from Republican families. They could hardly move in any other direction politically than toward being Democrats. A follow-up study by Newcomb showed a number of girls who had turned liberal during college reverting to more conservative views after graduation. "Persistence and Regression of Changed Attitudes: Long-Range Studies," *Journal of Social Issues*, XIX (1963), 3–14. If college teaching were responsible for the pro-liberalism shift during college, its results were not long-lasting, at least in the face of pulls in the opposite direction.

the average citizen, lacking political interest and knowledge, is not a strong foundation for democracy seem to some to imply that an elite should take over the political system. However, here again the implication is "read into" the finding, not "in" it.

That the political scientist has not allowed his values to contaminate his scientific study does not mean he is amoral. This is true despite claims that the relativism of value neutrality has left political science sterile, unable to defend the world against evil forces, and subject to use for nefarious schemes and totalitarian purposes, such as making it easier for rulers to manipulate those over whom they rule, thus assuring their perpetuation in office. Political relativism developed during a period, around the turn of the twentieth century, when there was a general agreement on basic values, but its impact supposedly was not clear until the growth of Fascism, Bolshevism, and Nazism around 1920. The inability "morally to condemn [these 'isms'] in unconditional terms is . . . the tragedy of twentieth-century political science, a tragedy as deep as any that has ever occurred before in this history of science," according to Arnold Brecht.[31] We are also told that a conservative bias exists in political science simply because we have adopted the fact-value distinction: by describing what is, we are allegedly saying that what is, is correct. Statements that certain activities contribute to the stability of political arrangements are supposed to be comments that the activity is "good." And, by being preoccupied with "reality," we are alleged to have less time to deal with the gap separating the real from the ideal.

These arguments and their corollary that political scientists without values might sell information to the highest bidder are based on a misreading of social scientists' intent and a refusal to accept the possibility of an objective social science. Statements of what is do not necessarily imply any particular value-position. If we adopt the position that science is "public," which it must be if scientific advance of any major sort is to occur, then we do have a risk that data will, from the point of view of citizens, be misused. The fact-value distinction is a scientific canon; the purpose of the value-free stance is to safeguard political science from ideological infiltration. If this scientific canon should, however, be transmuted into a personal ideology by the scientist, in which the individual completely surrenders any judgment over the uses to which he and his skills or information is put or in which he does not speak out in defense of his values, then he definitely may find himself morally implicated in the uses to which the material is put.

Advocates of the distinction between descriptive and normative statements are also accused of adopting science as a value, and rejecting other values, instead of placing all values to one side. They are also accused of making science their Utopia. Science does rest on certain basic, unprovable assumptions. If one chooses to call these values, then science is a value. How-

[31] Arnold Brecht, *Political Theory: The Foundations of Twentieth-Century Political Thought* (Princeton, N.J., 1959), p. 8. See also, by the same author, "Beyond Relativism in Political Theory," *American Political Science Review*, XLI (1947), 470–488.

ever, we agree with the philosophers who hold that "truth is not a value in the same sense as are the values at the basis of political activity, such as . . . individual freedom or economic security." [32] One can distinguish truth and objectivity as instrumental values, helping in the task of discovery, from substantive values, which are particular life-goals being sought.

Even if one accepts the idea that, for analytical purposes at least, definitional or logical statements, descriptive statements, and normative statements should be kept separate, he must recognize the difficulty of achieving the distinction in practice. As David Butler has stated, "Although the aim of every academic writer on politics should be a detached search for the truth, *objectivity is only a goal that can be striven for; it is not one that can be achieved.*" [33] In the way we actually write, the difference between detachment and involvement may be very small. However, it is not unreasonable to argue that we should exercise care in trying to remain detached as scientists, even if we are involved as citizens.

BIBLIOGRAPHY

Political Science

Discussions of political science, its boundaries, limitations, and future, abound. As political science can be defined in terms of what political scientists do, historical surveys and surveys of what they are doing (like the UNESCO and Robson works) become relevant. Discussions, like the volumes by Dahl, Hacker, and Meehan, of how to analyze politics also help provide definitions of political science. Others concentrate on the emphasis or outputs of the discipline; for example, Easton urges that we move away from historicism and toward theory-building. Attacks on current developments in approach and urgings that we hold fast to old ways, for example, the Vogelin volume, parts of Crick's argument, and the Moore article, help make clear by way of contrast what the discipline contains, as do complaints about shifts in subject-matter, like Cobban's article. The ruminations of Presidents of the American Political Science Association, two of which, by Redford and Truman, are noted, often deal with the content of political science. Eulau's article is a survey of approaches in the discipline; Young's collection has the same purpose.

BAILEY, STEPHEN K., ed. *Research Frontiers in Politics and Government.* Washington, D.C., 1955.

BUTLER, D. E. *The Study of Political Behaviour.* London, 1958.

CHARLESWORTH, JAMES, ed. *A Design for Political Science: Scope, Objectives, and Methods.* Philadelphia, 1966.

COBBAN, ALFRED. "The Decline of Political Theory." *Political Science Quarterly,* XLVIII (1953), 321–337.

CRICK, BERNARD. *The American Science of Politics: Its Origins and Conditions.* Berkeley, 1959.

[32] Hans Kelsen, "Science and Politics," *American Political Science Review,* XLV (1951), 642.

[33] D. E. Butler, *The Study of Political Behaviour* (London, 1958), p. 25. Emphasis supplied.

DAHL, ROBERT A. *Modern Political Analysis.* Englewood Cliffs, 1963.

——. "The Science of Politics: New and Old." *World Politics,* VII (1955), 479–489.

DE JOUVENEL, BERTRAND. "On the Nature of Political Science." *American Political Science Review,* LV (1961), 773–779.

EASTON, DAVID. *The Political System: An Inquiry Into the State of Political Science.* New York, 1953.

EULAU, HEINZ. "Political Science." *A Reader's Guide to the Social Sciences,* ed. Bert F. Hoselitz. New York, 1959. Pages 89–127.

HACKER, ANDREW. *The Study of Politics.* New York, 1963.

HANDY, ROLLO, and PAUL KURTZ. *A Current Appraisal of the Behavioral Sciences.* Great Barrington, Mass., 1964. Chapter V, "Political Science," pp. 57–68.

HYNEMAN, CHARLES S. *The Study of Politics: The Present State of American Political Science.* Urbana, 1959.

LASSWELL, HAROLD D. *The Future of Political Science.* New York, 1963.

MEEHAN, EUGENE. *The Theory and Method of Political Analysis.* Homewood, Ill., 1965.

MOORE, BARRINGTON. "The New Scholasticism and the Study of Politics." *World Politics,* VI (1953), 122–138.

REDFORD, EMMETTE S. "Reflections on a Discipline." *American Political Science Review,* LX (1961), 755–762.

ROBSON, WILLIAM A. *The University Teaching of Social Sciences: Political Science.* Paris, 1954.

SORAUF, FRANK J. *Perspectives on Political Science.* Columbus, 1965.

——. *Political Science: An Informal Overview.* Columbus, 1965.

TRUMAN, DAVID. "Disillusion and Regeneration: The Quest for a Discipline." *American Political Science Review,* LIX (1965), 865–873.

UNESCO. *Contemporary Political Science: A Survey of Methods, Research and Teaching.* Paris, 1950.

VAN DYKE, VERNON. *Political Science: A Philosophical Analysis.* Stanford, 1960.

VOGELIN, ERIC. *The New Science of Politics: An Introduction.* Chicago, 1952.

YOUNG, ROLAND, ed. *Approaches to the Study of Politics.* Evanston, 1958.

Science

Partial answers to the question, "What is Science?", are provided in some of the books listed above. Of most help will be the volumes by Easton, Meehan, and Van Dyke. Of the books listed below, those by Kaplan, Gibson, and Nathanson are most directly concerned with the scientific method in the social sciences. The Kaplan volume has become the "Bible" of many social scientists on this matter. Examination of the Campbell, Bridgman, and Eddington books, although not new, will give the student a better grasp of the philosophy underlying the physical sciences. The Churchman volume and the collection of readings edited by Feigl and Brodbeck, as well as the older classic by Cohen and Nagel, deal with philosophy of science in a broad sense. The Myrdal selections are an important separate contribution to the discussion of the fact/value problem in the social sciences. A number of the volumes are available in recent paperback editions.

BRIDGMAN, P. W. *The Nature of Physical Theory.* Princeton, 1936.

CAMPBELL, NORMAN. *What Is Science?* New York, 1952 [1921].

CHURCHMAN, C. WEST. *The Theory of Experimental Inference.* New York, 1948.

COHEN, MORRIS, and ERNEST NAGEL. *An Introduction to Logic and Scientific Method.* New York, 1934.

EDDINGTON, A. S. *The Nature of the Physical World.* New York, 1928.

FEIGL, HERBERT, and MAY BRODBECK, eds. *Readings in the Philosophy of Science.* New York, 1953.

GIBSON, QUENTIN. *The Logic of Social Inquiry.* London, 1966.

KAPLAN, ABRAHAM. *The Conduct of Inquiry.* San Francisco, 1964.

MYRDAL, GUNNAR. *An American Dilemma: The Negro Problem and Modern Democracy.* New York, 1944. "A Methodological Note on Facts and Valuations in Social Science," pp. 1035–1064, and "A Methodological Note on Valuations and Beliefs," pp. 1027–1034.

NATHANSON, MAURICE. *The Philosophy of the Social Sciences.* New York, 1963.

2 / APPROACHES TO THE STUDY OF POLITICAL SCIENCE

Normative and Empirical / Philosophical, Institutional and
Behavioral / The Study of Democracy:
Several Approaches

Political science, we noted earlier, is not distinguishable by its methods. Its approaches are also not a distinguishing feature. At any point in the recent history of political science, the existence of at least several approaches has been noticeable. While different approaches have from time to time seemed to be predominant, their time has also passed as some other way of going about the study of politics has come to the fore. As the difference between the approaches has been significant, and the heat generated by partisans of each way battling to prove the supreme virtues of their approach has been great, we need to examine the approaches and then see how they might be applied.

It is possible to categorize approaches to the study of politics in several ways, although our attention will be devoted mainly to two. One, based on stances taken toward the fact-value problem, is a division into a normative approach, on the one hand, and the empirical and analytical approaches, on the other. The other is based on the objects of study which the scholar prefers to emphasize. Within political science, this produces a three-fold division: the philosophical and ideological approaches, the institutional and structural approaches, and the behavioral approach.

The methods used in studies might serve to structure another classification. One could thus talk about legal, historical, and scientific approaches. In political science, an overlap has existed between the legal and historical approaches and the institutional approach, and the historical approach has also been used with regard to philosophical materials. The scientific approach has closely overlapped the behavioral approach. Approaches to the phenomena of politics might also be labelled in terms of other disciplines from which particular methods of study are borrowed, or from which emphasis on specific aspects of politics is taken. (See pp. 87–95.) One could also apply labels based on the age of a particular approach and its predominance in the field. In these terms, the label "traditional" has been attached to almost all the approaches except the behavioral and scientific, which have come to be synonymous with "recent" and, to some extent, "revolutionary."

NORMATIVE AND EMPIRICAL

The distinction between normative and empirical statements has already been developed in Chapter 1, and it has been noted that much early writing on politics was normative in character. Even when writers claimed to be describing "human nature," they were often dealing with transcendent ideals embodying their different views of what should be. Theorists writing from this point of view have been displaced from the center of the discipline, as the weight of the discipline has shifted from the normative to the empirical approach; however, they are not extinct. They are, in fact, very much alive—and vocal. Perhaps their principal representative at the present time is Leo Strauss, and he and a number of his students from his days at the University of Chicago present their position forcefully. Normative criticisms of existing states of affairs are certainly not dead, being produced in great volume, as are proposals for political action. To the extent the latter are explicitly based on a well-developed philosophy, rather than produced from unarticulated assumptions, they are properly classified as political *doctrine*.

One reason that the normative approach has not been completely displaced is that the normative and empirical traditions of thought have ignored each other; advocates of each have found something important on their own, without feeling it necessary to eliminate the other side. Many political scientists also realize that both approaches can be useful in daily life, even if they do not think both have an equal place within political science.

The lessened role of normative work in the discipline came about in part when contemporary science destroyed some of the assumptions which served as props to the Natural Law theory which undergirded much of normative

> **Natural Law.**   A body of transcendental, permanent principles which can be discovered by "right reason" and which is supposed to govern man's activities; for those who believe in Natural Law, man-made ("positive") law is proper only to the extent it is based on Natural Law. Natural Law should be distinguished from the "laws of nature," that is, rules indicating the actual behavior of the universe and its elements.

writing. For example, the discovery that the universe is moving toward increasing randomness contradicted the Natural Law philosopher's presumption of a fixed fundamental order. These scientific findings did not by themselves bring about the downfall of normative political philosophy; they merely helped to put in proper perspective an approach which had earlier begun to lose intellectual stature as a result of other shifts in philosophical outlook, such as the emphasis of Dialectical Materialism on the dynamic rather than the static in the world.

> **Dialectical Materialism.**   Marx's combination of the Hegelian dialectic, meant to explain the development of ideas, with material (social and economic) factors. In the dialectic, one position (the thesis) results in the for-

mation of its opposite (the antithesis) and the combination of the two results in a third position (the synthesis). For Marx, the bourgeoisie (owners of the means of production) represented the thesis, the proletariat the antithesis, and the classless society the synthesis.

Although the empirical approach has to a large extent superseded the normative, political science is not without its philosophizing, but with the normative aspect removed. There has been an increasing integration of theorizing and research through the development of what has come to be called "modern empirical theory." It is distinguished from the older utopia-developing political philosophy by its attempt to develop a set of interrelated value-free statements descriptive and explanatory of common properties of human behavior. On the surface, writers of the philosophy of old and philosophers of the modern empirical school may seem quite similar in their attempts to describe human behavior. However, each builds on a different set of assumptions about the procedures for developing such descriptions and on a different degree of consciousness about the possible impact of values on such description. It should be noted that some empirical theorists do not restrict themselves to contemporary work, but in addition are willing to attempt to develop their theory from classical works, such as those of Aristotle. However, the questions they ask of this older material and the manner in which they ask it are not the same as those employed by the political philosophers.

The intimate relationship between theorizing and research can also be shown by the connection between facts and theory. Much early empiricism was largely a collection of facts, perhaps based on the hope that "facts speak for themselves." This approach has been entitled "brute" or "raw" or "barefoot" empiricism. It does not have a high standing among most leading political scientists. As we have noted, facts cannot be collected without theory and facts exist only as the result of a theory, however implicit it may be and however unaware the researcher may be of its existence in his mind. This being the case, it is argued that theory ought to be made explicit, and the consensus among empirically-oriented political scientists conducting research today is that empiricism ought to be enlightened by theory. The temptation to revel in vast masses of new data, including the raw data collected as a result of the continuing activities of the government, such as masses of voting statistics and information obtained by the U.S. Census Bureau, has to be resisted. In fact, attention to theory may be the only way to avoid being trapped by a mass of facts.

There was a time in the history of political science when it was possible to master the facts essential to the available level of understanding of political phenomena. But as in all other areas of life, the increasing specialization of labor in scientific inquiry has proceeded at such a pace that today the absorption of known facts has passed beyond the capacity of any individual or small group. The belated recognition of the function of theory is itself a response to what would otherwise be an impossible situation. It is a means of rescuing the study of political life from the need to be the master of all the facts that he might possibly wish to survey.[1]

Thus, in order for empiricists to carry out their work properly, they need to become involved in a variety of activities such as concept development prior to the gathering of data. This discussion should show that the empirical political scientist is a philosopher as well as a "fact-grubber," although not a philosopher in the same sense as the man who spins normative theories. This integration of fact and theory has led some to say that what has been called here the empirical approach to political science should be called the analytical approach. Regardless of the term used, the difference from the normative approach is quite clear.

PHILOSOPHICAL, INSTITUTIONAL AND BEHAVIORAL

Philosophical.   Probably the oldest approach to the study of politics is the philosophical. Defining philosophy as "the study or science of the truths or principles underlying all knowledge and being (or reality)," [2] we can see that the philosophical approach is not narrowly focused but takes in all aspects of man's political activities, and has as its goal a statement of underlying principles concerning those activities. For centuries, the interest in the actual political activities of man was principally derived from a desire to find out why he did not live up to the ideal postulated in Natural Law, or to postulate utopias such as Plato's *Republic,* Harrington's *Oceana,* Hobbes' *Leviathan,* and Butler's *Erewhon.* Other writers, like Locke in his *Treatise on Civil Government,* postulated the existence of "states of nature" which, if not uto-

> **State of Nature.   A time prior to the formation of government or before the formation of society. As a result of conditions in the state of nature, people supposedly come together to form a "social contract" providing the basis of the State and government. Whether writers meant to assert that a state of nature really existed is unclear.**

pias in the sense of what the writer preferred, were clearly intended to show an ideal in the sense of an abstract state of affairs portraying "pure" human nature.

While this type of exploration into general principles underlying the political activity of man has never ceased, it does not bulk large in the period covered by modern political science. For one thing, Americans, despite their adherence to what they think the most superior political philosophy in the world, democracy, have not been people highly oriented to abstract philosophy. The pragmatism of Americans also gets in the way of efforts at broad

---

[1] David Easton, *A Systems Analysis of Political Life* (New York, 1965), p. 471.
[2] *The American College Dictionary* (New York, 1948), pp. 910–911.

political philosophy. One can talk of "American political philosophy," but one is hard put to find source materials written solely as political philosophy, rather than for some contemporary partisan purpose. Perhaps John Calhoun's *Disquisitions on Government*, in which he developed the theory of the "concurrent majority," qualifies, but even that work stemmed in part

> **Concurrent Majority.**   **The idea that a numerical majority is made up of a series of minorities. Calhoun felt that each minority ought to approve a policy before it could be enacted.**

from Calhoun's dissatisfaction with the impact of national tariff policies on his home state of South Carolina. (A more recent example of home-grown political philosophy is Walter Lippmann's *The Public Philosophy*.)

Lest we overemphasize the origin in practical politics of the materials of American political philosophy, we must recognize the partisan involvement of many of the writers of the "Great Books" of older political philosophy. John Locke, it is claimed, wrote to justify the new middle class of England; Machiavelli wrote for a specific Prince; and Hobbes wrote to justify the monarchy of his day. Our distance in time from these philosophers may make us see their work only as philosophy and not as partisan argument, while our proximity in time to the writings of American politics, even at the founding of the Republic, may blind us to their timeless aspects.

To say contemporary political science does not produce much political philosophy of the classical type is not to say that much attention is not paid to political philosophy and to the recognized great works. A prime emphasis in the political science of America as well as other countries has been on political philosophy. However, works of political philosophy were (and are) not studied so that more political philosophy could be produced, but so that the ideas contained could be analyzed and the history of the writers' ideas traced, with the latter receiving more emphasis. While the use of historical method in political science is not limited to the subfield of political philosophy, it certainly has found one of its widest uses there. In fact, some writers claim that classic works of political philosophy, important because they "faced up to many important problems in ways which have never been bettered," have been used for nearly everything but the purpose for which they were written.[3] The "Great Books," according to Andrew Hacker, have been explained through a number of disparate approaches, historical and quasi-historical. These include "*Capital* and Carbuncles,"[4] basically biographies of a book's author; "Intellectual Plagiarism," or who was influenced by whom; "Who Said It First;" "Mind-Reader," or what the author *really* meant; "Camera-Eye," in which a book is used to give us a view of what was being thought about at the time it was written; "Influencing the Intelligent-

[3] Andrew Hacker, "*Capital* and Carbuncles: The 'Great Books' Reappraised," *American Political Science Review*, XLVIII (1954), 784.

[4] The allusion is to Marx' *Das Capital* and to the painful carbuncles from which Marx suffered and which may have influenced his outlook on life.

sia;" and "Influencing the Masses." As one can see from these titles, much of our present writing is a re-examination of what past writers have done. However, not all political philosophy of the present day is of this type, because philosophers are still attempting original work on political theory's traditional problems.

What has to some extent served to revive interest in political philosophy is a study of the political ideologies individuals hold. Ideologies deal with questions like "Who will be the rulers? How will the rulers be selected? By what principles will they govern?" They "embrace a program for the defense or reform or abolition of important social institutions" and are "normative, ethical, moral in tone and content." [5] The study of ideologies is by definition not restricted to the study of ideas alone, but encompasses their impact and interrelationships between ideas and political activity as well. A supposed lessening of the impact of ideology on the world, with a corresponding shift to other factors as motivators of men, has been forcefully argued by sociologist Daniel Bell in *The End of Ideology*. Zbigniew Brzezinski and Samuel Huntington, in *Political Power: USA/USSR*, also talk of the institutionalization of ideology in Russia and its static quality in the United States. Their arguments are correctives to a tendency among political scientists, because they constantly deal with ideas, to overestimate the impact of ideas on the behavior of individuals and the rationality of the average citizen's thought process, stressed in normative democratic philosophy (at least the high school civics variety), which states that the citizen should cast his vote on the basis of candidates' positions on issues, of which the citizen should be aware. The assumption that the pen (or the tongue) is mighty is easy for the social scientist to believe. Similarly, because the scientific thought process requires rationality, it is easy by extension to think that others think politically in the

> **Rationality.** Usually construed to mean an ability to think logically, to reason from certain premises to conclusions on the basis of facts supplied. It can also mean the ability to take action which will best suit an individual in terms of his goals; the action taken may not be decided upon logically. The former is sometimes called "formal rationality," the latter, "substantive rationality," a distinction made by Karl Mannheim, *Ideology and Utopia*.

same fashion. However, there are large numbers of people for whom ideas have little direct impact and who do not rationally figure out what their next political move should be. In many instances these individuals do not even have awareness of ideas. However, even individuals without an awareness of ideas do have an ideology or philosophy which a researcher can construct from responses to questions.

Institutional.   The second major focus of long standing embodies the institutional or structural approaches. While its roots extend back in time to

[5] Robert Lane, *Political Ideology: Why the American Common Man Believes What He Does* (New York, 1962), p. 15.

Aristotle's description and classification of the constitutions of Greek city-states, its place in the study of politics comes after the philosophical approach and it is still either *the* predominant approach to the contemporary study of politics or of equal rank with the much newer behavioral approach.

The emphasis of the institutional or structural approach is almost exclusively on the formal aspects of government and politics; it has been described by Somit and Tanenhaus as "a routine description and pedestrian analysis of formal political structures and processes, based on the more readily accessible official sources and records." [6] Attention ranges from constitutions and other basic documents on which government is supposed to rest, through the structure of legislatures, courts, and executive branches, to the rules by which political parties are run, registration and election laws, and the intricacies of different forms of municipal government. Institutionalists are not unaware that people must "inhabit" institutions if the institutions are to exist and function, but they emphasize the rules and structure, not the people. Individuals are, in effect, treated as undifferentiated, as constant units, and different effects which the rules might have on different individuals are not examined, on the grounds that the institution must be understood before its effect can be studied.

Concentration on objects of study like those just named means, at the same time, an emphasis on legal matters. At least government's metes and bounds have been established by law, and we have enshrined the slogan of a "government of laws, not men." There also has been an American tendency noted by deTocqueville (and perhaps characteristic of advanced stages of political development) [7] to turn all social and political issues into legal ones, giving greater emphasis to things legal.

Just as the legal and institutional approaches have been used in complementary fashion, the same has been true of the historical and the institutional. Historians interested in political phenomena, or political scientists with an institutional bent, have spent much time examining the origins and development of the United States Constitution, and its interpretation over the years by the Supreme Court. The history of our major political parties has also been written, as has administrative history. Despite their efforts at political history, historians have paid less attention to political institutions than they have to political ideas and have tended to include political matters in their general chronicles of past events rather than to give them special emphasis.

Attention to the structure of governments and political groups brought with it, on the whole, a shift away from the normative approach. Even those who continued to look for the best mechanisms with which to implement democracy moved away from the purely normative to a more empirically-directed search. Whether or not political scientists were involved in reform-

---

[6] Albert Somit and Joseph Tanenhaus, *The Development of American Political Science: From Burgess to Behavioralism* (Boston, 1967), p. 70.

[7] I am indebted to Joann Paine for this suggestion.

oriented study, that portion of Aristotle's approach dealing with data-collection and classification again came to the fore. And great attention was placed, in the Aristotelian style, on classifying types of governments. The empirical attitude of the institutionalists was not, however, one principally directed to theory-building. For them, data-collection and categorization, with greater stress on the former, was enough. The development of generalizations was not a principal concern, and was to come to full flower only with the behavioral approach. The shift from idealism to the detailed study of material forces, which characterized early empiricism, was also a shift from a naive utopianism to a naive cynicism, with political scientists suspicious of speculative theory.[8] Empiricism brought emphasis on law, organization, structure, and machinery where facts were easily available. The early empiricists' aversion to theory meant they produced description, not explanation: classification was supposed to make facts speak for themselves. This ostracism of theory meant that all facts were equal, and left no way to choose among them.

The task of political scientists in teaching served to entrench the institutional approach. Teachers of political science, even if they disagreed as to whether they should teach their students to be good citizens, seemed to take for granted that the students should understand the basic structure of the governmental system in which they were to take their place. Overemphasis on the American political system, and on comparable modern systems such as those of Western Europe, also reinforced the stress on institutions. When the student of political science undertook a comparative examination of several countries, his attention was likely to be directed to Great Britain, France, Germany, and perhaps Russia, all of which possessed well-developed formal government systems. In the process, political systems with less formal apparatus were neglected. Similarly, lessened attention to the activity of individuals within and outside formal government systems meant that such groups as political parties and interest groups came within the ambit of political science long after the study of legislatures, courts, and executive branches, and the study of voting behavior was taken up by political scientists only after the sociologists had started to explore it on their own. Other important aspects of politics relatively ignored by the institutionalists were international politics, because of the absence of formal institutions, and violence, taken to be the denial of politics despite its relevance to on-going governments.

Just as a dissatisfaction with an overconcentration on the philosophical approach to the study of politics had, along with other factors, brought a shift toward the study of institutions and formal structures, with an accompanying move from normative to empirical outlooks, so there was increasing realization that the institutional approach did not encompass all of the world of politics. Scholars began to recognize problems in the use of the "State" con-

[8] Sigmund Neumann, "Comparative Politics: A Half-Century Appraisal," *Journal of Politics*, XIX (1957), 377.

cept. Other basic emphases were also questioned. Because not all rules or structures have been reduced to law, the legal approach to politics and the institutional approach had never completely coalesced. Political scientists of an institutional bent, freed from the European location of political science within Faculties of Law, recognized that there is much material within political science not subject to legal examination. This helped bring about the development of new approaches, including an emphasis on the *process* of politics (with particular attention to interest groups) which served as a transitional focus between the institutional approach and the behavioral approach, the field's most recent.

Behavioral.   The behavioral approach came on the scene amid a large amount of turmoil and controversy within the profession, now somewhat reduced but not totally subsided. Evron Kirkpatrick, the Executive Director of the American Political Science Association, has pictured the scene well:

> Between World War II and the mid-fifties, the term political behavior represented both an approach and a challenge, an orientation and a reform movement, a type of research and a rallying cry, a "hurrah" term and a "boo" term. Debate about behavioral techniques and methods was often accompanied by vituperation; discussions were more often aimed at vanquishing adversaries than at clarifying issues.[9]

According to some early behavioralists, the political behavior approach:

> 1. . . . . specifies as the unit or object of both theoretical and empirical analysis the behavior of persons and social groups rather than events, structures, institutions, or ideologies. . . .
>
> 2. It seeks to place theory and research in a frame of reference common to that of social psychology, sociology, and cultural anthropology. . . .
>
> 3. It stresses the mutual interdependence of theory and research. Theoretical questions need to be stated in operational terms for purposes of empirical research. And, in turn, empirical findings should have a bearing on the development of political theory. . . .
>
> 4. It tries to develop rigorous research design and to apply precise methods of analysis to political behavior problems. . . .[10]

Using a somewhat different tactic, David Easton identifies what he thinks are the major assumptions of behavioralism. These are:

- That regularities exist which are discoverable and which can be expressed in generalizations.
- Such generalizations must be testable with reference to behavior.
- "Means for acquiring and interpreting data cannot be taken for

[9] Evron Kirkpatrick, "The Impact of the Behavioral Approach on Traditional Political Science," *Essays on the Behavioral Study of Politics*, ed. Austin Ranney (Urbana, 1962), p. 11.

[10] Heinz Eulau, Samuel J. Eldersveld, and Morris Janowitz, eds., *Political Behavior: A Reader in Theory and Research* (Glencoe, 1956), pp. 3–4.

granted. They are problematic and need to be examined self-consciously."
- Measurement and quantification are necessary, but only where such measurement makes sense in terms of other purposes.
- "Ethical evaluation and empirical explanation" should be kept separate.
- ".Research ought to be systematic. . . . Research untutored by theory may prove trivial, and theory unsupportable by data, futile."
- The understanding and explanation of political behavior should precede application of this knowledge.
- Material from the various social sciences should be integrated.[11]

Although these lists may suggest that every behavioralist subscribes to all elements, it would be more accurate to call behavioralism "less a tightly structured dogma than a congeries of related values and objectives," [12] from which behavioralists select, although which few adopt *in toto*. While the behavioralists appeared to be conveying new doctrine, many of their arguments about establishing the scientific character of the study of politics were old. As Somit and Tanenhaus point out, "between its proponents and opponents, almost all the major arguments for and against a science of politics were voiced during the 1920's and 1930's." [13]

Reliance on the other social sciences, particularly heavy at first, meant that the behavioral approach took on some of the characteristics of the work in the fields on which it drew. Among these were an emphasis on perfection of technique and an avoidance of attention to social institutions larger than the small group. It is now recognized that the focus of the behavioral approach on the individual is not sufficient; how individual decisions are aggregated is also vital, because individual preferences cannot by themselves explain collective decisions. In explaining the individual we must turn to the social setting in which he is found; perhaps it is more accurate to talk of a focus on the "individual in his social environment," as when social psychologists talk of "personality *in* culture," not "personality *and* culture."

While there is no inherent reason why the behavioral approach should be more scientific in outlook than the institutional approach, this has been the case. As already noted, while the institutionalists in many cases shared with the behavioralists an empirical outlook, they did not often have the latter's desire to search for regularities and to formulate generalizations which might ultimately be placed in some over-arching theory. In addition, even some empirically-oriented institutionalists relied on impressionistic work rather than studies in which they attempted systematically to validate or disprove their speculations. This utilization of impressions instead of more systematic

[11] David Easton, "Introduction: The Current Meaning of 'Behavioralism' in Political Science," *The Limits of Behavioralism in Political Science*, ed. James C. Charlesworth, pp. 7–8. Another statement of the "behavioral creed," coupled with a summary of the "anti-behavioralist" position, is to be found in Somit and Tanenhaus, pp. 177–182.

[12] Somit and Tanenhaus, p. 176.   [13] *Ibid.*, p. 87.

findings is likely to lead toward an emphasis on the particularistic rather than the general; the latter is what the behavioralists generally emphasize. Most behavioralists are also more skeptical in their approach than are the institutionalists. This skepticism can help prevent over-commitment to particular findings or ways of developing data.

One characteristic by which behavioralism has come to be identified in the eyes of many political scientists is its use of numbers and its emphasis on methodology. Many if not most of the early political behavior studies involved quantification, and led some critics to refer to the approach as "numerology." The use of tables and graphs to present data and the use of tests of statistical significance does not indicate, say the behavioralists, a lack of thought or a substitution of counting for theorizing.

Whether quantification is necessary for behavioralism is still a very real question, to which most behavioralists would answer "yes," claiming that it is needed both for precision and for the handling of large bodies of data. However, insofar as behavioralism is an outlook rather than a set of specific techniques and to the extent it is equated with a scientific attitude toward the data of politics, we can perhaps speak of behavioralism without quantification. In other words, to be a "non-mathematical behavioralist" is a possibility; such a person would focus on political behavior, but would emphasize verbal description and analysis of the behavior, or might be the one who emphasizes the building of theory from generalizations rather than conducting the studies from which the generalizations are produced.

Because of the heavy emphasis by behavioralists on methods, the criticism that they are more interested in techniques than the results they obtain does strike home with a certain accuracy. Some, although clearly not all, behavioralists, appear to have chosen topics for study solely or largely on the basis of the applicability of available techniques rather than for their theoretical importance. The drawback of this habit is that there is a delay in the development of new techniques needed to examine some theoretically important questions. Valid data will not be obtained without proper instruments, and instruments do not just "happen" but must be developed through testing. In all other fields of scientific inquiry, attention to methods and techniques is considered legitimate and may even be granted the status of a separate sub-field, called methodology, as it has been in sociology but not yet in political science. The emphasis on techniques in the behavioral approach also means that behavioralists need to be committed to constant retooling so that they may be equipped to use the most recently developed effective techniques, a commitment which involves much hard work because of the lag of even graduate curricula behind current needs.

The political behavioralist has drawn on sociology, psychology, and, to a lesser extent, anthropology. Whether he did this at first by choice is unclear, although behavioralists today strongly advocate inter-disciplinary sharing. The sociologists and psychologists forced the political scientist to pay attention to their work when they took up subjects clearly related to politics. The first studies in the area of voting behavior, which has constituted a substantial component of the work of the political behavioralists, were performed by sociologists. Some political scientists realized that sociologists were explaining voting only in terms of such concepts as socio-economic status, and thus "leaving the political out of politics." They thus took up the subject, utilizing both the sociologists' tools and concepts drawn from their own experience, like party identification. They also recognized that the impact of factors like

> **Party Identification.** The psychological identification an individual feels with a particular political party. In the absence of formal party membership, this becomes quite important in explaining decisions to vote for certain parties or candidates.

socio-economic status (SES) on voting was not uniform or constant, and that SES variables affect people in different positions differentially. Just as the early voting behavior analysts had over-emphasized that which was not directly political, early students of community power structure, particularly sociologists, similarly de-emphasized the importance of politics and government in local community decision-making, prompting political scientists to begin study of this subject to see whether government and politics was so unimportant in crucial matters across the board. In addition to community power structure and voting behavior, the behavioralists have been concerned with such subjects as political socialization, the attitudes underlying

> **Political Socialization.** The inculcation of political values into younger generations by family, school, and peer groups; more specifically, the transmission of political attitudes and preferences from one generation to the next.

the decisions of judges, public opinion, and factors which explain the activity and voting patterns of legislators; for the study of these subjects, the political scientists drew heavily on psychology rather than, or in addition to, sociology.

Behavioralists have tended to avoid use of legal and historical materials, something which serves to differentiate them further from the institutionalists. While the avoidance of law and history was perhaps initially a reaction against the reliance on these fields by those emphasizing governmental structure, the behavioralists tended to avoid history because of its emphasis on the uniqueness of events. They also felt that historical emphasis brought about historicism, an attempt to explain phenomena only in terms of the historical period in which the events took place, which clashed with the desire for generalizations which were not time-bound.

The behavioralists have been criticized for concentrating on description of static situations. They undoubtedly felt justified in limiting their initial efforts to the study of "normal" and static situations to remedy the deficiencies they perceived in the picture of politics and government left by the institutionalists. However, in recent years, considerable effort has been devoted to studies of political change, particularly by those behavioralists in the field of comparative government, and to studies of what was once considered the pathological. Walter Lippmann is quoted as saying that, when he attended college, "it was not considered necessary to discuss the politician. . . . The boss and the district leader, the caucus and the conference, spoils and deals were regarded as belonging to the pathology of politics. . . . We studied the unperverted political system as it was presumed to exist . . ." [14] Political scientists now attempt to understand the subjects Lippmann talks about, rather than rejecting them out of hand.

The behavioral approach to the study of politics has now become fully established, and many of those initially hostile have come to use behavioral concepts and techniques regularly. Major front-line battles between the behavioralists and the "traditionalists" have receded into minor skirmishes, although the fighting has not totally died down. As this has happened, a more objective examination of the accomplishments and advantages of the behavioral approach became possible. It has been recognized that behavioralists at times concentrated so heavily on aspects of political phenomena previously neglected that they went from the institutionalists' failure to consider behavior to no consideration of institutions. Studies of voting behavior have at times lacked examination of factors such as registration requirements and ballot forms, which might affect, respectively, the rate of turnout or the direction of the vote, although the behavioralists now often incorporate structural variables in many of their studies. The fact that almost all early studies of voting behavior took place in the United States or within single communities or states made it easy for researchers to forget the possible effect of the institutional environment on electoral activity.

Relative Emphases. As the behavioral approach has become more fully accepted, it has been tied less and less to specific subject matters. However, the emphasis given to the various approaches is not uniform throughout political science. The subfields of political parties, public opinion, interest groups, and voting behavior are heavily behavioral, while constitutional law is far less so, the principal exception being studies of judicial attitudes. The area of international relations is perhaps the one in which conflict between traditionalists and behavioralists still most often breaks into open conflicts; the peace has been made more readily in the study of comparative government. Others have their own varying balances.

While silent peace between the various approaches in many areas of political science and active cooperation in some characterizes American political science, the balance is not the same as it is in other countries. The philosophical and institutional approaches are still dominant outside the United States; the behavioral approach is not much in vogue except in Britain and in new Institutes of Politics on the European Continent, and in Scandinavia, perhaps connected with Gallup Poll operations there. For example, in Brit-

[14] Quoted in Heinz Eulau, "Political Science," *A Reader's Guide to the Social Sciences,* ed. Bert F. Hoselitz (New York, 1957), p. 53.

ain, money has not been available for large-scale behavioral research, and other disciplines have not forced political scientists in this direction, as happened in the United States. Britain's religious and ethnic homogeneity also made less pressing some questions which stimulated behavioralists elsewhere. In other words, although America's philosophical consensus depresses interest in the writing of political philosophy, America's political pluralism stimulates behavioral research.

Each approach still has its convinced partisans, and no doubt the issues between them will never be fully settled. However, we need to recognize that the study of almost any given subject in the field of politics can profit from the application of a "mix" of approaches. The political philosopher can benefit from examining the attitudes of individuals to see what impact certain philosophies have. The behavioralist can utilize history in his study of community power structure, to find out whether the structure has changed over time. Information about empires of days gone by can provide relevant data for the study of supra-national governmental forms today. Behavioralists interested in political change may find history most useful, and nicely complementary to their own tools. The student of constitutional law can examine the reaction of officials to decisions of the Supreme Court, to see if the pronouncements of that body are in fact "the law of the land." The scholar trying to explain present-day politics may find that political philosophers developed ideas useful to him.

Scholars will find that they can mine certain fields better with emphasis on one approach, and other fields with a concentration on a different approach. Which approach will be applied is to some extent determined by the "state of the art." The susceptibility of some areas to scientific treatment is not as much a question of some data being inherently scientific while others are not, but of how far methods, techniques, and concepts have been developed. That political scientists will want to utilize one approach more than the other is perhaps natural as a result of such factors as their training, their interests and personal inclinations, and the outlook of their colleagues.

THE STUDY OF DEMOCRACY: SEVERAL APPROACHES

The study of democracy has attracted much attention from American political scientists for a variety of reasons. Probably the most important is that America is considered to have a democratic form of government and democracy is a value which ranks high for most American citizens. Democracy is also a subject which has been examined by political philosophers for centuries. The difficulty of keeping democracies, e.g., Weimar Germany, alive, or of establishing them as in many of the world's "new nations," has drawn increasing attention to the subject, but with more emphasis on the setting in which democracy is to be found or can survive than on its purely normative aspects. In order to obtain the fullest perspective possible on democracy, we can examine it in several different ways, with the purpose of showing how different approaches to the study of political science can be applied to a single subject.[15]

In discussing democracy, we must first isolate it analytically from extraneous phenomena with which it is often confused. Because Americans think of their nation as a democracy, they often consider all aspects of American political arrangements to be necessary to or inherent in democracy, or all aspects of American political thought to be part of democratic theory. Neither is the case, although some facets of American government contribute to the maintenance of democracy in this country. Neither federalism nor the separation of powers is basic to democracy, as is illustrated by the case of Great Britain, a democracy which has a unitary system of government (one without states) and a Parliament without separation of powers. Even in America, separation of powers does not exist at the local level of government, which many feel to be the most "democratic." There is similarly no requirement that capitalism, dear to the hearts of many Americans, accompany democracy. Just as specific economic arrangements are not inherent in democracy, the same is true of religions: although one can point to values inherent in democracy which can also be found in the Judeo-Christian tradition, such as an emphasis on the dignity of man, Christianity is not an imperative for democracy.

Perhaps the most common confusion of those who examine democracy is between what can be called basic democratic theory and specific forms the philosophy has taken at different times and places. In these specific forms, ideas not central to "pure" democracy, such as progress and humanitarianism, become added to democratic theory. That democracy will contribute to our continuous advance, or that it is the only way by which we may achieve progress, is a relatively new idea in the history of democratic philosophy, because the acceptance of the concept of progress itself is recent, developing in the nineteenth century and the rationalism of the Enlightenment. The idea of humanitarianism, that man is essentially good, also adheres to contemporary democratic thought, where it is argued that man must be good for democracy to succeed. While the prospects for democracy may be better if man is considered to be good and capable of improving his own situation, democracy can be considered possible (as well as necessary) if man is thought to be bad and tainted with original sin. While philosophers have often used the concept of sinful man to justify elite rule, it can be argued that a few sinful men should not be ruling over others, leaving democracy the only acceptable arrangement.

Having briefly said what democracy does not entail, we should examine what political philosophers have said of democracy in its ideal form. Perhaps the most central thought is that democracy involves certain values and procedures. Among the values which democracy has been thought to embody are the importance of individual man, the peaceful voluntary adjustment of

[15] Among the approaches which will not be discussed in detail is the logical analysis of normative theories.

disputes, the insuring of peaceful change in a changing society, the orderly succession of rulers, a minimum use of coercion, recognition of diversity and pluralism, and the attainment of justice. While all political systems claim to be just in their own terms, and while no system can avoid isolated instances of injustice, democracy, through the possibility of change which political freedoms provide, can at least make a request for continued obedience to laws people feel to be unjust while they work for a change in those laws. The multiplicity of these values can result in a number of different theories of democracy, as shown by Dahl's comment that "there is no democratic theory— there are only democratic theories." [16] The attempt to tie democracy down to a fixed set of principles—what a friend has referred to as "Thirty-Three Things to Remember While Brushing Your Teeth"—is also contrary to its character and makes it difficult to explain. Its ambiguity and lack of precise rules may have contributed to its long life, but frustrate the person looking for a clear statement of that in which he is supposed to believe. While communism has as its goal the establishment of a classless society, democracy entails no specific policy goals, although people using democratic arrangements adopt such goals and attempt for varying lengths of time to implement them. To some, democracy means definite goals, but these are general or abstract ones like freedom and equality, and the emphasis of democratic theory tends to be on the *process* of attempting to secure these goals instead of on the goals themselves.

The principal idea in democratic theory is that of rule by a majority, of all the people or of their representatives who would in turn be chosen by majority vote. It has been said that "democracy is the recurrent suspicion that more than half of the people are right more than half of the time." [17] While philosophers do not concede that what the majority decides is truth, in effect that equation is made in democratic systems. In order to avoid the problem of measuring the varying intensities with which people hold opinions and preferences, we also equate "preferred by most" with "most preferred." To some, democracy *is* majoritarianism; there are no further identifying characteristics. The difficulty with this position is that it does not take the long run into account. Thus, under a simple majoritarian definition of democracy, the Soviet Union (as well as the United States) might qualify as a democracy, as its officials are elected by a majority. However, it has been noted that:

> There is all the difference in the world between giving the population what the majority of the representatives will approve in the give and take of a free political process, and compelling and conditioning them to approve what is given to them by a few at the top in a state without free elections and political liberties. [18]

Agreement therefore exists that "majority rule . . . does not refer to a single determinate majority formed at a particular time in relation to a particular

[16] Robert Dahl, *A Preface to Democratic Theory* (Chicago, 1956), p. 1.
[17] Henry Mayo, *An Introduction to Democratic Theory* (New York, 1960), p. 175.
[18] *Ibid.*, p. 186. Much of the remainder of this discussion of the basic elements of democracy draws heavily on Mayo's work.

issue. Instead, majority rule is a general way of arriving at decisions." [19] The types of choices placed before a people for a vote and the presence or absence of a formal opposition and what happens to that opposition when it is unpopular or is defeated must be considered.

Other elements beyond majority rule are usually considered to be distinguishing principles of democracy. Political equality and political freedoms are basic, and, in contemporary democracy, popular control of policy-makers is also essential. Political equality means equality in voting: being granted equal participation in voting and having one's vote counted equally with those of others. Thus, universal suffrage is a part of democracy. Political freedom entails at least an opportunity to participate in political activity. The opportunity to pose alternatives to present policies and to seek to elect representatives to replace those presently in office is most important here. The degree to which political freedoms are *effective* will determine whether democracy really exists. It is not enough for the freedoms to exist on paper; if they are not exercised, they may atrophy.

The notions of political equality and political freedoms raise the issue of minority rights vis-à-vis majority rule. Although both are part of democracy, reconciling them is difficult if not impossible. They have made at least a partial peace with the recognition that the majority rule principle does not require that every majority wish be enacted in the face of intense opposition. The key question concerns which rights should be included as a limitation on the majority rule principle. Because of our attachment to the Bill of Rights of the U.S. Constitution, we sometimes tend to point to all the items included there as rights of the minority which should be protected within a democratic system of government. However, from the point of view of democratic theory, the right to counsel at trial or to a jury of our peers does not stand on the same footing with freedoms of speech, press, assembly, and petition, all of which are more directly relevant to political activity. In defining which should be protected in a democracy, it has been suggested that the only necessary right is "the right to try to become a majority." This right would entail the First Amendment political freedoms just noted.

Even if these rights are recognized in the abstract, controversy is likely to exist over the breadth of their application. Should they be exercised in all situations and without regard to the content of what is advocated, or should they be limited, either as to time or content? Some governments impose both time and content limitations, allegedly allowing discussion of alternatives up to the time a policy is adopted, after which discussion and criticism are to be cut off. In the Soviet system, this is known as "democratic centralism." In the United States, we limit the content of speech by punishing certain kinds of statements about political officials, obscene writing, and advocacy of overthrow of the government when accompanied by specific incitation to violence.

[19] Howard Dean, *Judicial Review and Democracy* (New York, 1966), p. 46.

The idea that there should be popular control of policy-makers was not found in the first development of democratic theory, because there was no distinction between citizens and policy-makers. In the ancient Greek city-state, the citizens were the policy-makers; democracy was "direct" rather than representative in character. Except for the town-meeting form of government in which all citizens attend an annual meeting and lay down the policy for the town, democracy has been adapted from its origins by the addition of representatives, chosen by the citizens, who make the decisions but are accountable to the populace. It has been stated that "no democratic system operates on the principle that voters directly decide public policies at elections. The control over policy is much more indirect—through the representatives." [20] While no system is set up so that *all* policies are voted upon by the public, the "direct democracy" movement in the United States did bring about direct popular decision-making on at least a limited number of policies, through the initiative and referendum. This shows that the Greek

> *Initiative* and *Referendum.* The *initiative* allows citizens to circulate petitions to place proposed legislation on the ballot without the intervention of the legislature; the measure becomes law upon receiving a majority vote at an election. *Referendum* involves either legislative submission of certain measures to the people for a vote, or allows voters to place measures already passed by the legislature on the ballot for approval or rejection. Along with these is often found *recall*, a device whereby voters can remove an elected official from office before the end of his term; after petitions with a specified number of signatures are collected, a special election is held to determine whether the official shall be "retired."

development of democratic theory has had a great impact on our ideas of what democracy should be, even if few historical examples can be found in which Greek theory was put into practice. We must take into account differences in scale and institutions between Athens and modern nations in considering Greek arguments in favor of democracy. Our shift to representative democracy has come about because of the vastly greater scale of our governmental units, although, of course, not solely for this reason. For example, intense criticism has been made of the competence of voters to judge the complexities of specific policies, and for many this is sufficient justification for a representative system. However, the idea that participation ought to be direct still has great impact. For example, people are still concerned about the degree of mass participation in elections, and about rates of non-voting, even when the public participates only in periodic elections of officials rather than in policy-making.

Majority rule, popular control of officials, political equality and political freedoms—such are the basic elements of democracy as stated by political philosophers. Our emphasis has thus far been primarily on the philosophical approach to democracy, whose practitioners have historically accounted for

[20] Mayo, p. 62.

the greatest amount of work on the subject. We have considered some institutional aspects of the subject in our mention of "direct democracy." In adopting an empirical approach to democracy, political scientists' focus has shifted to these institutional factors and to behavioral phenomena related to democracy. One study which has contributed to our knowledge of these facets of the subject is that conducted during the 1950's by the political sociologist Seymour Martin Lipset. He attempted to discover the characteristics accompanying stable democracies, on the one hand, and unstable democracies and dictatorships, on the other.[21]

Lipset defined as democratic those European countries in which there had been an uninterrupted period of political democracy from World War I to the time of his study, as well as the absence during the previous twenty-five years of a major political movement opposed to the democratic rules of the game (such as Fascism or Communism) which received 20% of the vote at any election. In Latin America, his requirements were less stringent; a country was considered democratic if there was a history of more or less free elections since World War I. One can quarrel with his use of a dichotomy, arguing that a continuum ought to be used to represent the degree to which countries possess democratic characteristics, and Lipset himself suggests the desirability of this in remarking, "democracy is *not* a quality of a social system which either does or does not exist, but is rather a complex of characteristics which may be ranked in many different ways." Lipset also noted that the conditions frequently accompanying stable democracies would not always bring about democracy where it did not previously exist. Democracy in particular situations may result from special constellations of factors and thus might exist even in the absence of many of the factors we are about to note. We must recognize that factors which assist in the birth of a phenomenon are not necessarily the same ones which assist in its continuation.

Combining examination of institutional and behavioral items, Lipset found a number of major differences between the two categories of countries. Two-party systems, like that in the United States, seemed to assist in the maintenance of democracy more than multi-party systems, which contributed to the difficulties which occurred in the Fourth French Republic. While majorities can be achieved in a multi-party situation by coalitions, the coalitions are not as stable as parties and each party in a multi-party system tends to be more rigid in its approach than parties in a two-party system, making compromise more difficult. Lipset also found the type of political party to be important in affecting democracy's stability. He distinguished between parties of representation, limited by and large to the political arena, and parties of integration, which, by setting up auxiliary organizations, try to encompass all of their members' lives, and found the former contributing more to democratic stability. Because the members of parties of integration are not

[21] Seymour Martin Lipset, "Some Social Requisites of Democracy: Economic Development and Political Legitimacy," *American Political Science Review*, LIII (1959), 69–105. The material in the following paragraphs is based in large part on this article.

subject to cross-pressures, they are less likely to compromise or to change positions.

> *Cross-Pressures.* Conflicting pulls on an individual from more than one source, e.g., groups to which he belongs or whose views he tends to follow. People in a cross-pressured situation tend to be less consistent with regard to such matters as voting preference, and often react to the cross-pressures, of which they may not be conscious, by withdrawing from the situation. The classic case of cross-pressure with its resulting ambivalence involves the donkey equi-distant between two bales of hay who starved to death because he could not decide to which one to go first.

One of Lipset's findings which seems to run directly counter to the ideology of democracy, with its heavy emphasis on individualism, is that the existence of "intermediary organizations," including such institutions as the family, the church, and interest groups, is helpful in maintaining the stability of democracy. These organizations serve as potential opposition to the government, as a training ground for new leadership and a place for the development of new ideas, and as a buffer between the government and the individual, between the elite and the "masses." [22] The cross-pressures caused by multiple memberships in these organizations are helpful in reducing the temperature of democratic conflict. If people are pulled in different directions by competing forces, they may very well wish to de-fuse the situation.

The individualism of democracy seems to deny not only the importance of the interest group but also the importance of bureaucratic organization, yet Lipset also finds that efficient bureaucracy is a condition for the modern

> *Bureaucracy.* A concept developed by the German sociologist Max Weber to indicate what Weber felt was the most rational form for the administration of large-scale organizations. A bureaucracy is hierarchical (pyramidal) in structure and impersonal. The term has come to be used to refer to the administrative structure of organizations, both public and private, whether or not they are "bureaucratic" in the Weberian sense.

democratic state. If democracies do not possess a mechanism by which the will of the majority as determined through the representatives or as equated with the accepted actions of the representatives can be effectively implemented, the majorities which enact policy may become frustrated, reducing the stability of the system. However, an efficient bureaucracy without a government the people consider legitimate is not sufficient to bring about stable democracy; both the efficiency and the legitimacy are necessary.

While the aspects of democracy just discussed are crucial to its maintenance, Lipset argues they are not as important as the social structure underlying democracy. Among the social and economic factors Lipset found to be characteristic of stable democratic situations were:

---

[22] The concept "masses" implies an aggregate of isolated individuals rather than a group of interacting persons, as such, it is said to characterize mid-20th-century life.

- an advanced state of economic development;
- higher wealth, more industrialization and urbanization, and a higher level of education than in other countries;
- an increase in wealth and education;
- a large middle class;
- Protestantism;
- the absence of minorities with values contrary to those of the system; and
- "universalistic" religions, that is, those which do not believe they are "the only true way."

The increase in wealth indicates to those low in socio-economic status that improvement in their condition is possible, while the increase in education tends to expose those same individuals to moderate political views; both thus help in maintaining democracy. A large middle class can serve to moderate conflict between the very wealthy and the very poor. Protestantism is important because of its emphasis on individual responsibility, consonant with democratic values.

Lipset did not suggest the sequence in which the social factors he discussed occurred in the development of democracy. One relevant study of several which have now been written is that by Daniel Lerner, who, in writing of the Middle East, suggested a likely partial chronology. He felt that urbanization came before literacy, and literacy before the development of the mass media. While perhaps the second is easier to understand than the first, although television and radio could exist in the absence of literacy, Lerner's explanation is that only the cities have developed "the complex of skills and resources which characterize the modern industrial economy." [23] It is within the "urban matrix" that literacy develops, to be further advanced with the coming of mass media.

Lipset also indicated that situations in which social cleavages line up one on top of the other are dangerous for democracy, because they can produce severe and protracted conflict. An example is the situation in Belgium, where the various social cleavages reinforce each other rather than mitigate conflict. In the North are the Flemish, of Dutch origin, Catholic in religion, and backers predominantly of the Right party; in the South are the Walloons, of French extraction, agnostics, and supporters of the Liberal and Socialist parties.[24] Cleavages based on language coincide with national distinctions, reinforced by religious divisions, and topped by political differences; each adds to the others. By contrast, Catholics, Protestants, and Jews are not found only in neatly defined areas of the United States, and the same is true of Democrats and Republicans, despite the "solid South." However, one can see the conflict that will be created if rich and poor in the United States

[23] Daniel Lerner, *The Passing of Traditional Society* (Glencoe, 1958), p. 60.
[24] Felix Oppenheim, "Belgium: Party Cleavage and Compromise," *Modern Political Parties: Approaches to Comparative Politics*, ed. Sigmund Neumann (Chicago, 1956), pp. 155–168.

should follow the cleavages between white and black, as it does in many large cities.

In addition, three major issues which have a considerable impact on democracy's life-chances have to be resolved everywhere. These are the place of the church and/or religions; the admission of lower strata, particularly workers, to full political and economic citizenship through universal suffrage and the right to bargain collectively; and the struggle over the distribution of national income. Resolving these issues one at a time contributes to stability, but if they are carried over from one period to another, tension, frustration, and potential instability may result.

Among types of behavioral analysis which have been conducted concerning democracy are those dealing with, first, the type of individual who can contribute most to its maintenance, and, second, the degree to which there is a consensus on the ideas and ideals of democracy in this country. Studies of political personality have never been totally satisfying to many, and the attempt to develop "personality types" which would best fit a particular political system has not been greeted with great enthusiasm. However, such efforts can be extremely useful in sharpening our thinking and in suggesting the relevance of the personality for political analysis. Recent discussions of the importance of political alienation and the danger it poses for a demo-

> **Alienation. A disaffection with the present political system, including feelings of powerlessness and normlessness (that no clear standards exist). Alienation may bring about withdrawal from the system or activism aimed at changing the system; the former is thought to be more likely.**

cratic system show the value psychological concepts can have for political science.

One listing which may be indicative of attempts to define the democratic personality was made by Henry Mayo.[25] According to him, the ideal democrat (small "d") would:

- desire to be self-governing ("The democrat will value political freedoms for themselves, as well as for the objectives which he wishes to achieve by using them.");
- possess an "inquiring, independent, rational attitude";
- be confident in the political system of which he is a part, and have a feeling of "political efficacy";
- sympathize with the claims of others, and not desire to dominate others ("A democrat need not and probably will not, in any personal sense, love or be charitable toward his political enemies, but he will tolerate them or at least not wish to suppress them and their political proposals.");
- willingly express opinions;
- have an ability to compromise and to accept compromise;

[25] Mayo, pp. 265–267.

- value peace and order achieved through democratic political freedoms; and
- not be extremely pessimistic or optimistic.

Another list, using language more clearly drawn from personality theory, was developed by Lasswell.[26] For him, democratic character involved

- "the maintenance of an open as against a closed ego";
- a person who was multi-valued rather than single-valued, and "disposed to share rather than to hoard or to monopolize";
- "deep confidence in the benevolent potentialities of man"; and
- "the specification that the self-system shall have at its disposal the energies of the unconscious part of the personality."

Either list will probably seem to the reader to describe a personality so ideal that no one person could possibly possess all the enumerated characteristics. However, we must recognize that democracy does demand much of its citizens, as Lane points out well:

Democracy is an odd system. It requires that most men tolerate freedom and that some men hold it dear. Yet men are born unfree, infants with only such choices as their parents offer them, and with a world of choice foreclosed. Though as adults they are required to tolerate some degrees of equality, and are entreated to believe in the equality of man, they inevitably emerge from families in which, as children, they learn inequality long before they learn equality. Democracy asks men to support the rights of others to be heterodox, to say things that violate their moral and political codes, but they are brought up to believe in propriety and convention. . . . It is little wonder that democracy is a late product of history, and a painful achievement for some individuals.[27]

While there is general agreement in the United States that the nation *ought* to be a democracy, there is far less agreement on what it means to have a democracy, i.e., what democracy requires in specific situations, and we tend to be ambivalent about applying democracy everywhere. Our ambivalence is seen in two recent episodes. During the late 1950's and early 1960's, there was a cry, in Congress and out, for more democracy within unions. The *bête noir* of the legislators was the Teamsters Union and its President, James Hoffa, who it was thought would be ousted as a result of increased internal union democracy. When it became clear that "clean" elections resulted in Hoffa's retention in office by greater margins than he had received before, the goal of internal union democracy was de-emphasized and people started to seek other methods to get rid of Hoffa. The reaction of the public to Fidel Castro's pre-eminence in Cuba was of much the same order. "He never would be *elected* to office," said many. "Let's go hold free elections there." But it became increasingly clear to observers of the Cuban situation that

[26] Harold D. Lasswell, *Democratic Character,* in *The Political Writings of Harold D. Lasswell* (Glencoe, 1951), pp. 495–503.
[27] Lane, pp. 39–40.

Castro, if allowed to run in a supervised election, might very well win, despite the displeasure of those whose property had been expropriated. Again, we moved on to a search for other methods to contain Castro. In both of these examples, democracy was approved only for instrumental reasons, not for itself. In any democratic society, there are undoubtedly both people who are democrats for instrumental reasons and those who back it on principle.

Exploration of Americans' belief in democracy has been undertaken by a number of scholars, among them Robert Dahl and the team of James Prothro and Charles Grigg. Dahl, in his study of decision-making in New Haven, Connecticut, *Who Governs?*, pointed out that most Americans believe in democracy at a high level of abstraction and feel that democracy is the best governmental arrangement, while agreement on the specific institutions of American government embodying those democratic ideals is somewhat lower.[28] When specific applications of democracy become the subject of controversy, noticeable numbers of citizens disagree with what the democratic philosophers would prescribe as correct application. Those most active in politics are, however, more in agreement about the norms and support them more highly than does the average citizen, a finding substantiated by Prothro and Grigg. Citizens also have the view that what is, is democratic. If there are gaps between the democratic ideal and American practice which a philosopher of democracy might point out, the average citizen is not aware of them or seems not to be disturbed by them. In effect, what the officials do is considered to be democratic unless shown to be otherwise.

Prothro and Grigg, who tested the hypothesis that a high degree of consensus on basic principles is necessary to the maintenance of democracy, like Dahl found that consensus existed on basic principles but not on specifics.[29] Specifics which produced more disagreement than consensus included the extension of democratic freedoms to Communists, the right of all citizens to vote, the right of a professional group to improve its voting position, and the right to criticize churches and religion. More pro-democratic responses came from the Midwestern community studied than from the one in the South. Income and education both affected responses, with education the more important factor; the higher the education or income, the more democratic the response. Prothro and Grigg concluded that consensus on fundamental principles "in a highly abstract form" was a necessary condition for democracy, although "the implication of political theory that consensus includes more specific principles is empirically invalid."

To conclude our examination of various approaches to the study of democracy, we turn to a discussion offered by Robert Lane of possible explanations for the hold democracy has on Americans, developed as part of an in-depth study of the beliefs of fifteen men in "Eastport." While few of the his-

[28] Robert Dahl, *Who Governs?: Democracy and Power in an American City* (New Haven, 1961), p. 316.
[29] James W. Prothro and Charles M. Grigg, "Fundamental Principles of Democracy: Bases of Agreement and Disagreement," *Journal of Politics*, XXII (1960), 276–294.

torical factors he cites affect the individual directly or indirectly, they are "in the air" and their effect is no less pervasive for being part of the culture. Lane offers eight possible explanations: [30]

- The American frontier helped mold democratic man.
- America's economic abundance has provided support for democracy; in the absence of such prosperity, the elite would be less willing to accommodate itself to the "lower classes."
- Land distribution in colonial America, with each man (Jefferson's "sturdy yeoman") holding his own plot, provided a property basis for popular government.
- America's isolation from Europe and the resultant escape from involvement in the political wars of that continent fostered stability, allowing popular government to gain a firm foothold.
- Self-government in early churches assisted later popularly-governed institutions.
- Similarly, the freedom of choice in our "free enterprise" system, with men largely on their own to search for work and employers free to assume the risks of running their own businesses, leads men to ask for involvement in the public government of their affairs.
- Those fleeing tyranny abroad who came to this country have served to refresh our democratic idealism.
- The way in which we raise our children, "wherein the child is taught his own worth, responsible independence, and how to share in family government," also is supposed to contribute to citizens who can better participate in democratic government.

The existence of so many explanations might mean we had little or no idea why democracy had such strength in America. However, it is also possible that each item listed by Lane has had some impact. De-emphasis on single-factor explanation for particular phenomena would lead us to accept the potential relevance of each of these explanations, and to recognize that it may be the cumulative significance of all the items which explains why democracy exists as it does in America.

BIBLIOGRAPHY

Approaches to Political Science

Somit and Tanenhaus's history of American political science traces the development of the various approaches in the discipline. The Riddle and Cleary volume contains elementary discussions of the philosophical, institutional, and behavioral approaches. The shift from political philosophy to political theory is attacked by Jaffa, while Rothman deals with the attempt by Leo Strauss and his followers to return to classical philosophy. Bluhm deals imaginatively with parallels between

[30] Lane, pp. 86–88.

classical political philosophy and contemporary political theory. The conflict between the philosophers and the behavioralists is also dealt with in "Political Theory and the Study of Politics" and in Dean's article, as well as by Prothro and Dahl.

The philosophy of behavioralism is expounded by Eulau, one of the earliest behavioralists. The collections edited by Eulau and by Eulau, Eldersveld, and Janowitz contain representative behavioral studies. A number of political scientists discuss how far behavioralism can be extended in the Charlesworth collection. The most virulent attack on the behavioral approach is that contained in the volume edited by Storing, which is analyzed by Schaar and Wolin.

BLUHM, WILLIAM. *Theories of the Political System: Classics of Political Thought and Modern Political Analysis.* Englewood Cliffs, 1965.

CHARLESWORTH, JAMES C., ed. *The Limits of Behavioralism in Political Science.* Philadelphia, 1962.

DAHL, ROBERT A. "The Behavioral Approach in Political Science: Epitaph for a Monument to a Successful Protest." *American Political Science Review,* LV (1961), 763–772.

DEAN, HOWARD E. "Blowing the Horns of a Counterfeit Dilemma." *Western Political Quarterly,* XVII (1964), 5–9.

EULAU, HEINZ. *The Behavioral Persuasion in Politics.* New York, 1963.

———, ed. *Political Behavior in America: New Directions.* New York, 1966.

———, SAMUEL J. ELDERSVELD, and MORRIS JANOWITZ, eds. *Political Behavior: A Reader in Theory and Research.* Glencoe, Ill., 1956.

JAFFA, HARRY V. "The Case Against Political Theory." *Journal of Politics,* XXII (1960), 259–275.

"Political Theory and the Study of Politics: A Report of a Conference." *American Political Science Review,* L (1956), 475–487.

PROTHRO, JAMES W. "The Nonsense Fight Over Scientific Method: A Plea for Peace." *Journal of Politics,* XVIII (1956), 565–570.

RIDDLE, DONALD H., and ROBERT S. CLEARY, eds. *Political Science in the Social Studies.* Washington, D.C., 1966. [36th Yearbook, National Council for the Social Studies]

ROTHMAN, STANLEY. "The Revival of Classical Political Philosophy: A Critique." *American Political Science Review,* LVI (1962), 341–352. A response is Joseph Cropsey, "A Reply to Rothman." *American Political Science Review,* LVI (1962), 353–359.

SCHAAR, JOHN H., and SHELDON S. WOLIN. *"Essays on the Scientific Study of Politics:* A Critique." *American Political Science Review,* LVII (1963), 125–150. "Response." *American Political Science Review,* LVII (1963), 151–160.

SOMIT, ALBERT, and JOSEPH TANENHAUS. *The Development of American Political Science: From Burgess to Behavioralism.* Boston, 1967.

STORING, HERBERT J., ed. *Essays on the Scientific Study of Politics.* New York, 1962.

Democracy

In addition to the material cited in the footnotes, a number of volumes and articles are important for the student interested in examining democracy more thoroughly. Thorson discusses the problem of justifying democracy. Dahl subjects several theories of democracy to intensive logical analysis, casting them into theorems and propositions. Downs develops a formal model of political rationality and explores the effects of certainty and uncertainty. Kendall and Carey, along with Dahl, deal with the problem of taking into account citizens' intensity of feeling on issues. Neubauer (and the articles he cites) continue the discussion of socio-economic correlates of democracy Lipset started. McCrone and Cnudde try to develop the sequence in which such factors occur. Kornhauser's volume is relevant to Lipset's discussion of intermediary organizations in contemporary society. Lane adds to the discussion of democratic personality.

DAHL, ROBERT. *A Preface to Democratic Theory.* Chicago, 1956.

DOWNS, ANTHONY. *An Economic Theory of Democracy.* New York, 1957.

KENDALL, WILLMOORE, and GEORGE W. CAREY. "The 'Intensity' Problem and Democratic Theory." *American Political Science Review*, LXII (1968), 5–24.

KORNHAUSER, WILLIAM. *The Politics of Mass Society.* Glencoe, 1959.

LANE, ROBERT. "Notes on a Theory of Democratic Personality." *Political Ideology: Why The American Common Man Believes What He Does.* New York, 1962. Pages 400–412.

MC CRONE, DONALD J., and CHARLES F. CNUDDE. "Toward a Communications Theory of Political Development: A Causal Model." *American Political Science Review*, LXI (1967), 72–79.

NEUBAUER, DEANE. "Some Conditions of Democracy." *American Political Science Review*, LXI (1967), 1002–1009.

THORSON, THOMAS LANDON. *The Logic of Democracy.* New York, 1962.

3 / BUILDING THEORY IN
POLITICAL SCIENCE

Introduction / Concept-Formation / Hypotheses / Theories /
On the Operationalization of "Power" and "Class"

INTRODUCTION

For working purposes, "theory" can be defined as *a system of generalizations based on empirical findings or testable empirically.* Theory is, or can be, based on, that is, developed from, practice; the theory serves to describe, in generalizations, and to explain what actually happens, not what should happen as in the phrase "theory versus practice." Some sets of statements, completely in hypothetical form, qualify as theory before empirical generalizations are developed. They remain hypotheses perhaps because they cannot be tested, as when access to necessary information may be blocked. As long as they are testable in principle, they may be considered theory.

A more complete definition of theory is that a theory basically involves *a set of (at least two) statements, called either laws or propositions, which are related to each other and which express relationships between variables under varying states of the system.* Laws or propositions are based ultimately on *facts* which are found by the testing of hypotheses. Laws are statements of invariant relations, stated in "if . . . then . . ." or relational (an amount of X is associated with a certain amount of Y) form. Propositions, usually stated in probabilistic form, are of lesser generality than laws. Hypotheses are speculative statements of relationships between items; they are propositions cast in specific form, with the terms of the proposition operationalized. This is why a hypothesis has been called a "model (or theory) sticking its neck out." Facts result from the testing of hypotheses. The distinctions between these terms are not as clear-cut as they may appear here. For example, facts have been held to differ from hypotheses only in degree. And it has been argued that attempts to distinguish concepts like hypothesis, theory, and law are not worthwhile because the concepts have so much in common.

At the discipline's current stage of development, we can talk more accurately about the "frames of reference" or "quasi-theories" we use than about "theories," because most of our collections of statements are not developed to the latter stage. To distinguish between theories and frames of reference is perhaps to say that something is not a theory until it has satisfied criteria for what is a "good" theory, and it can be argued that we can and should talk about theories of varying degrees of rigor or sophistication rather than limiting the meaning of "theory."

Perhaps influenced by earlier political philosophers who built grand, abstract structures, we tend to feel that the more general and all-encompassing a theory is, that is, the larger the number of classes of events it predicts (or to which it is applicable), the better the theory. However, we have developed little broad-gauge theory. Those interested in developing empirically-oriented theory are still, by and large, trying to establish frames of reference they think will be productive or to draw together into systematic but partial theory the valid generalizations, perhaps having different bases, which other political scientists have produced about some area of political existence.

Examination of things "in the large" (macroanalysis) and of more minute units of phenomena (microanalysis) are complementary, and both proceed side-by-side. Those political scientists with an interest in the politics of developing countries have been in the forefront in use of the macro approach, perhaps because developing countries lacked Western (developed) countries' internal differentiation, which had allowed microanalysis of particular institutions. Researchers were forced to develop more encompassing frameworks in order to work with developing nations' lesser internal differentiation.

In the short run, we are likely to develop mainly a series of "middle-range" theories and a far greater number of lower-level generalizations which are potential components of theories. By "low-level" (or "particular") theories are meant those dealing with or predicting a subclass of events, such as occurrences of world wars under certain conditions; "middle-range" theories have a wider compass, a class rather than a subclass of events, for example, all wars under specified conditions; and "general theory" has a still broader scope, including several classes of events, e.g., various types of conflict including but not restricted to wars.

Regardless of the level of theory at which we operate, we will be utilizing a multiplicity of factors rather than searching for a single factor which will explain all of politics. Attempts to explain political activity solely in terms of the groups with which people are affiliated or the geographical location of nations, social action by people's relationship to the means of production, or human activity solely in terms of body form, make their contributions to knowledge by highlighting problems and providing interesting perspectives. Yet such single-factor theories are not satisfying because of their lack of completeness and they lack validity because, in their construction, invariably data are forced into the theoretical framework or the framework is stretched to include errant data, as in the theories of Marx and Freud.

Before discussing specific frames of reference, quasi-theories, or theories (see Chapters 4 and 5), we need to examine further what theory is and particularly how it is constructed.[1] Only selected aspects of the process will be covered here, to provide the student with an introduction, particularly to terminology. Before we begin we must recognize that there is more than one philosophy of science. Although there are other views,[2] the one underlying what is put forward here is representative of much current thinking in the social sciences.

CONCEPT-FORMATION

The first and to many the most important part of theory-building is the development of concepts. While we talk about "facts" apart from theories, facts are constructed from concepts, which are the building blocks of theory. The concept and the fact are, however, clearly different things. Brodbeck says that a concept is a "term referring to a descriptive property or relation, (while) to state a fact . . . is to state that a concept has an instance or number of instances."[3] Reality is like a seamless web; activity does not come neatly broken down into categories, which must be constructed. Although theories must be based on adequately developed concepts, concepts are not developed or defined once and for all, although continuity is provided by prior work in a given field. A prime difficulty in theory-formation can be concepts accepted as fixed which do not properly encompass phenomena the observer is trying to describe or analyze. However, concepts and definitions must be fixed in the sense that they remain constant throughout a theory.

To some extent, concepts used by scientists are arbitrary, and are only more or less *useful* rather than true or false. Concepts are arbitrary in the sense that there are undefined terms in any definition or set of definitions, but they are not totally arbitrary. Kerlinger, for example, defines a concept as "a word that expresses an abstraction formed by generalization from particulars,"[4] thus indicating that not only is reality structured by concepts, but that reality (as seen by the scientist) affects the scientist's concepts. (He adds that "a *construct* is a concept with the additional meaning of having been created or appropriated for special scientific purposes.") A particular type of concept which combines the features of arbitrariness and relatedness to the real world is the "ideal type," a logical construct the purpose of which is to identify clearly, by simplifying, significant aspects of an event or institution. The ideal type, although "never found in reality, being ideal precisely in the sense that it is an abstraction, accentuation, and extension of relations found

[1] This chapter is based in large measure on the treatment of the subject by Robert Dubin in his lectures on "Theory-Building" delivered during 1961 at the University of Oregon and developed more fully and amended in *Theory Building* (New York, 1969).

[2] Eugene J. Meehan, *Explanation in Social Science: A System Paradigm* (Homewood, Ill., 1969).

[3] May Brodbeck, "Models, Meaning, and Theories," *Symposium on Sociological Theory*, ed. Llewellyn Gross (New York, 1959), p. 377.

[4] Fred N. Kerlinger, *Foundations of Behavioral Research* (New York, 1964), p. 4n.

in social life," [5] provides us with a useful baseline against which to judge and explain phenomena. Sometimes the ideal type is referred to as an "extreme" or "polar" type, particularly when used in pairs as opposites.

In the social sciences, new concepts have not often been developed for research purposes, in part because of resistance to new terms and coined language. Hyneman has, however, charged that "much of the objection to new terms which comes out under the charge of jargon is simple unwillingness to face the need for quick and easy ways of identifying a precise and firm set of ideas which promise usefulness in pushing inquiry ahead." [6] Because of the reluctance to develop new terminology, concepts are frequently borrowed, often from the everyday political world. The meanings these concepts have acquired through use in common political discourse often interfere with their effective use in scholarly work.

An example of the difficulty of using words from common political discourse is "pressure group," a term which has acquired negative connotations because "pressure" is considered by many to be improper in a democratic system, where legislators are supposed to make decisions without being coerced. The term "interest group," now more frequently used by political scientists, is also subject to somewhat the same problem, as "interest" to many means "self-interest." Another example is "neurotic," which, because it is used derogatorily by many laymen, causes difficulties when used in the study of political psychology, although it need not be value-laden if specific standards for its use are developed.

Concepts available in other disciplines or in other countries have at times been imported into political science wholesale. Many European concepts, among them "elite" and "mass," and "left" and "right," have been imported for use in American social science. The latter two, developed to describe "liberal" and "conservative" and based on the seating arrangement in the French Parliament, are far more useful in analysis of an ideologically-oriented political system than in the more result-oriented American polity. "Elite" and "mass" are terms far more applicable to societies with a division into nobility and peasantry than to one which developed without any such sharp division.

Difficulties such as the above have made even more clear the need to devote time to developing concepts, although it has been argued that an extraordinary amount of time has already been devoted to this endeavor. Despite the concern of some social scientists with this problem, they usually accept language as it comes to them, with all the implicit theories which may be built into the syntax and semantics of that language. Even when they are concerned about operationalizing, they usually do not deal with the structure and meaning of the language they use in building their theories.

That we have not been able better to conceptualize may also be related to

[5] Don Martindale, "Sociological Theory and the Ideal Type," *Symposium on Sociological Theory*, ed. Gross, p. 77.

[6] Charles Hyneman, *The Study of Politics*, p. 68.

the discipline's preoccupation with teaching. It has been accepted that communicating with students requires a "simpler" set of concepts, although often these are less precise. In arguing that "we must keep separate the criteria for deciding on how our knowledge is to be transmitted or packaged," [7] Richard Snyder is asserting that research conceptualization should come first, to be followed by conceptualization for teaching, instead of the former being determined by the latter. However, this does not answer the question of why the two should be kept separate and different. The result of the present situation is that the students are not able to share an understanding of political science research and that the material communicated to them is often vague and "soft."

Operationalization. Because concepts are needed for empirical research, an essential step in their development is their operationalization. They need to be tied to measureable elements in the political world to be useful. The preoccupation of social scientists with operationalizing has been noted by several observers. One of them, Gideon Sjoberg, attributes the urge to operationalize to the prestige given the natural sciences, and states that "many social scientists have felt that adoption of a rigid operationalist approach was one procedure by which they could rid themselves once and for all of the stigma of subjectivism." He also says that a number of social forces, among which were requirements of modern bureaucracies, such as "demands for added instrumentation in government, education, and the armed forces," and the employment of social scientists as technicians for large-scale organizations, reinforced the trend.[8]

Operationalization is not as difficult a matter as it may at first seem, and we may engage in it without being aware of it when we argue about the meaning of words, as the students overheard in the following discussion were doing:

A: " . . . the important thing is a measure of motivation."

B: "But you have to have a measure which is relevant. Productivity is a relevant measure of motivation."

C: "Oh, come now—don't make *that* mistake!"

B: "But you have to be motivated to produce."

A: "You do not!"

The specific problem with which these students were dealing was the one of developing "independent" concepts. If concepts are operationalized so as to include *a priori* generalizations (e.g., motivation increases productivity), then tests of hypotheses utilizing those concepts are not likely to be valid.

How directly concepts must be tied to measureable elements is a matter of debate. Some assert that the operationalization must be direct; thus, "opin-

---

[7] Richard C. Snyder, "A Decision-Making Approach to the Study of Political Phenomena," *Approaches to the Study of Politics*, ed. Young, p. 7.

[8] Gideon Sjoberg, "Operationalism and Social Research," *Symposium on Sociological Theory*, ed. Gross, pp. 612, 621.

ion" might be defined as a response to a questionnaire item. Others feel measurement may be less direct. They accept "hypothetical constructs," developed to account for unobservable activity; these are reflected ultimately but not immediately in measurement. "Attitudes," for example, would be more basic than the immediate response to questionnaire items. Dubin, in dealing with this problem, distinguishes between "real" and "nominal" units; empirical indicators are available for the former, but not the latter. "The distinction . . . rests solely upon the probability of finding an empirical indicator for the unit," so that a nominal unit can be converted into a real one when an indicator is found. Dubin indicates that many theories contain nominal units, whose "essentiality rests on the fact that knowledge about the real units and their behaviors is increased when the nominal units are included in the theory." [9]

Recognition that concepts must be operationalized directly or indirectly does not provide criteria for determining how best to operationalize a term, particularly as several possible operationalizations of a single term are possible. These differing operationalizations create problems for the social scientist trying to develop generalizations by integrating research findings developed by differing researchers each doing his own operationalizing. If agreed-upon valid concepts could be developed, some of this problem would disappear.

The problem of *validity*—of measuring what we say we are measuring—continually confronts us in the course of operationalizing; in seeking valid concepts, we are really asking whether our concepts, as operationalized, are meaningful or realistic. We want to include neither more nor less than we feel should be in a concept. The continuing debate about measurement of "intelligence" suggests the difficulties. For many years, it was generally accepted that "intelligence" was adequately measured by "IQ tests." Continuing research and debate produced the feeling that the "intelligence" measured was only that of Caucasian middle-class children; many pointed out that the tests emphasized verbal facility over manual dexterity and did not measure "social intelligence," that is, one's ability to handle interpersonal situations. Thus the initial operationalization was too narrow. The concept of "alienation" provides an example of a term possibly invalid as originally operationalized because it included too much. A person who felt powerless was generally considered alienated. However, there are some citizens for whom this is not a negatively-valued state of affairs, and who do not feel estranged from the government or society when they do not possess power, for example, if they feel the government is in good hands; to the extent they were included among the "alienated," the concept covers more than it should.

Discussion of the concepts "class" and "power" (see pp. 81–84) is intended to show part of what is involved in the development of crucial concepts of social science for analytical use. The difficulty of obtaining an operational-

[9] Dubin, *Theory Building*, pp. 42, 44.

ized definition of "power" provides a commentary on the problems of developing empirically-oriented political theory, as well.

Variables. In dealing with concepts, we often talk about "variables." A variable has at least two measurements, not necessarily arithmetical, along a given dimension; for example, the vote has the measurements Democratic and Republican (in most elections). Dubin notes a difference between "attributes," where a characteristic is either present or not, and a variable, where the characteristic is present in degree. Being Negro might be an example of the former; intensity of party preference, of the latter. For our purposes, both would be variables. Variables may be classified as independent, dependent, and intervening, and can be dependent at one time and independent at another, depending on the objective of analysis. An independent variable is one from which we work to see how it affects other, dependent, variables. For example, studies of voting behavior often use frequency of voting as a dependent variable and such items as education, income and occupation as independent variables. An intervening variable is supposed to affect the relationship between an independent and a dependent variable. "Amount of political discussion" might be an intervening variable between education and the vote. Thus, if levels of education are positively related to frequency of voting, examination of the amount of political discussion might refine the relationship, indicating that, for example, among the highly educated, those who frequently discuss politics vote more often than those who seldom discuss politics. In doing this, we would be "controlling" for or "holding constant" for level of discussion, although it may sound strange to talk about holding variables constant. When we say we are holding something constant, we are in effect putting it to one side so that we can watch the relationship of other variables more closely without the intervening variable's "interference." Thus, if, in examining the impact of socio-economic factors on voting, we wished to examine the relationship of education and the direction of the vote, without the possibly interfering effect of income, by holding income constant we could examine the relationship between education and the vote for each broad category of income.

Typologies. Concepts are often utilized in sets rather than individually. These sets may have developed through the definition of terms, when one term led directly to complementary or supplementary terms. For example, defining a "liberal" as one favoring greater government intervention in the private sector of society might lead to defining as a "conservative" one who believed in less such intervention. More thoroughly developed, these sets of terms become known as typologies. Typologies are *not* theories, although they are most useful in the development of theories by providing sets of categories from which research can proceed. Nor do they make statements about what is occurring in the world; even when operationalized, typologies are only logical constructs.

There are a few basic rules for constructing typologies. Each category must be internally homogeneous. The categories must be mutually exclusive, i.e., no overlapping between categories should exist. Finally, the entire set of categories must be exhaustive of the items being studied, which sometimes requires setting up a "residual category" to take care of left-over items.

An example might be developed from "liberal" and "conservative," defined more broadly than above. They would be fit into a typology of four categories which would also include "radical" and "reactionary." A liberal would be one generally content with the current governmental system but who believed in the need for change in policies; a conservative also would be content with the system, but reluctant to change policies unless an absolute necessity to preserve certain central values arose. The radical and reactionary wish to be rid of the system, but differ as to what they wish to see replace the current arrangement; the radical would move to a system not previously experienced, while the reactionary would return to a real or imagined previous arrangement. The distinction can be tentatively shown in Table 1.

Table 1

		ATTITUDE TOWARD SYSTEM	
		Accept	Reject
ATTITUDE TOWARD	Accept	Liberal	Radical
INNOVATION	Reject	Conservative	Reactionary

One drawback of typologies should be mentioned here. As Braibanti notes,

> The creation of classificatory schemes gives an illusion of permanence and may thereby mute subtleties of distinction. They may also compel nuances to become sharpened shadows cast in "proper" places in contrived schema. This obscures new and more subtle classifications which are continually being forged and which can rarely be identified or comprehended.[10]

HYPOTHESES

Once concepts are developed, theory-building can proceed to the development of hypotheses which relate concepts to each other. Hypotheses are often derived deductively from a theory or model, and some think they can be developed only within the confines of a theoretical framework. However, in practice this is not the only way hypotheses for testing are found. They can be taken from existing research studies, from which they can be either refined or re-used. They may even be taken from works of classical political philosophy, in which case they must often be converted into hypothetical form. Intuition and personal experience can also be the source of hypotheses. While social scientists have at times been criticized for confirming the obvi-

[10] Ralph Braibanti, "Comparative Political Analytics Reconsidered," *Journal of Politics*, XXX (1968), 41.

ous, hypotheses based on "conventional wisdom," on accepted generalizations, or on the "obvious," often provide fruitful (and unexpected) findings. For example, it was recently discovered that people of higher education were less cynical about politics than those of lower education,[11] a finding which does not fit with the common expectation that as people find out more about politics, they will become disenchanted (and more cynical). In any event, no definite rules exist for determining hypotheses for use.

Research may be carried on without theory and accompanying hypotheses, particularly at the "exploratory" stage, despite the stipulation that research must be started with hypotheses and the recognition that concepts guide the gathering of facts. When research is carried out initially without hypotheses, it is hoped that they will be developed *ex post facto* so that they can be tested later. Whether conducting research without hypotheses will be the best way to proceed will depend on the previous level of information we possess about a problem and the clues we have to further information.

Regardless of where they are found, hypotheses cannot all be tested simultaneously. Just as one starts research using a limited number of factors, and continues by retaining some, rejecting others, and adding more, so one has to start research with some hypotheses and work toward others. The initial ones may be chosen because they seem intuitively to make more sense than others available. The use of intuition, or *a priori* assumptions, is permissible as a rough working criterion for deciding the order of hypothesis-testing.

When an hypothesis is tested, it is often not possible to test it under all the varied conditions in which the relationship it embodies might occur. That is, it cannot be tested under all states of the system. In many cases, conditions

> **State of the System.** A theory's "background," the basic conditions under which relations stated in the theory take place. Dubin defines it as a condition of the system "in which there are persistent values of the variables . . . of the system. Each system is distinguished from all others by the unique configuration of values for the variables in that state." [12]

cannot be controlled, as might be possible in a laboratory situation, or necessary methods may not yet have been developed. If it is not possible to develop generalizations for all states of the system, in the short run we will have to state the theory, specifying the particular state(s) of the system applicable or the population on which the hypotheses have been tested. Because of the limited way in which the testing of theories proceeds, some portions of a theory are likely to be better "filled in" or verified than others.

Often the "null hypothesis" is used in research, particularly when little certitude exists about the possible relationship between certain variables. A null hypothesis is a statement that no relationship exists between two variables, e.g., X is not related to Y. Use of the null hypothesis stems from the

[11] Robert Agger, Stanley Pearl, and Marshall Goldstein, "Political Cynicism: Measurement and Meaning," *Journal of Politics*, XXIII (1961), 484.

[12] Dubin, p. 14.

principle of statistical theory that it is easier to reject a statement of a relationship than to confirm it. When we accept an hypothesis, we always do so subject to future *dis*confirmation. If we reject a null hypothesis, we know, beyond chance probability, that the variables *are* related, although further tests will be necessary to determine with greater precision the character of the relationship. To test a statement of a positive relationship (X is related to Y) would be inconclusive, because we would not be able to determine from a rejection of the hypothesis if no relationship existed or if only a weak one did. All that rejection of the hypothesis would prove is that an invariant 1:1 relationship did not exist. Few if any such relationships exist in political life, which explains why we do not have to worry about a single case contrary to an expected relationship destroying the stated relationship; it merely alters the probabilities that the expected relationship will occur.

While initially we may be satisfied with findings which demonstrate that two items or phenomena occur together (statement of correlation), we usually want to go beyond that to other types of statements. We want to move, in other words, from statements of conjunction or correlation to those which relate the direction and amount of change in one unit to a fixed direction and amount of change in another. We want to know whether A occurs all the times B does and vice versa. Is A, found with B, merely a result of a third item, C, which brings both A and B? We also want to know whether a certain item is a necessary or a sufficient condition for another or others, although

> **Necessary and Sufficient Conditions.**   A fact, A, which is a sufficient condition for an event, X, will always be accompanied by X. If A is only a necessary condition, then X will always be accompanied by it, but A may occur by itself at other times.

such statements do not tell us completely about cause.

The clear difference between causal and correlational types of statements must always be kept in mind. Correlations help us toward causation, but do not substitute for it; they corroborate our suspicions of invariant relations between phenomena, but do not ultimately confirm such connections. Whether political scientists at some later date will feel they can move from statements of correlation to statements of causation remains unclear. Many scientists reject the idea that we can have causal theory in any strict sense. The most we can do, they say, is to state correlations of a high order of probability. Certainly in political science, current work would seem to require agreement with this statement, although some have begun to attempt showing causal paths from sets of correlations between variables.

THEORIES

Ideally a theory would be made up solely of laws. In the social sciences, however, there are very few (if any) laws. The search to develop them is continuous, despite the conflict between our abilities to verify and to generalize.

What we can verify is usually at a low level of generality, while statements of high orders of generality are not easily verified. A theory made up solely of laws would be relatively permanent; however, one made up even partly of other components such as propositions is always subject to alterations. Even if some laws existed, our work would hardly be finished, because with them we encounter several additional problems. True propositions may turn out to be uninteresting as soon as they are proved, because they are then closed issues. And, given our relative inability to generalize in the social sciences today, our more general relationships may seem trivial.

As a result of the lack of laws, social science theories include mostly propositions. In order to determine where we stand in the development of theory, it is often useful to collect inventories of propositions. Having the propositional inventory allows us to see which areas of a subject or theory need to be examined before theory-building can continue. Propositional inventories are not equivalent to theory, because the propositions are not fully related to each other. As long as one does not try to make theory out of the inventory, it can serve the function of presenting a picture of the development of a subject-matter area.

Theories also contain unanalyzed parts, called *presuppositions*, temporarily accepted as valid, although one might want to treat them as neither true nor false. In any case, they should be explicit and unambiguous. Over time, there will be fewer and fewer presuppositions in a theory, although almost every theory rests on at least a limited number of them. Presuppositions are equivalent to the axioms of a mathematical proof. They are taken as given, not in the sense that their proof has been demonstrated so often that they are accepted automatically, but for the sake of building theory which will be judged by its results. May Brodbeck indicates that "the axioms are such only by virtue of their place in the theory. Neither 'self-evident' or otherwise privileged, they are empirical laws whose truth is, temporarily at least, taken for granted in order to see what other empirical assertions . . . must be true if they are." [13]

The acceptance of axiomatic presuppositions is disputed by some who argue that nothing can be accepted without an empirical basis; they would accept only presuppositions inductively established. Even if one accepts this argument initially, the problem of needing postulates prior to carrying out of inductive reasoning remains: some theory-formation occurs even prior to the collecting of facts.

Presuppositions are often based on metaphors drawn from the world around us. Gross notes that "metaphors and analogies ranging from loose correspondences to near isomorphisms are pervasive features of every scientific theory." [14] For a long time, models, both explicit and implicit, were drawn most heavily from the physical sciences, and mechanical analogies prevailed. In the last century, the biological sciences have become a prime

[13] Brodbeck, p. 378.
[14] Llewellyn Gross, *Symposium on Sociological Theory*, p. 9; italics in original.

source of metaphors and the machine has been supplanted by the organism. Organismic metaphors have been quite useful, for example, in directing people's attention to the interdependence and growth of social institutions. While a metaphor may stimulate thinking, help us organize our thoughts, or reveal new attributes of the phenomena we are studying, we must be careful to treat it as having only a general resemblance to the subject under study until its direct applicability has been verified. Because they have been easy to visualize and because their resemblance to political phenomena seems, intuitively, to be close, metaphors have been accepted readily rather than treated as tentative.

Deduction and Induction.   Both deduction and induction play a role in theory-building, as may now be clear. As we move from theory to law to proposition to hypothesis to the testing of that hypothesis, we move from statements of a higher order to those of a lower order, an essentially deductive operation. This sort of deduction is to be distinguished from *a priori* deduction, in which we move from assumed relationships to selected facts to prove our case. Deduction, besides helping us move from theory to hypothesis-testing, also is involved in seeing whether the parts of a theory are properly related to each other internally. Theory verification involves both empirical tests of propositions and logical tests of the consistency of the propositions; the former is not sufficient. One difficulty with deduction is that the logic used in deduction may imply determinism, that is, we may take a deterministic view of the world from a deterministic mode of inference. But even if this is partially true, it is a difficulty common to any theory, because generalizations tend to follow the pattern of the theory, rather than being totally independent of it.

The feeding of generalizations based on hypothesis-testing up into a theory is part of the inductive side of theory-building. If the hypothesis tested is not upset, one infers that the proposition which is its analog is all right, and that the laws of interaction embodied in the proposition are acceptable, and so on upward. However, because any proposition leads to many hypotheses, confirming any single hypothesis does not by itself establish the proposition, but only lends support to it. The inductive and deductive parts of theory-building are closely related in operations beginning with theory formulation, continuing through theory testing and resulting in theory modification.

Quality of Theory.   The quality of a theory can be determined, and there are criteria in addition to validity which scientists utilize regularly in so judging. The "elegance" of a theory is one criterion with clearly aesthetic connotations. Other, non-aesthetic, criteria are parsimony, size of domain, and completeness. The criterion of parsimony requires that a theory be stated in as few generalizations as possible. In addition, the simpler the underlying assumptions, the better the theory. Two theories covering the same set of data can be ranked in terms of the brevity with which they are stated. Size of domain refers to the amount of data covered by the statements within the theory, with the better theory being that which has a larger domain. Completeness refers to the internal logic of the theory as opposed to domain's external reference; the more tightly knit the parts of a theory, the better.

Perhaps even more important than those criteria is predictive ability. The predictions take the form of hypotheses generated from the theory to be confirmed by testing against empirical data. The precise behavior of a particular individual or group is not specified in predictions, but the probabilities of certain types (categories) of action occurring are indicated. If well constructed from generalizations based on properly gathered data, a theory should be the source of predictions about empirical phenomena additional to those on which the theory's generalizations are based. To provide a severe test of the "expandability" of the theory, the phenomena should be outside the theory's present boundaries.

Models. Theories are by definition somewhat formal. While not permanent, they are in a sense static; at a given time, they encapsulate reality. One can have theories of change, but even they abstract relationships and "freeze" them in much the same way a photograph "freezes" a subject. In the very act of stating a theory, we make it a closed system and to that degree isolate the factors within the theory from those not included; it is thus, as an analytical structure, always only partial. A model is somewhat like a theory. As defined by Dawson, a model is "a physical or symbolic representation of that object, designed to incorporate or reproduce those features of the real object that the researcher deems significant for his research problem." [15] Although some tentative or untested theories are too hastily called models, a model and a theory are roughly identical, although model has a more static connotation. Models, unlike concepts, are not arbitrary, and can be confirmed or disconfirmed. They differ in the degree of isomorphism (the degree to which elements of the model correspond on a one-to-one basis with elements of the modeled, and the degree to which relations between the elements are preserved) they have with the modeled phenomena. In the social sciences, a model is not a concrete or "real" structure, for that would be complete and idiosyncratic, from which developing generalizations would be difficult. One possible distinction between theory and model is that the model has primarily predictive power, while a theory has both predictive and explanatory power. Models, apart from their validity, direct us toward new materials and ground not yet covered, and help us to discover more relationships, thus serving a heuristic function.

Much effort has been devoted lately by mathematicians as well as social scientists to development of models and to their formalization although formal model-building has proceeded further in economics than in political science. Formal models, particularly when mathematics is used, are rejected by many social scientists on the grounds that formalization eliminates much of the relevant detail from the phenomena being investigated, but others re-

[15] Richard E. Dawson, "Simulation in the Social Sciences," *Simulation in Social Science: Readings*, ed. Harold Guetzkow (Englewood Cliffs, 1962), p. 166.

spond that models "have a more unambiguous extractable content than do most verbal theories." [16] Formalization, whether called "mathematical modelling" or not, is something which has usually come only very late in the process of theory-building. However, an increasing number of political scientists have been developing formal models deductively, working out the implications of a set of assumptions about behavior. However, even they must have clearly developed and unambiguous concepts and their assumptions usually have some grounding in either the findings of past studies or in relationships the model-builder perceives.

A Representative Model.   One model which has appealed to many political scientists is the "funnel of causality" developed by Angus Campbell and his associates as a basis for the study of voting behavior. Their explanation of the structure, which is an ideal in terms of clarity and organization, is presented here for the reader as an example of a model useful in guiding research efforts.

"A Structure for Theory: the Funnel of Causality" [*]

The particular explanatory problem that we have chosen has certain important characteristics. We wish to account for a single behavior at a fixed point in time. But it is behavior that stems from a multitude of prior factors. We can visualize the chain of events with which we wish to deal as contained in a *funnel of causality.*

The notion of a funnel is intended merely as a metaphor that we find helpful up to a certain point. That is, like all physical analogies for complex and intangible processes, it becomes more misleading than clarifying if pressed too far. With these cautions in mind, then, let us imagine that the axis of the funnel represents a time dimension. Events are conceived to follow each other in a converging sequence of causal chains, moving from the mouth to the stem of the funnel. The funnel shape is a logical product of the explanatory task chosen. Most of the complex events in the funnel occur as a result of multiple prior causes. Each such event is, in its turn, responsible for multiple effects as well, but our focus of interest narrows as we approach the dependent behavior. We progressively eliminate those effects that do not continue to have relevance for the political act. Since we are forced to take all partial causes as relevant at any juncture, relevant effects are therefore many fewer in number than relevant causes. The result is a convergence effect.

Now let us take a cross section of the cone of the funnel at any point, erecting a plane at right angles to the axis. Let us imagine that we can measure all events and states as they stand at the moment they flow through this plane. We would expect two results. First, we would have a congeries of variables that would be, in a peculiar and limited sense, of the same "conceptual order," that is, owing to their simultaneity. Second, this array of variables should be able to predict the dependent behavior perfectly, provided that we know the necessary combining laws.

One way of maintaining conceptual clarity, therefore, is to restrict our measurements to states as they exist at one "slice of time." For example, we would not say

[16] Hayward R. Alker, Jr., *Mathematics and Politics* (New York, 1965), p. 10.

[*] SOURCE: Angus Campbell, Philip E. Converse, Warren E. Miller, and Donald E. Stokes, *The American Voter* (New York, 1960), pp. 24–32. Footnotes deleted. Reprinted by permission of John Wiley & Sons, Inc. Copyright 1960 by John Wiley & Sons, Inc.

that the 1956 preference of [a] woman . . . was "caused" in 1860 and that of [another] in 1954. Instead, if we chose to make 1954 our point of measurement, we might measure the so-called "cause" of [one] directly, but the "cause" at a coordinate conceptual level for [the other] would lie in a certain state as it existed in 1954—strong attachment to the Republican party, for example.

We do not wish to preserve conceptual order at the price of restriction in the scope of our theory. We want a theory that will help us assess the current political effects of remote events like the depression or the Civil War. Now the funnel is bounded at its narrow end by the event that we are trying to explain. If we are dealing with the 1956 election, then we think in terms of a funnel terminating on Election Day, 1956. If we wish instead to study the 1960 election, we think of a new funnel that narrows to a point in 1960; events and states of Election Day, 1956, now represent one cross section of time four years prior to the dependent behavior. Yet, there is no fixed boundary for the funnel earlier in time. In effect, we can range freely in time back through the funnel.

To think of a funnel in this way greatly enlarges our explanatory chore, for in the ideal case we want to take measurements that refer to states not at one cross section alone, but at a great number. Each cross section contains all the elements that will successfully predict the next, and so on, until we have arrived at the final political act. Nevertheless, in such an expanded theory, we must remain cognizant of the temporal area in the funnel to which any particular measurement refers. The "conceptual status" of each measurement of an independent variable involves, as one element, location on a time dimension.

But time alone is not sufficient as an ordering dimension. The states that must be measured at any cross section in time to permit perfect prediction would be extremely heterogeneous. Since qualitative differences in content are involved, a great number of ordering dimensions could·be established. Let us take note of three important ones.

Exogenous factors versus relevant conditions. First, any single cross section will be divisible into (1) exogenous factors and (2) relevant conditions. Exogenous factors are those eliminated from consideration by fiat at the outset. They include all those conditions that are so remote in nature from the content interest of the investigator that their inclusion in a system of variables, even if possible, would be undesirable. A potential voter who has a flat tire on the way to the polls may fail in his intention to vote. In this instance, failure to vote would be due to certain accidental circumstances. Sufficient motivation was present and effort was expended that would normally have led to the casting of a ballot. The immediate cause of nonvoting involved a flat tire. Once we have located this circumstance, we do not wish to pursue the matter further, tracing out the chain of events in the funnel that led to the mishap with the tire. We shall have no difficulty agreeing that such concerns are alien to our interest.

We will be obliged to understand what happens within our system of relevant conditions when exogenous factors impinge upon it. If "accidental" obstacles such as flat tires and bad weather block the way to the polls, we would like to be able to specify how much motivation will be required to surmount obstacles of varying magnitude, as well as the general incidence of such obstacles in the election situation. At the same time, we are not obliged to construct a theory that will indicate when and where flat tires will occur, or make long-range predictions about the weather on Election Day.

This relegation of some factors to an exogenous status, even though they affect the system at a time close to the dependent behavior, stands in sharp contrast to treatment of other forms of non-voting. In many cases, for example, the immediate cause of failure to vote may be a low motivational state readily linked to general indifference toward political matters. Here we are interested in seeking determinants of apathy that lie deeper in the funnel. A flat tire may be as efficient in preventing a vote as apathy, but the causes of apathy remain within our content interest. The causes of the flat tire do not.

The distinction between exogenous factors and relevant conditions is quite relative; that which is an exogenous factor for a narrow conceptual system may become a relevant condition within the terms of a more inclusive system. Ordinarily, the boundary is dictated by the level at which units of analysis are chosen and by the subject matter of the discipline in which investigation is conducted. But there is always room for choice on the breadth of the system that is to be employed.

Hence we may imagine that an outer ring of conditions within the funnel is left unobserved as exogenous. This fact has an important implication. As long as every cross section in the funnel has some exogenous factors, our predictions will never be perfect. *How* excellent they will be depends upon the proportion of the total cross section that such factors occupy. We can presume that this proportion increases the deeper we recede in the funnel, away from the dependent behavior.

The distinction between exogenous and relevant factors, though left to the discretion of the investigator, can be maintained with clarity under all circumstances. A given factor, if measured and treated within the conceptual system applied to the phenomenon, is thereby defined as relevant. We may make some other distinctions as well, which, if less clear-cut, will be of value in thinking about the nature of events in the funnel.

Personal versus *external conditions.* For some purposes it is convenient to subdivide relevant and exogenous factors according to whether or not they enjoy a subjective reality for the individual at a given point in time. We shall call *personal conditions* those events or states within the funnel of which the individual is aware, although he need not conceptualize them as the investigator does. *External conditions* are those that warrant a place in the funnel because they are causally significant for later behavior, yet which currently lie beyond the awareness of the actor.

This distinction is most useful in a consideration of the political stimuli that can affect behavior only when perceived by the actor. Suppose, for example, that we were to trace events backward in time through the funnel conceptualized for a given election. We would soon encounter a point at which the individual is unaware of the existence of the candidate-to-be, although events that will lead to that candidate's nomination and that ultimately will exert profound influence on the individual's behavior are crystallizing rapidly. At such a point in the funnel, the conceptual status of the candidate as potential stimulus object is that of an external condition. When the individual knows who the candidate is, the conceptual status shifts to that of a personal condition.

By and large we shall consider external conditions as exogenous to our theoretical system. We want to understand the individual's response to politics by exploring the way in which he perceives the objects and events of the political world. Our approach is in the main dependent on the point of view of the actor. We assume that most events or conditions that bear directly upon behavior are perceived in some form or other by the individual prior to the determined behavior, and that much of behavior consists of reactions to these perceptions.

Nonetheless, the distinction between exogenous factors and external conditions will command attention at some points. For example, we shall make use of the fact that differences in legal forms that surround the conduct of elections serve to parcel the nation into electoral subcultures. It is likely that some of these legal forms affect behavior without being reacted to as objects or even cognized. In effect, they define the limits of possible behavior; they are the external "givens" of the situation, and actors make choices within these boundaries with little sense that other "givens" are conceivable. Hence many of the legal forms, as measured and related to behavior, are external conditions; yet they are not exogenous, for we have deemed it important to include them within our current explanatory system.

Tracing the antecedents of such external conditions deeper into the funnel is the obligation of institutional analysis. Why one aspirant wins the party nomination rather than another and why one legal form was instituted in preference to another are questions beyond the scope of our inquiry. Such antecedents we therefore consider exogenous. But to recognize that conditions exist in the funnel at any point in time, which are external for the actor yet which affect current or ultimate behavior, leaves our theoretical structure open for increasingly firm liaison with institutional analysis. As these bridgeheads become established, we may deal with convergent chains of external and personal conditions, neither of which will be discarded as exogenous.

Responses toward most objects are prefaced by attitudes toward those objects, which, in a proximal sense, determine the response. Therefore, the understanding of external conditions becomes more and more important as we attempt to anticipate behavior over longer and longer intervals. When we predict at short range, few events or conditions not already personal can intervene to deflect behavior to a new course. The deeper we range into the funnel, the larger the proportion of external factors with which we must cope.

Political versus *non-political conditions.*   Finally, conditions in the funnel may in a rough way be classified into those that are political and those that are not. If we may locate factors as central or peripheral within any cross section, according to our interest in them and their presumed importance as determinants of ultimate behavior, then conditions that are political form the core, or central artery, running longitudinally through the funnel. This central position of the political in the funnel follows quite naturally from the fact that the subject of inquiry is political. The nonpolitical relevant conditions form a shell around this political core. What portion of non-political conditions shall also be considered relevant depends again on the scope of the investigation.

When is a specified condition political, and when is it not? In everyday thinking we readily categorize events and objects in this fashion. Various individuals, groups, public problems, and current happenings are considered to be more or less political. And the relationship of such objects to politics can be seen to change in time. A person may decide to "go into politics"; a public controversy is "made a political issue"; a group should "get out of politics."

More formally, classification can be made on either an objective or a phenomenological basis. Once again, an objective set of criteria would be most appropriate for some institutional types of analysis. A factory shut down in Kankakee may or may not have political reverberations. An institutional approach might provide specifications of the conditions under which such a shutdown is most likely to "become political."

But whatever the objective definition of the situation, some individuals affected may link the shutdown with political objects such as parties, issues, and candidates, whereas others will not. Thus we may depend on a phenomenological definition of the degree to which an event, state, or factor is political. If the object or event is not cognized at all (an external condition), then no such determination can be made. But as soon as a condition is made personal, then determination of its political or non-political status can rest upon the individual's particular perceptions. Wherever possible, we shall treat this distinction here as it occurs phenomenologically.

We have said that at each juncture in the flow of events, effects that are not relevant for understanding the voting act are eliminated, thus creating the shape of a funnel. This fact now has a further implication; the proportion of events that are political (objectively or subjectively) increases as we take our cross sections closer and closer to the final behavior. Relevant measurements just prior to the act will be almost completely political. At a greater distance we will have to consider a larger proportion of other social and economic factors, unless we eliminate them by definition at the outset.

Process variables: communication and "political translation." Enough of the composition of the funnel has been outlined to suggest that as events approach the narrow end of the funnel, they are more completely relevant, personal, and political. Now the boundary line between the exogenous and the relevant is drawn at the discretion of the theorist. But when we use a phenomenological approach, the way in which external events become personal, and the way in which non-political events become political, depend on processes that operate within the funnel itself. The analyst does not intervene to make a citizen aware of an external condition. Nor does he point out the political implications of objects or events that the subject perceives as non-political. These are perceptual and cognitive changes that occur naturally as events unfold. Their timing and scope depend on individual conditions and hence must be predicted within the terms of the theory itself.

Figure 2-1 shows the four possible ways in which events may be categorized according to these two distinctions. An event may at some point in time be external and non-political (A); personal and non-political (B); external and political (C); or personal and political (D). The second portion of the figure provides a schematic

Fig. 2-1. Change in status over time of events affecting behavior. (*a*) The situation at a point in time remote from the behavior; (*b*) the situation at a point in time close to the behavior.

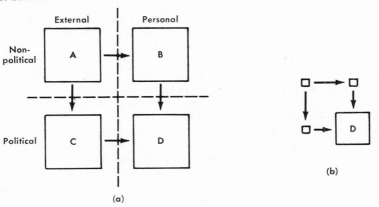

indication of the situation just before the vote to be predicted is cast. By this point in time, personal and political elements predominate: most events and conditions that are going to affect the behavior have come into the voter's awareness and have acquired political meaning.

The mechanisms involved in these categoric changes of elements over time are critical to our understanding of events in the funnel. If the vote to be predicted is that occurring in 1956, an example of an external, non-political sequence of events (A) lying within the funnel at a point early in the 1940's would be the emergence of Dwight D. Eisenhower as a major military figure. As we move forward in time, the consequences of these events can proceed from A toward D by one of two routes. In this case, the normal route was A→B→D. Early in the war few voters were aware of the rise of Eisenhower or would have attributed to it any political significance. By 1945, most Americans were aware of General Eisenhower. But for very few was this a fact of even potential political significance (B). During the mid-1940's, awareness led to some emotional content; for most Americans in this case the affect was positive. If we were measuring a cross section in time in 1947, it is likely that we could find a relationship between affect toward General Eisenhower shown at that time, and the individual's 1956 vote, even if traditional party preference were held constant. As Eisenhower began to receive mention as a possible presidential candidate, processes leading from B to D were set in motion. The object, Eisenhower, began to take on political coloration. This was faint, until his announcement that he would run for the Republican nomination. The affect that the individual felt for Eisenhower now was placed in contact with all the political cognitions and predispositions that had been formed independently in the core area of the funnel.

The second possible route from A to D lies through C (Fig. 2-1). In the illustration under discussion, this route was more rare. But there were undoubtedly a number of Americans who were personally unaware of the figure of Eisenhower until the point at which he broke into their consciousness as a political candidate. In this case, Eisenhower's movement into politics was an external event.

The major process by which an external event becomes personal is that of communication. That part of our theory that deals with the conditions under which an object or condition moves from a non-political area of the funnel to a political area will depend upon examination of communication vehicles such as the mass media and interpersonal communication. There are other more direct processes that can effect this transformation: loss of a job in 1930 may have turned the depression from an external to a personal event without mediation of a communication system in the normal sense. But most of the beliefs that come to affect political behavior are probably developed by way of communication processes.

A non-political event becomes political by a process we shall call *political translation*. As Fig. 2-1 suggests, political translation may occur externally; it also may occur within the individual himself. For some people, the fact of a depression in the 1930's immediately took on political meaning, with a minimum of outside suggestion. It was perceived directly as something that the government could and should do something about. The role of the Hoover Administration was evaluated accordingly. For others, with a different set of existing perceptions regarding the potential of governmental activity, the translation was made outside, by other agents in the society. The labor unions contended that the depression was subject to governmental control; during the Hoover Administration, Democratic Party spokesmen bore down hard on the same point. Thus the fact of depression was presented to many Americans with a political meaning already attached.

ON THE OPERATIONALIZATION OF "POWER" AND "CLASS"

Power.   Power is a relational concept, not a personal characteristic; it is exercised with respect to others. For there to be a leader, there must be followers; for someone to have power, there must also be those over whom power is exercised. Power is bilateral as well as relational. In order to lead or to have power, someone must take into account the needs/desires/demands of those he would command. As Lasswell and Kaplan noted, "those whose acts are affected also participate in decision-making: by conformity to or disregard of the policy they help determine whether it is or is not in fact a decision." [17] This also makes more difficult the identification of who is powerful and who is not.

Power is also situational. A teacher who has power to fail a student does not often have power over the content of the student's social life. Power also may inhere in certain specific positions or roles. Thus, all Presidents of the United States, even if they do not actively attempt to utilize all the instruments at their disposal, are powerful compared to other government officials. That some utilize more of the available tools than do others allows us to rank Presidents as "weak" or "strong" (or "more powerful" and "less powerful") in relation to other Presidents.

To say that power is situational and relational is still not to define the concept directly. One can start by saying that power exists when someone gets someone else to do something. A wants X done, B does it, therefore A has power with respect to B. But is this really an adequate operationalization? At first, it would appear that A has to want something done before we can talk about his having power. But that may not always be the case. If B decided to do something because he thought A wanted it done, A might have power over B's actions even if A had not communicated any orders or suggestions. As Cardozo said, the power of the Supreme Court is not measured solely by the number of times it is exercised. This "rule of anticipation," that people act on the basis of expected consequences of failing to do what they think other people want, helps to make operationalizing power difficult. Similarly, early students of community power structure felt that a person's power could be defined in terms of his reputation for power. If people act on the basis of that reputation, then it is relevant to a definition of power, even if they might be proved wrong were there an actual test.

Another problem is that, if A wants something done, B may have done it anyhow, or he may have been unaware that A wanted it done: in neither case would we be able to say that A has power with respect to B. Some feel we must include in a definition of power the communication of A's desire to B, after which, for power to exist, B would have to do something he would not otherwise have done. However, the communication need not be direct. Writers mention *manipulation*, which entails the idea that the person doing

[17] Harold D. Lasswell and Abraham Kaplan, *Power and Society: A Framework for Political Inquiry* (New Haven, 1950), pp. 74–75.

someone else's bidding is not aware he is doing so. A, in other words, engineers a situation so that B does A's bidding without any feeling of being coerced. In attempting to define community power structure, some political scientists have found that the most powerful people in the community may be those who remain "behind the scenes" or who control the "atmosphere" and the issues which are raised, rather than who openly participate in settling issues actually raised.

In any case, it is clear that consequences which follow from performing or failing to perform an action are necessary to the concept of power. Certainly the availability of some sanction, positive or negative, helps A to get B to do what A wants done. Lasswell and Kaplan, for example, talked of power as *effective* participation in the making of decisions, in turn defined as policies involving severe sanctions. If the participation is not effective, we can talk about attempts at power, but not about power itself.

Class.   Class, or, as more frequently used by social scientists, *socioeconomic status* (SES), can be operationalized in a variety of ways. Questions of objective or subjective definitions of class and the importance of "style of life" are at the heart of contemporary examinations of the subject. Emphasis by American sociologists has been on objective measures of class, that is, ones which an observer could apply after study; by contrast, subjective definitions are based on where people place themselves in the class structure. There has been a general recognition that class is more an objective than a subjective matter in the United States. "Class—I don't believe in them" is not an uncommon answer to the question, "To what class do you belong?" Sometimes, researchers attempt to combine measures of both objective and subjective class. For example, W. Lloyd Warner combined what he called Evaluated Participation (EP), which dealt with where individuals and groups stood according to their reputation in a community, with an Index of Status Characteristics (ISC), which included objective items of the type of which we have been speaking.[18]

Perhaps the earliest definition of importance was that of Karl Marx, for whom class was determined by one's relationship to the means of production. For Marx, there were two classes, the bourgeoisie (the owners of the means of production) and the proletariat (the workers). But Marx felt that class also had a subjective basis; a class did not exist, according to him, until its potential members developed "class consciousness" and associated to pursue common aims.

While Marx defined class in relation to the means of production, the economist Thorstein Veblen, in *The Theory of the Leisure Class*, related it to consumption. Conspicuous consumption, rather than production, was the important element for Veblen. In speaking of the non-material goods, e.g., knowledge and manners, that result from the use of leisure time, Veblen was really defining class in terms of what we have come to call "style of life."

[18] W. Lloyd Warner, Marcia Meeker, and Kenneth Eels, *Social Class in America* (Chicago, 1949).

The importance of the concept is shown in distinctions between the *nouveau riche* (newly rich) or *parvenu* (newly arrived), on the one hand, and the individual whose wealth is several generations old. The former are not accepted into the "upper class" because they have not had enough "experience" in living at that financial level.

Most Americans, if they perceive that classes exist, identify with the middle class. Richard Centers has shown that the form in which the question of class membership is asked has a noticeable impact on the results. "Do you consider yourself a member of the upper, middle, or lower class?" produces an overwhelming "middle" response. If one instead asks, "Do you consider yourself a member of the upper, middle, working, or lower class?," many who previously answered "middle" respond "working," which does not have the negative connotations of "lower" class.[19]

In dealing with objective social class, researchers have relied most heavily on levels of formal education, income, and occupation (ranked by prestige of the job). An index of socio-economic status is usually some compound of the three, although social scientists want to know which single factor will predict behavior most powerfully. They now find, for example, that occupation rather than income is the best single indicator of the direction of a person's vote,[20] although the combined index is better. While one's income and occupational rank were once fairly closely related, with blue-collar workers earning less income than white-collar workers, this is often no longer the case.

A current definition of socio-economic status based on style of life is the rather elaborate scheme developed by Arthur Vidich and Joseph Bensman.[21] Examining "Springdale," a small New York State community, they identified "rational farmers," who re-invest profits to expand their enterprises; professionals and skilled industrial workers, who, as employees, have fixed income ceilings, and engage in consumption competition; a "marginal middle class," including "aspiring investors," who have part-time business or farm ventures which cannot get off the ground for lack of capital or experience; the "old aristocracy," living off a steadily decreasing supply of inherited wealth; and the "shack people," who spend on immediate needs because of the irregularity of their income.

Most systems for examining SES were developed in terms of a particular community. We find some analytical schemes with three categories (upper, middle, and lower), some with four (Centers' scheme), and some with more. Warner, in his early studies of "Yankee City," developed a six-class categori-

---

[19] Richard Centers, *The Psychology of Social Classes* (Princeton, 1949); see also his Nominal Variation and Class Identification: The Working and Laboring Classes," *Journal of Abnormal and Social Psychology*, XLV (1950), 195–215, particularly 196.

[20] Angus Campbell, Philip E. Converse, Warren E. Miller, and Donald E. Stokes, *The American Voter* (New York, 1960), p. 344.

[21] Arthur Vidich and Joseph Bensman, "The Major Dimensions of Social and Economic Class," *Small Town in Mass Society: Class, Power, and Religion in a Rural Community* (Garden City, 1960), pp. 49–79.

zation (or a three-class system with sub-classes).[22] Thus one has upper-upper, lower-upper, upper-middle, lower-middle, upper-lower, and lower-lower (try saying that in one breath!); others have added middle-middle. Warner drew distinctions between the classes and sub-classes quite carefully. For example, the upper-upper class was composed of old families, possessing both wealth and the prestige which results from long-standing position in the community; the lower-upper group has wealth but not standing. Warner later modified his categories, reducing the six to five, with the original upper-upper and lower-upper being combined, because young communities simply did not have "old" wealth.[23]

BIBLIOGRAPHY

Theory-Building

While not directly aimed at political science, the Dubin volume and the Gross collection are probably the best basic introductions, although they are not easy reading. The several articles in the volumes edited by Lerner contribute to important aspects of the problem. Gregor's article deals in part with models and theories. Browning's article and Guetzkow's collection deal with the experimental side of theory-building. A good example of how a leading social scientist deals with theory-building and related methodological problems is found in Blalock. Baar deals with the role of *Verstehen* (understanding) in theory-building.

The works by Duverger and Downs are examples of systematic but partial theory, while the Apter volume and the Almond-Coleman collection are examples of macro-theory. Hyman's book is basically a collection of propositions and hypotheses; Lasswell and Kaplan's venture is also such a collection, although it is as well an example of an attempt to develop a broad formal deductive theory concerning political phenomena. Mitchell's *The American Polity* is an application of the framework of sociologist Talcott Parsons, one of social science's grand theorists; Mitchell's exposition of Parsons' political theory is also noted.

ALMOND, GABRIEL, and JAMES S. COLEMAN, eds. *The Politics of Developing Nations*. Princeton, 1960.

APTER, DAVID. *The Politics of Modernization*. Chicago, 1965.

BAAR, CARL. "Max Weber and the Process of Social Understanding." *Sociology and Social Research*, LI (1967), 337–346.

BLALOCK, HUBERT H., JR. *A Theory of Minority-Group Relations*. New York, 1967. Particularly Chapter 1, pp. 1–36.

BROWNING, RUFUS P. "Computer Programs as Theories of Political Processes." *Journal of Politics*, XXIV (1962), 562–582.

DAHL, ROBERT A. "Cause and Effect in the Study of Politics." *Cause and Effect*, ed. Daniel Lerner. New York, 1965. Pages 75–90. See also "Discussion," pp. 91–98.

---

[22] W. Lloyd Warner and Paul S. Lund, *The Social Life of a Modern Community* (New Haven, 1941).

[23] Warner, *et al.*, *Social Class in America*, and Warner and Associates, *Democracy in Jonesville* (New York, 1949).

DOWNS, ANTHONY. *An Economic Theory of Democracy.* New York, 1957.

DUBIN, ROBERT. *Theory Building.* New York, 1969.

DUVERGER, MAURICE. *Political Parties.* 2nd English edition. Translated by Barbara and Robert North. New York, 1959.

FAGEN, RICHARD R. "Some Contributions of Mathematical Reasoning to the Study of Politics." *American Political Science Review,* LV (1961), 888–900.

GREGOR, A. JAMES. "Political Science and the Uses of Functional Analysis." *American Political Science Review,* LXII (1968), 425–439.

GROSS, LLEWELLYN, ed. *Symposium on Sociological Theory.* New York, 1959. 2nd ed., 1968.

GUETZKOW, HAROLD, ed. *Simulation in Social Science: Readings.* Englewood Cliffs, 1962.

HYMAN, HERBERT. *Political Socialization.* Glencoe, 1959.

KAPLAN, ABRAHAM. "Noncausal Explanation." *Cause and Effect,* ed. Lerner. Pages 145–155.

LASSWELL, HAROLD. "The Qualitative and Quantitative in Political and Legal Analysis." *Quantity and Quality,* ed. Daniel Lerner. New York, 1961. Pages 103–116.

——, and ABRAHAM KAPLAN. *Power and Society: A Framework for Political Inquiry.* New Haven, 1950.

LAZARSFELD, PAUL F. "Evidence and Inference in Social Research." *Evidence and Inference,* ed. Daniel Lerner. Glencoe, 1959. Pages 107–138.

MITCHELL, WILLIAM C. *The American Polity.* New York, 1962.

——. *Sociological Analysis and Politics: The Theories of Talcott Parsons.* Englewood Cliffs, 1967.

RAPOPORT, ANATOL. "Various Meanings of 'Theory'." *American Political Science Review,* LII (1958), 972–988.

"Power" and "Class"

In addition to the items already cited in footnotes, the Bendix and Lipset reader contains a multiplicity of approaches to research on social class. The Bachrach-Baratz article is a good discussion of the points mentioned in the chapter. The March articles are of somewhat greater formality. An early attempt to measure power was that by Shapley and Shubik; the Brams and Russett pieces are recent contributions to the efforts to provide formal measurement of influence, particularly in terms of its concentration among the powerful.

BACHRACH, PETER, and MORTON S. BARATZ. "Decisions and Nondecisions: An Analytical Framework." *American Political Science Review,* LVII (1963), 632–642.

BENDIX, REINHOLD, and SEYMOUR MARTIN LIPSET, eds. *Class, Status, and Power: A Reader in Social Stratification.* Glencoe, 1953.

BRAMS, STEVEN J. "Measuring the Concentration of Power in Political Systems." *American Political Science Review,* LXII (1968), 461–475.

MARCH, JAMES G. "An Introduction to the Theory and Measurement of Influence." *American Political Science Review,* XLIX (1955), 431–451.

——. "Measurement Concepts in the Theory of Influence." *Journal of Politics,* XIX (1957), 202–226.

RUSSETT, BRUCE M. "Probabilism and the Number of Units Affected: Measuring

Influence Concentration." *American Political Science Review*, LXII (1968), 476–480.

SHAPLEY, L.S., and MARTIN SHUBIK. "A Method for Evaluating the Distribution of Power in a Committee System." *American Political Science Review*, XLVIII (1954), 787–792.

4 / SOME FRAMES OF REFERENCE: A

Disciplinary Approaches / Structural-Functional Analysis /
Political Systems / The Group Approach

In this chapter, an attempt will be made to examine some of the frameworks political scientists use to order political phenomena. Discussing each separately is simply a device of convenience; these approaches will often be found together in actual use. While it may be difficult to find frameworks in "pure" form in the literature, separating them analytically for the reader's first exposure is helpful.

DISCIPLINARY APPROACHES

A number of frames of reference used in political science are quite general and are based on the concepts of particular related disciplines; in political science, these would include the sociological, psychological, and anthropological frames of reference. At times these have been used when scholars trained in other disciplines turned to study political phenomena. In addition, political scientists have found that their colleagues in sister disciplines have already developed and tested frames of reference which have seemed promising. It may be easier to try to apply these already-developed outlooks than to invent totally new ones, despite the possible lack of applicability of concepts developed in a different setting. There has been sufficient continuing pay-off from the application of these frames of reference to warrant their use.

While the borrowing from sociology by political scientists has been extensive and fairly specific, there has been more borrowing of a vague and general sort with regard to the other social sciences with which political scientists are, on the whole, less familiar, such as (cultural) anthropology, (social) psychology, and (human) geography, so that one can talk of a psychological, anthropological, and geographical approach to politics. We will first consider the anthropological and geographical approaches, used least in political science, after which an extended discussion of the use of psychology in political science will follow. Sociology will be treated last.

Anthropology. The anthropological frame of reference in political science has been most useful in identifying and locating political functions in less developed political systems, which political scientists had ignored for years, and in exploring the way in which these functions are performed. While anthropologists have not been as interested in political phenomena as have sociologists, their concern with "control" in society is of long standing. Anthropologists have wanted to know the effect of political institutions on other aspects of society, a focus almost the reverse of that of the political scientist, whose primary interest has been in the effect of other aspects of society on political institutions.

When political scientists borrowed an outlook which was basically anthropological, they still did not concern themselves with communal groups below the level of the country or nation. As two anthropologists indicated ten years ago, "political scientists are concerned almost exclusively with the highly complex systems of historically known states and have barely nodded in the direction of nonliterate societies," [1] a situation not changed drastically since. While there is now a specialty known as political anthropology, primarily under the direction of the anthropologists, there is still relatively little interchange between anthropologists and political scientists. However, among the items with which the political anthropologist is concerned are integrative devices for muting conflict and the sources of the conflict; law's nature and functions; and the ways in which complex societies affect less "modern" ones with which they come in contact.

Geography. Interest in geography by writers about politics extends back at least to Montesquieu, who, in *The Spirit of the Laws,* attempted to relate political activity to geographical location and climate. The hypotheses of geopolitics are of much the same type today, explaining political power as a function of geographical configurations, climate, and access to physical resources. The geographical factor has been given varying weight as a determinant of national activity by students of international politics, who have used it more than other political scientists. One who gave geography great weight was Sir Halford Mackinder, who argued that whoever controlled the "Heartland" (central Europe, including Western Russia) would control the world.

Use of a geographical framework is also shown in the concern of public administration students about the size and type of area which can be administered reasonably by government organizations, and in the work of those who have concentrated on ecology, the relationship between the physical and social environment and man, an emphasis introduced to public administration by John Gaus.

Despite these geopolitical interests, geographers and political scientists have generally inhabited their own spheres. While "sharing of interest in the state serves as a major link between political science and political geography," [2] geographers have concentrated on "geographic patterns and rela-

[1] Douglas Oliver and Walter B. Miller, "Suggestions for a More Systematic Method of Comparing Political Units," *American Anthropologist,* XLVII (1955), 118.

[2] W. A. Douglas Jackson, *Politics and Geographic Relationships: Readings on the Nature of Political Geography* (Englewood Cliffs, 1964), pp. 2–3.

tionships," without paying equivalent attention to the institutional structure of government related to those patterns. Most geopolitical theories have seemed to overemphasize geographic factors and failed to consider technology and change.

Psychology. Political scientists have been concerned with what we now call psychology for many years, as indicated by the treatment of "human nature" by political philosophers. Only in recent years have political scientists, following the lead of Harold Lasswell, been explicitly concerned with such concepts as "personality," "attitude," and "perception." The study of public opinion is, of course, based on concepts such as "attitude" and "opinion," but even that branch of political science did not entail a notably psychological orientation until recently; although the relationship of an opinion-holder's social characteristics to his opinions was examined, opinions were analyzed for their content rather than related to psychological characteristics of the individual holding them. Similarly, early voting studies emphasized the influence of socio-economic factors on the vote, but only later were individuals' perceptions of their political world used for explanatory purposes. Political scientists' treatment of psychological elements in politics has been limited in other subfields. Obtaining adequate materials about the personality of political participants is difficult. The study of political socialization, with particular emphasis on the role of the family as a transmitter of political values, has brought political science closer to psychological materials. In addition, some scholars have written "psychological biographies." Many Americans consider such attempts to explain important figures in psychological terms generally unacceptable, even when it is admitted that the individuals contributed to their own failures, as in the case of Woodrow Wilson's defeat over the Versailles Treaty, or when the individual committed suicide, as in the case of Secretary of Defense Forrestal. The immediate negative reaction to a recently published Bullitt-Freud study of Wilson shows this even more clearly.

Alexander and Juliette George's study, *Woodrow Wilson and Colonel House: A Personality Study,* illustrates quite well the utility of psychological explanations in the study of political events. Many biographers of Wilson had written about the effect of Wilson's "temperament" on what he was able to accomplish, and had even remarked about his apparent inner conflicts, but could not explain either the content or genesis of those conflicts. By discussing Wilson's upbringing, particularly his father's harsh insistence on perfection, backed by ridicule, the Georges show at least some of the reason for Wilson's inflexibility, his insistence on "doing it himself," and his unwillingness to compromise, all of which directly affected his relations with legislators, first in New Jersey and then in Congress. The Georges also show that Wilson's inner fear of being aggressive made him embroider aggressive plans with high morality, as in his justification for America's entry into World War I, or caused him to insist his position represented overwhelming public opinion. By examining House as well as Wilson, and showing the origins of House's needs and wants (to be an advisor of high officials in lieu of being one himself), they do not attempt to explain all in terms of the psyche of one man, but show the effect of interaction, and they integrate the psychological with other, previous explanations, not neglecting political factors.

We need more systematic materials if we are to know about the impact of personality and other psychological variables in politics. In *Human Nature in Politics,* James Davies has steered us in the right direction by systematically relating the needs of an individual to his political behavior. Working from a system of needs postulated by Abraham Maslow (physical; safety; love, affection, belongingness; self-esteem; and self-actualization), Davies goes beyond others in exploring what (if any) needs must be satisfied *before* political activity occurs. According to Davies, physical needs must be at least minimally satisfied before politics will take place. Challenging the broad assertion that poverty will always bring revolution, Davies suggests that if poverty (or fear of poverty) comes *after* people are accustomed to satisfaction of their physical needs, political action to protest or restore acceptable conditions is much more likely. Davies' treatment of the need for self-actualization, reproduced here, indicates the potential of a psychological framework for political science.

"The Need for Self-Actualization" *

. . . The need for security is basic but not of the same order as the physical, social, and equality needs. It does not appear that people pursue security for its own sake, in contrast to the way they seek to satisfy the other basic demands of their organisms. They seek for security *in* the predictable, controllable satisfaction of the other needs. They want to feel secure in getting enough to eat, in the affection of others, and in the self-respect that derives from being regarded as equal. But they do not normally seem to want to be secure for the sake of being secure. Indeed, most people become politically concerned only when their security in meeting basic needs is threatened. For most people politics is thus almost purely instrumental.

This assertion as to the largely apolitical—though not asocial—character of the general public is based on several factors. For one thing, most people do in fact seem to turn their attention to politics when they are a little unsure about being able to pay for the next meal, the next pair of pants, or the winter fuel supply—or when they fear domestic insurrection or war which threatens them or their kin. For another, relatively few people seem to get concerned with politics even when tyranny threatens them with arbitrary government, perhaps because tyranny seldom, if ever, seeks to gain or maintain control on any platform other than full employment, full stomachs, and protection from all enemies foreign and domestic. Again, it seems evident that most of the relatively few who do get concerned with tyranny that threatens individual autonomy become so in consequence of some event which threatens their own individual security or which tends to ostracize them from their normal group relations in the broadest sense. (Aside from politicians, generally it is the scientist, engineer, or other employee ousted from his job as a security risk—or

* SOURCE: James Davies, *Human Nature in Politics: The Dynamics of Political Behavior* (New York, 1963), pp. 53–60. Footnotes deleted. Reprinted by permission of John Wiley & Sons, Inc. Copyright 1963 by John Wiley & Sons, Inc.

the individual who becomes a social pariah when stigmatized as a foreigner or Communist—who develops an unusual degree of political involvement.) And lastly, most of those who are political leaders are much above average in income and social integration: for them, the needs for physical security and a sense of social belonging are well satisfied.

If it sounds alarming to suggest what appears to be a selfish, inhuman, stomach-and-herd motivation pattern for the politics of most people, we need only consider the dismal alternative of the entire general public taking part in politics in order to determine by democratic majorities who should go into which occupations, what religion should be the legal one, and the maximum or minimum number of hours that must be spent daily in watching television. How then would we dispose of the wretched apolitical deviant who worked, worshiped, and relaxed contrary to law?

Although most people are apolitical most of the time, the large majority of people do at election time consider politics to be relevant to being *secure* in the satisfaction of their basic needs. But the overwhelming majority do not relate to politics their interest in those activities which are not directed toward securing the satisfaction of physical, social, or esteem needs but are pursued for inherent satisfaction—activities engaged in for their own sake, in the pursuit of happiness. The patterns of individual self-actualization are so varied that the group seeing political and governmental action as related thereto may become so small as to be politically impotent or inactive.

The person interested in recreational fishing will vote against a ballot proposition designed to open more fishing areas to commercial operation. As a fisherman, he may not be expected to have any political attitude on whether or not freedom of intellectual inquiry and expression should be restricted by sanctions against unorthodoxy. The businessman politically concerned with maximizing his freedom of action in economic matters may not be expected as a businessman to get aroused against investigations of teachers who are accused of devious indoctrination. There need be no surprise at the workingman who is secure on his job and who shows no spontaneous agitation at the fact that his union boss may have to sign a loyalty oath in order to hold his job. Only if the fisherman, businessman, or workingman is required to attest his own loyalty in order to engage in his chosen activity may he be expected to form a political opinion and engage in political action for or against oaths. If taking such action threatens his own security he very likely will not oppose oaths.

If these speculations are reasonable, they indicate limits to the amount of political action that individuals will take to *prevent* action by their governments. They may be expected to get aroused when state action threatens realization of their particular individual or group values. To expect more is to assume a measure of involvement, perspicacity, farsightedness, and perhaps meddlesomeness that is not the endowment of ordinary mortals. The implication of this is that the achievement and preservation of restrained political institutions which maximize the opportunities for individual self-actualization are a responsibility of relatively small groups influencing the action of public officials, each of which groups may be expected to engage in action designed to gain or maintain freedom from governmental interference for the group alone. In this sense, "free" as distinguished from "popularly responsible" government is the product of conflict between pairs of small groups— teachers vs. school boards; editors, writers, clergymen, and (paradoxically) government workers as individuals or as group members vs. congressional committees; and

Jehovah's Witnesses vs. local police departments—as much if not more than free government is the consequence of political participation by the general public.

There is one sense in which perhaps the large majority of people do relate their political participation to self-actualization. On any comparative basis it is clear that the standard of living in the industrialized Western world is high and that people, by and large, are relatively secure in what they have. Yet they want more and some-times seek more through their government. The relatively poor Frenchman who seeks a higher housing subsidy, the similar American who votes for the candidate who advocates a higher minimum wage or shorter hours, and any citizen who votes for a candidate who promises a reduction in personal income taxes are all well-off when compared with the unindustrialized, poor, and politically inactive Persian or Arab.

In these situations, the motivation appears to be related indirectly to the need for self-actualization, in the sense that they want a better living standard and more security generally: not for the inherent satisfaction of better quality food or steadier retirement income but in order to be able to buy a (newer) car, take a trip (or a longer one than they did last year), get a new fishing rod, or replace the table radio with a high-fidelity instrument on which they can enjoy fine music. Their political activity ostensibly has the same purpose as that of the insecure. They seek many of the same things that are sought by the insecure (minimum-wage and maximum-hours legislation, lower taxes, etc.). Yet in wanting more, one ultimate motivation appears to be a demand that government provide conditions under which they may pursue a line of activity which is related not to security but to self-actualization—to fishing rather than to fish or other food.

The relation between politics and self-actualization is here deemed largely negative for the large majority of people not just in America, with its ideological adherence to the principle of laissez faire, but in other industrial countries as well. People do agitate politically for legislation that will provide them not only security but also the time and money to pursue inherently satisfying activity. But they pursue this goal in nonpolitical ways. They look to government to provide the ground rules and sometimes the machinery, but they get their increase usually by negotiating directly for higher wages, shorter hours, etc., with employers. Or they get their increase by becoming skilled scientists, engineers, lawyers, doctors, or by a business venture.

They may turn to government to settle labor-management disputes by mediation, adjudication, or violent force. They may turn to government for a state-supported law school or a veterans' education subsidy. But the actual getting process is most of the time for most people a matter of interaction between individuals and private groups, or between different private groups, rather than between these two categories and the government. Yet it is ordinarily only when people feel insecure in the provision of food, clothing, shelter, health, and safety—when they fear arbitrary dismissal from a job, when private economic enterprise is unstable or breaks down, or when war threatens—that they turn to government.

There remains for consideration the very small minority of the general public—precinct workers, elected officeholders, and so on—for whom political participation is not readily explicable primarily in terms of the needs for security. Although this category of people is proportionally very small—as a guess, perhaps 5 or 10 million out of an adult population of 100 million in the United States in 1960—

their significance is great because they are the exceptionally active individuals and almost by definition the leaders in politics.

It would be possible to explain their extraordinary political involvement as being only quantitatively different from that of the great majority if it were evident that the exceptional individuals differ from the average only in the greater intensity with which they feel the necessity of being secure in food, clothing, shelter, health, and safety, and of being accepted and loved by the groups to which they belong. In the University of Michigan Survey Research Center's study of the 1952 election there is evidence that tends to validate the paradox that those who are most active in politics are not those who by an objective judgment are most in need of more security. People with the highest incomes, the most intricately skilled occupations, and the most education almost without exception are the ones who vote most regularly and frequently and who express the belief that voting is worth the trouble and that they have an obligation as citizens to do so. Similarly, the opposites of these people—the ones with least income, skill, and education—generally vote the least and care about it the least. It is, also, now rather clearly evident that elected public officials, ranging from President to governors to congressmen to state legislators, much more often than not are among the wealthiest, most highly skilled, and highly educated people in the society. Why do proportionally more of them become very active politically?

Lasswell's early study of agitators and administrators as political personality types was a pioneering effort in analysis of the motivation for political elites. One limitation of the analysis, however, is that describing motivation for politics as the displacement of private aggressions on public objects or as the extraordinary need for deference or as the urge for power does little to distinguish politicians from others—or to compare them with one another. Can it not with equal validity be claimed that Karl Marx displaced his private aggressions on public objects, that movie actresses have an extraordinary need for deference, and that Nicholas Biddle enjoyed power? And cannot wide differences be seen between the relatively serene personal background of Jefferson and the turbulent one of Jackson? Did they both equally have private aggressions, the former suppressing them or giving vent to them quietly, while the latter differed only in the volume of noise he made? Did John Quincy Adams and Theodore Roosevelt equally share the desire for public deference? Did Woodrow Wilson and Warren Harding equally share the desire for power?

Individual politicians like Peter the Great, Stalin, Jackson, Lincoln, Gladstone, Churchill, Bismarck, Hitler, Petain, and de Gaulle are a very heterogeneous lot. They tempt one to the occasionally voiced statement that there is no common set of factors characterizing people of extraordinary political activity. This is an easy and plausible generalization which contains a disturbing amount of truth. Both the politician, because of his subjective image of himself, and the biographer, because of his intimate involvement with the politician, are likely to encourage this impression of uniqueness.

There are large environmental influences on those people that make it incredible to imagine the often cruel techniques of Peter the Great being employed in early nineteenth-century America, or Jefferson successful in establishing parliamentary government in early eighteenth-century Imperial Russia. And the striking individuality of some political leaders makes it hard to imagine Germany being unified quite in the way it was without the particular personality of Bismarck, or to envision the temporary defeat of divisive forces within the American union in the 1830s without the unique figure of Andrew Jackson, who, in a style different from Peter the Great, offered to hang as high as Haman the leaders of a group that descended on Washington to demand restoration of government funds to the Bank of the United States. In a sense it seems to be true that the political events of a particular period are a unique and never-repeated consequence of the interaction of a vast array of forces, which include among other things individual political leaders, who in turn are personally shaped by almost as vast an array.

Many motivations for intense political participation do appear to be individual yet causally plausible. One person may be a precinct worker because he feels a particular loyalty to the candidate for whom he is working. Another such worker may distribute campaign literature because he wants to learn the game of precinct politics so that he can more effectively run for office himself. Still another may do so because he is compensating for guilt feelings induced by the shadow of his father, who was a corrupt political boss. Still another may feel that the particular political issues involved demand his active participation, even though he is cool toward the candidate, has no ambition to hold office, and his father is a universally respected member of the city council. Some or all of these individuals may also be partly motivated by a strong desire to be of public service, to do good.

Along this path of motivational investigation lies madness. Categories of motivation could be abstracted and classified in a manner that would be either meaninglessly simple and general or so complex as to addle the latest electronic computer. This is not to say that such idiosyncratic motivations are not a real part of the complex of causes for intense political activity in a particular individual. But they are so numerous, different, and likely to be so individually intertwined as to defy any kind of quantitative analysis.

The only factor which appears to be a reasonable postulate for common motivation of intense political participation is the need for self-actualization. Its manifestations, political or nonpolitical, are as varied as the number of human beings on earth and are only rarely political. Its characteristic is that it is activity in which the individual happily loses himself—getting so absorbed that, at certain times and in some situations, he is able to forget himself in the performance of activity which he enjoys primarily for its own sake and not primarily because he thereby feeds or protects himself, his family, his community—or because he can give socially acceptable vent to his aggressions, gain great deference, or bend people to his will. The choice of this activity may be conscious or unconscious, intentional or accidental, made by the individual himself or, perhaps, even for the individual by others. It is inseparable from competence, because a person cannot develop his potentialities in activity in which he is regularly a failure, and from energy level—both of which are conceptually though not behaviorally separable from motivation. Consequently some people who have competence for physical sport and a low energy level may get great inherent satisfaction out of watching a ball game on television. Others may love music, be tone deaf, and have a high energy level—all of which lead them to sponsor and subsidize a local symphony. Others get their greatest inherent satisfaction from politics, ending up as precinct workers, state legislators, constitutional heads of state, or dictators.

There might be a temptation to regard the need for self-actualization as a residual category, used to explain political activity when there is inadequate evidence that an individual is participating because of the needs for security or a place in the group. This makes the need for self-actualization either a card catalog of phenomenal, overtly expressed needs like the compensation for a corrupt father or the desire to do a favor for an old friend; or else a very empty void. Evidence for political manifestations of the need for self-actualization should be found by determining what it is that an individual likes to do best after his elemental needs for food, shelter, etc., are reasonably well secured. It is not just a matter of hobbies, because many individuals are basically happy with their work, whether it be as a machinist, business administrator, or full-time professional politician. For a substantial majority of people, politics does probably have some inherent interest, for example, during a political campaign or crisis. But for those few who do participate intensely in politics, the most reasonable, common, fundamental, and basically organic factor appears to be the inherent and profound pleasure which, for them, the game of statecraft contains.

We need not be misled by the statements of politicians that they really want to go back to the farm or edit a newspaper. If this is what they wanted more than politics, they would indeed have become farmers or editors. Charles V of the Holy Roman Empire became the equivalent after some thirty-seven years of power; Edward VIII of England after only eleven months. Most politicians prefer to die in harness or at least to serve out their full constitutional terms. There are few if any occupations, at least in our era, that give an individual a more abundant chance to realize his fullest potentialities for good or evil than politics. And it is to politics that highly ambitious people turn in the twentieth century, as such people turned to the Catholic Church in the Middle Ages and to the business world in late nineteenth-century America.

Sociology.   There has been less a borrowing of a broad "sociological frame of reference" than of specific emphases or outlooks within sociology, such as the attempt to explain behavior through examination of the dynamics of small groups or through analysis of the roles political participants take. Structural-functional analysis is the aspect of sociology which has been used most heavily and fruitfully by political scientists; it will receive separate treatment (pp. 98–108). Considerable use of the concepts and variables with which sociologists are most at home has also been made. Of most obvious note is the borrowing of what are called demographic variables, particularly

> *Demography.*   The study of the distribution of social characteristics in the population, including "vital statistics" (births, deaths, marriages), in order to find patterns of such characteristics and explanations for the patterns.

education, income, and occupation. Used heavily by early students of voting behavior, they have been put to use more recently by students of urban government, where writers are increasingly likely to open textbooks with a discussion of the effect of population movements on the growth and characteristics of cities and metropolitan areas. Demographic variables have also been

> *Metropolitan Area.*   A central city and its surrounding suburbs. Technically, a county containing a central city of at least 50,000 population, plus

> all adjacent counties with similar cities or which are related to the first county and "metropolitan in character"; the census designation is Standard Metropolitan Statistical Area (SMSA).

of valuable use in the study of the background and recruitment of political officials. Perhaps as a result of populistic suspicions that those from the

> *Populism.* A political and social movement in the United States, particularly during the late nineteenth century, although with earlier roots in Andrew Jackson's time. Its hero is the little man; it is opposed to bigness, particularly in business, and to aristocracy and special privilege. Some contemporary politicians are clearly identifiable as Populists.

higher economic strata held a disproportionate number of elective positions, some political scientists have studied the social backgrounds of office-holders. Most of these studies have simply described the background characteristics of the office-holders, including their parents' occupations, the type of community in which they were born and raised, the quality of the institutions at which they obtained their higher education, and their previous political and governmental careers, and have shown the increased "political life-chances" of white, Anglo-Saxon Protestants for most elective offices.[3] However, more sophisticated studies have related the demographic data to behavior in office, as when Supreme Court justices' propensity to dissent and to ignore precedent were shown to be related to their previous judicial experience or lack of it.[4]

A concept which has been borrowed from sociology and used to great effect is *role*, defined basically as a set of expectations about a person's behavior. A role is not to be confused with an individual's actual behavior, although some sociologists talk of "role behavior," that is, behavior resulting from a certain set of expectations. Distinguishing analytically between the expectations and the behavior is useful because not everyone acts the same way even within a clearly defined role; also, many roles are not precisely defined, leaving the individual considerable choice of behavior to meet the expectations. In addition, an individual has a number of roles, either serially or simultaneously. We are accustomed to talking of the President of the United States as chief executive, commander-in-chief of the armed forces, and party leader, indicating several of the different roles he has; he is also a husband and father. That individuals have a number of roles (in a "role set") brings about the possibility of "role conflict," in which the demands of two or more roles are felt by the individual to be irreconcilable, although some roles may be complementary rather than conflicting.

Role is basically an interpersonal concept. The expectations which make

[3] Donald Matthews, *The Social Background of Political Decision-Makers* (Garden City, 1954).

[4] John Schmidhauser and David Gold, "*Stare Decisis*, Dissent, and the Background of the Justices of the Supreme Court of the United States," *University of Toronto Law Journal*, XIV (1962), 194–212.

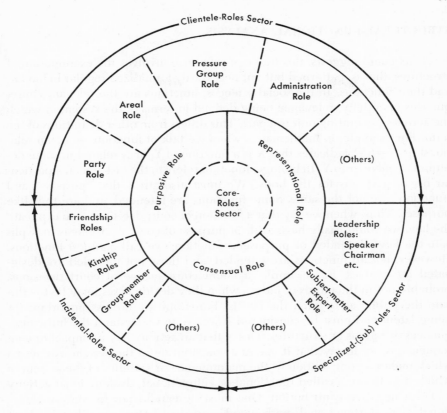

Figure 1. The Role of Legislator.

SOURCE: John Wahlke, *et al., The Legislative System* (New York, 1962), p. 14. Used by permission of John Wiley & Sons, Inc.

up the role are either those held by others of what the individual should do, or, if internalized by the individual, are of what others want the individual to do. Those who hold expectations of a legislator, for example, would include his fellow-legislators, his party leaders, and his constituents. The legislator would also have roles vis-à-vis the press, interest group representatives, and executive branch personnel. Thus, the "others" who hold the expectations of the individual are not simply an undifferentiated mass, but are themselves members of specific social groupings and holders of specific social positions; that is, roles are usually "institutionalized." The variety of groups or sectors of the population with which a person in a given role has relationships which determine his set of roles are shown in Figure 1. At the present time, role is more a useful concept which has provided explanatory power than it is the basis for a fully developed and connected set of propositions constituting a theory, despite references in the literature to "role theory."

STRUCTURAL-FUNCTIONAL ANALYSIS

As its name suggests, this frame of reference involves the examination of structures, that is, patterned but not necessarily formalized regular behavior, and their functions. In the social sciences, functions are the relevant consequences of activity, relevance being defined in terms of the system of which the activity-generating unit is a part. This differs from other definitions of the term. For example, in mathematics when we talk of function we mean relationship. $X = f(Y)$ indicates that X is a function of Y, or is related in some determinate manner to Y. In biology, function refers to the task which a particular organ performs for the body. We must also stress that "purpose" and "function" are not the same. Some functions are intended, and are thus like purposes. Thus, when we say that a function of court decisions is to explicate the law, we could easily have said, "a purpose of court decisions is to explicate the law." Intended or purposeful functions we call *manifest* functions. However, not all functions are intended, and those not intended are designated *latent* ones. For example, a latent consequence of court decisions, probably not in the minds of judges when they decide cases, may be to educate the public as to what the law is. Functions are no less important for being latent and must be considered if we are to understand the full consequences of actions or structures. To say that an activity has an impact or consequence is not to say that it makes a contribution to the system. An action which makes a contribution to the maintenance or stability of the system of which it is a part is called functional or eufunctional; dysfunctional activity makes a negative contribution. One must be careful not to confuse "functional" and "dysfunctional" with "good" and "bad." One can only talk about functional activity as good if one makes the prior normative assumption that maintenance of a particular system is good.

Until the growth of behavioralism, there had been a tendency in political science to confuse form and function. Perhaps enamored of our governmental system of separation of powers, we talked of the legislative, executive, and judicial branches, presuming that only legislatures made laws, only executive branch agencies enforced them, and only the courts interpreted them. The basic framework was maintained even though no one was sure how to classify the multi-purpose independent regulatory commissions and despite admissions that both the executive and the courts made policy.

In structural-functional analysis, one determines the important structures and then attempts to trace out the functions of those structures, as in Figure 2, or one notes certain actions and traces them back to the structures producing them, without being wedded in advance to a particular conjunction between certain structures and certain functions. Thus, one no longer confuses the legislature with policy-making or the executive branch with administration, and one has a far better idea of what results are produced by social institutions and why they continue to exist. If one knows the contributions made

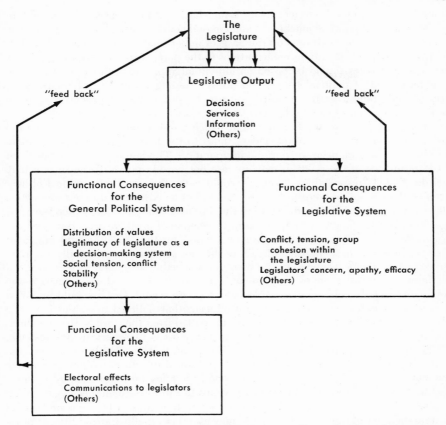

Figure 2. Legislative Output and the End Variables of Political Inquiry.

SOURCE: John Wahlke *et al.*, *The Legislative System* (New York, 1962), p. 27. Used by permission of John Wiley & Sons, Inc.

by an institution, one may better understand why the institution survives. A well-known example of the application of functional analysis to the latter sort of problem is the work of Robert Merton on the political "machine," presented here. Until Merton, most people looked at the machine solely in moral terms or claimed that its purpose was to fatten the pocketbooks of the bosses. Merton's analysis provides a quite different perspective.

"The Latent Functions of the Machine" °

. . . In [large] sectors of the American population, the political machine or the "political racket" is judged as unequivocally "bad" and "undesirable." The

° SOURCE: Robert Merton, *Social Theory and Social Structure* (Glencoe, 1957), pp. 71–81. Footnotes deleted. Reprinted by permission of The Macmillan Company. © 1957 by The Free Press A corporation. Copyright 1949 by The Free Press.

grounds for such moral judgment vary somewhat, but they consist substantially in pointing out that political machines violate moral codes: political patronage violates the code of selecting personnel on the basis of impersonal qualifications rather than on grounds of party loyalty or contributions to the party war-chest; bossism violates the code that votes should be based on individual appraisal of the qualifications of candidates and of political issues, and not on abiding loyalty to a feudal leader; bribery and "honest graft" obviously offend the proprieties of property; "protection" for crime clearly violates the law and the mores; and so on.

In view of these manifold respects in which political machines, in varying degrees, run counter to the mores and at times to the law, it becomes pertinent to inquire how they manage to continue in operation. The familiar "explanations" for the continuance of the political machine are not here in point. To be sure, it may well be that if "respectable citizenry" would carry through their political obligations, if the electorate were to be alert and enlightened; if the number of elective officers were substantially reduced from the dozens, even hundreds, which the average voter is now expected to appraise in the course of local, county, state and national elections, if the electorate were activated by the "wealthy and educated classes without whose participation," as the not-always democratically oriented Bryce put it, "the best-framed government must speedily degenerate", if these and a plethora of similar changes in political structure were introduced, perhaps the "evils" of the political machine would indeed be exorcized. But it should be noted that these changes are not typically introduced, that political machines have the phoenix-like quality of arising strong and unspoiled from their ashes, that, in short, this structure exhibits a notable vitality in many areas of American political life.

Proceeding from the functional view, therefore, that we should *ordinarily* (not invariably) expect persistent social patterns and social structures to perform positive functions *which are at the time not adequately fulfilled by other existing patterns and structures,* the thought occurs that perhaps this publicly maligned organization is, *under present conditions,* satisfying basic latent functions. A brief examination of current analyses of this type of structure may also serve to illustrate additional problems of functional analysis.

Some Functions of the Political Machine. Without presuming to enter into the variations of detail marking different political machines—a Tweed, Vare, Crump, Flynn, Hague are by no means identical types of bosses—we can briefly examine the functions more or less common to the political machine, as a generic type of social organization. We neither attempt to itemize all the diverse functions of the political machine nor imply that all these functions are similarly fulfilled by each and every machine.

The key structural function of the Boss is to organize, centralize and maintain in good working condition "the scattered fragments of power" which are at present dispersed through our political organization. By this centralized organization of political power, the boss and his apparatus can satisfy the needs of diverse subgroups in the larger community which are not adequately satisfied by legally devised and culturally approved social structures.

To understand the role of bossism and the machine, therefore, we must look at two types of sociological variables: (1) the *structural context* which makes it difficult, if not impossible, for morally approved structures to fulfill essential social functions, thus leaving the door open for political machines (or their structural equivalents) to fulfill these functions and (2) the subgroups whose distinctive needs are left unsatisfied, except for the latent functions which the machine in fact fulfills.

Structural Context.   The constitutional framework of American political organization specifically precludes the legal possibility of highly centralized power and, it has been noted, thus "discourages the growth of effective and responsible leadership. The framers of the Constitution, as Woodrow Wilson observed, set up the check and balance system 'to keep government at a sort of mechanical equipoise by means of a standing amicable contest among its several organic parts.' They distrusted power as dangerous to liberty: and therefore they spread it thin and erected barriers against its concentration." This dispersion of power is found not only at the national level but in local areas as well. "As a consequence," Sait goes on to observe, "when *the people or particular groups* among them demanded positive action, no one had adequate authority to act. The machine provided an antidote."

The constitutional dispersion of power not only makes for difficulty of effective decision and action but when action does occur it is defined and hemmed in by legalistic considerations. In consequence, there develops "a much *more human system* of partisan government, whose chief object soon became the circumvention of government by law. . . . The lawlessness of the extra-official democracy was merely the counterpoise of the legalism of the official democracy. The lawyer having been permitted to subordinate democracy to the Law, the Boss had to be called in to extricate the victim, which he did after a fashion and for a consideration."

Officially, political power is dispersed. Various well-known expedients were devised for this manifest objective. Not only was there the familiar separation of powers among the several branches of the government but, in some measure, tenure in each office was limited, rotation in office approved. And the scope of power inherent in each office was severely circumscribed. Yet, observes Sait in rigorously functional terms, "Leadership is necessary; and *since* it does not develop readily within the constitutional framework, the Boss provides it in a crude and irresponsible form from the outside."

Put in more generalized terms, *the functional deficiencies of the official structure generate an alternative (unofficial) structure to fulfill existing needs somewhat more effectively.* Whatever its specific historical origins, the political machine persists as an apparatus for satisfying otherwise unfulfilled needs of diverse groups in the population. By turning to a few of these subgroups and their characteristic needs, we shall be led at once to a range of latent functions of the political machine.

Functions of the Political Machine for Diverse Subgroups.   It is well known that one source of strength of the political machine derives from its roots in the local community and the neighborhood. The political machine does not regard the electorate as a vague, undifferentiated mass of voters. With a keen sociological intuition, the machine recognizes that the voter is primarily a man living in a specific neighborhood, with specific personal problems and personal wants. Public issues are abstract and remote; private problems are extremely concrete and immediate. It is not through the generalized appeal to large public concerns that the machine operates, but through the direct, quasi-feudal relationships between local representatives of the machine and voters in their neighborhood. Elections are won in the precinct.

The machine welds its link with ordinary men and women by elaborate networks of personal relations. Politics is transformed into personal ties. The precinct captain "must be a friend to every man, assuming if he does not feel sympathy with the unfortunate, and utilizing in his good works the resources which the boss puts at his disposal." The precinct captain is forever a friend in need. In our prevailingly impersonal society, the machine, through its local agents, fulfills the important so-cial *function of humanizing and personalizing all manner of assistance* to those in need. Foodbaskets and jobs, legal and extra-legal advice, setting to rights minor scrapes with the law, helping the bright poor boy to a political scholarship in a local college, looking after the bereaved—the whole range of crises when a feller needs a friend, and, above all, a friend who knows the score and who can do something about it,—all these find the ever-helpful precinct captain available in the pinch.

To assess this function of the political machine adequately, it is important to note not only the fact that aid *is* provided but *the manner in which it is provided.* After all, other agencies do exist for dispensing such assistance. Welfare agencies, settlement houses, legal aid clinics, medical aid in free hospitals, public relief de-partments, immigration authorities—these and a multitude of other organizations are available to provide the most varied types of assistance. But in contrast to the professional techniques of the welfare worker which may typically represent in the mind of the recipient the cold, bureaucratic dispensation of limited aid following upon detailed investigation of *legal* claims to aid of the "client," are the unprofes-sional techniques of the precinct captain who asks no questions, exacts no compli-ance with legal rules of eligibility and does not "snoop" into private affairs.

For many, the loss of "self-respect" is too high a price for legalized assistance. In contrast to the gulf between the settlement house workers who so often come from a different social class, educational background and ethnic group, the precinct worker is "just one of us," who understands what it's all about. The condescending lady bountiful can hardly compete with the understanding friend in need. In *this strug-gle between alternative structures for fulfilling the nominally same function* of pro-viding aid and support to those who need it, it is clearly the machine politician who is better integrated with the groups which he serves than the impersonal, profes-sionalized, socially distant and legally constrained welfare worker. And since the politician can at times influence and manipulate the official organizations for the dispensation of assistance, whereas the welfare worker has practically no influence on the political machine, this only adds to his greater effectiveness. More colloqui-ally and also, perhaps, more incisively, it was the Boston ward-leader, Martin Lomasny, who described this essential function to the curious Lincoln Steffens: "I think," said Lomasny, "that there's got to be in every ward somebody that any bloke can come to—no matter what he's done—and get help. *Help, you under-stand; none of your law and justice, but help.*"

The "deprived classes," then, constitute one subgroup for whom the political machine clearly satisfies wants not adequately satisfied in the same fashion by the legitimate social structure.

For a second subgroup, that of business (primarily "big" business but also "small") the political boss serves the function of providing those political privileges which entail immediate economic gains. Business corporations, among which the public utilities (railroads, local transportation companies, communications corpora-tions, electric light) are simply the most conspicuous in this regard, seek special political dispensations which will enable them to stabilize their situation and to near their objective of maximizing profits. Interestingly enough, corporations often want to avoid a chaos of uncontrolled competition. They want the greater security of an economic czar who controls, regulates and organizes competition, providing this czar is not a public official with his decisions subject to public scrutiny and public control. (The latter would be "government control," and hence taboo.) The political boss fulfills these requirements admirably.

Examined for a moment apart from any "moral" considerations, the political apparatus of the Boss is effectively designed to perform these functions with a minimum of inefficiency. Holding the strings of diverse governmental divisions, bureaus and agencies in his competent hands, the Boss rationalizes the relations between public and private business. He serves as the business community's ambassador in the otherwise alien (and sometimes unfriendly) realm of government. And, in strict business-like terms, he is well-paid for his economic services to his respectable business clients. In an article entitled, "An Apology to Graft," Steffens suggested that "Our economic system, which held up riches, power and acclaim as prizes to men bold enough and able enough to buy corruptly timber, mines, oil fields and franchises and 'get away with it,' was at fault." And, in a conference with a hundred or so of Los Angeles business leaders, he described a fact well known to all of them: the Boss and his machine were an *integral part* of the organization of the economy. "You cannot build or operate a railroad, or a street railway, gas, water, or power company, develop and operate a mine, or get forests and cut timber on a large scale, or run any privileged business, without corrupting or joining in the corruption of the government. You tell me privately that you must, and here I am telling you semi-publicly that you must. And that is so all over the country. And that means that we have an organization of society in which, *for some reason,* you and your kind, the ablest, most intelligent, most imaginative, daring, and resourceful leaders of society, are and must be against society and its laws and its all-around growth."

Since the demand for the services of special privileges are built into the structure of the society, the Boss fulfills diverse functions for this second subgroup of business-seeking-privilege. These "needs" of business, as presently constituted, are not adequately provided for by "conventional" and "culturally approved" social structures; consequently, the extra-legal but more-or-less efficient organization of the political machine comes to provide these services. To adopt an *exclusively* moral attitude toward the "corrupt political machine" is to lose sight of the very structural conditions which generate the "evil" that is so bitterly attacked. To adopt a functional outlook on the political machine is not to provide an apologia, but a more solid base for modifying or eliminating the machine, *providing* specific structural arrangements are introduced either for eliminating these effective demands of the business community or, if that is the objective, of satisfying these demands through alternative means.

A third set of distinctive functions fulfilled by the political machine for a special subgroup is that of providing alternative channels of social mobility for those otherwise excluded from the more conventional avenues for personal "advancement." Both the sources of this special "need" (for social mobility) and the respect in which the political machine comes to help satisfy this need can be understood by examining the structure of the larger culture and society. As is well known, the American culture lays enormous emphasis on money and power as a "success" goal legitimate for all members of the society. By no means alone in our inventory of cultural goals, it still remains among the most heavily endowed with positive affect and value. However, certain subgroups and certain ecological areas are notable for the relative absence of opportunity for achieving these (monetary and power) types of success. They constitute, in short, sub-populations where "the cultural emphasis upon pecuniary success has been absorbed, but where there is *little access to conventional and legitimate* means for attaining such success. The conventional occupational opportunities of persons in (such areas) are almost completely limited to manual labor. Given our cultural stigmatization of manual labor, and its correlate, the prestige of white-collar work," it is clear that the result is a tendency to achieve these culturally approved objectives *through whatever means are possible*. These people are on the one hand, "asked to orient their conduct toward the prospect of accumulating wealth [and power] and, on the other, they are largely denied effective opportunities to do so institutionally."

It is within this context of social structure that the political machine fulfills the basic function of providing avenues of social mobility for the otherwise disadvantaged. Within this context, even the corrupt political machine and the racket "represent the triumph of amoral intelligence over morally prescribed 'failure' when the channels of vertical mobility are closed or narrowed *in a society which places a high premium on economic affluence, [power] and social ascent for all its members."* As one sociologist has noted on the basis of several years of close observation in a "slum area:"

> The sociologist who dismisses racket and political organizations as deviations from desirable standards thereby neglects some of the major elements of slum life. . . . *He does not discover the functions they perform for the members* [of the groupings in the slum]. The Irish and later immigrant peoples have had the greatest difficulty in finding places for themselves in our urban social and economic structure. Does anyone believe that the immigrants and their children could have achieved their present degree of social mobility without gaining control of the political organization of some of our largest cities? The same is true of the racket organization. *Politics and the rackets have furnished an important means of social mobility for individuals, who, because of ethnic background and low class position,* are blocked from advancement in the "respectable" channels.[*]

This, then represents a third type of function performed for a distinctive subgroup. This function, it may be noted in passing, is fulfilled by the *sheer* existence and operation of the political machine, for it is in the machine itself that these individuals and subgroups find their culturally induced needs more or less satisfied. It refers to the services which the political apparatus provides for its own personnel. But seen in the wider social context we have set forth, it no longer appears as *merely* a means of self-aggrandizement for profit-hungry and power-hungry *individuals*, but as an organized provision for *subgroups* otherwise excluded or restricted from the race for "getting ahead."

Just as the political machine performs services for "legitimate" business, so it operates to perform not dissimilar services for "illegitimate" business: vice, crime and rackets. Once again, the basic sociological role of the machine in this respect can be more fully appreciated only if one temporarily abandons attitudes of moral indignation, to examine with all moral innocence the actual workings of the organization. In this light, it at once appears that the subgroup of the professional criminal, racketeer, gambler, has basic similarities of organization, demands and opera-

[*] *William F. Whyte, "Social Organization in the Slums,"* American Sociological Review, VIII (1943), 34–39. *Italics supplied.*

tion to the subgroup of the industrialist, man of business, speculator. If there is a Lumber King or an Oil King, there is also a Vice King or a Racket King. If expansive legitimate business organizes administrative and financial syndicates to "rationalize" and to "integrate" diverse areas of production and business enterprise, so expansive rackets and crime organize syndicates to bring order to the otherwise chaotic areas of production of illicit goods and services. If legitimate business regards the proliferation of small business enterprises as wasteful and inefficient, substituting, for example, the giant chain stores for the hundreds of corner groceries, so illegitimate business adopts the same businesslike attitude, and syndicates crime and vice.

Finally, and in many respects, most important, is the basic similarity, if not near-identity, of the economic role of "legitimate" business and "illegitimate" business. *Both are in some degree concerned with the provision of goods and services for which there is an economic demand.* Morals aside, they are both business, industrial and professional enterprises, dispensing goods and services which some people want, for which there is a market in which goods and services are transformed into commodities. And, in a prevalently market society, we should expect appropriate enterprises to arise whenever there is a market demand for given goods or services.

As is well known, vice, crime and the rackets *are* "big business." Consider only that there have been estimated to be about 500,000 professional prostitutes in the United States, and compare this with the approximately 200,000 physicians and 200,000 nurses. It is difficult to estimate which have the larger clientele: the professional men and women of medicine or the professional men and women of vice. It is, of course, difficult to estimate the economic assets, income, profits and dividends of illicit gambling in this country and to compare it with the economic assets, income, profits and dividends of, say, the shoe industry, but it is altogether possible that the two industries are about on a par. No precise figures exist on the annual expenditures on illicit narcotics, and it is probable that these are less than the expenditures on candy, but it is also probable that they are larger than the expenditure on books.

It takes but a moment's thought to recognize that, *in strictly economic terms*, there is no relevant difference between the provision of licit and of illicit goods and services. The liquor traffic illustrates this perfectly. It would be peculiar to argue that prior to 1920 (when the 18th amendment became effective), the provision of liquor constituted an economic service, that from 1920 to 1933, its production and sale no longer constituted an economic service dispensed in a market, and that from 1934 to the present, it once again took on a serviceable aspect. Or, it would be *economically* (not morally) absurd to suggest that the sale of bootlegged liquor in the dry state of Kansas is less a response to a market demand than the sale of publicly manufactured liquor in the neighboring wet state of Missouri. Examples of this sort can of course be multiplied many times over. Can it be held that in European countries, with registered and legalized prostitution, the prostitute contributes an economic service, whereas in this country, lacking legal sanction, the prostitute provides no such service? Or that the professional abortionist is in the economic market where he has approved legal status and that he is out of the economic market where he is legally taboo? Or that gambling satisfies a specific demand for entertainment in Nevada, where it is one of the largest business enterprises of the largest city in the state, but that it differs essentially in this respect from movie houses in the neighboring state of California?

The failure to recognize that these businesses are only *morally* and not *economi-*

cally distinguishable from "legitimate" businesses has led to badly scrambled analysis. Once the economic identity of the two is recognized, we may anticipate that if the political machine performs functions for "legitimate big business" it will be all the more likely to perform not dissimilar functions for "illegitimate big business." And, of course, such is often the case.

The distinctive function of the political machine for their criminal, vice and racket clientele is to enable them to operate in satisfying the economic demands of a large market without due interference from the government. Just as big business may contribute funds to the political party war-chest to ensure a minimum of governmental interference, so with big rackets and big crime. In both instances, the political machine can, in varying degrees, provide "protection." In both instances, many features of the structural context are identical: (1) market demands for goods and services; (2) the operators' concern with maximizing gains from their enterprises; (3) the need for partial control of government which might otherwise interfere with these activities of businessmen; (4) the need for an efficient, powerful and centralized agency to provide an effective liaison of "business" with government.

Without assuming that the foregoing pages exhaust either the range of functions or the range of subgroups served by the political machine, we can at least see that *it presently fulfills some functions for these diverse subgroups which are not adequately fulfilled by culturally approved or more conventional structures.*

Several additional implications of the functional analysis of the political machine can be mentioned here only in passing, although they obviously require to be developed at length. First, the foregoing analysis has direct implications for *social engineering.* It helps explain why the periodic efforts at "political reform," "turning the rascals out" and "cleaning political house" are typically short-lived and ineffectual. It exemplifies a basic theorem: *any attempt to eliminate an existing social structure without providing adequate alternative structures for fulfilling the functions previously fulfilled by the abolished organization is doomed to failure.* (Needless to say, this theorem has much wider bearing than the one instance of the political machine.) When "political reform" confines itself to the manifest task of "turning the rascals out," it is engaging in little more than sociological magic. The reform may for a time bring new figures into the political limelight; it may serve the casual social function of re-assuring the electorate that the moral virtues remain intact and will ultimately triumph; it may actually effect a turnover in the personnel of the political machine; it may even, for a time, so curb the activities of the machine as to leave unsatisfied the many needs it has previously fulfilled. But, inevitably, unless the reform also involves a "re-forming" of the social and political structure such that the existing needs are satisfied by alternative structures or unless it involves a change which eliminates these needs altogether, the political machine will return to its integral place in the social scheme of things. *To seek social change, without due recognition of the manifest and latent functions performed by the social organization undergoing change, is to indulge in social ritual rather than social engineering.* The concepts of manifest and latent functions, (or their equivalents) are indispensable elements in the theoretic repertoire of the social engineer. In this crucial sense, these concepts are not "merely" theoretical (in the abusive sense of the term), but are eminently practical. In the deliberate enactment of social change, they can be ignored only at the price of considerably heightening the risk of failure.

A second implication of our analysis of the political machine also has a bearing upon areas wider than the one we have considered. The "paradox" has often been noted that the supporters of the political machine include both the "respectable" business class elements who are, of course, opposed to the criminal or racketeer and the distinctly "unrespectable" elements of the underworld. And, at first appearance, this is cited as an instance of very strange bedfellows. The learned judge is not infrequently called upon to sentence the very racketeer beside whom he sat the night before at an informal dinner of the political bigwigs. The district attorney jostles the exonerated convict on his way to the back room where the Boss has called a meeting. The big businessman may complain almost as bitterly as the big racketeer about the "extortionate" contributions to the party fund demanded by the Boss. Social opposites meet—in the smoke-filled room of the successful politician.

In the light of a functional analysis all this of course no longer seems paradoxical. Since the machine serves both the businessman and the criminal man, the two seemingly antipodal groups intersect. This points to a more general theorem: *the social functions of an organization help determine the structure (including the recruitment of personnel involved in the structure), just as the structure helps determine the effectiveness with which the functions are fulfilled.* In terms of social status, the business group and the criminal group are indeed poles apart. But status does not fully determine behavior and the inter-relations between groups. Functions modify these relations. Given their distinctive needs, the several subgroups in the large society are "integrated," whatever their personal desires or intentions, by the centralizing structure which serves these several needs. In a phrase with many implications which require further study, *structure affects function and function affects structure.*

There is more to structural-functional analysis than Merton's type of work, however. Following the lead of Talcott Parsons, sociologists have attempted to identify society's functional requisites, that is, the functions which must be performed if the society is to continue to operate. The four usually noted are goal attainment, the principal function performed by the polity; adaptation, involving activities which provide resources for the social system's operation; integration, entailing holding the system together; and pattern maintenance. Pattern maintenance, also called allocation, involves the transmission of major values, the application of sanctions for violations of values, and operation of a "tension management process . . . to prevent the development of situations that increase the probability that large numbers of actors will violate basic norms." [5]

Applying structural-functional analysis to political science, some researchers have developed lists of political functional requisites. One such list was developed by Gabriel Almond, who divides them into four input and three output (or "governmental") functions. [6] The latter are rule-making, rule-application, and rule-adjudication, equivalent to what we conventionally

[5] Robert T. Holt, "A Proposed Structural-Functional Framework for Political Science," *Functionalism in the Social Sciences: The Strengths and Limits of Functionalism . . .* ed. Don Martindale (Philadelphia, 1965), pp. 92–93.

[6] Gabriel A. Almond, "Introduction: A Functional Approach to Comparative Politics," *The Politics of Developing Areas,* ed. Almond and James S. Coleman (Princeton, 1960), p. 17.

think of as the tasks of the three branches of our government. As such they have been criticized for not getting far enough away from the framework of modern, complex societies. Almond's four input functions are political socialization and recruitment, interest articulation, interest aggregation, and political communication. The last is the easiest to explain, because all political functions require communication, and at times the communication network appears to have a life of its own. Accordingly, political socialization is carried out largely within the family and other primary groups. This is at a

> **Primary Group.** **A collection of people interacting frequently on the basis of face-to-face relations. Family and friendship groups are examples.** *Secondary groups,* **or** *associations,* **have less frequent internal interaction, and are characterized, at least in part, by the use of impersonal means of communications between members.**

"pre-political stage," that is, before the individual is participating directly in political affairs. As a learning process, it continues until adulthood. "Political recruitment" is later, more explicitly political, adult socialization; it involves the training of members of society in the skills needed for specialized political roles.

Interest articulation is connected with statements of demands. We in America tend to associate the performance of this function with interest groups (what Almond calls "associational interest groups"), formal organizations which specialize in communicating members' desires. However, Almond points out that interests can also be articulated through "institutional interest groups," institutions such as churches and armies established for purposes other than advocating interests but which articulate their own interests; "non-associational interests," including ethnic groups and kinship groups; and "anomic interest groups," that is, riots and demonstrations. Interests must be aggregated as well as articulated, that is, they must be brought together and sifted at some point in the system, resulting in ideas more general than those embodied in the originally and individually articulated interests. While suggesting that the "functions of articulation and aggregation overlap," because "the narrowest event of interest articulation . . . involves the aggregation of the claims of even smaller groups or of firms," [7] Almond designates them as separate functions.

POLITICAL SYSTEMS

An analytical scheme which provides a broad framework for the examination of politics is that of the "political system." [8] Not truly a model, it provides

---

[7] *Ibid.*, p. 39.

[8] Not to be confused with "systems analysis," a decision-oriented method of inquiry for aiding a decision-maker in assessing alternative courses of action. See E. S. Quade, *Analysis for Military Decisions*, ed. Quade (Chicago, 1964), p. 4.

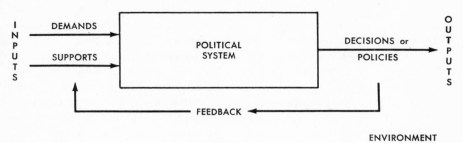

Figure 3.

SOURCE: David Easton, "An Approach to the Analysis of Political Systems," *World Politics*, IX (1957), 384. Used by permission.

the theoretical equipment both for looking at political phenomena on a macroscopic level and the setting in which micro-analysis can be carried out, by providing an opportunity for the political scientist to relate the more specific work he is doing to the larger political world. The political system idea serves to keep us attuned to the broad implications of political acts and institutions, and to the interrelatedness of events rather than to their idiosyncratic or particularistic aspects. Until the systems approach was developed, political scientists studying one area of politics or government had no way in which to place in context the phenomena they were studying or to relate institutions to each other systematically. Not only does the political systems framework encourage political scientists to check for such interrelationships, but also it provides a large-scale map of the political world so the researcher can see which areas remain unexplored. Its leading exponents claim that the systems framework "represents a genuinely important step in the direction of science" for political science and provides a new paradigm for the discipline.[9]

The first important presentation of the systems approach in political science was made by David Easton. In his first model (See Figure 3), he was primarily concerned with portraying the relationships between a system and the environment in which it was located. He directed attention to the boundary between politics and other aspects of social life and postulated the existence of a close relationship between system and environment. The boundaries of a system were to be inferred from the frequency of relations between units. But if a unit interacted with other certain variables in the system with only erratic infrequency, should it then be included? Some have argued that one should distinguish between (relatively) self-contained or closed systems and open systems, while others assert that an "open system" is a contradiction in terms, because no way would exist to distinguish it from its environment. If, as Easton noted earlier, "all those variables essential to an

[9] Gabriel A. Almond, "Political Theory and Political Science," *American Political Science Review*, LX (1966), 875.

understanding of a significant area of social behavior constitute a determinate system,"[10] the criterion of frequency of relationship between units at least provides a way of setting up some admittedly arbitrary cutting points between system and environment and between system and system.

Easton divided the basic components of his model into inputs, consisting of "demands" and "support," and outputs, connected by feedback. Support derives from satisfaction with the system's outputs, and from more generalized or diffuse support or approval for the system itself. The latter is necessary because a system's outputs cannot satisfy everyone. Easton distinguishes between external demands coming from the environment and internal ones from within the system. There are also three objects of support: the "political community," defined as a "group that seeks to settle differences or promote decisions through peaceful action in common"; the "regime," equivalent to the constitutional order, including arrangements for the processing of demands and implementation of decisions; and the government, which undertakes concrete tasks. The relationship between these levels is portrayed in Figure 4.

The difficulty with Easton's diagrammatic presentation (Figure 3), although not with his textual explication, is that one cannot tell what occurs within the "Black Box." It seems mysteriously to process the demands and support into decisional outcomes. The problem may be resolved by portraying the original model with an internal modification, which makes clear that activity does occur within the system, that the system itself generates demands and support, and that some of the outcomes are "consumed" within the system without having an immediate impact on the environment. (See Figure 5.)

Once Easton had presented his original "box model," others were soon to follow with different ways of depicting the system. As Figure 6 shows,

Figure 4.

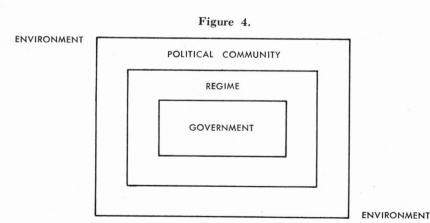

[10] David Easton, "Limits of the Equilibrium Model in Social Research," *Political Behavior: A Reader in Theory and Research,* ed. Eulau, *et al.,* p. 398.

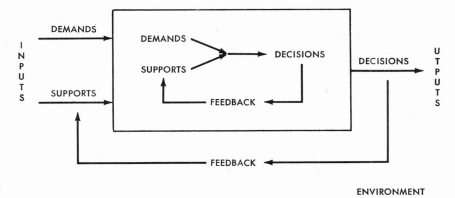

Figure 5.

Mitchell divided inputs and outputs somewhat differently from Easton, indicating that demands and support do not account for all the system's inputs; expectations (what individual members of the society desire, but short of demands and perhaps not even conscious) and resources, on which the system operates, are also necessary. Mitchell also refines the outputs of the system into three categories: goals, values and costs, and controls. Values in a sense are positive outputs, and costs, negative ones; what is a value for one person usually involves costs for himself or others. Controls are the ways in which the goals, values, and costs are implemented. Easton himself has also presented a number of additional versions of his original model, one of which is presented in Figure 7.

Frequently connected with the system concept has been the idea of equilibrium. If the parts of a system develop a set of relationships to which the system returns when disturbed, so that a steady-state exists, equilibrium is said to occur; in the physical sciences, this is known as homeostasis. In the social sciences, where subjects studied undergo constant change, an equilib-

Figure 6.

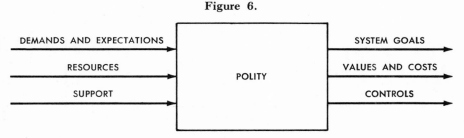

SOURCE: William C. Mitchell, *The American Polity* (New York: The Free Press, 1962), p. 6. Used with permission of The Macmillan Company. © by The Free Press of Glencoe, a Division of The Macmillan Company, 1962.

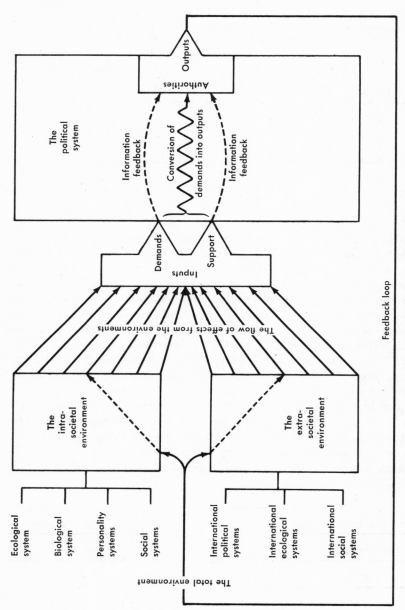

Figure 7. A Dynamic Response Model of a Political System

SOURCE: David Easton, *A Systems Analysis of Political Life* (New York, 1965), p. 30. Used by permission of John Wiley & Sons, Inc. (For a more elaborate version, see the same volume, pp. 74–75.)

rium would be a special case, not a general occurrence. However, equilibrium, as an analytical concept applied by the observer, not a goal in the minds of the system's actors, can be used to provide a base-line from which movement can be measured, thus allowing observers to ascertain how far a system can move from a posited point without serious strains being produced.

The idea of disequilibrium may provide an escape from equilibrium's static connotations. To Easton it suggests more than change but contains recognition that events occur to block a full return to or arrival at equilibrium. Disequilibrium, while containing a more accurate description of political reality than does equilibrium, by shifting emphasis from stability to disturbance, does not adequately provide for "forward motion." To surmount this problem, some have talked of a "dynamic equilibrium," in which the entire system moves with respect to its environment and no single steady-state even occurs, "with the position of equilibrium of the system itself always shifting." [11]

THE GROUP APPROACH

The group approach is basically an attempt, often overdone as occurs with single-factor analysis, to describe political life in terms of groups to which people belong as formal members, groups from which they take cues or which provide the frames of reference within which they take action (reference groups), and the informal groups within which they interact at work and play. Thus citizen John Doe is raised in one primary group, the family, in which certain political values are transmitted to him; he lives in another primary group, his own family, whose needs may affect his political outlook; at work he regularly comes in contact with a certain group of men, with whom he may discuss politics; in addition, Doe may belong to certain formal organizations—a labor union, a church, a rifle association, or a neighborhood improvement group—which deal directly with important social and political issues.

The subject of the group has been central to the study of politics for many years. Within political philosophy, the group has been considered important in terms of its relationship to government; whether government is more important or less important than major interest groups or social institutions or is on the same plane with them is a question which has long agitated students of pluralism. At one extreme, some political philosophers have taken the posi-

Pluralism. A state of affairs in which a multiplicity of groups or institutions are operative within society. Observers of American politics often talk of its pluralistic quality because of the number and diversity of participants. Pluralism can be contrasted with *monism*, in which one institution

[11] *Ibid.*, p. 399.

or group is predominant, and *dualism*, in which two, e.g., church and state, are controlling.

tion that government is passive, a *tabula rasa* (blank slate) on which interest groups write their wishes, with government policy merely reflecting the relative strengths of the groups. Others see government as only an umpire or referee between contending parties, still with no particular position or will of its own, or as only *primus inter pares* (first among equals), with no more power than any one of the major institutional groupings in society. However, still others have recognized that government's role is more active and that government is predominant, with groups placed in a position of petitioning the government for action favorable to the group or attempting to get the government to decide on such action.

It is difficult to pinpoint exactly the beginning of the modern "group approach" in political science. Some date it from the publication in 1951 of David Truman's *The Governmental Process;* however, Truman's work was not without predecessors, and Arthur Bentley, to whose *The Process of Government* much homage has been paid, is often cited as the originator of attention to the group. (How closely Bentley's approach has been followed by those who claim descent from him is another matter.) The group approach has been used mainly to explain legislative action, because the legislature is where interest groups have tended to exert much of their effort. The increased efforts of interest groups to achieve their goals through the administrative process and the courts has also been recognized. This emphasis on group action in various political arenas has led to the suggestion that group theory of the type developed by Truman is really more a "group theory of politics" than it is a "theory of interest groups," with relatively little attention paid to problems of group formation and group internal processes.[12]

Truman's definition of interest group provides a useful starting point for a discussion of modern group theory. An "interest group" is a collection of individuals which

> on the basis of one or more shared attitudes, makes certain claims upon other groups in the society for the establishment, maintenance, or enhancement of forms of behavior that are implied in the shared attitudes. . . . The shared attitudes constitute the interests.[13]

To talk of shared attitudes is too limiting; any shared characteristic, whether an attitude or not, is sufficient as the basis for an interest group. To talk of attitude focuses attention too narrowly on "purpose groups" or "principle groups" like the National Association for the Advancement of Colored People (NAACP) and the American Civil Liberties Union (ACLU) to the neglect or exclusion of groups like the National Association of Manufacturers (NAM),

---

[12] Robert Salisbury, "An Exchange Theory of Interest Groups," *Midwest Journal of Political Science*, XIII (1969), 2–3. Salisbury also suggests that one effect of the success of Truman's volume may have been to shut off research on interest groups for many years.

[13] David Truman, *The Governmental Process* (New York, 1951), pp. 33–34.

the American Medical Association (AMA), and the American Federation of Labor-Congress of Industrial Organizations (AFL-CIO), whose members have objective, e.g., economic or occupational, characteristics in common. In any case, what is crucial, as Truman points out, is not the shared attitude (or characteristic) but the interaction within the group which takes place based on what is shared. This interaction or activity was the key to interest groups to Bentley, for whom a group was

> a certain portion of the men of a society, taken . . . not as a physical mass cut off from other masses of men, but as a mass activity, which does not preclude the men who participate in it from participating likewise in many other group activities.[14]

Thus the activities *are* the groups, and each group is an interest, with the group being inseparable from its interest. As Charles Hagan put it, "interest group is a tautologous expression." [15]

Political scientists have often departed from Bentley's approach to the subject by emphasizing the group as if it were a concrete independent entity and de-emphasizing the analytical element of activity. This resulted from almost exclusive attention to long-lived, formal interest groups with permanent offices in Washington, D.C., and large corps of lobbyists. Sociologists and more behaviorally-oriented political scientists have, however, been more willing to recognize informal groups and their impact on individual political behavior. That other types of groups exist which have relevance for politics is clear. The most elementary type mentioned in the literature is the "categoric group," a collection of individuals with no other marks of identification than a common characteristic. "Statistical groups," to which they are equivalent, have no organization, no social relations between members, and no consciousness of kind.[16] In "incipient groups," mentioned by Latham, a common interest exists but is not recognized by the members of the group; until such a group has manifested some activity, it, like Truman's "potential group," is difficult to identify in behavioral terms. A conscious group has a sense of community between its "members," and an organized group is a "conscious group which has established an objective and formal apparatus to promote the common interest." [17] As Truman points out, formal organization is only one stage of group interaction. "The existence of neither the group nor the interest is dependent upon formal organization, although that feature has significance, particularly in the context of politics." [18] For an interest group

[14] Arthur Bentley, *The Process of Government* (Evanston, 1908; reissued in 1935, 1949), p. 212.
[15] Charles Hagan, "The Group in Political Science," *Life, Language, Law*, ed. Richard W. Taylor (Yellow Springs, Ohio, 1957), p. 117.
[16] Richard Bierstedt, "The Sociology of Majorities," *American Sociological Review*, XIII (1948), 703.
[17] Earl Latham, "The Group Basis of Politics: Notes for a Theory," *American Political Science Review*, XLVI (1952), 384n.
[18] Truman, p. 36.

to be a "political interest group," the claims or demands it makes must be made on or through government; however, because of the variable involvement of many groups in the political arena, the term is not particularly useful.

Efforts to distinguish between interest groups on the basis of degree of organization have brought analysts face-to-face with the question of "membership" in groups. While there are some groups which have elaborate formal membership procedures, formal membership is not the only relationship people have with groups. They may be non-members in a formal sense and still be relevant to the group's activities. Thus, for some purposes government officials can be considered members of interest groups on the basis of their regular interaction with other members of the group or their adoption of the group's desires. Those who, although not formal members, sympathize with a group and identify with it clearly are relevant for the group's position in the political system, and may actually be of greater importance than some of the formal but inactive members.

That individuals have relations with groups other than through formal membership also increases the chances of multiple "memberships" or affiliations, particularly ones which conflict with each other and create situations of cross-pressure. With very few exceptions, men do not devote all of their efforts to a single group; they participate, formally or informally, in several. Groups are neither monolithic nor exclusive. A theory has been developed that these multiple and overlapping memberships reduce the amount of conflict in society, by providing limits to the action and demands of each of the groups; supposedly no group, with members who have relationships in other groups, would want to push so hard as to alienate those with conflicting allegiances. Conflict resulting from cleavages in society is reduced, but not eliminated, by this overlapping of membership. The conflict shifts from the intergroup level to intra-individual conflict (within the individual's mind).

While this theory has been challenged at least as applied to formal interest groups on the basis that Americans, particularly at lower socio-economic levels, are not the joiners our conventional wisdom suggests they are, the theory concededly has some validity if groups are defined in terms of informal and/or primary groups. However, multiple memberships must overlap for the conflict-reduction to take place, so the simple fact of multiple membership is not sufficient; the memberships could be cumulative, thus reinforcing conflict rather than reducing it.

BIBLIOGRAPHY

The volumes by Meehan and Oran Young discuss the frameworks covered in this chapter, and will be valuable supplements for the reader. Roland Young's collection deals with these and a number of other frames of reference.

The anthropological approach is discussed by Eisenstadt, by Easton in his article in the *Biennial Review of Anthropology*, and is represented in the work by Fortes and Evans-Pritchard. Jackson's collection of readings is illustrative of the application of geography to politics. Davies' volume, from which a selection was reprinted in this chapter, and Rieff's article give a perspective on the use of psychology in political science, as does the Appendix of Gottfried's biography of Cermak. Edinger's work is another example (in addition to those cited in the chapter) of a psychological biography.

Drawing on sociology, Mitchell illustrates the application of the concept of "role." Marion Levy's volume is a full-scale theoretical development of functional theory, based on and paralleling Talcott Parsons' functional requisites for society, but far more understandable than Parsons' work. Apter's article deals with political functional requisites, and Martindale's collection contains articles discussing the relevance of the functional approach to political science as well as other social sciences. Gregor's article contains some trenchant criticism of functionalism.

Easton's *Systems Analysis of Political Life* is his most complete development of the political system idea, first broached in his *World Politics* article and carried forward somewhat in *A Framework for Political Analysis*. The Almond-Coleman volume is based on Almond's typology of the functions performed within political systems. Almond's separate article shows a more recent approach that author has used in analyzing political systems.

Truman's book is perhaps the recent classic of group theory, while the Monypenny and Latham articles also develop the theory incisively. Gross was one of the earliest to utilize it. Rothman's article is a criticism of some aspects of Truman's theory, particularly the "overlapping membership" idea, which is also discussed by Verba. The White and Lippitt volume is an example of attempts to extrapolate from "small group" laboratory experiments to the larger political arena. Zeigler has integrated and summarized what we have learned about groups.

ALMOND, GABRIEL. "A Developmental Approach to Political Systems." *World Politics*, XVII (1965), 183–214.

———, and JAMES S. COLEMAN, eds. *The Politics of Developing Areas*. Princeton, 1960.

APTER, DAVID E. "A Comparative Method for the Study of Politics." *American Journal of Sociology*, LXIV (1958), 221–237.

DAVIES, JAMES. *Human Nature in Politics: The Dynamics of Political Behavior*. New York, 1963.

EASTON, DAVID. "An Approach to the Analysis of Political Systems." *World Politics*, IX (1957), 383–400.

———. *A Framework for Political Analysis*. Englewood Cliffs, 1965.

———. "Political Anthropology." *Biennial Review of Anthropology*, ed. Bernard J. Siegel. Stanford, 1959. Pages 210–262.

———. *A Systems Analysis of Political Life*. New York, 1965.

EDINGER, LEWIS. *Kurt Schumacher: A Study in Personality and Political Behavior*. Stanford, 1965.

EISENSTADT, S.N. "Primitive Political Systems: A Preliminary Comparative Analysis." *American Anthropologist*, LXI (1959), 200–220.

FORTES, M., and E.E. EVANS-PRITCHARD. *African Political Systems*. London, 1940.

GOTTFRIED, ALEX. *Boss Cermak of Chicago: A Study of Political Leadership*. Seattle, 1962. Particularly, Appendix II, "Leadership and Psychosomatic Analysis," pp. 365–378.

GREGOR, A. JAMES. "Political Science and the Uses of Functional Analysis." *American Political Science Review*, LXII (1968), 425–439.

GROSS, BERTRAM. *The Legislative Struggle*. New York, 1953.

JACKSON, W.A. DOUGLAS, ed. *Politics and Geographic Relationships: Readings on the Nature of Political Geography.* Englewood Cliffs, 1964.

LATHAM, EARL. "The Group Basis of Politics: Notes for a Theory." *American Political Science Review,* XLVI (1952), 376–397.

LEVY, MARION. *The Structure of Society.* Princeton, 1952.

MARTINDALE, DON, ed. *Functionalism in the Social Sciences . . . .* Philadelphia, 1965.

MEEHAN, EUGENE J. *Contemporary Political Thought: A Critical Study.* Homewood, Ill., 1967.

MITCHELL, WILLIAM C. "Occupational Role Strains: The American Elective Public Official." *Administrative Science Quarterly,* III (1958), 210–228.

MONYPENNY, PHILIP. "Political Science and the Study of Groups." *Western Political Quarterly,* VII (1954), 183–201.

RIEFF, PHILLIP. "Psychology and Politics: The Freudian Connection." *World Politics,* VII (1955), 293–305.

ROTHMAN, STANLEY. "Systematic Political Theory: Observations on the Group Approach." *American Political Science Review,* LIV (1960), 15–33.

TRUMAN, DAVID. *The Governmental Process.* New York, 1951.

VERBA, SIDNEY. "Organizational Membership and Democratic Consensus." *Journal of Politics,* XXVII (1965), 467–497.

WHITE, RALPH K., and RONALD LIPPITT. *Autocracy and Democracy: An Experimental Inquiry.* New York, 1960.

YOUNG, ORAN R. *Systems of Political Science.* Englewood Cliffs, 1968.

YOUNG, ROLAND, ed. *Approaches to the Study of Politics.* Evanston, 1958.

ZEIGLER, HARMON. *Interest Groups in American Society.* Englewood Cliffs, 1964.

5 / SOME FRAMES OF REFERENCE: B

by Joann Poparad Paine [1]

Conflict Theory / Decision Theory / Communications Theory /
Comparison of Three Theories

Three sets of empirical theory-building activities in political science will be considered in both their inductive and more axiomatic deductive forms in this section: conflict theory, decision theory and communications theory. A systematic analysis of these efforts cannot proceed, however, without explicit criteria. Two sets of criteria will guide our analysis: (1) the degree to which a set of logical and empirical requirements have been fulfilled and (2) the stage of theoretical development which has been attained. In other words, we not only want to know whether a particular theory fulfills certain requirements irrespective of its stage of development; we also want to compare its stage of development with that of other theories before making tentative judgments about the theory's usefulness to political scientists.

The set of logical and empirical requirements may be translated into the following set of questions that will be directed to each of the theoretical approaches:

1. What are the units of analysis?
2. Are the definitions and/or conceptualizations of these units logically consistent and operational?
3. Are the basic explicit and implicit assumptions or axioms logically consistent with the selection and definition of the units?
4. Do the propositions logically follow from the assumptions and definitions of the units selected?
5. Are the main hypotheses testable, i.e., formulated so as to be subject to rejection, and do they follow logically from the definitions, assumptions, and propositions? [2]
6. Has testing the hypotheses produced findings consistent with the predictions and/or suggested modifications of new theory?

[1] The author wishes to acknowledge and thank Stephen L. Wasby for his substantive and editorial advice in the preparation of this chapter.

[2] What we are calling a "proposition" in Question 4 is sometimes called a hypothesis. The term "hypothesis" in Question 5 may be called an "operational hypothesis." Question 4 refers to statements predicting a general set of events and/or behaviors, while Question 5 refers to statements subsumed by the proposition predicting sub-classes of events and/or behaviors under explicitly stated empirical conditions.

7. Does this theory subsume sets and/or subsets of political events, behaviors, and/or situations that are subsumed by other theories?
8. In what other ways does this theory relate to other theories? Through the selection of similar units, definitions, assumptions, propositions, hypotheses, and/or types of situations? [3]

At least two generally concurrent theory-building strategies can be identified. The more implicit inductive theory-building strategy can be characterized by its "scatter-gun appearance" and the tendency of those consciously or unconsciously employing this strategy to particularize with respect to time, events, and/or behavior. By "scatter-gun appearance" we are suggesting the tendency of inductive theorist-researchers to include large numbers of units all of which have not been explicitly related to one another theoretically. In the process of focusing on specific sets of empirical events or behaviors, these more inductive theory-builders often appear to be unaware that they may be contributing to theory-building and that their strategy, however ambiguously and implicitly defined, holds certain consequences for obtaining generalizations that are less time-, event-, and/or sample-bound. For this reason, it may be more accurate to call these political scientists "theory contributors" or "theorist-researchers" rather than theory-builders.

In contrast, the more axiomatic deductive theory-builders are characterized by their purposive selection and explicit interrelating of a more limited number of units. The selection and interrelating of the units are usually determined by the theorist's tentative answer to the question of the behavioral consequences of certain posited conditions. The axiomatic deductive theorists make more use of non-statistical content-free mathematical models, e.g., game theory, graph theory, and matrix algebra, than do their inductive counterparts. While they may well consider criteria of efficiency and/or pay-off in selecting these models, it is also likely that the aesthetic appeal of mathematic modeling is an important factor in selecting a deductive theory-building strategy. If we insist that axiomatic-deductive theorists include a specification of empirical indicators linking their theories to the empirical world or referent system, the products of their efforts can be considered empirical theories.

Although the axiomatic-deductive strategy is rapidly gaining adherents, the more frequent appearance of primarily inductive reasoning suggests the influence of sociological modes of theory-building on political scientists.[4] As yet, however, there appears to be little communication between these two

[3] Questions 7 and 8 are included to provide a basis for determining which theory is "best." The best theory is one that predicts and/or explains the most sets and/or subsets of political events and behaviors. If one desires control and manipulation rather than prediction and explanation, the criteria for determining the "best" theory would have to be changed correspondingly.

[4] See William C. Mitchell, "The Shape of Political Theory to Come: From Political Sociology to Political Economy," *The American Behavioral Scientist*, XI (1967), 8–20, 37.

groups of empirical theorists. The omission of cross-referencing citations in their published research implies that they may not be aware of cases of shared common substantive and/or methodological interests.

After the appearance of both types of theory-builders in a particular theoretical or substantive area, a third type of empirical theory-builder may appear. For want of a more descriptive term, they will be called deductive probabilists.[5] They are concerned with discovering and elaborating the linkages between regularities in the empirical findings of the inductive theorist-researchers and the assumptions and propositions of the axiomatic deductive theorists in order to produce an integrated and probabilistic reformulation. Concisely, their goal is to retain coherence and explicitness while increasing the numbers of units and relationships so that complex political behavior may be better predicted and explained. Given the variations in definitions, measures, and findings of selected units, this more eclectic theory-building strategy contains many more opportunities for error, but it may well maximize the balance between parsimony, high predictive capacity, and greater generality.

We will find that there is a tendency for theorists to stay close to the stages implied in their selection of a theory-building strategy. Consider this rough delineation of theory-building stages:

1. Theoretical and empirical discovery of relationships among hitherto unrelated units
2. Conceptualization of these units of analysis
3. Breakdown of larger units into subunits
4. Selection of "relevant" units
5. Statement of relationships
6. Theoretical and/or empirical exploration of these relationships to others previously discovered
7. Continued manipulation of units and/or relationships by aggregating or subdividing them in the process of verifying the hypotheses.

We would expect the more inductive theorist to be less systematic and explicit in stages (5) and (6) while the more deductive theorist would tend to focus more on producing explicit theoretical statements at each of these stages. The deductive probabilist would focus primarily on stage (7). The general point to be remembered is that none of these three types of theorists totally ignore any of the stages; rather they differ as to which stages they attack explicitly and rigorously and which stages they consider much less systematically. The process of theoretical development through the above stages may recycle at any stage and will not reach a stage of absolute universal laws in the social sciences. Our universal laws will be probabilistic laws.

[5] This term is not entirely accurate, for few using this strategy consistently follow the logic of probability theory in building their deductive-probability models. Eugene J. Meehan also notes this discrepancy, *The Theory and Method of Political Analysis* (Homewood, Ill., 1965), pp. 141–144.

That different theorist-researchers may be working at different stages of development in the same theoretical area should warn the reader that the use of the term "theory" implies an integrated coherence that is not found in the areas of conflict, decision-making, or communications theory. Therefore, our analysis will imply greater systematization and regularity than would the theoretical efforts with which the analysis is concerned.

CONFLICT THEORY

That the above is so can be seen immediately in the conceptualizations and strategies found in conflict theory. Conflict has been conceptualized as an outcome of exchanges between individuals, as a spatial relationship, as dissensus or conflicts of values, as competition or conflicts of interest, as incompatibility of role expectations, and/or as a game. In the exchange models constructed by some contemporary sociologists, conflict in a political system takes the form of competition, which is conceptualized as the exchange by which reciprocal relationships between individuals and/or groups are transformed into unilateral or superior-subordinate relationships. While both Homans and Blau relate competition to mobility and leadership selection, their main emphasis is on competition for the goods or values to be allocated in a political system. Since scarcity of values is assumed, the elimination of any of the participants is viewed as incidental to the primary focus of political behavior, the allocation of values.[6] Presumably, the scarcer the values, the higher the intensity and frequency of competitive conflict behavior among the members of a political system. Coser distinguishes this "realistic" type of conflict, i.e., one arising out of rival ends, from non-realistic conflict in which drives for tension-release become the "ends" of the conflict.[7]

Boulding, on the other hand, conceptualizes conflict as a spatial relationship rather than as an exchange process. He defines a competitive situation as one in which two or more individuals may or may not perceive that they are both seeking a mutually incompatible goal. Boulding reserves the term "conflict" for objective competitive situations which are perceived as competitive by the participants; i.e., when two or more individuals seek a goal that can only be attained by one of them, a conflict results when and only when the individuals affected perceive this and attempt to do something about it.[8] Dahrendorf treats competition, however, as a more regulated subtype of conflict, but he limits his use of the term conflict to situations involving a

[6] George Homans, *Social Behavior* (New York, 1961), and Peter Blau, *Exhange and Power in Social Life* (New York, 1964). This basic conceptualization of politics as an exchange process has given rise to a relatively new theoretical area in political science, namely, exchange theory.

[7] Lewis Coser, *The Functions of Social Conflict* (Glencoe, Ill., 1956), p. 156.

[8] Kenneth E. Boulding, *Conflict and Defense* (New York, 1962), pp. 4–5.

scarcity of resources and/or positions.[9] Boulding and Dahrendorf account then for two possibilities: (1) the situation is objectively competitive and it is perceived that way by the participants and (2) the situation is not objectively competitive and it is not perceived to be competitive by the participants. The theorist-researcher can only ask if different types of behavior can be found, each of which is characteristic of only one of the above possibilities; otherwise, these categories will not be meaningful.

Some theorists also question whether these categories exhaust the possible types of conflict situations. In other words, do conflicts occur in which the elimination of competitors for the attainment of scarce resources and positions is not the goal of the participants? Debates and other conflicts involving differing perceptions may be examples of conflicts that cannot be subsumed under the above categories. The characteristics of a more complete set of conflict types are displayed in Table 2.

All of the authors recognize that conflicts, with the possible exception of debates, typically involve both competitive and non-competitive elements, though one type of conflict may dominate the others at different stages of a conflict. The behavior patterns of competitive conflicts are likely to dominate the conflicts of values and non-competitive conflicts in all interaction situations where the rules for resolving leadership succession have not been legitimated and institutionalized and are not equally visible to all participants or where the competitive rules have been institutionalized.[10] The appearance of violent or non-violent behaviors will likely depend as much on the cultural setting as on the form of conflict.

By assuming that different types of conflict will appear in a conflict and that competitive rules will dominate in at least two major types of political interaction situations, we have the basis for examining the less complex game theoretic literature for a more rigorous and general conflict theory. In zero-sum games, one player's loss is the other player's gain; in non-zero-sum games, both may win or lose. The election of the President of the United States exemplifies a zero-sum situation; that is, only one candidate can attain the position of President at any one time. The Prisoner's Dilemma is one of the most frequently studied non-zero-sum conflicts. Briefly, this is a situation involving two non-communicating prisoners who must decide whether to admit their commission of a crime. If both trust each other and refuse to admit their guilt, they will receive a light prison sentence. If they tell on each other, they will both receive a longer prison term. If only one tells on the other one, the "squealer" will not receive a prison sentence and the "sucker" will be sentenced to an even longer prison term. The paradox or dilemma is that if both act "rationally," i.e., squeal, they will get an undesirable outcome.

[9] Ralf Dahrendorf, *Class and Class Conflict in Industrial Society* (Stanford, Calif., 1959), pp. 208–210.

[10] The former interaction situation characterizes leadership selection in the Soviet Union, and the latter type of situation characterizes the dependence of the party in power on votes of confidence in Britain.

Table 2.   The Type, Form, and Characteristics Defining the Forms of Conflict

TYPES OF CONFLICT	FORMS OF CONFLICT	CHARACTERISTICS DEFINING THE FORMS OF CONFLICT
Competitive (interest)	Games (zero-sum)	Certainty or uncertainty Perception of mutually incompatible goal Objective: outwit and eliminate competition or compromise by saddle-point determination [11] Use of threats and sanctions
	Games (non-zero-sum)	Uncertainty Option of perceiving goals as mutually incompatible or temporarily mutually shared Perception of the alternative rules of the games, but discrepant values leading to disagreement over selection of rules which shall be considered binding Objective: if goals mutually exclusive, outwit and eliminate competition; if goals temporarily shared, incur a minimum level of risk and cost Use of threats and sanctions
Value	Fights	Uncertainty Mutually incompatible goals Discrepant values leading to disagreement over selection of rules which shall be considered binding Objective: eliminate competitor Use of threats and sanctions
Non-Competitive	Debates	Uncertainty Mutually shared problem Discrepant cognitive processes in the beginning stage(s) Objective: change opponent's mind; do not eliminate him Absence of threats and sanctions

Except in games incorporating mixed strategies, it is generally assumed that each participant's strategy is predicated on the strategy selected by the opponent. Information about all possible strategies, rules, and payoffs or

[11] "Saddle-point determination" is a term in game theory designating a row-column position in a game matrix which is both a minimum and maximum strategy choice. Anatol Rapoport, *Two-Person Game Theory* (Ann Arbor, 1966), pp. 59–60.

their probabilities enables each player to maximize benefits while minimizing losses. These games describe a process of interaction in which the players' or decision-makers' [12] ability to rank their preferences, estimate probabilities, and make interpersonal comparisons is assumed. Predictions are made by the participants about the outcomes of future competitive and/or cooperative interactions; the interaction, cooperative or competitive, is determined by this comparison. A number of interesting findings have come from this research. Increases in pay-offs and the amount of power, for example, have tended to increase the frequency of competitive responses. Depending upon the number of trials and other variations in the experimental situation, however, authoritarian F-scale scores, internationalism, ambiguity tolerance, motivation, and sex have correlated both positively and negatively with competitive response tendencies.

A number of other assumptions and characteristics related directly to the theoretical requirements of game theory and to the practical requirements of experimental research have led, however, to an unfortunate dichotomization of conflict and cooperation. Static one-stage experiments limited to two players preclude the simultaneous development of cooperative and competitive relationships within a larger set of political interactions. These limitations are due in part to the absence of satisfactory, i.e., deterministic, mathematical solutions for a larger number of players or decision-makers without collapsing all players or decision-makers into two teams. Limiting the number of alternative strategies and controlling the "mix" of the strategies also contribute to the dichotomization of cooperation and competition. Often the only likely "rational" behavior in the experiments is either a cooperative play or a competitive play; a strategy alternative incorporating coalition formation for competitive plays is not found outside of the theory and research on triads (three-person groups) or tetrads (four-person groups), which do not conform to the strict theoretical requirements of game play.

The studies incorporating iterate games, which are static one stage occurrences in which the outcomes of one interaction game do not become the inputs in the next playing of the game, do not approximate dynamic processes of decision-making. Thus, there is little opportunity for combining cooperative and competitive plays in a strategy.[13] In addition, the assumption that competition under certain conditions is ultimately punished and cooperation rewarded ignores at least two possible alternatives: competition may be rewarded and cooperation punished; and particular combinations of cooperation and competition may be rewarded by payoffs while other combinations are punished.

[12] In mathematics, game theory is a part of decision theory. In the behavioral sciences, game theory has been incorporated in the models and experiments of both conflict and decision theorists concerned with decision-making in a conflict situation.

[13] An exception to this statement can be found in Martin Shubik's derivation of a dynamic theory of oligopoly from the extensive form of a game, *Strategy and Market Structure* (New York, 1961).

Other assumptions [14] basic to the mathematic formulation of game theory also lead one rather naturally to considering cooperation and competition antithetical. However, in any interaction set involving more than two persons, teams, groups, or nations, these assumptions have not led to the derivation of hypotheses having a high predictive value.

To predict and explain complex empirical conflicts, we need to relax some of the game theoretical restrictions. Before continuing with our analysis, however, it may be helpful to state our problem more concisely and to indicate what we would consider desirable types of theoretical "answers." We are interested in the political situation in which one decision-maker can attain his goal if and only if other decision-makers attain their goals *and* other decision-makers do not attain any of their goals. This political situation includes competitive and cooperative aspects and specifically introduces coalition potentialities into the conflict situation. Moreover, we want to make more specific predictions about which actors are likely to form subsets or coalitions and the strategies that they are likely to select in this predominately competitive conflict situation.

The theorist-researchers attempting to resolve this theoretical problem in their research on triads and tetrads begin with the following set of assumptions:

1. The actors can be ranked by resources (votes), position, or by some other characteristic.
2. The actors have the same information about the initial distribution of resources and the payoff for any coalition.
3. All coalition strategies are equally difficult or costly.
4. No actor can be eliminated from the group or added to the group, and no actor has veto power.
5. Each actor will expect the other actors to demand a share of the payoff proportional to the amount of resources which each has contributed to the coalition.
6. The "chooser" will seek a maximum advantage or minimum disadvantage of strength relative to his coalition partner.
7. The "chooser" will seek a "minimal winning coalition," which is characterized by the fact that the defection of any member will make the coalition no longer winning.
8. The payoff matrix is in the zero-sum form, i.e., no single alternative will maximize the payoff to all participants and the decision to be

---

[14] For example, perfect information; complete certainty; stable rank orderings of preferences throughout the game; comparable utilities; equally distributed rationality and skills in bargaining; complete symmetry; finite termination points; stability of payoffs; voluntary participation; costs, threats, and sanctions considered only as attributes of the payoff; and the availability of unambiguous maximizing or minimax strategies.

made involves more than two members attempting to maximize their payoff.

9. The decision rule is a simple majority.[15]

Some predictions derived from these assumptions by different scholars are displayed in Table 3. In Type I Gamson predicted any coalition as equally

Table 3. Coalition Formation in a Triad

		COALITIONS PREDICTED BY		
TYPE	RANKING	CAPLOW	GAME THEORY	GAMSON
I	$A_1 = A_2 = A_3$[a]	any	any	any
II	$A_1 > A_2$, $A_2 = A_3$,[b] $A_1 < (A_2 \cup A_3)$[c]	$(A_2 \cup A_3)$	any	$(A_2 \cup A_3)$
III	$A_1 < A_2$, $A_2 = A_3$	$(A_1 \cup A_2)$ or $(A_1 \cup A_3)$	any	$(A_1 \cup A_2)$ or $(A_1 \cup A_3)$
IV	$A_1 > (A_2 \cup A_3)$, $A_2 = A_3$	none	none	none
V	$A_1 > A_2 > A_3$, $A_1 < (A_2 \cup A_3)$	$(A_1 \cup A_3)$ or $(A_2 \cup A_3)$	any	$(A_2 \cup A_3)$
VI	$A_1 > A_2 > A_3$, $A_1 > (A_2 \cup A_3)$	none	none	none
VII	$A_1 > A_2 > A_3$, $A_1 = (A_2 \cup A_3)$	$(A_1 \cup A_2)$ or $(A_1 \cup A_3)$	°	°
VIII	$A_1 = (A_2 \cup A_3)$, $A_2 = A_3$	$(A_1 \cup A_2)$ or $(A_1 \cup A_3)$	°	°

[a] A_1, A_2 and A_3 designate members of the triad.
[b] Read "greater than" for $>$ and "less than" for $<$.
[c] Read "A_1 union A_2" for $(A_1 \cup A_2)$. Although the use of mathematical set theory and notation in coalition theory is not yet widespread, it should be. See William H. Riker, *The Theory of Political Coalitions* (New Haven, 1962), 279–292.
° No prediction made.

SOURCE: Except for the "Game Theory" column, this table is based on a table in W. A. Gamson, "A Theory of Coalition Formation," *American Sociological Review*, XXVI (1961), 377. The "Game Theory" predictions are included in a table in W. E. Vinacke, *et al.*, "The Effect of Information about Strategy on a Three-Person Game," *Behavioral Science*, II (1966), 181. Reprinted by permission.

likely; no member has an initial advantage over any other, yet some combination of two members is a prerequisite to receiving a payoff. He inexplicably found that coalitions formed more often between (A_1, A_2) and (A_2, A_3), although the differences were not statistically significant. In Types II and V, A_1 has an initial advantage over A_2 or A_3, but A_2 and A_3 together can best A_1. It is predicted that actors will form a coalition against an actor enjoying an initial advantage. In Type III, A_1 is the disadvantaged actor. It is predict-

[15] These assumptions are delineated most clearly in W. A. Gamson, "A Theory of Coalition Formation," *American Sociological Review*, XXVI (1961), 373–382 and 565–573.

ed that competition is more likely to occur between peers than between un-equals unless other actors have the initial advantage. Consequently, A_2 and A_3 will each seek to form a coalition with A_1 against each other. Since A_1 is ahead in Types IV and VI even if A_2 and A_3 form a coalition and A_2 and A_3 both know this, there is no basis for coalition formation. That is, a coalition will only form if it places each of the members of the coalition in a better position vis-à-vis their competitors than each would have alone. The coali-tions predicted by Gamson in Types II, III, IV, V, and VI were either statisti-cally significant or in the predicted direction.[16] Caplow predicted that the highest ranking member must be a part of any coalition formed in Types VII and VIII if an advantage is to be gained.[17]

The focus in this brief outline of the theory and findings has been on coali-tion formation or who will cooperate with whom to achieve a goal that cannot be attained any other way. We could extend the findings in Table 3 to obtain a modified set of assumptions from which predictions about both conflict and cooperation may be derived. Such predictions would provide the basis for linking conflict, coalition, and integration theories. It is apparent from the content of our discussion, however, that cooperation in the form of coalition formation is one type of competitive strategy. Having identified the "enemy," the actors form a coalition to outrank him and ultimately eliminate him from the competition. Seeing that he is about to be eliminated, the "enemy" actor will tend to pursue a competitive expansion strategy to enlarge the size of the group to regain supremacy.[18] This process may continue until one coalition can no longer recruit new supporters or until viable rules call an end to the competition.

Explicitly linking conflict and cooperation implies that all types of con-flict are not "bad" and that both cooperation and competition are integral to most conflicts involving more than two actors or units. Thus, cooperation leading to integration within a group may be at least initially an outgrowth of conflict between this group and another group.[19] In fact, it has been hypothe-sized that stability of political relations is not maintained by cooperation alone but rather by an overlapping pattern of conflicts. This overlapping pat-tern of conflicts is defined by the presence of conflicts of approximately equal intensity [20] in which no actor(s) consistently wins or loses, and no set of con-flicts makes the same members consistently friends or enemies. Thus, no cleavage can develop, because the behavior of two members competitive with respect to one particular conflict issue tends to be partially determined by the joint expectation that they may be cooperative in a future conflict situ-

[16] Ibid., 568.

[17] T. A. Caplow, "A Theory of Coalitions in the Triad," American Sociological Review, XXI (1956), 489–493.

[18] This proposition is similar to one developed by E. E. Schattschneider, The Semi-Sovereign People (New York, 1960), p. 16.

[19] Coser, pp. 87–95, 139–149.

[20] Schattschneider considers this a necessary assumption. Pages 67–68.

ation.[21] In these circumstances the theorist-researcher expects the members to consider future situations, risks, costs, and rewards in selecting their strategies.

When cleavages develop that make the same people and/or groups continually winners and losers, the more non-competitive or ideological aspects become increasingly important and tend to dominate the perceptions and behavior of the contestants. In the stages through which a conflict may pass, (1) an event becomes a conflict issue; (2) the specific conflict issue "gives rise to general issues;" (3) unrelated issues are introduced by the participants; (4) a shift from disagreement to antagonism involving a "reciprocal reinforcement of psychological and political polarization" of the participants occurs; (5) combat or partisan organizations are organized and new leaders rise to direct these organizations in carrying on the conflict; (6) increasing use is made of non-formal primary communications channels; and (7) the conflict "takes off" independent of the issues.[22]

For a partially hypothetical example, we could consider as a conflict-producing event Russian trawlers fishing in waters off the coast of Oregon where American and Canadian fishermen have agreed not to fish. This event is perceived initially as depriving United States and Canadian fishing fleets of future fish catches. The fishermen, consequently, appeal to their political leaders to intercede in their behalf. The fishing trawlers are then boarded by the United States Coast Guard. In the meantime, discussion of the presence of camouflaged Russian electronic communications ships in Russian fishing fleets appears in the newspapers. In this manner, issues of foreign policy, general international behavior, and the "aggressiveness" of a communist system are introduced into the conflict. If some agreement resolving the initial conflict issues does not occur by this time, the Russian leaders are portrayed and perceived as communists for which this incident is only one of a series of representative behaviors of a "vile, criminal" set of leaders. American and Canadian leaders are distorted in a corresponding way in the Soviet Union. If the three sets of leaders call upon other national leaders to support them in the conflict and if the support is organized into combat groups, such as NATO or the Warsaw Pact, the conflict takes off, i.e., it becomes a cleavage.

Often the specific issues involved in the early stages of the conflict are forgotten in the latter stages as the contestants have decreasing contacts with those who disagree with them and increasing contacts with those who agree. Perception of the opponent is increasingly distorted to make him symbolic of all that is bad or evil. Both cooperative and competitive aspects remain, but the elimination of the antagonists becomes the goal replacing competition for goods and/or other values. An important consequence of this shift in goals is

[21] The reader may wish to compare this proposition and the conception of "overlapping conflict patterns" with that of "overlapping membership" developed by the group theorists; see p. 116.

[22] This outline of conflict stages is based on James Coleman, *Community Conflict* (Glencoe, Ill., 1957), p. 11.

that no matter what the combatants do, they perceive themselves to be in a zero-sum type conflict and, therefore, seek ulterior motives in each other's behavior.

Much less attention has been focused on how events become conflict issues. Coleman convincingly hypothesizes that a conflict-producing event will be salient, affect the potential contestants differentially, and not prohibit their taking action. Resting as it does on inferences drawn from community studies, Coleman's hypothesis must be tested on numerous conflicts. Another factor and possibly the catalyst in intergroup conflicts is the presence of intragroup conflicts threatening the leadership. In other words, the leadership, fearing its overthrow, attempts to channel and displace the aggressiveness of the group's members onto other groups. This hypothesis has been popular in international relations for some time, as when analysts suggest that Chinese international behavior is dependent upon conflict between Chinese leaders and their supporters over economic policy. However, empirical testing of this hypothesis on domestic and international conflicts has shown both positive and negative relationships.[23] Another hypothesis, that intergroup conflict is primarily determined by relations between the groups, has predicted behavior in small group experiments, but it has not been tested on the same data as the hypothesis which relates intergroup conflict to intragroup conflict.[24]

Notwithstanding the existence of a *Journal of Conflict Resolution*, a great deal is still not known about processes of resolving conflicts. Most of the more systematic theories are theories of bargaining and negotiating behavior.[25] These theories assume that an agreement to negotiate or bargain is contingent on the belief of the potential negotiators that they can both do better by negotiating than they can without it. This belief does not preclude one actor from pursuing goals which conflict with those of other actors, such as wanting to get more from the negotiation than the other(s). Sawyer and Guetzkow hypothesize that negotiators try to modify the degree to which the other party values his initial goals (his utilities) through communication and persuasion to achieve an advantageous modification of the alternatives available to the other party by the use of threats, promises, and *faits accompli*, and by the creation of new alternatives. The outcomes of negotiations may range from further aggravation of the conflict through a "mere self-restraint consciously contingent upon the other's behavior" to formal specific agreements providing for the punishment of violators. As in the other stages through which a conflict may pass, the number of individual participants and groups,

[23] R. J. Rummel, "The Dimensions of Conflict Behavior Within and Between Nations," *General Systems Yearbook*, VIII (1963), 1–50, and "Dimensions of Conflict Behavior Within Nations, 1946–1959," *Journal of Conflict Resolution*, X (1966), 65–73; R. A. Tanter, "Dimensions of Conflict Behavior Within and Between Nations, 1958–1960," *Journal of Conflict Resolution*, X (1966), 41–64.

[24] M. Sherif, *et al.*, *Intergroup Conflict and Cooperation: The Robbers Cave Experiment* (Norman, Okla., 1961), p. 38.

[25] The literature on deterrence theory would also be relevant here if we define conflict resolution to include conflict-containment.

information about the others' valued outcomes, situation stress, presence of trust, and timing of actions may all affect the process and outcomes of negotiation.[26]

Unlike Coleman's latter stages of conflict, the process of conflict resolution, if it takes the form of negotiation, requires that the conflicts be of the non-zero sum type. Hypotheses about the tendencies to pick the cooperative rather than the competitive response when personality factors, information, threats, and trust are varied have been tested extensively in the Prisoner's Dilemma research. Thus far, the findings, except for the recent ones by Rapoport and Chammah, in which the tendency was reversed after 50 to 150 trials, indicate that the participants in the experiments pick the competitive response most frequently, but increases in information about outcomes and the other's utilities increase the frequency of trusting or cooperating responses.[27]

DECISION THEORY

Conflict theory and decision theory overlap in many of the units selected and the situations subsumed by each. They differ, however, in one of their major characteristics. In conflict theory, an actor's behavior is assumed to be at least partially determined by the behavior of others. This relationship may be but is not necessarily assumed in decision theory. This difference becomes clearer when we consider the common conceptualization of decision-making.

Decision-making is usually defined as a process or sequence of activities involving stages of problem recognition, search for information, definition of alternatives, and the selection by an actor(s) of one from two or more alternatives consistent with the ranked preferences identified in the first three stages that will maximize or "satisfice" the actor's goal.[28] In many instances the last stage has been further defined to include a relationship (additive or multiplicative) between possible alternatives, preferences or utilities attached to each of the alternatives, and the probabilities of alternatives becoming the outcomes. These probabilities may or may not include or depend upon the actions of others.

This conceptualization of decision-making has prompted the decision theorist-researcher to attempt to deduce patterns and/or to infer patterns from the data gathered to answer the following questions:

[26] Jack Sawyer and Harold Guetzkow, "Bargaining and Negotiation in International Relations," *International Behavior*, ed. H. C. Kelman (New York, 1965), pp. 466–501.

[27] See A. Rapoport and A. H. Chammah, *Prisoner's Dilemma* (Ann Arbor, 1965); B. M. Bass and G. Danteman, "Biases in the Evaluation of One's Own Group, Its Allies and Opponents," *Journal of Conflict Resolution*, VII (1963), 16–20; J. S. Mouton and R. R. Blake, "The Influence of Competitively Vested Interests on Judgments," *Journal of Conflict Resolution*, VI (1962), 149–153, and "Comprehension of Own and of Outgroup Positions Under Intergroup Competition," *Journal of Conflict Resolution*, V (1961), 304–310.

[28] *The Making of Decisions*, ed. W. J. Gore and J. W. Dyson (New York, 1964), pp. 1–63.

1. Who made the decision?
2. What was the decision?
3. When was the decision made?
4. How was the decision made?
5. Where was the decision made?
6. What were the characteristics of the decision situation?
7. To what class or subclass of decisions does this decision belong?
8. Why was the decision made?

The reader should note that the conceptualization and guiding questions imply that the theorist-researchers assume that decision-makers act *as if* they were capable of rational calculation, i.e., they can rank alternative preferences and consciously select the most efficient or feasible means consistent with their rank preference orderings of the alternatives for attaining explicitly stated goals. This assumption of rational behavior, preferred most consistently by decision theorists, obviously implies that a decision-maker's personal idiosyncrasies do not determine the form of the process of selecting alternatives.

The conceptualization of decision-making as irrational, on the other hand, implies that non-logical pressures emanating perhaps from childhood traumas or a need to release tension often do determine the form of the process of alternative selection. In the irrational model the decision-maker's aggressive response will not be the result of a logical calculation of risks and pay-offs relevant to the decision situation, but will be the result of unrelated personality conflicts or frustration.[29] If this assumption of irrationality is selected, the theorist-researcher will need to know the conscious and unconscious personal histories of all the decision-makers before he can hope to describe a decision situation. More importantly, he must give up the hope of prediction and explanation based upon frequencies of decision-making behavior. If each decision-maker and situation is unique in all its aspects, an empirical decision theory is impossible.[30]

It is this writer's view that dichotomizing behavior into irrational and ra-

---

[29] To distinguish in empirical research between rational and irrational behavior and motivations is difficult. For example, a decision-maker may discuss factors logically related to the decision problem, while "actually" reacting to the resemblance of one of the other decision-makers to his autocratic father. One may decrease the chances of confounding the rational and irrational; thus, Snyder, Bruck and Sapin exclude "because of" motives from their analysis and include "in order to" statements made by decision-makers. "In order to" motives are those reasons given by decision-makers before a decision is made, while the "because of" statements are the reasons or rationalizations of decision-makers that follow the making of a decision. See R. C. Snyder, *et al.*, "Motivational Analysis of Foreign Policy Decision-Making," *International Politics and Foreign Policy*, ed. J. N. Rosenan (New York, 1961), pp. 247–253. L. Festinger's theory of cognitive dissonance predicts changes in the evaluation of alternatives after a decision is made. *A Theory of Cognitive Dissonance* (New York, 1957).

[30] By assuming that decision behavior is entirely random, however, we can construct a probability model predicting outcomes. Outside of mathematics, few decision theorists have considered this alternative.

tional behavior is not necessary to the development of generalizations about decision-making behavior. Rather, predictive and/or explanatory generalizations can depend upon the theorist-researcher finding a pattern of behavior, e.g., a frequent response to decision situation characteristics which may and probably does involve both rational and irrational components. There is no *a priori* reason to believe that only rational behavior will provide the empirical theorists with patterned behavior. Groups of individuals in certain types of decision situations, e.g., crises, may typically behave in other than strictly rational ways. Thus, the relevant question is not whether or not the individuals behave rationally, but instead is: In what types of decision situations would we predict that psychological or other non-rational factors tend to be significant determinants of decision-making behavior?

Verba has examined this latter question for international relations. He suggests the following propositions:

1. The greater the (personal) involvement of an individual in a situation, the greater will be the effect of non-logical and pre-dispositional influences.
2. The more information an individual has about [the problem at hand], the less likely it is that his behavior will be based upon non-logical influences.
3. The higher the level of skill in handling [a particular type of decision problem], the less likely it will be that attitudes on [the problem area] will be free to form personality-oriented functions.
4. The more an individual values rationality as a decision-making process, the less personality factors will play a role in his decision.
5. The more influence a person believes himself to have over events, the less he will orient himself toward those events in terms of personality variables.
6. Those who are expected to be responsible for the consequences of their decisions will be more inhibited in admitting criteria that are not supposed to be relevant.
7. The more detailed a decision an individual is expected or required to make, the less likely it is that personality variables will have an effect.
8. The more ambiguous the cognitive and evaluative aspects of the decision-making situation, the more scope there is for personality variables.[31]

In other words, non-rational behavior that is patterned can be predicted.

There are others who reject the primarily rational conception of decision-making on grounds other than non-rational personality variables. Lindblom

[31] Sidney Verba, "Assumptions of Rationality and Non-Rationality in Models of the International System," *The International System*, ed. K. Knorr and S. Verba (Princeton, 1961), pp. 99–105. Also see J. A. Robinson, "Decision Making in the House Rules Committee," *Administrative Science Quarterly*, III (1958), 73–86.

argues that decision-making does not regularly involve the selection of courses of action involving radical changes in past policies or in the selection from among alternatives that might be described as "all or nothing" alternatives, i.e., either we do something or we do not decide to do something. On the contrary, decision-making typically involves small incremental changes by what he terms "successive limited comparison." [32] What he means is that only a small change is made and then the decision-maker compares the results of the small change with his expectation(s). The small change selected is most often one that has been tried in the past in what the decision-maker perceives to be similar decision-making situations. The decision-maker does not consider any new changes without making this comparison with experience. Thus, radical changes in the direction or course of policy are quite rare. The observer's awareness of a change usually comes only after a number of such small incremental changes.

This is obviously a rather conservative description of decision-making based on the assumption that the results of present and past policies have in the main tended to be satisfactory to the decision-makers and the public(s) upon which they depend for support. Marginal changes are considered by them to be sufficient for achieving an acceptable rate of improvement in the policy. This conception of decision-making would seem to better fit a system where conditions of political and/or social stability prevail. Highly unstable systems often appear to be unstable precisely because the results of past decisions have been unsatisfactory to significant segments of the decision-makers or aspiring decision-makers and to their supporting publics. In this case, some of these decision-makers may be looking for radical changes and intend to select from alternatives which might be described as all or nothing alternatives. Rather than past experience providing a guide for the selection of alternatives, the alternatives may be drawn from political and/or economic theory and/or models provided by other political systems.[33] Lindblom's conception, therefore, may be a good starting point for investigating how a decision is made in a more stable political organization or system, but we must apparently look elsewhere for conceptions more relevant to the more unstable system, such as in developing and international systems.

Certain theoretical units are common to both the rational and nonrational or patterned behavioral assumptions. All theoretical efforts begin with decision-makers, their preferences or utility functions, the decisions, decision participation, rules for making decisions, types of decision situations and decision outcomes. There are, however, a number of differences in the definition and operationalization of these units.

Decision-makers are variously defined as those individuals who have public or legal responsibility for certain classes of political decisions; those

[32] C. E. Lindblom, "The Science of Muddling Through," *The Making of Decisions,* ed. Gore and Dyson, pp. 155–179.

[33] Yehezkel Dror, "Muddling Through—'Science' or Inertia?" *Public Administration Review,* XXIV (1964), 153–157; Wolf Heydebrand, "Administration of Social Change," *Public Administration Review,* XXIV (1964), 164.

who actually participate or share in decision-making; those who contribute information to individuals participating in decision-making; those who decide which decisions or alternatives will be considered; those who belong to the more powerful economic, political, military, and/or social elites; those who participate in the most types of decision issues; those who are leaders of interest groups; those who administer or carry out the decision; those who have veto power on a decision; and/or those who select the decision rules. The particular definition of decision-makers by a theorist-researcher appears to be at least partially determined by his perception of the issue area which he wishes to investigate.

It seems clear that over a period of time not every one of these definitions, operational or not, will consistently identify the decision-makers at the local, state, national, or international level. The particular characteristics of the decision situation itself may partially determine the identity of the decision-makers. For example, the more technical, complicated, and sophisticated an understanding is required to make a decision and the more indirect the effects perceived by most individuals, the more probable that the group making the decision will be smaller.[34] Consequently, it may be safest in the beginning to define decision-makers by their formal position, particularly in less economically developed and role-differentiated political systems (including the international system) until one can infer or ascertain from the data that this is not a useful definition.

We have already indicated that a decision at a minimum is a choice of one from two or more alternative future courses of action, which includes the alternative of doing nothing. If we look at a political decision, however, we often find that it consists of a number of smaller decisions. Thus, we approach the problem of defining time and other boundaries of a decision. For example, interaction between the Soviet Union and the United States decision-makers has lasted for varying lengths of time, but the decision to invoke a blockade of Cuba in 1962 may be perceived as having a beginning with the discovery by United States decision-makers that missile bases were being constructed in Cuba and ending with the Soviet decision-makers' decision to remove the missiles. The persistence of an issue, therefore, may involve a number of decisions by a changing number and composition of decision-makers.

Decision participation is a particularly difficult unit to define and operationalize. Is the individual who votes in a general election or one who bribes the administrator to change the application of a decision to be considered a participant in the making of a decision? Is the international civil servant who translates a message from Russian to English a participant in a decision to alter relations with the Soviet Union? Are the civil rights groups that participate in an economic boycott of segregated businesses also participants in a

[34] See, for example, R. C. Snyder and G. D. Paige, "The United States Decision to Resist Aggression in Korea: The Application of an Analytical Scheme," *International Politics and Foreign Policy*, ed. Rosenau, pp. 193–208.

community decision to desegregate? These hypothetical examples suggest some of the problems that confront the theorist-researcher trying to construct an operational definition of decision-making participation.

Except in game theory research and studies on voting and registration as they are related to party competition in the United States, the theoretical literature on decision-making also largely ignores the consequences of political competition on participation or decision outcomes. While the decision models include the constituent parts of interaction patterns, they implicitly rely on undefined drives, traits, motivations, or other personality attributes to provide the "goad" or "spur." This is particularly characteristic of decision-theory in the foreign policy area. It must be inferred that these drives and traits transform the static descriptions of states into dynamic processes of decision-making. Part of the problem is the failure to make explicit whether the models depend for their dynamics on the decision-making process itself and/or motivations of the individual participants. If the models depend upon interaction for their dynamics, then there has clearly been a failure to define the dynamics of the process.

A decision rule is a formal or informal criterion accepted by the relevant decision-makers specifying the procedures necessary to transform an alternative into a binding decision of the group, e.g., majority vote, unanimity, or a required number of readings of a bill. Voting decision rules have been studied most systematically by the more deductive theorists. They have been particularly concerned with Arrow's Paradox of voting.[35] Citizens John, Jim, and Jack have the following ranked preferences:

John prefers policy a to policy b, policy b to policy c, and policy a to c;
Jim prefers policy b to policy c, policy c to policy a, and policy b to a;
Jack prefers policy c to policy a, policy a to policy b, and policy c to b.

If we assume majority rule and a transitive relation holds between preferences,[36] it can be shown that for every alternative preferred by any of the above two citizens there remains another alternative preferred by another combination of two. Recently Tullock has tried to show that the theorem is inconsequential if the number of voters is large and if it is assumed that the voters' preferences are interdependent.[37]

Other types of decision rules have not played an important role in decision theory. Even less attention has been focused upon negotiation of decision rules or the consequences of changing from one set of rules to another. That is, the theoretical and empirical consequences of dynamic decision-making in less institutionalized settings have not been studied extensively by political scientists.[38]

[35] Kenneth Arrow, *Social Choice and Individual Values*, 2nd ed. (New York, 1963).
[36] Transitivity refers to John's implied preference for policy "a" over policy "c" if he prefers policy "a" to policy "b" and policy "b" to policy "c."
[37] Gordon Tullock, *Toward a Mathematics of Politics* (Ann Arbor, 1967), pp. 37–49.
[38] However, James Buchanan and Gordon Tullock consider the problem of choosing a constitution in *The Calculus of Consent* (Ann Arbor, 1962).

Although considerably more thought has been devoted to decision out-comes than decision rules, many political scientists define outcomes in different ways. For some, it is a policy outcome which has authoritative and legal sanctions. For others, a decision outcome refers to the "consequences" of having selected a particular alternative. These consequences may include (1) what happens to the decision when it is administered, (2) what advantageous and disadvantageous effects it has on what groups in the political system, and (3) how the decision and its administration affect the political system's ability to maintain itself, resolve conflict, integrate the system, and/or allocate values. For the more mathematically-inclined decision theorists, it is a payoff which results in an allocation of theoretically divisible goods, e.g., rewards (money, rank, and position) and costs (the loss of any of these) to the decision participants.

Perception is another theoretical unit that appears frequently, although not universally, in decision theory. Theorists including this unit attach primary importance to it, because they assume that understanding decision-making depends on the reconstruction of the particular decision-maker's "world" during the decision situation. Basic to this assumption is the phe-nomenologists' belief that the "real world" exists only through our senses. Most of the decision theorists have accepted the importance of perception but assume the existence of a "real world" or reference system independent of perception. How someone perceives "objects" will limit, and some would say determine, his alternatives and his responses. Factors hypothesized as affecting perception are numerous: political socialization; ideology; person-ality characteristics, such as risk-taking propensities or authoritarian ten-dencies; institutionalized role expectations; past political experience with equivalent decision situations; decision situation characteristics; potential decision rewards and costs; demands from clienteles or other outside groups and agencies; information; and/or semantic problems.[39]

Level of aspiration is a subfactor of perception that has been receiving increasing attention from decision theorists. Level of aspiration may be de-fined as the probability of a decision-maker's attaining his future goals or pre-ferred decision outcomes. Unlike the more stable units of perception, level of aspiration may undergo comparatively rapid change when failure or success is experienced by the decision-maker. One possible hypothesis is that failure will lower a decision-maker's level of aspiration while success will maintain or raise it. This is one of the units that makes a decision theory dynamic.

While there have been some attempts to conceptualize and measure util-ity by assigning interval scale values to a decision-maker's alternatives, most theorizing about preferences assumes an ordinal ranking of alternatives. With present measuring devices, we can generally secure data that allows us to infer that decision-maker A prefers alternative x to y; however, we cannot

[39] Richard C. Snyder, *et al.*, "Decision-Making as an Approach to the Study of Inter-national Politics," *Foreign Policy Decision-Making*, ed. Snyder, *et al.* (New York, 1962), pp. 65–73.

always infer that this decision-maker prefers x twice as much as y. In the instances where the decision theorist cannot assign interval scaled values, he has great difficulty estimating the decision-makers' utilities or interval values of alternatives. This has been one of the chief criticisms of theorizing using game theory models for predicting decision outcomes.

The decision situation, the last unit that will be considered here, has been categorized by several different dimensions. Those interested in crisis or non-crisis conflict decision behavior have specified the following dimensions: structured—non-structured; threatening—non-threatening; hostile—friendly; short term—long term; familiar—unfamiliar; planned—non-planned; and zero-sum—non-zero sum. Most of the theorizing and research on crisis conflict decision behavior in international relations is concerned with the effects of changes in the above factors on selected psychological variables.

Holsti has hypothesized these relationships between situation characteristics and perception from his work on World War I:

1. As stress increases in a crisis situation: (a) time will be perceived as an increasingly salient factor in decision-making and (b) decision-makers will become increasingly concerned with the immediate rather than the distant future.

2. In a crisis situation, decision-makers will tend to perceive (a) their own range of alternatives to be more restricted than those of their adversaries and (b) their allies' range of alternatives to be more restricted than those of their adversaries.

3. The higher the stress in a crisis situation: (a) the heavier the overload upon channels of communication; (b) the more stereotyped will be the information content of the messages; (c) the greater the tendency to rely upon extraordinary or improvised channels of communication of intra-coalition as against intercoalition communication.

4. The higher the stress in a crisis situation: (a) the fewer decision-makers will be included in the decision group; (b) the fewer decision-makers that disagree will be included in the decision group.[40] Thus, we expect that in crisis conflict decision situations the hierarchical channels of communication and decision-making will collapse into horizontal ones, that search behavior for information will be sharply curtailed, and that a much smaller group of individuals will be involved in making the decision. This appears to have been the case in the decision to commit United States troops to participation in the Korean conflict in 1950.

Decision situations have also been categorized by location: community;[41] committee and small group; national; legislative; judicial; executive; foreign; military; organizational; and international. In other words, the environment and organization in which decision-making takes place are hy-

[40] Ole R. Holsti, "The 1914 Case," *American Political Science Review*, LIX (1965), 366.
[41] See pp. 192–195 for discussion of relevant research methods.

pothesized to be among the determinants of decision-making and decision outcomes.

Task leaders as well as popular leaders have been identified in committee and small group decision-making processes. One of the most suggestive propositions that has been tested in small group research is that those who interact most frequently with the largest number of participants tend to be the most popular and active decision-making leaders and, consequently, the most visible.[42] Studies on the effects of group size indicate that, except in groups of two (dyads), the larger the group, the less frequently individuals voice their opinions.[43] Much work remains to determine the limits, if any, of generalizing these and other propositions to small and large political groups.

While some systematic theory-building on decision-making in legislatures and the judiciary, primarily those of England and the United States, can be found, it seems amazing that so little has been done on the federal executive. Apart from some informative descriptions and foreign policy case studies, few attempts have been made to test hypotheses derived from crises and incremental decision-making studies on decision-making in the Office of the President.

Research on national political development has revealed, however, a number of findings of interest to the study of national decision-making processes. If one is willing to assume that progress is linear and that the stages of development through which the advanced countries have passed are relevant to most political systems, a number of countries can be said to exhibit similar characteristics at the same stage of political development irrespective of their democratic, authoritarian, or totalitarian nature. Decision-makers in traditional political systems will occupy their positions on the basis of custom and tradition. Class, race, religion, ethnic group, and family instead of skill are their qualifications for position. They will tend to perform many political and non-political roles, because specialization is not yet developed.

Decision-makers in transitional political systems depend primarily on loyalty and their charismatic relationships with their supporters for their positions. Aspiring decision-makers are perceived as revolutionary. Age differences between the younger and older decision-makers appear to be related to sharp differences in perception in general and political orientation in particular. There is overlap in decision-making between the political, economic, and social systems. Because the general population is still not organized for making demands of the political decision-makers, decision-makers tend to have more latitude in determining policies. This lack of policy-making limitations is reinforced by the basis of their authority, i.e., their supporters are loyal to them personally, not because of positions taken on specific issues.

[42] J. D. Barber, *Power in Committees: An Experiment in the Governmental Process* (Chicago, 1966), pp. 83–100, and T. K. Hopkins, *The Exercise of Influence in Small Groups* (Totowa, N.J., 1964), pp. 51–98.

[43] See R. F. Bales and E. F. Borgatta, "Size as a Factor in the Interaction Profile," *Small Groups*, ed. A. P. Hare, *et al.*, rev. ed. (New York, 1965), p. 500.

We would expect, therefore, that decision-makers in modern political systems would take more defined positions on issues, for their positions depend upon their fulfilling a universal achievement criterion which has a rational-legal basis. They must exhibit skills, particularly managerial and bureaucratic skills, to hold their positions. Unlike the transitional political system where citizens tend to participate in the administration but not the formulation of policy, e.g., through bribery to assure that a policy is applied to the citizen's liking, citizen groups in modern political systems tend to play a more important role in the formulation stage of policy by making their demands known to the decision-makers in non-crisis decision situations.

Although there are no examples of automated political systems, Organski has speculated about the citizen's role in decision-making in such a system.[44] If we can visualize a computer in each family's home hooked up to a central communications center in Washington, D.C., we can also visualize much greater participation in decision-making. Every time an issue appeared salient to the citizen, he would push buttons calling forth additional information, communicating his agreement or disagreement, and/or specifying modifications or other alternatives to the national administrators. Legislators would no longer act as representatives. Such advances in technology, however, would require greater technological sophistication by both political leaders and citizens. Decision-makers would have to rely on technical experts or become knowledgeable themselves in systems analysis, information retrieval, and other uses of the computer. The need for expertise to understand and evaluate what is going on might discourage the participation of most laymen. One might even envision wars being fought on computers, but it is not necessary to go this far to be impressed by the potential effects of automation on decision-making at all levels.

Two forms of decision theory have been developed in the foreign policy and international areas. The one form, decision theory in a conflict crisis situation, we have already examined. The other form has remained at the pre-theory level of classification or framework. Because it appears to include the universe of factors that may impinge on foreign policy decision-making or on the decision-making process of a group of international actors, the framework developed by Snyder, Bruck, and Sapin is presented (see Figure 8). Although the interaction lines (→) trace the expected patterns of interaction, the limited number of studies beginning with this framework precludes a specification of generalizations beyond the obvious one that these factors are somehow related to the process of decision-making.

The same authors suggest that foreign policy decision-making *may* differ from other types in the following ways:

1. Wider range of possible objectives and projects subject to a wider range of possible interpretations.

---

[44] A.F.K. Organski, *The Stages of Political Development* (New York, 1965), pp. 186–211.

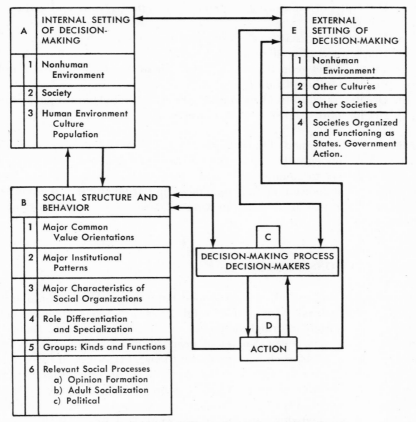

Figure 8. State "X" as Actor in a Situation

(Situation is comprised of a combination of selectively relevant factors
in the external and internal setting as interpreted by the decision-makers.)

SOURCE: Richard C. Snyder, *et al.*, "Decision-Making as an Approach to the Study
of International Politics," *Foreign Policy Decision-Making* (New York: The Free
Press, 1962), p. 72. Used with permission of The Macmillan Company.© by the Free
Press of Glencoe, a Division of The Macmillan Company, 1962.

2. Greater heterogeneity of "clientele" and thus more potentially hostile or dissatisfied reactions and demands.

3. A greater number of perspectives have to be integrated before consensus is achieved.

4. The "setting" and "situation" of decisions are more complex, less certain, less stable; the consequences of action are therefore harder to predict and control.

5. Sources of information are broader and less reliable, and the necessity of "classification" constitutes a special problem.

6. Relative lack of "experimental opportunity" and infrequency of replicable situations.

7. Difficulty of measuring organizational effectiveness and policy results.
8. Necessity of discussing alternatives in terms which do not meet the simplest test of verifiability.
9. Time-lag between the arising of problem-situation and the unfolding of its full implications.
10. Greater possibility of fundamental value conflicts and hence necessity for more extensive compromise.[45]

The increasing discussion of these factors in all national decision-making policy areas and the beginnings of an attempt to apply theory developed at the international level to communities suggests that our conception of community and national decision-making may need up-dating and that these factors may be characteristic of decision-making in most large complex organizations or systems.

COMMUNICATIONS THEORY

Of the three theoretical areas examined here, the content of communications theory is the least coherent. One might even argue that it consists of (1) a model drawn from information theory and cybernetics, (2) a theory of communications nets, and (3) a set of propositions partially derived from other theoretical areas, such as democratic theory, organization theory, and decision theory, about the characteristics and effects of communications and their media on attitude change, public opinion formation, voting behavior, maintenance and stability of a political system, consensus, coercion, political socialization, political development, perception, and ideology. Ambiguity and confusion are compounded by the use of similar terminology with different definitions. Perhaps the best way to avoid confusion is to differentiate their foci by describing each separately.

Mathematical information theory is essentially a physical theory of signal transmission concerned with problems of efficiency in the transmission of electrical impulses. Cybernetics is a theory of information, self-regulating machines, computers, and the physiology of the nervous system. An important concept in cybernetics is that of a machine which recognizes stimuli, "learns," adjusts itself automatically upon receiving feedback about its performance, and moves through a determined number of possible states.[46] This conception calls forth notions of a capacity to adjust automatically to pre-programmed and feedback information so as to maintain a state of stability or equilibrium. Information theory provides a means of analyzing messages into

[45] Snyder, *et al.*, p. 104. Italics omitted.
[46] Karl W. Deutsch, *The Nerves of Government* (New York, 1963), pp. 80–85. Also see Gregory Batesson, "Cybernetic Explanation," *American Behavioral Scientist*, X (1967), 29–32.

small discrete units, e.g., alphabet, dots and dashes, or points on a television screen, and measuring the efficiency, distortion, or noise in transmission of these units from the sender to receiver.[47] The physical basis of cybernetics (including information theory) is apparent in the definitions of communication, information, channel capacity, communication network, noise, and feedback.[48]

In applying cybernetics to a description of a political system and government as a process of steering, Deutsch transfers concepts defined in terms of a physical closed system to a more open system, the political system. It can be argued that as long as Deutsch limits his theory to information, knowledge can be gained about more open, indeterminate systems. Deutsch, however, does not limit his concern to the communication of information; in addition, he wants to apply communications theory to the "way in which attitudes and images are built up in minds of political decision-makers," to the role and relative weight of mass media compared with past memories, stereotypes and other media,[49] and to areas of attention, perception and orientation, values and evaluation, goal-seeking, and decision-making.[50]

Communications linkages or flows also play a major role in Deutsch's work on a theory of integration. Ratios of internal to external flow, e.g., domestic and foreign mail and tourists, are used as indicators of integration and cohesion. Deutsch theorizes that political integration develops as facilities are developed for handling increased communications, particularly demands. The institutional capacity to handle these communications is considered by Deutsch to be analogous to the channel capacity of a communication system for coding and decoding messages.[51] When institutional capacity is equivalent to the communications flows, the political system is maintained; when there is an overload on facilities, disintegration may ensue. These propositions have been generated in the context of international and national relations, but there is no a priori reason to believe that they will not tell us something about metropolitan and urban communities.

Deutsch is clearly no longer talking about only ". . . the transfer of messages containing quantities of information." [52] In the process of translation to political science, much of the original meanings of the units have been lost. Can we define information states, channel capacities, amplification, fidelity, and feedback in a large complex political system? Surely, feedback is not a

[47] Karl W. Deutsch, *Nationalism and Social Communication* (Cambridge, Mass., 1953), pp. 64–65.

[48] These definitions can be found in Deutsch, *Nationalism and Social Communication*, p. 228n.

[49] Karl W. Deutsch, "Mass Communications and the Loss of Freedom in National Decision-Making: A Possible Research Approach to Interstate Conflicts," *Man and International Relations*, ed. J. K. Zawodny (San Francisco, n.d.), Volume I, p. 697.

[50] Karl W. Deutsch, "Shifts in the Balance of Communication Flows," *Politics and Social Life*, eds. Nelson W. Polsby, *et al.* (Boston, 1963), p. 727. See also Karl W. Deutsch, "Communications Models in the Social Sciences," *Public Opinion Quarterly*, XVI (1952), 356–380.

[51] Deutsch, *Nationalism and Social Communication*, p. 90.

[52] Meehan, pp. 334–335.

substitute for equilibrium, although it may allow a system to maintain equilibrium.

Deutsch is equally, if not more concerned, with the communication of intention and the perceptions and interpretations of the messages by those receiving them. A model such as the one illustrated in Figure 9 [53] will not handle these additional variables without major modification.[54] We are saying that the cybernetics model loosely adapted by Deutsch for analyzing the stability and instability of political systems as coupled communications systems is not rich enough to do all that he intends to do with it. The curse of the innovator is always criticism, but Deutsch, in introducing cybernetics to political scientists and others, must yet show that the interesting questions that he has raised can be "answered" with the theory and tools of cybernetics.

The research on communication nets is concerned with the effects of structure on group behavior, particularly the selection and identification of leaders, efficiency in problem solving and learning, and the morale or satisfaction of group members. Structure and communication nets are generally assumed to be isomorphic or equivalent. This assumption follows from the definition of communications structure as a set of positions with specified two-way, one-way, or no channels linking them. "A channel is the probability that a message can pass a given direction between two positions." [55] "Message" and "position" are primitive or undefined terms. Direct communication of written messages is used in experimentation, which may imply that the findings are not relevant to indirect communication.

Hypothesis testing is concentrated on two-, three-, four-, and five-position nets arranged in a number of different forms, e.g., Wheel, Y, Chain, Circle, and All-Channel. (See Figure 10.) Most of the hypotheses tested thus far have involved predictions concerning the effects of various types of communications restrictions on behavior. Measured by the index of relative centrality,[56] the Wheel, Y, Chain, and Circle are the most to least centralized,

Figure 9.

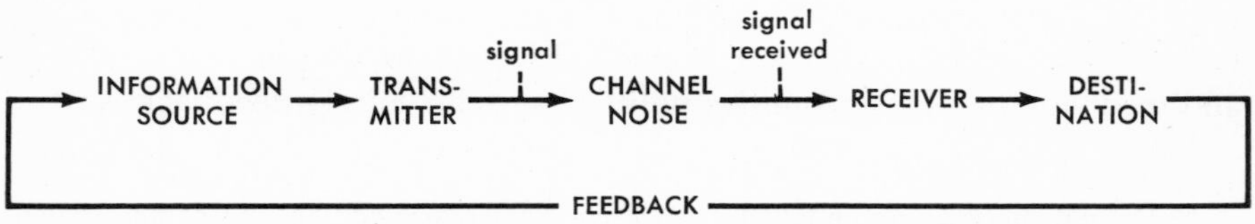

53 Based on Warren Weaver, "The Mathematics of Communication," *Communication and Culture*, ed. A. G. Smith (New York, 1966), p. 17.

54 This also appears to be true for Deutsch's diagrammed model, *The Nerves of Government*, p. 258.

55 M. Glanzer and R. Glaser, "Techniques for the Study of Group Structure and Behavior," *Small Groups*, ed. Hare, *et al.*, p. 400.

56 The index of relative centrality of a position is defined as "the ratio of the sum of the minimal distances of all positions to all others over the sum of the minimal distances of [that position] to all others." Glanzer and Glaser, pp. 401–402.

| WHEEL | CIRCLE | CHAIN | ALL-CHANNEL | Y |

Figure 10.

respectively. The same ranking has been hypothesized and not rejected for the speed of development of an organization for problem handling, agreement on identification of group leaders, and satisfaction with the group. However, Guetzkow and Simon hypothesized and confirmed the prediction that restrictions on communication would only affect the speed with which a group could organize. Testing their hypothesis on the Chain, Wheel, and All-Channel communications nets, they found few differences in problem-solving efficiency once the nets were organized.[57]

Glanzer and Glaser argue that these findings cannot be generalized to small groups, because in the experimental situation membership in a communications net is not voluntary, many of the participants are ignorant of each other's position, and many of the channels are arbitrarily closed. They suggest that these laboratory characteristics may be similar to ones found in larger organizations,[58] but no one has attempted to show the relevance of the hypotheses for predicting behavior in non-experimental larger organizations. If we assume that problem-solving efficiency is logically similar to selecting the least complex strategy, the development of a theory of communications nets may be relevant to decision and conflict theories. Certainly political scientists are interested in the effects of communications nets on the speed of organizational development in organization theory.

Unlike the other two subareas of communications theory, the theory of communications nets is much more particular and limited. If, as Glanzer and Glaser suggest, the theory of communications nets is waiting more general development, the concepts and hypotheses derived from mathematical graph theory may be useful in building a more general theory encompassing groups and organizations of varying size and complexity.

Unlike the definition of communications nets, the concept of mass communication in the third subarea of communications theory has numerous definitions. Mass communication is defined as (1) an act or process of "the transmission of information, ideas, emotions, skills [and the like] by the use of symbols—words, pictures, figures, graphs," gestures, and facial expressions; [59] (2) media through which flow information and persuasion; (3) the

[57] H. Guetzkow and H. A. Simon, "The Impact of Certain Communication Nets Upon Organization and Performance in Task-Oriented Groups," *Management Science*, I (1955), 240.
[58] Glanzer and Glaser, p. 418.
[59] B. Berelson and G. A. Steiner, *Human Behavior* (New York, 1964), p. 527.

linkages between individuals and groups; and (4) "the mechanism through which human relations exist and develop." [60] Sets of hypotheses are associated with each definition, but there are no identifiable coherent, logical theories.

The act of communication is described by Lasswell:

Who
Says What
In Which Channel
To Whom
With What Effect? [61]

Numerous studies have focused on opinion leaders and the press, to discover characteristics of the "Who?" and "Which Channel?" At least a comparable number have tried to associate changes in events, behavior, and leadership with changes in the frequencies of certain symbols using the technique of content analysis. We have already noted in the sections on conflict and decision theory that the use of stereotyped messages, face-to-face communications, and horizontal as opposed to hierarchical communications channels increases as stress increases in a conflict decision situation.

The question of effect has been examined primarily in voting studies, community studies, international relations, and small group research. Face-to-face communication is commonly distinguished from mass communications in this literature, but findings supporting Katz's two-step flow hypothesis [62] mitigate against a conception of members of a mass audience linked only to the mass media and not to each other. Similarly, simplistic notions about the direct effects of mass media on attitude change and beliefs must be tempered by findings indicating that people tend to filter out selectively unfavorable and hostile communications that do not reinforce and support their predispositions, particularly if they are subject to cross pressures.[63] Interest and the prestige and popularity of the communicator are important determinants of receptiveness to any particular communication. Even a monopoly of communications media will not make all people change their minds in the short run; such a monopoly is much more likely to reinforce pre-existing beliefs.[64]

Some effects of communication on audiences are summarized by Klapper:

[60] C. H. Cooley, "The Significance of Communication," *Reader in Public Opinion and Communication*, ed. B. Berelson and M. Janowitz, 2nd ed. (New York, 1966), p. 147.

[61] Harold Lasswell, "The Structure and Function of Communication in Society," *Reader in Public Opinion and Communication*, ed. Berelson and Janowitz, 2nd ed., p. 178.

[62] Elihu Katz, "The Two-Step Flow of Communication: An Up-to-Date Report on an Hypothesis," *Reader in Public Opinion and Communication*, ed. Berelson and Janowitz, pp. 293–303.

[63] James G. March and H. A. Simon, *Organizations* (New York, 1958), pp. 150–154. Davies, *Human Nature in Politics*, pp. 104–140; Angus Campbell, *et al., The American Voter*, pp. 59–60, 293–303.

[64] Berelson and Steiner, p. 541.

1. Mass communication ordinarily does not serve as a necessary and sufficient cause of audience effects, but rather functions among and through a nexus of mediating factors and influences.
2. These mediating factors [e.g., group norms, loyalty, cross-pressures, role-playing] are such that they typically render mass communication a contributory agent, but not the sole cause, in a process of reinforcing the existing conditions. . . .
3. On such occasions as mass communication does function in the service of change, one of two conditions is likely to obtain. Either:
   a. the mediating factors will be found to be inoperative, and the effect of the media direct; or
   b. the mediating factors, which normally favor reinforcement, will be found to be themselves impelling toward change.
4. There are certain residual situations in which mass communication seems to wreak direct effects, or to directly and of itself serve certain psychophysical functions.
5. The efficacy of mass communication, either as contributory agents or as agents of direct effect, is affected by various aspects of the media themselves or of the communication situation (including, for example, aspects of contextual organization, the availability of channels for overt action, etc.).[65]

Marshall McLuhan argues, however, that the researchers on communications effects have missed the main point: "the medium is the message," not what is transmitted by the medium.[66] McLuhan divides communication media into "hot" and "cool" media. A cool medium is one which requires the receiver to involve himself by filling in for missing data, e.g., television; a hot medium, such as radio, allows the receiver to remain detached.[67]

Tracing the rise of nationalism to the effects of typography, McLuhan states:

. . . Political unification of populations by means of vernacular and language groupings was unthinkable before printing turned each vernacular into an extensive mass medium. The tribe, an extended form of a family of blood relatives, was exploded by print, and is replaced by an association of men homogeneously trained to be individuals.[68]

Now he predicts:

. . . we are in great danger of wiping out our entire investment in the pre-electric technology of the literature and mechanical kind by means of an indis-

---

[65] Joseph Klapper, "What We Know About the Effects of Mass Communications: The Brink of Hope," *Public Opinion Quarterly*, XXI (1957–58), 457–458.
[66] Marshall McLuhan, *The Medium Is the Massage* (New York, 1967), p. 26. Jimmy L. Riley suggested McLuhan's relevance to the question of media effects on political behavior in "Communication: What Is the Message," unpublished paper (1967).
[67] McLuhan, *Understanding Media: The Extensions of Man* (New York, 1964), p. 36.
[68] *Ibid.*, pp. 218–219.

criminate use of electrical energy [because] . . . [t]oday's television child is attuned to up-to-the-minute "adult" news—inflation, rioting, war . . .—and is bewildered when he enters the nineteenth-century environment that still characterizes the educational establishment, where information is scarce but ordered and structured by fragmented, classified patterns, subjects, and schedules.[69]

Although (or perhaps because) McLuhan states that his propositions about media effects cannot be tested using empirical techniques, his critics are having a field day with his ideas. Whatever the outcome, McLuhan has forcefully suggested to the political scientist that the medium itself may be an important determinant of audience effects.

This brief review of communications theory has not dealt with all of the implications for future theory-building nor all of the areas in which theorist-researchers have assigned communications a central or key role, e.g., communications and political development. If, as it is often stated, the verbal communication of abstract ideas distinguishes human beings from other creatures, then clearly communication permeates all aspects of political life. It is not surprising, therefore, that something so encompassing has not yet been made amenable to coherent theory-building.

COMPARISON OF THREE THEORIES

A comparison of conflict, decision, and communications theories reveals that conceptualization and deductive modeling are on-going activities in all three areas.

What we can see developing in the theoretical work on development of conflicts and conflict resolution are two different, but not necessarily incompatible, formulations of the conflict situation. One formulation conceives of the conflict situation as essentially a decision problem, while the second formulation focuses on the interaction of conflict behavior. The first formulation is found more frequently in studies of conflict resolution and Coleman's early conflict stages. As the conflict becomes more "non-rational," interaction models are most often employed. A general theory of conflict behavior would incorporate variables from both formulations and from theories of change and revolution to predict and explain patterns of behavior and changes in these patterns under varying conditions as conflicts move through formative, advanced, and resolution stages. Conflict theory and decision theory appear to be at a similar stage of development or, depending upon one's view, underdevelopment. There have been fewer and less successful attempts at deductive theory-building and the linking of subareas in communications theory than in conflict or decision theory.

The presence of units common to two or all three theoretical areas tan-

[69] McLuhan, *The Medium Is the Massage*, pp. 18, 276.

talizes the theory-builder with the possibility of formulating a more general theory by relating the units and their dimensions to one another under varying conditions. At the same time, the complexities of such an undertaking are overwhelming without a computer to handle the number of units and relationships.

Remembering that we have been concerned here with empirical theory, we must ask about any differences in the availability of data and the ease of testing hypotheses generated in each of the three areas. Conflict theory would appear to be more amenable to testing, because less perceptual data is required. On the other hand, computerized content analysis and other techniques, e.g., the semantic differential, may enable decision and communications theory testers to overcome this initial disadvantage. It is possible, however, that amenability to testing and logical coherence will not decide the relevance of these particular theories for future political scientists. If empirical theorists are affected by many of the same concerns as others in their societies, the nod may go to conflict theory as it relates to change.

BIBLIOGRAPHY

The format of this bibliographical essay is developmental; that is, within each of the theoretical areas, the materials are organized by the anticipated degree of theoretical difficulty and/or the required level of mathematical sophistication.

Conflict Theory

In the general area of conflict theory, these works introduce the reader to hypotheses relating scope, intensity, types, and/or functions of conflict behavior to patterns and changes in individual and group behavior:

LEWIS COSER, *The Functions of Social Conflict* (Glencoe, Ill., 1956) and *Continuities in the Study of Social Conflict* (New York, 1967);

E.E. SCHATTSCHNEIDER, *The Semi-Sovereign People* (New York, 1960);

MORTON DEUTSCH, "A Theory of Co-operation and Competition," *Human Relations*, II (1949), 129–152; and

R. C. NORTH, *et al.*, "The Integrative Functions of Conflict," *Journal of Conflict Resolution* [hereafter: *JCR*], IV (1960), 355–374.

The discussion by R.W. MACK and R.C. SNYDER, "The Analysis of Social Conflict —Toward an Overview and Synthesis," *JCR*, I (1957), 218–248, covers a wide range of types of conflict behavior and offers a rich source of bibliographical material.

Those wishing to pursue role conflict behavior should begin with NEAL GROSS, *et al., Explorations in Role Analysis* (New York, 1958).

PETER BLAU, *Exchange and Power in Social Life* (New York, 1964), and WILLIAM C. MITCHELL, "The Shape of Political Theory to Come: From Political Sociology to Political Economy," *American Behavioral Scientist*, XI (1967), 8–20, 37, both present the essential aspects of exchange theory and help illuminate the conception of conflict as a consequence of specific types of exchange processes.

Game Theory

In order to understand the game theory used in exchange theory, decision theory, and/or conflict theory, begin with ANATOL RAPOPORT, "The Use and Misuse of Game Theory," *Scientific American*, 207 (1962), 108–118, which is both entertaining and a good introduction. The essentials of mathematical game theory are simply and well presented in J. D. WILLIAMS, *The Compleat Strategist*, 2nd ed. (New York, 1968). From there, the reader may go on to:

R. C. SNYDER, "Game Theory and the Analysis of Political Behavior," *Politics and Social Life*, eds. Nelson Polsby, *et al.* (Boston, 1963), pp. 130–145;

ANATOL RAPOPORT, *Fights, Games and Debates* (Ann Arbor, 1960) and *Two-Person Game Theory* (Ann Arbor, 1966), as well as his "Critiques of Game Theory," *Behavioral Science*, IV (1959), 49–66;

MARTIN SHUBIK, ed., *Game Theory and Related Approaches to Social Behavior* (New York, 1964); and

HAYWARD R. ALKER, JR., *Mathematics & Politics* (New York, 1965), pp. 130–146.

If interest in game theory has been sustained, see WILLIAM H. RIKER, *The Theory of Political Coalitions* (New Haven, 1962), followed by:

W. A. GAMSON, "A Theory of Coalition Formation," *American Sociological Review*, XXVI (1961), 373–382 and 565–573;

W. H. RIKER, "Bargaining in a Three-Person Game," *American Political Science Review*, LXI (1967), 642–656;

CHARLES R. ADRIAN and CHARLES PRESS, "Decision Costs in Coalition Formation," *American Political Science Review*, LXII (1968), 556–563; and

H. H. KELLEY and A. J. ARROWHEAD, "Coalitions in the Triad: Critique and Experiment," *Sociometry*, XXIII (1960), 231–244. These items will form a basis for attacking similar topics that appear regularly in *JCR* and *Sociometry*. These materials may also provide the motivation for using or learning additional mathematical skills.

KENNETH E. BOULDING, *Conflict and Defense* (New York, 1962);

THOMAS C. SCHELLING, *The Strategy of Conflict* (New York, 1963);

J. K. ZAWODNY, ed., *Man and International Relations* (San Francisco, n.d.), Volume I;

C. G. MC CLINTOCK, *et al.*, "Internationalism-Isolationism, Strategy of the Other Player, and Two-Person Game Behavior," *Journal of Abnormal and Social Psychology*, LXVII (1963), 631–635;

MARC PILISUK, *et al.*, "War Hawks, Peace Doves: Alternative Resolutions of Experimental Conflicts," *JCR*, IX (1965), 491–508;

R. A. TANTER, "Dimensions of Conflict Behavior Within and Between Nations, 1958–1960," *JCR*, X (1966), 41–64; and

R. J. RUMMEL, "The Dimensions of Conflict Behavior Within Nations, 1946–1959," *JCR*, X (1966), 67–73, should stimulate interest in game theory applications and/or general conflict behavior in international relations.

Decision Theory

A general foundation in non-mathematical decision theory is provided by:

R. C. SNYDER, "A Decision-Making Approach to the Study of Political Phenomena," *Approaches to the Study of Politics*, ed. Roland Young (Evanston, Ill., 1958), pp. 3–38;

HAROLD D. LASSWELL, *The Decision Process* (College Park, Md., 1956);

HERBERT SIMON, *Administrative Behavior*, 2nd ed. (New York, 1957);

C. E. LINDBLOM, "The Science of Muddling Through," *Public Administration Review*, XIX (1959), 79–88;

B. E. COLLINS and HAROLD GUETZKOW, *A Social Psychology of Group Processes for Decision-Making* (New York, 1962);

W. J. GORE and J. W. DYSON, eds., *The Making of Decisions* (New York, 1964);

PAUL DIESING, "Non-Economic Decision-Making," *Ethics*, LXVI (1955), 18–35;

JAMES BATES, "A Model for the Science of Decision," *Philosophy of Science*, XXI (1954), 326–339; and

PETER BACHRACH and MORTON BARATZ, "Decisions and Nondecisions," *American Political Science Review*, LVII (1963), 632–642.

Applications of decision theories can be found in RICHARD C. SNYDER and GLENN D. PAIGE, "The United States Decision to Resist Aggression in Korea: The Application of an Analytical Scheme," *Administrative Science Quarterly*, II (1958), 341–378, and OLE R. HOLSTI, "The 1914 Case," *American Political Science Review*, LIX (1965), 365–378.

In addition to the materials cited under game theory, more logical and/or mathematical theories of decision-making can be found in:

O. A. DAVIS, *et al.*, "A Theory of the Budgetary Process," *American Political Science Review*, LX (1966), 529–547;

ANTHONY DOWNS, *An Economic Theory of Democracy* (New York, 1957);

JAMES BUCHANAN and GORDON TULLOCK, *The Calculus of Consent* (Ann Arbor, 1962);

KENNETH ARROW, *Social Choice and Individual Values*, 2nd ed. (New York, 1963); and GORDON TULLOCK, *Toward a Mathematics of Politics* (Ann Arbor, 1967). Davis, *et al.* share Lindblom's conception of incremental decision-making.

To relate cognitive variables to decision and/or conflict behavior, read:

NATHAN KOGAN and M. A. WALLACH, *Risk Taking: A Study in Cognition and Personality* (New York, 1964);

DAVID FINLAY, *et al.*, *Enemies in Politics* (Chicago, 1967);

MILTON ROKEACH, *The Open and Closed Mind* (New York, 1960);

B. M. BASS and GEORGE DANTEMAN, "Biases in the Evaluation of One's Own Group, Its Allies and Opponents," *JCR*, VII (1963), 16–20;

SIDNEY SIEGEL, "Levels of Aspiration and Decision-Making," *Psychological Review*, LXIV (1957), 253–260;

S. SIEGEL and L. A. FOURAKER, *Bargaining and Group Decision-Making* (New York, 1960); and

LEON FESTINGER, *et al.*, *Conflict, Decision and Dissonance* (Stanford, Cal., 1964).

Communication Theory

EUGENE MEEHAN, *Contemporary Political Thought* (Homewood, Ill., 1967), pp. 328–335;

R. C. NORTH, "Communication as an Approach to Politics," *American Behavioral Scientist*, X (1967), 12, 21–23.

GREGORY BATESSON, "Cybernetic Explanation," *American Behavioral Scientist,* X (1967), 29–32; and

WALTER BUCKLEY, ed., *Modern Systems Research for the Behavioral Scientist* (Chicago, 1968), discuss the application of cybernetics (communications theory) to political science.

KARL W. DEUTSCH, *The Nerves of Government* (New York, 1963) and *Nationalism and Social Communication* (Cambridge, Mass., 1953) are probably the best known attempts to apply this type of communications theory to politics.

In the area of communications nets, MURRAY GLANZER and ROBERT GLASER, "Techniques for the Study of Group Structure and Behavior: Empirical Studies of the Effects of Structure in Small Groups," *Small Groups: Studies in Social Interaction,* eds. A. PAUL HARE, *et al.,* rev. ed. (New York, 1965), pp. 400–426, have written an overview of the empirical findings and theory to date.

HAROLD GUETZKOW and H. A. SIMON, "The Impact of Certain Communications Nets Upon Organization and Performance in Task-Oriented Groups," *Management Science,* I (1955), 233–250, and A. R. COHEN, "Upward Communication in Experimentally Created Hierarchies," *Human Relations,* IV (1955), 39–56, are representative of the type of research in this area. The possible relevance of graph theory for further development of the theory of communications nets can be explored after reading FRANK HARARY, *et al., Structural Models* (New York, 1965).

B. BERELSON and G. A. STEINER, *Human Behavior* (New York, 1964), pp. 527–555;

B. BERELSON and M. JANOWITZ, eds., *Reader in Public Opinion and Communication,* 2nd ed. (New York, 1966); and

LUCIAN PYE, ed., *Communications and Political Development* (Princeton, 1963), and "Communications Patterns and Problems of Representative Government in Non-Western Societies," *Public Opinion Quarterly,* XX (1956), 249–257, provide a basis for evaluating the present potential for developing a theory of mass communications.

6 / SOME ASPECTS OF METHODOLOGY AND METHODS

Introduction / Problem Formulation and Development / Data Collection and Analysis / Documentary Analysis / Survey Interviewing / Participant-Observation / Experimentation / Methods and Community Power Structure

INTRODUCTION

As more emphasis has been placed on the scientific aspects of political science, concern and sensitivity about research methods has increased, and new methods have been developed. Pressure has also increased for the separate study of research methods and techniques, particularly at the graduate level. Separate discussion of research methods does not mean the problems of applying a given method in a particular field are to be ignored. However, if students are to be trained in their use and if the methods are to be made more precise, they must be examined independently of particular subject-matter concerns. The present chapter will contain a general discussion of a number of problems connected with research, and an elementary examination of some of the principal methods used in political science research. Although examples will be used to illustrate general points, the details of how to carry out particular techniques will not be presented.

An examination of the methods used by social science researchers indicates that traditionally certain methods are used in connection with a particular subject, such as interviewing in connection with voting behavior studies. Many methods have been "field-specific," that is, they have been developed and applied in one particular area of knowledge. For example, roll-call analysis was developed in connection with the study of legislation, and

> **Roll-Call Analysis.** Analysis of the votes of public officials, based on the official records of the roll-calls during which the votes were cast.

survey research was refined in the voting behavior field. In addition,

> **Survey Research.** A generic term used to encompass research undertaken by means of interviews. Sometimes loosely equated with "public opinion polling."

153

methods may have remained field-specific because of earlier intensive resistance to their examination separate from those fields. Once developed in one area, methods can often be used in another, although adaptation is sometimes necessary, and we have seen this extension of methods from one field to another. For example, roll-call analysis has been applied to the United Nations, and survey research has been utilized widely, including in the study of judicial behavior. Until recently, few people would have attempted to interview judges in connection with studies of judicial behavior. Similarly, while for many years students of judicial activity concentrated on analysis of the judges' written opinions for the legal principles enunciated there, many have shifted their attention to the judges' votes in cases. Such sophisticated techniques as bloc analysis, Guttmann scaling, and factor analysis have been used

> *Bloc Analysis.*   A method for determining which members of a group tend to be associated most regularly with which others, accomplished by comparing their rates of interaction, such as their frequence of voting together. Clusters of individuals are said to form a "bloc," and the method is sometimes referred to as "cluster-bloc analysis."

> *Guttmann Scaling.*   Used to ascertain whether a common dimension, such as an attitude, underlies the behavior of a collection of individuals or members of a group, based on the individuals' actions (votes or statements). If unidimensionality exists, the individuals will be arranged along a continuum according to their relative position on that dimension.

> *Factor Analysis.*   A method for determining the smallest number of dimensions (factors) underlying the activities of individuals, such as their voting on legislative bills or court cases. It is developed from correlations between variables and requires electronic data-processing equipment.

in attempts to define patterns in judges' votes, as well as in other areas of political science.

In considering methodology, one must be aware that some scholars, perhaps carried away with the apparent success of their early work, have used research devices without much thought about the theoretical significance of the problems to which they were applying the device, in some instances turning out work which could be called statistically significant but substan-

> *Tests of Statistical Significance.*   Formulae which provide answers to the question whether an observed frequency can be expected to occur solely on the basis of chance. Statements are made in terms of "confidence levels," which indicate how likely it is that the frequency occurred on the basis of chance. To say that a result is significant at the .05 level is to say that it could have occurred on the basis of chance 5 times or less out of 100 times.

tively meaningless. Criticism arose that method determined choice of subject, instead of selection of tool following choice of subject-matter. A better balance between method and theoretical relevance now has been achieved than existed in behavioralism's earliest years. While emphasis on a particular method at the expense of subject-matter may be valid when attempts are being made to "de-bug" the technique, an increasing proportion of political scientists recognize that methods must be kept subordinate, particularly if we are to develop theory.

That methodology does not mean only quantifying or that it is not dominated by a specific method, like survey research, also needs to be made clear. Those who first became interested in methods in contemporary political science were generally those engaged in voting behavior research; they administered questionnaires to large numbers of people, transferred the responses to punch-cards, and quantified the results, using percentages and tests of statistical significance. But while the behavioral approach gave early emphasis to one method and to quantification, it is now clearly recognized that many methods can be utilized in political science, and that methodology does not equal survey research.

There are some well-recognized priorities in research, although there is no complete consensus on the necessity of each step or on the order in which the steps should take place. A preliminary list might include:

- problem formulation
- review of knowledge
- research design
- preliminary observation
- data collection.

To these items one might add choice and pre-testing of research instruments and hypothesis development, both part of the construction of the research design, as well as analysis and interpretation of data. We turn to an examination of some aspects of these elements of the research process now.

PROBLEM FORMULATION AND DEVELOPMENT

Clearly the first step is the formulation of a problem and specification of one's research goals. What is a "relevant" or "significant" problem depends largely on the view of the researcher (see pp. 24, 28), although the views of those in the private foundations and government who dispense needed research funds may have an effect on the researcher's views, particularly for large projects for which out-of-pocket financing is inadequate. Goals might include adding to our store of facts, testing a theory, or providing a policy-maker with material on which he might base a decision. The wide range of standards for determining what is a legitimate problem and the wide variety of possible goals have meant that few political science studies are comparable, because each researcher generally has gone off in a direction which has interested him. In addition, our stress on originality has restrained people from repeating (replicating) in different settings research projects carried out by others, to see whether the earlier findings are borne out.

Review of Literature.   A review of the literature is generally considered to be the next step after preliminary formulation of the problem. The review will show whether and how the problem has been dealt with before. The literature search will also provide possible propositions and hypotheses for testing. A search of the literature should not be equated with a grasp of all research on a subject, because hypotheses which did not "pan out" are often not reported. Some researchers feel that they have not discovered something unless they find a positive relationship along expected lines. A researcher may want to re-test an hypothesis which had brought negative results earlier, but he cannot do this if his colleagues have not reported their negative results.

Research Design.   A research design must next be developed; while varying considerably in complexity and detail, these include certain minimal items, such as the hypotheses to be tested, a specification of the data to be gathered, and a description of the methods to be used. While specific attention has to be paid to development of hypotheses, in practice their development is not an isolated step. The researcher is likely to have had some in mind when he formulated the problem, and he will have gathered others while reviewing the literature. The hypotheses probably will remain somewhat undeveloped until it has been determined what data are to be examined and research methods have been chosen. Research tools are developed after hypotheses have been spelled out in preliminary form but the hypotheses may be modified as attempts to develop precise tools expose ambiguities in their wording. Specification of the data to be gathered is an important step at this stage, one which is easily overlooked. One cannot simply take hypotheses in hand, march out into the world, and expect valid research results. Among other things, it is imperative to state how people will be chosen for a study, for sampling methods used will affect both the procedures used in analyzing the data and the generalizations which can legitimately be made from them.

The development of a research design and its component parts is perhaps the most difficult as well as the most crucial part of the research process. Much hard thought is necessary to clarify a problem and make instruments precise. Lack of clarity in the earlier stages of the research process will substantially decrease the validity of what goes after. There are, however, instances when considerable time spent on developing a design may not be productive. This is particularly true with "exploratory studies" where the only way to begin research may be to go out to collect data with only a skeleton design and some rough boundaries for one's project. From this preliminary study, ideas for future testing can be refined, and useless data discarded once the universe of data is better known. Analysis of preliminary findings may also help generate hypotheses, called *ex post facto* hypotheses, which can then be plugged into later studies done "according to the book."

Similarly, in fast-breaking situations, a researcher may have to collect data before his research design is fully developed.

As part of the development of the research design, a decision must be made as to the scope of the study. What domain of data is to be studied? Is one, for example, to study the political process in interest groups? Or in one type of interest group, such as a labor union? If one wants to examine electoral behavior, is the subject to be behavior in a particular election or in Presidential elections of the past twenty years? Is the study to be examination in detail of a particular election or labor union, or of only some aspects of either? Or is it to be a comparison of several elections or several labor unions? And, if the latter, will it be a comparison of all aspects or only some aspects of the groups?

Case and Comparative Studies.   One of the matters which is at issue here is whether to conduct a *case study* or a *comparative study*. Because both terms have been given a variety of meanings, it is important to specify what each involves. We may start by saying that a case study is an in-depth study of a single unit of analysis, while a comparative study involves attention to the similarities and differences between two or more such units; the units could be decisions, groups, or government institutions.

> A single case is taken to be a body of factual statements at a low level of abstraction pertaining to a single unit of analysis or number of interacting units and limiting conditions which the researcher considers relevant for the explanation of a particular outcome. . . . A single case is a "construct" whose empirical boundaries vary with the analytical choice—explicit or implicit—of the observer.[1]

One could conduct a case study of labor unions as a particular type of interest group, or one could use a single union as the basis for a case study. Similarly, one election could be the subject of a case study, while particular collections of voters in that election could also be the basis for still another. The same items can be the subject of both case studies and comparative studies. While a case study, regardless of its scope, emphasizes the particularities of the unit being examined, a comparative study, on the other hand, emphasizes similarities and differences and deemphasizes the compared items as discrete units.

Without some additional characteristics, a study which involves two or more organizations or situations is not necessarily a comparative study and may be little more than a case study of both (or all), with material on each presented in parallel fashion. Without an emphasis on similarities and differences, a study, no matter how many political units are involved, is not truly comparative. And even a study of one election can be comparative, if the emphasis is on differences and similarities between voters or categories of voters within that election. This explains why many of the early voting studies, although they concentrated on only one election in one community, were not case studies so much as comparative studies undertaken with emphasis on

[1] Glenn Paige, "Problems and Uses of the Single Case in Political Research," pp. 6–7.

developing generalizations. As this suggests, the distinction between "case studies" and "comparative studies" is not a totally hard-and-fast one. Some studies partake of elements of both, and what has been intended as a comparative study may very well be seen by someone with different theoretical interests as a case study. For example, the above-mentioned study based on a particular election in a particular community, although not intended as a case study, might be seen by an historian of elections as one. Similarly, a case study, particularly when joined to other case studies, may seem to contain implicit comparisons or provide data for comparative findings—subject to the warning that the data of each case study may have been collected by researchers with different implicit frameworks.

Initially, case studies were descriptive and factual, with no explicit explanatory matter, as in the studies developed by the Inter-University Case Program (ICP) for use in the teaching of public administration. "Comparative study" generally came to be associated with the study of foreign governments, initially those of Western Europe, on a country-by-country basis, with each country's governmental institutions described in considerable detail, and with little or no comparison. Both these associations unnecessarily limit the two terms. While traditionalists, particularly in public administration, have used the case study as a prime working method, case studies can contain many research tools, including "behavioral" ones. Reflecting a shift within the comparative government field to a more genuinely comparative approach, more political scientists now pay attention to explicit comparison of particular institutions, such as legislative bodies, from several countries. (See Chapter 15.) Identification of similarities and differences becomes a part of the description, and description of the units being compared is integrated; this had led some to call comparers the general theorists of political science. In what has been called a methodological revolution in the study of comparative politics, a need to develop cooperative research and shared conceptual frameworks has been recognized. And efforts have been made to develop concepts which "(1) facilitate systematic comparison across cultures, (2) permit more abstract analysis . . . and (3) apply to all, or almost all, extant polities." [2]

Existing theory may be used to explain (not just describe) what has occurred, or a case study can be used to test theory or to develop hypotheses for further testing. In this connection, Lipset, Trow, and Coleman, authors of a classic case study of the International Typographical Union (ITU), assert a difference between "particularizing" and "generalizing" analysis. In the former, while there is "description and explanation of the single case, to provide information concerning its present state, and the dynamics through which it continues as it does," generalizations are *used* in carrying out the analysis of the particular case.[3] This is not to suggest that all the factual

[2] Arthur L. Kalleberg, "The Logic of Comparison: A Methodological Note on the Comparative Study of Political Systems," *World Politics*, XIX (1966), 70.

[3] Seymour Martin Lipset, Martin A. Trow, and James S. Coleman, *Union Democracy: The Internal Politics of the International Typographical Union* (Glencoe, 1956), pp. 419, 420.

statements made in the case study can be explained by the generalizations. As another user of case studies notes,

> Since the social scientist's ability to describe far outruns his ability to account for what he has described in terms of general laws, a discrepancy between the total range of empirical phenomena reported in a case study and the amount of data which can be accounted for in terms of *explicit* theory seems inevitable.[4]

"Generalizing" analysis, on the other hand, involves "development of empirical generalizations or theory through the analysis of the single case," using the case "as an empirical basis either for generalization or theory construction." [5] This is particularly useful at the "exploratory" stage of work on a subject. However, "very few cases have been chosen for any specific theoretical purpose" and, "although one of the most frequently heard justifications for the case study is that it is suggestive of hypotheses for future research, the subsequent research of the authors of case studies has not often pursued the alleged advantage." [6]

Analysis of unusual situations or "deviant cases" through the case study device may cast further light on the "mine run" of situations than would occur if the "normal" situations were the only ones analyzed. Moreover, only one case may be available in order to study a particular theoretical point; thus, the ITU studied by Lipset *et al.* was the only American labor union with a fully-developed two-party system on a national basis, crucial for those interested in discovering factors supporting internal union democracy. The ITU might very well be the only (as well as the best) place to start. Findings based on a single case cannot provide us with high-level generalizations, but they take us further than we otherwise could go in the absence of additional units to study. One difficulty with case studies of deviant situations is that so many have been written that there are few descriptions of ordinary situations with which to compare them. As James Robinson remarks concerning case studies of Congressional activity, "the cases have been selected for virtually every reason except for the illustration of the most typical patterns of legislative activity. . . . Most of the cases concern dramatic, important, and novel decisions." [7] While a man biting a dog is news, a dog biting a man is not (unless the Post Office develops a new way of repelling the canines). The greater proportion of studies which have been produced are of the factual variety, although not necessarily without explanation. They may have been written simply to preserve historical material, to provide details for those interested in the substance of the study (as against generalizations which might be developed), or to assist in teaching by familiarizing the student with materials to which he could not easily have access and awakening him to relationships which he can then explore in other settings. This last purpose is particularly

---

[4] Paige, p. 10.
[5] Lipset, *et al.*, pp. 419–420.
[6] James A. Robinson, *Congress and Foreign Policy-Making: A Study in Legislative Influence and Initiative*, rev. ed. (Homewood, Ill., 1967), pp. 24, 71.
[7] *Ibid.*, p. 24.

relevant when the situation studied is supposed to be in some way "representative" of a large number of others.

Preliminary Observation.   Preliminary observation was noted above as a step in the research process, although it usually occurs continually once a researcher has become interested in a problem. He will be attuned to the phenomena in which he is interested and, almost naturally, will begin to "keep an eye out" for events around him which might cast light on "his" problem. Preliminary observation also has other, more definite, meanings. One is that the researcher will check to see whether adequate data are available. Once it is determined that data are available, checking the research instruments, pre-testing, is necessary to remove "bugs" in a particular research tool. Questionnaire items which produce little response can be modified or dropped. Ambiguous instructions can be rewritten or categories changed. Where all the peculiarities of research instruments which may affect data cannot be removed, they often can be identified through the pre-testing process so that they can be discounted when data are analyzed. Pre-testing also allows researchers to determine whether the tools they are using are both valid and reliable. A research method is *valid* if it actually measures what it is said to measure. For example, a set of questions designed to measure the degree to which a person has "authoritarian" views which measured only one of several types of authoritarianism would be said to be lacking in "content validity." If responses to the set of questions were not highly correlated with actions which our hypotheses indicated should be performed by authoritarians, we would say the measure did not have "construct validity." [8] A research method is *reliable* if it produces the same results at different times or the same results when used by different people. If two researchers interview the same set of individuals with the identical research tool and obtain largely different results, the tool is likely to be unreliable.

Although the method used will affect the data collected, there has been relatively little emphasis within political science on testing particular methods for validity. Once the basic validity of a method has been ascertained, it can be used with much more certainty that it will not distort data and resulting findings. Yet many political scientists use methods which may bias or distort data or provide data which are an artifact of the method. Particular methods have been refined through continual use, and the fact that some researchers tend to choose a subject for study because it lends itself to a particular method (rather than a method because of its applicability to the subject-matter) has provided some useful methodological information. However, the systematic application of several methods to the same data, in order to determine the differential effect of the methods, has occurred seldom, even when a field produces conflicting findings which may be the result of varied methods. This is discussed at the end of the chapter with particular reference to the study of community power structure. Unless one is using a method whose

[8] Fred N. Kerlinger, *Foundations of Behavioral Research,* pp. 444 ff.

validity has been tested and shown, it is useful (if not imperative) to employ two or more methods "in tandem" in order to improve the chances that one's findings are not simply the results of a single particular method. However, use of a single method is clearly considered legitimate, particularly if it is described so that other researchers can consider its possible effects on the data.

DATA COLLECTION AND ANALYSIS

Data collection, analysis, and presentation are equally important steps in the research process. Even if a research instrument is precise, failure to act carefully in the collection of data can impair its effect. Particularly where interpersonal relations are involved in the collection of data, as in interview situations, careful attention to the task at hand is necessary if the impact of extraneous or interfering factors is to be kept to a minimum. In data analysis and interpretation, the principal problems generally are, first, keeping generalizations in line with data, and second, presenting material in clearly understandable form. Particularly when we are striving to develop generalizations from which theory can be constructed, the temptation is to push our data as far as possible, to develop the broadest generalizations given the data we have. While the researcher wants to obtain from his data all that is possible, he must be quite careful that generalizations are based on what has been discovered, not on what he might have discovered or he would like to have discovered. He must not forget the problems involved in getting the data to the stage where he could analyze it, and must not fall prey to the temptation to consider as completely "hard" all data in numerical form. Thus Herbert Hyman notes that we accept without question census figures about the number of homes with interior plumbing, although a census enumerator does not walk past his respondents to check on the presence of a bathroom nor does he walk around the outside of the house looking for a privy. If the respondent is embarrassed by not having interior plumbing in his residence, he might say "yes" when the answer should be "no." If this sort of question about an inanimate object provides difficulties, one can imagine the problems provided by questions about a person's views of the political world around him, and we should remember them when analyzing our data.

Problems of Access.   One aspect of the research process which may be more serious than developing the research problem is that of access to data, involved in data collection. While not in principle a new problem, it has become of increasing importance as more use has been made of survey research techniques. When research in political science meant mostly documentary analysis, the problem was far less great, particularly in the United States, where researchers were not faced with the burdens of Great Britain's Official Secrets Act, which severely restricts the availability of public documents. Although the "classification" of certain documents in the interest of national security has restricted access to some materials, access to American government documents political scientists want has usually been largely a matter of time.[9] For example, certain papers relating to our foreign policy are released only after a period of years, making the writing of "contemporary history" more difficult but ultimately providing the documents for analysis. Decisions of administrative bodies or regulatory agencies, and of the courts, are published in such profusion that the problem is usually one of determining which to use rather than of finding enough to work with. The papers of important public officials are usually considered private but often are made available through some university library upon the man's death. While access to public records is by and large not difficult, the completeness of those records may be in question to some extent, and the records may have been "manufactured" with a view to subsequent history.

Although obtaining consent to interview someone has always been a problem, conducting research through interviews has in recent years become related to some problems of professional ethics, increased concern about personal privacy, and lack of trust of the social sciences. Many people welcome the chance to express their views on political matters to an interviewer, so that access to most members of the general public is not difficult. The Gallup and Roper Polls, despite their famed failure to predict the 1948 Presidential election, have considerable prestige, and perhaps there is "glamor" in being asked to participate in a survey, although people may mistrust them because they have not been interviewed, or because they have been harrassed by people conducting marketing surveys. There are, however, members of the public who feel strongly that political views are private matters and that the interviewer, despite his promises to the contrary, will reveal what he is told to unknown individuals.

Questions have been raised as to whether members of the general public, uneducated concerning social science and survey research, understand clearly what they are getting involved in when asked to participate in a survey, and that they may not be able to give "valid" consent. This concern is reinforced by the social scientists' claim that they cannot inform their potential respondents about all their reasons for asking questions without prejudicing the responses. Thus we have a conflict between the researcher's right to search for information and add to our knowledge, and the individual's right not to be manipulated. While this question first arose in connection with the testing of drugs on unaware patients, the relevance for social science has now received attention. A prominent social scientist recently described a project in which the cultural level of high school graduates is raised by having them watch special educational TV programs under a pretext, e.g., of timing commercials. After some time has elapsed, the researcher checks to see whether they continue to watch the programs to which they have been

[9] However, see the comment by Arthur Waskow about the Department of the Army's refusal to release, in 1965, a report of a 1919 race riot. *From Race Riot to Sit-In* (Garden City, 1967), p. xiv.

exposed. A research problem is involved in this project, but one principal purpose is clearly not research.

Another type of problem is this: A researcher tells a respondent a falsehood, e.g., that the respondent has injured someone, in the interest of determining the respondent's reaction to the statement, and the false statement is disturbing to the respondent. What should be done? Is it enough to tell the respondent the truth after the study is over, hoping to extinguish the disturbance? Or is the matter serious enough so that this sort of study should not be carried out in the first place? While this type of problem is of more immediate import to the field of psychology, which relies more heavily on experimental stimuli than does political science, the implications for political science are clear. What if a political scientist wanted to know the public's reaction to an announcement of an atomic attack on a distant city? Might not personal disturbances be long-lasting, even if the fraudulent nature of the statement were later revealed?

Even when experimental stimuli are not being administered, the types of questions asked raise issues. Are questions about sexual behavior and sexual attitude acceptable? Their inclusion in a study of sexual attitudes is one thing. But if one includes sex-related items in a series of questions because of an interest in the relationship between a person's psychological makeup and his voting behavior, what then? To announce the purpose of the questions may produce a response tailored to what the respondent thinks the researcher wants. Nor can we ignore the statement that

> Any attempt to insure that no questions are asked that are embarrassing or offensive to some person would so impede creative research that much . . . investment in the behavioral sciences will be wasted, or worse, the knowledge which our society expects and needs will not be obtained.[10]

Perhaps as the public becomes more aware of social science and comes to accept its validity, and if a greater understanding of psychology develops, questions of the type mentioned here will become more acceptable, although they may be offset by an increasing sensitivity of the public about its constitutional rights.

The question, "How far shall a person's identity be protected?" is at the heart of the present controversy about anonymity of persons contributing data to research projects. When a researcher promises anonymity or at least confidentiality as most individuals conducting interviews do, what does this mean?[11] Does it mean that only statistical interpretation of data about a mass of individuals will be presented, so no one individual can be separated from

[10] Office of Science and Technology, Executive Office of the President, *Report on Privacy and Behavioral Research* (Washington, D.C., 1967), p. 55.

[11] "*Anonymity* and *confidentiality* are related. Anonymity refers to preventing the identity of the subject from ever being known to anyone. Anonymity merges into confidentiality when the research design permits the identity to be known at one point in time or to a limited number of investigators, but is otherwise protected from dissemination." *Ibid.*, p. 34.

the others, much less identified? Or does it mean only that some action will be taken to prevent easy identification? The problem is made more serious because the issue often turns on whether the individual thinks he has been identified, not on whether he has been in fact. While interviewers might be able to obtain much information "on the record" which they now receive by granting anonymity, they are honor-bound to respect the grant if they make it.

Researchers studying community power structure frequently disguise the names of the towns being studied and the individuals who constitute what they allege to be the power structure. But should they also disguise, for example, an individual's occupation? If they do, the individual might not be recognizable, but the picture presented might then not be accurate, if occupation has an effect on the participant's actions. One compromise is to disguise quite completely in publications, while making detailed and accurate information, properly identified, available to legitimate researchers for follow-up studies and cross-checking.

The difficulties which can arise, and their relation to professional ethics, are shown by the aftermath of *Small Town in Mass Society*, by two sociologists, Arthur Vidich and Joseph Bensman. The authors were accused of having used data from a related study whose directors had promised confidentiality to those studied. The inhabitants of "Springdale" were also quite unhappy about Vidich and Bensman's portrayal of the town and "negative" characteristics of some of its people, who considered themselves recognizable. It was claimed that the town would be "useless" for research purposes for many years.[12] Lengthy exchanges in professional journals resulted, with the authors denying the charges against them. They claimed in turn that those managing the earlier research project were "censoring" data to protect vested interests, a situation which Vidich and Bensman felt did not comport with an "open social science." "At certain stages the community may become a more important reference group for the project than is the scientific community to which the research is ostensibly addressed," they wrote later.[13] They also claimed that "negative reaction to community and organizational research is only heard when results describe articulate, powerful, and respected individuals and organizations." [14] As Becker has put it, "trouble occurs primarily . . . because what the social scientist reports is what the people studied would prefer not to know [or to have known], no matter how obvious or easy it is to discover." [15]

---

[12] The initial charge was made in the editorial, "Freedom and Responsibility in Research: The 'Springdale' Case," *Human Organization*, XVII (1958), 1–2. Further comments by Vidich and Bensman and others appeared in *Human Organization*, XVII (1958–1959), 2–7 and XVIII (1959), 49–52. Vidich and Bensman make a final full statement in "The Springdale Case: Academic Bureaucrats and Sensitive Townspeople," *Reflections on Community Studies*, ed. Vidich, Bensman, and Stein, pp. 313–349.

[13] Vidich and Bensman, "The Springdale Case . . . ," p. 334.

[14] Vidich and Bensman, " 'Freedom and Responsibility in Research': A Comment," *Human Organization*, XVII (1958–1959), 4.

[15] Howard S. Becker, "Problems in the Publication of Field Studies," *Reflections on Community Studies*, ed. Vidich, et al., p. 273.

The problem becomes more complex with public officials, who generally have little time to devote to answer interviewers, but whose responses may be crucial for some research projects. Such people are especially reluctant to reveal their "private" views to an interviewer if they think that publication of an article detailing those views might invite criticism or be embarrassing. Because many view political scientists as supporting reform, they may also be wary of participating in a project they see as serving as the basis for changing the system in which they operate. Promises of anonymity are harder to carry through with public officials, because readers will often recognize those who have participated in key decisions, even if the researcher goes to great lengths to camouflage identities. When the researcher does not reveal his purpose, suspicion may be heightened. The controversy occasioned by the revelation in 1967 that the Central Intelligence Agency had provided funds to organizations conducting research, in addition to raising questions about the CIA's involvement in domestic politics, raised for political scientists the additional problem that potential respondents might feel that they were being asked to participate in a study financed, directly or indirectly, through such funds. Even if the researcher were himself not aware of the source of his money, the problem would remain.

The increasing role of government in social science research has served to bring all these problems to the fore, as government agencies have begun to insist that certain guidelines be followed by researchers using government money, and as these guidelines have then been adopted on a wider basis. At issue here is not only the question of the merits of individual guidelines, but also the question of the propriety of government issuing any guidelines. As can be expected, professional associations in the various social science disciplines tend to take the position that individual professions should develop their own codes of ethics or that institutions administering research money should be the ones to develop (and enforce) guidelines. A recent government panel made up principally of social scientists stated: "We do not believe that detailed governmental controls of research methods or instruments can substitute for the more effective procedures which are available and which carry less risk of damage to the scientific enterprise"; and recommended that "legislation to assure appropriate recognition of the right of human subjects is neither necessary nor desirable if scientists and sponsoring institutions fully discharge their responsibilities in accommodating to the claim of privacy." [16] One might ask, of course, "but where have they been until now?" Government development of guidelines concerns much more than simply ethics. It concerns the freedom of researchers to spend research money as they see fit, without government controls; it involves the paperwork and "red tape" necessary to apply for funds which will be denied if proper procedures are not followed. In short, it raises the whole question of research administration (not only a government problem, although perhaps more visible there) and the larger issue of who or what institution, if any, should have the right to set specifications for researchers' work. This brings the charge that the organiza-

[16] Office of Science and Technology, *Report* . . . , pp. 10, 13.

tion with the guidelines, like any organization, will begin to demand what is convenient for it, rather than for the researcher. With government we can see the values which compete with the researcher's desire for independence, values which have to be considered: satisfying taxpayers that money is not wasted and perhaps choosing projects of most use to the government (where government officials and social scientists differ on evaluations of usefulness). Whether or not government is directly involved, the social scientist, who has been used to operating under conditions of quasi-anarchy, has difficulty seeing the need for restrictions imposed by administrators he perceives as unknowledgeable. Even when the social scientist wants money for large projects he could not finance on his own, he often takes the position that the money should be available for him without any reciprocal responsibilities on his part.

In the last analysis, the individual researcher, on the basis of his own (personal and professional) set of values, has to determine how to handle these questions. The lack of a code of ethics for political science and what many consider to be inadequate training of potential social scientists concerning these matters, even in the form of raising questions to be considered, makes the matter more difficult. (In 1968, the American Political Science Association did adopt two statements as "expressions of principle" for the time being, rather than as specific codes.) The existence of a code of ethics, such as that developed by the American Psychological Association, does make people aware of concern about problems even if they aren't sure of the precise terms of the code. The indirect effect of the code is that it becomes part of graduate students' training, thus becoming more or less internalized.

Aggregate and Individual Data.   In analysis of data, census material and official statistics raise special problems, and give rise to the question of the difference in the use of individual data and aggregate data. Census data, an example of the latter, are presented as total figures for a given unit of area —a municipality, a state, a census tract. Thus, for a particular city, one can determine what percentage of residences are owner-occupied, how many homes have interior plumbing, what the average income is, and what percentage of the people are foreign-born. But these figures do not tell us about individuals. Clearly not everyone in the city has the same income, not all people own their own homes, and not the same proportion of each family is foreign-born. This becomes important to political scientists when they are trying to determine factors influencing the vote.

Imaginative interpretation of aggregate data has added much useful information to our knowledge of political behavior. This has been possible because electoral statistics, which invite analysis of voting patterns, are elaborately recorded and publicly available in aggregate form for basic local governmental units, such as counties and municipalities (cities and towns), minor civil divisions (townships), and election districts (wards and precincts). One of the best-known uses of aggregate data is V. O. Key's study of politics in the South, *Southern Politics in State and Nation,* in which he related the percentage of the vote cast (by the then almost entirely white electorate) for the Democratic and Republican parties to the percentage of the population which was Negro, on a county-by-county basis. He showed that the vote for Hoover in 1928, that is, defection from the Democratic Party, was greatest in those areas with the lowest percentages of Negroes and in the cities, and that the vote for the Dixiecrat ticket in 1948 was greatest in the counties with the heaviest proportion of Negro residents; his conclusion was that the race issue was the basis for Southern political unity.[17]

Our temptation, on the basis of such studies, is to try to relate census figures to voting statistics, in order to explain why *individuals* vote as they do. When census areas and units for which election statistics are reported are congruent, the task appears easy. If we find that a district 70% Negro votes predominantly Democratic, and a district including 80% native-born whites votes Republican, we may be tempted to begin to talk about native-born whites voting Republican and Negroes voting Democratic. Perhaps it might be legitimate to use these as hypotheses, but, in the absence of further research, difficulties might easily arise. For example, the Democratic majority in the Negro area might be largely a result of a nearly unanimous pro-Democratic vote among the white residents of the area, with the Negroes split between the two parties. Or the Republican majority in the native-born district might result from a heavy Republican vote cast by immigrants, with the native-born actually favoring the Democrats. Without suggesting that either of these results is plausible in real life, the possibility of misleading conclusions from aggregate data is considerable.

One example concerns the "coattail-effect" in Presidential elections, that is, the degree to which the Presidential candidate is able to pull into office with him other members of his party. Examination of this phenomenon in the press has usually been in terms of the President's total vote compared with the votes of those running with him. Supposedly, if the President ran ahead, it showed the President's pulling power; if he ran behind, his coattails were useless to those running with him. This conventional wisdom has been challenged with the argument that, to the extent the President runs ahead he has not been able to attract votes to others of his own party—thus, the greater the President's margin over his "teammates," the *worse* his coattails.[18] But, even more important, it has been shown that "it is clearly very difficult to estimate accurately the extent to which a Presidential nominee influences the vote for his fellow candidates, if all one has to go on is the aggregative election returns."[19] Aggregate figures do not reveal what proportion of the voters cast ballots for the President's entire ticket, what proportion voted for him but not his running-mates, or what proportion voted for them (or some of

[17] V. O. Key, Jr., *Southern Politics in State and Nation* (New York, 1949), Ch. 15, "Hoovercrats and Dixiecrats," pp. 317–344.

[18] Warren E. Miller, "Presidential Coattails: A Study in Political Myth and Methodology," *Public Opinion Quarterly*, XIX (1955–1956), 353–368.

[19] Angus Campbell and Warren E. Miller, "The Motivational Basis of Straight and Split-Ticket Voting," *American Political Science Review*, LI (1957), 309.

them) but not for him. Thus, even where the President and his running mates received an identical percentage of the vote, we should be wary about inferring straight-ticket voting unless we can actually see the ballots or talk to the voters individually. Significant numbers of cross-party voters ("ticket-splitters") may be hidden beneath the surface of the gross returns.

If we are to find answers to the questions posed above, we need to obtain data for individuals rather than collective figures for aggregates. Survey research has allowed us to do this. However, particularly in the absence of survey findings, but also even when they are available, we should not discard aggregate data, because of its advantages, stated clearly by Austin Ranney:

> . . . By contrast with survey data, they are available for a wide variety of electorates and [are] relatively easy and inexpensive to obtain and analyze. Most democratic nations have for some time published election returns broken down by various subconstituency units. Also, most units periodically conduct censuses and publish reports presenting veritable avalanches of social and economic information about their populations. The result is an immense body of data, rich in its variety and coverage, and easily and cheaply accessible to individual scholars anywhere in the world . . .
>
> . . . The accessibility and inexpensiveness of aggregate data invite replicative and comparative studies on a wide scale.
>
> . . . For finding answers to many questions about electoral behavior, they are the "hardest" data we can get, in the sense that their meaning and comparability vary less from area to area, from time to time, and from study to study than do most survey data.[20]

And Retzlaff has suggested that not only is survey research new in many countries, but it is also particularly expensive, difficult, and even suspect, in the "developing nations." He also notes that not all aggregate measurements have their counterparts in individual measurements; for example, per capita figures permit standardization to control for variations in population size between countries. And, echoing Ranney, he suggests that, even where survey research is now being conducted, aggregate data are available over longer periods of time.[21]

Primary and Secondary Analysis. Until recently, particularly with the coming of survey research, it was taken for granted that each researcher would develop his own data. As long as data was collected neither systematically nor rigorously, the materials of any one researcher were of relatively little use to anyone else. The researcher reported what he had "found," but his data were largely "in his head" or in a form which, while it suited the researcher's own habits, did not make sense to other researchers. As emphasis in the social sciences shifted to more precise methods of data-gathering, not only was the reliability of findings increased, but data became available

[20] Austin Ranney, "The Utility and Limitations of Aggregate Data in the Study of Electoral Behavior," *Essays on the Behavioral Study of Politics*, ed. Ranney, pp. 95–96.

[21] Ralph H. Retzlaff, "The Use of Aggregate Data in Comparative Political Analysis," *Journal of Politics*, XXVII (1965), 797–817.

in a form that others could use. Survey research, particularly in the study of voting, began to result in sizeable amounts of data in a form which could be made available without considerable difficulty—in decks of punch-cards. The question arose as to the possible further use of that material by people other than the individual(s) who originally collected it. Through "secondary analysis," that is, analysis of data which another researcher has collected *and prepared,* the later users might attempt to "milk" more or different information from the data than had the original researchers, predominantly those who had the financial and other resources available to conduct large surveys, particularly on a nation-wide basis. A few research units came to do much of the data-collecting in this area. Thus, the work of the Inter-University Consortium for Political Research, based at the University of Michigan's Survey Research Center, has provided the basis for many "satellite" projects on voting behavior based on SRC data; comparable centers exist for public opinion data. Data banks reinforced the trend toward secondary analysis. The data banks coupled survey research material with distribution facilities under one roof, and were based on an ethic that a researcher, after a certain minimum time for primary analysis of "his" data, had a professional obligation to make his data available to others.

The availability of SRC-type material has, however, not eliminated the difficulties of secondary analysis, and the facility with which one can obtain data may blind one to its possible limitations, which depend on what one is trying to do. No major difficulties arise simply in checking findings the primary researchers have reported, if the work in preparing ("coding") the raw data (the original interview forms) for the punch-cards is accepted as accurate. Difficulties are more likely to arise when an attempt is made to do more than the primary researchers did or to do something different. At this point the secondary researcher is likely to find that the primary data do not contain answers to questions he wants answered, or that they were asked or coded in somewhat different form from what he would prefer. Someone interested in the relation between age and conservatism might find that the data he was using contained items on age and the political views of the respondents, as well as certain standard demographic items, but not the respondent's opinion on the desirability of change or answers to questions about the respondent's general flexibility/rigidity. If he had hypothesized that the latter was relevant to the age-conservatism relationship, he would have no way to test it through the secondary analysis. The researcher attempting comparative analysis on a secondary basis finds his problems compounded. Each primary researcher, in addition to collecting his information in a form not ideal for the secondary analyst, will likely have collected it in somewhat different form, creating hazards both in construction of tables from such data and interpretation of the data.

Secondary analysis can be particularly useful when a researcher is making preliminary tests of his hypotheses to determine which of several alternatives seem to be worth pursuing. He may be able to save himself much time by checking his hypotheses on the data of available studies. Nevertheless, in the long run, however helpful secondary analysis may be for some purposes, it will probably have to be supplemented by more primary research if theoretically important questions are to be answered.

Secondary analysis is most likely in the areas of voting behavior and public opinion, because the original researcher has directly affected the shape and form of the data before it becomes accessible to others. When data is conveniently accessible to all in document form, each researcher can perform his own primary analysis, without having to rely on the intermediary steps performed by some other researcher. But, even here, questions of time, effort, and resources intervene. Thus, someone interested in the votes of Congressmen in support of their party or in support of the President will be tempted to use the "Party Support Score" and "Presidential Support Score" compiled by *Congressional Quarterly*, even if he might compile the figures somewhat differently if he had to do it himself. Also, the line between primary and secondary analysis is one which cannot be drawn too sharply. Data from the Bureau of the Census, while often considered "primary," depends upon the Bureau's work in presenting the data in its published form, thus in effect making its use secondary analysis. One sees this clearly when trying to find census-type information for areas which do not follow census tract lines, for example.

A Note on Statistics in Political Science. It is extremely important for the researcher to think about the characteristics of his data before applying (or attempting to apply) statistical measures, so that not only will he avoid using statistics more "powerful" than his data will support, but also so he can use statistics as powerful as the data *will* support. His difficulty will be that statisticians in the social sciences are not themselves completely agreed on when certain measures are appropriate, indicated by recent controversy over the use of tests of significance. (The principal controversy concerns *inductive* statistics, that is, those used to test generalizations, rather than *descriptive* statistics, used to describe the characteristics of data.) [22]

Statistics is only an aid to political science. As Meehan argues, "statistics is a formal device, a logic of numbers, that demonstrates the properties of relationships among numbers and no more." He goes on to add, "mastery of statistics . . . implies nothing whatever about knowledge of subject matter; when there is a conflict, it is always the latter that holds." [23] And others warn against ignoring large numerical differences even when statistical significance does not exist, or ignoring them when numerical differences are small. Common sense—or rather common sense educated by knowledge about political phenomena—must play a role in ultimate interpretation.

In determining what statistics are appropriate, it is necessary to know whether one's data takes the form of *nominal, ordinal, interval,* or *ratio* scales. In a nominal scale, values have been assigned to items which do not themselves have any particular arithmetic values, e.g., Democratic = 1 and

[22] Hayward R. Alker, Jr., *Mathematics & Politics*, p. 55.
[23] Eugene Meehan, *The Theory and Method of Political Analysis*, pp. 209, 212.

Republican=2. This assignment of numbers, like the assignment of numbers to players on a football team, is simply for purposes of designation; it does not mean that a Republican is worth twice as much as a Democrat, or even that he is worth any more. In order to treat the data without having to repeat "Democrat" and "Republican," we assign numbers arbitrarily. With an ordinal scale, we are able to say that one item is "more than" or "less than" or "the same as" another item, but we are not able to say anything about the amount by which they are more than or less than each other. For interval scales to exist, equal distances on the scale must represent equal distances on the property measured, as on a temperature thermometer. The difference between the interval scale and the ratio scale is that the latter has a fixed zero point. With a ratio scale, we can say that something is "twice as much as" something else, or "half as much as," while, with an interval scale, we can only say it is "five units more" or "three units less," although it may be possible to treat an average as a zero-point for some purposes even when we technically have only interval data. Each succeeding type of scale has the property of the preceding type(s), in addition to its own distinguishing characteristic.

Another problem with the use of statistics occurs in the presentation of data. Much care must be exercised in order to make the data comprehensible, but also because data can be made to show noticeably different results, depending on the way in which they are arranged. For example, students of British politics have been interested in the "working class Tory," that is, laboring people who vote for the Conservative Party rather than the Labour Party. Some British newspapers present their analysis by dividing the electorate by party, and then figuring the class composition of each party's vote, as the following table shows: [24]

	Middle Class	Working Class	
Conservative	51%	49%	100%
Labour	19%	81%	100%

On the basis of this table, it would appear that substantially more members of the working class vote Conservative than members of the middle class vote Labour. If, however, we talk of the party vote of each class (divide by class, then distribute by party), we get a different picture:

	Middle Class	Working Class
Conservative	77%	29%
Labour	23%	71%
	100%	100%

[24] From a paper by Donald Stokes, American Political Science Association meetings, Chicago, September, 1964.

This arrangement of the data reduces the difference between working-class Tories and middle-class Labourites considerably.

DOCUMENTARY ANALYSIS

The analysis of documents, private and public, has consumed much of the effort of scholars in the social sciences. Those documents have varied from writings of ancient philosophers to speeches by the President of the United States, from declarations of medieval kings to recent rulings of the Supreme Court. These documents have been analyzed for many reasons: to verify their authenticity, to determine their historical antecedents, to examine their style, to check logical and doctrinal consistency, and to ascertain their implications. All these types of research can be carried on according to accepted canons of interpretation. Specific techniques exist for tracing the roots or results of a particular document. For example, in the field of legal research, it is possible to trace the use of a particular court case, so that one can determine when the principle (or holding) enunciated in that case has been followed by later judges, avoided, or overruled; similarly, one can trace the earlier uses of a case cited in a current judicial statement. A principal although not absolutely essential aid in this process is *Sheppard's Citator,* in which are recorded in abbreviated form the uses to which a case has been put by subsequent judges. The process of tracing out a case's past or future, known as "Sheppardizing," has particular usefulness in determining the impact of Supreme Court decisions.

In the last few decades, an increasing interest in language and its uses has directed attention to more systematic methods of studying political statements and documents. This interest, related at first to the use of propaganda,

> *Propaganda.* "The manipulation of symbols as a means of influencing attitudes on controversial matters." [25] The term can be used in a neutral sense, but most often has a pejorative connotation; thus, statements of the enemy are propaganda, while statements from our side are education or information.

started with the rise of the Nazi regime in Germany and with World War II, and was nurtured in part by the American government. Later, interest shifted to include the study of symbols and the symbolic use of political acts, reinforced by a renewal outside of political science in linguistics. That language did more than assign formal meaning to words was recognized.

> The terms in which we name or speak of anything do more than designate it; they place it in a class of objects, thereby suggest with what it is to be judged and compared, and define the perspective from which it will be viewed and evaluated.[26]

[25] Harold Lasswell, Nathan Leites, and Associates, *Language of Politics: Studies in Quantitative Semantics* (New York, 1949), p. 177.
[26] Murray Edelman, *The Symbolic Uses of Politics* (Urbana, 1964), p. 131.

And, in addition, the words' impact and meaning became paramount. This shift in emphasis led to "content analysis" as a more systematic means of analysis.

Content analysis, the purpose of which is to categorize parts of a written text, and to allow symbols to be related to deeds, has been defined as

> referring to any technique a) for the *classification* of the *sign-vehicles,* b) which relies solely upon the *judgments* . . . of an analyst or group of analysts as to which sign-vehicles fall into which categories, c) on the basis of *explicitly formulated rules,* d) provided that the analyst's judgments are regarded as the reports of a *scientific observer.*[27]

Content analysis is a way of defining with greater clarity a political system's predominant "political myth" or political ideology. The precise descriptions of communications provided by content analysis assist investigations of the relationship between communication content and characteristics of communicator, audience, or communication itself. As its foremost advocates make clear,

> Content analysis will not tell us whether a given work is good literature; it *will* tell us whether the style is varied. It will not tell us whether a paper is subversive; it *will* tell us if its contents change with the party line. It will not tell us how to convince the Russians; it *will* tell us what are the most frequent themes of Soviet propaganda.[28]

Content analysis begins with the construction of a series of categories into which statements (or parts of statements) are to be placed, along with rules for making decisions as to the category in which to place a statement. This part of the process is more crucial than the actual classifying. If the procedural rules bring about faulty classification, systematic errors will result from the analysis. If the categories constructed are ambiguous or not exhaustive of the types of material to be analyzed, several types of statements will be placed in the same category. If the categories are not relevant to the questions to which an answer is wanted, then the content analysis will not be either theoretically or practically useful. Categories are not automatic because the researcher's interests may vary from the frequency with which certain subject-matters are mentioned ("designations analysis") to the manner in which certain objects are characterized ("assertions analysis") to the frequency of the characterizations ("attribution analysis").[29]

All the problems of content analysis do not, however, relate to the category construction stage. The actual categorizing must be done with every effort to achieve high reliability. To assist in achieving such a high standard, identical samples of materials to be analyzed can be given to different re-

---

[27] Irving Janis, "The Problem of Validating Content Analysis," *Language of Politics,* p. 55. Emphasis in original.

[28] Harold Lasswell, Daniel Lerner, and Ithiel deSola Pool, *The Comparative Study of Symbols: An Introduction* (Stanford, 1952), p. 45.

[29] Janis, p. 57.

searchers for them to code (sort into the constructed categories) to determine if they arrive at roughly the same decisions. If divergent results occur, further training of the workers or further clarification of procedures or categories must be necessary. Individual coders can also be asked to code the same documents at different times to determine consistency, but this test is less effective because initial work may affect the coder's subsequent coding.

SURVEY INTERVIEWING

Survey interviewing is important because it provides a large proportion of the data used by contemporary political scientists. While the term is often restricted in meaning to questions asked directly of respondents by interviewers, and thus is considered to be different from telephone interviews or mail-questionnaire studies, the term is used here to cover all these methods. Whether or not to use survey research at all is, of course, the first question to ask. Because of its overuse, one must guard against using it hastily before considering other techniques. For example, Paul Lazarsfeld imaginatively suggests we could determine liquor consumption in a "dry" town by counting bottles in trash cans, and the popularity of paintings by worn spots on art gallery rugs.[30] This draws our attention to the need for ingenuity (and "unobtrusive measures").

While problems differ somewhat from written questionnaires to face-to-face interviews, the preparation stage for both is comparable. The principal questions which the researcher must ask himself are: "To whom shall I ask these questions?" (sample construction); "What questions shall I ask?" (questionnaire construction); and "How shall they be asked?" (interview technique).

Sampling. Choice of those of whom the researcher will ask the questions or to whom he will send a written questionnaire will depend on what is being sought. If he wants a picture of public opinion in a particular community concerning a pressing community issue, the respondents may be drawn from all adults in the community. If, instead, he wants to know what community leaders think on some subject, then "community leaders," after the researcher has defined them, will be interviewed. In short, the relevant *population* (or *universe*) from which the *sample* is to come must first be determined.

> *Sampling.* **The procedure for selecting a number of people (the sample) from whose characteristics the characteristics of a larger number of people (the population) can be inferred.**

Once the population has been determined, the sample size needs to be chosen. This will be in part a function of the population size, one's resources, and the degree of accuracy desired. If the population is small, e.g., leaders in

[30] Paul Lazarsfeld, Seminar, Department of Sociology, Southern Illinois University, Carbondale, Ill., October, 1967.

a state legislature, one might decide to interview all of them. However, samples involving public officials have not often been used because social scientists have tended unnecessarily to write them off in advance as unapproachable. If the population is large, e.g., all state legislators in four states or all citizens eligible to vote in a city of 25,000, then, from a practical point of view, some device for choosing a smaller number becomes necessary. This is also permissible methodologically. If the sample chosen is representative of the population, then a relatively small sample should produce results not particularly different from those which would be obtained if the entire population were interviewed. The Gallup Poll, for example, uses a national sample of approximately 3,000 persons. While the accuracy of the Poll's results might be increased by doubling the sample size, with the size now used there is only a small possibility that results will diverge from the results for the entire population. Even a smaller sample would be quite reliable. Thus, a sample of only 600 will produce results with an error of $\pm 4\%$ in 95 samples out of 100.[31] The reliability of a sample is related to its size in a curvilinear rather than linear fashion. Thus, a sample of 1,500 is not half as reliable as one of 3,000, and one of 1,500 is not twice as reliable as one of 750, although an increase from one figure to the next will increase the reliability of the results. One must ask, "is additional reliability worth the additional cost?" Because interviewing with trained, paid interviewers is not inexpensive, this is an important question.

The *type* of sample wanted must be examined next. Often discussed is the "random sample," in which each member of the universe has an equal chance of being selected. "Random" in this case does not mean "haphazard" or "accidental." Accidental choices might have a pattern or bias, albeit an unplanned one. Random sampling is carefully planned, so that bias or distortion will be avoided. For example, a random sample might be obtained by drawing from a census list by using either every n^{th} name or a table of random numbers available in a statistics book. A telephone book might be the source of names, if everyone had a telephone, or if those who did not have them were not from a particular stratum of the population. An example of the bias possible from using a telephone book as a basis for a survey is the famed *Literary Digest* poll of the 1936 election, in which Landon's victory was predicted over Roosevelt. Another way of obtaining a sample, known as cluster sampling, would be to divide the area in which interviewing is to take place, and then to interview at every n^{th} house in every x^{th} block. Situations in which specific groupings of the population known to be representative are taken to stand for the population as a whole are area sampling. The Census Bureau uses this device in some of its special reports. The theory is that it will produce the same results as a random sample.

The researcher may want to be sure that certain characteristics, e.g., certain income or occupational levels, are represented sufficiently in his sample.

[31] Charles H. Backstrom and Gerald D. Hursh, *Survey Research* (Evanston, Ill., 1963), Table 1, p. 33.

In stratified random sampling, the population is divided (stratified) on the basis of the variables to be studied, and then sampling is random within each category. Another device (but less reliable) is quota sampling, in which interviewers are instructed to interview until they have obtained interviews from so many people with each of several designated characteristics; in this method, interviewers may choose those who are easiest to contact, usually unrepresentative of the population. A special method described by James Coleman, called "snowball sampling," helps to eliminate a problem caused by the interview's emphasis on the isolated individual, which takes him out of the social context in which he exists. Coleman suggests the inclusion of sociometric questions (Who are your friends? From whom do you seek advice?) in the questionnaire. The interviewing would start with one person, continue with those listed as friends or advice-givers, then the ones they name, and so on.[32]

For some research purposes, less systematically chosen samples may be adequate. College professors, for example, often utilize students in their classes, even for studies not dealing specifically with college students. If a study is at the exploratory stage, it may be more convenient to ascertain what relationships exist in the response of the college students than to go beyond the campus to interview. Checks can be applied to determine to what extent the group actually interviewed is representative of the population as a whole. If the college students possess some of the same characteristics as the ultimate sample, so much the better.

Response Rates.   Constructing a sample is not the same thing as actually obtaining responses, and different devices tend to produce different rates of response. A mail questionnaire, for example, is considered to produce a high rate of return when 50% of the sample returns are completed, although use of follow-up letters and second and third "waves" of mailings can coax the return rate up somewhat; 35% would not be an unreasonably low rate. Those responding are likely to have more interest in the subject-matter than the sample as a whole. Personal interviews, conducted by trained interviewers instructed to call back several times before giving up, can result in a response rate of better than 80%.

The panel type of interview device, in which a sample is chosen and interviewed several times in succession, causes special problems in obtaining responses. Used frequently in voting studies, its principal purpose is to obtain information about development, stability, crystallization, and change of political attitudes during and immediately after a campaign. Normal problems of contacting members of the sample are compounded because those first interviewed must be seen again two or three times. In addition to the "drop-out" problem, there is a possible distortion in responses caused by re-interviewing with the same interview instrument. If a significant portion of the panel is replaced each time to guard against familiarity with the questions, one no longer has a panel. Participation in a panel might force respon-

[32] James S. Coleman, "Relational Analysis: The Study of Social Organizations with Survey Methods," *Human Organization*, XVII (1958–1959), 28–36.

dents to make up their minds on questions they would not otherwise be prepared to answer; whether or not this happens depends on whether fact questions (on which respondents could inform themselves between interviews) or questions on personal behavior and attitudes are being used; the latter seem to be less affected.

Questionnaire Construction. The structure of the interview form requires considerable attention. While normally problems related to processing data are deferred until after the data are collected, one does have to think about the form in which the data is to be used when constructing questionnaires, because the form which answers are allowed to take determines the work necessary to put them in usable form. For example, if a question requires a yes/no response, no further coding need be done before the response can be used. But if the question is open-ended, allowing a rambling, discursive answer, considerable work may be necessary to put responses into categories which can be used in analysis of the data, and an additional element of potential human error is injected into the data-gathering/preparation process.

To be sure that answers are comparable from respondent to respondent, "forced-response" questions in which all possible answers are indicated can be used. The risk with such questions is that the respondent will choose an inappropriate response because an appropriate one is not available. To ask that he pick the "best" or "most appropriate" answer solves only part of the problem. This is symptomatic of the type of problem facing the researcher, who must often balance competing considerations such as codability and individualization of response in constructing his questionnaire.

When open-ended questions are being used, the interviewer can be sure he collects specific types of information by using "probes," supplementary questions used to elicit material the respondent has not volunteered. In an interview, these can be adjusted to the response, although they depend on the skill, training, and sensitivity of the interviewer to the interview situation, as well as his ability to react quickly. In a written questionnaire situation, there is no way for the researcher to stop the person filling out the questionnaire and ask him to clarify certain information, thus requiring that the researcher reduce all the matters in which he is interested to specific questions.

The inability to probe is not necessarily a drawback, if we remember that not all information obtained through probing is equally valid. While some people will not volunteer information unless asked specific questions, but have such information to give, others have no more to offer than what they volunteer initially. In the latter case, to probe is to procure material "manufactured" as a response to the question asked. Hyman's remarks on this general point deserve quotation:

> The belief prevails too widely that the richer and deeper and lengthier the remarks of the respondent, the more likely is this to be the genuine picture of the attitude. Interviewers are encouraged to keep probing and to question the valid-

ity of a thin answer. Certainly there is much truth in this point of view, and we may miss the full complexity of a deep, tortuous attitude structure in a given respondent by not pursuing the answer far enough. But conversely, we may distort the situation just as much if we forget that there are some people in this world with no hidden depths and only superficial attitudes on certain issues. In such instances, repeated probing may only suggest dimensions that were never operative in the first place.[33]

The degree to which a questionnaire is structured will depend to some extent on the purpose for which the data is being collected. If interviews are being used largely to collect "background" views or "local color" to use in connection with a case study based primarily on documentary material, then a relatively unstructured questionnaire with many open-ended questions may be sufficient. Unstructured interviews may also be particularly appropriate when one is beginning research in a new field and wants to know what respondents consider most salient. If, on the other hand, one wishes to be able to compare large numbers of respondents on certain specific items, primary use of forced-response questions, offered in a set order, will be more appropriate. If a researcher wishes to try to preserve a definite order in which questions are asked, a written questionnaire may be a better device than a personally-asked set of questions, although, even in the former situation there is nothing to prevent the respondent from skipping pages and answering the questions in any order he chooses.

Much criticism has been leveled against data collected through interviews because it is alleged that the interpersonal nature of the interview produces biased results. While this occasionally happens, and must be guarded against, we must be careful to separate bias which occurs as a result of the interpersonal aspect of the interview situation from bias which might result even if the person were filling out a printed questionnaire in complete solitude. (Absence of the interviewer does not always mean the absence of an interpersonal situation: a wife filling out a mail questionnaire might ask her husband which answers to give.) Whether one uses professionally trained interviewers, usually mature women, or volunteers, usually unreliable in terms of job completion, or students, whose potential enthusiasm and interest may offset their age, can and does make a difference in results. And we must further separate respondent reactions to the general interview situation from those caused by the *modus operandi* of specific interviewers. Respondents may stereotype the interviewer, with the characteristics of the stereotype affecting the respondent's reaction to the interview situation. Thus an interviewer, particularly if connected with a university, may be stereotyped as an "egghead" or liberal, so that the respondent either reacts negatively to the perceived higher intelligence of the interviewer or perhaps, if a liberal, presumes that the interviewer agrees with him. Visible characteristics of the interviewer will also structure the interview situation: Males may refuse to be

[33] Herbert H. Hyman, with others, *Interviewing in Social Research* (Chicago, 1954), p. 24.

questioned by females (whose "place is in the home"), and females may be more deferential to males than to other females, *if* they allow the males in the house. Using whites to interview Negroes and Negroes to interview whites may cause problems the reader can well imagine. The interviewer's style of dress, as a possible indication of where he stands on the social scale, is also important.

A number of other problems stem from the interpersonal aspect of survey research (although also present with written questionnaires). One involves the respondent's "answering for the sake of answering." He may feel it is improper not to fill in all the spaces on a questionnaire or to indicate to an interviewer that he does not care to answer a particular question, a tendency reinforced because it is "socially correct" to give an answer to a question when it is asked. So the respondent answers, to be polite, to speed up the interview and "get it over with," perhaps putting little thought into his response. A related problem is the answer given to hide ignorance, when a respondent indicates he has heard of a political event about which, in fact, he has never heard. Some responses of this type can be detected. For example, if someone had been asked at the beginning of World War II, "What do you think of Lend-Lease?", and the respondent had said it was something the Germans should not have done, it would be clear that he did not know what Lend-Lease was. If, however, the respondent gave an answer such as "That was a fine decision," it would be more difficult to determine whether the respondent knew about Lend-Lease or was covering up his ignorance with a general response. Somewhat related, but not necessarily conscious, is the problem of "response set," the tendency to answer "yes" consistently or "no" consistently regardless of the question. To avoid this, one can reverse the "direction" of specific questions, that is, ask some in negative form and others in positive form.

Another type of response which can cause problems is the "appropriate" response, the answer everyone is "supposed" to give, thus reinforcing the conventional wisdom. Surveys conducted immediately after elections almost invariably produce a larger percentage of respondents who say they have voted than the election reports show have voted, indicating the result of a feeling that one is a "bad citizen" if he doesn't vote. Similarly, a "bandwagon" effect operates to make people indicate they have voted for the winner in an election; thus, if the percentage of people who said they voted for John F. Kennedy for President in 1960 had actually done so, he would have won by a landslide instead of a "squeaker." Not everyone is affected by this response-bias, to be sure. Obviously, people do say they did not vote, and people still admit to voting for Nixon in 1960 (more respectable after his 1968 victory) or Goldwater in 1964.

There has been a tendency to presume that the interviewer transmits his views about what answers are desirable, either through the manner in which he asks the questions or through specific off-hand remarks. Even if the interviewer were to act in this way, many respondents would be immune to such statements because they are "task-involved," i.e., concerned with doing the job of answering the questions, or because the strength of their own opinions acts as a barrier to any attempts by the interviewer to communicate his views. As this may indicate, the most desirable interview situation is not the one in which the respondent feels completely removed or apart from the situation; his involvement is wanted.

The interview situation can have its positive aspects for the respondent. Most interviewers are strangers to their respondents, which provides the respondent with an opportunity to say things in confidence which he would not say to his friends, because he knows he will not see the interviewer again and that the interviewer does not know his friends to be able to report to them what he said. The interview may thus be cathartic, that is, permit the respondent to express emotions and relieve himself of tension in a way which cannot be done in everyday life, where one must be careful not to tell others of one's worries and fears, or at least be able to bear them without visible strain.

One further problem which should be noted is that of recall. Frequently respondents are asked to provide information about themselves at earlier times: "How did you vote in 1964? In 1960?" Or they must provide information about people they know; for example, young adults may be asked to provide information about their parents' political party preferences. Not only is there a lack of memory, but memory is creative, the more so as events are further in the past or ambiguous. Not all events are remembered with equal accuracy; displeasing events may be retained less well than events which were pleasing at the time they occurred or which had beneficial effects for the respondent. The inaccurate (biased) reporting is most often not done purposefully; the respondent may not even be aware he is doing it. But for a variety of reasons, the bias does occur. Corrections of at least a rough sort can be made if we know that biases in responding are systematically in one direction. Enough studies have been made so that we do know the direction (if not the exact magnitude) of many of the most obvious biases in response and can learn to be on the watch for them.

PARTICIPANT-OBSERVATION

A method used less frequently than the interview or questionnaire, although sometimes incorporating them, is that of participant-observation, borrowed from the anthropologists and used particularly in studies of communities and organizations. It is a method in which a unit or area is studied intensively, as contrasted with the extensive coverage which interview studies generally provide. Participant-observation requires much skill and sensitivity to carry out well, because the researcher becomes a part of the ongoing social grouping (organization, community, business firm) he wishes to study, and at the same time conducts research on that grouping. That he is a researcher may not be known by those observed.

The researcher may be satisfied to be a participant in his group during its regular activities, returning to his residence to record his observations "after hours," without ever revealing his research role. However, he is usually interested in more: he will, for example, want to talk to the members of the social grouping he is studying to obtain their views of the situation, to get the insight of the "insider." This usually requires that the researcher, after he has become "accepted," reveal his identity and purposes in order to obtain further information. He can only hope that the individuals with whom he has been working, having had an opportunity to see he is an "OK guy," will not feel something has been put over on them. He can use "informants" from the group—if chosen properly, people knowledgeable about the group's inner workings but willing to talk about them. They can be used to help explain matters which on the surface do not appear obvious and which would be misunderstood by the participant-observer or which might never be mentioned to him because of a presumption that he knows and understands them. One drawback of informants is that the researcher is seeing the group through their eyes (and thus from their social location). Another is that their wish to please the researcher makes them report what they think he wants to hear. Informants are not the only source of information outside the observer's role. If the participant-observer's research role is accepted as proper by the group, interviews of a more formal sort can be used to supplement his other material.

Even if the desired *entree* to the community or organization is obtained, participant-observation has a number of drawbacks. In the first place, one comes to see the community or organization from the point of view of the social role which he has adopted or been assigned within the group. If the researcher is interested in studying the group from that perspective, perhaps that is not a drawback, but if he is interested in a broader picture, then his findings will be limited. It is possible that a broader view may be obtained by working with the organization as a researcher and being known in that capacity. However, there are situations when this is not possible or research would be prevented, making participant-observation imperative as a last resort.

The researcher is expected to perform his participant role adequately, thus limiting time for the collection of research material outside of the settings into which that role takes him. The responses of other members of the community will to some extent be dependent on the researcher's participant role within the group. He may find that his informants are not well placed in the community, and that the first people with whom he has associated have led to his being typed in a way that limits obtaining useful information. If the participant-observer enters into his participant role enthusiastically, there is the danger he will "go native." The term, drawn from problems faced by anthropologists studying "exotic" cultures, denotes over-involvement in the situation and acceptance of the values of those with whom the researcher is participating. "Going native" can bring resentment on the part of those studied, and the researcher's role will be obstructed by his seeing things only through the eyes of those he has joined. These drawbacks must, of course, be balanced against the virtues of the method: ability to study a community or organization from the inside, and a decreased likelihood of the observer's imposing his own theoretical preconceptions on the grouping.

Participant-observation is not the only role which a researcher can take with respect to the social unit he wishes to study. He can, at one extreme, be a full participant, recording research notes in his spare time and not using any research tools in addition to his own eyes and ears. At the other extreme, he can be a non-participant observer (without labelling himself as such), simply collecting information. Even his presence, however, may affect the behavior of those he is observing. The participant-observation role fits somewhere in between. Babchuk has suggested still another role, that of "participant-as-observer," which he claims has many advantages over the participant-observer research role.[34] "Participant-as-observer" means that the researcher participates in the organization as an observer, as more than a passive on-looker. He is known as an observer, is accepted as such, and has regular relations with the members of the group in that capacity. Because he is accepted as a researcher, he may have access to material with which the participant-observer is not entrusted.

EXPERIMENTATION

The research methods discussed thus far are ones which are applied in non-experimental situations. The situation being examined or the set of attitudes being studied is given. The population to be studied is already determined; it is "self-selected" because of characteristics which the researcher wants to examine. The researcher attempts to encompass the situation as best he can, with whatever manipulations he can impose on the data; "the researcher starts with the observation of a dependent variable or variables. He then studies the independent variables in retrospect for their possible relations to, and effects on, the dependent variable or variables."[35] By contrast, an experiment involves *control* by the investigator over at least one of the independent variables in the study; however, the independent variables the experimental researcher can manipulate in the laboratory are not notably strong.

Experimental work, broadly defined, is not totally foreign to political science.

If we adopt a strict definition of "experiment," i.e., controlled observation, repeated trials, and systematic manipulation of crucial variables, this basic scientific procedure—for the present at least—has relatively little application to

---

[34] Nicholas Babchuk, "The Role of the Researcher as Participant-Observer and Participant-as-Observer in the Field Situation," *Human Organization*, XXI (1962), 225–228.

[35] Kerlinger, p. 360; italics in original.

the study of human behavior outside of psychology. . . . If we allow for *degrees* of rigor and for *quasi-experimental* exploration, the trial and error of everyday political and social life and the semicontrolled exercises in contrived situations may fall within our purview.[36]

Simulation of political situations, which might be called indirect experi-

> **Simulation.** Reproduction of real or possible political or social situations, in scaled-down or simplified form, covering periods of time, usually carried out with "real-life" variables represented by individuals or symbols. A simulation is said to be valid if one system replicates properties of another accurately. Simulation can be all-human (usually termed *gaming*), man-machine, or all-machine (computer) in nature.

mentation, has increased the amount of experimental political science research. Simulations of city councils and courts have been undertaken, although the most frequent application has been to the realm of international relations. Simulations, while "indirect," *are* experiments, with variables controlled and manipulated before rather than after the fact. Problems which frequently frustrate direct experimentation in politics, such as lack of situations permitting experiments where variables can be controlled, norms against the manipulation of individuals, or the lack of sufficient frequency of a situation so that comparison of variables can be made, are avoided.

A portion of an excellent discussion of experimentation and simulation in the present political science literature is that by Richard Snyder. He deals with both direct experiments and simulation. One comment is necessary: simulation can be used for more than the experimental purposes of which Snyder writes here, concentrated, as he notes elsewhere, "in the discovery phase of science-building, not in the verification phase." [37] It can be used for verification, and for post-diction as well as prediction. It has also been used successfully as a teaching device and it has important uses in the building of theory in political science.

"Experimental Techniques and Political Analysis: Some Reflections in the Context of Concern Over Behavioral Approaches" *

Kinds of experiments.   Exactly what is implied by "experimental techniques"? Generally speaking, experimentation consists of a contrived series of observations of phenomena which are under more or less controlled conditions and which are re-

---

[36] Richard C. Snyder, "Some Perspectives on the Use of Experimental Techniques in the Study of International Relations," *Simulation in International Relations: Developments for Research and Training*, by Harold Guetzkow and others (Englewood Cliffs, 1963), p. 6.

[37] *Ibid.*, p. 7.

* SOURCE: Richard C. Snyder, "Experimental Techniques and Political Analysis: Some Reflections in the Context of Concern Over Behavioral Approaches," *The Limits of Behavioralism in Political Science*, ed. James C. Charlesworth (Philadelphia, 1962), pp. 102–114. Reprinted with the permission of the author and the American Academy of Political and Social Science. Footnotes numbered as in original.

peatable and verifiable. Usually, such observations are made in some sort of laboratory where conditions can be more easily manipulated. The basic idea is, as we all know, that repeated exercises permit the researcher to vary certain factors while holding others constant (or as nearly so as possible) for the purpose of seeing what changes are induced as a result of the variance. (For those who take a puristic view of science, repeated controlled observation is the essence of the scientific method; there can be no scientific knowledge unless it is generated by this fundamental procedure.)

A number of possibilities are accessible to us because the basic idea can be expressed in many forms. Hence, a crude classification is needed.

(1) One important distinction has been suggested . . . quasi experiments which permit some of the advantages of repeated observations under changing conditions in natural social settings without entailing the greater degree of control by the experimenter we associate with the laboratory. A prime example is Gosnell's classic study *Getting Out the Vote: An Experiment in the Stimulation of Voting* (1927), which has not been replicated (to this writer's knowledge). Equally noteworthy is the fact that those committed to a more rigorous political science rarely cite Gosnell's work. Two other examples of interest to political analysts are Sherif and Others, *The Robber's Cave Experiment* (1961) and White and Lippitt, *Autocracy and Democracy: An Experimental Inquiry* (1960). The former focuses on patterns of co-operation and conflict in a boys' camp; the latter focuses on patterns of leadership in after-school activity groups. A common characteristic of all these studies is that experimental controls are imposed on real-life situations, with the aim of disturbing spontaneous behavior as little as possible.

(2) Artificial experimental situations, on the other hand, may be divided for our purposes into two types: those which use computers and those which use human subjects. Both often involve *simulation*, that is, the attempt to induce realistic effects and to reproduce properties of reality.

Computer simulation of immediate interest to political scientists is exemplified in the successful effort to program national political campaigns and elections by Pool,[2] McPhee,[3] and others. Benson [4] has developed a computer simulation of international relations and diplomacy, and Coleman [5] has adapted his developmental model of community political conflict processes to a machine program. Essentially, the computer makes possible a much more complex set of starting conditions and variables whose interrelationships are expected to determine outcomes and a much greater opportunity to examine the different long-and-short-term consequences of changes introduced at various stages. It becomes feasible to explore many more dynamic possibilities inherent in initial models, as in the case of the "campaign simulator" which permits the introduction of new voter appeals to see how opinion formation processes are affected and how these, in turn, influence voting behavior. Pool reports considerable success in predicting the 1960 presidential election. "Simul-

[2] *Ithiel Pool and Robert Abelson, "The Simulmatics Project,"* Public Opinion Quarterly, Vol. 25 (1961), 167–183.

[3] *William McPhee, "Note on a Campaign Simulator,"* Public Opinion Quarterly, Vol. 25 (1961), 182–193.

[4] *Oliver Benson, "Simulation of International Relations and Diplomacy," in* Computer Applications in the Behavioral Sciences, *ed. H. Borke (Englewood Cliffs, N.J.: Prentice-Hall, 1961).*

[5] *James Coleman, "The Simulation of Processes in Social Controversy," in* Simulation in Social Science, *ed. Harold Guetzkow (Englewood Cliffs, N.J.: Prentice-Hall, 1962).*

matics," as his computer program is called, has been put on a semipermanent basis.

A second basic type of laboratory experimentation uses human subjects. In turn, these must be subdivided in order to reveal the range of choice:

(a) Small face-to-face groups. Most of us tend to think first about the extensive literature and research on small groups when laboratory techniques are mentioned. It seems fair to say that this rapidly accumulating work has not yet been combed thoroughly and systematically by and for political scientists. Until recently, there were only a handful of examples of attempts at constructive political applications, and the general reaction has been a somewhat negative skepticism. Fortunately, two valuable books go a long way toward filling an important gap in our own literature: Verba, *Small Groups and Political Behavior: A Study of Leadership* (1961) and Golembiewski, *Organization and Behavior* (1962). Both authors build bridges between a domain of psychological and sociological inquiry, on the one hand, and the interests of political analysts, on the other. Verba, in particular, discusses many of the problems which have caused the skepticism just mentioned and it is, therefore, not necessary for me to repeat his major points. Together with Guetzkow's fine essay in Young, *Approaches to the Study of Politics* (1958), the reader has a much more reliable introduction than has been available in the past.

. . . A large number of items are ordinarily lumped under this category [small groups] and it is misleading to assume that laboratory groups performing trivial tasks cover the terrain (see Sprott, *Human Groups*, 1958, especially chapters 4–6).

Accordingly, we must draw distinctions between kinds of primary groups—for example, a primary group actually embedded in a social milieu which performs a specific political function on a face-to-face basis (a jury) and a primary group associated with an institution which is thrown together sporadically without continuity (a clique in Congress). In turn, these two differ from a primary or face-to-face small group which is a site for studying political phenomena—for example, husband and wife interaction over political issues.[6] So far as *experimental* small groups are concerned, it is important to note that, on the whole, the interest is to *produce* the phenomena to be observed—the assembled group plus its immediate operating environment *is* reality. This stands in contrast to the *reproduction* of phenomena and aspects of reality *indirectly* through various representational devices.

(b) Simulation of institutions, organizations, systems, and processes. It would be a mistake to assume automatically that if one saw a relatively small group of subjects going through certain motions in a laboratory that a small face-to-face group experiment was under way. Neither primary groups nor face-to-face interactions are necessarily involved in observing social behavior under controlled conditions. Single business firms,[7] international systems,[8] or strategic encounters and diplomatic negotiations [9] can be simulated. To the extent that experimentation has entered a branch of political science, it has been mainly through the simulation of international relations. Simulation and one of its major species, "gaming," have be-

[6] *James March, "Husband and Wife Interaction Over Political Issues," Public Opinion Quarterly, Vol. 17 (1953–1954), pp. 461–470.*

[7] *Harold Guetzkow and Ann Bowes, "The Development of Organizations in a Laboratory," Management Science, Vol. 3 (1957), pp. 380–402.*

[8] *Charles McClelland, "A World Politics Game" (San Francisco: San Francisco State College, International Studies Project, 1959, mimeo).*

[9] *Herbert Goldhamer and Hans Speier, "Some Observations on Political Gaming," World Politics, Vol. 12 (1959), pp. 71–83.*

come significant teaching [10] as well as research techniques, though only the latter will be discussed.

As already mentioned, simulation exercises *reproduce* some portion or aspect of reality—a "likeness" if you will. Because many kinds and degrees of likeness are possible, still further distinctions among forms are indicated. . . . An example will illustrate both distinctions. If we used experienced officials, including Soviet experts, from the State Department and Defense Department to act out Soviet and American responses to a current problem—some phase of the Cold War or the negotiation of an inspection agreement—if, in constructing the "game," we employed all the relevant knowledge at our disposal, and if we asked the Soviet experts to take the part of the Soviet Union and act as real Soviet representatives would act, we would have a realistic, role-playing simulation. If, on the other hand, we created fictitious nations operated by nonexperts, if we built in only certain features of the international system, and if we presented the players with a minimal set of rules (for example, general objectives, modes of communication, and so forth), asking that they take off from a particular set of starting conditions and let actions and interactions flow as they will, then we would have a nonroleplaying, nonrealistic simulation. As a matter of fact, these overly simple descriptions differentiate between two actual simulation programs: the first kind has been undertaken by Rand [11] and the second by a group at Northwestern University.[12] The Rand version of gaming is more adapted to policy research, to determining how national policy-makers might respond to various moves and situations and what alternative consequences will result from the interplay of political strategies. The Northwestern version is more adapted to basic research, to answering questions like: Under what conditions will coalitions form and how cohesive will they be? What will be the effects of distrust on communication patterns?

A further necessary distinction is [that] . . . machine simulations are obviously programed by definition, but man-machine and man-man simulations differ with respect to how much is left to the participants to decide—the limitations incorporated in the rules, and/or whether some determinate "solution" is expected. Strategic gaming is, of course, a more programed type of simulation. The key difference lies in the availability of greater knowledge and "harder" variables (such as military factors) which programing requires.

(c) Bargaining and negotiation experiments.[13] Research into bargaining behavior has increased rapidly. While much of it has been focused on economics and economic theory, several projects have been inspired by, or are geared to, political

[10] Chadwick F. Alger, "Use of the Inter-nation Simulation in the Under-graduate Teaching of International Relations," in Simulation in International Relations: Developments for Research and Teaching, ed. Harold Guetzkow and Others (Englewood Cliffs, N.J.: Prentice-Hall, 1962); Lincoln Bloomfield, "Political Gaming," United States Naval Institute Proceedings, Vol. 86 (1960), pp. 57–64; Proceedings of the Conference on Business Games, ed. W. Dill and J. Jackson (New Orleans: Tulane University, 1961).

[11] Joseph Goldsen, The Political Exercise, an Assessment of the Fourth Round (Washington, D.C.: The Rand Corporation, D-3640-RC, 1956, mimeo).

[12] Harold Guetzkow, "A Use of Simulation in the Study of Inter-Nation Relations," Behavioral Science, Vol. 4 (1959), pp. 183–191; Guetzkow and Others, Simulation in International Relations, op. cit.

[13] Thomas Schelling, The Strategy of Conflict (Cambridge: Harvard University Press, 1960), especially chaps. 2, 6; Sidney Siegel and Lawrence Fouraker, Bargaining and Group Decision-making: Experiments in Bilateral Monopoly (New York: McGraw-Hill, 1960).

analysis—notably international relations. It is here that some aspect or form of game theory is manifest in the design of experiments. To delimit bargaining from related phenomena, two characteristics may be regarded as essential: first, a conflict of interest (opposing needs) between parties cannot be satisfied separately, completely, or simultaneously—their fates are intertwined; second, a possibility of mutual gain through co-operation—gain meaning more than each party could achieve by going it alone. Bargaining experiments can be categorized as a variation under both (a) and (b) above, for face-to-face contacts among subjects may or may not be involved and exercises are not usually constructed as small group studies per se.

The purposes and designs of experiments vary, with the following targets of inquiry typical: [14] (i) a comparison of choicemaking in zero-sum and nonzero-sum game situations; (ii) the relative significance of rational and irrational motivations on solutions reached; (iii) effects of social-structural, personality, informational, and communication variables on bargaining strategies and pay-offs; and (iv) changes in strategies and pay-offs through time as a result of learning and alteration of conditions or rules.

Though political content has not been built into bargaining experiments on any great scale, a leading exponent, economist Thomas Schelling (*The Strategy of Conflict*, 1960), is exploring his notion of "tacit" bargaining (indirect communication) between nations and a corollary notion of "prominent solutions." Schelling's general intent is to interpret or extend elements of game theory so as to embrace what he calls "mixed motive" conflicts in which nonmilitary strategic moves are interdependent under less limited conditions than are specified by the pure zero-sum version of the theory. Others (Ratoosh, Scodel, Willis, and Joseph) are also interested in applications to international relations. However, the basic structure of bargaining experiments is equally applicable to decision-making within governments and the role of bargaining in domestic policy formation is widely recognized though thus far not researched extensively.

One of the chief advantages of current work on bargaining is that it seems to provide a likely prospect of useful adaptation of game theoretic analysis to the political arena through the manipulation (and loosening) of conditions which hitherto have been too restrictive to be found often in real life.

LIMITS AND POTENTIALITIES OF EXPERIMENTAL TECHNIQUES

Even this sketchy discussion suggests there are a number of experimental modes to choose from once we admit the general technique to a place in a multiple strategy. I have glossed over some very difficult technical problems in the design and execution of experiments. In particular, there are problems of internal validation— for example, processes of change within human subjects resulting from the passage of time between trials—and external validation—for example, generalizability. I cannot begin to give these important factors the treatment they deserve. However,

[14] *For example: Richard Willis and Myron Joseph, "Bargaining Behavior I: Prominence as a Predictor of Games of Agreement," Journal of Conflict Resolution, Vol. 3 (1959), pp. 102–113; Alvin Scodel and Others, "Some Descriptive Aspects of Two Person Nonzero Sum Games," Journal of Conflict Resolution, Vol. 3 (1959), pp. 114–119; Scodel and Others, "Some Personality Correlates of Decision-making Under Conditions of Risk," in Decisions, Values, and Groups, ed. D. Willner (New York: Pergamon Press, 1960), pp. 37–40.*

invalidating factors have been identified and ways of handling them have been proposed. Nothing could be worse for the development of politically relevant experimentation than naive amateurism. At least three requirements enter, aside from statistical sophistication: (1) knowledge of the behavior to be produced or reproduced; (2) experience in rigorous use of the technique; and (3) imagination.

Are there unique advantages for the political scientist which would justify increased experimentation? I shall attempt to state my reasons for a qualified, yet strongly affirmative, answer to this question.

Limitations and objections.   The nature and significance of limitations on the utility of experimentation depend greatly on our keeping misunderstanding, and false expectations to a minimum.

In order to clear the record, let me anticipate certain objections, knowing the reader might not raise them seriously in this form:

(a) The richness of political reality is beyond the reach of the laboratory.

Reply: If taken literally, this objection is both valid and irrelevant. The controlled experiment can never replace, say, a political ethnography, but *cultural elements* can be introduced. Although a surprising degree of richness can sometimes be produced, the primary aim of laboratory representations is to set key variables and their interrelationships *in motion* and to create, explicitly, imitations of and substitutes for the hidden explanatory or conditioning factors assumed to operate in life. Moreover, the experimental situation is usually designed to achieve *not actual effects* observed outside the laboratory but *equivalent kinds of effects* using the most economical representation of causal variables. For example, if we have reason to believe that the behavior of political actors is affected by their need to respond to voters or superiors or elite supporters, it is not necessary *for certain experimental purposes* to build in *all* of these possible sources of influence. Instead, *a validation function* can be injected which will accurately reflect the *gross impact* of a many-sided factor. Finally, it will be recalled that a quasi experiment in a natural setting does permit the observer to impose "extras" on reality without fundamentally disturbing it.

(b) Observing small numbers of people in contrived situations cannot tell us anything about the behavior of aggregates of large numbers or about institutional patterns.

Reply: Again, by definition, yes, *unless* one draws a distinction between a small face-to-face group experiment and one employing a small number of subjects. Apart from insights to be drawn from the former, complex organizational behavior can be simulated and nonface-to-face relationships can be reproduced artificially. Furthermore, because most small-group experiments per se have emphasized endogenous variables and nonpolitical behaviors, it does not mean that exogenous, political variables cannot be the focus of analysis. There is no reason *in principle* why a city council or a foreign office or a court cannot be imitated *in certain particular respects*. It is not numbers of participants by itself which is important but the structural features and mechanisms we choose to manipulate. For example, we could watch the differential effects of precedent, group size, channels of communication, and allocations of power and responsibility on either group or organizational policy deliberations.

(c) No proposition concerning the real world can be directly tested in the laboratory.

Reply: At this stage of the game and given the nature of political phenomena, probably not. However, two things must be added. First, "test" is an ambiguous word, and much depends on how propositions are stated—which goes to the word "directly." If by "test" one means rigorous proof, then clearly experiments will not do the job. If one adopts the position that *probing* theories—for example, disqualifying inadequate hypotheses or operationalizing variables—is required, then experimental techniques can help. As noted, the contrived situation is only one phase of a multiple strategy in which preliminary controls permit greater clarification than is possible by observation in natural settings. Second, there seems to be no way to test *directly* through experiment the proposition that legislatures assume relatively little initiative in external affairs as compared to the executive. But, if this proposition is logically derived from one (among others) which states that in complex organizations initiative tends to coincide with control over relevant information, then experimental exploration to discover the conditions under which the relationship between information and initiative holds or does not hold is feasible.

(d) Real world incentives cannot be simulated.

Reply: In effect, this says (i) that declaring war in a simulated international system does not have the consequences it does in reality and (ii) that epiphenomenal factors contaminate or destroy the validity of the experiment—the "gaming" really becomes a game for its own sake. This is a tricky question and one that implies conditions to be overcome. Is this sufficient reason not to use the technique as an adjunct to other research methods? To begin with, it is a warning not to base even tentative conclusions *solely on laboratory exercises* unless the behavioral situation is homologous. On the other hand, there are reasons for not overestimating the difficulty. Evidence indicates that subjects do become deeply involved in contrived situations and have a capacity for acting "as if" the exercise were actuality. And subjects can be pretested for general attributes deemed important as governing responses within the rules and parameter established by the experimenter. Thus, to put the matter in sharp perspective, the problem is not whether a college student acting as, say, a high-level policy-maker really sees the world as the latter does but whether, within the conditions imposed by the experimenter's theory, the college student is compelled to react to the same kinds of constraints which confront the policy-maker. Artificiality of subjects' motivation will be directly related to the degree of role-playing and programing manifest in a simulation. Generally speaking, we would not expect an average student to play President de Gaulle with much realism, though an expert might. To look at it from the other side, we know that political actors often must act contrary to their personal preferences. We do not therefore, assert that the individual is incapable of being motivated qua policy-maker. How far the incentive factor is a handicap depends in part on how the participants are chosen for the purposes of the experiment, and on the experimenter's cleverness in devising ways of either inducing motivation or rendering inconsequential the lack of actual experience. This is one case where the proof of the pudding is in the eating—if equivalent effects are achieved despite the seeming lack of realistic incentives, then the lack is not fatal to the purposes of the exercise.

The objection is plausible, but its *a priori* acceptance is not warranted and the limitation can be accommodated.

I have made no attempt to deal with the foregoing arguments in the depth they deserve, nor would I wish to suggest these are the only questions which arise. The tone I have tried to convey is that quick answers based on inexperience or overly stringent conceptions of what experimentation can accomplish may slam the door before we can determine its utility by empirical means.

The problem of extrapolation.   A fundamental issue of external validity is: to what universe of reality can we generalize, assuming the criteria of sound experimental design have been met? We frequently hear the phrases "reduction of politics to psychology" or "reduction of institutions to small groups" in connection with this problem. Premature or unnecessary reduction from one level of description or explanation to another is surely to be avoided. Moreover, White and Lippitt, who try to be helpful to the student of government, frankly acknowledge that "A nation involves many qualitatively different things—economics, propaganda, foreign policy, a nationalistic tradition—that do not exist, except possibly in an embryonic form, in a small group of eleven-year-old boys meeting after school" (*op. cit.*, p. vii) —in other words, large groups and small groups are patently quite different. Moreover, most small group experiments are not undertaken with political phenomena in mind (the White and Lippitt study is a glaring exception) and are almost exclusively concerned with endogenous variables, with the *internal* properties of groups, rather than with context variables and interplay between the two.

It would seem possible to steer around the often attractive pitfalls of overgeneralization in several ways, but it should be noted first that the irrelevance of small-group research may be due more to the special interests of the researchers than to any basic disability inherent in the use of human subjects in contrived situations. We might also note that extrapolation presents a generic problem not confined to generalization from the laboratory—the nature of the fit between a proposition and an instance recurs in many of our pursuits and is, of course, embedded in analogous thinking. If analogies are linguistic experiments conducted by putting words together whose language structure is similar to that of another assertion known or thought to be true, laboratory experiments of the sort we are discussing are nonspeculative efforts to produce structural likenesses between the real and the artificial.

Consonant with our earlier rule requiring political content in propositions and experiments, we might add a "closeness" rule, that is, in order to reduce slippage in the jump from the laboratory (or natural-setting experiments) to reality, we ought to adhere as closely as possible to political variables, to features of political structures and processes, and to counterpart levels and units of analysis. This is why our knowledge of the real world must be fed into experimental designs. If we can differentiate between the individual and group levels on other occasions, we can certainly avoid such absurdities as experimenting with individual attitude changes respecting violence as a mode of conflict accommodation and then purporting to make meaningful statements about the conditions under which a group of national policymakers might change their attitudes toward war as an instrument of policy.

Let us illustrate what "closeness" might mean in practice by a series of graded instances, starting with the more distant:

(a) We simulate Osgood's *Graduated Reciprocation in Tension-Reduction: A Key to Initiative in Foreign Policy* (1960) by having two individuals or groups follow rules aimed to demonstrate whether the mechanism of tension-reducing acts followed by equal similar responses, followed by further acts, followed by further responses, really operates in a very general way, that is, there is no effort to put the experiment in an international context.

(b) Fiedler's laboratory experiments using Catholic and Protestant subjects in the Netherlands and in the United States to discover what types of leaders and leadership styles will produce what degree of co-operative political problem-solving in bifurcated social systems. Groups are constituted to reflect the actual distribution of the two religious groups in the Netherlands.[16]

(c) Two experiments by Bevan and Others to see the extent to which the personality of a jury foreman influences the decisions reached by individual members of the group.[17]

(d) Turner's *The Child Within the Group: An Experiment in Self-Government* (1957)—a quasi experiment (as earlier defined) in a natural setting to ascertain the preconditions and effects of political learning. (White and Lippitt would be another example.)

(e) The unicameral Nebraska legislature agrees to permit a controlled experiment to determine whether, on a specific kind of issue, models of rational or irrational conduct are better descriptions (or predictors) of political compromise during the regular course of legislative business.

Note that (a) is prompted by an interest in a *politically relevant* phenomena—as the title of Osgood's monograph implied—at the international level, but the unit observed is not simulated as an international system. Note also that it could be brought a step closer by casting the exploration in the inter-nation simulation mold —which in fact will be done during 1962–1963 at the Western Behavioral Sciences Institute. The second example (b) reproduces a key feature of the Netherlands' political culture and the subjects try to reach agreements of a broadly political character. Hence the phenomena studied are political, but the unit created in the laboratory is not concretely political—for example, a legislature. The jury experiments are obviously embodied in a *simulated* political unit but not in a natural setting. Political content and a natural setting are both represented in (d), yet the unit is obviously not a public body. Number (e)—if executed—would combine the observation of political phenomena in an actual governing unit.

Clearly, the examples do not exhaust possibilities and each has its own peculiar extrapolation limits and its own uses. Thus, the first step in experiments should be to ask: What are we simulating and for what purposes? Whether a congressional committee or subcommittee should be replicated as a small face-to-face group depends on what phase of the unit's activity we are interested in and on how we conceptualize the unit. A city council meeting might be very realistically reconstructed in the laboratory, but a nation will be quite differently represented. Because "nation" is essentially a construct, we need to determine what concrete actions or properties or events will constitute focuses of applications of experimental results. . . . Extrapolations can be improved over time.

[16] *References to these studies are to be found in University of Illinois Department of Psychology,* Research in Social Psychology, Second Annual Report (*Urbana, December 1961), pp. 19 ff.,* 28.

[17] *William Bevan and Others, "Jury Behavior as a Function of the Prestige of the Foreman and the Nature of His Leadership,"* Journal of Public Law, *Vol. 7 (1958), pp. 429– 440.*

METHODS AND COMMUNITY POWER STRUCTURE

One of the fields of study in which much controversy has developed over proper methods, and over the effect of those methods on the results obtained, is that of community power structure. Community has usually referred to a municipality, a city or town. "Structure" refers to the existence of a regular pattern of relationships between those with power in the community. Use of the phrase "community power structure" may prejudice the study of power in the community, because of the implication that some structure is there, leaving the researcher only the job of finding it. The logically prior question should be, "Is there a power structure?"; if that question is answered in the affirmative we can then ask, "What form does the structure take?" In short, community power structure refers to the patterning of power relations in the local community.

Community studies, often dated from the Lynds' studies of *Middletown* (Muncie, Indiana), have been conducted by sociologists for several decades, although they were concerned with matters besides power structure. The controversy over methods developed largely in the aftermath of Floyd Hunter's study of Regional City (Atlanta, Georgia), *Community Power Structure*, and as a result of political scientists' subsequently entering into the study of community power. Hunter developed the first easily replicable method for determining what he thought was a community's power structure, thus making cumulative findings from such studies possible. From the managers of civic associations, he obtained the names of business, government, civic, and status (society) leaders; he then had a panel of people knowledgeable about the community nominate from each of his four lists the ten they thought were most influential. Hunter interviewed this top forty, who were given an opportunity to name others to the list. Through this procedure, known as the "reputational" method, Hunter found that an economic elite dominated the life of Regional City, and that politicans and government officials played a relatively minor role in the city's "power elite." [38] Actually, Hunter's method combines both the "reputational" and another method, which can be called the "positional" or "formal leadership" method, in which those holding formal positions of importance in the community are designated as the power elite.

A number of other methods are available, to be used either independently or in some combination. One, used principally by political scientists, is the "decision-making" or "event-analysis" approach, called here the "decisional" approach. Making no assumptions about power in a community, advocates of this approach examine particular important decisions in the community, or specific "issue-areas," to determine who actually made de-

[38] His findings were contradicted in a later study of Atlanta. M. Kent Jennings, *Community Influentials: The Elites of Atlanta* (New York, 1964).

cisions. For example, Robert Dahl, in his study of New Haven, *Who Governs?*, examined the issue-areas of political party nominations, education, and urban renewal. Several other methods are subsidiary; they are the "social-participation" method, in which social interaction between the powerful is examined to ascertain the degree of unity of the power structure; the "personal-influence" or "opinion-leadership" method, in which it is determined who obtains advice or information from which other members of the leadership; and the "social background" approach, in which such matters as formal education, father's occupation, and organizational memberships are examined to determine to what extent the already-identified members of the leadership share certain characteristics.

The two methods over which controversy has raged are the reputational and decisional methods, largely because they tend to produce different results. Those who have used the reputational method, as in Hunter's study, generally found a well-knit if not necessarily monolithic, power structure, with heavy representation by economic leaders. The political scientists have more frequently found a situation in which, while there is some overlapping of leadership between issue-areas, there are leaders predominant in one area but not another, leaving a picture of a pluralistic or "polylithic" structure; they also find a fairly important place for the political and governmental leaders in the picture they paint. Thus, "the disciplinary background of the investigator tends to determine the image of the power structure that results from the investigation." [39] Of course, the results obtained extend over a vast range, depending on the communities studied and particular refinements in methodology used. Historical evidence has been used by both Dahl and Schulze, the latter showing what he calls the "bifurcation" of the power structure over time, with a shift from dominance by the economic leaders to a separation between economic and governmental/political spheres.[40] Some more recent studies have also indicated that, in addition to a "top" leadership, there are a variety of leadership roles which must be performed; these include initiators, experts, publicists, and brokers ("go-betweens").

Political scientists, particularly those involved in the New Haven study, have leveled heated charges against the sociologists of the "reputational school." They state that "the heavier the weight of evidence against it, the more uses its champions find for it, and the more ambitious are the theories based on its findings." With respect to the ease of using the method, they note that "this is somewhat analogous to the popularity of frozen dinners that may not taste like much, but are marvelously easy to prepare." [41] They charge that the propositions resulting from reputational studies are no more than deductions from the assumptions about power in "stratification theory,"

[39] John Walton, "Discipline, Method, and Community Power: A Note on the Sociology of Knowledge," *American Sociological Review*, XXXI (1966), 687, 688.

[40] Robert O. Schulze, "The Bifurcation of Power in a Satellite City," *Community Political Systems*, ed. Morris Janowitz (New York, 1960), pp. 19–80.

[41] Raymond Wolfinger, "A Plea for a Decent Burial," *American Sociological Review*, XXVII (1962), 841, 843.

that the community is divided into ranked layers with the highest layer holding the most power.

Among the other principal charges made are that power and status are confused by the nominators and that the selection of the initial formal leaders from whom the "influentials" are to be nominated brings what is known as "premature closure," that is, influentials are not likely to be named from outside the basic list. The areas the researcher chooses as important will be the ones in which influentials are named. Thus, Hunter, in starting with the areas of status, civic, business, and governmental leadership, emphasized non-governmental leadership and proportionately downgraded governmental leadership. In addition, those nominated are only those who have the *reputation* for power, not necessarily actual power. However, we must remember that if people *think* certain individuals are powerful, they will act in such a way as to reinforce that power, regardless of what a real test or confrontation might produce. Here the advocates of a decisional approach argue forcefully that their method provides a real test to determine whether those with the reputation also actually are the decision-makers. They challenge the "reputationalists" with data showing that the reputed leaders don't always win on key matters. Wolfinger goes so far as to say that the findings of the reputational method "are often invalidated and never confirmed." [42] In response to this challenge, some say there is an elite "behind the scenes," or that, on a given issue, the leadership "wanted to lose" so as not to give the impression of having too much power. While these arguments are not totally implausible, they are not empirically based.

Sociologists advocating the reputational approach have also attacked the event-analysts. Against them is leveled the charge that they, "like the elitists, utilize an approach and assumptions which predetermine their conclusions," [43] and particularly that the issue-areas they choose to examine help determine the structure of community power which is found. It is also claimed that the advocates of an event-analysis approach, in assuming that power is seen only in specific acts, have concentrated on visible decisions without examining what decisions have *not* been made and what issue-areas have been "kept quiet." If only "safe" issues are contested in the public arena, the interests of certain individuals in the community may be protected. The followers of the decisional approach are also said to emphasize individual, rather than community, power because of their emphasis on specific issue-areas. Thus we have the assertion that they do not come to grips with the notion of community: they deal with power and its structure, but only within subcommunities (for example, those concerned with education or urban renewal).

There have been relatively few studies testing the results of one method against those of another in the same community and few tests dealing with other methodological criticisms. Schulze and Blumberg applied the rep-

---

[42] *Ibid.*, 847.
[43] Peter Bachrach and Morton S. Baratz, "Two Faces of Power," *American Political Science Review*, LVI (1962), 948.

utational and formal position methods to the community of Cibola (Ypsilanti, Michigan). Initially using the heads of voluntary associations as nominators, they found little overlap between those picked by the reputational method and those identified through their formal position. The nominators "definitely make a distinction between those persons who occupied the top formal political and civic offices and those who, in their opinions, wielded the most influence and exerted the greatest public leadership in the community."[44] When they used different nominating panels (public leaders or economic dominants), they found that the lists produced were not noticeably different. Presthus, in *Men at the Top*, a study of two communities, found that the reputational method produced a list of leaders with important economic and political formal positions, while the decisional method uncovered subsidiary "leg-men" the reputational method had not revealed. He suggests that the reputational method shows those with power potential, even though that potential is not always used. D'Antonio and Erickson, through studies of El Paso, Texas-Ciudad Juarez, Mexico, and six Mexican-American border cities, claim that nominators in reputational studies *do* know the difference between general influence and influence in a particular area and that "Key Influentials" are influential for more than the reason of the salience of a particular issue at a given time.[45] Similarly, when asked to name separately those influential in business and those influential in government, nominators did not give the same names for general community decision-making as they did for those influential in government and politics or in business, although some overlap exists. The reputational method is used by D'Antonio and Erickson over time to show that nominators "are keenly aware of the dynamics of power and power change as measured in a three to four year period,"[46] meeting the challenge that it produces a static picture.

The debate is not likely to end soon, nor is the use of differing methods by individuals highly committed to those methods and to the findings of their studies likely to vanish. The debate thus far has, however, cast some light on the relationship between method and findings and should make us more aware of the implications of differing methods and of the lack of consensus over which ones should be used in some areas of the discipline.

BIBLIOGRAPHY

General

The Research Process.   The volumes by Duverger, Festinger and Katz, Kerlinger, Lazarsfeld and Rosenberg, and Selltiz, *et al.* contain discussions of ways to go about research as well as material on particular methods. The Lerner-Lasswell col-

[44] Robert O. Schulze and Leonard U. Blumberg, "The Determination of Local Power Elites," *American Journal of Sociology*, LXIII (1957), 293.

[45] William V. D'Antonio and Eugene C. Erickson, "The Reputational Technique as a Measure of Community Power: An Evaluation Based on Comparative and Longitudinal Studies," *American Sociological Review*, XXVII (1962), 362–376.

[46] *Ibid.*, 371.

lection is one of the earliest dealing with methods in political science. The Ranney volume contains articles evaluating some methods and summarizing the findings obtained by use of those methods. Blalock has written an important recent methodological work. Janda is one of the discipline's experts on data-processing. The sophisticated techniques of bloc analysis, factor analysis, and Guttmann scaling are discussed by Schubert, and Guttmann himself describes scaling. The Anderson-Watts-Wilcox volume is probably the best available introduction to roll-call analysis; the authors discuss other research techniques as well.

The ways of going about research are portrayed thoroughly by Lipset and Mills in their respective articles. Doing research on short notice is discussed by Back and Saravay. Carrying out research unobtrusively, in order to reduce the effect of the research on what is studied, is examined imaginatively by Webb and his associates.

Types of Research.   Press's article is an example of the use of aggregate data, the application of which to comparative studies is discussed by Retzlaff. Robinson's article is an important discussion of the problem of trying to make statements about individuals when one has only aggregate data from which to work. Bisco discusses the places through which data is made available for secondary analysis. The Campbell, *et al.*, and Jacob-Vines volumes and Key's *Southern Politics* are examples of comparative research in American politics; the first is longitudinal comparison, the second and third "horizontal." Alger and Eulau also deal with different aspects of comparative research in their articles. Kalleberg's piece discusses the methodology of comparative research. Stein's article and the essays edited by Bock give a thorough picture of aspects of the case-study as a research tool.

ALGER, CHADWICK F. "Comparison of Intranational and International Politics." *American Political Science Review,* LVII (1963), 406–419.

ANDERSON, LEE F., MEREDITH W. WATTS, JR., and ALLEN R. WILCOX. *Legislative Roll-Call Analysis.* Evanston, 1966.

BACK, KURT, and JUDITH SARAVAY. "From Bright Ideas to Social Research: Studies of the Kennedy Assassination." *Public Opinion Quarterly,* XXXI (1967), 253–264.

BISCO, RALPH L. "Social Science Data Archives: A Review of Developments." *American Political Science Review,* LX (1966), 93–109.

BLALOCK, HUBERT. *Causal Inferences in Non-Experimental Research.* Chapel Hill, 1964.

BOCK, EDWIN A., ed. *Essays on the Case Method in Public Administration.* New York, 1961.

CAMPBELL, ANGUS, PHILIP CONVERSE, WARREN E. MILLER, and DONALD E. STOKES. *Elections and the Political Order.* New York, 1966.

DUVERGER, MAURICE. *An Introduction to the Social Sciences, with Special Reference to Their Methods.* New York, 1964.

EULAU, HEINZ. "Comparative Political Analysis: A Methodological Note." *Midwest Journal of Political Science,* VI (1962), 397–407.

FESTINGER, LEON, and DANIEL KATZ, eds. *Research Methods in the Social Sciences.* New York, 1953.

GUTTMANN, LOUIS. "The Basis for Scalogram Analysis." *Measurement and Prediction, Studies in Social Psychology in World War II.* Princeton, 1949. Vol. 4, pp. 60–89.

JACOB, HERBERT, and KENNETH VINES, eds. *Politics in the American States: A Comparative Analysis.* Boston, 1965.

JANDA, KENNETH. *Data Processing: Applications to Political Research.* Evanston, 1965.

KALLEBERG, ARTHUR L. "The Logic of Comparison: A Methodological Note on the Comparative Study of Political Systems." *World Politics,* XIX (1966), 69–82.

KERLINGER, FRED N. *Foundations of Behavioral Research.* New York, 1964.

KEY, V.O., JR. *Southern Politics in State and Nation.* New York, 1949.

LAZARSFELD, PAUL, and MORRIS ROSENBERG. *The Language of Social Research.* Glencoe, 1955.

LERNER, DANIEL, and HAROLD D. LASSWELL, eds. *The Policy Sciences: Recent Developments in Scope and Method.* Stanford, 1951.

LIPSET, SEYMOUR MARTIN. "The Biography of a Research Project: *Union Democracy.*" *Sociologist at Work,* ed. Philip E. Hammond. New York, 1964. Pages 96–120.

MILLS, C. WRIGHT. "On Intellectual Craftsmanship." *Power, Politics and People: The Collected Essays of C. Wright Mills,* ed. Irving Louis Horowitz. New York, 1963. Pages 25–53.

PRESS, CHARLES. "Presidential Coattails and Party Cohesion." *Midwest Journal of Political Science,* VII (1963), 320–335.

RANNEY, AUSTIN, ed. *Essays on the Behavioral Study of Politics.* Urbana, 1962.

RETZLAFF, RALPH H. "The Use of Aggregate Data in Comparative Political Analysis." *Journal of Politics,* XXVII (1965), 797–817.

ROBINSON, W.S. "Ecological Correlation and the Behavior of Individuals." *American Sociological Review,* XV (1950), 351–357.

SCHUBERT, GLENDON. *The Judicial Mind: The Attitudes and Ideologies of Supreme Court Justices, 1946–1963.* Evanston, 1965. See pp. 22–31 for factor analysis, and pp. 31–37 for scaling.

SCHUBERT, GLENDON. *The Quantitative Analysis of Judicial Behavior.* Glencoe, 1959.

SELLTIZ, CLAIRE, MARIE JAHODA, MORTON DEUTSCH, and STUART W. COOK. *Research Methods in Social Relations.* Rev. ed. New York, 1959.

STEIN, HAROLD. "Preparation of Case Studies: The Problem of Abundance." *American Political Science Review,* XLV (1951), 479–487.

WEBB, EUGENE J., DONALD T. CAMPBELL, RICHARD D. SCHWARTZ, and LEE SECHREST. *Unobtrusive Measures: Nonreactive Research in the Social Sciences.* Chicago, 1966.

Mathematics in Political Science

Alker's book is a good introduction, as is Key's little primer, and Charlesworth's collection is also useful in dealing with some of the relevant issues. Selvin's article is an important attack on the use of statistics in social science; McGinnis answers Selvin. Bernd's collection is one of several he has edited on applications of mathematics to political science. The Lazarsfeld-Henry and Massarik-Ratoosh volumes are for advanced reading.

ALKER, HAYWARD R. *Mathematics and Politics.* New York, 1965.

BERND, JOSEPH, ed. *Mathematical Applications in Political Science.* Dallas, 1966.

CHARLESWORTH, JAMES C., ed. *Mathematics and the Social Sciences.* Philadelphia, 1963.

KEY, V.O., JR. *A Primer of Statistics for Political Scientists.* New York, 1954.

LAZARSFELD, PAUL, and N.W. HENRY, eds. *Readings in Mathematical Social Science*. Chicago, 1966.

MC GINNIS, ROBERT. "Randomization and Inference in Sociological Research." *American Sociological Review*, XXIII (1958), 408–414.

MASSARIK, F., and P. RATOOSH, eds. *Mathematical Explorations in Behavioral Science*. Homewood, Ill., 1965.

SELVIN, HANAN C. "A Critique of Tests of Significance in Survey Research." *American Sociological Review*, XXII (1957), 519–527.

Content Analysis

HOLSTI, OLE R. "Content Analysis." *The Handbook of Social Psychology*, ed. Gardner Lindzey and Elliott Aronson. 2nd ed. Cambridge, Mass., 1969.

HOLSTI, OLE R., *et al. Theory and Measurement of Interstate Behavior: A Research Application of Automated Content Analysis*. Stanford, 1964.

LASSWELL, HAROLD, NATHAN LEITES, and Associates. *Language of Politics: Studies in Quantitative Semantics*. New York, 1949.

LASSWELL, HAROLD, DANIEL LERNER, and ITHIEL DE SOLA POOL. *The Comparative Study of Symbols: An Introduction*. Stanford, 1952.

Survey Interviewing

The issue of *American Journal of Sociology* is devoted in its entirety to various aspects of interviewing. Backstrom and Hursh is probably the best introductory handbook on the subject. Hyman's volumes are far more detailed and are definitive works on the subject. Riesman's article is an interesting discussion of types of interviewers. Dexter, Robinson, and Grey deal with the problems faced by those who wish to interview public officials. Carlson discusses the issue of privacy in interviewing.

American Journal of Sociology, LXII (September, 1956), entire issue.

BACKSTROM, CHARLES H., and GERALD D. HURSH. *Survey Research*. Evanston, 1963.

CARLSON, ROBERT O. "The Issue of Privacy in Public Opinion Research." *Public Opinion Quarterly*, XXXI (1967), 1–8.

DEXTER, LEWIS ANTHONY. "The Good Will of Important People." *Public Opinion Quarterly*, XXVIII (1964), 556–563.

GREY, DAVID L. "Interviewing at the Court." *Public Opinion Quarterly*, XXXI (1967), 284–289.

HYMAN, HERBERT H., with others. *Interviewing in Social Research*. Chicago, 1954.

HYMAN, HERBERT H. *Survey Design and Analysis: Principles, Cases, and Procedures*. Glencoe, 1955.

MC CLOSKY, HERBERT. "Survey Research in Political Science." *Survey Research in the Social Sciences*, ed. Charles Y. Glock. New York, 1967.

RIESMAN, DAVID. "Some Observations on the Interviewing in the Teacher Apprehension Study." In Paul Lazarsfeld and Wagner Thielens, *The Academic Mind*. Glencoe, 1958. Pages 266–370.

ROBINSON, JAMES S. "Survey Interviewing Among Members of Congress." *Public Opinion Quarterly*, XXIV (1960), 127–138.

Participant-Observation

BABCHUK, NICHOLAS. "The Role of the Researcher as Participant Observer and Participant-as-Observer in the Field Situation." *Human Organization*, XXI (1962), 225–228.

BECKER, HOWARD S., and BLANCHE GEER. "Participant Observation and Interviewing: A Comparison." *Human Organization*, XVI (1957), 28–32.

MANN, FLOYD C. "Human Relations Skills in Social Research." *Human Relations*, IV (1951), 341–354.

PAUL, BENJAMIN D. "Interviewing Techniques and Field Relationships." *Anthropology Today: An Encyclopedic Inventory*, ed. A.L. Kroeber. Chicago, 1953. Pages 430–451.

VIDICH, ARTHUR J. "Participant Observation and the Collection and Interpretation of Data." *American Journal of Sociology*, LX (1955), 354–360.

VIDICH, A., and J. BENSMAN. "The Validity of Field Data." *Human Organization*, XIII (1954), 20–27.

Experimentation

BLOOMFIELD, LINCOLN P., and NORMAN J. PADELFORD. "Three Experiments in Political Gaming." *American Political Science Review*, LIII (1959), 1105–1115.

BROWNING, RUFUS P. "Computer Programs as Theories of Political Processes." *Journal of Politics*, XXIV (1962), 562–582.

GOLDHAMER, HERBERT, and HANS SPIER. "Some Observations on Political Gaming." *World Politics*, XII (1959), 71–83.

GUETZKOW, HAROLD, ed. *Simulation in Social Science: Readings.* Englewood Cliffs, 1962.

GUETZKOW, HAROLD, et al. *Simulation in International Relations: Developments for Research and Teaching.* Englewood Cliffs, 1963.

HERMANN, CHARLES F., and MARGARET G. "An Attempt to Simulate the Outbreak of World War I." *American Political Science Review*, LXI (1967), 400–416.

POOL, ITHIEL DE SOLA, ROBERT P. ABELSON, and SAMUEL L. POPKIN. *Candidates, Issues, and Strategies: A Computer Simulation of the 1960 and 1964 Presidential Elections.* Cambridge, Mass., 1965.

ROBINSON, JAMES A., et al. "Teaching with Inter-National Simulation and Case Studies." *American Political Science Review*, LXI (1966), 53–65.

STRODTBECK, FRED L. "Social Process, the Law, and Jury Functioning." *Law and Sociology*, ed. William Evan. New York, 1962. Pages 144–164, particularly pages 149–152.

VERBA, SIDNEY. *Small Groups and Political Behavior.* Princeton, 1961. Chapter 3, "Experiments and the Political Process," pp. 63–89, and Chapter 4, "Experiments and the Political Process: 2," pp. 90–109.

ZEISEL, HANS. "Social Research on the Law: The Ideal and the Practical." *Law and Sociology*, ed. William Evan. Pages 124–143.

Community Power Structure

In addition to the items already cited in the footnotes, the following items provide a fairly thorough coverage of the subject. Rossi's articles and those by Anton and Bonjean and Olson provide good summaries of existing studies, as does Chapter

12 of Presthus' volume. The Kaufman and Jones article is a discussion of Hunter's book. Polsby and Wolfinger, who follow the decisional approach, are its prime "Defenders of the Faith." The Presthus and Agger-Goldrich-Swanson volumes are multi-community studies. Articles by Pfautz and Barth and Abu-Laban deal with the Negro sub-community.

AGGER, ROBERT E., DANIEL GOLDRICH, and BERT E. SWANSON. *The Rulers and the Ruled: Political Power and Impotence in American Communities.* New York, 1964.

ANTON, THOMAS J. "Power, Pluralism, and Local Politics." *Administrative Science Quarterly,* VII (1963), 425–457.

BARTH, ERNEST A.T., and BAHA ABU-LABAN. "Power Structure and the Negro Sub-Community." *American Sociological Review,* XXIV (1959), 69–76.

BONJEAN, CHARLES M., and DAVID M. OLSON. "Community Leadership: Directions of Research." *Administrative Science Quarterly,* IX (1964), 279–300.

DAHL, ROBERT. "A Critique of the Ruling Elite Model." *American Political Science Review,* LII (1958), 463–469.

D'ANTONIO, WILLIAM V., HOWARD J. EHRLICH, and EUGENE C. ERICKSON. "Further Notes on the Study of Community Power." *American Sociological Review,* XXVII (1962), 848–854.

FISHER, SETHARD. "Community Power Studies: A Critique." *Social Research,* XXIX (1962), 449–466.

FREEMAN, LINTON C., THOMAS J. FARARO, WARNER BLOOMBERG, JR., and MORRIS H. SUNSHINE. "Locating Leaders in Local Communities: A Comparison of Some Alternative Approaches." *American Sociological Review,* XXVIII (1963), 791–798.

HERSON, LAWRENCE J.R. "In the Footsteps of Community Power." *American Political Science Review,* LV (1961), 817–830.

KAUFMAN, HERBERT, and VICTOR JONES. "The Mystery of Power." *Public Administration Review,* XIV (1954), 205–212.

PFAUTZ, HAROLD W. "The Power Structure of the Negro Sub-Community: A Case Study and a Comparative View." *Phylon,* XXIII (1962), 156–166.

POLSBY, NELSON. *Community Power and Political Theory.* New Haven, 1963.

———. "Community Power: Some Reflections on the Recent Literature." *American Sociological Review,* XXVII (1962), 838–841.

———. "How to Study Community Power . . ." *Journal of Politics,* XXII (1960), 474–484.

———. "Three Problems in the Analysis of Community Power." *American Sociological Review,* XXIV (1959), 796–803.

PRESTHUS, ROBERT. *Men at the Top: A Study in Community Power.* New York, 1964.

ROSE, ARNOLD M. *The Power Structure: Political Process in American Society.* New York, 1967. See in particular Chapter 8, "Issues in the Study of Local Community Power," pp. 255–297.

ROSSI, PETER. "Community Decision-Making." *Administrative Science Quarterly,* I (1957), 415–443.

———. "Power and Community Structure." *Midwest Journal of Political Science,* IV (1960), 390–401.

WALTER, BENJAMIN. "On the Logical Analysis of Power-Attribution Procedures." *Journal of Politics,* XXVI (1964), 850–866.

WOLFINGER, RAYMOND. "Reputation and Reality in the Study of 'Comunity Power'." *American Sociological Review,* XXV (1960), 636–644.

Part II / POLITICAL SCIENCE AS A PROFESSION

7 / POLITICAL SCIENCE:
GENESIS AND GROWTH

A Short History of the Discipline / Political Science and the
Social Sciences / Political Science and the Public

A SHORT HISTORY OF THE DISCIPLINE

Political science is both an old and a new discipline, extending historical roots back to Plato and Aristotle, yet always absorbing new material and, more recently, attempting to reorient itself. The reason that it is both old and new stems from a separation or division of labor within the social sciences over a hundred years ago. Political science and the other social sciences are quite young, having begun to move toward their present status only with the increasing complexity of life which had its roots in the Industrial Revolution. No one previous area of knowledge had a scope large enough to cope with all social and political phenomena, forcing scholars to create new tools, and with them new fields, through which to analyze the world around them. Many use as a benchmark for the origin of modern political science the establishment at Columbia University in 1856 of a separate chair of political science, occupied by the German émigré, Francis Lieber. From that time, American political science has grown immensely. By 1969, over 15,000 individuals were members of the American Political Science Association, and the Association has been growing by 10% or more each year. (The 15,000 figure is an understatement of the number of political scientists, because not all belong to the APSA.) Yet, despite political science's roots and increasing age and size, it is only recently that political scientists have shown much interest in their discipline and its development. Most are probably still generally unfamiliar with such details, and, according to the profession's leading historians, "have paid a heavy price in time, effort, and controversy for their failure to attend more closely to their past." [1]

The study of politics had origins in the centuries before the birth of Christ, particularly in ancient Greece. Although Plato and Aristotle in general treated knowledge holistically instead of recognizing separate disciplines, the subject of politics was central to the work of both men. Plato attempted in the *Republic* to examine justice through the depiction of the Ideal

[1] Albert Somit and Joseph Tanenhaus, *The Development of American Political Science*, p. 3.

State. The development of Utopias, in the tradition of Plato, was the central feature of the examination of politics for many centuries. While Aristotle also wrote about ideal forms of government and clearly indicated preferences for certain types over others, he began another trend: the systematic study of existing forms of government, which he did through classification of the constitutions of the Greek city-states and neighboring nations. While the empirical approach to politics used by Aristotle is now of great importance, clearly outshining Plato's philosophical method, the two ways of going about the study of politics did not proceed evenly or simultaneously.

For many centuries, the study of politics remained submerged in philosophy, which at the time contained almost all knowledge. This helps explain why political scientists find so many items of relevance in the works of the early philosophers. A separate literature on politics began to develop in the fifteenth and sixteenth centuries, stimulated by the establishment of separate university faculties of law, where professors wrote about international law, and by a change in philosophical outlook away from passivity toward the world. The view that events are totally predetermined may produce quiescence and a lack of interest in studying those events. When men feel they have at least some power over events, or some control over their own behavior, they are more likely to undertake an examination of that behavior.

Many point to Machiavelli's *The Prince*, written in the early sixteenth century, as the starting point for a pragmatic examination of politics, because

> *Pragmatism.* **A philosophical position that ideas or actions are to be judged by their results, instead of, for example, in terms of their logic, morality, or consistency with other ideas or actions. Whether something works is the question the pragmatist asks.**

of the advice Machiavelli provides for the best way of running a state.[2] The writing of political materials, whether tracts or philosophy, by those involved in practical matters occupied a major place in writings about the politically relevant for many years and has continued until the present day. Sometimes the writing was merely the afterthoughts or public writings of men deeply involved in the practice of politics. Collections of American political thought almost entirely contain these types of writing. A long time was still to pass between this practical concern and the establishment of political science as an independent academic discipline. During the intervening years, writing took a variety of forms—more Utopias, specific advice to lawmakers, and, although less frequently, general speculation about the real working of the world of politics and government.

Political science was a result both of certain philosophic trends and developments within fields of knowledge and university structure. Philosophy

---

[2] Recently, a writer has drawn parallels between the writings of Machiavelli and that of a contemporary political scientist, Richard Neustadt, writing about the preservation of power in the American Presidency. William T. Bluhm, *Theories of the Political System* (Englewood Cliffs, 1965), Ch. 7, "Naturalistic Prudence: Machiavelli and Neustadt."

began to lose control of the study of social and political life. In addition, other disciplines, including history, showed a lack of interest in the investigation of politics as a concern. While law schools on the European continent taught materials which were close to political science, they excluded much that was relevant to the subject. Despite the concern of some early law professors with international law, they tended to ignore administrative law and constitutional law, which, as is natural for a developing field, political science took over. In this country, the disappearance of the European-style faculty of law also assisted the development of political science. While some present-day law schools provide a broad orientation, training for the law in America is largely technical. It can be argued that had the European-style law faculty existed in this country, such a faculty would have undertaken political science study. The existence of an institutional location for the study of politics would have made it difficult for a separate discipline of political science to develop.

At least initially, modern political science could best be defined negatively: it covered what some other fields did not. Certainly departments of political science in the United States, where political science's independence has been predominant, did not grow from well-ordered ideas about the scope and boundaries of political science. Instead, "they reflected the negative attitude of other academic disciplines." As Morgenthau sums it up: "Political science grew not by virtue of an intellectual principle germane to the field, but in response to pressures from the outside. What could not be defined in terms of traditional academic disciplines was defined as political science." [3] This appears to have been true with respect to both content and the methods and approaches used by political scientists.

During the more than a century of its existence, and the more than half-century of its official institutionalized existence, American political science has passed through a number of moods, involving the use of various emphases. Transition from one phase to another is often prolonged; differences in approach often co-exist, with only relative emphases varying. One could divide political science into "periods" in a number of ways, such as that into four periods suggested by Merriam.[4] Up to 1850, a philosophical emphasis and the use of deductive methods characterized what could at that time be called political science. For the next half-century, historical and comparative methods were predominant. The third period, from 1900 to 1923, is identified by an emphasis on observation, survey, and measurement. Merriam dates the last period, which is marked by greater use of a psychological treatment of politics, from 1923. Many other observers of political science, while perhaps not disagreeing about the content of the periods, would place both the third and fourth much later. As late as 1940, one observer noted that "we have only

[3] Hans Morgenthau, "Power as a Political Concept," *Approaches to the Study of Politics*, ed. Young, p. 67.

[4] Cited by William A. Robson, *The University Teaching of Social Sciences: Political Science* (Paris, 1954), p. 27.

begun to break through on the social and psychological frontiers." [5] In addition, more periods might be added, most particularly one beginning with the end of World War II in which an empirical and clearly interdisciplinary approach began to move to the fore. This might in turn be broken into three subperiods: World War II-1949, 1950 to the mid-1950's, and from that time to the present.

Some have noted that political science as we presently know it, while affected by what went on before 1900, draws its present scope and content from only the period since then. This means that basic approaches appeared within the last seventy years, and it also means that the scope of the discipline has not changed radically in that period. While we have deepened our study substantially, we did not broaden it noticeably, at least not until after World War II, and many of the newer items to which attention was then given had been examined on a limited scale earlier.

Some of the "moods" in the discipline deserve mention. A number of observers mention a "reformist" orientation in political science, most prevalent before World War I and lasting until the growth of the totalitarian powers and the collapse of the League of Nations. At first this reform was often simply moralism. One commentator even suggests that the first grouping of political scientists we could call a "school" came about through "the deep dissatisfaction among some young academicians who measured the reality of their American community against the ideals of an imagined polis and found it wanting." [6] They believed, he commented, in the assured spread of democracy, harmony of interests among people, and the basic rationality of man. Later a shift occurred; while the idea of reform remained paramount, objective study, directed toward finding means to obtain the ends of the reformers, replaced some of the moralism, or at least began to undergird it. The "objective" study was also based on the rationalistic assumption that if the citizenry had more facts, then they would almost automatically help bring about reform, a point of view quite clearly the basis of such organizations as the League of Women Voters. Political scientists of that time apparently failed to realize that what they regarded as problems might not be recognized as such by others or that people, even when they did recognize problems, might wish to ignore them.

Municipal reform, legal realism, direct democracy (initiative, referen-

> **Legal Realism.**   A jurisprudence based on the idea that law is not simply judges' statements of what they do, but what judges in fact do in cases. In a broad sense, it is a behavioral jurisprudence.

dum, recall, and the direct primary), the short ballot, and world peace through world law all were concerns of the political science profession for at

[5] Benjamin E. Lippincott, "The Bias of American Political Science," *Journal of Politics*, II (1940), 129.

[6] Sigmund Neumann, "Comparative Politics: A Half-Century Appraisal," *Journal of Politics*, XIX (1957), 372. "Polis" is the Greek word for city-state (here, nation-state).

least the first two decades of the twentieth century. However, the optimism of the reformers was shattered by America's failure to join the League of Nations and the League's ultimate passage from the scene, the rise of Hitler and Mussolini, and, in America, the election of Warren Harding as President.

> The total defeat of Woodrow Wilson, *the* political scholar in politics, and the election of Warren Gamaliel Harding were more than symbolic of the passing of the ethos of the Progressive Era. Progressives had worked hard to return politics to the people, and the people had returned Harding. These events, together with the "Red Scare" of 1919 and the fierce anti-intellectualism of the popular press in the early twenties, must have convinced men like Merriam that they were only burning their fingers in practical politics.[7]

Political scientists began to take cover in objective study of a different sort, hoping through a greater collection of facts and generalizations to be able ultimately to provide reform. From this it was not a long step to a study without reform attached. Wars, depressions, and the shifts in the world power structure also changed the emphasis of political science away from state and local problems and toward national government and international affairs. That we have not moved completely away from reform is shown by the idea of political science as a "policy science." The idea that we should take our subjects for study from those which are current policy problems or which affect current policy does not automatically entail a reformist orientation, but it does bring political science closer to living politics than if other criteria of subjects to study are used.

The tone of American political science has always been "middle-class." Little explicit root-and-branch challenge has been made of the basic values of the political system in which most political scientists live, namely that of the United States. To the social critic, findings made by the political scientist undoubtedly suggest criticisms, but it is the critic supplying the values. This is not to suggest that political scientists are totally happy either with the present arrangement of politics or with the state of their discipline and its approach(es). There are political scientists who are extremely upset with the present state of the world and their nation, just as there are others who are quite satisfied with the *status quo*. But while the former may allow their values to help them determine what they shall study, they have not, as political scientists, been demanding change in loud tones. Perhaps this can be explained by the amount of effort spent attempting to realign and re-orient the discipline; time spent on internal reform is not available for external changes.

Another crucial mood in political science, the most recent one, is that of behavioralism. Behavioralism is more than just one of several approaches to the study of politics (see pp. 38–48); it is almost a personal philosophy or way of life for many of those who utilize it. Coming into their own after World War II, behavioralists, unlike most other political scientists, drew heavily and un-

[7] Bernard Crick, *The American Science of Politics: Its Origins and Conditions* (Berkeley, 1959), p. 134.

ashamedly from other disciplines, emphasized the individual as the basic unit for analysis, and sought to make political science more scientific. Their attempt to develop a value-free political science clearly distinguishes them from the reformers. At least at first, survey research was their trademark and methodology was a major concern; an interest in theory became prominent as the movement grew older. A number of forces contributed to the development of this important mood in political science, which had its antecedents at the University of Chicago in the 1920's, with Charles Merriam and his students. Stimuli which affected its development were arrival of sociologically-oriented European scholars during the 1930's; World War II, in which a number of academic political scientists were involved in large-scale government research projects; support from the Social Science Research Council (SSRC) and the Carnegie, Rockefeller, and Ford Foundations; and the growth of the survey method, permitting study of voting behavior and public opinion in ways not previously possible. Behavioralism has now made its mark on all the subfields of the discipline, although it has not been comfortably accepted in all.

One of the principal salient features of political science, as of any discipline today, is the amount of its specialization, accentuated by the behavioral approach. We have moved from having political science a branch of philosophy (as was every other presently separate field) to having political philosophy a branch of political science. And we have moved further, for example, from political philosophy to the separation of classical political thought and modern empirical theory. It has become more and more difficult for political scientists to keep "on top" of their own field and to talk to each other as specialization has spread; we narrow our individual attention as the amount of material from other sub-specialties increases at a phenomenal rate. In the words of one observer,

> It is probably not too much to say that any essay which some political scientists regard as really significant and first-rate work hardly communicates at all to most political scientists; and an essay which most political scientists understand and approve is regarded by some of us as unimportant.[8]

Specialization, in the eyes of some, has brought political science to the point where there is fear for the future of the discipline: "While specialization and professionalization create problems of communication and synthesis at the periphery . . . they create problems of homogeneity at the core," [9] and raise the spectre of disintegration. Problems are overlooked because the results of specialization are uncoordinated and no one can prevent important areas of analysis from "falling between two stools." Methods and concepts do not circulate from the subfield in which they originated to other areas of the discipline where they might also be fruitful. This returns us to the meaning of

[8] Charles B. Hagan, "The Group in a Political Science," p. 39.
[9] Dwight Waldo, *Political Science in the United States of America: A Trend Report* (Paris, 1956), p. 13.

political science. Are we talking only about a congeries of separate enterprises or about something more cohesive? That there is some hope for a unified discipline is voiced by those who emphasize theory-building on the level of the political system as a whole, which may begin to break down the isolation of sub-fields within the discipline. Nonetheless, we still do not clearly know who or what we are: "Ambiguity and confusion betray the inner tensions that have accompanied the rapid development in the field." [10]

In a recent work, Bernard Crick, an English political scientist, has argued that political science is heavily influenced by the society in which it is located and by that society's values.[11] Concentrating his analysis on American political scientists, Crick asserts that events in the political system affect political studies. He points out that the range of accepted values in this country is relatively narrow. According to Crick, "the study of politics is everywhere a response to a belief that there is a crisis." [12] Crises there have been, including the Civil War, but, by comparison with other countries, they have been crises about minor frictions resting on a "massive surface confidence" about "problems to be clearly solved so as to maintain the validity of the old beliefs in new circumstances." However, beyond this, he feels political science to be itself an ideology, even when it is thought to be objective. Political science has not been political philosophy (which Crick apparently thinks should be the "mother" part of the discipline, as philosophy itself was once the mother of other disciplines), but instead has been "citizenship education." Political science became "mere method," Crick writes, "a technique for sustaining a pre-existing American liberalism, not . . . a critical or speculative discipline."

Crick's explanation of the development of American political science is at least plausible as an hypothesis. He argues that the "fictions of adjustment and growth" suffered by America have seemed to make political science needed, "on a uniquely large scale." In addition, political life in the first half of the nineteenth century had ceased to attract men of ability, who then, according to Crick, re-created within the classroom the practiced science of politics of some of the Founding Fathers. Through all this, Crick constantly repeats, the extremely high consensus on the purposes and values of American life served as a conditioning influence. Crick errs in not distinguishing between reasons why an academic field comes into being, and factors explaining its current operation. They may or may not be the same, and in this case are not. Even if Crick is correct concerning origins, the attempt being made by many political scientists in the 1960's is to produce an objective political science; whether they are succeeding is another matter, but that is their motivation.

[10] Harold Lasswell, *The Future of Political Science*, p. 35.

[11] The study of the relationship of ideas to their social and cultural setting is generally known as "the sociology of knowledge." Among its foremost developers was Karl Mannheim.

[12] The material in this and the following two paragraphs is based on Crick, particularly pp. 8, 36.

Whatever the reasons for the initiation of a separate discipline of political science in America, one did develop, and grew with rapidity after the appointment of Lieber at Columbia. Some time passed after Lieber's appointment before the training of political scientists took place in this country, an indication of the considerable foreign influence which had existed for many years, as shown by the earlier contribution to the examination of American political practices made by foreign observers such as Alexis deTocqueville, whose *Democracy in America* is the outstanding example. The establishment in 1880 by John Burgess of a School of Political Science with a graduate program, also at Columbia, was a landmark of the trend toward the domestic training of political scientists; the first American political science journal, *The Political Science Quarterly*, was published at Burgess' school. One measure of the change in training is that, "whereas nearly half of those making up the 1904 Establishment had pursued formal graduate study on the Conti-

Establishment. A group of individuals who control, or are considered to control, an organization. Sometimes used as shorthand for the outstanding or dominant social or political figures in a country or community.

nent, less than a third of those holding Association posts in 1914 took any training abroad." [13] However, it was some years more before the graduate schools were displaced as the center of focus of the discipline by the American Political Science Association.

The American Political Science Association.   Although the American Academy of Political and Social Science, started in 1899, antedates it, the American Political Science Association (APSA), founded in 1903, is the principal professional organization of political scientists. The APSA's birth was both proof that political science was a discipline independent of others and a stimulus to further growth. In the ensuing years, a number of regional associations have been formed within the United States, the most active being the Midwest, Western, and Southern Political Science Associations. In the Southwest, political scientists participate in the Southwestern Social Science Association. All of these organizations, like the APSA, publish journals.[14] Subregional and state groups exist in many parts of the country. The International Political Science Association (IPSA) dates from only 1949, at which time only Canada and India, in addition to the United States, had national political science organizations, although several more, including ones in France and England, have since been formed.

Annual meetings of the APSA serve to bring together American political scientists for the presentation of technical research and theoretical papers, and for some limited discussion of issues within the discipline, as well as for hiring of personnel and renewal of friendships, the latter continuing the early use of the *American Political Science Review* as a device for transmitting in-

[13] Somit and Tanenhaus, p. 61.

[14] Respectively, *The Midwest Journal of Political Science, The Western Political Quarterly, The Journal of Politics,* and *Southwestern Social Science Quarterly* (now *Social Science Quarterly*).

formation about members of the profession.[15] (Recently, a number of political scientists, discontent with what they perceived to be the lack of relevance of topics considered in the papers presented at the annual meeting, formed a Caucus for a New Political Science to present their own panels.) The APSA serves more to reflect what is happening within the discipline, primarily within the colleges and universities, than itself to initiate developments, although its actions may serve to reinforce trends. It is a service rather than a reform or activist type of professional organization, generally not much concerned with political scientists' day-to-day problems such as academic freedom or teaching loads, which are left by default to other groups such as the American Association of University Professors (AAUP) and the accrediting associations. As a service organization, the APSA has conducted fellowship programs to allow political scientists, journalists, and federal career employees to learn more about Congress and to permit Congressional staff personnel to continue special academic studies away from Washington; held seminars for freshmen Congressmen in Washington and for freshmen state legislators; and has helped in development of summer Civics Institutes for secondary school teachers under the National Defense Education Act.

An indication that the organization does from time to time deal with matters of broad professional concern is shown by its continuing interest in increased funds for the support of political science research. Thus, the Executive Director of the APSA, Dr. Evron Kirkpatrick, has carried on a long campaign to have political science accorded the same status as other behavioral sciences by the National Science Foundation, and the Association has shown concern about the problem of government involvement in research, in the aftermath of the "Camelot" furor. (See pp. 259–271.) In addition, committees are appointed to look into particular matters raised within the group. Thus, a Committee on Professional Standards and Responsibilities was appointed in 1967 to deal on a continuing basis with problems of political scientists' relations to government research and connected matters, and it began almost immediately to issue recommendations concerning activities of members, officers, and employees of the Association. In recent years, committees have been used far less than previously because of their earlier divisive effect resulting from independence of the organization, reinforced by the difficulty the part-time officers of the Association had in overseeing the committees' work, although there has been an increase in the number of committees in 1967 and 1968 as some members of the Association have pressed demands for examination of matters within the profession. The APSA committees whose reports are best known are those in which particular political institutions, e.g., political parties or legislatures, have been examined and recommendations for reform made. These research committees have been less frequently utilized in recent years, partly because foundations seem more interested in funding research through individuals in universities than through the committees.

[15] Such information is now transmitted to the Association's membership in a separate publication, *P.S.*, initiated in 1967.

For all these reasons, the APSA does not usually figure prominently in discussions of political scientists' daily activities and of the issues within the discipline, which tend to be resolved primarily at the level of the individual institution. The organization's lack of political involvement does not, however, indicate lack of political interest or partisanship among its members, although the fact that political scientists' political preferences (dominantly Democratic) are not reflected in the APSA's actions is quite probably the result of the attitudes of political scientists as members of a profession. In addition, the Association's Constitution does not allow the Association to take positions on matters of public policy, although in 1968 it was amended to allow the taking of positions on academic freedom issues, and was also amended to encourage research in and concern for significant contemporary political problems regardless of their controversiality. The Association's members' collective interest in contemporary politics is shown by, among other things, the fact that important figures in both major political parties have spoken to national conventions of the APSA.

POLITICAL SCIENCE AND THE SOCIAL SCIENCES

That the relationship between political science and the other social sciences and related disciplines demands exploration is stressed in statements like the following:

> Political science is now less parochial than before the war, but this exercise in togetherness has demonstrated all too clearly that there is little difference between the social science disciplines, save only as they are shaped by their intellectual history, the vested interests of the departments and of book-publishers, and the budgets of academic deans.[16]

One major question is whether, on the one hand, a "master" or unifying social science exists, or, on the other, the social science disciplines contribute equally and independently to our knowledge. An answer to this question depends in part on what one considers a desirable goal for the study of politics (or of any other aspect of human behavior). For those who feel that our goal should be a general theory of all behavior, each component of the social sciences is valuable to the extent that it contributes to such a general theory, and findings true in only one area of human behavior are less valuable than findings duplicated with respect to other aspects of life. Thus, any one component of the social sciences that can contribute, or has contributed, more to such general theory qualifies as the master social science.

Economics and sociology, at their present stages of development, would be considered more qualified for the title than would political science, anthro-

---

[16] Roland Young, "Comment on Professor Deutsch's Paper," *A Design For Political Science: Scope, Objectives, and Methods,* ed. James C. Charlesworth (Philadelphia, 1966), p. 193.

pology, or history. Economics would be the leading candidate because the development of formal theories of behavior has proceeded furthest in that field. Sociology is a candidate because of the breadth of its concerns, which include politics, law, and religion. If "society" is all-encompassing, then sociology, as the study of society, necessarily integrates the other, more specialized studies such as economics and political science. However, if we consider social relations only one aspect of human life, distinct from rather than enveloping the polity and economy, sociology is only a coordinate social science rather than the superior one.

Geography, not usually considered part of the social sciences, has begun to contribute to a general theory of human behavior through its subfields of human geography, economic geography, and cultural geography, which are concerned with relating behavior to the characteristics of the locations in which the behavior is found. Psychology, through its subfield of social psychology, also makes a profound contribution to theories of social behavior. For some, psychology is the basic science of behavior. However, this position involves the explanation of all behavior in terms of personality and other psychological concepts. Most social scientists consider this a forced reductionism, because they feel social and psychological elements in behavior cannot be completely separated, even if they can be isolated analytically. While some see social phenomena as deriving from an individual's subjective experiences, others find social structure to be independent of the individual. They draw support from studies which show that individuals with similar personalities behave differently in different social situations. In addition, regardless of the relative virtues of particular disciplines, many scholars would reject the idea that any one field, either as presently or possibly constituted, could be the master social science. To the extent a general theory of behavior is emphasized, individual disciplines would be reduced in importance, although each could contribute to general social theory (or broader behavioral theory) in varying degrees, as well as to each other.

Some do consider that political science is *primus inter pares* in the social sciences, both because Aristotle called politics the master art and because modern social scientists have felt that the polity performs the goal-attainment function for the society as a whole. If this is the polity's function, what more important social science could there be than the one which examines the way in which we set and achieve our goals? Without goals, it could be argued, no society could exist. In addition, political science compares well with other fields in the degree to which it encompasses all of social behavior. For example, the sociologist Talcott Parsons takes the position that political science utilizes a broader portion of a "general theory of action" than does economics. David Truman, however, analogizes the relation between behavioral science and political science as "roughly [to] that between 'basic' and 'applied' research." [17] Behavioral science would emphasize general

---

[17] David Truman, "The Impact on Political Science of the Revolution in the Behavioral Sciences," *Research Frontiers in Politics and Government*, ed. Bailey, p. 224.

principles of human behavior, without respect to context, but utilizing relevant findings from political science research; the political scientist would concentrate on a specific aspect of behavior, the political and governmental, at the same time it aimed at findings of broader relevance. Another way of viewing this relationship is to see political science as taking a different point of view toward events which are the same as those examined by other social sciences.

If the various disciplines included within either the social or behavioral sciences provide concepts, methods, findings, and approaches for each other, the stance of the scholar toward these disciplines other than his own comes to have increased importance. He has several options: he can be a generalist, concentrating on what the fields have in common; he can be a specialist in a single field, leaving it to others to extract from his work findings which may be of value to them; or he can be a borrower, familiar enough with related fields to use their techniques, findings, and hypotheses and to adapt them to his own "acre of soil."

Until recently, the political scientist has been a specialist. He has concentrated on matters clearly political or governmental, although he has not been able to avoid giving attention to other fields, which may have intruded unasked into his line of vision. Given the partially blurred lines between the disciplines, he is likely to have acquired some extra-disciplinary knowledge as a student, and contact with members of the other social sciences will have added more, even if not acquired willingly. Now an increasing number of political scientists are borrowers. Perhaps one important factor in this change was the war-time experience of many political scientists as government employees, working on multi-faceted problems. They recognized that they needed to be a combination of political economist, political geographer, and political psychologist, because, as administrators, they did not find problems neatly divided into political science, economics, sociology, *et al.*; the problems had to be handled in their totality. Those political scientists leaning in the direction of more general theories of politics were among the heaviest and earliest users of other fields. Those who felt we could legitimately aim for a "science" of politics (often the same as those interested in general theory) also leaned heavily on developments in other disciplines, primarily sociology. Some of the items borrowed were already second-hand, as the neighboring social sciences had in turn found them elsewhere.

Whether the items taken from other fields were appropriate for political science was often unclear at the time they were taken, because political scientists often did not state their problems or needs clearly or in a way which would make it easier for them to find out what they wanted to borrow. Until borrowed items were tested, one could not tell definitely how useful they would be. However, the temptation to borrow almost at random from other fields items which appeared to be successful may have been irresistible. As more borrowing has taken place, a greater recognition has come about of the need to scrutinize other fields carefully so that materials chosen will be appropriate for political science, and so that the place of the borrowed materials within the field from which they come, as well as their limitations, would be properly understood.

Political Scientists and Lawyers. While a large proportion of lawyers are trained in political science as undergraduates because political science is the basic part of most "pre-law" programs, after their undergraduate days lawyers' training and experience take them on routes separate from those followed by political scientists. American legal training is essentially "technical." Case-centered rather than based on abstract generalizations, legal education is aimed at preparing the lawyer for the practice of law, either through instruction in the law of a particular state or a more general approach later supplemented by intensified preparation for admission to the bar. Although a few law schools do attempt to provide a thorough understanding of the processes which bring law about, the primary orientation of law schools and the principal interests of their students tend to submerge this in favor of material of more immediate vocational relevance, clearly different from the approach of most political science graduate training. Once out of law school, the lawyer finds himself in professional associations which have little contact with equivalent political science organizations. As a result, the lawyer's outlook and thought process are different from the political scientist's. While both are concerned with facts and generalizations from those facts, their goals differ. What each produces from his work is therefore also different; lawyers are more interested in marshalling facts to make an argument than in developing scientific generalizations from those facts.

Most political scientists are academicians, but the largest proportion of lawyers are outside university walls. Even lawyers teaching in law schools, many of whom have been practicing lawyers, fit in a separate "professional school" within the university structure, and thus are divorced from political scientists. In the past, lawyers frequently have been convinced that political scientists were improperly trained to study the law, although they were perhaps willing to make exceptions for those possessing both an LL.B. and Ph.D. Despite the serious use of legal analysis by many political scientists, the attitude has been voiced that political scientists who undertake to study the law are charlatans. A late Supreme Court Justice allegedly refused to be interviewed by a political scientist, a leading scholar in constitutional law, because the political scientist did not have a law degree and was thus "not qualified." And a law professor once told the author, in all seriousness, that "no one should teach a course with the word 'law' in the title unless he has a law degree," a sentiment not likely to be appreciated by political scientists teaching Constitutional or Administrative Law. Despite these feelings, within the last few years there has been increasing contact between lawyers, particularly those teaching, political scientists, and sociologists. Factors which have helped bring this about are exposure of some lawyers to sociology and political science in law school; establishment of a Law and Society Association; articles in the law reviews by political scientists and sociologists; the schools

of "Sociological Jurisprudence" and "Legal Realism"; the long-standing interest of sociologists in criminology and the increasing interest of political

> *Sociological Jurisprudence.* **The philosophy that law should be devel-
> oped in terms of its effect on a variety of interests in society. Some have
> said it is merely a device for classifying interests rather than a theory of
> jurisprudence.**

scientists in law-enforcement problems, stemming from the Supreme Court's
"fair trial" decisions of the 1960's; [18] and the introduction of courses in the
undergraduate political science curriculum dealing with the legal process.

One of the most articulate statements about the relationship between political science and its neighboring disciplines is David Easton's essay, "Alternative Strategies in Theoretical Research." A long excerpt is reproduced
here.

"Alternative Strategies in Theoretical Research" [°]

It has often been said that wars do not change basic intellectual or political
trends, that they simply delay or modify what in any case would eventually have
occurred.[1] Whether or not this is true for all wars, World War II in fact did mark a
major turning point in the history of political science, one that defied recognition
until a decade or more after the fact. It is true that before World War II, there were
some hints of the pattern of future developments in political theory. But after 1945,
a number of new currents were set in motion, the earlier detection of which would
have taxed the ingenuity of even the most insightful and careful observer. Among
these innovations, we find a slowly growing body of political theory unlike anything
that had preceded it in the previous 2000 years.

Prior to World War II, theory almost exclusively implied moral philosophy in its
various forms, or, at the very least, the history and analysis of the moral systems of
the great political thinkers of the past. Only the barest glimmerings of the modern
kind of theory were visible. For most students of politics, the little that did exist was
scarcely recognizable as such; very seldom was it clearly identified and labelled.

Since World War II, however, there has gradually accumulated a small but distinguished inventory of this new kind of theoretical inquiry, what we may call descriptive, or empirical, theory.

Empirical theory is by no means homogeneous; it varies widely in its scope and
degree of abstractness. Much of it is confined to very limited hypotheses about small
fragments of political behavior; other parts of it pertain to somewhat broader ranges

---

[18] Among the most important were *Mapp* v. *Ohio,* 367 U.S. 643 (1961), in which the
Court said that illegally seized evidence could not be admitted in state courts; *Gideon* v.
Wainwright, 372 U.S. 355 (1963), providing the right to counsel to indigent defendants;
and *Escobedo* v. *Illinois,* 378 U.S. 478 (1964), and *Miranda* v. *Arizona,* 384 U.S. 436 (1966),
detailing a suspect's rights prior to trial.

[1] *For the effects of wars on basic ideas, see* J. U. Nef, War and Human Progress (*Cambridge, Mass.: Harvard University Press,* 1950).

[°] SOURCE: David Easton, "Alternative Strategies in Theoretical Research" in *Varieties of Political Theory,* ed. David Easton (Englewood Cliffs, 1966), pp. 1–8. © 1966. Reprinted by
permission of Prentice-Hall, Inc., Englewood Cliffs, New Jersey.

of political phenomena such as we find in particular sets of political institutions and parties, administrative behavior, or electoral choices, for example. But the kind of empirical theory which represents the most striking and promising innovation since World War II seeks to illuminate the whole domain of political interaction. That is to say, the new theory which has special significance in political science seeks to systematize and lend coherence and direction to the whole field of political science as a discipline. It represents in political science what in other fields—such as economics or sociology—has been called general as against partial or special theory.[2]

Modern theory, in the form of general theory, has a number of important functions. It gives guidance to empirical research by summarizing what has been discovered and by suggesting the relevance or significance of new, proposed investigations. It acts as an economical means for storing and retrieving larger bodies of apparently discrete information about political behavior. But general theory also serves as an incentive for the creation of new information, insofar as logical operations can be performed on its theoretical propositions to extend the horizons of our understanding and explanation. In this function lies the truly creative and most rewarding potential of general theory, one that we can expect will assert itself increasingly in political science as theoretical enquiry acquires a deeper sense of security, and a greater appetite for innovative boldness.

Significant as the body of modern political thought has been, it has made a mere beginning in the decades since World War II. Nevertheless, even in its paucity it represents a break with the past, the enormity of which is only slowly being absorbed into the consciousness of political scientists. We are not yet fully aware of the fact that as part of the general scientific revolution under way in the area of methods and techniques—usually described as the study of political behavior—political science is also experiencing a revolution in the field of theory that is of comparable proportions and significance.

THE IMPACT OF THE THEORETICAL REVOLUTION

The implications of this theoretical revolution are varied and profound . . . [and] it will be helpful to explore some of these implications.

Theory and "the Myth of Methodology." The revolution in political theory testifies to the fact that in political science we have been able to address ourselves directly to substantive construction in theory. This may seem to be a strange statement, since presumably, once we undertake to build theory, no other path would seem to be open. But the fact is that in political science we are largely unaware of the distractions and wasteful motions that we have mercifully been spared.

Unlike sociology or psychology, political science, as the doors to scientific method have finally been opened wide, has been able to avoid a long and agonizing period in which its theoretical efforts might have been buried in what has been called "the myth of methodology." [3] We have been able to take advantage of the history of other disciplines, in which all too easily theory could imperceptibly slip from substantive analysis into methodological discussion. Methodology often masqueraded under the title of theory. In exploring theoretical alternatives in political

[2] *For extended comments on this new theory, see my* A Framework for Political Analysis (*Englewood Cliffs, N.J.: Prentice-Hall, Inc., 1965*), *especially Chapter One.*
[3] Abraham Kaplan, The Conduct of Inquiry (*San Francisco: Chandler Publishing Co.,* 1964), p. 24.

science, we have usually succeeded in distinguishing clearly between methodology and the substantive treatment of theoretical issues, assigning to each its proper place and weight.

This self-conscious awareness of the difference between substantive theory and methodological analysis has gone hand in hand with a balanced appreciation of the relative importance of rigorous fact-gathering as against theorizing. All too often, inadequate distinction between methodological discussion and theoretical analysis has been accompanied by an undue emphasis on the rigorous collection of data undirected by theoretical criteria of relevance; each reinforced the other. Preoccupation with methodology led to experimentation with varying techniques for gathering hard data; the investment of great amounts of time and labor in collecting data encouraged continued exploration of the methods used and their implications. In the period between the two World Wars, fact-gathering unregulated by theory—"hyperfactualism," as I have called it elsewhere [4]—reached its peak in the social sciences as a whole.

Although the reception of scientific method in political science did not occur until after World War II, our discipline also participated in the hyperfactualism of the 1920's and 1930's, however impressionistic our techniques were. But by the time scientific method did begin to make serious inroads into political research, after World War II, political science was spared the sins of the other social sciences. It could learn from the errors of their ways.

By the end of World War II, a new era had opened up for the other social sciences: hyperfactualism had come under sharp criticism and was already on the wane. From this new spirit, as political scientists became increasingly hospitable to scientific method, we were quickly able to appreciate the dangers of strengthening our techniques of empirical research in the collection and interpretation of data without at the same time testing the relevance and significance of the results by reference to empirically oriented theory. The consequences of neglecting theory had become too apparent to be ignored. Thus, although in its prescientific period political science had had its own hyperfactual phase, it dropped this emphasis once it began to enter fully into its own scientific age.

Because political science has come under the full sway of scientific method as the so-called behavioral revolution has been taking hold [5] we have fortunately been able to develop the capacity to pursue a dual but parallel course. We have been successful in simultaneously sharpening our tools of empirical research and bolstering our substantive, theoretical understanding, at the highest conceptual levels. We have found it neither necessary nor desirable to substitute methodological discussion for theoretical contributions or to mistake rigorous fact-gathering for explanatory knowledge and understanding.

The Bond Between Theory and Research. The theoretical revolution in political science has had other vital implications for the place of theory in the structure of the discipline as a whole. From time immemorial, political theory has presumed to offer intellectual leadership within political science. For reasons recounted elsewhere,[6] as political science moved tentatively in the direction of a rigorous science

[4] David Easton, The Political System (*New York: Alfred A. Knopf, Inc., 1953*), p. 66 ff.

[5] *For a full discussion of this, see David Easton, "The Current Meaning of 'Behavioralism' in Political Science," in* The Limits of Behavioralism in Political Science, *ed. J. C. Charlesworth (Philadelphia: American Academy of Political and Social Science, 1962), pp. 1–25.*

[6] *Easton,* The Political System.

in the first half of this century (seeking explanations rather than asserting prescriptions), the preoccupation of traditional theory with moral evaluation and with the history of ideas helped to divorce the subfield of political theory from the mainstream of research in political science as a whole. Today, however, for the first time in this century, the emergence of empirically oriented theory holds out the promise that theory can begin to reassert its intellectual leadership. Even as the techniques of rigorous research are increasingly improved and sharpened, the new political theory has defined its own tasks in such a way that it seeks to provide propositions that are ultimately testable through these very techniques. Theory seeks to march side by side with empirical research.

But of even greater significance, modern theory seeks to follow in the grand tradition of moral theory. It poses fundamental questions about the nature and direction of political enquiry, even though for modern theory this means probing deeply into the nature and direction of the new scientific research as it spreads through the discipline as a whole. It is clear that modern theory has already begun to act as a major and severe solvent of the numerous unexamined assumptions prevalent in empirical research. New dimensions of political life have been uncovered; new units of analysis have been proposed; alternative over-all conceptualizations of the discipline have been invented; and new objectives for research have been suggested. Theory no longer brings up the rear, but rather seeks to act as the vanguard of research.

Modern Theory as a Link to the Basic Social Sciences. From the long perspective of history, perhaps the major contribution of this theoretical revolution will prove to be its attaining for political science a permanent place in the ranks of the so-called basic social sciences. Political science has not always been accepted in this way. In the recent past, for example, other social scientists have not only entertained strong doubts about where political science stands in the social science establishment; they have at times gone so far as to construe political science as only a discipline for the application of basic knowledge acquired by the other social sciences. For them it has been an area of applied rather than of theoretical knowledge.[7]

As a result of its new theoretical tendencies, political science, for the first time, is arriving at a full appreciation of itself as a discipline with a theoretical status equivalent in every respect to those of the other social sciences. Although in the past, political science was able to define an institutional area of interest distinct from the other disciplines, it had difficulty in showing that its understanding of political phenomena possessed a theoretical coherence as isolable as political interactions themselves. Modern theory has had to do precisely that in order to establish its own validity and justify its own existence as an area of enquiry. In other words one of the major tasks of theory has been to identify a set of behaviors that it could describe as political, and, in the process, to construct an analytic system or a theory that would help to explain the behavioral reality. A political theory is but a symbolic system useful for understanding concrete or empirical political systems.

Whether or not political theory has been successful in inventing a conceptual system that explains the operations of political systems may be debatable. But what is unmistakably clear, even at this early stage in the development of modern political theory, is that political science has become aware of its own potential theoretical

---

[7] See *Talcott Parsons*, The Social System (*New York: Free Press of Glencoe, Inc., 1951*), pp. 126–27; H. L. Zetterberg, Sociology in the U.S.A. (*Paris: UNESCO, 1956*), pp. 45–46.

autonomy, that is, of a capacity for creating its own general theory applicable to the phenomena it normally includes within its scope. In this sense, it is a basic theoretical science equivalent in every respect to the other major social sciences.

From this conclusion, we need not of course infer that, as an area of understanding, political science stands independent of the other disciplines and can therefore explain political phenomena without reference to other major areas of behavior. The interrelatedness of behavior and of most knowledge can today be taken for granted. But the assertion that political science has become a theoretically autonomous discipline does mean that we can conceptualize the subject matter of political science so that theories of political interaction will have equal status with theories of culture, the economy, social structure, and other basic modes of social interaction.

It is no longer plausible to suggest that political science is just a field in which basic knowledge acquired in other disciplines is applied for the understanding of political institutions. Rather, through the new optique of empirical theory we are able to reinforce a fundamental truth: that each discipline cuts through a unique even though interrelated aspect of social life, one that is no less "fundamental" than any other aspect in the understanding of social interaction in its entirety.

· *The Road to Integration of the Disciplines.*   A final noteworthy consequence of the theoretical revolution in political science is that it has opened the door to a new and more meaningful relationship between political science and the other disciplines. In the past, when political science enquired into the relationship between itself and the other disciplines, it was able, at the very most, to assert that it could borrow the findings and methods of the other social sciences and apply them toward a richer understanding of political phenomena. Indeed, in the older fashion, the methods of research were characteristically described as psychological, sociological, historical, and the like. In practice, little in the way of techniques was borrowed. At most, political science imported limited amounts of data and findings from the other disciplines so as to temper the assumptions upon which political interpretations proceeded. In essence, as the social sciences spun off from their parent discipline, philosophy, and as professional specialization intensified toward the end of the nineteenth century, political science, more than the other social sciences, tended to follow a separate path. It maintained its original close association with philosophy and was indifferent if not hostile to many of its neighboring disciplines. During most of the first half of the twentieth century, it almost pursued a course of splendid isolation.

But with the growth of empirical theory, political science has begun to send out new and deep roots into the other social sciences. In part, these new ties spring from the efforts of political scientists themselves to strengthen the theoretical base of their discipline.

One of the peculiar features about the development of political science, understandable because of its long connection with philosophy, is that it was unable to cultivate very much in the way of general theory from its own internal resources. We might be tempted to deny this by pointing to a single, distinguished exception—equilibrium analysis—as it emerged in the group approach to politics.[8] Even this, however, owes a great deal to sociology and its group theorists

[8] *See Easton,* The Political System, *Chapter Eleven.*

in Germany and Austria at the end of the last century, particularly as their ideas were interpreted in the United States by Albion Small and others. But aside from group analysis, which could be interpreted as more a product of pluralist philosophy than of group sociology, and therefore as a home-grown product of political science, there was very little general theorizing, of an empirical sort, within political science.

Since political science lacked a tradition from which to draw inspiration for theoretical innovation, we can appreciate why, as the scientific revolution made inroads into political science, it began to reach out to the other social sciences for help. This is particularly understandable when we look at the rapid rate of change in political science as a whole since World War II. Because of this, political science, unlike other disciplines, has lacked the time to speculate about a variety of independently generated alternatives, or to move slowly, on the basis of trial and error, toward some minimal consensus on a few selected promising approaches winnowed out of a larger body of experimentations. Rather, in retrospect, it appears that as we political scientists have searched for ways to conceptualize our discipline, we have understandably scanned the theoretical models of other scientific disciplines, natural as well as social, especially where these models helped a discipline to achieve that level of over-all self-awareness and organization expected of a maturing scientific field. If for no other reason, the combined pressures of time and necessity have imposed this strategy on us.

Through such explicit theoretical borrowing, at the very least, some interpenetration of political science with the other disciplines has begun to occur. Decision-making theories from the organizational field, the structural-functional approach from anthropology and sociology, action theory from sociology, and systems analysis from the communications sciences have offered vast reservoirs of fairly well-developed concepts and even, to a more limited extent, of theorems that have seemed cogent to students of political science.[9]

But the integration of political science with other disciplines has not been left to the initiative of political science alone. Students from the other social sciences have helped to hasten the process. And here we come upon a phenomenon strange in the annals of science. . . . Social scientists outside the field of political science itself have felt impelled to invent new theoretical devices for conceptualizing politics as a whole. Without doubt, the history of the social sciences, whenever it is written, will reveal the extraordinary nature of this influx of theoretical models into political science from adjacent disciplines. Sociologists, economists, and anthropologists, among others, have turned their skills to systematizing the study of political phenomena, at a high level of theoretical generality. . . .

There are undoubtedly many reasons why other social scientists should feel driven to do for political science what the discipline has been slow in doing for itself. Among them, the growing urgency of the political crisis in the modern world looms very large. The substitution of political for economic primacy in the United States and in most parts of the developed world could not help but impress on many social scientists the inescapable consequences of politics for all other aspects of society. In the present epoch, it has become increasingly clear among other social sciences that a minimally adequate understanding of the phenomena at the center of their own interests would be hastened if the existing knowledge

[9] *For additional comments on this, see Easton, "The Current Meaning of 'Behavioralism' in Political Science."*

of political behavior were shaped into some systematic form. Since the other social sciences had waited many decades for political science to begin to provide them with this generalized conceptualization of itself, we can appreciate why students in those disciplines should feel impatient and take matters into their own hands, even if lack of *expertise* should hamper their efforts.

Because of guild spirit in the disciplines prior to World War II, a political scientist who valued his professional honor might have cried out: "Hold! Trespassers beware! These grounds are reserved for professional political scientists alone." Although there are still some who might utter this injunction, the temper of the times has changed dramatically. We are gradually becoming accustomed to an image of ourselves as an integral part of the total scientific enterprise that pursues an understanding of man in society.

In this new spirit, since World War II many bridges have been built to link political science with the other disciplines at all levels, from the crudely empirical to the broadly theoretical. Many techniques are identical for all social science; many theorems are now shared; and even training in research overlaps. There is little of the old fear left in political science that incursions by others will result in intellectual losses. Rather, the conviction has now begun to prevail that such invasions can benefit all. There is little reason, therefore, to resist theories of politics proffered by other social scientists, simply because they bring a different kind of knowledge and *expertise* with them. This new attitude toward the increasing exchange of ideas between political science and the other social sciences receives its stimulus, then, from outside the field as well as from within.

POLITICAL SCIENCE AND THE PUBLIC

Political scientists cannot adequately describe what impact political science has had outside the profession or to what use their findings have been put. Politicians occasionally refer to the work done by political scientists. A Supreme Court Justice, talking to a group of political scientists and others recently, mentioned off-handedly that he didn't know where he would appear on a Guttmann scalogram, showing awareness of a sophisticated political science technique, and then went on to talk about the usefulness of classifying judges as "liberal" or "conservative." *Presidential Power*, by political scientist Richard Neustadt, has been referred to as a how-to-do-it book on the care and use of Presidential power (it is also extremely reputable from a scholarly point of view); its impact on President Kennedy, who relied on its author as an adviser, has been noted. The findings of students of voting behavior have had an effect on politicians, it is alleged, through advisers who read the studies looking for clues as to how to win more votes, or public relations men selling their services to would-be winning candidates. The impact on the average voter is thus indirect rather than direct, but nonetheless quite important.

The very fact of a study may have a broad impact, something the social scientist is less likely to be aware of because it is not his central concern, which is the study's scientific, not social, consequence. Because the social scientist deals with human beings, a study is not without effect on those studied. At a minimum, their attitudes about researchers are altered to some degree, with implications for later researchers, who may find themselves, for nothing they have done, either welcomed warmly or left in the cold. Questions asked by the researcher, e.g., on race relations, may start in motion a thought-process which may change the community or group studied; thus, he may be considered to have a professional responsibility to weigh the consequences of his study (insofar as he can estimate them in advance) before beginning his work.

That some of the language of the social scientist has been borrowed by journalists and others, and has had an effect on the way in which we talk about political phenomena, is clear. No election night television returns in America are now without discussion of the "ethnic vote" or the "middle-class vote." The phrase "power structure" used by sociologists in their studies of communities is a common word in the civil rights movement. Whether more than the language has been transmitted is the big question. If the language but neither the meaning of that language nor a systematic way of looking at political phenomena has been passed from the academic world to those outside it, no great changes have been brought about. In fact, Harold Lasswell argued, slightly more than fifteen years ago, that the social sciences had had very little if any impact, and that people didn't even know what a political scientist was.

What is read by those outside the profession of political science may not give them a complete picture of what is being done in the profession, and much of what political scientists are trying to say may be "lost in translation." In addition, materials written for political scientists by political scientists are often difficult for the average layman to understand, particularly where mathematics is used; this seems to bother people more than it has with respect to the physical sciences, where few expect technical papers to be understood by the layman. It can be argued that if the materials we produce do have social relevance, apart from our own intentions in the matter, we should exert more effort to provide our materials in a form so that they can be more widely used. That this problem is not true of political science alone is shown by the establishment several years ago of the periodical, *Trans-Action*. The purpose of the new venture was to rewrite technical articles of social scientists into a language which the educated layman could understand; the magazine now presents much new material, but it is still written for the same audience.

Educational television has exposed more Americans to formal political science, its way of looking at the world, and its findings, through the late Peter Odegard's presentations on Continental Classroom and a similar course series broadcast as part of the Sunrise Semester and led by Paul Tillett. Political commentators have remarked on the greater political sophistication of the American voter, to which political science may or may not have contributed. However, there is little question that the impact of political science is greater on leaders than on the "masses."

Neustadt's volume on the Presidency is one example. The adoption of program budgeting, developed in part by scholars in the area of public administration, is another. Both are examples of the impact of political science on public administration at the federal level, perhaps a function of both political scientists' alleged alignment with, rather than criticism of, federal interests, and of the more practical orientation of the public administration subfield.

Perhaps the use made of social science materials will become greater as more social scientists are employed within the government or are granted government funds to explore subjects government officials consider relevant. Until now one obstacle has been the difficulty of finding middle ground between scholars interested in developing theory and the government employee searching for operating maxims. This difficulty is accentuated by political scientists' professionalization, which has reduced the discipline's impact by not rewarding those who show a sense of responsibility for the policy implications of their work.

That political science has had a relatively limited impact on the world around it does not mean that its potential has not been recognized by many. There has been a concern that social scientists could control people, a fear about the (liberal) political tendencies of social scientists, and hesitancy about the state of development or maturity of the social sciences. However, in recent years, the picture has changed noticeably, in part because of a feeling that social scientists might be objective, to the point where

> By the early 1960's there seemed to be a general acceptance of the social sciences, including a recognition both of their status as sciences and of their utility for mission-oriented government agencies. Negative attitudes persisted and social science research programs tended to be scrutinized more closely than others by congressional committees, but social research *per se* no longer generated the disdain and suspicion it once had.[19]

However, this acceptance did not mean that those in government expect much of political science, or know what to expect. They may be simply revering from afar. But respect has been shown for the social sciences generally, and political science in particular; there have been instances where the use to which behavioral sciences have been put, but not the behavioral sciences themselves, have been criticized, and a desire to increase the level of funding for social science research has been shown by a number of legislators. They must believe something good is there, even if all do not understand exactly what. It is also clear that officials differ in the degree to which they are open to social science and to intellectual concerns. The Kennedy administration,

[19] Kathleen Archibald, "Federal Interest and Investment in Social Science," *The Use of Social Research in Federal Domestic Programs,* Subcommittee on Research and Technical Programs, Committee on Government Operations, U.S. House of Representatives (Washington, D.C., 1967), Part I, pp. 337–338.

with close ties to academia, was more likely to come in contact with political science (and therefore to have an opportunity to use it) than was, for example, the Johnson administration.

Others have noted that the social science work is there, but that its potential is not used because government officials do not know how to use it. Beals has remarked that government "lacks the administrative organization to secure such aid as it needs and it generally makes poor use of such research as it gets." [20] It has also been asserted that the administrators do not know what type of help they can expect to receive from social scientists. The lack of impact might be documented by showing cases where data relevant to the concerns of the public or its leaders existed, but was ignored. A recent example involves the alleged impact on voters in the Western United States of early election returns (and predictions of victory) broadcast over radio and television. Many suggestions have been made that such broadcasts ought to be banned until all the polls are closed, yet studies which show little if any impact are not mentioned.[21] Even if these studies were examined, a decision might still be made to restrict the early media reports, but at least the data would have been considered. However, even when data is "bought and paid for," it may not be used—or may be used only if it fits in with the policy-maker's preconceived notions, being debunked if it runs contrary to them. Thus, when a group of Stanford professors presented the results of a poll showing less support for the Vietnam war than many had previously believed to be the case, it was claimed (by the latter) that the pollers were simply trying to reinforce their (allegedly dovish) view of the war.[22]

Because of its subject-matter, which many consider inherently controversial, it has been alleged that support for political science has been restricted. For example, the reluctance of the federal government to support political science research, well after other disciplines including other social sciences like sociology were supported, was attributed by some to the fact that the government did not want itself studied. (An alternative explanation, of course, is that those providing the money did not think political science well enough developed to produce good research, a judgment voiced by some political scientists as well as by others.) Because the findings of political scientists have from time to time challenged the conventional wisdom by which we live, those supporting the *status quo* have not been overjoyed with this field of endeavor. Even the political scientist who is not immediately concerned with developing data directly relevant to a particular policy goal may have more substantial effect on the status quo than those who work to-

[20] Ralph L. Beals, Response to Inquiry, *The Use of Social Research*, Part III, p. 27.
[21] Harold Mendelsohn, "Election-day Broadcasts and Terminal Voting Decisions," and Douglas A. Fuchs, "Election-day Radio-Television and Western Voting," *Public Opinion Quarterly*, XXX (1966), 212–225 and 226–236, respectively, show no impact of the early returns, both because they weren't heard by large numbers of those who had not yet voted and because, even if heard, they did not change the voters' stated intentions.
[22] See Nelson W. Polsby, "Hawks, Doves, and the Press," *Trans-Action*, IV (1967), 35–41.

ward a particular policy goal. The latter can "be discounted almost immediately as a partisan operator," but "the institutionally detached scholar who simply reports and theorizes on what he sees, especially if he can prove it, can unintentionally undermine an entire culture." [23] However, even if the basis on which a policy or program rests can be shown to be factually invalid, people will by no means immediately accept the research findings and reject ways of operating to which they have become accustomed. As Leiserson has noted, "the authority of scientific opinion rests upon its impact upon people's experience in their everyday lives." [24]

BIBLIOGRAPHY

The materials cited in the bibliographies for Chapters 1 and 2, while not repeated here, are relevant to the matters taken up in this chapter.

BAILEY, STEPHEN K., ed. Research Frontiers in Politics and Government. Washington, D.C., 1955.

CORWIN, EDWARD S. "The Democratic Dogma and the Future of Political Science." American Political Science Review, XXIII (1929), 569–592.

CRICK, BERNARD. The American Science of Politics. Berkeley, 1959.

CROPSEY, JOSEPH. "On the Relation of Political Science and Economics." American Political Science Review, LIV (1960), 3–14.

EASTON, DAVID. The Political System. New York, 1953.

HAWLEY, CLAUDE F., and LEWIS A. DEXTER. "Recent Political Science Research in American Universities." American Political Science Review, XLVI (1952), 470–485.

HERRING, PENDLETON. "On the Study of Government." American Political Science Review, XLVII (1953), 961–974.

LASSWELL, HAROLD. The Future of Political Science. New York, 1963.

LEPAWSKY, ALBERT. "The Politics of Epistemology." Western Political Quarterly, VII (1964), pp. 21–52 of Proceedings of Western Political Science Association.

LIPPINCOTT, BENJAMIN E. "The Bias of American Political Science." Journal of Politics, II (1940), 125–139.

LOWI, THEODORE J. "American Government, 1933–1963: Fission and Confusion in Theory and Research." American Political Science Review, LVIII (1964), 589–599.

MAC PHERSON, C. B. "World Trends in Political Science Research." American Political Science Review, XLVIII (1954), 427–449.

ROBSON, WILLIAM A. The University Teaching of Social Sciences: Political Science. Paris, 1954.

SOMIT, ALBERT, and JOSEPH TANENHAUS. The Development of American Political Science: From Burgess to Behavioralism. Boston, 1967.

[23] Stephen K. Bailey, "New Research Frontiers of Interest to Legislators and Administrators," Research Frontiers in Politics and Government, ed. Bailey, p. 4.
[24] Avery Leiserson, "Science and the Public Life," Journal of Politics, XXIX (1967), 253.

SPENGLER, J. J. "Generalists Versus Specialists in Social Science: An Economist's View." *American Political Science Review*, XLIV (1950), 358–379.

TRUMAN, DAVID B. "Disillusion and Regeneration: The Quest for a Discipline." *American Political Science Review*, LIX (1965), 865–873.

WALDO, DWIGHT. *Political Science in the United States of America: A Trend Report* (Paris, 1956).

8 / POLITICAL SCIENTISTS:
VIEWS AND ROLES

Traditionalists v. Behavioralists / Teaching and Research / The
Political Scientist as Citizen / Relations with Government

We are challenged to be more systematic and scientific and at the same time
to impress students with the rightness of democracy and inspire them to participate in government. We are adjured to be high-flying theorists, to be down-to-
earth practical men sharing in our community's government, and to devote time
to workshops with high school teachers. . . . We are to cultivate real distinction in our special areas, resist narrow specialization, be stunning teachers of
sophomores, learn the use of visual aids, and be rigorous in the training of graduate students. We are to collaborate fully with sister disciplines but remain loyal
to political science.[1]

In these words, a political scientist commented on a 1950 report of an
American Political Science Association committee which had attempted to
develop goals for the political science discipline. The large number of goals
mentioned and the tone of the critic's remark suggest the lack of consensus
among members of the profession about what they should do. In fact, the
commentator went on to say that the failure of the committee to reach a consensus was less a fault of the committee "than an evidence of the present
state of political science and an index to the difficulty of the task,"[2] a more
charitable evaluation than the remark that the report "managed to face in all
directions on all issues."[3] That some political scientists are not interested in
knowing about their discipline, consensus or not, is shown by the reaction
that the internal organization of the political science discipline is "house-
keeping" and thus not worthy of attention and the unwillingness of a large
proportion of scholars to respond to an inquiry about federally financed federal research, provoking the remark that "by no means all but by all means
some among them evidently believe that government officials have a duty to
respond when a scholar asks something of them, but the scholar has no duty
to respond when officials ask something of him."[4] Despite this feeling, we

[1] James Fesler, "Goals for Political Science: A Discussion," *American Political Science
Review*, XLV (1951), 1000–1001.
[2] *Ibid.*, 1001.
[3] Albert Somit and Joseph Tanenhaus, *The Development of American Political Science*, p. 188.
[4] Harold Orlans, in *The Use of Social Research in Federal Domestic Programs*, Part
III, Introduction, p. 2.

will explore some aspects of what political scientists do and how they view their chosen profession.

Consensus? What political scientists think about their field was demonstrated more than ten years after the above-mentioned "goals" report, when Albert Somit and Joseph Tanenhaus conducted a study based on questionnaires sent to a sample drawn from the APSA directory. They documented the relative lack of consensus among members of the profession, although they did find high levels of agreement on some questions.[5] 80% of those answering felt that political scientists think of themselves only figuratively as scientists and 85% agreed that political scientists were increasingly concerned about the adequacy of the discipline's methodology. There was similar consensus on disagreement with the statement that involvement in nonscholarly activities has impeded the progress of the discipline. Over 70% thought that research was undertaken to use a specific research tool or because money was available to finance the research. 65% agreed that much of what passes for scholarship in the discipline is trivial and superficial, and an equal percentage agreed on the lack of agreement in the field about methods and techniques. There were also key issues on which agreement clearly did not reach even these levels, and on which a lack of consensus must be noted. Slightly over half the respondents felt that political scientists are unhappy about the state of the discipline. Division was almost equal between those who feel that political scientists are sophisticated about the scientific method and those who feel they are not, with 11% indicating a strong feeling that their brethren are unsophisticated in such matters. Over half thought that doctoral programs overstressed research. Slightly less than two-fifths felt not enough attention was being given to policy matters. Sharp disagreement was registered over questions concerning the development of general theory and the utility of the behavioral approach. 38% agreed and 53% disagreed that attempts to develop a general theory of politics are premature; 38% agreed and 45% disagreed that the behavioral approach cannot successfully attack significant problems of political life. These data of Somit and Tanenhaus reinforced what many observers had felt for some time and have, in many cases, decried: that political scientists' views reflect the entire spectrum of possible approaches to and views of the subject, and then some. While matters are perhaps not as severe in political science as it is said they are in French politics ("for every two Frenchmen, three political parties"), the range of positions is wide and the distribution over that range diffuse.

TRADITIONALISTS V. BEHAVIORALISTS

The adoption by individual political scientists of differing positions on the discipline's philosophical issues has probably been the chief source of di-

[5] The following figures are taken from Somit and Tanenhaus, *American Political Science: A Profile of a Discipline* (New York, 1964), Table I, pp. 14–17.

vision within the profession. The field's three major approaches—philosophical, institutional, and behavioral—came to prominence at different times, and the latter two did not gain a foothold easily. None was successful either in supplanting its predecessors or eliminating challengers. Advocates of each approach have been committed, and willing to expend much energy on internal disciplinary battles. Perhaps having been trained for so long before becoming "working members" of the political science "fraternity," they have a particularly great investment in the way they go about doing things. They take and fight for positions on issues within the discipline in much the same fashion as political partisans in the "real world" of politics, although it might seem that a profession which emphasizes the question of rationality, for example, concerning the rational voter and rational administration, might use calm discourse about the best ways in which to go about the business of studying politics.

While the "battle" is not over, the harshness of the split within departments has begun to soften. This has happened as the validity of a division of labor based on the existence of enough work for all has been recognized, and as departments, however grudgingly, have realized the need to have in their ranks those competent in behavioral techniques and familiar with aspects of the subject with which behavioralists regularly deal. While some departments, particularly in the larger universities, with the more advanced programs, have reached a balance of synthesis between older and new approaches, we still have the phenomenon of the "house behavioralist(s)," the one or more individuals hired to uphold the behavioral approach, based on the assumption that behavioralism is a sub-field of the discipline rather than an approach to it. The practice leads some behavioralists to feel that they are tolerated rather than accepted, like the "company black" hired by a business to show (token) compliance with non-discriminatory hiring practices. Certainly behavioralists often do not feel they are accepted as they would like to be, and one can easily disagree with the suggestion that their "movement" has been completely successful. Further evidence that traditional-behavioral cleavage still exists comes from a recent study, in which chairmen of Political Science Departments offering the Ph.D. degree were asked about the extent of divisiveness in their departments. Only slightly over one-quarter answered "none," almost half said "very little," one-fifth said "somewhat," and 2% said "much." [6] One can interpret this data to mean that the division is moderate; however, one could emphasize the large proportion indicating at least some friction, a proportion which is understated at least to the extent that department chairmen do not like to "wash their dirty linen in public."

The essay by William and Joyce Mitchell, "Behavioralists and Traditionalists: Stereotypes and Self-Images," which follows, gives an indication of how adherents of both the traditional and behavioral approaches have dealt with this conflict.

---

[6] Norman R. Luttbeg and Melvin A. Kahn, "The Ph.D. Program in Political Science" (mimeo, 1967), Table 3, p. 5. As noted, this does not include by far the greater number of departments in the country *not* offering the Ph.D.

"Behavioralists and Traditionalists: Stereotypes and Self-Images" °

Political scientists, students of the very human subject of politics, are human, too, when it comes to conduct within their own profession. The dedication to intellectual values and the quest for knowledge by no means sever us from the less noble needs and goals. Graham Wallas was saying nothing essentially new when he emphasized in his memorable way that politics incorporates more than a purely rational quest for public goals. So, too, must we recognize the problem of reconciling the consequences of all-too-human professional and personal needs with the more rationally-affirmed substantive goals of our science.

It is not intended, here, to discuss our professional behavior in order to "unmask" or expose "improper" motivation. Rather, it is our intention to analyze the current debates between the so-called "behavioralists" and "traditionalists" in order to show how a most unprofessional practice of "stereotyping" has taken the place of rational debate. More specifically, we wish to explore the content of the stereotypes, their sources (social and psychological), and the techniques by which stereotyping is conducted. We also intend to complement the stereotypes with the self-images of the relevant groups.

Before we begin the analysis proper, it should be said that most stereotyping in the academic world takes place not in the learned journals and books, but in private conversations over the coffee table, at departmental meetings, conventions, and in the club cars. To be sure, some sophisticated forms are found in print, especially in book review sections, but the norms of scholarship work to minimize the amount and the crudeness. Accordingly, our presentation of the content of the stereotypes and self-images will rely more upon our impressions of actual life situations than it will upon systematic data of those situations or of a detailed content analysis of printed materials.[1]

THE NATURE OF STEREOTYPING

Stereotyping is a form of behavior recognized by social scientists since Walter Lippmann's classic work, *Public Opinion* (1922), in which he described stereotypes as "the pictures in our heads." Lippmann's major concern over such behavior was its effect in limiting public rationality. He treated stereotyping as a deterrent to effective awareness and discussion of public issues, just as faulty and inadequate information were also deterrents.

In his work on prejudice, Gordon W. Allport [2] has termed stereotyping not so much as a category of perception itself, as the fixed ideas held about groups or classes of people, due to selective perception and forgetting.[3] These ideas are simplified, over-generalized and exaggerated characterizations of the category of objects perceived. They are the value-oriented type of assertion, not admitting of internal distinctions, or a minimizing of their importance.

Stereotyping is shown not to be just an innocent pastime. It serves needs of ego-defensiveness in several ways. It is a means of justifying hostility toward a group and

---

[1] *We are fully aware of the possibility that we are merely substituting our own stereotypes for those of colleagues. The reader must decide after he has read the paper.*

[2] The Nature of Prejudice (*New York, 1958*).

[3] Ibid., *pp. 187–188.*

° SOURCE: William C. and Joyce M. Mitchell, "Behavioralists and Traditionalists: Stereotypes and Self-Images." This article is published for the first time here. The "Postscript, 1968" was written especially for this volume.

the rejection by various means, of that group. Further, it reinforces the self-estimation or esteem of the person(s) doing the stereotyping. The stereotyper is not a member of the category being characterized; in fact, he is the presumed opposite —the "white" side of the well-known dichotomy. In the words of Lippmann a stereotype is

> . . . the guarantee of our self-respect; it is the projection upon the world of our own sense of our own value, our own position and our own rights. The stereotypes are, therefore, highly charged with the feelings that are attached to them. They are the fortress of our tradition, and behind its defenses we can continue to feel ourselves safe in the position we occupy.[4]

There is another function of stereotypes—one recognized by Lippmann and others—that is of great importance to the political scientist. It is the function of economy, i.e., stereotyping serves to allocate scarce time and energy for the busy political scientist.[5] Like the other professionals, political scientists are overwhelmed by work and information relevant to that work. Some kind of specialization of interest is the normal and legitimate means for reducing these demands, but it is hardly the only one, for even within a specialty it is necessary to allocate time and energies. We all devise little techniques for accomplishing this end; one of these techniques is to rely upon a set of principles for structuring the "universe." In many cases, this set of "principles" amounts to a stereotype of research. We learn to select from the multitudinous materials certain symbols, including the names of authors, jargon, and the reputation of various journals for the types of materials published. On the basis of these symbols we proceed to scan the table of contents of the latest issue of a journal and make decisions. If our stereotype is a rigid and clear one, we are also likely to utter various groans and praises for what is contained in the issue.

Still another function served by stereotypes and closely related to the first two functions was also noted by Lippmann. The world frequently appears as sheer anarchy; the only way in which it can be made understandable and comfortable is to order it in some way. A stereotype is a means of ordering, even if a distorted one. Again, we may quote Lippmann:

> They [stereotypes] are an ordered, more or less consistent picture of the world, to which our habits, our tastes, our capacities, our comforts and our hopes have adjusted themselves. They may not be a complete picture of the world, but they are a picture of a possible world to which we are adapted. In that world people and things have their well-known places, and do certain things. We feel at home there. We fit in. We are members. We know the way around. . . .[6]

Political scientists are no different from other humans in their need for a structured universe of meaning, and a sense of knowing their way around. In fact, as teachers, political scientists require an even greater amount of order, for it is expected of them that they will aid others in the building or drawing of their own cognitive and evaluative maps of the political world. And, the more one studies the more he realizes the complexities of the universe and the greater the realization of the complexity the greater the need for order. A stereotype is, then, an ordering device.

It may seem a bit exaggerated to say that ignorance exists in the profession, but

[4] Public Opinion (New York, 1922), p. 96.
[5] Ibid., p. 88.
[6] Ibid., p. 95.

in a very real sense ignorance and barriers to communication do flourish even among a generally well-educated and literate group. Departments do tend to become "inbred" and in so doing erect barriers to effective communication of truth. Many members of the profession do not know, by their own admission, very much about what behavioralism, e.g., is all about. Ignorance is increased and sustained by the reward and penalty system that works in each department, for most members and especially the younger ones capable of learning are in no economic position to challenge the entrenched, if they happen to be of the old school. And, where behavioralists dominate, they are not likely to hire traditional scholars, if they can help it. Their zeal and reforming values are too powerful. Thus, are ignorance and barriers to learning created and sustained.

Stereotyping is likely to increase wherever the minority group is either large or increasing, or both. On the basis of impression this would seem to hold in our field as well as in racial and religious situations. The departments in which the feud is hottest are those in which the traditionalists and behavioralists are fairly evenly matched in numbers. Where but a single-member minority is found, the fight is unequal to begin with and not worth fighting, for either side. In fact, in such a case, the minority may have been hired in the first place for window-dressing. So long as he does not pose a threat, which is unlikely, he will remain welcome. "Some of my best friends are behavioralists," or "traditionalists" as the case may be. In the profession as a whole, the number of behavioralists is increasing, and while they are still a minority, it is a powerful one. As such its power may even be exaggerated as is the case with certain religious and racial minorities.

It hardly requires proof that direct competition and realistic threats exist over the distribution of positions in political science and the allocation of article space in the journals. Traditionalists and behavioralists may be interested in and competent in different areas, but they compete over which areas are to be stressed in the form of jobs, income, and research funds. The number of battles over such problems are considerable and occur in almost every department and journal office, as well as within the foundations. No doubt some of these fights are given more attention than they are due, but they are real and not imagined. As such, and even were they exaggerated by paranoids, they still serve to increase prejudice and stereotyping, if for no other reason than the fact that the disappointed must find a rationalization.

As we have suggested above, there are a variety of social and cultural devices to ensure loyalty to the group. Both the behavioralists and traditionalists employ these devices, largely in an unconscious manner. The very language each uses tends to structure the situation against the other fellow and the continual interaction of members of the same school tends to reinforce prejudices as each repeats the same slogans to his colleagues. We all are too familiar with the endless social gatherings in which shop-talk takes the form of lambasting the silly work of someone else. And, we are all too familiar with the endless nodding of heads in agreement. Birds of a feather flock together and in flocking together they breed the same old stereotypes.

No doubt many political scientists believe that variety is the spice of research and intellectual life, but many, when it comes to hiring and firing and promotion policies, are not apt to believe in assimilation or cultural pluralism. At best, but one of the other "camp" will be hired because it is the fashion just now. And, life may be made miserable for him as he is forced to be self-reliant and defensive. A real belief in advancing knowledge by all methods is not widespread, for such a belief is a fundamental one and not easily accepted by most men, even the most humble and generous. It is for this reason that behavioralists are not evenly distributed throughout the universities of the country. They tend, rather to concentrate at particular campuses where one of them managed to come into control. We have here a similar condition to that found in the voting studies where Republicans tend to talk only to Republicans and Democrats to Democrats.[7] The in-group talk further confirms attitudes and prevents the fruitful meeting of minds across group lines. Each group is blamed for not understanding the other, but they seldom have the opportunities to confront one another except in the cold pages of a journal issued every three months. The time-honored dialectical method seldom really comes into practice in the professional world of political science. And, when it does, neither party to the controversy is likely to know how to participate and so arguments of the fruitless methodological type predominate and discourage further discussion.

THE STEREOTYPE OF THE BEHAVIORALIST

The traditionalist stereotype of the behavioralist, like all stereotypes, contains elements of ridicule and humor; and, like all stereotypes it has elements of a far more serious nature that express, more openly, the fears of the traditionalist—fears that the newcomer may be right, but that in any case he appears to have vertical mobility or greater opportunities. And, like all stereotypes, portions are correct or reasonably accurate; but, again, like all such images much is distorted, exaggerated and generalized. All behavioralists are not alike as only behavioralists know so well.

The image of the behavioralist is, of course, intended to be a derogatory one. What is not achieved in substance is achieved through stylistic means. This image is also a confused one, i.e., contains contradictory elements or assertions, some of which simply are untrue. But, contradiction and confusion are no obstacles to the development and perpetuation of the ideas.[8] The major elements (beliefs and labels) can be easily summarized. We do not claim that the following listing is complete or accurate in the sense of containing all the possible variations on the theme, but we do believe it representative. Terms such as the following suggest and convey the behavioral stereotype:

- obvious
- pretentious
- trivial
- dangerous
- fad or vogue
- jargoneering
- meaningless

- deterministic
- "what have they done?"
- "what about values?"
- "neo-scholasticism"
- pseudo-science
- positivistic
- model-builders

According to the traditionalist, the behavioralist is some of these "things" and guilty of all of them. He is a victim of the latest fad, that of numbers or statistics and jargon. While this vogue holds sway for the moment with the foundations and some professional organizations, its day will be short and political science will return to sanity. The behavioralist is engaged in a great numbers game, literally and figuratively; in the former instance he seems to believe that nothing is meaningful unless it has been "reduced" to statistics or equations. In the figurative sense, he is a con-man for he confounds the innocent, especially businessmen, with his special form of magic and mumbo-jumbo.

[7] Bernard R. Berelson, et al., Voting (Chicago, 1954), pp. 88–117.
[8] Allport, pp. 190–191.

A stereotype not only suggests positive characteristics, but certain negative ones as well. The behavioralist is not supposed to be a very literate person, nor is he supposed to be interested in "ideas," "values," "history," "individual" events and persons. This leaves out not only the most interesting aspects of life for the traditionalist, but the most important. Even if an exception to the case is pointed out, it is still argued that his methods are ill-suited to elicit the truth. Political science has the great resources of its past and need not depend upon the sister social sciences, most of which are held in contempt in any case. Political science is idiographic and value-bound. The behavioralist does not seem to recognize this fundamental fact and therefore goes wrong.

The traditionalist tends also to believe that the behavioralist is pretentious, even as he goes about dealing with trivialities, commonplace observations and jargoneering. Indeed, it is the jargon which allows the behavioralist to deceive himself and some others. Behavioralists are seldom given credit for any "insights" or "understanding," favorite terms of the traditionalist. About all that they provide are collections of definitions, endless models of unrealistic assumptions and complexities, and meaningless correlations about insignificant matters. The behavioralist cannot, according to this image, have insight because he treats men as mechanical entities, motivated by interests and not values and norms.[9]

The charge of jargoneering is a crucial and popular one, not only with reference to behavioralists, but with all the behavioral sciences. Jargon is, according to the traditionalist, not only unnecessary, but misleading and unaesthetic as well. Jargon makes for unpleasant reading, and worse, it misleads in that it encourages the careless reader to believe that something is actually said. Nothing is added to the body of political science but more definitions. Hans Morgenthau in reviewing Lasswell and Kaplan's *Power and Society* claimed that the definitions "are obviously either platitudinous, circular, or tautological, and at best, convey information which Aristotle would have taken for granted." [10] About the only remark one ever hears about Talcott Parsons from a traditionalist is that he is incomprehensible and cannot write a simple sentence. Additional comments about behavioralists and their schemes and language usually note that little of it is or can be applied to real-life situations.

Traditionalists also seem disturbed by the brashness of the young behavioralist who parades around his recently acquired competence in the tools of research as though no one had come before him. The behavioralist seldom acknowledges his indebtedness to the great tradition; in fact, he sometimes gives the appearance of being unaware of it, or so say the traditionalists. Few kind words are ever spoken of past scholarship. Thus, one searches, almost in vain, through two recent works, March and Simon's *Organizations,*[11] and Downs' *An Economic Theory of Democracy*[12] for references to the great traditions of public administration and political theory. If references are made in behavioral productions, they are usually critical or at best condescending. Traditionalist thinkers are hardly so inclined to dismiss the past.

[9] *The point has been made countless times. For a representative statement see Louis Hartz, "The Problem of Political Ideas," Approaches to the Study of Politics, ed. Roland Young (Evanston, 1958), pp. 78–87.*
[10] *Hans Morgenthau, "Reflections on the State of Political Science," Dilemmas of Politics (Chicago, 1958), p. 20.*
[11] *James G. March and Herbert A. Simon, Organizations (New York, 1958).*
[12] *Anthony Downs, An Economic Theory of Democracy (New York, 1957).*

STEREOTYPE OF THE TRADITIONALIST

The behavioralist's view of his more traditional colleagues is no more complimentary than the latter's image of the former. While the behavioralist is quite likely
to be impatient with the emotive descriptions of traditional work, he is highly emotional and eloquent concerning the failures of the traditional school. We can cata-
logue the elements of his stereotype with the same ease as that of the traditionalist.
When the "Young Turks" want amusement or a morale-building activity they are
prone to attack their colleagues by calling them:

- sloppy and imprecise
- literary
- unsystematic
- legalistic
- reformer

- untheoretical
- historian
- impressionistic
- metaphysical

Like the traditionalist and all stereotypers, the behavioralist generally treats his
objects as undifferentiated, although he will make room for two sub-types, for neither of which he has much respect. The two are: the "brute empiricists" and the
"theorists." Different labels and criticisms are voiced of each, but both are unscien-
tific in approach and methods. The brute empiricists are those political scientists
who collect facts about everything but behavior. Typically, the behavioralist believes that these facts are of a legalistic and historical kind, interesting, but of little
value in constructing a science. When the behavioralist considers such matters he
also enters a protest against the giant, impressionistic, value-laden studies in which
entire societies are described and analyzed.

While the empirical scholars are treated rather badly, they are at least commended for their sensitivity to reality. It is the "theorist" who comes in for the
greatest contempt. The "theorists" are special targets of the behavioralist because
they meet so few of the behavioralist's criteria, but also because it has been the
"theorists" who have done battle more often and more vehemently with the new approaches. The behavioralist tends to believe that the "theorists" are really historians
and not builders of theory, even of the type done by their heroes, the great philosophers. The historians have themselves preferred to be called theorists and describe
their work and courses as theory. Whatever they do, the behavioralist sees them as
idle speculators about human nature, "navel-gazers," and essayists. They are regarded as primarily interested in recording the uniqueness of the world, values, and
not in the construction of a scientific body of empirically verified propositions. Their
search for "meaning," "insight," "essences" are regarded as old-fashioned and even
primitive. And, nothing bothers the behavioralist more than the language of the traditional scholar. In a well-known debate between Herbert Simon and Dwight
Waldo [13] some years ago, Simon observed that

> . . . I do not see how we can progress in political philosophy if we continue to
> think and write in the loose, literary, metaphorical style that he [Waldo], and
> most other political theorists adopt. The standard of unrigor that is tolerated in
> political theory would not receive a passing grade in the elementary course in
> logic, Aristotelian or symbolic.[14]

[13] "Development of a Theory of Democratic Administration: Replies and Comments,"
American Political Science Review, XLVI (1952), 494–503.
[14] Ibid., 496.

In the work of the theory man, "facts" are confused with "values" and logical with empirical proofs, according to the behavioralist. The behavioralist is inclined to believe that theory students act more as a debating club in which the trappings of learning are considered the major criterion of work. Since traditionalists, generally, are unfamiliar with the use of modern tools of analysis and computing machines, the behavioralist feels they know very little. In any case, their contribution to science is nil.

The tendency of the theorists to deal in the "big" issues and to do so with little regard for the boundaries of empirical and logical inference amuses and occasionally irritates the behavioralist. Even so modest and traditional a scholar as V. O. Key, Jr., has commented on this tendency. In the Foreword to *The Voter Decides*, Key, in an appreciative mood, notes: "At point after point the scholar of speculative bent will observe that the authors have stonily ignored opportunities to soar out through the boundless blue in imaginative explication of the possible immediate or future significance of particular bits of data." [15] Further on he writes, ". . . it can only be said that habituation to explicit methods of analysis tends to dampen intellectual boisterousness." [16] Key's deadpan humor points out significant elements of the behavioralist's image—their feeling that traditionalists do not discipline their imaginations by the use of rigorous conceptual schemes, empirical propositions, tests of validity and reliability. The traditional scholar would rather coin a moving sentence, a sweeping generalization, a plea for some course of action. In crude terms, the traditionalist is sloppy where behavioral research is concerned, although he may be meticulous in his scholarly references and documentations.

Interestingly, the behavioralist stereotype is not based on the same rigorous standards he admires in the abstract or imposes on traditional work. The stereotype is just that—an impressionistic, value-oriented, selective, and over-generalized portrait of his colleagues. Nevertheless, the stereotype is a fact of behavior—the behavior of behavioralists.

THE STYLE OF STEREOTYPING

Stereotypes, especially in the academic world, cannot be detected solely, if at all, by their content. This is so because stereotypes are based, to some extent, upon reality. What makes a stereotype most apparent is the manner in which it is derived and expressed. In the world of daily affairs, stereotypes are likely to be rather crude, but in the world of the intellectuals, they are frequently very sophisticated, and conveyed with great verbal skill. This must be the case, for the intellectuals, and this includes most political scientists, place a high premium on both truth and verbal facility or dexterity.

Stereotyping among political scientists is generally done via the use of parody, satire, burlesque, and the derisive remark.[17] The juxtaposition of quotations, the use of frequent quotation marks, and, above all, in the conversation, the precise little intonation of the voice, the smile, the doubt, the amusement, and the query are standard means.

Still another means of conveying one's image of an approach is to expose its

[15] *Angus Campbell*, The Voter Decides (*Evanston, 1954*), *pp. xii–xiii*.
[16] Ibid., *p. xiii*.
[17] *The point has been made with respect to intellectuals, generally, by Bennett M. Berger, "Sociology and the Intellectuals: An Analysis of a Stereotype,"* Antioch Review, *XVII* (1957), 275–290.

origins. Traditionalists are particularly fond of tracing the pedigrees of ideas; this is done to embarrass the behavioralist—to show that everything worth saying has been said before.[18] Likewise, to expose origins is to cast doubt on the truth of the assertion and its range of application. Since a part of the traditional stereotype of the behavioralist is the unoriginality of his ideas and their very limited applicability, this means of stereotyping is especially popular.

Behavioralists have their favorite techniques, too. The usual means is to point up the confusion of the traditionalist by demanding that he operationalize everything he says, and since traditionalists frequently do not know what the word means, or accept such a definition of meaning, they are embarrassed.

Stereotypes are created and communicated for the most part under conditions that minimize respect for truth, but which maximize sophisticated talk and criticism. Style is of the utmost importance for it serves to disarm, amuse, and provide quotable labels. The norms of the genteel academic tradition serve to reward the clever and so stereotyping is encouraged.

SELF-IMAGES

The "reciprocal" of a stereotype is a "self-image." By knowing the contents of one we can better understand the contents of the other and their interrelationships. A stereotype, we have argued, serves to economize, provide meaning and order, and ego-maintenance, as well as to create and sustain group morale. Self-images serve similar functions for the individual and group, but do so in a more positive sense by focusing attention on the self rather than the other, the "out-group," as the stereotype does invariably. Self-images may not be complimentary, but even so, some kind of identity is established and it is this identity that interests us. Of course, the self-image may not be clear-cut, nor very secure and stable. But, in the cases we are dealing with they tend to be both clear-cut and stable and firmly held.

If one's self-image is firmly based and realistic, the tendency to indulge in vicious stereotyping is not likely to be very great. But, if self-doubts and hatred enter, the probability of stereotyping as well as other asocial actions is much greater. The insecure cannot afford the luxury of group and individual differences; for him, conformity is a necessity and stereotyping a means of reducing and handling unwelcome distinctions. While a major distinction among groups is established, all the minor differences within the groups are obliterated.

While self-images generally relate to one's total life pattern and experiences, a substantial part of the image stems from the work a person performs and the rewards he acquires therefrom. This work identification is, perhaps, inevitable in a work-oriented society such as the American. The academic profession shares in this ethic of work. Political scientists have self-images distinct from the other social sciences, and they also have a set of images within their profession and some of these, perhaps the most important ones, relate to one's methodological approach to the study of politics. Thus, political scientists, today, are likely to identify themselves with respect to this methodology and refer to themselves as either traditionalists or behavioralists.

The behavioralist image tends to be somewhat more clearly drawn than the traditional; the reason is simple, for the behavioralist is a kind of "revolutionist" and therefore very self-conscious of his rebellion and differences with the representa-

---

[18] See Andrew Hacker, "Capital and Carbuncles: The Great Books Reappraised," American Political Science Review, XLVIII (1954), 775–786.

tives of the "status-quo." The traditionalists lack the same self-awareness for they have long accepted the order and see little reason to question its foundations. But, the challenge is making the traditionalist aware of himself and what is at stake. It is interesting to note that most of the methodological writings and the best ones are done by the behavioralists. They see differences and attack them, while the traditionalist has been forced to defend himself. But, we may expect that a traditionalist will, in the near future, produce a first-rate methodology of his position that will command much attention. Just as Mannheim noted that political necessity forces the conservative to become articulate, so the methodological challenge of the behavioralists will force the traditionalists to become more articulate about their values and norms.[19]

The behavioralist generally sees himself as the opposite of the traditionalist as pictured in the stereotype. Thus, the behavioralist likes to see himself as precise, neat, logical, systematic, empirical, theoretical, and above all, scientific. He sees himself as a kind of "heretic," a "pioneer," a member of an exclusive group, united by its difference and special vocabulary and symbols of science. He sees himself the reader of esoteric journals that are beyond the comprehension of the traditionalist.[20] He likes to see himself as "doing things," of being "hard-nosed," and in command of his variables and methods. And, he loves to speak the language of mathematics and research, particularly before an audience of traditionalists, or of practical men of the world, businessmen, and military officers at the Pentagon. The behavioralist wants to be a scientist, but a practical one in order to demonstrate his competence.

Traditionalists, likewise, consider themselves the opposite of their antagonists. The traditional scholar, if he is a theorist, likes to see himself as a humane man of letters, a product of and a conveyer of the great truths of the past and of great men. He prides himself on being acquainted with and perhaps competent in good writing, the kind of writing one finds in classic literature. He likes to think of himself and his particular heroes as having "understanding," "insight," "feeling for," and "sensitivity" to life and politics. What counts is not an elegant equation, a complete research design, an accurate sample, but an insight, or profundity or depth of understanding. Usually this means a comprehension of the ideas and ideals that men have held and expressed in beautiful language that moves the reader. What interests the theorist is the "condition of man" with all its paradoxes and ironies. What interests the behavioralist is the elimination of these "paradoxes" and "ironies" which are only products of hazy thinking and unoperational ways of research. If the traditionalist is enamored of the more mundane branches of political science such as local government or parties, he is likely to see himself as more realistic than the theorists, because they are so metaphysical, but also to see himself as more realistic than the behavioralist because the latter is a model-builder and has never even met a real-life politician or worked in an election.[21] The brute-empiricist is frequently a man of action, unencumbered by the apparatus of science and prides himself on direct acquaintanceship with the facts of life, rather than through the artificial concepts and methods of the scientist. Like the theorists, in many cases, the brute empiricist really believes the world is made up of unique events and personalities and that a science is impossible. The brute empiricist really tends to think that he studies poli-

---

[19] Essays on Sociology and Social Psychology (*New York, 1953*), p. 106.
[20] Behavioral Science *and* Econometrics *are good examples.*
[21] *The business of research or doing things out in the field is noted by Andrew Hacker,* "Political Behaviour and Political Behavior" Political Studies, *XII* (1959), 32–40.

tics, while the behavioralists, because they have been so influenced by sociology and psychology, no longer have contact with "politics." Politics they say has been eliminated from the voting studies, for example, as well as the study of administration.

We noted above that elements of doubt may enter the self-image. Doubts have come to be more frequent among the traditionalists than the behavioralists for the simple reason that the latter have not been around long enough to experience them. The attrition rate among traditionally educated scholars appears far greater at present, but perhaps, in the distant future we will hear confessions of error from the behavioralists. The status-quo is bound, whether in politics or the academic world, to experience the greater number of deviations for the sources of dissatisfaction are to be located there, while the promises of utopia come from outside and are beyond immediate check. Behavioralism is still largely a utopian venture; as it develops, its limitations will become more apparent, and the movement will lose its emotive appeal. As revolutionists become administrators, so behavioralists will become working rather than crusading scientists. And, behavioralists will then come to have doubts, doubts which can be publicly admitted without embarrassment as happens in mature sciences. At present, the behavioralists, fighting for recognition, must present a self-image of supreme confidence. Such are the self-images of the behavioralist and traditionalist.

POSTSCRIPT, 1968

When we first wrote this essay, we were still graduate students and the "behavioral movement" was well under way at the major institutions across the land. Today, that issue has subsided and the behavioralists have prevailed. In the words of Robert A. Dahl, it has been a "successful protest," rather than a genuine full-scale revolution. The victory is symbolized by the fact that most of the leading political scientists are behavioralists, several leading political science journals now carry mostly behavioralist-inspired articles and research notes, and the heated methodological arguments of a decade ago are seldom heard. In place of the latter we hear technical discussions concerning the improvement of research tools.

While the behavioral revolution is now over, change has not stopped and a new orthodoxy set in; indeed, important shifts may be noted in both the subject-matter of research and theory, and the tools of analysis. For example, whereas the early behavioralist specialized almost exclusively in the study of individual beliefs, norms, values, and attitudes (mostly of Americans), behavioral work is now showing increasing concern for *interaction* and *system level* problems. The earlier behavioralism could not easily describe and explain the workings of entire systems such as nation-states, nor the international system simply by "adding up" attitudes of individuals. No matter how well done, such analyses could not cope with such system level problems as the allocation of resources, distribution of benefits and costs among a populace, nor how and why political systems change or remain stable through time. The great processes of interaction—competition, bargaining, coalition-formation, hierarchy—require analysis of behaviors other than the attitudinal properties of the actors. Contemporary research is manifesting far more concern for these problems.

As the questions have shifted from the micro- to the macro-level, political scientists have found it necessary to adapt their methods. Whereas simple descriptions and statistical techniques served well for the early studies it now becomes necessary to employ more sophisticated analysis to handle vastly greater numbers and combinations of different variables. Various mathematical models have become the prototype, in forms derived from game theory, economics, communication theories, and the more experimental approaches in psychology.

Not all political scientists, including behavioralists, will welcome these drastic changes, for they come, as do all things, with varying threats and costs. Some political scientists will behave in response to these changes as did the behavioralists and anti-behavioralists in earlier battles; there are indications this is already the case, except that now many older behavioralists will join the defensive "resistors." Again, it is not easy to "retool," but the rejection of the new can be rationalized in stereotypical terms, with such labels as "inhuman," "abstract," "mechanistic," "useless," or "esoteric." Yet younger recruits to the profession will find the newer approaches increasingly attractive, and, to a great degree, will find pleasure in the discomfort of the elders, whom they may in turn view as "crude empiricists," "simple-minded quantifiers," as well as "ritualistic traditionalists," and the like.

More significant, however, are the broader effects on professional performance, in terms of recruitment, training, and the distribution of rewards. Again, there is a training gap, for the new skills can seldom be taught by those who earned their degrees in political science. With a few notable exceptions, the new generation of scholars must acquire their special training from other disciplines, and the recruitment of talented personnel from the other relevant professions will increase, both at the beginning graduate level, as well as for teaching and research staff. The competition will be felt keenly by the student who has invested in the conventional political science now dominated by older behavioralists. In major and crusading institutions, the structure of rewards thus shifts. We are beginning to see dramatic offers and promotions for that relatively small minority able to apply the new approaches to political subjects, as well as new societies and journals, even research centers and programs catering to the futurists. And the structure of prestige rewards has subtly shifted, too. This new political analyst finds his "great men" more frequently in the other disciplines: Arrow and Boulding, Converse and Coombs, Buchanan and Diesing, Lazarsfeld and Guttmann, Blalock and Black—to name but a few from outside, as compared to the lonely crusading "natives," Simon and Riker, whose books can stand alongside the contributions of these many others.

But there is another issue cutting across this professional divide which may serve to pluralize the profession, rather than further stratify or polarize it. It is more a public and collective issue, which divides both the new and older professionals, and challenges their self-images and roles from another perspective. First, it concerns the nature of the professional commitment, whether to theoretical and technical gains for the sake of "pure knowledge," or to public applications and uses. Secondly, it involves the reference group: are the supports and rewards for performance expected from fellow professionals, or from public officialdom and political groups? Thirdly, it entails the choice of channels of communication and arenas of performance: does one choose to address one's professional peers, or see his ideas and findings used in the "political marketplace"? In all, it is an issue of professional activism or insulation, and secondly, one of support or dissent in terms of the established system. The issue divides the profession in new ways—and also brings together formal professional antagonists. Because they are related to great public issues, war and civil rights especially, the passions stirred can intensify divisiveness, but may also be quite productive in terms of the talents joined on particular problems. Some of the new analysts serve the Defense Department or join its "think tanks," while others join peace research societies and publish in such issue-oriented media as the *Journal for Conflict Resolution*. In contrast with the consultancies and conferences of our older behavioral "elites," one finds the newer breed as willing to experiment in political action groups as in the simulation laboratory. And the older humanists have now the choice of devoting their life to the great thinkers and classics, or re-evaluating the issues of the day as to how revolutions and violence, civil disobedience and mass appeals, relate to the concepts of peace, freedom, order, and justice.

However events may unfold, and they do much to shape political science, it would seem that the next decade will be as exciting as the past one. Students entering political studies can now look forward to a vital and far more politically relevant and sophisticated political science than has heretofore been the case.

TEACHING AND RESEARCH

The Conflict.   Another division has been over the appropriate weights to be given to teaching and research. For many years, political science was predominantly a profession of teachers and government administrators. While political scientists did write books and articles, this activity was carried on as a "sideline;" however, as the necessity for empirical studies began to be accepted within the discipline, this began to change. Research was no longer an armchair sport but required large amounts of time and financial assistance. With the development of the behavioral approach, the issue was even more clearly defined. A number of foundations, particularly the Ford, Carnegie and Rockefeller Foundations, began to provide massive financial assistance for research efforts. In addition, the Social Science Research Council (SSRC), composed of the principal professional organizations in the fields of anthropology, economics, history, political science, psychology, sociology, and statistics, provided funds for projects in particular areas, such as political behavior and comparative government. As the availability of these funds stimulated more research, it became clear that additional courses were going to be needed.

At the same time the necessity for research in the study of politics was recognized, research came to be considered more important within the academic community. Much of the reason for this was external: the result of government funds for research. It has been said that "governmental participation in social science research, at the university end, shows little understanding of the priorities of universities." [7] Thus, in the words of the same critic, "N.S.F. [National Science Foundation] and all the other research agencies of the federal government are together contributing measurably to the bureaucratization of higher education in America." [8] The absence of a substantial number of well-established commercial organizations in the social science research field meant that "the expanded Government activity in

[7] Alfred DeGrazia, "The Government in Behavioral Science: Some Critical Notes," *The American Behavioral Scientist*, VII (1964), 26.

[8] Alfred DeGrazia, Response to Inquiry, *The Use of Social Research*, Part III, p. 75.

social science research was exceptionally heavily concentrated in the universities," although it would be difficult to agree that "the social science staffs of many universities have been flooded, some overwhelmed, by the inflow of research from the Federal Government." [9] All this money did tend to mean another kind of shift of balance, with the selection of research problems on which to work changing from the social scientist to the government, which had the money. This came about because social scientists working on the more highly technical problems required funding of a sort which could be provided by agencies wanting the researcher to study public issues. It has also been suggested that government research sponsorship overemphasizes certain methods of research. And, particularly in earlier days when a heavier proportion of research conducted on university campuses was Defense Department-sponsored, research was often classified, with resultant restrictions on its publication, although university administrators generally resisted controls over freedom to publish results. Such restrictions would fly in the face of the "open" character of scientific research. Another complaint is that basic research may be sacrificed to more immediate, problem-centered or "action-oriented" research. And this orientation is supposed to pull political scientists away from research into "political engineering." As Pool recently noted, "more and more political scientists are becoming not just detached observers . . . but also participant technicians in the management of public action." [10] Lest these distortions be overemphasized, it should be pointed out that far less of university research in the social sciences is financed by the federal government than is true with respect to university research as a whole (including physical sciences), although the social sciences are more rapidly increasing their "take" from federal research funds than are the natural sciences.

Increasing emphasis on research has been reflected in the idea that professional competence was to be shown through conducting research and having the results published in professional journals or books, known as "publish or perish." If jobs do not depend on publication, promotion and salary increases may. Perhaps publications are easier for administrators to measure than is the quality of teaching, but there is considerable agreement that the present system is one providing lesser rewards for the best teaching. According to Somit and Tanenhaus, political scientists rank, in descending order, the following factors contributing to career success:

- volume of publication
- school at which doctorate obtained
- connections
- ability to get research support
- textbook authorship
- luck or chance
- school at which first job is held
- self-promotion
- teaching ability.[11]

[9] Alex Inkeles, Testimony, July 19, 1966, *Hearings:* "Federal Support of International Social Science and Behavioral Research," Subcommittee on Government Research, Committee on Government Operations, U.S. Senate (Washington, D.C., 1967), p. 182.

[10] Ithiel De Sola Pool, "Foreword," *Contemporary Political Science: Toward Empirical Theory* (New York, 1967), p. xii.

[11] Somit and Tanenhaus, *American Political Science*, p. 79.

The behavioralists, with their heavy emphasis on research, have thus made a virtue of necessity.

Research Positions.   The lack of full-time research positions in the social sciences has helped compound the research v. teaching problem. In the physical sciences, a large number of full-time research jobs, either in industry or with the federal government, are available. Someone primarily interested in research and not wishing to teach can often find a job to suit his interests. If he wishes to teach full-time and not do any research, his situation is more difficult, as the expectation of research-*cum*-publication may be difficult to avoid. But in the social sciences, if you want to do research, you must take a teaching job. The growth in government research jobs has been primarily for "in-house research," and jobs have generally gone to economists, sociologists, and psychologists, not to political scientists. In any case, they are not jobs involving the opportunity to perform "basic research," at least if some immediate payoff is not foreseen. A number of schools have been able to develop jobs involving a combination of teaching and research, usually in connection with an institute or bureau for the study of governmental affairs.

These bureaus had their origin in the American reform movement, as the movement began to give great attention to the way in which municipal functions were performed. The New York Bureau of Municipal Research, established in 1906, was the first. Despite close ties to the academic community, bureaus were not formally part of it until 1909 at the Universities of Wisconsin and Kansas. Bureaus seemed to fit in well in the universities, because they implied such things as research, service to the community, libraries, and training, all to be carried out objectively. When the number of bureaus increased considerably between the two World Wars, their focus shifted to include higher levels of government, and research interests broadened in terms of other types of subject-matter as well. In addition, they were less closely tied to extension divisions and took on a new role in public service training. By 1960, however, the movement had lost most of its steam, and existing bureaus had no single common pattern, although they were still strongly service-oriented. Because of this orientation, the work they have done has been extremely detailed with very little theoretical apparatus, and has often consisted of consulting with local governments on proposals for new programs or governmental reorganization. However, the research bureaus at a few of the state universities have recently begun to share personnel with Departments of Political Science instead of relying solely on state or local government technicians. Research bureaus will to some extent be supplanted by the growing number of specialized study institutes, on such topics as national security policy, urban affairs, transportation, and area studies, the emphasis of which is on basic research rather than constituency-oriented effort.

The lack of a large number of research positions and the relative unavailability of research money has meant that most research has been done on an individual basis, frequently on an "as-time-is-available" basis. Political scientists are an individualistic lot and do not like to work together on research projects, but they can hardly work together on large projects, even if they want to, in the absence of support. There has, surprisingly, been some co-operative research even under these conditions, sponsored by the founda-tions. The study of the 1952 Presidential nominating conventions, conducted by Paul David and others, is one example.[12] The Fund for the Republic un-derwrote a major study of Communism in American Life, but this was more a series of individual studies than simultaneous cooperative research by sev-eral individuals.[13] The Study of Congress (now in progress) funded by the Carnegie Foundation is of the same genre. A study of legislators in four states has indicated what is possible in regard to cooperative research,[14] and Harold Lasswell has argued in favor of a broad project he calls the Basic Data Survey, which would involve political scientists and their students across the country in a collective venture.

Types of Researchers. "Researcher" has so far been treated as a neatly defined, homogeneous category. It is not. For one thing, political scientists vary in the relationship between their work and that already done in the field. Several styles of researchers can be identified, of which the two basic ones are "pioneer" and "mopper-upper." The first characterizes the individ-ual whose work is always at the forefront of the profession; he is constantly embarking on forays into previously unexplored areas, not remaining in one place long enough to do more than indicate that the field is worthy of study. He then seems desirous of moving on to another area. The following descrip-tion of Lasswell is illustrative:

> Professor Lasswell is . . . not a settler, he is a pathfinder and a border scout. He has either led in person nearly every migration into the "field" in con-temporary political science or else the project-leader has borne his authenti-cated charts, and also his passports to tribes and disciplines along the route. He has blazed the trail for small armies of settlers, but, as the wagons stop moving and the ploughs are dragged out, he always gallops off to yet more virgin soil. . . . He leaves us dazed by the many accounts of the many border-lands he has explored for a while, but his general direction is always the same, the West of Science. . . . His movements do become a little bewildering for those who want not merely to do "research," but to do research with the latest concepts and the newest tools. They are apt to appear outmoded before they have had time even to unpack.[15]

The work of men like Lasswell, through whom the profession is probably best known, accounts in some measure for the impression that the field is rel-atively uncoordinated and even incoherent. The pioneers strike off on their own, away from other political scientists and away from other pioneers as

12 Paul David, Ralph Goldman, and Richard Bain, *The Politics of Presidential Nomi-nating Conventions* (Washington, D.C., 1960).

13 Among the books in that series are Theodore Draper, *The Roots of American Com-munism* (New York, 1957), and Clinton Rossiter, *Marxism: The View from America* (New York, 1960).

14 John Wahlke, Heinz Eulau, William Buchanan, and LeRoy Ferguson, *The Legisla-tive System* (New York, 1962).

15 Bernard Crick, *The American Science of Politics*, pp. 180–181.

well. However, the amount of new territory to be explored also helps to account for the relatively large proportion of "pioneers" in relation to more "pedestrian" researchers.

The work done by the "pioneer" creates the need for another type, the "mopper-upper." However inelegant the title may sound, his is the important function of studying an area which a pioneer has laid open to view, of mining the ore about which the pioneer has told us, thus producing the real "pay-off" from an area of research. In addition, he may show that what the pioneer thought was useful needs much reworking before it will produce any results. The research situation for political scientists is generally such that small, limited projects, ideal for the "mopper-upper," are encouraged instead of work on a broad scale. Lasswell himself notes that in the physical and biological sciences, individual researchers are not tied to a single target, but are given elbow room; they can explore general problems, and research support contains a margin for such general exploration. He argues that political scientists don't have the self-confidence to adopt this approach, but even if they did, grant-giving agencies might be reluctant to go along.[16]

At times, because of the publicity which the pioneer receives, other researchers may feel that unless they develop a new field or an "original" set of findings, they are (relative) failures. This is not so; no profession could operate without both types of researchers. Nor could it be productive without still other types. Somit and Tanenhaus, noting the recognition given to those who develop new tools or concepts, spell out the value of those who bring order into a field (the "systematizers" or "synthesizers"), those who serve to help others on toward new findings (the "catalyzers"), and those who disseminate knowledge to students (the "textbook-writers").[17] Not all are researchers, but all play a large part with respect to the initiation of research and the uses to which it is put after it is conducted. If the results of research tasks are to be utilized in the development of theory, the work of the synthesizers is necessary; at their best, their consolidation sparks new hypotheses. If the research already conducted is to be made known to future generations of scholars so that they may decide in which direction they are to move, writers must be able to communicate to them.

Teaching.   Even if a political scientist says that he is only a teacher, that does not resolve all problems, because the teaching role is not easily defined. Some professors choose to keep their values as far outside the classroom as possible, except perhaps for the values that knowledge is good and that politics is worth studying. While, as private citizens, they may be concerned about their students' present or ultimate political views and participation, as professors they do not consider it their job either to encourage or discourage political participation or the holding of any set of specific views. This view runs counter to the position that the educational institution has among its functions the instilling of "proper" values in the student and instruction in

[16] Harold Lasswell, *The Future of Political Science*, p. 149.
[17] Somit and Tanenhaus, *American Political Science*, pp. 67–69.

"citizenship education." While it is clearly understood that primary and secondary educators bear the greatest responsibility for these functions, and that public institutions of higher education might be expected to do it more than private ones, the issues are never distant, particularly for political scientists, who from their profession's beginning, have taken on the task of transmitting knowledge of our government and the basic elements of patriotism. The expectations of clientele, both state legislators and parents, reinforce (or perhaps, in some cases, cause) the views of the political scientists.

Minimally, educators are expected to deal with "important" issues even if they do not indoctrinate. And not only are certain issues thus brought to the fore for teachers of political science to cover in their classes, but certain aspects of government and politics also gain dominance. Thus, the argument goes, the student should know about registration requirements, forms of the ballot, the two-party system, how Congress operates, and what the President does, as well as forms of municipal government, so that he can cope with the world of politics when he reaches the age at which he is legally allowed to participate fully, although he need not be made a specialist. Political scientists are also expected to help train students to run the government, either as public administrators, city managers, or foreign service officers. That a broader understanding of the political system as a whole might allow the student to grasp better the political world around him generally does not occur to the non-academic advocate of citizenship education, who may not really be sure he trusts "education for education's sake." That he is not sure is shown by the attacks which come when professors are alleged to have taught things with which the individual citizen disagrees or which he feels run counter to his (and, by extension, the country's) most deeply held values.

That citizenship education has led to attacks on political scientists, on the field itself, and on academic freedom within universities, seems clear. However, rejection of citizenship education will not still attacks on political science. Social scientists in general, and political scientists in particular, have been most often among those subject to infringements on academic freedom. That the attacks made, particularly during the period of "McCarthyism" in

McCarthyism.   A generic term used to refer to attacks on the political beliefs and associations of individuals, including wide-spread labelling of beliefs considered unorthodox as "leftist," "pink," and "Communist." The term derives from the activities of the late Senator Joseph McCarthy (R-Wis.), although many other individuals and groups were (and are) involved.

the 1950's, have caused political scientists to become more cautious in what they have said and done is quite clear, and has been well documented.

Lazarsfeld and Thielens, in a 1955 study of a cross-section of social science professors, wrote that "American social scientists felt in the spring of 1955 that the intellectual and political freedom of the teaching community had been noticeably curtailed, or at least disturbingly threatened." [18] 63% of those responding to the study felt a greater threat to intellectual activity in America than a generation before, and 79% thought there was greater concern by the public and groups outside the classroom with teachers' political views and with political matters taught in the classroom than six or seven years previously. Two-thirds of those who said that the public was showing greater concern felt it to be harmful. Lazarsfeld and Thielens also noted that the type of ideas attacked had changed—they were political rather than religious, evolution having been a point of major controversy in earlier years —and the scope of ideas attacked was greater.

That outsiders initiating attacks are not the only ones influencing the atmosphere is also clear; hesitation and anxiety resulted from the willingness of some college and university administrators to respond to the attacks, not in defense of the rights of the faculty, but in support of those making the charges against the faculty. One author has written that college boards of trustees "foster timidity and caution, not independence and a critical spirit," and that the position of the faculty member is not a secure one, economically or otherwise.[19] Lazarsfeld and Thielens found that the better the school, the more the administration did to defend the social scientists' academic freedom. This was particularly important, because it happened that attacks occurred more frequently at better institutions of higher education.[20]

A fact which is important is that many political scientists are *not* the subject of attack, rather than that a certain number are. The amount of disagreement within the profession on matters like approaches to the study of politics is not also found concerning the values of the society. Instead, "the political order has been 'accepted.' . . ." [21] While being a true political scientist does not automatically make one unpopular with the powers-that-be,[22] the political scientist honestly going about his work must face up to the possibility that his findings will irritate the existing "power structure."

Undergraduate Programs.   Because of the extremely high percentage of political scientists in academic life, and because of their involvement in teaching, a presentation of the field of political science must include at least a brief discussion of political science in our colleges and universities. A recent study indicates a total of almost 500 independent political science departments, with over 300 additional departments in which political science and some other discipline were combined.[23] While certain common patterns do

[18] Paul F. Lazarsfeld and Wagner Thielens, Jr., *The Academic Mind: Social Scientists in a Time of Crisis* (Glencoe, Ill., 1958), p. 37.

[19] Benjamin Lippincott, "Political Theory in the United States," *Contemporary Political Science*, p. 137.

[20] Lazarsfeld and Thielens, p. 166.

[21] Dwight Waldo, *Political Science in the United States*, p. 17.

[22] See, for example, Hans Morgenthau, "The Purpose of Political Science," *A Design for Political Science*, ed. Charlesworth, p. 63, and the discussion following, pp. 80–145 *passim.*

[23] Somit and Tanenhaus, *The Development of American Political Science*, p. 145, extrapolating from Committee on Standards of Instruction, American Political Science Association, "Political Science as a Discipline," *American Political Science Review*, LVI (1962), 418.

exist in political science programs, there is much which is fuzzy about what should be included at the undergraduate level and a lack of clarity about what is to be expected from graduate students. As one commentator noted, "it does little good to insist on the unity of our subject if we have no concept of the minimum qualifications of a political scientist or of the proper scope of an undergraduate major program." [24] Such programs and the way they are structured have been roundly criticized by some leading political scientists in recent years. A long-time department chairman at a Midwestern university has written that "an extraordinary amount of guesswork, personal prejudice and highly personal judgment is allowed to determine what is contained in courses of political science," [25] a judgment affirmed by Lasswell in his comment that the field is "populated by professors who enjoy courses full of descriptive detail, semi-rigorous legalisms, and semi-defined affirmations of preference on questions of public policy." [26] Lasswell also has alleged that political science departments do not appeal to first-rate and creative students because the departments are "highly pedestrian when evaluated in intellectual terms," a point echoed by Apter, who argues that the best students "often tend not to go into political science, but into those disciplines where a genuine body of research theory is emerging." [27]

A principal reason why the undergraduate program suffers from lack of clarity and is frequently a collection of courses rather than a major with an underlying rationale is a tradition of long standing giving professors virtual independence concerning teaching methods and course content, coupled with conflicts over goals to be achieved from teaching. Should students be "taught to think," that is, to exercise their own initiative in going about the solving of problems? Or, in the alternative, should they be taught the conceptual schemes which are current in the discipline at the time? The difficulty with taking the latter approach is that what is taught may then become out-of-date or inapplicable to new problems, even if it serves a training function. Perhaps the fundamental problem is the cleavage between "understanding" and training as principal goals. The conflict between the development of understanding of things political and training for public careers is not automatic or foreordained; it depends on the type of training involved. In Britain, where training for the public service, particularly at the higher levels, has meant a broad background in a number of subjects, the conflict is minimal. However, American training for the public service is not usually aimed at producing generalists ("amateurs" in the British sense) but at instilling technical information and skills in would-be administrators, thus bringing the conflict to the surface.

Another sort of training in which the political scientist is involved is teacher education. Because many college graduates, particularly at state-supported institutions of higher education, enter teaching at the elementary and

[24] Fesler, 1000.
[25] Walter H. C. Laves, "Goals for Political Science: A Discussion," 1017.
[26] Lasswell, p. 170.
[27] David Apter, "Theory and the Study of Politics," *American Political Science Review*, LI (1957), 748.

secondary levels, political scientists have been given the responsibility of preparing them to teach grammar school and high school social studies. As social studies courses at the high school level have generally been only descriptive and institutional in orientation, with affirmation of key societal values as an underlying purpose, preparation of students to teach these courses has often meant the propagation of material not at the heart of the discipline's current concerns and not in keeping with the newer approaches in the field. While efforts are now being made to transmit newer views of political phenomena and while students preparing for teaching are now more likely to be studying a standard undergraduate political science curriculum, the problem has not been fully solved.

Graduate Training. While undergraduate education continues on its more or less (dis)organized basis, graduate study in political science has been growing greatly in size in recent years and has received increased attention. Somit and Tanenhaus noted an increase in the number of Ph.D. degrees granted, from 464 in the 1943–1949 period to 1289 in 1950–1956, as well as an increase in the number of schools granting them; the ten schools giving the largest number of degrees accounted for 60% of those degrees in 1936–1942, but only 53.5% (608 of 1137) in 1957–1962.[28]

Graduate education in any field is a period, more or less long, in which students who wish to attain the status of "professionals" within the field undergo serious and intensive training, during which time they are brought to share existing methods of looking at the phenomena of the field in which they are studying and during which they acquire additional facts and theories to use in their later work. As Somit and Tanenhaus point out, "graduate education . . . has two quite different objectives," transmission of subject matter and inculcation of values, beliefs, and roles connected with the field.[29] This is why it is said that "the whole purpose of scientific training . . . is to produce a particular kind of conformity in the scientific community." [30]

Which goals will be emphasized within graduate training is in large measure a function of the views of universities' graduate faculty. Berelson, examining all the social sciences, found that those instructing in the social sciences at the graduate level give highest value to training college teachers. Doing basic research was weighted less highly, and both training professional practitioners and doing applied research ranked far behind. While proportionately more of those questioned thought the balance within graduate education should be more toward research than thought it should be toward teaching (37% and 16% respectively), 43% thought the two should be balanced or about equivalent. On the other hand, 63% thought the balance *was* more toward research; 15%, more toward teaching; and 18% about equivalent. In specific mention of political scientists, Berelson found that 48% of the graduate faculty in political science were dissatisfied with graduate training in their

[28] Somit and Tanenhaus, *American Political Science*, pp. 29, 30.
[29] *Ibid.*, p. 162.
[30] Eugene Meehan, *The Theory and Method of Political Analysis*, p. 81.

field, the most dissatisfied group except for economists. Only 6% of graduate faculty political scientists described the present state of their discipline as very satisfactory, and only 13% of then-current recipients of graduate degrees were similarly inclined, in both instances the lowest level of all fields examined.[31]

In a recent study, Luttbeg and Kahn, interested in factors related to the orientation of political science Ph.D. programs, found that more chairmen in departments offering the Ph.D. viewed their departments as behavioral than saw them as traditional, but relatively few felt their programs were strongly committed in either direction.[32] Of the various subfields, American Government and Politics was felt to be the most behaviorally-oriented, with Public Law and Political Theory the least so directed. Luttbeg and Kahn found little relationship between the quality of a department, as measured by the American Council on Education's 1966 assessment,[33] and whether its program was behaviorally- or traditionally-oriented.

In terms of graduate curriculum, the researchers found that behavioral areas (Use and Limits of Scientific Method, Empirically Oriented Political Theory, Political Science as a Discipline, Empirical Research Methods) were required more frequently than traditional areas (Legal and Historical Research Methods, Philosophically Oriented Political Theory, History of Political Thought). Behaviorally-oriented departments tended to require behavioral subjects in addition to rather than instead of traditional subjects. It is also interesting to note their finding that schools of higher reputation imposed fewer course requirements.

Luttbeg and Kahn found a relatively high degree of attrition among those entering the Ph.D. programs, but also found that relatively little of this attrition was initiated by the departments. They found, not surprisingly, that the dissertation was the biggest hurdle to be cleared by Ph.D. candidates. The median figure for completion of the program was four-and-one-half years.

THE POLITICAL SCIENTIST AS CITIZEN

Part of academic freedom is the freedom to pursue knowledge. Another aspect—the right to participate in the local community on the same terms as everyone else—brings us in touch with another of the political scientist's roles, that of citizen in the community. At times, those political scientists who advocate a value-free social science abjure political participation even "off-the-job." Others are willing and even eager to participate actively in politics, but try to keep this part of their life separate from their academic life. Still

[31] Bernard Berelson, *Graduate Education in the United States* (New York, 1960), pp. 46, 205–212.
[32] Norman Luttbeg and Melvin Kahn, "Ph.D. Training in Political Science," *Midwest Journal of Political Science*, XII (1968), 303–329.
[33] Allan M. Carter, *An Assessment of Quality in Graduate Education* (Washington, D.C., 1966).

others believe that the knowledge of politics they have as political scientists and the objective manner they use in looking at political phenomena can be beneficial to their communities, and perhaps even feel an obligation to contribute that knowledge and skill. Mulford Sibley has even suggested the development of a specialized role, that of the professional politicist, who would bridge the gap between theoretical and practical, and assist the citizen in decision-making.[34] There has also been talk in political science (although less than in sociology and anthropology) of applied social science to bring together pure social science and government officials.

There has been a tendency, perhaps stemming from the days of the reform movement, for political scientists to participate in politics. For example, "perhaps two-thirds of those initially appointed to the offices and standing committees of the American Political Science Association had already been, or were soon to become, more than casually involved in public affairs." [35] The temptation to help provide leadership when existing leadership is seen as weak is apparently more than many political scientists can resist. (And if they wish to participate, they can easily convince themselves of the weakness of the leadership.) If they do not run for office, they may work for local organizations supporting the values they hold or they may offer expert advice. For example, a political scientist well versed in the operation of federal agencies might assist a community in attempting to obtain federal grants. It has been claimed that very few political scientists have not served as an adviser, formally or informally, to some community group at some time in their careers.

Whether being a political scientist does give one an advantage in politics is an open question, which many answer in the negative. However, regardless of the answer, whether he *should* be able to participate is a real issue in many places. Certain views, even if somewhat out of conformity with prevailing values, may be acceptable when discussed on the campus, but become anathema to both the public and, in some instances, college administrators, when discussed "in public." The administrators fear the wrath of the trustees and the fund-giving alumni; the public seems to feel that those who receive their pay from the public ought to keep quiet if they cannot mouth views consonant with those of the current majority.

In addition to the matter of fearful townspeople or timid administrators, there is a question of professional responsibility. If a person who is a political scientist talks about politics, he may be expected by his profession, as well as the general public, to act in a "responsible" manner, that is, to recognize that what he says may be given extra weight because people know he is a political scientist. There is general agreement among teachers' associations that an individual professor should make clear that he is not speaking for an institution if he happens to use his institutional affiliation for purposes of identification. Nor should he let his argument extend beyond his evidence or attempt

---

[34] Mulford Q. Sibley, "The Limitations of Behavioralism," *The Limits of Behavioralism in Political Science*, ed. Charlesworth, p. 89.

[35] Somit and Tanenhaus, *The Development of American Political Science*, p. 43.

to appear to be speaking on the basis of sound, verified knowledge when in fact there is no such information to support his position. This issue is clearly not one involving only political scientists; all teachers, particularly at public institutions, and all government employees are affected.

A question remains as to the pay-off for the political scientist *as a political scientist* from his community participation. The profession has accepted the fact that research of high quality can be performed by political scientists who have not themselves participated in politics; however, such participation may serve as a corrective against "wild goose chases" in research and give the researcher a clearer picture of a portion of political reality than he would receive only through interviews, questionnaires, and even observation.

RELATIONS WITH GOVERNMENT

Even if not involved in political activity, the political scientist may have working relations with government. These are basically of three types—as employee, as consultant, and as beneficiary of research grants.

Employee. Many political scientists have participated in the government service as full-time employees, on either a temporary or career basis. The New Deal programs of President Franklin Roosevelt brought the first major influx of political scientists to government as rapid expansion of the government provided many new administrative positions and many New Deal programs fit the sympathies of many political scientists. The influx continued with World War II. Until then, government officials did not know what political scientists were, or suspected that their contributions would be abstract and irrelevant to the work of government. An APSA committee indicated in 1942 that political scientists were not competing successfully for appointments and were not being recognized in job descriptions. The disadvantage was attributed to the fact that "too few political scientists have got around enough to make themselves attractive to operating chiefs. Appointing officers prefer men who have demonstrated their prowess off the campus." [36] The idea held by political scientists that having taught public administration courses proved their competence for administrative tasks simply was not accepted in Washington. As the years have passed, and more recently with the development of the "New Frontier" and "Great Society," more positions which political scientists could fill have opened.

That political scientists should participate in government as administrators, even in periods of national crisis, has not been totally accepted by political scientists themselves, although "not until the post-1945 period did a sizable segment of the profession begin seriously to reflect on the possible incompatibility between the scientific pursuit of knowledge and participation

[36] Committee on War-Time Services, American Political Science Association, "The Political Scientist and National Service in War-Time," *American Political Science Review*, XXXVI (1942), 933.

in programmatic and applied policy undertakings." [37] However, even before the end of the war, it was recognized that active participation in government was not the only way in which the discipline could serve the country. The APSA Committee on War-Time Services indicated that "the primary task of the political science profession, other than that of teaching young people, is to provide specialized thinking on public affairs," and asserted that political scientists could serve their country "by carrying on systematic inquiry and disciplined thinking upon the more critical issues that face the country." Political scientists could do this by giving up "the customary individualism of the profession," which the committee considered "a luxury that cannot be maintained in war-time." [38] Establishing priorities in scholarly work, the assumption of more training for the public service, and attempts to reach a broader audience (beyond the classroom) would also be necessary.

Despite these comments, another APSA committee noted that while considerable use was being made of political scientists within the government, far less use was being made of those who remained on the campus.[39] William Anderson, then APSA president, argued that better service to the nation, as well as to political science, would come when political scientists held positions close to, but outside the government. Writing during the war, he felt that "the science of politics is already suffering because so many of our able colleagues are so much engaged in doing public work"; what particularly upset him was that the time of these men was often being taken up with "routine and unimportant work." [40] More recently, a political scientist has taken an even stronger stand. George Blanksten has argued that when a social scientist gives up his own terms and accepts those of an employer, he does a disservice both to his discipline and his employer.[41] This does not mean that all political scientists who work for the government automatically lose their professional integrity, but that they must guard against giving up their work standards as social scientists.

In addition to serving as administrators, political scientists have helped restructure the government. The President's Committee on Administrative Management, composed of three political scientists headed by Louis Brownlow, in 1937, made recommendations for providing the President with needed staff, thus leading to the growth of the "modern Presidency." Political scientists helped conduct the basic studies for the two Commissions on the Organization of the Executive Branch (known as the "Hoover Commissions" after their Chairman, former President Herbert Hoover). More recently, political scientists have served as aides to Presidents: Malcolm Moos

[37] Somit and Tanenhaus, *The Development of American Political Science*, p. 45.

[38] Committee on War-Time Services, 939, 940.

[39] Committee on Research, American Political Science Association, "War-Time Priorities in Research," *American Political Science Review*, XXXVII (1943), 505–514.

[40] William Anderson, "The Role of Political Science," *American Political Science Review*, XXXVII (1943), 10.

[41] Statement, Panel on Ethics in Research, Midwest Conference of Political Scientists, Lafayette, Indiana, April 28, 1967.

in President Eisenhower's administration and Richard Neustadt and Richard Goodwin in President Kennedy's are examples. Generally, however, the appointment of political scientists to positions in the top levels of the administration is more the result of political activity than their skill as political scientists. A number work for the Congress, as staff assistants to Representatives and Senators or on the staffs of legislative committees.

Despite an increasing amount of "lateral entry" into the government service or "horizontal mobility" between government and academic life, there has not been the smooth transition between university life and the upper levels of government true in England, where a number of Oxford and Cambridge "dons" have held cabinet positions. However, despite the increasing number of openings in government, the proportion of political scientists in academic life has increased in recent years, at government's expense, from 60% in 1953 to 70% in 1961, with the rise continuing during the 1960's.[42] Perhaps the principal reason that more political scientists are not involved in government work of any type is that the outlook of the academician and of the decision-maker are dissimilar. Bailey has put it well:

> The real hiatus between scholars and decision-makers is not that one deals with generalizations and the other with specifics. Every specific decision is based on a multitude of general working propositions. . . . The differences . . . are to be found in the respective environments in which they operate, the speed with which knowledge must be synthesized and applied, the degree of immediacy of value considerations, the degree of explicitness of assumptions and logic, and the nature of respective attitudes toward the use of language.[43]

Perhaps this explains why political scientists-turned-administrators (whether government, university or private) act more like administrators than like political scientists. Their work as political scientists is sufficiently different from that as administrators that they generally bring little from the former to the latter.[44] In addition, there has been a separation between researchers and "doers" in government. There has been little bridge from the former to the latter except for situations where policy researchers study day-to-day problems, e.g., in the State Department and the Council of Economic Advisers. The idea of research leaves for policy-makers or policy-observation posts for scholars, to reduce the gap, has not taken hold on a large scale, although the Civil Service Commission has instituted programs for advanced academic work for government employees and has provided some temporary positions for academically-based political scientists.

Consultant. A role which the political scientist has been occupying with increasing frequency in recent years, primarily at the federal level, is that of consultant. Political scientists in academia may not wish to work full-time for the government but may be willing to provide their expertise under some

---

[42] Somit and Tanenhaus, *The Development of American Political Science*, p. 8.
[43] Stephen K. Bailey, "New Research Frontiers," pp. 5–6.
[44] I am indebted to Victor Thompson for this insight.

other arrangement. From the government's point of view, knowledge can be expanded without having to increase the full-time payroll, and having leading academicians performing consulting services is a way of gaining prestige. Some political scientists, like some academicians in other fields, spend a large proportion of their time in consulting work. The story is told of the professor involved in so much consulting that he was teaching only one seminar. He was asked by the government to undertake another consulting job, and his dean agreed when the professor said he would tape material for the remaining class. One day, the professor-consultant was on campus when the class was supposed to meet, and decided to attend. He found sixteen tape recorders "listening" to his tape recorder.

In some circles within political science, it is alleged that a continuing consultative status creates a potential conflict of interest for the political scientist which makes it awkward for him to study certain areas or to produce research findings offensive to the agency with which he has a relationship. It is also alleged that those desiring consultantships may "fudge" their work to improve their eligibility for such positions. While the Devil's Advocate, the question-asker, the "Abominable No-Man" is considered by many to be needed at various stages of the policy-making process, government officials may be unwilling to have him, particularly as a consultant. And it is easy to argue in response that those who compromise (or prostitute) their work for the government would do so even in the absence of the consulting relationship. However, the fact that the government does have the money and the positions to hand out, coupled with the fact that the positions can contribute honor to the individual and the institution with which he is affiliated, does create a potential problem requiring extreme care on the part of both the individual political scientist and the government which is using his services.

A controversy which developed in early 1967 illustrates the problems which can be created by the greater involvement of political scientists in government, with increased use of an "in-and-out" pattern. Under an endowment from the Kennedy Library established at Harvard University, an Institute of Politics was set up within the newly-named John F. Kennedy School of Government. The Institute's Director, Richard Neustadt, had worked closely with President Kennedy. The purposes of the Institute were to create a new intellectual source for the use of future government officials and to break down the isolation of academia vis-à-vis the federal bureaucracy. Exposure of undergraduate students to people who had worked in the government was to be another benefit. A British reporter, Henry Fairlie, raised the issue of whether the real purpose behind the Institute was to provide a manpower pool for use by the late Robert Kennedy in his supposed pursuit of the Presidency, as many of the first Fellows of the Institute were former members of the Kennedy and Johnson administrations. He also suggested that the Kennedy family would control the Institute.[45] Needless to

[45] Henry Fairlie, in *The London Sunday Telegraph*, January 15, 1967. The article was carried as "Is Harvard's Institute of Politics a Kennedy Recruiting College?" *The Boston Globe*, January 15, 1967, pp. 4–5.

say, the Harvard administration denied the allegations, pointed out that former Eisenhower staff men were also Fellows, and went on to say that they
did not think that government and the universities should be kept separate.[46]
"The University will of course continue to put first priority on the advancement of knowledge," Dean Price wrote.[47] "But in its professional schools . . .
it will surely continue to work toward the use of basic knowledge for applied
purposes." Whether one shared Fairlie's suspicions or agreed with Harvard's
point of view, the issue existed. There is no question of government funds
here, but the controversy would not have come about had there not been the
interchange between the formerly "ivory tower" university and the "real
world" of daily government. It is quite difficult for the university, like Cae-
sar's wife, to keep its reputation for unsullied knowledge intact under such
arrangements; the university's product may be untouched, but the reputation may not be.

  Government Support of Research.   While the government until recently
has not been in the business of supporting research in the social sciences, this
is no longer the case. With the establishment of the National Science Foundation (NSF) after World War II, the government began to provide money
to individual researchers, usually within a university setting. The grants
awarded by NSF were primarily in the physical sciences, although some social science awards were made, primarily to sociologists. Only in the last several years, after considerable effort by political scientists, has the NSF begun
to provide even limited research funds for political scientists. When the NSF
was first established, in 1950, the social sciences were included within its
domain as "other sciences," but on a permissive basis: NSF did not have to
support them. (By comparison, the National Defense Education Act of 1958
placed no limitations on disciplines.) In 1958, an Office of Social Sciences
was created within NSF, and, in 1960, this Office was elevated to Division
status. But, at least until 1964, when many restrictions on political science
were removed, this increased formal status for social scientists meant largely
increased status for sociologists, economists, and psychologists. Even in Fiscal
Year 1966, of 47 grant applications received (with a value of $1,937,000), only
17 grants of $335,650 were activated, with 15 more ($612,400) in process at the
end of the period. By comparison, 125 grants in anthropology (value: $3,981,-
890), 51 in economics ($2,345,210), and 83 in sociology and social psychology
($3,658,600) were activated in the same period.[48] In 1968, Congress did
amend the NSF Act to include the social sciences (including political science) among those fields explicitly designated for support. Excuses by NSF
officials for the low funding of political science in relation to other social sciences included those that political science had not been sufficiently scientific
until recently, and few grants were made because few proposals were re-

<hr>

[46] Fred Pillsbury, "Behind the Smiles, Shock and Anger at Harvard," *The Boston
Globe,* January 18, 1967, pp. 1, 6.
  [47] "Harvard Rebukes Critic," *The Boston Globe,* January 19, 1967, pp. 8–9.
  [48] National Science Foundation, Annual Report, Division of Social Services, Fiscal
Year 1966; reprinted in *The Use of Social Research,* Part I, p. 149.

ceived. However, "the Foundation's policies and procedures simply were not designed to induce on the part of political scientists the confidence, trust, and expectations that would lead to the submission of proposals. . . ." [49]

In addition to NSF, some other federal agencies, such as the Public Health Service and the National Institutes of Health, have provided some social science research money, but, again, usually not to political scientists. The recent interests of the Department of Health, Education and Welfare have led to some grant money from that source, but the funds are minimal in terms of what those conducting research consider necessary.

Proposals were made in Congress starting in 1966 to establish a National Foundation for the Social Sciences which would provide substantially greater amounts of money for research than had previously been available. One of the matters which brought considerable attention to the need of the social sciences for adequate research funds was government involvement in research projects abroad. The government had for some time sponsored in-house research, particularly in the area of national security, and each branch of the military establishment sponsored an organization, like the Air Force's RAND [Research and Development] Corporation and the Defense Department's Institute for Defense Analysis, to perform objective research on topics of interest to the services. The Army had its Operations Research Office and the Navy its Operations Evaluations Group. Despite continuous argument about the possible distorting effects of military sponsorship, the relationship between the sponsoring organization and the researcher was at least fairly clear. And it was clear in the case of other research directly contracted for by the government to an individual or a university, although the possibility of being involved in research the results of which had to remain classified existed. Then, shortly after the American intervention in the Dominican Republic, it was found that the federal government had been involved in some research projects in Latin America which on the surface appeared to be conducted by social scientists performing legitimate independent study but which were related to military interests and were done under contract from the Department of Defense. Given the sentiment of many Latin Americans toward the United States government, the reaction to discovery of the situation was severe. From the point of view of social scientists, the results could easily be disastrous, making it difficult for them to conduct research abroad because they would not be able to convince people they were not a front for some government agency.

The project which served as a catalyst for a thorough discussion, both in and out of government, of the problems involved in social science research abroad was Project Camelot, discussed here by Irving Louis Horowitz. Those who reacted to the procedures by which Camelot and related projects were carried out felt that if overseas research were "civilianized," part of the

[49] James D. Carroll, "Notes on the Support of Political Science Research Projects by the Division of Social Sciences of the National Science Foundation, Fiscal Years 1958–1965," *The Use of Social Research*, Part IV, p. 94.

problem would be solved. The problem of research "mining" of another country, in which political scientists come for a few months, collect data, and leave with all their data, would still exist, and wounds left by this "intellectual colonialism" are not easily healed. President Johnson's 1965 directive to the Secretary of State, that all overseas social science research conducted by military, foreign affairs, and intelligence agencies should be cleared so as not to interfere with or embarrass the conduct of United States foreign policy, did not please many social scientists, particularly those who took a dim view of the State Department's cautious attitude toward anything new.

With the possibility of increased funds to support research go certain problems, such as government regulation of research or the possibility that research into certain subjects might not be approved. Political scientists might well be concerned about the latter, in view of the earlier reluctance of the government to support political science research, and in view of such actions as the requirement that the Bureau of the Budget "clear" all questionnaires to be administered to ten or more people, if the questionnaires are sponsored by the government, i.e., carried out under contract, usually at the government's request. The imposition of research procedures not presently required by present grantors of funds is also bound to produce resentment within the social science field, perhaps as much because social scientists are independent and like to have only self-restraint instead of externally-imposed limitations as from a feeling that the specific procedures imposed are improper.

"The Life and Death of Project Camelot" *

In June of this year—in the midst of the crisis over the Dominican Republic—the United States Ambassador to Chile sent an urgent and angry cable to the State Department. Ambassador Ralph Dungan was confronted with a growing outburst of anti-Americanism from Chilean newspapers and intellectuals. Further, left-wing members of the Chilean Senate had accused the United States of espionage.

The anti-American attacks that agitated Dungan had no direct connection with sending US troops to Santo Domingo. Their target was a mysterious and cloudy American research program called Project Camelot.

Dungan wanted to know from the State Department what Project Camelot was all about. Further, whatever Camelot was, he wanted it stopped because it was fast becoming a *cause célèbre* in Chile (as it soon would throughout capitals of Latin America and in Washington) and Dungan had not been told anything about it—even though it was sponsored by the US Army and involved the tinderbox subjects of counter-revolution and counter-insurgency in Latin America.

Within a few weeks Project Camelot created repercussions from Capitol Hill to the White House. Senator J. William Fulbright, chairman of the Foreign Relations Committee, registered his personal concern about such projects as Camelot because

* SOURCE: Irving Louis Horowitz, "The Life and Death of Project Camelot," *Trans-Action* (November–December, 1965), 3–7, 44–47. Copyright © 1965 by Washington University, St. Louis, Mo. Reprinted from *Trans-Action* Magazine by permission of the author and the editors.

of their "reactionary, backward-looking policy opposed to change. Implicit in Camelot, as in the concept of 'counter-insurgency' is an assumption that revolutionary movements are dangerous to the interests of the United States and that the United States must be prepared to assist, if not actually to participate in, measures to repress them."

By mid-June the State Department and Defense Department—which had created and funded Camelot—were in open contention over the project and the jurisdiction each department should have over certain foreign policy operations.

On July 8, Project Camelot was killed by Defense Secretary Robert McNamara's office which has a veto power over the military budget. The decision had been made under the President's direction.

On that same day, the director of Camelot's parent body, the Special Operations Research Organization, told a Congressional committee that the research project on revolution and counter-insurgency had taken its name from King Arthur's mythical domain because "It connotes the right sort of things—development of a stable society with peace and justice for all." Whatever Camelot's outcome, there should be no mistaking the deep sincerity behind this appeal for an applied social science pertinent to current policy.

However, Camelot left a horizon of disarray in its wake: an open dispute between State and Defense; fuel for the anti-American fires in Latin America; a cut in US Army research appropriations. In addition, serious and perhaps ominous implications for social science research, bordering on censorship, have been raised by the heated reaction of the executive branch of government.

GLOBAL COUNTER-INSURGENCY

What was Project Camelot? Basically, it was a project for measuring and forecasting the causes of revolutions and insurgency in underdeveloped areas of the world. It also aimed to find ways of eliminating the causes, or coping with the revolutions and insurgencies. Camelot was sponsored by the US Army on a four to six million dollar contract, spaced out over three to four years, with the Special Operations Research Organization (SORO). This agency is nominally under the aegis of American University in Washington, D.C., and does a variety of research for the Army. This includes making analytical surveys of foreign areas; keeping up-to-date information on the military, political, and social complexes of those areas; and maintaining a "rapid response" file for getting immediate information, upon Army request, on any situation deemed militarily important.

Latin America was the first area chosen for concentrated study, but countries on Camelot's four-year list included some in Asia, Africa, and Europe. In a working paper issued on December 5, 1964, at the request of the Office of the Chief of Research and Development, Department of the Army, it was recommended that "comparative historical studies" be made in these countries:

- (Latin America) Argentina, Bolivia, Brazil, Colombia, Cuba, Dominican Republic, El Salvador, Guatemala, Mexico, Paraguay, Peru, Venezuela.
- (Middle East) Egypt, Iran, Turkey.
- (Far East) Korea, Indonesia, Malaysia, Thailand.
- (Others) France, Greece, Nigeria.

"Survey research and other field studies" were recommended for Bolivia, Colombia, Ecuador, Paraguay, Peru, Venezuela, Iran, Thailand. Preliminary consideration was also being given to a study of the separatist movement in French Canada. It, too, had a code name: Project Revolt.

In a recruiting letter sent to selected scholars all over the world at the end of 1964, Project Camelot's aims were defined as a study to "make it possible to predict and influence politically significant aspects of social change in the developing nations of the world." This would include devising procedures for "assessing the potential for internal war within national societies" and "identify(ing) with increased degrees of confidence, those actions which a government might take to relieve conditions which are assessed as giving rise to a potential for internal war." The letter further stated:

> The US Army has an important mission in the positive and constructive aspects of nation-building in less developed countries as well as a responsibility to assist friendly governments in dealing with active insurgency problems.

Such activities by the US Army were described as "insurgency prophylaxis" rather than the "sometimes misleading label of counter-insurgency."

Project Camelot was conceived in late 1963 by a group of high-ranking Army officers connected with the Army Research Office of the Department of Defense. They were concerned about new types of warfare springing up around the world. Revolutions in Cuba and Yemen and insurgency movements in Vietnam and the Congo were a far cry from the battles of World War II and also different from the envisioned—and planned for—apocalypse of nuclear war. For the first time in modern warfare, military establishments were not in a position to use the immense arsenals at their disposal—but were, instead, compelled by force of a geopolitical stalemate to increasingly engage in primitive forms of armed combat. The questions of moment for the Army were: Why can't the "hardware" be used? And what alternatives can social science "software" provide?

A well-known Latin American area specialist, Rex Hopper, was chosen as director of Project Camelot. Hopper was a professor of sociology and chairman of the department at Brooklyn College. He had been to Latin America many times over a thirty-year span on research projects and lecture tours, including some under government sponsorship. He was highly recommended for the position by his professional associates in Washington and elsewhere. Hopper had a long-standing interest in problems of revolution and saw in this multi-million dollar contract the possible realization of a life-long scientific ambition.

THE CHILEAN DEBACLE

How did this social science research project create a foreign policy furore? And, at another level, how did such high intentions result in so disastrous an outcome?

The answers involve a network spreading from a professor of anthropology at the University of Pittsburgh, to a professor of sociology at the University of Oslo, and yet a third professor of sociology at the University of Chile in Santiago, Chile. The "showdown" took place in Chile, first within the confines of the university, next on the floor of the Chilean Senate, then in the popular press of Santiago, and finally, behind US embassy walls.

It was ironic that Chile was the scene of wild newspaper tales of spying and academic outrage at scholars being recruited for "spying missions." For the working papers of Project Camelot stipulated as a criterion for study that a country "should show promise of high pay-offs in terms of the kinds of data required." Chile did not meet these requirements—it is not on the preliminary list of nations specified as prospects.

How then did Chile become involved in Project Camelot's affairs? The answer requires consideration of the position of Hugo G. Nutini, assistant professor of anthropology at Pittsburgh, citizen of the United States and former citizen of Chile. His presence in Santiago as a self-identified Camelot representative triggered the climactic chain of events.

Nutini, who inquired about an appointment in Camelot's beginning stages, never was given a regular Camelot appointment. Because he was planning a trip to Chile in April of this year—on other academic business—he was asked to prepare a report concerning possibilities of cooperation from Chilean scholars. In general, it was the kind of survey which has mild results and a modest honorarium attached to it (Nutini was offered $750). But Nutini had an obviously different notion of his role. Despite the limitations and precautions which Rex Hopper placed on his trip, especially Hopper's insistence on its informal nature, Nutini managed to convey the impression of being an official of Project Camelot with the authority to make proposals to prospective Chilean participants. Here was an opportunity to link the country of his birth with the country of his choice.

At about the same time, Johan Galtung, a Norwegian sociologist famous for his research on conflict and conflict resolution in underdeveloped areas, especially in Latin America, entered the picture. Galtung, who was in Chile at the time and associated with the Latin American Faculty of Social Science (FLACSO), received an invitation to participate in a Camelot planning conference scheduled for Washington, D.C., in August 1965. The fee to social scientists attending the conference would be $2,000 for four weeks. Galtung turned down the invitation. He gave several reasons. He could not accept the role of the US Army as a sponsoring agent in a study of counter-insurgency. He could not accept the notion of the Army as an agency of national development; he saw the Army as managing conflict and even promoting conflict. Finally, he could not accept the asymmetry of the project—he found it difficult to understand why there would be studies of counter-insurgency in Latin America, but no studies of "counter-intervention" (conditions under which Latin American nations might intervene in the affairs of the United States). Galtung was also deeply concerned about the possibility of European scholars being frozen out of Latin American studies by an inundation of sociologists from the United States. Furthermore, he expressed fears that the scale of Camelot honoraria would completely destroy the social science labor market in Latin America.

Galtung had spoken to others in Oslo, Santiago, and throughout Latin America about the project, and he had shown the memorandum of December 1964 to many of his colleagues.

Soon after Nutini arrived in Santiago, he had a conference with Vice-Chancellor Alvaro Bunster of the University of Chile to discuss the character of Project Camelot. Their second meeting, arranged by the vice-chancellor, was also attended by Professor Eduardo Fuenzalida, a sociologist. After a half-hour of exposition by Nutini, Fuenzalida asked him pointblank to specify the ultimate aims of the project, its sponsors, and its military implications. Before Nutini could reply, Professor Fuenzalida, apparently with some drama, pulled a copy of the December 4 circular letter from his briefcase and read a prepared Spanish translation. Simultaneously, the authorities at FLACSO turned over the matter to their associates in the Chilean Senate and in the left-wing Chilean press.

In Washington, under the political pressures of State Department officials and Congressional reaction, Project Camelot was halted in midstream, or more precisely, before it ever really got under way. When the ambassador's communication reached Washington, there was already considerable official ferment about Project Camelot. Senators Fulbright, Morse, and McCarthy soon asked for hearings by the Senate Foreign Relations Committee. Only an agreement between Secretary of Defense McNamara and Secretary of State Rusk to settle their differences on future overseas research projects forestalled Senate action. But in the House of Representatives, a hearing was conducted by the Foreign Affairs Committee on July 8. The SORO director, Theodore Vallance, was questioned by committee members on the worth of Camelot and the matter of military intrusion into foreign policy areas.

That morning, even before Vallance was sworn in as a witness—and without his knowledge—the Defense Department issued a terse announcement terminating Project Camelot. President Johnson had decided the issue in favor of the State Department. In a memo to Secretary Rusk on August 5 the President stipulated that "no government sponsorship of foreign area research should be undertaken which in the judgment of the Secretary of State would adversely affect United States foreign relations."

The State Department has recently established machinery to screen and judge all federally-financed research projects overseas. The policy and research consequences of the Presidential directive will be discussed later.

What effect will the cancellation of Camelot have on the continuing rivalry between Defense and State departments for primacy in foreign policy? How will government sponsorship of future social science research be affected? And was Project Camelot a scholarly protective cover for US Army planning—or a legitimate research operation on a valid research subject independent of sponsorship?

Let us begin with a collective self-portrait of Camelot as the social scientists who directed the project perceived it. There seems to be general consensus on seven points.

First, the men who went to work for Camelot felt the need for a large-scale, "big picture" project in social science. They wanted to create a sociology of contemporary relevance which would not suffer from the parochial narrowness of vision to which their own professional backgrounds had generally conditioned them. Most of the men viewed Camelot as a bona fide opportunity to do fundamental research with relatively unlimited funds at their disposal. (No social science project ever before had up to $6,000,000 available.) Under such optimal conditions, these scholars tended not to look a gift horse in the mouth. As one of them put it, there was no desire to inquire too deeply as to the source of the funds or the ultimate purpose of the project.

Second . . . one man noted that during the 1950's there was far more freedom to do fundamental research in the RAND corporation (an Air Force research organization) than on any campus in America. Indeed, once the protective covering of RAND was adopted, it was almost viewed as a society of Platonist elites or "knowers" permitted to search for truth on behalf of the powerful. In a neoplatonic definition of their situation, the Camelot men hoped that their ideas would be taken seriously by the wielders of power (although, conversely, they were convinced that the armed forces would not accept their preliminary recommendations).

Third, many of the Camelot associates felt distinctly uncomfortable with military sponsorship, especially given the present United States military posture. But their reaction to this discomfort was that "the Army has to be educated." This view was sometimes cast in Freudian terms: the Army's bent toward violence ought to be sublimated. Underlying this theme was the notion of the armed forces as an agency for potential social good—the discipline and the order embodied by an army could be channeled into the process of economic and social development in the United States as well as in Latin America.

Fourth, there was a profound conviction in the perfectibility of mankind; particularly in the possibility of the military establishment performing a major role in the general process of growth. They sought to correct the intellectual paternalism and parochialism under which Pentagon generals, State Department diplomats, and Defense Department planners seemed to operate.

Fifth, a major long-range purpose of Camelot, at least for some of its policy-makers, was to prevent another revolutionary holocaust on a grand scale, such as occurred in Cuba. At the very least, there was a shared belief that *Pax Americana* was severely threatened and its future could be bolstered.

Sixth, none of them viewed their role on the project as spying for the United States government, or for anyone else.

Seventh, the men on Project Camelot felt that they made heavy sacrifices for social science. Their personal and professional risks were much higher than those taken by university academics . . . (as indeed was the case). . . .

In the main, there was perhaps a keener desire on the part of the directing members of Camelot not to "sell out" than there is among social scientists with regular academic appointments. This concern with the ethics of social science research seemed to be due largely to daily confrontation of the problems of betrayal, treason, secrecy, and abuse of data, in a critical situation. In contrast, even though a university position may be created by federally-sponsored research, the connection with policy matters is often too remote to cause any *crise de conscience*.

THE INSIDERS REPORT

Were the men on Camelot critical of any aspects of the project?

Some had doubts from the outset about the character of the work they would be doing, and about the conditions under which it would be done. It was pointed out, for example, that the US Army tends to exercise a far more stringent intellectual control of research findings than does the US Air Force. As evidence for this, it was stated that SORO generally had fewer "free-wheeling" aspects to its research designs than did RAND (the Air Force-supported research organization). One critic inside SORO went so far as to say that he knew of no SORO research which had a "playful" or unregimented quality, such as one finds at RAND (where for example, computers are used to plan invasions but also to play chess). One staff member said that "the self-conscious seriousness gets to you after a while." "It was all grim stuff," said another.

Another line of criticism was that pressures on the "reformers" (as the men engaged in Camelot research spoke of themselves) to come up with ideas were much stronger than the pressures on the military to actually bring off any policy changes recommended. The social scientists were expected to be social reformers, while the military adjutants were expected to be conservative. It was further felt that the relationship between sponsors and researchers was not one of equals, but rather one of superordinate military needs and subordinate academic roles. On the other hand, some officials were impressed by the disinterestedness of the military, and thought that far from exercising undue influence, the Army personnel were loath to offer opinions.

Another objection was that if one had to work on policy matters—if research is to have international ramifications—it might better be conducted under conventional State Department sponsorship. "After all," one man said, "they are at least nominally committed to civilian political norms." In other words, there was a considerable reluctance to believe that the Defense Department, despite its superior organization, greater financial affluence, and executive influence, would actually improve upon State Department styles of work, or accept recommendations at variance with Pentagon policies.

There seemed to be few, if any, expressions of disrespect for the intrinsic merit of the work contemplated by Camelot, or of disdain for policy-oriented work in general. The scholars engaged in the Camelot effort used two distinct vocabularies. The various Camelot documents reveal a military vocabulary provided with an array of military justifications; often followed (within the same document) by a social science vocabulary offering social science justifications and rationalizations. The dilemma in the Camelot literature from the preliminary report issued in August 1964 until the more advanced document issued in April 1965, is the same: an incomplete amalgamation of the military and sociological vocabularies. (At an early date the project had the code name SPEARPOINT.)

POLICY CONFLICTS OVER CAMELOT

The directors of SORO are concerned that the cancellation of Camelot might mean the end of SORO as well in a wholesale slash of research funds. For while over $1,000,000 was allotted to Camelot each year, the annual budget of SORO, its parent organization, is a good deal less. Although no such action has taken place, SORO's future is being examined. For example, the Senate and House Appropriations Committee blocked a move by the Army to transfer unused Camelot funds to SORO.

However, the end of Project Camelot does not necessarily imply the end of the Special Operations Research Office, nor does it imply an end to research designs which are similar in character to Project Camelot. In fact, the termination of the contract does not even imply an intellectual change of heart on the part of the originating sponsors or key figures of the project.

One of the characteristics of Project Camelot was the number of antagonistic forces it set in motion on grounds of strategy and timing rather than from what may be called considerations of scientific principles.

The State Department grounded its opposition to Camelot on the basis of the ultimate authority it has in the area of foreign affairs. There is no published report showing serious criticism of the projected research itself.

Congressional opposition seemed to be generated by a concern not to rock any foreign alliances, especially in Latin America. Again, there was no statement about the project's scientific or intellectual grounds.

A third group of skeptics, academic social scientists, generally thought that Project Camelot, and studies of the processes of revolution and war in general, were better left in the control of major university centers, and in this way, kept free of direct military supervision.

The Army, creator of the project, did nothing to contradict McNamara's order cancelling Project Camelot. Army influentials did not only feel that they had to execute the Defense Department's orders, but they are traditionally dubious of the value of "software" research to support "hardware" systems.

Let us take a closer look at each of these groups which voiced opposition to Project Camelot. A number of issues did not so much hinge upon, as swim about, Project Camelot. In particular, the "jurisdictional" dispute between Defense and State loomed largest.

State vs. Defense. In substance, the debate between the Defense Department and the State Department is not unlike that between electricians and bricklayers in the construction of a new apartment house. What union is responsible for which processes? Less generously, the issue is: who controls what? At the policy level, Camelot was a tool tossed about in a larger power struggle which has been going on in government circles since the end of World War II, when the Defense Department emerged as a competitor for honors as the most powerful bureau of the administrative branch of government.

In some sense, the divisions between Defense and State are outcomes of the rise of ambiguous conflicts such as Korea and Vietnam, in contrast to the more precise and diplomatically controlled "classical" world wars. What are the lines dividing political policy from military posture? Who is the most important representative of the United States abroad: the ambassador or the military attaché in charge of the military mission? When soldiers from foreign lands are sent to the United States for political orientation, should such orientation be within the province of the State Department or of the Defense Department? When under-cover activities are conducted, should the direction of such activities belong to military or political authorities? Each of these is a strategic question with little pragmatic or historic precedent. Each of these was entwined in the Project Camelot explosion.

It should be plain therefore that the State Department was not simply responding to the recommendations of Chilean left-wingers in urging the cancellation of Camelot. It merely employed the Chilean hostility to "interventionist" projects as an opportunity to redefine the balance of forces and power with the Defense Department. What is clear from this resistance to such projects is not so much a defense of the sovereignty of the nations where ambassadors are stationed, as it is a contention that conventional political channels are sufficient to yield the information desired or deemed necessary.

Congress. In the main, congressional reaction seems to be that Project Camelot was bad because it rocked the diplomatic boat in a sensitive area. Underlying most congressional criticisms is the plain fact that most congressmen are more sympathetic to State Department control of foreign affairs than they are to Defense Department control. In other words, despite military sponsored world junkets, National Guard and State Guard pressures from the home State, and military training in the backgrounds of many congressmen, the sentiment for political rather than military control is greater. In addition, there is a mounting suspicion in Congress of varying kinds of behavioral science research stemming from hearings into such matters as wire-tapping, uses of lie detectors, and truth-in-packaging.

Social Scientists. One reason for the violent response to Project Camelot, especially among Latin American scholars, is its sponsorship by the Department of Defense. The fact is that Latin Americans have become quite accustomed to State Department involvements in the internal affairs of various nations. The Defense Department is a newcomer, a dangerous one, inside the Latin American orbit. The train of thought connected to its activities is in terms of international warfare, spying missions, military manipulations, etc. The State Department, for its part, is often a consultative party to shifts in government, and has played an enormous part in either fending off or bringing about *coups d'état*. This State Department role has by now been accepted and even taken for granted. Not so the Defense Department's role. But it is interesting to conjecture on how matter-of-factly Camelot might have been accepted if it had State Department sponsorship.

. . . Many social scientists doubtless see nothing wrong or immoral in the Project Camelot designs. And they are therefore more likely to be either confused or angered at the Latin American response than at the directors of Project Camelot. (At the time of the blowup, Camelot people spoke about the "Chilean mess" rather than the "Camelot mess.")

The directors of Project Camelot did not "classify" research materials, so that there would be no stigma of secrecy. And they also tried to hire, and even hired away from academic positions, people well known and respected for their independence of mind. The difficulty is that even though the stigma of secrecy was formally erased, it remained in the attitudes of many of the employees and would-be employees of Project Camelot. They unfortunately thought in terms of secrecy, clearance, missions, and the rest of the professional nonsense that so powerfully afflicts the Washington scientific as well as political ambience.

Further, it is apparent that Project Camelot had much greater difficulty hiring a full-time staff of high professional competence, than in getting part-time, summertime, weekend, and sundry assistance. Few established figures in academic life were willing to surrender the advantages of their positions for the risks of the project.

One of the cloudiest aspects to Project Camelot is the role of American University. Its actual supervision of the contract appears to have begun and ended with the 25 percent overhead on those parts of the contract that a university receives on most federal grants. Thus, while there can be no question as to the "concern and disappointment" of President Hurst R. Anderson of the American University over the demise of Project Camelot, the reasons for this regret do not seem to extend beyond the formal and the financial. No official at American University appears to have been willing to make any statement of responsibility, support, chagrin, opposition, or anything else related to the project. The issues are indeed momentous, and must be faced by all universities at which government sponsored research is conducted: the amount of control a university has over contract work; the role of university officials in the distribution of funds from grants; the relationships that ought to be established once a grant is issued. There is also a major question concerning project directors: are they members of the faculty, and if so, do they have necessary teaching responsibilities and opportunities for tenure as do other faculty members.

The difficulty with American University is that it seems to be remarkably unlike other universities in its permissiveness. The Special Operations Research Office received neither guidance nor support from university officials. From the outset, there seems to have been a "gentleman's agreement" not to inquire or interfere in Project Camelot, but simply to serve as some sort of camouflage. If American University were genuinely autonomous it might have been able to lend highly supportive aid to Project Camelot during the crisis months. As it is, American University maintained an official silence which preserved it from more congressional or executive criticism. This points up some serious flaws in its administrative and financial policies.

The relationship of Camelot to SORO represented a similarly muddled organizational picture. The director of Project Camelot was nominally autonomous and in charge of an organization surpassing in size and importance the overall SORO operation. Yet at the critical point the organizational blueprint served to protect SORO and sacrifice what nominally was its limb. That Camelot happened to be a vital organ may have hurt, especially when Congress blocked the transfer of unused Camelot funds to SORO.

Military.   Military reaction to the cancellation of Camelot varied. It should be borne in mind that expenditures on Camelot were minimal in the Army's overall budget and most military leaders are skeptical, to begin with, about the worth of social science research. So there was no open protest about the demise of Camelot. Those officers who have a positive attitude toward social science materials, or are themselves trained in the social sciences, were dismayed. Some had hoped to find "software" alternatives to the "hardware systems" approach applied by the Secretary of Defense to every military-political contingency. These officers saw the attack on Camelot as a double attack—on their role as officers and on their professional standards. But the Army was so clearly treading in new waters that it could scarcely jeopardize the entire structure of military research to preserve one project. This very inability or impotence to preserve Camelot—a situation threatening to other governmental contracts with social scientists—no doubt impressed many armed forces officers.

The claim is made by the Camelot staff (and various military aides) that the critics of the project played into the hands of those sections of the military predisposed to veto any social science recommendations. Then why did the military offer such a huge support to a social science project to begin with? Because $6,000,000 is actually a trifling sum for the Army in an age of multi-billion dollar military establishment. The amount is significantly more important for the social sciences, where such contract awards remain relatively scarce. Thus, there were differing perspectives of the importance of Camelot: an Army view which considered the contract as one of several forms of "software" investment; a social science perception of Project Camelot as the equivalent of the Manhattan Project.

WAS PROJECT CAMELOT WORKABLE?

While most public opposition to Project Camelot focused on its strategy and timing, a considerable amount of private opposition centered on more basic, though theoretical, questions: was Camelot scientifically feasible and ethically correct? No public document or statement contested the possibility that, given the successful completion of the data gathering, Camelot could have, indeed, established basic criteria for measuring the level and potential for internal war in a given nation. Thus, by never challenging the feasibility of the work, the political critics of Project Camelot were providing back-handed compliments to the efficacy of the project.

But much more than political considerations are involved. It is clear that some of the most critical problems presented by Project Camelot are scientific. Although for an extensive analysis of Camelot, the reader would, in fairness, have to be familiar with all of its documents, salient general criticisms can be made without a full reading.

The research design of Camelot was from the outset plagued by ambiguities. . . . It was difficult to determine whether it was to be a study of comparative social structures, a set of case studies of single nations "in depth," or a study of social structure with particular emphasis on the military. In addition, there was a lack of treatment of what indicators were to be used, and whether a given social system in Nation A could be as stable in Nation B.

In one Camelot document there is a general critique of social science for failing to deal with social conflict and social control. While this in itself is admirable, the tenor and context of Camelot's documents make it plain that a "stable society" is considered the norm no less than the desired outcome. The "breakdown of social order" is spoken of accusatively. Stabilizing agencies in developing areas are presumed to be absent. There is no critique of US Army policy in developing areas because the Army is presumed to be a stabilizing agency. The research formulations always assume the legitimacy of Army tasks—"if the US Army is to perform effectively its parts in the US mission of counter-insurgency it must recognize that insurgency represents a breakdown of social order. . . ." But such a proposition has never been doubted—by Army officials or anyone else. The issue is whether such breakdowns are in the nature of the existing system or a product of conspiratorial movements.

The use of hygenic language disguises the anti-revolutionary assumptions under a cloud of powder puff declarations. For example, studies of Paraguay are recommended "because trends in this situation (the Stroessner regime) may also render it 'unique' when analyzed in terms of the transition from 'dictatorship' to political stability." But to speak about changes from dictatorship to stability is an obvious ruse. In this case, it is a tactic to disguise the fact that Paraguay is one of the most vicious, undemocratic (and like most dictatorships, stable) societies in the Western Hemisphere.

These typify the sort of hygenic sociological premises that do not have scientific purposes. They illustrate the confusion of commitments within Project Camelot. Indeed the very absence of emotive words such as revolutionary masses, communism, socialism, and capitalism only serves to intensify the discomfort one must feel on examination of the documents—since the abstract vocabulary disguises, rather than resolves, the problems of international revolution. To have used clearly political rather than military language would not "justify" governmental support. Furthermore, shabby assumptions of academic conventionalism replaced innovative orientations. By adopting a systems approach, the problematic, open-ended aspects of the study of revolutions were largely omitted; and the design of the study became an oppressive curb on the study of the problems inspected.

This points up a critical implication for Camelot (as well as other projects). The importance of the subject being researched does not *per se* determine the importance of the project. A sociology of large-scale relevance and reference is all to the good. It is important that scholars be willing to risk something of their shaky reputations in helping resolve major world social problems. But it is no less urgent that in the process of addressing major problems, the autonomous character of the social science disciplines—their own criteria of worthwhile scholarship—should not be abandoned. Project Camelot lost sight of this "autonomous" social science character.

. . . They seem not to have thought about inquiring into the role of the United States in these countries. This points up the lack of symmetry. The problem should have been phrased to include the study of "us" as well as "them." It is not possible to make a decent analysis of a situation unless one takes into account the role of all the different people and groups involved in it; and there was no room in the design for such contingency analysis.

In discussing the policy impact on a social science research project, we should not overlook the difference between "contract" work and "grants." Project Camelot commenced with the US Army; that is to say, it was initiated for a practical purpose determined by the client. This differs markedly from the typical academic grant in that its sponsorship had "built-in" ends. The scholar usually *seeks* a grant; in this case the donor, the Army, promoted its own aims. In some measure, the hostility for Project Camelot may be an unconscious reflection of this distinction—a dim feeling that there was something "non-academic," and certainly not disinterested, about Project Camelot, irrespective of the quality of the scholars associated with it.

THE ETHICS OF POLICY RESEARCH

The issue of "scientific rights" versus "social myths" is perennial. Some maintain that the scientist ought not penetrate beyond legally or morally sanctioned limits and others argue that such limits cannot exist for science. In treading on the sensitive issue of national sovereignty, Project Camelot reflects the generalized dilemma. In deference to intelligent researchers, in recognition of them as scholars, they should have been invited by Camelot to air their misgivings and qualms about government (and especially Army sponsored) research—to declare their moral conscience. Instead, they were mistakenly approached as skillful, useful potential employees of a higher body, subject to an authority higher than their scientific calling.

What is central is not the political motives of the sponsor. For social scientists were not being enlisted in an intelligence system for "spying" purposes. But given their professional standing, their great sense of intellectual honor and pride, they could not be "employed" without proper deference for their stature. Professional authority should have prevailed from beginning to end with complete command of the right to thrash out the moral and political dilemmas as researchers saw them. The Army, however respectful and protective of free expression, was "hiring help" and not openly and honestly submitting a problem to the higher professional and scientific authority of social science.

The propriety of the Army to define and delimit all questions, which Camelot should have had a right to examine, was never placed in doubt. This is a tragic precedent; it reflects the arrogance of a consumer of intellectual merchandise. And this relationship of inequality corrupted the lines of authority, and profoundly limited the autonomy of the social scientists involved. It became clear that the social scientist savant was not so much functioning as an applied social scientist as he was supplying information to a powerful client.

The question of who sponsors research is not nearly so decisive as the question of ultimate use of such information. The sponsorship of a project, whether by the United States Army or by the Boy Scouts of America, is by itself neither good nor bad. Sponsorship is good or bad only insofar as the intended outcomes can be predetermined and the parameters of those intended outcomes tailored to the sponsor's expectations. Those social scientists critical of the project never really denied its freedom and independence, but questioned instead the purpose and character of its intended results.

It would be a gross oversimplification, if not an outright error, to assume that the theoretical problems of Project Camelot derive from any reactionary character of the project designers. The director went far and wide to select a group of men for the advisory board, the core planning group, the summer study group, and the various conference groupings, who in fact were more liberal in their orientations than any random sampling of the sociological profession would likely turn up.

However, in nearly every page of the various working papers, there are assertions which clearly derive from American military policy objectives rather than scientific method. The steady assumption that internal warfare is damaging disregards the possibility that a government may not be in a position to take actions either to relieve or improve mass conditions, or that such actions as are contemplated may be more concerned with reducing conflict than with improving conditions. The added statements about the United States Army and its "important mission in the positive and constructive aspects of nation building . . ." assumes the reality of such a function in an utterly unquestioning and unconvincing form. The first rule of the scientific game is not to make assumptions about friends and enemies in such a way as to promote the use of different criteria for the former and the latter.

The story of Project Camelot was not a confrontation of good versus evil. Obviously, not all men behaved with equal fidelity or with equal civility. Some men were weaker than others, some more callous, and some more stupid. But all of this is extrinsic to the heart of the problem of Camelot: what are and are not the legitimate functions of a scientist?

In conclusion, two important points must be clearly kept in mind and clearly apart. First . . . it was political expedience, rather than its lack of scientific merit, that led to the demise of Camelot because it threatened to rock State Department relations with Latin America.

Second, giving the State Department the right to screen and approve government-funded social science research projects on other countries, as the President has ordered, is a supreme act of censorship. Among the agencies that grant funds for such research are the National Institutes of Mental Health, the National Science Foundation, the National Aeronautics and Space Agency, and the Office of Education. Why should the State Department have veto power over the scientific pursuits of men and projects funded by these and other agencies in order to satisfy the policy needs—or policy failures—of the moment? . . .

We must be careful not to allow social science projects with which we may vociferously disagree on political and ideological grounds to be decimated or dismantled by government fiat. Across the ideological divide is a common social science understanding that the contemporary expression of reason in politics today is applied social science, and that the cancellation of Camelot, however pleasing it may be on political grounds to advocates of a civilian solution to Latin American affairs, represents a decisive setback for social science research.

BIBLIOGRAPHY

See the bibliographies for Chapters 1, 2, and 7 to supplement the items noted here.

American Political Science Association, Committee for the Advancement of Teaching. *Goals for Political Science.* New York, 1951.

American Political Science Association, Committee on Professional Standards and Responsibilities. Report: "Ethical Problems of Academic Political Scientists." *P.S.*, I (1968), 3–28.

ANDERSON, WILLIAM. "The Role of Political Science." *American Political Science Review*, XXXVII (1943), 1–17.

CONNERY, ROBERT H., ed. *Teaching Political Science: A Challenge to Higher Education*. Durham, N.C., 1965.

CRAWFORD, ELISABETH T., and GENE M. LYONS. "Foreign Area Research: A Background Statement." *American Behavioral Scientist*, X (1967), 3–7.

DAVIS, KINGSLEY, JR. "The Perilous Promise of Behavioral Science." In *Research in the Service of Man: Biomedical Knowledge, Development, and Use*. Subcommittee on Government Research, Senate Committee on Government Operations. Washington, D.C., 1967. Pages 23–32.

"Goals for Political Science: A Discussion." *American Political Science Review*, XLV (1951), 996–1024. "Replies and Comments." *American Political Science Review*, XLVI (1952), 504–511.

GRIFFITH, ERNEST S., ed. *Research in Political Science*. Chapel Hill, 1948.

HOROWITZ, IRVING LOUIS, ed. *The Rise and Fall of Project Camelot: Studies in the Relationship Between Social Science and Practical Politics*. Cambridge, Mass., 1967.

LAZARSFELD, PAUL F., and WAGNER THIELENS, JR. *The Academic Mind: Social Scientists in a Time of Crisis*. Glencoe, 1958.

MERTON, ROBERT K., and DANIEL LERNER. "Social Scientists and Research Policy." *The Policy Sciences*, ed. Lerner and Lasswell. Pages 282–307.

RAINWATER, LEE, and WILLIAM YANCEY. *The Moynihan Report and the Politics of Controversy*. Cambridge, Mass., 1967.

REISSMAN, LEONARD, and KALMAN H. SILVERT, eds. "Ethics and Social Science Research." *American Behavioral Scientist*, X (1967). Entire June, 1967, issue.

Research for Public Policy. (Brookings Dedication Lectures.) Washington, D.C., 1961.

ROSSITER, CLINTON. "Political Science 1 and Political Indoctrination." *American Political Science Review*, XLII (1948), 542–549.

SOMIT, ALBERT, and JOSEPH TANENHAUS. *American Political Science: A Profile of a Discipline*. New York, 1964.

——. *The Development of American Political Science: From Burgess to Behavioralism*. Boston, 1967.

Subcommittee on Government Research, Committee on Government Operations, United States Senate. *Hearings:* "Federal Support of International Social Science and Behavioral Research." Washington, D.C., 1967.

Subcommittee on Research and Technical Problems, Committee on Government Operations, United States House of Representatives. *The Use of Social Research in Federal Domestic Programs*. Washington, D.C., 1967. Four volumes.

TURNER, HENRY A., CHARLES G. MC CLINTOCK, and CHARLES B. SPAULDING. "The Political Party Affiliation of American Political Scientists." *Western Political Quarterly*, XVI (1963), 650–665.

"Undergraduate Instruction in Political Science." *American Political Science Review*, XLI (1947), 487–534. (A set of three articles.)

WALDO, DWIGHT, ed. *The Research Function of University Bureaus and Institutes for Government-Related Research*. Berkeley, 1960.

WALKER, ROBERT. "Citizenship Education and the Colleges." *American Political Science Review*, XLII (1948), 74–84.

WHITE, LEONARD, ed. *The State of the Social Sciences*. Chicago, 1956.

Part III / THE FIELDS OF POLITICAL SCIENCE

INTRODUCTION

In the eight chapters which follow, the reader will be introduced to eight fields of political science. He will not be presented with a short, neat summary of the findings in each of these fields; compressing our findings into the space available would result in an extremely superficial presentation. Instead, the author's purpose is to emphasize the scope of each field, the types of topics with which its scholars have concerned themselves, and their growth, development, and present status. In connection with this approach, *some* findings will be presented, but it must be stressed that they are selected and limited, and are presented primarily in connection with discussions of methods used and present emphases in a given field.

The stress on the scope and development in the eight fields presented is in keeping with the purpose behind this volume, to provide an "overview" of the discipline of political science, and to give the student a better "feel" for the discipline before he encounters courses dealing in detail with more limited segments of what we study. The book is meant to serve as background for later developments and as the basis from which the student can comfortably move to deal with new approaches and studies. The rapid growth of writings, both in book form and in the professional journals, would make the following chapters background in any case; between the time this is written and the time this volume is published, there will have been major additions to each of the fields discussed here. If the eight chapters are successful, however, the student will be better able to understand these new writings and to fit them within the intellectual development of the aspect of political science within which they fall.

The present portion of the volume is in one sense more traditional than Part I, because the earliest courses in Scope and Methods of Political Science often adopted this same field-by-field approach to the discipline; later courses took up subjects of the sort discussed in Part I. The eight-fold division used here is also a relatively traditional one. The division is, as follows, in the order presented:

- Political Theory
- Political Behavior and Public Opinion
- Parties and Interest Groups
- The Legislative Process
- Public Administration
- Public Law
- Comparative Government and Politics
- International Relations.

It should be made abundantly clear that other divisions or combinations, expansions or contractions in the number of fields, could easily be made, and that the fields will overlap at a number of places. The omission of a separate field of State and Local Government or Intergovernmental Relations may be noted; that material is covered elsewhere, particularly under the heading of Public Administration. For those concerned with the development of modern empirical theory, some of each of the other areas fits under the rubric of Political Theory. Similarly, if one holds to the position that all political analysis is becoming comparative study, the existence of a separate field of Comparative Government and Politics is brought into question. But, whatever the current developments in the field, relatively traditional divisions have been used in order to be able to account for the existing body of work in political science. While perhaps in another five or ten years political scientists will be commonly using an entirely different set of categories, the reorientation of the discipline has not yet progressed to the point where a basic survey of developments in the field can leave older, more familiar divisions.

The order of presentation follows a plan. In dealing first with Political Theory, we consider the role of political ideas in political science. We next move to the behavior which precedes formal, governmental action and the attitudes and opinions which underlie that behavior, first in a chapter on Political Behavior and Public Opinion, and then, at a more organized but still pre-governmental level, with Parties and Interest Groups. The following three chapters essentially parallel the legislative-executive-judicial division created by the "separation of powers" principle; we talk first about the Legislative Process, then about Public Administration (including the Presidency), and last, about Public Law. With the exception of the Political Theory chapter, the emphasis has been on American materials. This leads to the last two chapters, on Comparative Government and Politics and International Relations, including international law and organization. That such a division can occur is not simply a reflection of the author's interests, but a statement of how political scientists have carved up their chosen subject, leaving the discussion of non-American parties, interest groups, legislatures, courts, and the like to the student of Comparative Government, and taking the relations in the international arena to be at a different level from politics within individual countries.

Two other introductory remarks. First, no attempt has been made to follow a fixed common format in these chapters, in view of the fact that they are general surveys or discussions rather than exhaustive presentations, and in order to provide some change-of-pace from one chapter to the next. This also allows the three experts who have contributed chapters—in Political Theory, Comparative Government and Politics, and International Relations—to adopt their own format rather than be forced into one perhaps not appropriate for their fields. Second, after each of the chapters, a bibliography, basically annotated, will be presented for easy reference by the reader who wishes to obtain a basic exposure to the substantive materials of that field.

9 / POLITICAL THEORY

by William C. Baum

WHY POLITICAL THEORY SEEMS COMPLEX—AND IS

Someone once described a camel as a horse that had been built by a committee. Similarly, the corpus of political theory has many odd-shaped humps and bumps resulting from the fact that many hands have helped in developing its myriad forms and shapes. This should not surprise us when we are reminded that political theory in the West is *at least* 2300 years old and has been attended to by kings, philosophers, popes, rogues and highwaymen of every sort, stripe and denomination. The number of political "theorizers" is very large and when we consider the number of personal problems and private feuds that have been made into public issues (in addition to the number of genuine public issues which any society faces) one might then expect political theory to be the complex and varied field of inquiry that it is. The interests and commitments of those engaged in political theorizing are so varied and diffuse that we face a difficult task in answering the ostensibly simple question: What is political theory?

The advanced student of political theory is undoubtedly aware of the complexities associated with the study of political theory. But it would not take the beginning student very long to come to the same conclusion. For instance, some of the more important works recently published on the subject of political theory include: *A History of Political Theory* (Sabine); *Great Political Thinkers* (Ebenstein); *The Political System* (Easton); *An Introduction to Political Philosophy* (Murray); *Political Theory* (Hacker); *History of Political Philosophy* (Strauss and Cropsey); *Theories of the Political System* (Bluhm); *Political Science: A Philosophical Analysis* (Van Dyke); *Theory and Method of Political Analysis* (Meehan); *Politics and Vision* (Wolin); and *Men and Society* (Plamenatz).[1] A major source of the complexities already referred to stems from the fact that certain important recurring words, especially the words *philosophy* and *theory*, are used in significantly different ways in these volumes. For example, Sabine and Hacker employ the term

---

[1] More complete reference and comments on these and related works can be found in the closing paragraphs of the annotated bibliography at the end of this chapter.

theory in the same way that Murray and Strauss-Cropsey use the term *philosophy*. Wolin and Plamenatz have written essays on the history of political ideas. Van Dyke, Meehan, and Easton are primarily concerned with the condition of contemporary political science.

One of the main tasks of this chapter is to assess the condition of contemporary political theory. At the outset we can pronounce the condition as healthy and sound—if we judge the health on the basis of great activity and diversity. As a consequence, there is more than a small grain of truth to the allegation that political theory is an extremely unwieldy subfield of political science. Delaying for now a discussion of the substantive themes of political theory, we might first pause to reflect on how political theory got to the state of affairs which confuses us so. In a sense, *a* political theory has never existed. The air would be clearer if we stopped referring to political theory as though it were a singular entity. Political theory does not exist suspended above men like a cloud independent of their thoughts and desires. There are about as many different political theories as there are people who write about political theory. This does not mean that all those who write about political theory have anything original or important to say. Few people have an original or important idea in a lifetime. Most people, if they have any political ideas at all, have borrowed them from relatives, friends, newspapers, and bartenders. But those few people who unfailingly appear in political philosophy textbooks appear because they *do* have something new to say. Hence the inclusion of Plato, Hobbes, and Marx, *inter alia*, in these books. It is in this context that I suggest that there are as many different theories as there are writers.

Despite any alleged confusion, political theory does have a subject matter. From Plato to the present, substantial agreement as to what political theories should discuss has helped keep political theory free from chaos. Important changes have taken place over this long period of time. However, these changes have primarily involved *how* politics should be studied rather than *what* the subject matter is about.

Political theories are the inventions and creations of men. The naïve may have to be told that theories are *not* brought by philosophical storks. Historical and social changes—changes in the status quo—inspire both rationalizations in defense of the change and attacks on the change itself. Sometimes, however, historical necessity requires that a writer deliberately mislead his readers—or at least some of them. Many scholars are convinced that John Locke conveyed his real message between the lines to avoid arrest.[2] In time we may have further evidence that exigencies or a writer's own tastes led to symbolism, allegory or otherwise indirect presentations of political views.

Not only does confusion arise from this human element in theorizing, but the confusion has been compounded because, as a subfield subordinate to philosophy, political theory changed with its master, and because there have

[2] See William Bluhm, *Theories of the Political System* (Englewood Cliffs, 1965), pp. 302–314, and especially the footnotes to pp. 302–303, for a discussion of Locke's alleged subterfuge.

been changes in the general usage and acceptability of terms over a period of years. At times democracy and equality are used with the understanding that women cannot participate in politics while slavery is winked at. In recent years the popularity of democracy has been so great that every country claims to be a democracy. Thus, in a world with over 150 nations, there are almost that many democratic theories.

The Rule of Political Theory by Philosophy. A brief glance at the tables of contents in a few of the textbooks commonly used in political theory courses will impress upon us the fact that, until quite recently, political theory was political philosophy. The great philosophers of the Western world were great, in part, because of both the profundity and scope of their thought. Plato, Aristotle, Locke, and Hegel were major philosophers as well as prominent political thinkers. Political thinkers they were, but they were *more* than that. They wrote about whatever concerned them—whatever they deemed important. They would not fit comfortably into our present-day academic departments. Today they would be considered rascals. If they were filling out employment forms they would probably list themselves as philosophers, economists, sociologists, historians, theologians, *and* political theorists. What Dean could countenance such an outrage? The scope of their writings would bear them out. But it is important to recognize that they were economists or political theorists only when these "fields" (as we now define them) were relevant to the discussion at hand. During this long period of its "captivity," from Plato to the present, political theory was dominated by philosophy in three ways.

First, in the hand of philosophers political theory had a greater dimension than it has today.[3] The dimensions of political theory—as in many theories in many sciences—include description, explanation, prescription and evaluation. All political theories contain varying degrees of description and explanation. It could not be otherwise. Facts, labelled by concepts, are the raw material of any science. These concepts are necessary for the facts to be ordered into generalizations and for the explanation of phenomena. What distinguishes contemporary from earlier political theory is a reluctance on the part of most contemporary political scientists to work in what they deem the nonscientific areas, i.e., prescription and evaluation. This is largely due to the acceptance of the fact-value dichotomy by most scientists.[4] Accordingly, only facts and concepts are deemed relevant to the primary aim of science: explanation of phenomena. Traditional philosophy also had a deep interest in ethical and normative judgments. So, too, did political theory until very recently.

There is a second way in which philosophy dominated political theory. Until recently, there was no clear distinction between the burning philosophical, theological, and political issues. For centuries the Western world was a

[3] The major differences between contemporary and earlier political theory can be illustrated as shown in Table 4 on page 280.
[4] This point was discussed on pp. 26–32.

Table 4. Possible Dimensions of a Theory

A	B	C	D
DESCRIPTION	EXPLANATION	PRESCRIPTION	EVALUATION
On August 5, 1962 John Jones, broker, committed suicide. Ray Smith, insurance executive, committed suicide, October 15, 1963. Other suicides in 1962–1963 include: etc.	Ordering and explanation of fact, such as the concept of *anomic suicide*.	Relation of empirical finding to value in *if . . . then* form: *if* the state wants to minimize suicide, it *then* should provide a stable economy.	Discussion of what ought to be, e.g., suicide is morally wrong and should be outlawed because . . .
(Factual description takes place at this level. The "raw data" or evidence in a theory will be presented here.)	(Concepts are developed which order and explain the factual or descriptive material. Political scientists hope that laws and theories can be formulated so that events such as those described in Column A can be *explained* as well as described.)	(This is sometimes referred to as "social engineering." If political scientists are successful in formulating laws and theories of political behavior, they can advise the state what it should do if it wants . . .)	(Traditionally, political theory contained much evaluation. Many contemporary political scientists feel that we should devote less attention to evaluation *per se*, and concentrate on building solid, scientific explanation.)

Catholic christendom which sought Divine Grace. Thus when St. Thomas Aquinas endorsed monarchy, he was addressing himself to the still more fundamental problem of providing a Just Order for a Christian Community. Prior to that Plato had advocated rule by a philosopher-king in the name of Justice.

It would be an exaggeration to suggest that political theory was lost when it was subordinated to other matters. But unlike today, it was neither autonomous nor *primus inter pares;* it is autonomous today in academia and often first among equals when a Giovanni Gentile or an Alfred Rosenberg is manufacturing philosophical support for Mussolini and Hitler. Political Theory has survived some hard moments throughout its long history. But it has served many masters and *this* makes the difference.

A third area of influence pertains to logic and methodology. Here the relationship between philosophy and political theory is subtle and less direct but important nonetheless. In earlier years political theorists were guided by such things as the rules of formal logic and developments in theories of knowledge. Important recent developments which bear on political theory have been initiated in the philosophy of science. Ironically, an empirical political theory may be as dependent on philosophy (at least the philosophy of science) as theory more traditionally has been. This demonstrates that philosophy has an important role to play in the development of any significant area of inquiry. A very encouraging sign can be seen in the rash of extremely good books published in the last decade which deal with the major dimensions of political theory and their relationships to *both* philosophy and political science. (See bibliography, pp. 304–307.)

The Recent Development of a Professional Political Science. Another factor which complicates the content and status of political theory is related to the development of a professional and specialized political science in the Twentieth Century, which will be discussed more fully on pages 301–302.

At this point it is only necessary to indicate that a basic issue, increasingly the subject for debate within the political science profession, has to do with the very purpose (or purposes) political theory should serve. Those persons empathetic to traditional political theory feel that political theory can stand on its own two feet: probing into issues, asking the important questions, serving as a sort of conscience to political science. In this view, political theory is somewhat independent of political science. If there is a relationship it is largely one of leader to follower—political theory being the leader.

A different role for political theory is implicitly prescribed by behavioralists in recent years. In their judgment, political theory should have an empirical referent and stand to political science in the same way that Newtonian or Einsteinian theory stands to physics, e.g., as an *explanatory* device. Here the standard for evaluating theory is related directly to the range of its explanatory power. According to behavioralists, a good political theory will order, explain, and (some argue) predict political phenomena. One particularly lively issue which affects both political scientists and other social scientists concerns the question: at what range or level of general explanation can theories be constructed? There are those who maintain that *no* explanation of human behavior is possible, or even desirable. Behavioralists, on the other hand, point out—with good reason—that there are no logical grounds for maintaining that we *cannot* have explanations of human behavior. Social scientists debate over how extensive these explanations will be. The most optimistic hope that social science will someday develop theories of such range and scope this specific behavior can be deduced (and even predicted). For example, if the correlation between income and voting was invariant, then we could deduce how a man would vote if we knew his income. This goal will have to remain as something to look forward to, because, to continue our example, at the present time we know that some millionaires vote Democratic and some very poor Negro Catholics vote Republican.

Realistically, then, we should expect to find political scientists developing explanations of the "middle-range" or perhaps even more modest "low-level" range. Such explanations are, in part, a result of the fact that *not* all millionaires vote Republican; not all people with incomes below $3,000 per year vote Democratic. But most millionaires *do* vote Republican, most union members, Catholics, and people at lower income levels do vote Democratic. Information such as this is important and it appears that political scientists will generate theories of the low or middle-range based on such data. But it seems unlikely that political scientists will soon be able to generate theories beyond the low or middle range. Nevertheless, every theory represents progress, no matter how modest it might be. For the time being it appears that the real dispute will take place between the traditionalists who view political theory as a discipline devoted to *evaluation* and those who insist that political theory must be *descriptive* and *explanatory*. We shall, however, speak of three major traditions in political theory inasmuch as traditional theory can be conveniently divided into the classical and modern schools. After considering them we will assay the recent developments leading to a Contemporary Empirical Political Theory.

MAJOR TRADITIONS OF POLITICAL THEORY

Classical Political Thought

Introduction. In the previous section it was suggested that there are almost as many political theories as there are political theorists. In the sense that each writer brings a unique angle of vision to his creation we can properly speak of the considerable diversity in political theory. It is even more important, however, to point to the continuity in Western political theory. Political theory in the West is a dialogue extended over time. A meaningful dialogue requires that the participants share some degree of familiar attitudes and beliefs. (How strange it would be for one of us to discuss life, death, eternal salvation and train schedules with someone who had a different concept of time.) But the Western world does have a pattern and degree of homogeneity in its political concepts and beliefs. We shall now consider some of these concepts and commitments which make possible political dialogue in the Western world.

At the outset we need to examine the word that we have heretofore ignored: political. It is this word that focuses the dialogue, giving it a line, just as the key of a musical composition serves as a point of departure and point of return. The outer contours of the dialogue are shaped by a set of issues and perspectives that men in the West have found both exciting and perplexing.

The Political in Political Theory. We should acknowledge that only members of a self-conscious scientific endeavor care about pushing hard on definitions and terminology. The ancient greats in political theory were interested in politics as part of a comprehensive form of inquiry. Consequently, politics—the political of political theory—was always described and discussed in a rather elaborate context. Twentieth Century political scientists, on the other hand, are primarily interested in developing terms that have a firm empirical basis and are, ideally, measurable and operational. This means, of course, that any brief and succinct definition of politics must be imposed. Nonetheless, we can find a common denominator, a line to follow. Sheldon Wolin is correct in suggesting that "the task of defining what is political is a continual one." Despite the warning he offers a definition of politics which we can profitably use. Wolin defines "politics" to include the following:

(a) a form of activity centering around the quest for competitive advantage between groups, individuals or societies;
(b) a form of activity conditioned by the fact that it occurs within a situation of change and relative scarcity;
(c) a form of activity in which the pursuit of advantage produces consequences of such magnitude that they affect in a significant way the whole society or a substantial portion of it.[5]

The hard core of politics, then, is struggle for power and advantage, with only a small group of people being able to hold political power and advantage at a given time (making Kings and Presidents a scarce commodity); as a result, a society is profoundly affected by both the struggle for dominance and the results of the domination. Many of the major problems and issues which Western political theorists have debated for centuries are closely related to the definition of politics suggested by Professor Wolin. These questions include: What is the nature of man? What is the social or political nature of man? How can man be free and yet also be governed? What is the relation between political rights and political duties? Classical theorists repeatedly argued the question: Who should rule and *why?* A behavioral scientist today would only change the wording to who *does* rule, and *how?* Despite the continuity and agreement regarding certain features of the subject matter of politics, one should not be deceived into thinking that the bifurcation in political theory between those wedded to the traditional study of politics and those who label themselves the behavioralists is the result of a petty disagreement over minor matters. It is now time to consider this from a new vantage point. We shall briefly consider some of the concepts, and— most important—the world views (*Weltanschauung*) that have evolved in

Weltanschauung. Literally, a world view. It is an all-encompassing theory of history of the world. Most political theories contain such a sweeping theory of history. That of Karl Marx is certainly the most famous.

Western political theory, noting first some of the features of the classical tradition followed by a discussion of how and why this tradition has been undermined in the last three centuries.[6]

[5] See Sheldon Wolin, *Politics and Vision* (Boston, 1960), pp. 10—11.
[6] For discussion of the importance of the role played by *Weltanschauung* in theory and explanation, see Fred Frohock, *The Nature of Political Inquiry* (Homewood, Ill., 1967), Chapters II and IV, and Maurice Nathanson, *The Philosophy of the Social Sciences* (New York, 1963), pp. 3—26.

Prominent Themes in Classical Political Thought

Rationalism and Rational Man.　Western man has shown an insatiable urge for certainty. He might find little amusement in the exchange between A) "Only fools can be certain." and B) "How can you be so certain?" The first two subjects of many political theory books, Plato and Aristotle, probed deeply into the question of knowledge and attempted to answer for all time how one can know something for certain. Plato distinguished opinion from certain knowledge. Aristotle developed a system which would provide knowledge which was permanent and immutable.

Aristotle's "system" is commonly referred to as *rationalism*. Without doubt, this has been the most influential theory of knowledge in the history of Western thought. Put simply, rationalism represents the view that truth is knowable and that truth (reality) can be known for certain. Unlike the "radical rationalism" of Plato, Aristotle built his theory of knowledge on a firm

> *Radical Rationalism.*　Radical rationalism is a term sometimes used to describe the belief that there is a supra-sensible world which is more real than the world of sense. This unchangeable world of ideas constitutes reality and differs sharply from the changeable world of "sense data" or empiricism. Plato is an example of a radical rationalist. His famous student, Aristotle, took a more moderate road on this issue by emphasizing the role played by sense data in the process of knowing. Hence, Aristotle is sometimes referred to as a moderate realist or moderate rationalist. Rationalism of any kind represents a strong challenge to the modern and contemporary political theorists who primarily rely on empiricism as the valid theory of knowledge.

empirical base. Aristotle felt that from observation and experience we can see an orderliness, a symmetry—a Grand Pattern in the universe. Aristotle's explanation of this is presented in his doctrine of four-fold cause. Nothing can take place (i.e., the result or effect of a cause), Aristotle said, from a single cause. Instead, everything that happens is the result of four causes, including causes of being and causes of becoming. For example, if we were to study politics, our study would be incomplete if it did not include examination and analysis of each of the four causes. In Figure 11 we can see the comprehensiveness of a study of politics which examines all four of the Aristotelian causes.[7] Figure 11 indicates how Aristotle's interests extended to all areas of inquiry noted in Table 4. Note the empirical basis on which Aristotle conducted his investigation in *each* area. (Compare this with Table 4 where a distinction was made between those areas which were factual and those which had little or no factual basis.) It is precisely at this point that Aristotle's influence has been greatest (as we shall see in the discussion on natural laws) and where he has been much criticized. We should carefully examine

[7] See Bluhm, Chapter IV, for a fuller discussion.

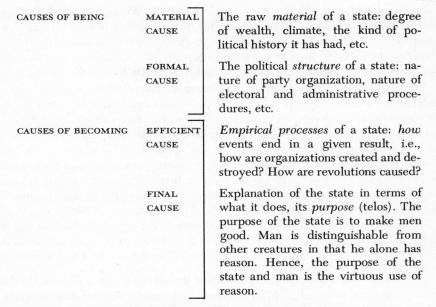

CAUSES OF BEING	MATERIAL CAUSE	The raw *material* of a state: degree of wealth, climate, the kind of political history it has had, etc.
	FORMAL CAUSE	The political *structure* of a state: nature of party organization, nature of electoral and administrative procedures, etc.
CAUSES OF BECOMING	EFFICIENT CAUSE	*Empirical processes* of a state: *how* events end in a given result, i.e., how are organizations created and destroyed? How are revolutions caused?
	FINAL CAUSE	Explanation of the state in terms of what it does, its *purpose* (telos). The purpose of the state is to make men good. Man is distinguishable from other creatures in that he alone has reason. Hence, the purpose of the state and man is the virtuous use of reason.

Figure 11. Aristotle's "Fourfold Causes" Applied to the *Polis*

this matter because where Aristotle is open to question, so is classical political theory. Such has been the magnitude of his influence.

Aristotle's claim—self-evident to some, outrageous to others—was that one could empirically demonstrate purpose (or value). Aristotle's argument is not difficult to comprehend. To him, we can empirically "see" the final cause of a thing. By careful study we can see the purpose of something. The purpose of an apple tree is to bear healthy apples; the purpose of a house is to provide shelter. What could be more clear?

It was clear to rationalists for centuries. The strength of Aristotle's case is great for those, who like the master, have a scientific bent and prefer scientific evidence over other forms. Rationalism means knowledge based on reason and it was viewed as the answer to claims for knowledge based on faith or intuition. Aristotelians, like Perry Mason, like their facts and their logic. The rationalists were convinced that the world we see is the real world —the world of being and the world of becoming.

Many modern philosophers and, it would seem, most contemporary scientists would grant Aristotle his empiricism but deny that we can *see* the purpose and order in the universe as the rationalists claim. If we could really see the good, political theory might have ended with Aristotle. (If we can truly see *telos*, what could we possibly do for an encore?)

The dispute over rationalism is sophisticated but not complicated. The strength of the Aristotelian argument would seem to depend on the examples one uses. If we use as our example the building of a house, we can probably see and comprehend *all* of the Aristotelian causes. We can say that the purpose of the house is to provide shelter. But the problem is this: Is this unquestionably, undeniably and necessarily the case? Isn't it conceivable that a house could be built for the purpose of burning it (the case of the wealthy pyromaniac)? Couldn't a fire department build cheap homes for the purpose of burning them so that firemen trainees could have some practice? Similarly, is the *true* purpose of an apple tree to bear apples? If we see a young deer eating the saplings, couldn't this be another purpose of apple trees— deer fodder? Once we open the door to doubt for alternate possibilities and admit that it *could* be otherwise, then the certainty—the necessity—is lost. Those in the rationalist tradition, however, were convinced that they could demonstrate a reason and purpose in nature. And until David Hume launched his famous assault on rationalism and necessity in the eighteenth century, most men were convinced by the Aristotelian argument.

A close corollary to rationalism as a theory of knowledge is the concept of rational man. The rationalism of Aristotle, in contrast to the radical rationalism of Plato or the mysticism of some others, maintains that knowledge is

> **Mysticism.**   Mysticism contends that the supreme source of truth (in this case real knowledge) is supersensory and superlogical intuition or revelation. There are many varieties of mysticism. Some allege that Plato was a mystic in the final analysis because the Philosopher King understood or comprehended real knowledge by some form of intuition or revelation. Mysticism and radical rationalism share one important characteristic in that they tend to be private or personal. Despite their differences, rationalism and empiricism are public. They claim that their knowledge is communicable.

both accessible and public. Practically every man has access to the knowledge of rationalism through his senses and his rational faculties. Opposed to the theories of knowledge which admitted few people to their privileged sanctuaries, rationalists insist that true knowledge is public. For them, the demonstration of truth is public. Furthermore, the public can comprehend it. The influence of rationalism and the concept of a rational man have several implications for Western political theory. Included among these are:

1. If man is rational and can know truth, he has a responsibility to live up to the standards revealed in truth.
2. Consequently, Western political theory has a gravity and seriousness to it that resembles seventeenth century American Puritan sermons. The prose is often turgid, the arguments are straightforward with a premium placed on clarity and logical development. Spice and wit are rare.
3. There is in the rationalist tradition a suggestion of democracy. If true knowledge is available to the public, why shouldn't the public participate in the making of policy? It would certainly be a serious

contradiction in rationalism to argue for public virtue and personal rule. This idea was not fully developed until at least the seventeenth century, but it served as a counterweight to rule by whimsy and caprice. Aristotle was firmly committed to the view of a *collective* wisdom.

Natural Law.   We have already mentioned that Aristotle helped to protect rationalism from its critics by placing it on grounds that correspond with science and common sense. Despite this difference with Plato, both Plato and Aristotle developed "standards of correctness . . . available to the human intellect which are universally true. Plato and Aristotle are rationalists, then, in the sense that they claim for the mind an ability to apprehend essential structures." [8] It is not surprising that rationalism, as an approach to knowledge, would dominate Western thought for so many centuries. After demonstrating to their satisfaction the possibility of certain knowledge, rationalists focused their attention on the objects of knowledge. Inspired by Aristotle's convincing and apparently conclusive argument that we can see the pattern of a purpose in nature, philosophers, theologians and jurists concentrated on discovering and ordering this pattern. The product of this collective effort we shall hereafter refer to as *natural law*. The principal features of natural law are:

1. There is a structured reality embedded in the very nature of things which man has the capacity to discover by his reason.
2. Each being has a natural purpose, or end, or goal.
3. There is an order of inclinations in each being which "pushes" it toward its end.
4. Goodness is the fulfillment and completion of this end.
5. Man thus can know not only what he is, he can also know what he is to do.
6. This knowledge is general and man can understand that there are certain fundamental principles of justice and morality which govern all human conduct.

The reader has undoubtedly concluded at this point that natural law and rationalism sound very much like the same thing. They are closely related inasmuch as rationalism provided a foundation for natural law. But as in the case of carpentry, buildings intended for a variety of functions could be built on a given foundation. For example, if we assume that man possesses the faculty of reason and can come to realize the pattern of order and purpose in the universe, we could then come up with many different things. Like Tom Paine, we could argue that the British were violating the "pattern" of self-rule to which all men are entitled. The British could counter that the Crown was obeying the proper order of things. Thomas Jenkin has shown us that many different specific political arguments can be built on the open-ended foun-

[8] Frohock, p. 39.

dations of traditional natural law.[9] It would therefore be more appropriate to speak of natural laws. But any great breakdown in natural law did not occur until the emergence of a modern and secular political theory after about 1500. Long before this breakdown, some major patterns and variations were taking shape. Two of these major features have been very important in Western political thought:

1. *The Utopian Future.* Aristotelian Natural Law stressed the idea of tendency—that each character or quality is tending toward something to be reached in the future. This concept of time was peculiarly atomistic and limited. Entities had a nature to fulfill and they were fulfilled during the course of growth and maturation, ceasing at a given point. This naturalistic view undoubtedly reflected the Greek belief that nature itself moved in cycles of conception, growth and decay.

Through adaptation and embellishment, Christian thinkers changed Natural Law in a manner which profoundly affected Western political theory. The change, simply, was to free purpose and fulfillment from the cycle which began with great hope but which included inevitable death and to tie it instead to a concept which progressively developed to a time of Divine Deliverance. Whether expressed radically for centuries by Millenarian sects

> *Millenarian Sects.* For centuries, beginning at the close of the eleventh century, small revolutionary groups appeared in northern Europe devoted to the realization of the Millennium. Believing in a future golden age and messianic kingdom on earth, the preachings and actions of these groups were usually volatile and controversial.

or more softly in the idea of attaining Grace, the Future As Progress is perhaps the point of departure in our political heritage. The "Good Vessel Natural Law" was loosened from its confining moorings by centuries of Christians who steered it toward a vision of distant fulfillment. This image is dominant in both ecclesiastical and secular political thought in the West. Whether expressed in the Utopian writings of a More or a Marx, in the totalitarian message of a Hitler, or the hopes outlined by a Jefferson, we can find the central idea of linear time.[10] In Western political theory, past and present are future.

2. *The Organic Community and the Common Good.* As we have seen, the doctrine of tendency is central to natural law. Nourished by reason, man can realize his purpose. Man cannot, however, attain his purpose apart from human association. In the span of fifteen centuries from Plato to Aquinas many different answers were offered in defending the idea that men are interdependently involved in the realization of common purpose. Two of these answers are dominant and warrant special attention. The idea of an *organic*

---

[9] See Thomas P. Jenkin, *The Study of Political Theory* (New York, 1955), pp. 12–14. A similar argument, with examples, is given by James Ward Smith, *Theme for Reason* (Princeton, 1957), Chapter 2.

[10] This theme is thoroughly discussed in Norman Cohn, *The Pursuit of the Millennium* (London, 1957).

community is closely tied to Aristotle's test: when *is* man self-sufficing? The other question, more difficult to resolve than the first, is: how can one know that there is a *common good* superior to the good of individuals?

The claim that the state or community is natural is given by Aristotle in his argument that "the proof that the state is a creation of nature and prior to the individual is that the individual, when isolated, is not self-sufficing; and therefore he is like a part in relation to the whole." [11] Arguing by analogy, Aristotle points out that the family is a natural outgrowth of man's efforts to survive, perpetuate himself and attain self-sufficiency. The state is only a natural and fuller expression of the family and is a consequence of the fact that even the family is not entirely self-sufficient. Aristotle does not confine his comments to economic self-sufficiency alone. In George Sabine's words, "what is distinctive about the state is, for Aristotle, that it first produces the conditions necessary to a really civilized life." [12] Emphasizing here the naturalistic side of natural law, Aristotle is telling us simply that man has a nature to fulfill which can only be fully realized in a civilized community life. It is only in such a setting that man's greatest accomplishments—science, art and philosophy—are possible.

Political theorists have long quarreled over the problem of individual and common good. Some have stressed the primacy and sovereignty of the individual and have argued that individual goodness is only the concern of the particular individual.[13] Others maintain that there is both an individual and a common good and that the latter is *useful* to the realization of the more important individual good.[14] (In view of the fact that most of us have been reared in a tradition that stresses individual worth, dignity and initiative, any mention of a common good sounds subversive. (How could there possibly be a *common* good superior to individual good?)

The strength and persuasiveness of the answer in classical thought is due to the absence of any minimization of the individual in that tradition. Critics of this view, a Thoreau or a Tolstoy, perceptively wrote that you can't have it both ways—a view prevalent in much modern and contemporary political thought. But for the formulators of the classical tradition, the Aristotelians and Thomists, there is an individual good which *is dependent* upon the reali-

> **Thomist.**   Those who follow in the theological and philosophical tradition of St. Thomas Aquinas (1225–1274). The contemporary theologian Jacques Maritain is sometimes referred to as a "neo-Thomist."

zation of the common good. According to one interpreter, the common good extends to men because of their diversity. ". . . This very diversity comes

[11] *Politics*, I, 2.

[12] George Sabine, *A History of Political Theory* (New York, 1953), p. 118.

[13] Henry David Thoreau and John Stuart Mill had a good time with this problem. Two of the most profound works ever offered on the subject are Thoreau's *Civil Disobedience* and the essay, *On Liberty*, by Mill.

[14] Discussed in Yves Simon, *The Tradition of Natural Law* (New York, 1965), pp. 97–109.

from the order of the parts in any whole; and thus the common good is the good of individuals as parts and members of society, and is sought by them precisely as *members of society and as being not all alike.*" [15] The common good is more complete than the private good of individuals and it is this completeness "which determines the greater excellence of the common good." [16]

As we have just seen, classical political thought revolves around the themes of potentiality and completion, the individual and his social fulfillment. It is the author's hope that this brief discussion has conveyed some of the strength of the classical political tradition without sowing too many misimpressions. To help in allaying any such distortion we might conclude the present discussion with a caveat: The classical political tradition—a tradition usually considered to include the eighteen or so centuries sandwiched between Plato and Machiavelli—was considerably richer and more varied than the present discussion indicates. But even more important differences and variations were yet to come. In the little more than two hundred years between the appearance of Machiavelli's *The Prince* and Hume's *Treatise of Human Nature,* new ideas and events shook the foundations of the Western world. During this period a new tradition of political theory was born. The products of this revolution we shall refer to as modern political theory (traditional).

Modern Political Theory: Traditional

When dealing with ideas, it is often difficult to pin-point when an idea was born and to whom we should credit the paternity. It is likewise difficult to designate certain periods of time as modern or pre-modern or classical. A case could even be made for the old adage that there is nothing new in the world of ideas since Plato and, consequently, that the history of Western thought is only a history of reinterpretations and reassessments of the old master. But this clearly is not the case.

The long spell that Plato, Aristotle, Cicero and other greats had cast over political dialogue was broken in several important ways by many persons, beginning even with Plato's student, Aristotle, and including such modern "greats" as Niccolo Machiavelli, Thomas Hobbes, John Locke, David Hume and Karl Marx. Many of the problems and issues which had bothered the ancients have continued as topics for political theorists to the present day. This gives Western political theory a certain continuity. But major changes affecting political theory occurred when thinkers began to alter radically the context and conditions under which any answers and solutions to the problems could be made. Plato, for example, was keenly interested in promoting a viable unit of political organization. He concluded that the proper size for a state was a population of about 5,000. Several of his contemporaries came to a similar conclusion. The problem of how one realizes a mean-

---

[15] Charles N. R. McCoy, *The Structure of Political Thought* (New York, 1963), pp. 51–52.

[16] Simon, p. 89.

ingful political atmosphere is acute for modern dictators (How can *I* rule?) as well as for modern democrats grappling with the problem of self-government (How can *we* rule?). Modern political thinkers write in an age of population explosion. They must consider groups of people numbering in the tens or hundreds of millions. The situation is far different from Plato's. Accordingly, new concepts must be developed. Here we are alluding to the peculiarly modern idea of nationalism.

To use another example, Plato and Aristotle saw the moral development of the individual and the evolution of the community as co-terminous. Many of the modern political thinkers rebelled against the monarchs and rulers who ruled in their own selfish interest with little or no regard for the material or moral betterment of their subjects. In order to break out of this tradition modern thinkers developed a concept of individual sovereignty which was *sui generis* in Western thought. It is this concept, individualism, which above all else distinguishes modern political theory from its classical predecessor. In fact, the bulk of modern political theory is a debate over the meaning and consequences of individualism.

Individualism. The concept of atomistic individualism is the most important single concept in modern Anglo-Saxon political thought. It was born

Atomistic Individualism. **The severest form of individualism. It connotes an autonomous individual who is his own master.**

in the pages of the writings of Thomas Hobbes (1588–1659), who was attempting to emphasize a point by using it. Not all writers used the term as did Hobbes, who, ironically, was a monarchist of sorts. In the mind of writers such as John Locke, Thomas Jefferson and Thomas Paine, individualism was seen as a necessary prerequisite to the liberation of man from tyranny, monarchical government, and nonrepresentative government.[17] It would be no exaggeration to say that such important concepts as natural rights, the social contract, government by consent and the right to revolution are all dependent on the concept of individualism. Put simply, the concept of individualism established the matter of priority. Who is ultimately supreme, a man and his conscience or the state? In Western democratic theory, emphasis is given to the priority of man. Man came first and was "endowed by his creator with certain unalienable rights." From this it follows that since man has natural rights at birth, the state is *not* the grantor of these rights. This means that the state can neither give man his rights nor take them away. (Any government which attempts to violate man's rights is acting unjustly.) Since man and his rights exist prior to the establishment of government, man and his rights cannot be bargained away when government is established. Man must be wary

[17] The long and tortuous history of man's struggles with tyranny is much too vast and complicated to be recounted here, but suffice it to say that the concept of individualism was focused and given a familiar context during the famous "Putney debates" held near London from 28 October to 11 November 1647 at the time of the Puritan resistance to Charles I. See Alpheus T. Mason, *Free Government in the Making* (New York, 1949), pp. 3–21, for a fuller account.

when setting up a government and obtaining the guarantee that the individual will not be swallowed up by government. The best guarantee, many believed, was to write a contract which would spell out the rights and duties of subject and state. The product of this contract is often referred to as constitutional government.

The Machine Theory of the State.   A consequence of the development of individualism and government based on contract was the notion that the state is an artifact—an artificial contrivance devised by man to do *only* what he wills it to do. In this simile, the state is accorded the status of a tool or machine.[18] The state is useful to man but he is clearly the master.

Individualism and the state viewed as machine vividly illustrate a major gulf dividing classical from modern thought. These concepts fly directly in the face of an idea of a common good and an organic community. The traditionalists of classical thought stressed the social side of man, indicating that man who did not participate in the affairs of his community was literally an idiot. Furthermore, the state and society were both civilizing and moralizing agencies. Modern democratic thinkers, following John Locke, have changed that. The success of these thinkers can be seen in the inability of Anglo-Saxons to be other than wary and cynical of government. Jefferson's dictum "that Government governs best that governs least" is part and parcel of this tradition. To us, the only *genuine* entity is the individual.

Modern democracy, the rise of Protestantism, and the development of capitalism are all associated with the emancipation of the individual in Western political thought. But not everyone applauded this development. Two of the more important criticisms of individualism and its alleged or real consequences have themselves become significant strains in modern political theory. Both these traditions, conservatism and Marxism, were created in the same country as the individualism they criticized. Consistent with the legacy they inspired, the first was prompted by a member of the aristocracy, the second by a wandering intellectual who carried his lunch in a brown paper bag to the London Museum where he wrote in behalf of the proletariat he befriended.

Conservatism.   The rhetoric of those proclaiming the rights and liberties of man were frightening to the famous eighteenth century English patrician, politician and writer, Edmund Burke (1729–1797). There is general agreement that Burke's criticisms of the intense political movements in behalf of democracy (or pretenses of democracy) in Europe during his time constitute the basis for the modern political tradition usually called conservatism. Most of Burke's more important thoughts are presented in his famous work *Reflections on the Revolution in France* (1790).

Burke's attitude toward ideology is helpful to an understanding of conservatism. Burke felt that the slogans being circulated in his day—"free-

---

[18] As far as I can determine, T. D. Weldon, a contemporary English political theorist, is the inventor of this useful concept which helps to explain what Locke and others were trying to do. See Weldon's *States and Morals* (New York, 1947), pp. 130–141.

dom," "liberty," and "natural rights"—presented great danger to society. Burke was against ideology as such because ideologies oversimplify and exaggerate actual social conditions. Worst of all, Burke feared that these slogans inevitably become the weapons of revolutionaries and social reformers who have little understanding or concern for the consequences. Do you believe in liberty for all? In one famous passage Burke mocked those who would answer yes:

> Is it because liberty in the abstract may be classed among the blessings of mankind, that I am seriously to felicitate a madman, who has escaped from the protecting restraint and wholesome darkness of his cell, on his restoration to the enjoyment of light and liberty? Am I to congratulate a highwayman and murderer, who has broke prison, upon the recovery of his natural rights?[19]

Burke's conservatism, then, represents an anti-ideology. At the very least it is strongly critical of most political ideas, especially those which urge social reform and social change.

But even an anti-ideology cannot be expressed without ideas. The primary notion or commitment of conservatism is literally that: to conserve. It has been pointed out countless times that conservatism works well for those who are "on top" of a society and want nothing more than to continue things as they are. That may be. Burke and his conservative followers would hardly be worthy of our attention, however, had they been nothing more than aristocrats who blindly defended the *status quo*. As a student of history and government, Burke felt that there were certain "truths" about which there could be little doubt. Included among these "truths" are the following: Man is fallen, doomed to imperfection. Moreover, men are *naturally* unequal and society requires "orders and classes" for the good of all. Man is a creature of appetite and will and is governed more by emotion than by reason. Man should shun the arrogance that would have him think that he is in command of his own destiny. Actually, society is governed by a divine being. The world that is governed by divine intent is incredibly complex and mysterious. In understanding the evolution of society, there is presumption in favor of that which has survived. Change has and will take place. But only necessary change (i.e., change necessary for the orderly continuation of a given society) should be allowed.[20] If and when changes are proposed, the burden of proof is on those urging the change to *prove* that the change is indeed necessary. These, in brief outline, are some of the important ideas of conservatism.

When compared to other "ideologies," conservatism seems flat and anything but exciting. This is the inevitable fate of those who say: "Show Me." In Western political theory, the excitement is caused by those—like the Marxists and Fascists—who present grandiose offers of a Utopia. There may also

[19] Edmund Burke, *Reflections on the Revolution in France* (London, 1910), p. 6.
[20] This presumably explains why Burke opposed the French Revolution while *favoring* the American Revolution.

be something here that is worthy of comment concerning political ideology—or the lack of it—in the United States.

A Note on Political Thought in America.   The United States has been a melting pot for more than ethnic, religious and racial groups alone. Many kinds of political ideas have been brought to these shores. Additional ideas have been generated to cope with our civil strife in the middle 1800's (a problem that never ends) and our various economic crises, including unionization. Yet with the exception of the decade or so preceding the American Revolution, the country as a whole has not pursued ideological dogmas. The conservative admonition of "show me" to those seeking change is little different from hard-headed American pragmatism. If Americans spoke of "life, liberty and the pursuit of happiness" in their Declaration of Independence, it was understood that this was Revolutionary rhetoric and should be accepted as such. The constitutional convention which followed the Revolution produced a document in which the word property was substituted for "the pursuit of happiness." When the revolutionary honeymoon was over, property was made secure.

The tone of American politics was clearly demonstrated at the constitutional convention in 1787. Some of this country's most brilliant and well-read men were in attendance at Philadelphia during that hot summer. Two things about that experience serve as a commentary on the nature of American political ideology.[21] First, these learned men had studied and considered the great political works of Western political philosophy. They were not convinced that there was any single great work with a guaranteed recipe for constitution-makers. Instead, they borrowed ideas from a variety of writers.[22] Despite the differences, even contradictions, in the works which most influenced the Founding Fathers, *none* of these influential works represents a program for Utopia. Hobbes, Locke and Montesquieu were men of this world who were interested not in devising blueprints for a paradise but rather in showing us how we can *avoid* having to live in a still worse world.[23] Locke

[21] I am herein using ideology to refer to a set of generalizations which rationalize or justify a given political system. Ideologies are usually highly abstract and emotional. An ideology will often contain assumptions and values which are passed off for facts, e.g., "All men are endowed by their creator with certain unalienable rights . . . ," "the Aryan race is naturally superior . . . ;" etc. *Cf.* Gustav Bergmann, "Ideology," *Ethics*, LXI (1951), 205–218, and Andrew Hacker, *Political Theory* (New York, 1961), Chapter 1.

[22] According to Saul Padover, Hobbes' *Leviathan* (1651); Locke's *Letter on Toleration* (1689), *Treatise on Government* and *Essay Concerning Human Understanding* (1690); and Montesquieu's *L'Esprit des lois* (1748) were "by far the most influential" sources of political ideas among the Founding Fathers. Saul K. Padover, *The World of the Founding Fathers* (New York, 1960), p. 36.

[23] Locke did write a Constitution for South Carolina, but it may not have been successful. H. C. Allen remarks:

In 1670 a small group of proprietors, who had been granted a charter by the King in 1663, founded Charleston; their effort, under the "fundamental Constitutions of Carolina," drawn up (ironically in some ways, in view of the later American opinion of him as a great democrat) by John Locke, to establish an elaborate system of social and political hierarchy, failed to take root in the actual soil of the New World, but it may possibly have helped to give South Carolina the aristocratic tone it long maintained. *The United States of America* (New York, 1964), p. 32.

and Montesquieu warned us of the danger of concentrated political power. This warning has been so firmly embedded in our collective psyche that Americans keep coming back to it as their *greatest* political problem. American political thought has one basic theme: How can we avoid the evil of centralized power? American political thought consequently takes on a negative and pragmatic quality. The problem is negative—how do we *avoid* too much governmental power? But any solution must be practical, it must work. The debates in the constitutional convention, the constitution itself, the splendid collection of essays circulated to defend the constitution (*The Federalist* papers) deal primarily with the fragmentation of political power. There is little room for ideology in such an enterprise.

A second feature of American political thought which serves to minimize ideology has to do with the manner in which Americans behave in political combat. One of the tacit ground rules in American politics is that differences of opinion stem from personal preference rather than from any success or failure to comprehend the truth. The style of American politics and rhetoric reflects the view that any person *could* be wrong! What *seems* true today will probably appear different tomorrow! State your opinions tentatively! Above all, adjust and compromise your differences! The Founding Fathers met at the Constitutional Convention as professional politicians who clearly understood that hard bargaining, negotiation, and compromise are the basic ingredients of democratic politics. These men considered many constitutional proposals before they agreed to compromise, giving and taking what was necessary to produce a document which both they and the public could accept. This spirit of compromise is deeply embedded in our behavior and we can only shudder to think of the consequences when the art of political compromise fails us, as it did prior to the Civil War.

In this commentary on American political thought, the emphasis thus far has been on style. Our *modus operandi* is that of practicality and compromise. This does not mean that American political thought lacks any substance or content. The content of this thought is the product of a happy marriage of Lockean ideas and American circumstances. In addition to the individualism already discussed, Locke's view that government must protect property, that men are equal with respect to rights, that governments obtain their authority from the consent of the governed are part of the American civil "credo." The adaptation of Locke to American politics and life was largely one of timing. His ideas on government based on consent were useful to colonists in fighting the crown. His concept of equality was agreeable to a bourgeois America who read Horatio Alger stories and believed in limitless social mobility. A vast and frightening wilderness could be conquered and occupied only by those who saw in themselves the rugged individual. Beyond this there is little more to add because American political thought rests on but a few foundation stones. Americans have added little to this foundation stone; accepting the basic ingredients of their "credo," they demand of any reformer or ideologue: "Show Me."

The amalgamation of European liberalism and a conservative domestic style in American politics has perhaps sheltered us from some of the harsher and more ideologically "pure" debates that have engulfed Europe from time to time. One reaction to the liberal individualism associated with the French and American revolutions is of special significance. Marxism has not only been a revolutionary ideology with tremendous strength and appeal, it has also proven to be a durable commodity.

Marxism.   Some readers might wonder why the term Marxism rather then Communism is being used here. Communism, like Nazism, Fascism and other modern authoritarian doctrines, is simply an apology for a totalitarian state. While details and specifics of terminology vary between these forms, we can readily see that the powerful dictators of the twentieth century, for example, Stalin, Hitler, and Mussolini, all commanded total allegiance to themselves in the name of some "higher doctrine." The megalomania, irrationalism, and ruthless suppression of opposition within these systems are factors which help illustrate the inseparability of these dictators from the ideology which explained and defended their actions. These doctrines waned on the passing of their masters. This is not to suggest that the close relationship between an ideology and a given ruler is a sign of weakness on the part of either the ideology or the ruler. The three men mentioned were most successful as dictators. It is just that it is difficult to consider Communism, Nazism and Fascism except in autobiographical and psychological terms. After Stalin's death, Khrushchev spoke in derision of the "cult of personality" that the Soviet Union had suffered under Stalin. Donald Zoll's crisp assessment of Fascism: "Fascism is an intestinal faith, not a cerebral theory . . ."[24] is a succinct summary of Fascism and Nazism, if not Communism also.

Marxism, on the other hand, is a cerebral theory with roots going back to such giants of modern Western philosophy as Kant and Hegel. Marxism is a paradigm of an ideology with a genuine *Weltanschauung*—which only adds to its appeal. At the heart of Marxism is a sweeping theory of history. Briefly, Marx argued that we can understand both the long pull of history and our specific place and role in that story by taking note that the organization, structure, mores—practically everything—of any society are the result of the tools (or mode of production) that men have available to them. What Marx is suggesting is that man is first and foremost an economic being, a worker, who builds his entire social life around how he makes his living. Nomadic man, for instance, wandered about because he had to. His livestock would continually move in order to graze more efficiently. But as improvements and innovations were made in man's tools—the wooden plow, the steam engine—a subsequent reordering and transformation of society took place.

Writing in a time when the industrial revolution was showing some of its worst side-effects, such as the employment of very young children for very long hours, Marx viewed capitalism as a system plagued by greed and ava-

[24] Donald Atwell Zoll, *Reason and Rebellion* (Englewood Cliffs, 1963), p. 319.

rice. Under capitalism the exploiting capitalists and the exploited proletarian are pitted together in a struggle which will end when the capitalists are defeated and the history of the exploitation of man by man is terminated. For Marx the low point in man's unsavory history came under capitalism where the doctrine of obsessive individualism led men to see in one another nothing more than another object to be exploited. Marx dubbed this milieu the "cash nexus."

But Marx did not despair; he felt that a psychological transformation, not unlike salvation in Western Christianity, would overtake man during the last stage of capitalism. Members of the working class, the proletariat, would one day realize their common plight, capitalism would be overthrown, and the road would be clear for a future of hope and promise. Marx did not give us a clear picture of this Utopia. He did, however, point out the need for man to find himself in meaningful work so that he might escape from his previous condition of alienation and lack of purpose.

This brief survey of certain aspects of Marxism is presented so that we might better understand something about the tremendous appeal that it has had in Western politics over the past hundred years.

After reading *Das Capital,* George Bernard Shaw is supposed to have said: "Karl Marx made a man of me." Shaw's long-standing affiliation with British Fabian socialism may offer a clue as to what he meant when he made that statement. While socialism extends back far beyond Marx's time, it was Marx who brought together many ideas about the ills of society and gave them a great sense of urgency and relevancy. The relevancy and popularity of Marx became a rallying point for many different kinds of social protest. And since social protest practically always comes "from below," Marx, the bitter critic of the captains of Western industry, became the symbol of protest for a host of social-political movements. Lenin saw in Marx the foundation (to which Lenin added many important details) for Russian Bolshevism. Many people could interpret World Wars I and II as the inevitable consequences of greedy capitalists who needed to sell weapons or starve. In many Western European countries, Marxism became the catalyst for general social reform. More than anything else, these reforms were designed to cure economic ills and to correct the social-political abuse which resulted from economic "injustice." Marx "made a man" of many, especially those who shared his sense of injustice and anger. As the famous French sociologist Emile Durkheim put it: "Socialism . . . is a cry of pain, sometimes of anger, uttered by men who feel most keenly our collective *malaise.*" [25] While the degree of Marxian influence on Western socialism may be impossible to measure, there can be little doubt but that Marx stands to socialism as do Hobbes and Locke to individualism.

But it remained for the father of Russian Communism, Lenin, to serve as the intellectual "mid-wife" who altered Marx's thoughts in a way that would

[25] Quoted in W. G. Runciman, *Social Science and Political Theory* (New York, 1963), p. 47.

make legitimate an elite ruling group—the Communist Party—and give Marxism a pointed edge in twentieth century international politics. Regarding the first matter, Lenin "clarified" an ambiguity in Marx's writings on the question: How will the revolution take place? Lenin answered that a group of intellectuals must provide the leadership and "spark" the revolution. Lenin truly gave birth to the Communist Party.

It is Lenin's theory of imperialism, however, which contains such explosive implications for international politics in our age. In this theory Lenin altered the Marxian view of exploitation of the proletariat by the capitalists to that of exploitation of the colonial nations by the capitalist nations. According to Lenin, the capitalists, having already plundered their own markets, looked greedily on the "underdeveloped" areas of the world where they could get their raw materials for next to nothing and, in turn, could sell their finished products. The capitalists could stave off internal problems by giving their own workers such "sops" as slightly higher wages and fringe benefits. Hence, Lenin suggested, the underdeveloped areas of the world have been forced to take the role of the proletariat in the twentieth century.

Supporting evidence for Lenin's theory of imperialism could easily be obtained from, say, a 1945 world map. The territorial and market holdings of such western nations as Great Britain, France, Holland and the United States were extensive.[26] As the idea of self-government and self-development spread to Latin America, Africa and Southeast Asia, many local political leaders saw in Marxism an explanation for their plight. For this very reason Marxism is taken seriously in much of the world.[27] In these movements toward self-rule there is both hope and danger. The hope, eloquently explained in a little book, is that no doctrine or dogma—even Marxism—can successfully capture the minds of men and make great ideological wars inevitable. According to this interpretation, the antidote to mass ideology and world conflict lies in national development.[28] National self-interest, as the case of Yugoslavia demonstrates, is stronger than a commitment to abstract Communism. The danger here, though, is that nationalism itself is a possible source of the greatest friction between nations.

Nationalism. In the last chapter of his notorious handbook for rulers (*The Prince*—1513), Niccolo Machiavelli pleads for a strong ruler who will finally bring together a united Italy "so that our fatherland may be raised up." In the closing lines of this work Machiavelli asks: "What doors would be closed against him [the strong ruler]? What people would refuse him obedience? What envy could oppose him? What Italian would withhold allegiance?" These words of Machiavelli summarize one of the most significant and volatile developments in modern political thought: Nationalism.

---

[26] A recent book by a non-Marxist demonstrates the plight of underdeveloped economies due, in part, to their role as suppliers to the industrial nations. See Robert L. Heilbroner, *The Great Ascent* (New York, 1963).

[27] See Adam Ulam, *The Unfinished Revolution* (New York, 1960).

[28] Edmund Stillman and William Pfaff, *The New Politics* (New York, 1961).

The nation state of our modern world is in sharp contrast to the Italian city states of Machiavelli's time which were petty dynasties run by bourgeois merchant princes whose *modus operandi* was intrigue, terror, and eternal warfare. Ironically, world politics today may be dominated by intrigue, terror and eternal warfare but, nationally, consolidation and centralization have replaced the reign of internal disorder which so disturbed two early giants of modern political theory, Machiavelli and Hobbes. Today, sovereignty often extends to large areas of land, peopled by millions with common language and culture.

The growth of nationalism in recent years illustrates the interdependence of forces which constitute any tradition of political thought. In the classical era, rationalism, natural law, a common good and an organic community were closely tied together. In modern thought nationalism is a by-product of individualism, popular sovereignty and secularization. One authority, Hans Kohn, suggests that nationalism had its first great manifestation in the French Revolution.[29] Nationalism is a force which involves general or mass participation of the population which, by definition, cannot be realized in an atmosphere of courtly life where the majority of people are literally subjects. In modern political thought and history, the subjects became objects.

Whether the trend toward secularization, individualism and nationalism in modern thought represents a blessing or a curse is a subject much debated. Nationalism, for instance, has a horrible side if the deeds of Hitler can be attributed to it. In a happier vein, some authorities feel that the post-World War II experience of two colossal forces teetering on the edge of brinkmanship may end as nations achieve greater internal strength and break away to develop their own national interests. In any case, modern thought itself represents a continuing dialogue over these and other questions. A different set of issues, those methodological rather than substantive, are now to be considered.

Modern Political Theory: Empirical-Scientific

This kind of degenerate learning did chiefly reign among the schoolmen: who, having sharp and strong wits, and abundance of leisure, and small variety of reading, but their wits being shut up in the cells of a few authors (chiefly Aristotle their dictator) as their persons were shut up in the cells of monasteries and colleges, and knowing little history either of nature or time, did out of no great quantity and infinite agitation of wit spin out unto us those laborious webs of learning . . . indeed cobwebs of learning, admirable for the fineness of thread and wars, but of no substance or profit.[30]

The above passage, written almost four centuries ago, is representative of another modern tradition in political theory. This tradition, based on empiri-

[29] Hans Kohn, *The Idea of Nationalism* (New York, 1944).
[30] Francis Bacon, quoted in Lee McDonald, *Western Political Theory: The Modern Age* (New York, 1962), p. 11.

cism, seeks to explain political behavior empirically. It has met increasing widespread acceptance and adoption and is now closely tied to the development and future of American political science. The success or failure of political science as an explanatory science will depend on the ability of political scientists to develop those major tools of scientific explanation—laws and theories. This is an inevitable consequence of any science which postulates scientific explanation as its goal.

Modern political theory, then, has two heads—although it appears that political scientists will give more food and support to the scientific head than it will to the other. Inasmuch as the classical normative tradition is usually associated and identified as political theory, it is not altogether surprising that in a recent survey, American political scientists ranked political theory at the bottom of seven fields in the profession judged on the basis of the significance of the work currently being done.[31] In other words, there is a basic dispute between those who view political theory as an area of moral-ethical inquiry, relevant to political inquiry and political science and those, following Bacon, who consider traditional political theory as "of no substance or profit."

The dispute over political theory is indicative of a basic conflict within the profession. In their recent assessment of American political science, Somit and Tanenhaus report, "political scientists consider behavioralism the most important issue facing the discipline. . . ."[32] At stake here are two important questions:

- What should political scientists be doing?
- Which type of political theory—normative or empirical—should play a prominent role in the development of political science?

The gulf which separates the two most prominent and antagonistic participants is both wide and deep because some see political theory as an *explanatory tool* for a political science while others feel that political theorists must lead, set standards, point out the problems to be considered—in short, to act as the conscience for a wayward discipline.[33] This conflict was born in that historic century and a half dating from the major work of Copernicus in 1543 to Newton's work at the close of the seventeenth century. During this period there was increasing optimism that man had the ability to comprehend his universe scientifically. Later—although it is possible to date the raw beginnings of a modern political science as early as the publication of *The Prince* in 1513—such eminent and influential thinkers as the Englishman Hobbes, the Frenchmen Montesquieu, Comte and Durkheim convinced themselves and

[31] Albert Somit and Joseph Tanenhaus, *American Political Science: A Profile of a Discipline* (New York, 1964), p. 56.

[32] *Ibid.*, p. 21.

[33] Some of the essays in *Approaches to the Study of Politics*, ed. Roland Young (Evanston, 1958), Part II, present eloquent defenses of the importance of the classical tradition. Other people have more aggressively brought battle to the camp of the opposition. See *Essays on the Scientific Study of Politics*, ed. Herbert J. Storing (New York, 1962).

persuaded others that they could, scientifically, comprehend and explain man and his social behavior as well.

Due to these efforts, the idea of a social science became fashionable and respectable in the eighteenth and nineteenth centuries. Social science has become so respectable in the twentieth century that few scholars find it worth questioning. In fact, this century is marked primarily by a sober commitment to finding the ways to speed up the accomplishment of a social science.

However, by 1900 it was apparent that the physical and natural sciences were light years ahead of the social sciences. Social scientists had little if anything to offer in the way of *general* laws and theories although they had developed interesting terms and concepts, e.g., alienation, anomie, mercantilism, class, bureaucracy, unconsciousness, insanity, culture, and many, many others. Consequently, it was agreed that specialization—a form of dividing and conquering—and professionalization would aid greatly in the development of a science of man's behavior.

The divisions and distinct areas of social science became more apparent as social scientists pursued their particular interests and began to differentiate between types and categories of phenomena. For example, culture was distinguished from contemporary political institutions, learning patterns in individuals were distinguished from behavior in the market place. As these specialized subject matter areas were refined, people began to seek out and communicate with their newly-found colleagues. In political science the event was symbolized by the founding of distinct departments later in the nineteenth century and the American Political Science Association in 1903.

Potentially, political theory now had a new master. At question was the role, if any, that the newly-founded political science profession *might* assign to political theory. Until recently, little concern was given to the question and political theory remained much as it had before—an area wherein study and investigation was largely confined to explaining and assessing the great masters of yesteryear: Plato, Aristotle, Rousseau, J. S. Mill, and the like.

Then, shortly after World War II, serious stock-taking was applied to political theory. Many of the young leaders in political science, intent upon developing an empirical science, raised the question: *Is* political theory, as it now stands, relevant to political science? In 1953 David Easton wrote: "Today in the United States . . . it has become increasingly difficult to appreciate why political theory should continue to be as a central part of political science. Theory has become increasingly remote from the mainstream of political research." [34] Easton set off a wave of action and reaction which has resulted, to use Meehan's term, in a "bifurcation of the discipline." [35] Although political scientists do not agree on the value of the more traditional and "classical" political theory, many political scientists, by their actions, reveal the belief that traditional theory is largely irrelevant to the study of politics.

[34] David Easton, *The Political System* (New York, 1953), p. ix.
[35] Eugene Meehan, *Contemporary Political Thought* (Homewood, 1967), p. 1.

The view here is simply that a theory is only meaningful to the degree that it is verifiable. In modern science, verifiability is determined empirically and intersubjectively.

The result of this is that a traditional political theory might be ignored, the highest form of contempt. There is nothing criminal in this; we should even expect it. There are many fine minds at work in this country eager to develop a science of politics. Sanguine about their prospects, they feel that time and effort will bring them those theories they need. There is no compelling logical reason why they won't succeed, given their willingness to be realistic about the range of the theories they might develop.[36] The parting wish, however, is that some consideration be given to matters such as those to be discussed in the epilogue.

EPILOGUE

In closing this chapter it seems appropriate to make explicit some of the reasons why a modern, empirical political science could profit from a closer relationship with political theory and philosophy than that which now exists. Clemenceau once remarked that wars are too important to be left to the generals. Likewise, politics is too important to be left entirely to the politicians for the simple reason that no group of individuals has a monopoly on wisdom. If Clemenceau meant by his remark that generals often lack the perspective of a statesman, his statement can also be read to mean that two heads are better than one.

One danger facing a field as broad as politics is that the politicians, the behavioral scientists of politics and the philosophers of politics might fail to communicate with one another. Worse still, they might not even try. The world of the politician is a tough one and he regularly faces many—if not most—of the crucial problems of his time. The problems that are too big and too complicated for people to resolve by themselves inevitably come to the politicians for resolution. These problems of our time—racial tension and bigotry, unemployment, decaying cities, an aging population which we won't allow to work, conflict between nations, to name but a few of the scores of problems—are such that we need every available brain to work on their solution. Students of politics might do well to ask themselves what Robert Lynd asked all of us some thirty years ago: Knowledge for what? Are the studies we engage in, whether they be speculative or empirical, relevant to the big problems of mankind? We could do no better than to begin here.

As political scientists produce more comprehensive explanations of how

[36] Sobering, constructive and useful are the works by Meehan, Abraham Kaplan, *The Conduct of Inquiry* (San Francisco, 1964), and Quentin Gibson, *The Logic of Social Enquiry* (London, 1966). These volumes clarify the kinds of theories which political scientists can help to develop in the near future. Useful accounts of contemporary political theory can be found in *Varieties of Political Theory*, ed. David Easton (Englewood Cliffs, 1966), and Eugene Meehan, *Contemporary Political Thought*.

and why things happen in the world of politics, there will undoubtedly be still greater pressure to separate and divide further empirical political theory from the speculative. This would be unfortunate because empirical political theory and normative political theory are interdependent. They can and should complement one another. The distinction between the realms of explanation and evaluation is not as clear as some people seem to think. As in the case of some couples, a separation or divorce is not in the best interest of either party.

Presently, many social and political scientists share the feeling that it is improper for scientists to be seen in public with the mistress, evaluation. Such an attitude is the result of a misunderstanding of the nature of science. It is increasingly clear that the conceptual tools used in scientific explanation cannot claim to have a 1:1 relationship to the empirical data they seek to explain. If there is *no* reality "out there" to be mechanically photographed and reproduced, we have to rely on the genius of scientists in constructing our picture of the political universe. This is not to argue that a science of politics is necessarily subjective or that explanatory laws and theories cannot be produced. I merely—and it may not be merely—want to indicate in addition that the concepts developed by scientists have a dimension that is frequently overlooked. On the one hand, concepts in scientific explanation are ultimately and necessarily tied to an empirical base. The scientist is restricted, as Kaplan reminds us, in that his concepts must "be capable of being checked by experience." [37] On the other hand—and this is a dimension of importance seldom discussed—the concepts developed by scientists contain implications and connotations as to what *should be* the case. In other words, the scientist selects from a practically limitless universe of phenomena what it is he will study. He, in turn, will develop those concepts which help him to order this data. The literature of social and political science is laden with these concepts: class, elite, power, alienation, freedom, anomie. The relevance of these concepts to science is dependent on empirical indicators which relate the phenomenon in question and the concept being used.

But concepts have an openness due to their indirect relationship to the data they *refer* to. Unable to generate *the* conceptual photograph of reality, the social and political theorist must create the concepts which to him seem empirically valid *and* significant or important (based on his own background and interests). The social and political theorist can develop many kinds of explanations for phenomena just as there are many ways to interpret and paint a landscape scene. The question always is: *What is it* you are trying to explain?

In Table 4, the "facts" in the far left hand column are meaningless until interpreted. In the second column, we find the concept of anomie which Durkheim employs in his work, *Suicide*. Durkheim, like any other social theorist, brought a great many predilections to his sociological studies. For one thing, as Robert Nisbet points out, Durkheim felt that "*society* is simply

[37] Kaplan, p. 79.

community written large." [38] According to Nisbet, Durkheim was caught up in the late nineteenth century revival which emphasized the intimacy, cohesion and depth of group and community life. More than three centuries earlier, Hobbes brought to his political theory an equally heavy array of conceptual baggage. Hobbes was impressed by just the opposite: the lack of intimacy, cohesion and depth in group and community life. And—what might seem strange—both Durkheim and Hobbes were right. A social scientist can develop explanations for social order, for social change, for anarchy. The social universe which the social scientist examines is almost impossibly complex. Hobbes chose to discuss the implications of a society on the verge of collapse. Durkheim, in *Suicide,* attempted to tie different kinds of suicide to different social contexts.

The message here for political science and political theory seems abundantly clear. The problems which seem important to a political scientist help him in selecting his "facts" and determining the concepts which order and explain these facts. Accordingly, normative thought *is* as relevant as ever. The normative inquiry produced in recent decades may be largely a barren wasteland. *This* criticism of traditional or classical theory *is* valid. But to criticize the works of a discipline as poor or useless is not the same as the charge that it is not needed. In any case political scientists should never forget that the level of achievement in any discipline is indicated by the nature and quality of the dialogue that takes place within its own ranks. It is heartening to note in closing that the level of the dialogue within political science has improved considerably during the past five years.

BIBLIOGRAPHY

The student of political theory often confronts the problem of choosing what to read from an almost limitless list of possibilities. This problem is compounded by the fact that some of the great political philosophers are relatively easy to comprehend while others can only be understood with great assistance from commentators and interpreters. With this in mind, the following bibliography includes references to some of the major works which speak most clearly for significant traditions in Western political thought. Additional reference is made to secondary sources which help to explain and interpret the masters.

The first major political thinker in the West, PLATO, is normally interpreted through his *Republic.* Two later works are often neglected but are important in an understanding of Plato's total view of politics. These works are *The Statesman* and *The Laws.* A collection of contemporary essays on Plato demonstrates just how controversial he still is. See THOMAS L. THORSON, *Plato: Totalitarian or Democrat* (Englewood Cliffs, 1963). ARISTOTLE's writings on ethics and metaphysics are important for those wanting a full understanding of Aristotle's political views. Nevertheless, a reading of his *Politics* is a good beginning. SIR ERNEST BARKER's *The Political Thought of Plato and Aristotle* (New York, 1959) is helpful in studying these two figures.

[38] Robert A. Nisbet, *Emile Durkheim* (Englewood Cliffs, 1965), p. 34.

Plato and Aristotle inspired the grand tradition of Natural Law in Western thought. This tradition is sympathetically treated by JOHN WILD in *Plato's Modern Enemies and the Theory of Natural Law* (Chicago, 1953). The revival of Aristotle in the thirteenth century was soon followed by his absorption into the rational system of ST. THOMAS AQUINAS in his massive *Summa Theologica*. Students may find St. Thomas and his period more accessible by way of A. P. D'ENTRÈVES, *The Medieval Contribution to Political Thought* (London, 1939).

The above tradition was broken abruptly with the appearance of MACHIAVELLI, *The Prince* in 1513. Machiavelli's naturalism is also expressed in the *Discourses* which include a modern case for democracy on naturalistic grounds. THOMAS HOBBES is without doubt a most important figure of the early modern period although his prose is less appealing than that of many others. Hobbes' interest in politics spills out of most of his works. The *Leviathan* is his best known political work and every student should at least browse through it at some time. Fortunately, there are several excellent interpretations of Hobbes including those by LEO STRAUSS, HOWARD WARRENDER and C. B. MACPHERSON which should be available in practically any college library.

JOHN LOCKE's influence on American thought has been nothing less than overwhelming. But of his *Two Treatises of Civil Government*, only the *Second Treatise* is important today. Every student should read it. Locke influenced a tradition of political essays which include THOMAS JEFFERSON, *Declaration of Independence* and TOM PAINE, *Common Sense*. The literature of and about American political thought is extensive. Two useful bibliographical sources can be found in CHARLES MERRIAM, *A History of American Political Theories* (New York, 1920), and THORNTON ANDERSON JACOBSON, *Development of American Political Thought* (New York, 1961). The bibliographical essay at the close of RICHARD HOFSTADTER, *The American Political Tradition* (New York, 1965), is excellent.

Other readable works of the modern period which are also representative of important traditions include: EDMUND BURKE, *Reflections on the Revolution in France*, an excellent introduction to conservatism; and JOHN STUART MILL, *On Liberty*, for an early statement of a libertarian view. JEAN JACQUES ROUSSEAU's profound effort to reconcile individual liberty with his feeling for communal fulfillment is expressed in *A Discourse on the Origins of Inequality* and *The Social Contract* (both readily available in a number of editions, as are most of the classics of political theory).

Standing against these writings—writings which constitute efforts to conserve traditions or modify them from within—are those modern works which would make society over out of new cloth. It is this total approach of some modern ideologies, e.g., revolutionary Communism, Fascism and Nazism, which provide the basis for modern totalitarianism. The scope of those ideologies is all-inclusive. No part of society is untouched. (This may help to explain the occasional popularity of an antidote, pluralism, during this period. Pluralists stress the advantages and virtues of differentiation and the autonomy of the group and the individual.) MARX and ENGELS' *The Communist Manifesto* is the best known of these totalitarian tracts. The tradition which Marx is generally considered to have inspired is both strong as an ideology and as a statement that radical change is the antidote to a too conservative Western tradition. An extremely important work here is MARX and ENGELS' *The German Ideology*. The bibliography on Marx and Marxism is so extensive that it practically staggers the imagination. For the beginner, ISAIAH BERLIN's biography, *Karl Marx: His Life and Environment* (New York, 1948), is a good place to start. So is ALFRED

MEYER, *Marxism: The Unity of Theory and Practice* (Cambridge, 1954). There seems to be a trend to interpret Marx as a humanist. This further distinguishes Marx from Communism in the twentieth century, notwithstanding the debt that the latter owes to Marx. See ROBERT C. TUCKER, *Philosophy and Myth in Karl Marx* (New York, 1961). The all-consuming features of modern totalitarian ideologies can also be seen in the famous work of a master practitioner of his own advice, HITLER and his *Mein Kampf*. Two excellent works on Nazism and Fascism are FRANZ NEUMANN, *Behemoth*, 2nd ed. (New York, 1944), and ERNST NOLTE, *Three Faces of Fascism* (New York, 1966).

Works such as those just cited give some indication of *some* of the various features of Western political thought as presented in this chapter. These suggestions refer primarily to *original* works and the list is spotty. Little mention was made of the twentieth century. Will the remainder of this century belong to the Marxists, the followers of racism, or the liberals? Or will the popularizer of non-violence, Gandhi, be later seen as the spirit of our age? It should be at least a bit exciting for the reader to contemplate that his reading, reflection and actions can play a part in answering these questions. In filling in the holes of this reading list, the reader is advised to consult secondary sources which interpret Western thought and are rich mines for additional reading suggestions. GEORGE H. SABINE, *A History of Political Theory* (New York, 1953), is the traditional classic in the field. Encyclopedic in scope, it is a very valuable reference to the study of the history of political ideas. Ebenstein's work is also something of a classic. Woven together are short introductory essays to and excerpts from the greats of political thought. WILLIAM EBENSTEIN, *Great Political Thinkers* (New York, 1960). Plamenatz has written some lengthy and provocative essays on important political thinkers dating from Machiavelli to Marx. JOHN PLAMENATZ, *Man and Society*, 2 vols. (New York, 1963). Murray's little volume is a relatively unknown gem. A careful reading of Chapter 1 should pay great dividends to any student of politics. Murray brilliantly explains why political thinkers tend to divide into scientists on one hand and philosophers on the other. A. R. M. MURRAY, *An Introduction to Political Philosophy* (London, 1959). Wolin has written some strikingly original essays on some of the major traditional figures. In Chapter 10, Wolin offers a challenging analysis of what he regards as the decline of political thought over the past three centuries. SHELDON S. WOLIN, *Politics and Vision* (Boston, 1960). Modern political thought is surveyed in LEE MC DONALD, *Western Political Theory: The Modern Age* (New York, 1962).

There are a few very fine works which critically evaluate theory and its role in contemporary political science. Easton's was one of the first and has been very influential. DAVID EASTON, *The Political System* (New York, 1953). An excellent work which attempts to connect classical inquiry with contemporary political analysis is WILLIAM BLUHM, *Theories of the Political System* (Englewood Cliffs, 1965). The foundations and problems of contemporary political theory are discussed in ARNOLD BRECHT, *Political Theory: The Foundations of Twentieth-Century Political Thought* (Princeton, 1959). A group of scholars discuss the integration of theory and current political analysis in a collection of essays, *Varieties of Political Theory*, ed. David Easton (Englewood Cliffs, 1966). A healthy trend can be noted in recent years in a number of works which critically evaluate the strengths and weaknesses of both political theory and political science. Some of these works reveal a solid background in the philosophy of science on the part of the author. These works consequently apply to practically any area of social science. Still at the head of the class of these efforts is ABRAHAM KAPLAN, *The Conduct of Inquiry* (San Francisco, 1964). QUENTIN GIBSON, *The Logic of Social Enquiry* (London, 1960), is interesting as well as useful. Works which are more specifically political include FRED FROHOCK, *The Nature of Political Inquiry* (Homewood, Ill., 1967), and two books by EUGENE MEEHAN, *The Theory and Method of Political Analysis* (Homewood, 1965), and *Contemporary Political Thought: A Critical Study* (Homewood, 1967). Meehan's works are especially germane to the discussion in this chapter. Another indication of the strength of this trend was the appearance of two more works at the close of 1967. W. J. M. MACKENZIE, *Politics and Social Science* (Baltimore, 1967), is a good companion to Meehan's work. DANTE GERMINO, *Beyond Ideology: The Revival of Political Theory* (New York, 1967), is comparable to the present chapter in subject matter, but not always in the conclusions reached. Another recent work worth investigating is W. G. RUNCIMAN, *Social Science and Political Theory* (New York, 1963).

10 / POLITICAL BEHAVIOR
AND PUBLIC OPINION

Voting Behavior / Public Opinion / Political Socialization /
Political Recruitment and Leadership / Community Politics

Many political behavioralists would quarrel with the designation of a specific subfield of political science as "political behavior," because of their strong feeling that the study of political behavior occurs (or should occur) in all fields of the discipline. This point is well taken; however, in the early years of the growth of the behavioral movement, the subject matter to which the approach was applied was largely in the area of voting behavior. Many courses were developed—and still exist—with the title "Political Behavior," and the designation of the field of voting behavior studies as political behavior continued. Perhaps one could designate the area "voting behavior" or "electoral behavior," but that would now be too narrow, because of the subjects, related to voting behavior, with which political behavioralists have more recently become concerned, such as leadership, political socialization, and community politics. Our attention in the first part of this chapter will be primarily on voting behavior, because it is on that subject that most effort has been expended. It should be noted, however, that voting is only one kind of *political participation,* which includes campaigning, political discussion, fund-giving, and running for office. Because of the close relationship between public opinion and those attitudes which have an effect on voting behavior, public opinion has been grouped with "political behavior" for the purposes of organization. However, the closeness in origins and approach, which will be discussed later, should not be over-estimated.

To consider political behavior and public opinion apart from political parties and interest groups, as the structure of this and the next chapter requires us to do, also introduces problems. One of the most important influences on voting behavior is an individual's affiliation with a political party; he may receive much political communication affecting his opinions through the groups of which he is a member. While recognizing this, we must make some attempt to "sort out" the various aspects of our political life. The present chapter arrangement is based on the fact that parties and interest groups have certain formal characteristics which distinguish their existence. This does not mean either that formal structure does not influence voting or our opinions, or that the opinions and the voting are not patterned. In fact, without such patterns, we could not make any generalizations about them.

VOTING BEHAVIOR

It has been noted at several earlier points in this volume that the first voting studies were heavily sociological in their orientation. Their authors relied on demographic variables, particularly income, education, and occupation, in explaining both voting turnout and the direction of the vote (which
candidate or party the voter chose). The use of such variables proved rewarding, because it was shown that they were related to frequency of participation and direction of the vote, as well as such items as interest in politics,
which itself had an impact on turnout. Thus, those with higher income, education, and occupational status were more likely to vote than those lower
with respect to those items, as well as to vote Republican. Higher turnout by
those disposed to vote Republican usually gave Republicans strength out of
proportion to their numbers. It was also found that urban dwellers voted in
greater proportions than did rural residents, and that whites (and males)
voted more frequently than Negroes (and females). Those of medium age
(usually defined as 35–55) voted in greater proportion than those either
younger (21–34) or older (56+), although the youngest did have a critical
effect on election outcomes despite having the lowest rates of voting. Increasing Republicanism was noted among the older voters. The relevance of religion was also seen, with Catholics voting heavily for Democratic candidates,
and Protestants voting in large measure for Republicans. (Jews were revealed to be strong supporters of the Democrats, despite the higher-than-
average education and income possessed by many of the religion's adherents.) As the foregoing may suggest, the emphasis in voting studies has been
on the causes of voting behavior, not on the effect of this behavior or on the
elections in which it takes place, although the latter has been considered by
students of public opinion interested in such questions as "When is an election a mandate to a candidate to pursue a given course of action?"

The emphasis on demographic variables in the early studies, which were
conducted in one community during one election (such as Erie County in
1940 and Elmira in 1948),[1] may be explained as a result of the fact that some
of the senior researchers were sociologists, working with political data,
rather than political scientists. In addition, research on the subject had to
start somewhere, and such demographic variables seemed to be a good jump-
ing-off point. Those who worked with such data did not stop at individual
correlations between each independent variable and the turnout or the vote
(the dependent variables); they worked them in combination, which meant,
among other things, the development by Lazarsfeld of an Index of Political

---

[1] The Erie County study is Paul Lazarsfeld, Bernard Berelson, and Hazel Gaudet, *The
People's Choice* (New York, 1944); the Elmira study is Bernard Berelson, Paul Lazarsfeld,
and William McPhee, *Voting: A Study of Opinion Formation in an Election Campaign*
(Chicago, 1954).

Predisposition (IPP). He reasoned that if education, income, and occupation were each related to turnout, then an index combining one's ranking on each should prove useful—as it did. Others worked with the effect of social mobility, examining the direction of the vote of those moving up and down the socio-economic ladder; one finding of interest was that those aiming upward were quite likely to vote like the group toward which they were moving rather than the group from which they came. On the other hand, those downwardly mobile continued to vote like those in the group *from* which they were moving down.

The idea of "cross-pressure," more thoroughly developed in the interest group literature, also was applied. If it was recognized that individuals of a certain religion were likely to vote in a certain direction, and that voters of a particular range of income would likely vote for one party rather than another, one came to the question: "What if these run in opposite directions?" The low income Catholic would not be buffeted in different directions, because both Catholics and those of less income tended to vote for the Democrats. Similarly, the wealthy Protestant (at least of certain denominations) would not be cross-pressured. But what of the indigent Protestant or the wealthy Catholic? Here it was found that the cross-pressure hypothesis was useful, even when the individual involved might not be aware of the "pressure" to which he was subject. Thus, wealthy Catholics would cast a higher proportion of their votes for Democratic candidates than would wealthy non-Catholics, but a lower proportion than low-income Catholics. These cross-pressured individuals also tended to vote less frequently, withdrawal being a not unusual response to the problems of ambivalence. The direction of their vote was also less consistent when they did vote. The suggestion has been made more recently that there is a difference between an "avoidance-avoidance" cross-pressure situation, where neither alternative is attractive and the result is non-participation, and the "approach-approach" situation, in which both attract the individual and are likely to result in activity.[2]

The anti-behavioralists have objected to the voting studies, on the grounds that the studies reject the "political" and explain everything in terms of the "sub-political," [3] by which they mean sociological or psychological variables. Even those sympathetic have raised such a criticism. Thus Philip Rieff has noted that "too frequently depth psychology has been used by political scientists to mask problems of objective social processes, reducing them to characterological problems." [4] The anti-behavioralists also claim

[2] Ithiel De Sola Pool, Robert P. Abelson, Samuel L. Popkin, *Candidates, Issues, and Strategies: A Computer Simulation of the 1960 and 1964 Presidential Elections* (Cambridge, Mass., 1965), pp. 76–77.

[3] Walter Berns, "Voting Studies," *Essays on the Scientific Study of Politics,* ed. Herbert Storing (New York, 1962), p. 42. Dissent from those clearly not anti-behavioralist comes from V.O. Key, Jr., and Frank Munger, "Social Determinism and Electoral Decision: The Case of Indiana," *American Voting Behavior,* ed. Eugene Burdick and Arthur Brodbeck (Glencoe, 1959), pp. 281–299.

[4] "Psychology and Politics: The Freudian Connection," *World Politics,* VII (1955), 304.

that the voting studies show that the vote is "selfish," when they feel it should be "rational" and "disinterested." But they confuse the correlation of two objective items (socio-economic status and the vote) with the conscious action of the voter.

While the over-emphasis on socio-economic variables at the expense of political variables *in the earlier studies* has already been noted, the anti-behavioralists continue to criticize almost all voting studies on the same basis. Perhaps they are unwilling to accept the fact that political opinion is not simply the result of a "unique human faculty," but that it reflects the social environment in which the individual finds himself. The critics, in asserting the "will" as the sole determinant of the voting decision, at every point reject psychology. And they reject sociology as well; if the background of the voters in each party were identical, then to pursue the relationship of socio-economic data to the vote would not be productive—but the point is that there *is* a difference in the backgrounds of Republicans and Democrats and, while perhaps overdone, the pursuit of such factors has been found to be worthwhile in explaining predispositions (not determinants) to vote in a cer-

> *Predisposition.*   A leaning or tendency in a certain direction. In the absence of other, complicating or contradicting, factors, and when properly stimulated, one will act in the direction of the predisposition. To say that someone is predisposed to do something is perhaps to say that, "other things being equal [which they often are not], he will do thus-and-such." A predisposition does not always result in identical behavior.

tain direction. And, as Greenstein points out with respect to psychology,

> Psychoanalytic hypotheses, especially those drawing upon the central notions of repression and ego defense, have the merit of offering non-obvious explanations of behavior that otherwise seems obscure and inexplicable, and especially of much of the "irrationality" and emotionalism that abounds in politics.[5]

The scope of the first studies did include more than turnout and direction of the vote. Thus the researchers explored political discussion, and began to find that people tended to talk with those who were like-minded, rather than with those of opposite views, requiring us to change our views of the amount of political "debate" which occurs. The relationship between the politics of the voter's parents and the voter's own politics was explored, at least in terms of party preference, thus establishing a foundation for later political socialization studies. It came to be recognized that the effect of age on the vote might not be simply a function of age, but might be more a result of the generation in which the voter first was exposed to politics. This has brought a shift to analyses of "cohorts" (a given age group examined through the years as it becomes older), rather than simply of those in a given age category at different times. In older studies, the voting behavior of those 65 and over in one

[5] Fred I. Greenstein, "Personality and Politics: Problems of Evidence, Inference, and Conceptualization," paper presented at American Political Science Association meetings, Chicago, September, 1967, p. 3.

election was examined and compared with the voting behavior of those 65 and over in another election; the second group was not the same age as the first (at *that* time) and had not been introduced to politics at the same time. A cohort study would, for example, take a group of voters aged 21–25 in 1940 and follow them when they were 31–35 in 1950, 41–45 in 1960, and so on. Party preference itself (aside from the vote for specific candidates) was also examined, as was the effect of different types of issues. A distinction was developed between "position issues" (bread-and-butter substantive matters) and "style issues" (such as political morality and Communism in government),[6] with positions on the former having a clearer relation to party preference. However, such matters as party preference, political interest, and opinions on issues tended to take a back seat to the basic elements already delineated. As a number of studies were carried out, it became possible to accumulate findings, to provide greater strength for the assertions which could be made, and to provide a thorough picture of political life. Obviously, if a finding from Erie County was repeated in Elmira, one could voice it with more assurance than if it did not recur.

The early work of the politics-oriented sociologists led political scientists to enter the voting studies area. With their entrance, and with the development of the Survey Research Center at the University of Michigan, we find a shift, albeit a gradual one, from the sociological variables (although they were certainly not discarded) toward more explicitly political variables. This led at first through a stage when the political variables (interest, orientation, opinion) were seen as reflections of the demographic variables, mediating between the latter and the turnout and vote-direction variables, as when Miller suggested that the independent variables of income, occupation, and education were funneled through an "economic outlook" or economic confidence variable before they had an impact on voting behavior. Then it came to be recognized that the intervening variables had their own impact, for example, that party identification had an impact independent of education or income, or that the socio-economic variables only supported the intervening variables rather than determined voting outcome. Thus, Miller has remarked that "the Index of Political Predisposition is latterly conceived to be an index of socio-economic *support* for the carrying out of an *intention* to behave."[7]

Psychological variables were also introduced into the analysis of voting. The role which perceptions played, as a mediating influence between what went on "out there" in the campaign and the voter's ultimate decision, was one item considered. The ideas of *identification* with groups, particularly

Identification. In its social-psychological sense, this term means a "feeling part of" or "akin to." Individuals *consider themselves* part of organi-

---

[6] Berelson, *et al., Voting*, pp. 184–185.

[7] Warren E. Miller, "The Socio-Economic Analysis of Political Behavior," *Midwest Journal of Political Science*, II (1958), 242. The introduction of intervening political variables between socio-economic items and the vote is analogous to the shift in psychology from a straight S→R (stimulus-response) position to one of S→O→R (stimulus-organism-response).

zations with which they have no formal attachment. It is on the basis of identification that we usually speak of people as Democrats or Republicans.

with a political party, and of *orientations* toward political phenomena (to-

> *Orientation.*   An outlook, either general in nature or focused on a limited aspect of one's surroundings. These outlooks, which cover more than individual attitudes or opinions, help the individual sort out, emphasize, and evaluate the stimuli coming from the world around him. A particular pattern or aggregate of political orientations becomes a *political culture.*

wards issues, party, and candidates, and to different levels of government) were borrowed from social psychology. An individual's identification with a political party—although it remained quite stable—did not mean he automatically voted for that party, but his identification was relevant to his evaluation of candidates' positions and the strength of his identification was related to his vote decisions. In addition, even when party identification was strongly related to the vote, it did not mean that the voters were necessarily casting their ballots on the basis of what the party espoused (the "responsible parties model"), because the voters might lack the information necessary to

> *Responsible Party.*   A type of political party in which leaders must follow the collective views of the party and are responsible to the party members who choose them. Often such groups are organized around particular legislative programs: thus they are sometimes called *programmatic parties.* Many Americans feel the British parties in Parliament are "responsible" in the sense indicated here.

link policy and party. The concepts of alienation, political efficacy ("Does my voice count in politics?"), and political cynicism were among those which proved useful—that is, they were shown to be related to people's participation. Alienation, which is supposed to characterize the age in which we live, has received particular attention, not only from a methodological point of view (What constituted alienation?), but also in terms of its effect on political activity. It has been suggested that, while withdrawal is one result of alienation, high rates of activism may occur as people attempt to change the alienation-producing situation.

The SRC involvement also meant nation-wide samples rather than those from individual communities. It also meant data on off-year elections as well as Presidential-year elections, and this has revealed differences in the composition of the electorate in different elections. We have known for some time that turnout (in gross figures) was greatest in Presidential elections, smaller in "off-year" elections for Senator and Representative, and smaller yet for county and municipal elections, but we did not know that the size of the turnout affected the composition of those participating. Now it appears that the electorate in Presidential elections is proportionately more female, less educated, and less wealthy than that voting in non-Presidential elections, and that those voting in party primary elections also are not representative of the total electorate or even of those usually voting for that party's candidates in the general election, being disproportionately the "strong partisans" of that party.

The use of nation-wide samples raised the question of what to do with the South, with its traditional one-party Democratic dominance, which could easily distort generalizations made about the nation as a whole. Many analysts have, in fact, excluded the Southern states (usually those which constituted the Confederacy) from their studies, or have treated them separately, because the region's one-party nature has decreased the effect of economic issues and class by comparison with other states. The SRC involvement in voting research did, however, still mean an emphasis on votes for candidates in partisan elections. Less attention was given to voting in non-partisan elections for candidates or to voting in referendum elections. While clearly there are no nation-wide referenda and nation-wide elections are partisan rather than non-partisan, the comparison might have proved helpful. It has been suggested that referendum and "people" elections cannot be compared because a matter is fixed once proposed in a referendum, and cannot be changed in the course of a campaign as candidates can change their arguments.[8] This misses the point that supporters or opponents of a referendum can shift their arguments during a campaign, and voters may shift their views during the same period, just as they would in considering candidates, and that, while candidates can change the issues they stress, the candidates (like the referenda) remain (physically) the same during the period of the campaign. The concentration on election campaign periods (intra-election) has also meant a relative disregard for the periods between elections (inter-election) when greater change of views may occur because people are less politically involved, less on their guard against politically relevant stimuli.

While the first studies under the SRC were, like their antecedents, single-election studies, this quickly changed, so that now we can talk about historical voting behavior studies, refuting the criticism, based on earlier studies, that voting behavior analysis was inherently ahistorical. In fact, there now is available through the SRC a vast amount of material on electoral behavior for a long series of elections, a resource which will continue to accumulate as further nation-wide studies are conducted at each election.

A type of "historical" concern in voting behavior studies—and a principal one—has been what transpires during the course of the campaign. Survey studies of voting behavior have not been based solely on one-shot interviews, but generally have utilized what are known as "panel studies" in which individuals are interviewed at several times during the campaign (as well as immediately before and immediately after) to determine shifts in views and to relate them to more constant factors, such as some of the demo-

[8] Gilbert Y. Steiner, "Bureau Research and Community Decisions: Some Points of Intercept," *The Research Function of University Bureaus*, ed. Dwight Waldo, pp. 139–140.

graphic items. The importance of the several-interviews-over-time approach is shown by the 1948 disaster of the commercial pollsters, who predicted the Presidential election outcome on the basis of a poll taken several weeks before Election Day; shifts in preference and intention to vote after the last poll date spelled the outcome in favor of Truman rather than Dewey.

The panel studies show that the principal effect during a campaign is not, as many believe, conversion from one position to another. Instead, crystallization of an intention to vote in a given direction and reinforcement of views already held are the principal effects of the campaign but, as 1948 and other elections show, they are crucial, particularly when the number of those turning out in support of their own party's candidate are divided about equally between the two parties.[9] The reinforcement is brought about in large measure by the informal groups of which the voter is a "member," and which serve an important mediating function in the electoral process. The panel studies have focused attention on the relevance of such "small groups" to politics. As Verba has noted,

> Primary groups of all sorts mediate political relationships at strategic points in the political process. They are the locus of most political decision-making, they are important transmission points in political communications, and they exercise a major influence on the political beliefs and attitudes of their members.[10]

The largest proportion of the voters do not remain in suspended animation until "all the evidence is in." The intention to vote is crystallized well before Election Day. Perhaps this explains why so much of the fear about the impact of the broadcast of early Presidential election returns on West Coast audiences is misplaced: Even if the late voters on the coast heard that the candidate for whom they did not intend to vote was winning heavily, their intention would be sufficiently set that it would not in most cases affect either their intention to vote or the direction of that vote.[11]

Through this accumulation of data, we have been able to see whether or not trends have developed, and whether the relationships found in the earlier voting studies still hold. Some changes are evident. The turnout of urban Negroes is sufficiently high to raise questions about the earlier statement that whites vote in higher proportions than blacks. While the Negro attachment to the Democratic party remains strong, history makes us remember that this attachment does not extend back in time beyond President Franklin Roosevelt. We now have more evidence of the effect of differences in generations in party attachment. Those who came to vote first during the New Deal are to a large extent remaining Democratic, even as they become

[9] Angus Campbell, "Surge and Decline: A Study of Electoral Change," Campbell, *et al., Elections and the Political Order* (New York, 1966), p. 44. [Originally published in *Public Opinion Quarterly*, XXIV (1960), 397–418.]

[10] Sidney Verba, *Small Groups and Political Behavior: A Study of Leadership* (Princeton, 1961), p. 4.

[11] Harold Mendelson, "Election-day Broadcasts and Terminal Voting Decisions," and Douglas Fuchs, "Election-day Radio-Television and Western Voting," *Public Opinion Quarterly*, XXX (1966), 212–225 and 226–236, respectively.

older. The increased participation of women, although still less than that of men, has been noted; certainly one found far less of the phenomenon noted by Gosnell in the 1920's, when women declined to vote because their husbands felt their position was in the home, a feeling particularly true in immigrant families. But we still find women more likely to follow the "lead" of their husbands than is true in the opposite direction.

The relevant effects of income and occupation on political behavior have also been found to have changed. Of the three basic items comprising socioeconomic status (SES), income, education, and occupation, income was originally the best *single* indicator of a person's vote. Now that the income of many skilled laborers exceeds that of many white-collar workers, the strength of income as an independent variable has been exceeded by that of occupation; one's place in the occupational prestige ladder tends to be a better indicator of one's vote. We also find that the introduction of more "style" issues as compared with "position" issues has had an effect on the relationship between SES and voting. When the basic issues were economic, the working class voted heavily Democratic, because the Democratic Party was "liberal" on such matters. Now, however, with civil rights (such matters as open occupancy) at the heart of much political discussion, these same working class people have often decreased their support of the Democratic Party. The Democrats were also the "liberal" party on this measure, but the liberalism of the working class on economic matters did not extend to liberalism on civil rights matters. The Johnson landslide of 1964, the Kennedy-Nixon "squeaker" of 1960, and the Humphrey-Nixon-Wallace contest of 1968, have shown us that each election does have its idiosyncratic aspects, and that while we can still test for generalizations within each election, we need a series of elections for our most solid findings.

Recent elections have led some analysts to question whether socioeconomic factors are having the same impact they had when the country was still fighting the battles of the New Deal and the Fair Deal; they point to the election of 1964, with a Democratic majority in almost every category in the population, as evidence for this. While perhaps the effect of SES variables has dampened compared to the period of the first voting studies, we can still find differences in the degree to which the Democratic Party is supported by those in various categories of income, education, and occupation. Almost every Gallup Poll on the subject of party identification reveals such differences, and they were apparent even in 1964 and 1968; while previously Republican suburbs may have voted for President Johnson, they did not do so by the same overwhelming margins as did certain central-city working-class districts. It may be that, in attempting to retain socio-economic categories in our explanations of voting behavior, we are being creatures of habit, insisting on old explanations and developing an increasing number of reasons to explain exceptions to our old generalizations. Perhaps we might better recast our basic outlook, rather than mask the basic developments going on around us, such as lessened control of the black vote, the increasing conservatism of the ethnic vote, and the lessened party vote in large cities. The increasing number of studies of voting behavior on a cross-national basis using a thorough-going comparative approach suggests that this re-casting is perhaps already going on.

Particular subgroups in the population have always attracted special attention and individual studies. Catholics and Jews have received much attention, the latter particularly in terms of the role of religion in both the 1928 and 1960 Presidential campaigns. Although earlier interpretations attributed Al Smith's 1928 defeat by Hoover largely to his religion, more recent (revisionist) history has suggested both that no one could have defeated Hoover

> **Revisionism.**   In history, the rewriting of history from a point of view different from that used by earlier "schools" of historians, like Charles Beard's economic interpretation of the writing of the United States Constitution. For a new approach to be labelled "revisionist," it must contain substantially different conclusions about the *how* or *why* of past events. In Marxist philosophy, the term is used to indicate, pejoratively, anyone who deviates from (one's own conception of) Marx's or Lenin's or Stalin's views.

in 1928 and that Smith's immigrant-urban background and his position on Prohibition were especially damaging to his cause, apart from his religion.[12] Studies of the 1960 election, based on national survey data, suggest that Kennedy may have lost 1,500,000 votes *net* because of his religion (subtracting those who voted for him solely because he was Catholic from those who voted against him for the same reason).[13] The degree of participation and involvement in the ethnic or religious subcommunity has also been shown to be quite important.

Republican suburbs raise another subject of "conventional wisdom" which has now been subject to analysis. The mythology has it that the suburbs are monolithically Republican, and that those moving to the suburbs from the central city are converted to that Republicanism. The data on social mobility would seem to support this hypothesis. However, even during the Eisenhower years, when the Republican Presidential vote was high, a number of suburbs voted Democratic, while others produced a Republican vote only for President, indicating that because voters voted for someone with the

---

[12] Ruth Silva, *Rum, Religion, and Votes: 1928 Re-examined* (University Park, Penn., 1962).

[13] Philip E. Converse, Angus Campbell, Warren E. Miller, and Donald E. Stokes, "Stability and Change in 1960: A Reinstating Election," *American Political Science Review*, LV (1961), 269–280. This statistic casts quite a different light on Nixon's narrow defeat, and suggests a much weaker "Republican vote" than was interpreted at the time. V.O. Key reinforces this view with data from *The Responsible Electorate: Rationality in Presidential Voting, 1936–1960*, with Milton Cummings (Cambridge, Mass., 1966), in which he shows that those shifting from past Democratic to present Republican vote in that election were quite unenthused about the Republican Party, about Nixon, and about Republican policy; he does not indicate directly whether their shift was a result of Kennedy's religion.

Republican label does not mean they voted for him *because* he was a Republican. The blue-collar (or industrial) suburbs, now present in addition to the white-collar ("bedroom") suburbs which characterized earlier suburban growth, may be as heavily Democratic as the Democratic areas from which those suburbanites who live there have come. Partisan identification survives people's residence-changing, even when their new neighbors have opposing political views.[14]

The Negro's political participation has been of long-standing interest. Students of constitutional law have examined the many legal hurdles, such as the "grandfather clause" and the white primary, placed in his way; those

> **Grandfather Clause.**   A provision indicating that if a person or his relatives had been eligible to vote prior to the passage of the Fifteenth Amendment, or prior to 1865, he himself was eligible; otherwise, he would have to pass a literacy test. It was used to disfranchise Negroes until struck down by the Supreme Court in *Guinn* v. *United States*, 238 U.S. 347 (1915). (Generically, a provision which continues an arrangement for those presently advantaged without subjecting them to the provisions of a newly enacted rule.)

> **White Primary.**   A primary election open only to whites; another means of disfranchising the Negro, where winning the primary is equivalent to election. Struck down in 1944, in *Smith* v. *Allwright*, 321 U.S. 649 (1944).

dealing with the electoral process have examined both the Negro's participation and his effect on political life around him. Thus, V. O. Key, in his classic *Southern Politics in State and Nation*, showed the unifying influence the Negro had on Southern Democrats. And Donald Matthews and James Prothro have systematically examined, in *Negroes and the New Southern Politics*, the factors, both political and socio-economic, affecting rates of participation by Negroes in politics, as well as the community settings in which Negro participation (or non-participation) is rooted. The Matthews-Prothro work serves to carry forward what Key started, into the period of the "sit-in" and the street demonstration. It should be noted that to study the Negro in politics does not mean that Negroes always act *qua* Negroes when they participate politically. What Key said about Negroes applied generally to the study of any identifiable category of people in the population:

> The fact that a person is . . . a Negro serves as an index to what he believes and to why he votes as he does only when an election concerns Negroes as Negroes and when the members of the group are aware of the issue and see it as basic among their concerns of the moment. Not every election generates group-related issues . . .[15]

---

[14] Frederick M. Wirt, "The Political Sociology of American Suburbia: A Reinterpretation," *Journal of Politics*, XXVII (1965), 647–666.

[15] Key, p. 70.

And it can be added that even when such issues are generated, making those who may be affected by them *aware* of their stake in the matter may be the largest part of the battle. For an issue to bear upon a person's vote: "1. The issue must be cognized in some form. 2. It must arouse some minimal intensity of feeling. 3. It must be accompanied by some perception that one party represents the person's own position better than do the other parties." [16]

The electoral analysis just discussed is dependent on the existence of survey data. Even without the Survey Research Center, there has been increasing interest in the history of elections and their patterns or cycles, particularly at the national level. Such analysis can be based on aggregate results. Thus we have had discussion of "critical elections," ones in which a new pattern of dominance by one party or the other begins to assert itself, and of the "surge and decline" both of parties and of election turnout. Burnham shows that, while turnout has increased in recent years, it has not returned to the levels which existed prior to 1896, and, in addition, the extent of "drop-off" (from Presidential to off-year elections) and "roll-off" (those voting for the highest spots on the ticket but not for less prestigious offices) has increased.[17] Elections have been categorized into maintaining, deviating, and realigning,[18] on the basis of shifts in the winning party. Shifts within particular sections of the country or particular states have been examined, although it may be difficult when working with only aggregate data to distinguish between partisan shifts which are the result of population movement and those which represent a change in sentiment on the part of the voters. Similarly, one is usually forced to operate with an "assumption of minimal change" in working with aggregate figures, that is, to assume that the only change is the net change between parties, because of the impossibility of determining what the gross change has been. Any such analysis of change requires a definition of a "normal" vote, else one has nothing from which to measure trends or deviations. Despite these difficulties, some regularities have been noted on the basis of aggregate data study, such as the off-year loss in Congress by the party winning the Presidency. But even here, survey data has been able to contribute much additional insight into the process behind such a phenomenon.

As this aggregate analysis and the survey research mentioned above suggest, participation and the direction of the vote have remained at the forefront of the interests of voting behavior scholars. Participation has perhaps been of such substantial concern because of the norm in the American political system that political participation, at least at the level of voting, is expected. The turnout in our Presidential elections has often produced harsh clucking from political moralists, who compare us unfavorably with the turnout in other Western democracies. The turnouts in state and local elections

[16] Campbell, *et al.*, *The American Voter*, p. 170.

[17] Walter Dean Burnham, "The Changing Shape of the American Political Universe," *American Political Science Review*, LIX (1965), 7–28.

[18] Campbell, *et al.*, *The American Voter*, pp. 531–538; also reprinted as "A Classification of the Presidential Elections," *Elections and the Political Order*, pp. 63–77.

horrify these individuals even more. It should be pointed out that several scholars, in recent examinations of voting data, have suggested that our turn-out is not as low as we have believed it to be particularly when measured in terms of those *eligible* to vote. Thus, William Andrews argues that, "in 1960, at least, probably between 80 and 85 per cent of persons who were legally and physically able to vote did so." [19] He suggests that some vote in Presi-dential elections, but not for the Presidential office (the latter vote being the usual basis for our turnout figures), while others vote in primaries, but not in general elections. The suggestion of Andrews and some others is that voting requirements may keep more people from voting than does unwillingness and apathy—a challenge to the behavioralists' findings.

The behavioral scholars have taken a different view of non-voting, to which their attention was directed by their interest in democracy. They have examined its extent and analyzed the reasons for its existence. Thus non-participation may be a function of pleasure with the *status quo*, or a feeling that there is no difference between the two candidates, or a lack of positive feelings about either (apathy in a relatively narrow sense), or a feeling of a lack of capacity to participate in politics, or of disgust or alienation at the political system. Similarly, participation is not always a result of positive feel-ings or a high sense of competence; it may be done as an habitual act with low salience and low affect, or someone may cast a vote for "the lesser of two evils" rather than "the best man." This suggests that the *style* of an individ-ual's political activity may be crucial for the polity. In this connection it is important to note that voting has been considered by some to be a minimal act, not requiring much effort, even though it is the most obvious act of citi-zenship in a democracy. There are many who *only vote*, but relatively few who participate actively beyond that level. They have received attention, but less than has been devoted to the act of voting.

Not only have behavioralists contributed to the discussion/debate con-cerning non-voting, they have added much to consideration of the question of the rationality of voters. Because the success of democracy supposedly rests on a full airing of important public issues, followed by voters' "free" decisions based on a thorough understanding of the issues and the candi-dates' positions on them, it has been presumed that the voter should be (and is) rational in the sense of coldly logical and dispassionate. Coupled with this has been the view that a person who votes a straight party ticket is either lazy (taking the easy way out) or emotional, and that he contributes little. Thus, the best person is the "independent," who votes on the basis of the issues, or perhaps for the "best man," but not simply on the basis of party preference. These assumptions have been challenged on several fronts.

Examination of ballot forms and their relation to voting behavior has showed that, while a straight-ticket cast on a party-column ballot might be an

Party-Column Ballot.   **A ballot in which all candidates running for office with the same party label are listed in one column, with other parties' can-**

[19] William Andrews, "American Voting Participation," *Western Political Quarterly*, XIX (1966), 639.

didates in parallel columns, and with a provision for voting for all of the candidates in one party by making one mark (in a circle or block at the top of the party list). On the other hand, an *office-block ballot* lists all candidates for an office in a block, without particular regard to party, although party labels are included; no single-vote-straight-ticket vote is possible. The office-block ballot is sometimes known as the Massachusetts ballot because of its apparent origin there.

easy (hence "lazy") vote, a voter has to be highly motivated to cast a straight-ticket ballot on an office-block ballot, which had been devised to encourage "independent," i.e., split-ticket, voting. Thus straight-ticket voting might be directly, rather than inversely, related to political motivation (a "good thing"). In addition, the rules, including ballot forms, have an effect on the voters' political self-perceptions.

Voters governed by rules most likely to promote partisanship are most likely to be strong party identifiers and least likely to classify themselves as Independents. Conversely the voters in states that provide minimal encouragement of partisanship are significantly more often self-classified Independents and less often strongly identified with a party.[20]

We have also seen that party can act as a useful cue so that the voter can organize the multiplicity of stimuli which bombard him, so that he is not immobilized by the task of sorting them out without such a device.

What voters respond to in their voting has also been of interest; clearly not all respond to the issues, at least not the issues about which the candidates speak. Thus, Campbell and his associates show that, although Adlai Stevenson claimed foreign policy was the most important issue in his 1956 campaign, relatively few voters could identify foreign policy as among the major issues. This was true even for those voters who were predisposed toward or identified with the Democrats—voters one would expect to "hear" the Democratic candidates more clearly. Earlier, Berelson, *et al.*, had shown how the Elmira voters often confused Truman's and Dewey's positions on the Taft-Hartley Bill, even though it was perhaps the most visible and controversial campaign issue in 1948.[21] If the reader finds this lack of information appalling, he should be aware that many voters have minimal amounts of knowledge about such matters as the name of their Congressman or Senator (much less state representatives), of the length of their terms, and the like. Those who did not "see" the candidates' positions clearly (by no means all the electorate) usually twisted it in the direction of their own preference, showing that the distortion had a selective basis, as did perceptions of what the candidates stood for; the material which disagreed with their own stands was more likely to be "screened out." Analysis of the 1960 Kennedy-Nixon television "Great Debates," when viewers saw both candidates at the same time, showed this phenomenon of "selective perception" operating; partisans

[20] Campbell, *et al.*, *The American Voter*, pp. 269–270.
[21] Pool, *et al.*, say that the 1964 election was determined by issue-attitudes, thus contrasting it with earlier elections. Page 165.

of Kennedy looked for the good things in him and the bad things in Nixon, while Nixon partisans did the reverse. (Stokes and Miller show that even lack of information has an effect on voting, bringing "fairly unrelieved party-line voting," while slight knowledge about the opposition candidate brings defections in his direction.[22])

Voters have seemed not to consider issues in terms of the "public interest" (a phrase perhaps more often used to rationalize a person's own position than as an independent criterion for judging between competing positions), but recent analysis has suggested that such a thing as the "public interest" may exist as a factor affecting voting. Wilson and Banfield, calling this "public regardingness," examined votes at the community level to determine whether individuals would vote for projects for which they stood to pay more in taxes than they would receive in benefits; they found that there was an identifiable group of voters who did so vote.[23] V. O. Key also attempted to show that the electorate was in fact rational and "responsible," that it did tend to shift in response to the raising of different issues.

> The perverse and unorthodox argument of this little book is that voters are not fools. To be sure, many individual voters act in odd ways indeed; yet in the large the electorate behaves about as rationally and responsibly as we should expect, given the clarity of the alternatives presented to it and the character of the information available to it.[24]

He found "switchers" (those moving from the Democrats at one election to the Republicans at the next, and vice-versa) moving in the direction of the party espousing the voter's opinion. "Vote switches occurred in directions consistent with the assumption that voters were moved by a rational calculation of the instrumental impact of their vote." However, he did not show that this was the *reason* they shifted, nor did he show that opinion explained "defections" from standard SES-vote correlations. Shifts in conjunction with differences in issues may be the reflection of other factors, something Key himself recognized.[25]

As noted earlier, behavioralists have not been particularly disturbed by their own findings. Some of them have argued that, while rationality in the sense of individual logic and "independence" may not have been shown to be pervasive, system-wide goals are adequately met through voter shifts in preference, and thus rationality in the broad sense exists—just as non-voting supposedly contributes to the flexibility of the polity. Thus, they feel that as

---

[22] Donald E. Stokes and Warren E. Miller, "Party Government and the Saliency of Congress," Campbell, *et al.*, *Elections and the Political Order*, pp. 204–205. [Originally published in *Public Opinion Quarterly*, XXVI (1962), 531–546.]

[23] James Q. Wilson and Edward C. Banfield, "Public-Regardingness as a Value-Premise in Voting Behavior," *American Political Science Review*, LVIII (1964), 876–887. They are criticized by Raymond E. Wolfinger and John Osgood Field, "Political Ethos and the Structure of City Government," *American Political Science Review*, LX (1966), 306–326.

[24] Key, p. 7.

[25] *Ibid.*, pp. 47, 60.

long as system-wide requirements are met, individual failure to adhere to the norm of rationality is not dysfunctional. The political "low-life" may have turned out to contribute some highly-desired characteristics to the system. This approach has upset a number of political scientists, who attack the conclusions as ideology. Some simply are unable to distinguish between possible implications of a described situation and the assumptions underlying it. Thus they feel that the behavioralists are assuming that the current ideal should be altered—that the behavioralists *prefer* the present state of affairs—instead of simply examining the possible consequences of what does exist. Surely if the ideal is not met, we might want to know how serious it is that it is not being met. The emphasis of political life has supposedly been shifted by the behavioralists from activity to stability, with the "passive virtues" being glorified. Perhaps virtue, like obscenity, is in the eye of the beholder, with the anti-behavioralists only *perceiving* that the behavioralists are glorifying political inactivity. They also claim that the behavioralists have adopted an "elitist theory" of voting behavior, supposedly by advocating the continuation of the present situation in which not all vote. To be sure, the behavioralists find that not all the electorate possess basic electoral information, skills, interest, and commitment, but it is a substantial (valuational) jump from that fact to the conclusion that the ideal of mass-participation democracy should be discarded, a jump the behavioralists clearly do not make explicitly. Some (but not many) political scientists, however, attack the behavioralists on their own ground, by building a case that the data of the voting studies does not support the behavioralists' inferences from that data. Thus Goldschmidt points out that those uncommitted concerning party preference may not have the flexibility Berelson claims for them, pointing to civil liberties ideology, and Stouffer's finding (in *Communism, Conformity, and Civil Liberties*) that the less educated are more, not less, rigid on these matters. Goldschmidt also suggests that Berelson himself shows the uncommitteds dividing the party preference in roughly the same proportion as do the partisans (although the uncommitted might register trends earlier than the partisans).[26]

The independent has been pictured in standard American fare as educated, aware, interested, rational, not committed to a particular party, as well as highly participant. This image has had to be recast; in the first place, we have seen that those with higher political awareness and interest were more likely to be political partisans than uncommitted; in the second, those who spread their votes around between the parties, either in a single election or by shifting from one election to the next, were often those with the *least* interest and knowledge about politics, and without an issue-orientation, as well as those least likely to vote regularly at all. Thus the ideal turned out to be a political "slob." To be sure, being an "independent" serves an important function for some: it allows them to move gradually from one party prefer-

[26] Maure Goldschmidt, "Democratic Theory and Contemporary Political Science," *Western Political Quarterly*, XIX (1966), Supplement, 5–12.

ence to another, using "independent" as a transitional stage, as Robert Agger
has illustrated with regard to the South. Analysis, particularly by Agger, has
shown that it is perhaps most accurate to talk of two types of "independents,"
one who does act as the ideal would have him do, with the other independent
of party because of apathy, lack of involvement, and lack of a feeling he can
perform effectively in politics.[27]

One aspect clearly neglected in earlier studies was the impact of the formal institutional aspect of voting. Traditional examinations of elections had
recited the details of such matters as registration requirements, the form of
the ballot, and absentee ballot provisions, and the topic of reducing the
voting age from 21 to 18 has been a favorite of college and high school debat-
ers from time to time. Tables showing the requirements of each state are
easily available, but apparently it was presumed that differences were minimal and/or had no effect, so, except for the work of the late V. O. Key, Jr., we
know little of the effect of these mechanisms. Key argued that each additional
requirement—long residency, closed registration, difficulty in obtaining ab-

> **Closed Registration.**   When the period in which citizens may register to
> vote is limited to specific times of the year, usually short in duration and
> ending well before the election occurs.

sentee ballots, and the like—would reduce the size of the electorate. It is not
until recently that we have had a more systematic presentation of the effect of
registration requirements on voting. Kelley found that the greatest proportion of the variance in voting participation rates across the country was accounted for by variations in the proportion of eligibles registered to vote.[28]
Kelley's work and work by Campbell and Miller on the effect of ballot forms
on straight- and split-ticket voting hopefully will bring about an integration
of institutional factors with behavioral factors in our examination of voting,
and thus counter the neglect of the former. Among the items which might
be examined, or examined more fully, are the relative effect of the "long
ballot" and "short ballot," the frequency of elections with the possibility

> **Long Ballot.**   A ballot containing many *positions* to which officials are to
> be elected. In a *short ballot*, only a few positions are filled by election; the
> elected officials then appoint other officials.

of "voter fatigue," and elections by single-member or multi-member legislative district. Proportional representation and cumulative voting have been

> **Proportional Representation.**   A complicated method for electing mem-
> bers of a multi-member legislative body, in which the voter indicates his
> preferences among the candidates ("1", "2", etc.), and each candidate re-

[27] Robert E. Agger, "Independents and Party Identifiers: Characteristics and Behavior
in 1952," *American Voting Behavior*, ed. Burdick and Brodbeck, pp. 308–329.

[28] Stanley Kelley, Jr., Richard E. Ayres, and William G. Bowen, "Registration and
Voting: Putting First Things First," *American Political Science Review*, LXI (1967), 359–
379.

ceiving a certain number of votes (called the "quota") is elected. Under this system, various groups in the population are supposed to be represented in rough proportion to their strength; it is easier for minority-groups to receive representation this way. This system has been used in the United States only at the municipal level and is no longer used in any major city.

Cumulative Voting.   A system for electing legislators, used in Illinois. In each legislative district, three representatives are elected. Each voter has three votes, but may give all three to one individual; two to one and one to another; one and one-half each to two; or one to each of three.

studied, perhaps because they are considered "exotic," but our information about the total effect of the complex of institutional arrangements we use is unsystematic and incomplete. Thus we are left with many civics-type arguments about the virtues of electing only a small number of officials, or of the advantages of separating national and state elections in order to avoid "contaminating" the latter, without being able to evaluate them empirically. It already has been suggested that "formal political institutions have their greatest impact on behavior when the attitudes relevant to that behavior are least intense" and that "informal environmental factors have the greatest direct relevance for political behavior when political motivations pertaining to that behavior are reinforced by formal institutional arrangements," [29] showing clear interrelationships between structural and behavioral factors.

PUBLIC OPINION

The earliest discussion of public opinion was philosophical. In a democratic system, "public opinion" (substitute "the will of the people" if you wish) was supposed to govern the action of government officials. What public opinion was and how it was to be determined were questions of some importance. To some, the result registered at election time reflected public opinion directly on the issues of the campaign. To others, it came from the communications of citizens to their elected representatives. To others, it was an almost mystical force (like Rousseau's "general will"), to be conjured up in support of all things good and pure. That the concept was to some extent a "will-o-the-wisp" and that it was not easily measured became clear. Walter Lippmann, in his classic *Public Opinion*, began to tie public opinion down to individual views, to transform it from a transcendent phenomenon with a life of its own, by talking about the "pictures in our heads" which affected our opinions.

The principal concern of political scientists with public opinion questions has been in connection with voting behavior studies, particularly with the

[29] Campbell, *et al.*, *The American Voter*, pp. 283, 287. Italics in original.

effect of opinions and attitudes on the direction of the vote. We also have a new interest in the ideologies held by individuals and in the internal structure of individuals' views, and the impact these might have on their behavior. No longer is ideology simply a subject for the political philosopher, whose job it has been to describe the content of ideologies. Its roots in a person's life and background are now closely examined, even though ideologies, in the sense of "a particularly elaborate, close-woven, and far-ranging structure of attitudes . . . cannot be thought to be widespread in the American population." [30]

In most current work, public opinion is defined in relation to issues, and many current definitions are so constructed. Key suggests that there must be at least two positions on a subject before we can talk about public opinion, because there is otherwise no "issue," no controversy. Thus Berelson points out that traditional custom must be distinguished from "dynamic" public opinion "(topical, based on the mass media, 'rational')," with only the latter considered to be public opinion, and the former left to the historian and anthropologist.[31] Another aspect of current definitions is that there must be a collection of individuals (the "public") concerned with, attentive to, or at least affected by the issue before we can talk about "public opinion." Key has defined the term as "those opinions held by private persons which governments find it prudent to heed." [32]

Interest in predicting the outcomes of events led to efforts to measure public opinion. One of the first, and extremely unsophisticated, efforts was *The Literary Digest's* 1936 election poll, based on a sample drawn from telephone directories. That this basis for a public opinion survey led to badly biased results was shown by the *Digest's* prediction, based on the survey, of a Landon victory. Stimulated by the interest of manufacturers in market research, polls began to develop on a commercial basis. And national public opinion polls were undertaken, not only on elections (although they have perhaps drawn the most attention), but also on political issues of moment. This emphasis on the polls has led some to define public opinion as simply the percentages appearing in polls.

The interest in measuring public opinion brought about radical changes in the study of the subject.

> In the academic discussion of public opinion there is a sharp discontinuity between the periods before and after the development of systematic opinion surveys. The world of public opinion in today's sense really began with the Gallup Polls of the mid-1930's, and it is impossible for us to retreat to the meaning of public opinion as it was understood by Tocqueville and Jefferson—or even by Walter Lippmann in 1922.[33]

[30] *Ibid.*, pp. 192, 202.
[31] Bernard Berelson, "The Study of Public Opinion," *The State of the Social Sciences*, ed. Leonard D. White (Chicago, 1956), p. 300.
[32] V.O. Key, Jr., *Public Opinion and American Democracy* (New York, 1961), p. 14.
[33] Leo Bogart, "No Opinion, Don't Know, and Maybe No Answer," *Public Opinion Quarterly*, XXXI (1967), 334.

However, the existence of the large commercial polling organizations—the Gallup (American Institute of Public Opinion), Roper (*Fortune*), and Harris surveys—as well as the highly reputed state polls, e.g., the Minnesota Poll and California Poll, and their increasing accuracy has not closed the door on all the philosophic questions about public opinion in a democracy. For those who believe that opinion should be "educated," a public opinion poll, in which many of the respondents may know little about the subject discussed,[34] is a travesty. However, the views of these individuals, who would in effect impose a test of political education as a qualification for political participation, are in a real sense anti-democratic.

Others have criticized the impact of polls on opinion (and action), claiming that the polls have themselves become an important (and irresponsible, in the sense of non-accountable) force in our political life. Thus we have the "bandwagon" and "underdog" effects, in which, respectively, an individual may decide to support a position because it is ahead or decide to back a loser to keep him from being too heavily defeated. Whether these two effects, and others the polls may cause, will cancel each other out in a particular situation is only problematical. We have also seen, particularly with former President Lyndon Johnson, the political uses of polls. Of course, if polls are conducted to provide information for political/governmental leaders, it could hardly be otherwise, but even those polls conducted for purposes ostensibly unrelated to politically partisan battles become themselves the subject of controversies.[35] Related to the political use of the polls is the question of government secrecy and news management; if the information available has an effect on views held, the government, by restricting (and filtering) the news it releases, can affect those views, or at least make it more difficult for people to come to clear conclusions.

Still others have suggested strongly that an answer to a question in a public opinion poll will by no means automatically result in behavior (either at the ballot box or in the public arena) commensurate with the stated opinion. The differences between our stated sexual morality and our actual behavior as indicated in the Kinsey studies (even if one discounts the statistics of those studies) show this, as does our willingness to agree with abstract statements in support of civil rights, for example, on open housing, coupled with our unwillingness to let minority group members purchase houses in our neighborhoods, as noted by the title, *But Not Next Door*. This discrepancy may arise because of a difference between our "public" and "private" views: What we tell the interviewer and what we "really" feel—in the sense of what we are

[34] The percentage of "Don't Know" or "No Answer" responses to a particular question is quite important in evaluating polls. It also has been shown that differences in knowledge on a subject may bring differences in opinion. William C. Rogers, Barbara Stuhler, and Donald Koenig, "A Comparison of Informed and General Public Opinion on U.S. Foreign Policy," *Public Opinion Quarterly*, XXXI (1967), 242–252.

[35] See the "Stanford poll" on Vietnam, reported in Sidney Verba, *et al.*, "Public Opinion and the War in Vietnam," *American Political Science Review*, LXI (1967), 317–333, and a discussion of the reaction, Nelson W. Polsby, "Hawks, Doves, and the Press," *Trans-Action*, IV (1967), 35–41.

willing to act on—may be different, or it may be a function of the effects of personal interaction, which may alter (or suppress) an attitude. Thus, we find cases of peoples who claim not to want to live near Negroes both accepting them, for example, when placed in the same housing project, and even defending their right to live where they are. This points up another drawback of public opinion polls, in that asking questions of individuals "lifts" the response out of its social context, including the individual's reference groups.

> *Reference Groups.*   Groups, of which an individual may or may not be a formal member, from which he draws views in terms of which he judges the world around him, and from which he also draws cues for thought and action. The groups need not be formal, but may simply be categories of individuals with a common characteristic, e.g., "other businessmen."

It is clear that "public opinion" does not bear a clear, uniform relationship to government activity. Thus Key suggests that public opinion may be permissive, demanding, or supportive in relation to government policy. When it is permissive, government may do a number of things (within broad limits) without incurring the public's displeasure; when it is demanding (what he calls a "consensus of decision"), a prompt, direct response from government specifically related to the public's feelings is expected; when it is supportive, it is "after the fact" of what the government has done, perhaps in a situation in which there was no developed "public opinion" because of confusion or lack of knowledge.

Basic elements, such as the mass media, which are held to contribute to public opinion have always received much attention. Attention to other than "mass media," for example, to neighborhood newspapers and suburban weeklies, suggests the importance of examining the media in terms of their components rather than as one monolithic entity with a uniform effect. The increasing concentration of the mass media in the hands of a smaller number of individuals and the possible impact of this concentration on the availability of a wide range of points of view to the citizen have been noted, reflecting in part a reformist orientation, and based in part on an over-emphasis on the part thought to be played by media without any mediating influence by individuals or groups. Because not all elements of politics are visible, the accuracy of the picture of the political world provided by the media is quite important in terms of the content of public opinion, although reinforcement of previously-held views, rather than change, is the media's principal effect. And that the media can have an impact on events—and not just on people's views of events—has also been noted. National party conventions have been altered for the benefit of television, and the constant pressure to have something to report causes some reporters to contrive "newsworthy" situations.

The relatively new role played by public relations organizations, such as Whittaker and Baxter, in "packaging" candidates for election campaigns or in promoting grass-roots public opinion on an issue of importance to particular groups, has also drawn attention. The presence of new specialists in politics, devoting full-time to political public relations (rather than handling it as a side-line) has also been noted. This activity is still viewed as opposed to "proper" politics, and we hear talk of *manipulation* and of the *engineering of consent,* clearly pejorative terms. Others are interested in the effect of public opinion in particular policy areas, e.g., foreign policy, while the effect of public opinion on particular institutions has concerned others. They have dealt both with Congress, where public opinion is considered as part of the system of communication between legislator and constituent, and the Supreme Court, where communication of the Court's opinions to its affected publics has been a serious problem.

Arising from an earlier interest in propaganda shown by the government in World War II, broader concern with the role of symbols and symbolic acts in politics has developed. In this connection, the functions which attitudes and symbols perform for the individual have received some attention; this social-psychological focus is almost completely opposite from the standard concerns of public opinion, which work from the individual's opinion *to* government, not from the opinion back "into" the individual. But we find that opinions can serve not only for "object appraisal"—to help the individual evaluate and organize the stimuli of the political world around him— but also for "externalization," the projection of individual psychological problems on the outside world, and the "mediation of self-other relations," that is, in dealing with one's relations with friends and acquaintances.[36]

It has become clear that, in talking about public opinion, we need to talk about public*s*, not *a* public—that those interested in and concerned about one specific subject will not necessarily be the same as those interested in the next subject, although some people are more "generalists" than others. It is also clear that we can distinguish between people on the basis of their levels of knowledge and interest in matters which become the subject of public opinion. We also have a distinction between "opinion leaders," who are "oversupplied" with information and views and sustain the circulation of opinion, and others who may be divided further into those attentive to public issues and those neither interested nor knowledgeable. Other relevant participants in the public opinion process are opinion-initiators and opinion-makers, those who have access to the means of communication; these in turn can be divided further, depending on the scope of their communications and the range of the impact of those communications.[37] According to a theory developed by Katz and Lazarsfeld in a study of opinion transmission on political as well as non-political subjects, there is a "two-step flow of communication," not simply a direct flow from media to recipient, the flow of communication which produces an influence on views is that from the opinion leaders,

[36] M. Brewster Smith, "Opinions, Personality, and Political Behavior," *American Political Science Review,* LII (1958), 1–26.

[37] The labels are developed in James Rosenau, *Public Opinion and Foreign Policy* (New York, 1961) and *National Leadership and Foreign Policy: A Case Study in the Mobilization of Public Support* (Princeton, 1963).

who are more highly attentive to, informed about, and articulate concerning events, ideas, or issues, and who have followed the media more closely than the general public, to the members of the public with whom they come in contact. The latter flow is usually initiated by the followers, not the opinion-leaders. This theory extends a long-standing concern with the content of what people see and read, their sources of news (from magazines and news-papers to radio and television), and the credibility they attach to these sources (in part a function of the prestige of the source). We find that people do not get their news from *either* the papers *or* the television, but that atten-tion to them is cumulative, that is, some of those who watch television also read newspapers and some of those also read magazines.

The distribution of opinion, its "shape," is clearly not uniform over time, nor is what Key calls its viscosity, its resistance to change. He postulates a number of distributions, running from a normal (or "bell") curve, with a sin-gle hump in the middle of possible positions on an issue, bi-polar and multi-polar distributions, as well as a J-distribution in which opinion is over-whelmingly one-sided on a given issue. But he does more than describe these distributions; he suggests that their shape is relevant for the resolution of conflict. Thus a bi-polar distribution, with the two modes both high and far apart, provides little basis for compromise, while a multi-polar W-distribu-tion, with a hump at the moderate position and other modal positions some-what more extreme, provides a good chance for compromise. The intensity with which views are held is quite relevant to conflict resolution because an intense-feeling minority can "triumph" over a majority composed of those with weakly-held views. Intensity, which Key does consider, greatly compli-cates the problem of measuring public opinion; when it is considered, one can no longer simply "count heads." With respect to viscosity (which Key prefers to the more frequently used "stability"), Key suggests that issues which involve knowledge beyond the immediate personal experience of the individual (such as foreign policy) are less viscous, that is, more subject to change on the basis of new information or new ideas, while those "closer to home" are most resistant to change.[38]

POLITICAL SOCIALIZATION

While an exploration into the genesis of individual political opinions and attitudes could easily fall within the scope of public opinion, a new subspe-cialization has developed in the last few years, called political socialization. The subject-matter of this area is the process by which people acquire politi-cal values, not simply during active political participation, but also in the period before they engage in any explicitly political activity. Findings that many individuals voted for candidates of the same party as that for which their parents had voted (V. O. Key said that 75% of American voters did this)

[38] Key, *Public Opinion and American Democracy*, pp. 235–237 ff.

stimulated some political scientists to look further into the process by which political values—not only political party preference, but also such other items as political interest and opinions—were transferred from one generation to the next.

The principal emphasis is on transmission *between generations,* and thus on continuity within the polity. The idea that rebellion is characteristic of adolescents in the political sphere has been shown by several studies, including those by Eleanor Maccoby, to be generally inaccurate, in part because politics is not sufficiently salient to be a major area of rebellion.[39] When rebellion does occur, it has been found to be related to the situation within the family, that is, the relations between children and parents, with more rebellion (or divergence from parents' views) on the part of those strictly disciplined than from those moderately disciplined.[40] The studies by Theodore Newcomb at Bennington College, which showed movement away from parents' views (in the direction of political liberalism) during college have also shown that, in later life, many of the students reverted to the views with which they had come to college, in part a function of the environment into which they moved after graduation and the views of the man they married.[41]

While it is widely recognized that whatever values are inculcated prior to active adult political participation may be modified or reinforced depending on the individual's work situation, friendship groups, and the like, obviously by the time the individual reaches that stage he is not a "blank slate" on which events and those around him write at will. The two institutions to which most attention has been paid in connection with political socialization are the family and education. In studying these two institutions, political socialization experts have been most interested in general orientations to authority and to various aspects of the political system, on the one hand, and specific items which might be transmitted, on the other. In the latter connection, they have found that political party preference is perhaps the aspect most easily transmitted from parents to children, even if the parents are making no explicit effort to do so. This is particularly true if the parents agree with each other and have strong views. Interest in politics is transmitted almost as readily as political party preference. When matters become more specific, they are less easily carried over from one generation to the next, partially because they *are* more specific (and thus less easily remembered), but also because specific items are more likely to lose their relevance to the child's political world when it becomes time for him to participate directly. Thus, we find that general attitudes which are relatively broad—such as an

[39] Eleanor E. Maccoby, Richard E. Matthews and Alton S. Morton, "Youth and Political Change," *Public Opinion Quarterly,* XVIII (1954), 23–39.

[40] Russell Middleton and Snell Putney, "Political Expression of Adolescent Rebellion," *American Journal of Sociology,* LXIII (1963), 527–535; "Student Rebellion Against Parental Political Beliefs," *Social Forces,* XLI (1963), 377–383.

[41] Theodore Newcomb, *Personality and Social Change* (New York, 1943); "Influence of Attitude Climates," *Journal of Abnormal and Social Psychology,* XLI (1946), 291–302; "The Persistence and Regression of Changed Attitudes," *Journal of Social Issues,* XIX (1963), 3–14.

outlook on the virtues of business or labor—may be carried by the child, but that views on particular legislation, such as the Taft-Hartley Act, will be less easily transmitted and less meaningful to the next generation. More general values are also transmitted, such as an appreciation of democracy or a view of respect for law enforcement officials. Much of this may be unintentional; when the father calls a policeman unpleasant names for having given him a ticket, it may make a greater impression on his young son than when the father tells his child, "the policeman is your friend." When the mother sends Johnny out to play with his friends, saying, "why don't you play what they want to play today?" she may simply want him out of her hair, but may be encouraging an acceptance of the majority view. That much of this occurs at an extremely early age, before there is any competing socializing agency, makes it all the more effective. However, as Verba warns, we should not allow ourselves to be seduced by what he calls a "simple primary group monism," in which we look to "the family, the peer group, and other primary groups" for explanations of political behavior.[42] The impact of the family as a molder of personality also has drawn recent attention, with particular attention given to personality abnormality resulting from an unhappy childhood, and its effect on political attachment. Much of the data for the latter has come from psychiatrists. Trying to broaden our theory of socialization and not to be limited to deviant cases, some political scientists, most particularly Lewis Froman, have tried to apply learning theory to the process by which political values are acquired.[43]

It may be more accurate to say that we have fewer studies of the effect of education than we do of the growth of values in children during the educational process. The availability of large numbers of primary and secondary school children to whom questionnaires can be administered has formed the basis for many of the political socialization studies which are now being produced. We can now make some generalizations about the changes which occur in the child's view of authority—from seeing the President as a glorified version of the child's father, and as one who can do no wrong, to a more clearly differentiated and realistic view of that official—and in his acceptance of some of the basic values necessary for effective participation in politics, such as a feeling of political efficacy.[44] We can also watch knowledge about politics increase as age increases. And certainly these studies have shown us that children have political views which do not simply reflect their parents' at a much earlier age than was thought to be true at one time.

The overly simplistic views that high school civics courses provided all the information a young citizen possessed, and that it properly inculcated the

[42] Sidney Verba, *Small Groups and Political Behavior*, p. 37.

[43] Lewis A. Froman, Jr., "Learning Political Attitudes," *Western Political Quarterly*, XV (1962), 304–313; Lewis A. Froman, Jr., and James K. Skipper, Jr., "An Approach to the Learning of Party Identification," *Public Opinion Quarterly*, XXVII (1963), 473–480.

[44] Fred I. Greenstein, *Children and Politics* (New Haven, 1965), and David Easton and Jack Dennis, "The Child's Acquisition of Regime Norms: Political Efficacy," *American Political Science Review*, LXI (1967), 25–38.

"correct" views toward political participation, have long since been rejected. That groups which compete with the educational institution can have a greater effect than that institution itself has become clear. For example, as (and to the extent that) teenagers become estranged from their parents and the educational system, and take part in a set of activities with their peers (the "adolescent culture") which is independent of what they do with their parents, the values received through that experience can play a large part in developing views toward authority. These views may not be explicitly political at the time they are developed, but there is no question that sooner or later they will be politically relevant.

POLITICAL RECRUITMENT AND LEADERSHIP

One specific aspect of political socialization is the induction of individuals into their specific adult political roles. Because Gabriel Almond considers this a separate "input" function in the political system, and because there has been a long-standing interest in political leaders, political *recruitment* can be discussed separately, despite the possible overlap. Thus, we find Wahlke and his colleagues examining the political socialization of state legislators, to determine whether they differ from the general public in terms of the ways in which they became familiar with politics; this study could fit under either head.[45] That the initial attainment of political office and advancement in office have become more regularized and formalized over the years has perhaps directed the attention of scholars to the subject. Thus "bureaucratic," "entrepreneurial," and "zig-zag" patterns have been identified. The professionalization of politicians—the separate styles they adopt once they have reached positions of some importance or which they use in dealing with each other and those around them—have also been noted in connection with leadership research.

Political leaders, most particularly those in formal positions, have always been of interest, even if only in terms of the adulatory biographies which have been written about the best known. That political leaders other than those in formal positions exist has been known at least since the time of the journalists who went looking for the "power behind the throne." However, the concern of contemporary political scientists over the meaning of power has led to a more systematic examination of those not at the top places in the formal governmental structure and about those outside the formal structure. This has led to a conception of politics as something other than merely a few leaders and a large group of the led; we are beginning to recognize a cake of at least three layers: top leaders, non-leader political activists, and the "average citizen." It is the first two categories that have been the subject of political recruitment studies, although the average citizen also has been examined so we can see to what extent leaders and activists differ from him.

[45] John Wahlke, *et al.*, *The Legislative System*, pp. 77–94.

Perhaps legislators have been the ones to whom most attention has been paid. In addition, however, there are studies of the patronage appointments of New York's Mayor; of the Assistant Secretaries in federal departments; of Supreme Court judges; political party activists and election campaign workers; and of community leaders. All are not examined in the same way or in equal detail, but all these studies combined do tell us much about a collection of political participants about whom we knew little a decade ago.

The studies of these individuals tend to be of several types. Perhaps the most basic is that which examines the social background of the individual, to determine his place of birth, occupation, education, and the occupation of his father, as well as sundry other demographic items. Donald Matthews' *The Social Background of Political Decision-Makers* is perhaps the earliest systematic collection of data to be stimulated by the behavioral approach. Matthews demonstrates that the "political life-chances" of a white Protestant whose father comes from a managerial or professional occupation are substantially higher than those from other combinations of categories, although political position is by no means closed to those not of that set of circumstances. That this has been true for some time is indicated in David Rothman's figures on backgrounds of United States Senators in the late nineteenth century, although it would appear that proportionately fewer Senators came from professional family backgrounds (as was probably true of the population as a whole).[46] John Schmidhauser has confirmed Matthews' findings with respect to the United States Supreme Court. He shows that a high proportion of the justices came from politically active families, repeating a finding produced elsewhere. It should be noted, however, that not all activists or office-holders are from politically active families and that, in fact, some come to politics relatively late in life. In some cases, those who are not from politicized backgrounds may actually be more highly motivated in their participation than those who are doing it out of family habit. That the simple historical examination of differences in backgrounds can tell us much about political recruitment is shown by Robert Dahl, who found that in New Haven, community leadership had passed from the gentry to the small businessmen to other leaders, as the political "shape" of the community had changed.[47] Dahl's work is typical of attention to the role of *organized* social strata in politics, principally examined at the community level. The great opportunities for social mobility which politics (then frowned on by "upstanding" citizens) provided for certain ethnic groups, such as the Irish, plus the advantage which accrues to those in particular occupations, such as the law, have contributed to the greater life-chances of the non-WASP elements of the population.

The lawyer has been a particular object of study. Early explanations of

[46] David J. Rothman, *Politics and Power: The United States Senate, 1869–1901* (Cambridge, Mass., 1966).

[47] Robert Dahl, *Who Governs? Democracy and Power in an American City* (New Haven, 1961).

lawyers' predominance revolved around oratorical skills and facility in "representing" clients. As it became clear that the great proportion of lawyers are not practicing criminal law in the nation's trial courts, thus radically reducing the number of Clarence Darrows, other explanations became necessary. The monopoly of certain public positions, e.g., county prosecuting attorney, by lawyers gives the lawyer a "leg up" in politics. The lawyers' work schedule, more flexible than that of many other occupations, at least for those in solo practice or small partnerships, may allow him the freedom to campaign and to spend several months at the legislature without damage to his occupation; this is true also of such other fields as real estate and insurance. That the young lawyer can in effect advertise himself by running for office may explain some candidacies.

Most studies of office-holders' backgrounds tell us much about others— of the same characteristics as those in office—who chose not to enter public life, or to enter it at some lesser level of involvement. What faces the potential candidate has thus not received as much attention as the place from which he comes. We do have some generalized explanations, but less systematic data. Lasswell argued some time ago that a combination of skill with opportunity was necessary, and, in a heavily psychological view, asserted that individuals became involved in politics by displacing private motives on public objects, and then rationalizing this in terms of the public interest.[48] Others have asserted that some people specifically seek positions in which they can exercise power over others. Starting with Lasswell, we have had much discussion of various psychological types in politics, such as David Riesman's "inner-directed," "other-directed," and "autonomous" individuals (in *The Lonely Crowd*); authoritarians; dogmatics; agitators; and bureaucratic types.

In looking at the opportunity side of Lasswell's equation (while perhaps the background studies and those of lawyers deal with the skill side), Joseph Schlesinger has systematically introduced the concept of ambition into the study of recruitment, but in a special way. "What is needed . . . is a theory of politics which explicitly accepts the assumption that politicians respond primarily to their office goals . . . rather than a theory which explains personal ambitions." [49] He has suggested that the availability of positions controls recruitment (and advancement). Thus, whatever the desire, the differential existence of opportunities directly affects political careers. Studies of lawyers have shown, in corroboration, that the greater availability of public positions "reserved" for lawyers in proportion to the lawyer population in rural areas greatly increases the lawyer's chance of an entrance into politics there over what would be available to him in the large city. For Schlesinger, this sort of study is much more valuable than one in which the availability of positions is equated with party competition; while more candidates may run

[48] Harold D. Lasswell, "Psychopathology and Politics," *The Political Writings of Harold D. Lasswell* (Glencoe, 1951), pp. 74–77.
[49] Joseph A. Schlesinger, *Ambition and Politics: Political Careers in the United States* (Chicago, 1966), p. 4.

for office in the primary of a party which has a realistic chance of winning a position, and more will gravitate to the majority party, this does not explain the availability of positions; in fact, Schlesinger shows a lower opportunity rate in the majority than in the minority party.[50]

Activists who do not occupy formal positions have been studied, as noted earlier. The public opinion studies of "opinion leaders" fall into this category. Others have looked at the degree to which those more active in politics uphold the values of the system, finding that they do a better job in this respect than the average citizenry. It is concluded from those findings that agreement on the tenets of democracy among all the public is unnecessary for democracy to continue to function, as long as those most active do so. Stouffer's study of attitudes toward Communism showed that public officials and those better educated in the ways of politics were likely to be more tolerant of the rights of minorities, e.g., in the area of freedom of speech, which was of particular concern to Stouffer. Another approach to the activists is to look at the "pay-off" (the "kicks") they get from politics. James Wilson's study of *The Amateur Democrat*, in which he examines New York City's Reform Democrats as well as the (Democratic) Independent Voters of Illinois and the California Democratic Council, shows the notable difference between the professional politician, who regards politics as a full-time (paid) job and who is interested in victories, not ideologies, and the (middle-class) amateur, who is more likely to be an ideologue and who does not know what to do with a full-time paid political job when he finally does oust the professional, as happened in New York.

COMMUNITY POLITICS

Perhaps the last major category of studies which come under the heading of "political behavior and public opinion" is that concerning community politics, although it could in turn be subdivided. Frequently, such studies are the pet projects of experts in the field of state and local government or municipal government rather than of voting behavior, but their relevance is nonetheless clear. We are not here talking about the early voting behavior studies, which did take place within the confines of a particular community. One can certainly learn much about Elmira, for example, from *Voting*, about what happens when one political party is predominant in a community; the majority party receives an advantage both in attracting the uncommitted and in weakening the commitment of the minority. This is known as the "breakage effect." However, the concentration in that study was on general, non-community-related facts which created voting predispositions rather than on the impact of the community on voting. Instead, we are referring to examination of decision-making in the local community and with respect to that local community—its issues and its organization. Thus we are also not talking

[50] *Ibid.*, p. 146.

about studies by municipal reformers, what Wallace Sayre and Nelson Polsby have called writing about "actor-defined problems," but instead about "observer-defined problems," work by those "who in recent years have begun to view urban communities as political systems capable of yielding answers to some of the enduring problems of political science as a discipline." [51]

In this connection, we now have a number of studies of the politics of individual cities, particularly the large central cities of our metropolitan areas; the politics of local governments other than municipalities have generally been neglected. Generalizations also have been pulled together, but they usually rest on single-city studies of the type produced by the Harvard-MIT Joint Center on Urban Studies (some of which are distilled by Edward Banfield in *Big City Politics*). Of course, here as elsewhere, whether the case studies contribute more knowledge about a specific unit of government or whether they provide material to fit into hypotheses depends in large part not only on the author but, more importantly, on the reader. If one reads the almost classic *Small Town in Mass Society*, by Arthur Vidich and Joseph Bensman, he may come away with many specific details about "Springdale"; but he may also come away with a feeling for such matters as class defined in terms of style of life, the relationship between the small community and the larger society, or the hold of a few individuals on political decisions in a small community. The same is true of *Small City Politics*, by Warren Mills and Harry Davis, where one may learn more about Beloit than about the political problems (and how they are handled) in medium-sized cities. Banfield's *Political Influence*, six case studies about Chicago, can tell much about the way in which civic committees can serve as "fronts" for a big-city mayor—or one may simply store details about Chicago.

While studies of the politics of metropolitan reorganization and local government reform emphasize the specific city, studies of community power structure (to the methodology of which much attention was paid earlier) tend to emphasize generalizations, perhaps in part because the names of the cities are concealed, thus drawing our attention away from the "real-life" situation. We are also less likely to know about the community, as smaller cities are often (but not always) emphasized, perhaps because of the greater ease of studying them. But, beyond that, the interest of the researcher is different: he is looking more for a general theory of community power structure. Despite all the various case studies of community power in particular communities— Regional City (Atlanta), Middletown (Muncie, Indiana), Cibola (Ypsilanti, Michigan), Springdale, the two Oregon and two North Carolina towns studied by Agger, Goldrich and Swanson, and Dahl's New Haven—we have no broad-scale theory. Why? In large measure because no two studies were performed with the same methods or with the same theoretical framework. Some, like Dahl and Schulze, have used history to great effect. Thus, we can

---

[51] Wallace S. Sayre and Nelson W. Polsby, "American Political Science and the Study of Urbanization," *The Study of Urbanization*, ed. Philip M. Hauser and Leo F. Schnore (New York, 1965), p. 127.

see that, over the years, what was once a monolithic type of power structure, with local businessmen having both economic and political dominance, becomes a bifurcated (or bipolar) structure, with the most powerful economic interests belonging to "outsiders" and with politics in the hands of the locals. (The managers for the absentee-owned corporations and the political role of both their corporations and themselves have received specific study, by Roland Pellegrin and others.) The variety of issues studied by the pluralists shows the scarcity of those who are important as "generalists" in the exercise of power, unless one or two key officials like the mayor be placed in that category. The power of city-wide elected officials like the mayor has been stressed by Dahl, in his discussion of the "executive-centered coalition" as a former of power structure, and by Salisbury, who speaks of the "new convergence of power." [52] We can also see in some situations that power is fluid, being little structured, while in others, the manner in which it is exercised is well defined, although several different forms to that definition may exist. But so long as a different theoretical view, which leads to a specific methodology, separates the "elitist" from the "pluralist" perspective, broad tight-knit generalizations will be hard to come by. Because there are so many different specific approaches to community power structure, some scholars have attempted totally different theoretical frameworks. One example is the work of Norton Long and Paul Smith, each of whom view the community as a set of "games" interlaced with each other.[53] Whatever hope these new approaches may bring for a better theory of local politics at a later date, the community power structure framework is still predominant.

Little attention has been paid to the process by which issues are raised in the community; predominant concern has been with who does what once an issue is raised. But some have shown interest in the topic of community conflict, despite the general allocation of "community organization" to the sociologists. James Coleman, in *Community Conflict*, portrays the process by which certain issues, instead of being resolved "peaceably," become the subject of much heat and emotion; social relations within the community are reshaped as a breach between the two sides to the controversy begins to widen; and finally, a new leadership arises which manages to provide at least a temporary resolution to the matter, the older leadership having been shown to be incapable of handling this crisis. Some of the work on fluoridation campaigns, which often provoke this type of response, has added to our knowledge on this subject. But we do not have a broad theory of community conflict with evidence from a broad spectrum of issues; we do not know whether the process with respect to certain types of issues is different from that concerning other types of controversies.

[52] Robert H. Salisbury, "Urban Politics: The New Convergence of Power," *Journal of Politics*, XXVI (1964), 775–797.

[53] Norton E. Long, "The Local Community as an Ecology of Games," *American Journal of Sociology*, LXIV (1958), 251–261, and Paul Smith, "The Games of Community Politics," *Midwest Journal of Political Science*, IX (1965), 37–60.

BIBLIOGRAPHY

Readings. Three broad collections of readings in this field are HEINZ EULAU, SAMUEL ELDERSVELD, and MORRIS JANOWITZ, eds., *Political Behavior: A Reader in Theory and Research* (Glencoe, 1956); NELSON W. POLSBY, ROBERT A. DENTLER, and PAUL A. SMITH, eds., *Politics and Social Life: An Introduction to Political Behavior* (Boston, 1963); and EDWARD C. DREYER and WALTER A. ROSENBAUM, eds., *Political Opinion and Electoral Behavior: Essays and Studies* (Belmont, Cal., 1966).

Voting Behavior

Summaries. Summaries of a number of the findings discussed in this chapter may be found, most conveniently, in ROBERT E. LANE, *Political Life: Why People Get Involved in Politics* (Glencoe, 1959), and LESTER MILBRATH, *Political Participation: How and Why Do People Get Involved in Politics?* (Chicago, 1965). Another summary is SEYMOUR MARTIN LIPSET, *et al.*, "The Psychology of Voting: An Analysis of Political Behavior," *Handbook of Social Psychology*, ed. Gardner Lindzey (Reading, Mass., 1954), Vol. 2, pp. 1124–1175. ANGUS CAMPBELL, PHILIP E. CONVERSE, WARREN E. MILLER, and DONALD E. STOKES, *The American Voter*, at pp. 13 ff., also provide a good summary of voting behavior research, as does CAMPBELL, "Votes and Elections: Past and Present," *Journal of Politics* [hereafter: *JOP*], XXVI (1964), 745–757.

Political Participation. WILLIAM ANDREWS, "American Voting Participation," *Western Political Quarterly*, XIX (1966), 639–652, and WALTER DEAN BURNHAM, "The Changing Shape of the American Political Universe," *American Political Science Review* [hereafter *APSR*], LIX (1965), 7–28, are important discussions, and both LANE, *Political Life*, and MILBRATH, *Political Participation*, provide valuable material on the subject. MORRIS ROSENBERG, "Some Determinants of Political Apathy," *Public Opinion Quarterly* [hereafter: *POQ*], XVIII (1954), 349–366, deals with reasons why people do not vote. Alienation is one such factor. MURRAY LEVIN, *The Alienated Voter* (New York, 1960), stresses it in his study of Boston politics, and LEWIS LIPSITZ looks at its causes, "Work Life and Political Attitudes: A Study of Manual Workers," *APSR*, LVIII (1964), 951–962. Much attention has been given to determining adequate measures for alienation; a leading attempt is MELVIN SEEMAN, "On the Meaning of Alienation," *American Sociological Review*, XXIV (1959), 783–791. Related to alienation and also used to explain voting participation is political cynicism; for a discussion, see ROBERT AGGER, STANLEY PEARL, and MARSHALL GOLDSTEIN, "Political Cynicism: Measurement and Meaning," *JOP*, XXIII (1961), 477–506.

Voting Studies. Classics in the voting behavior field, in addition to *The American Voter*, which is a study of the 1956 election, are STUART A. RICE, *Quantitative Methods in Politics* (New York, 1928); ANGUS CAMPBELL, GERALD GURIN, and WARREN E. MILLER, *The Voter Decides* (Evanston, 1954), the first study based on an SRC national survey [1952]; PAUL LAZARSFELD, BERNARD BERELSON, and HAZEL GAUDET, *The People's Choice* (New York, 1944), a study of Erie County; and BERNARD BERELSON, PAUL LAZARSFELD, and WILLIAM MC PHEE, *Voting: A Study of Opinion Formation in an Election Campaign* (Chicago, 1954), the oft-noted Elmira study. All four are summarized and discussed in PETER H. ROSSI, "Four Landmarks in Voting Research," *American Voting Behavior*, ed. Eugene Burdick and Arthur Brodbeck (Glencoe, 1959), pp. 5–54. Most of the items in the Burdick-Brodbeck volume are based on four voting studies: *The People's Choice; Voting; The Voter Decides;* and R.S. MILNE and H.C. MACKENZIE, *Straight Fight* (London, 1954), a British voting study. The 1964 election is discussed from the perspective of repetitive regional patterns in WALTER DEAN BURNHAM, "American Voting Behavior and the 1964 Election," *Midwest Journal of Political Science*, XII (1968), 1–40. A series of studies based on SRC data is collected in CAMPBELL, *et al., Elections and the Political Order* (New York, 1966). ARTHUR GOLDBERG, using SRC 1956 data, tests various models of factors leading up to the vote, emphasizing the role of partisan attitudes and partisan identification: "Discerning a Causal Pattern Among Data on Voting Behavior," *APSR*, LX (1966), 913–922.

As the foregoing list would seem to suggest, most voting studies have been American (or, to a lesser extent, British). We have recently seen a growth in comparative voting studies, such as ROBERT ALFORD, *Party and Society* (Chicago, 1963), and SEYMOUR MARTIN LIPSET and STEIN ROKKAN, eds., *Party Systems and Voter Alignments: Cross-National Perspectives* (New York, 1967).

Elections. Students of voting behavior talk about types of elections, dealing with the relationship between shifts in partisan identification and changes in the party holding power nationally. See particularly, V.O. KEY, JR., "A Theory of Critical Elections," *JOP*, XVII (1955), 3–18, and also his "Secular Realignment and the Party System," *JOP*, XXI (1959), 198–210, as well as many of the items in CAMPBELL, *et al., Elections and the Political Order*. The effect of elections on the larger political system is considered by TALCOTT PARSONS, " 'Voting' and the Equilibrium of the American Party System," *American Voting Behavior*, ed. Burdick and Brodbeck, pp. 80–120.

Class v. Party. Class and party are two variables used heavily in the voting studies, and the relationship between them is much explored. An article dealing with this is JAMES W. PROTHRO, ERNEST Q. CAMPBELL, and CHARLES M. GRIGG, "Two-Party Voting in the South: Class Vs. Party Identification," *APSR*, LII (1958), 131–139. Also on the subject of class and party, but not restricted to the South, is HEINZ EULAU, *Class and Party in the Eisenhower Years* (New York, 1962). Concerning political changes in the South, which might change the situation with regard to voting studies, see PHILIP E. CONVERSE, "On the Possibility of Major Political Realignment in the South," in CAMPBELL, *et al., Elections and the Political Order*, pp. 212–242. That one-party situations exist elsewhere than in the South and pose the same analytical problem is noted by WARREN E. MILLER, "One-Party Politics and the Voter," *APSR*, L (1956), 707–725.

Institutional Factors. While institutional factors have not been much dealt with by students of voting behavior, they are considered by ANGUS CAMPBELL and WARREN E. MILLER, "The Motivational Basis of Straight and Split Ticket Voting," *APSR*, LI (1957), 293–312, and by JACK L. WALKER, "Ballot Forms and Voter Fatigue: An Analysis of the Office Block and Party Column Ballots," *Midwest Journal of Political Science*, X (1966), 448–463. The effects of registration are considered by STANLEY KELLEY, JR., RICHARD E. AYRES, and WILLIAM G. BOWEN, "Registration and Voting: Putting First Things First," *APSR*, LXI (1967), 359–379.

Sub-Groups. The effect of ethnic, religious, and racial identifications on voting behavior and other forms of political participation has been examined at some length. LUCY S. DAWIDOWICZ and LEON J. GOLDSTEIN look at the effects of ethnicity in the 1960 election in *Politics in a Pluralist Democracy* (New York, 1963); the effect of religion in that campaign is handled by PHILIP E. CONVERSE, "Religion and Politics: The 1960 Election," in CAMPBELL, *et al.*, *Elections and the Political Order*, pp. 96–124. LAWRENCE H. FUCHS, *The Political Behavior of American Jews* (Glencoe, 1956) and WERNER COHN, "The Politics of American Jews," *The Jews: Social Patterns of an American Group*, ed. Marshall Sklare (Glencoe, 1958), pp. 614–626, are thorough treatments of the role of Jewish identification in politics, and JAMES Q. WILSON, *Negro Politics* (Glencoe, 1960) and HARRY BAILEY, ed., *Negro Politics* (Columbus, Ohio, 1966), deal fully with Negroes in politics. An exciting recent study of Negro politics in the South is DONALD MATTHEWS and JAMES PROTHRO, *Negroes and the New Southern Politics* (New York, 1965).

Public Opinion

General Treatment. Text considerations of public opinion include HARWOOD CHILDS, *Public Opinion* (Princeton, 1965); BERNARD HENNESSY, *Public Opinion* (Belmont, Cal., 1965); and V. O. KEY, JR., *Public Opinion and American Democracy* (New York, 1961). Hennessy has summarized recent findings in the field, "Public Opinion and Opinion Change," *Political Science Annual*, ed. James Robinson (Indianapolis, 1966), Vol. 1, pp. 243–296. Key's is clearly the most important attempt to place our knowledge in a theoretical framework. ROBERT LANE and DAVID O. SEARS, *Public Opinion* (Englewood Cliffs, 1964), provide a succinct and sophisticated introductory treatment. Collections of polling data are to be found in HADLEY CANTRIL, *Public Opinion 1935–1946* (Princeton, 1951), and in a special section devoted to that purpose in *Public Opinion Quarterly*.

Communication. Many students of public opinion have dealt with the subject in the larger framework of communications and the mass media. A collection of relevant readings is BERNARD BERELSON and MORRIS JANOWITZ, eds., *Reader in Public Opinion and Communication*, 2nd ed. (New York, 1966). JOSEPH KLAPPER, *The Effects of Mass Communication* (New York, 1960), provides a good summary of the studies of the impact of communications. CHESTER NEWLAND, "Press Coverage of the United States Supreme Court," *Western Political Quarterly*, XVII (1964), 15–36, is a good example of an examination of a part of the mechanisms by which information is communicated to relevant publics, as is DAN NIMMO, *Newsgathering in Washington* (New York, 1964). The effects of a mass medium on politics is HERBERT WALTZER, "In the Magic Lantern: Television Coverage of the 1964 National Conventions," *POQ*, XXX (1966), 33–53. The role of interpersonal relations in the dissemination of communication is handled in the famous exposition of the "two-step flow of communication," ELIHU KATZ and PAUL LAZARSFELD, *Personal Influence* (Glencoe, 1955).

Public Opinion and Democracy. One of the early theoretical statements of this relationship was BERNARD BERELSON, "Democratic Theory and Public Opinion," *POQ*, XVI (1952), 313–330. Much of the concern about the relationship centers in the field of foreign policy. Examples of work in this area are GABRIEL ALMOND, *The American People and Foreign Policy* (New York, 1950); JAMES ROSENAU, *Public Opinion and Foreign Policy* (New York, 1961); and BERNARD C. COHEN, *The Press and Foreign Policy* (Princeton, 1963). The Rosenau volume is more a general theory of the public opinion process; ROSENAU carried his work forward in *National Leadership and Foreign Policy: A Case Study in the Mobilization of Public Support* (Princeton, 1963). NORMAN LUTTBEG has collected articles which bear on the question of the linkages between leaders and publics, and a number relate to public opinion; the volume is *Public Opinion and Public Policy: Models of Political Linkage* (Homewood, Ill., 1968). Those dealing with public opinion in a democracy usually are concerned with possible manipulation of the public through growing use of political public relations: STANLEY KELLEY's *Professional Public Relations and Political Power* (Baltimore, 1956) was the first full-scale treatment of this problem. Earlier writing on public opinion and propaganda provides the base from which current concerns about manipulation of opinion comes. LEONARD W. DOOB, *Public Opinion and Propaganda*, 2nd ed. (Hamden, Conn., 1966) is a standard text on the subject. See also SAMUEL J. ELDERSVELD, "Experimental Propaganda Techniques and Voting Behavior," *APSR*, L (1956), 154–165, as well as HAROLD GOSNELL's earlier study, *Getting Out the Vote: An Experiment in the Stimulation of Voting* (Chicago, 1927), for another side of the interest in propaganda, which has been based primarily on international themes.

Political Socialization

For summaries of the literature, see HERBERT HYMAN, *Political Socialization: A Study in the Psychology of Political Behavior* (Glencoe, 1959); STEPHEN L. WASBY, "The Impact of the Family on Politics: An Essay and Review of the Literature," *Family Life Coordinator*, XV (1966), 3–23; and ROBERTA SIGEL, ed., "Political Socialization: Its Role in the Political Process," *Annals of the American Academy of Political and Social Science*, Vol. 361 (1965). Another summary is RICHARD E. DAWSON, "Political Socialization," *Political Science Annual*, ed. Robinson, Vol. 1, pp. 1–84. JACK DENNIS deals with "Major Problems of Political Socialization Research," *Midwest Journal of Political Science*, XII (1968), 85–114.

Most recent research has dealt with the political socialization of children. FRED GREENSTEIN's *Children and Politics* (New Haven, 1965) is a presentation of important research findings. The orientation of children to various parts of the political system is covered in DAVID EASTON and ROBERT D. HESS, "Youth and the Political System," *Culture and Social Character*, ed. Seymour M. Lipset and Leo Lowenthal (New York, 1961), pp. 226–251; M. KENT JENNINGS, "Pre-Adult Orientations to Multiple Systems of Government," *Midwest Journal of Political Science*, XI (1967), 291–317; and DAVID EASTON and JACK DENNIS, "The Child's Acquisition of Regime Norms: Political Efficacy," *APSR*, LXI (1967), 25–38.

The instrument of socialization most concentrated upon has been the family. In a recent article, M. KENT JENNINGS and RICHARD G. NIEMI present findings which raise questions about the scope of items transmitted from parent to child: "The Transmission of Political Values from Parent to Child," *APSR*, LXII (1968), 169–184. Another important agent of socialization is examined by KENNETH P. LANGTON in "Peer Group and School and the Political Socialization Process," *APSR*, LXI (1967), 751–758.

Recruitment and Leadership

The connection between socialization and recruitment is shown by the examination of the socialization to politics of legislators: KENNETH PREWITT, HEINZ EULAU, and BETTY H. ZISK, "Political Socialization and Political Roles," *POQ*, XXX (1966–1967), 569–582.

WENDELL BELL, RICHARD J. HILL, and CHARLES R. WRIGHT, *Public Leadership* (San Francisco, 1961) is a useful summary of leadership research and DWAINE MAR-

VICK, ed., *Political Decision-Makers* (New York, 1961) is a good collection of recent empirical research on the subject. SIDNEY VERBA's oft-cited *Small Groups and Political Behavior* deals with the small-group leadership studies. A framework for leadership studies, which has generally been lacking, is proposed by LEWIS EDINGER, "Political Science and Political Biography: Reflections on the Study of Leadership," *JOP*, XXVI (1964), 423–439 and 648–676.

DONALD MATTHEWS, *The Social Background of Political Decision-Makers* (Garden City, N.Y., 1954) is typical of the early studies of leadership by political scientists. ANDREW HACKER's "The Elected and the Anointed," *APSR*, LV (1961), 539–549, compares the characteristics of United States Senators and corporation executives. JOHN SCHMIDHAUSER deals with the background of judges in *The Supreme Court: Politics, Personalities, and Procedures* (New York, 1960).

More attention is now paid to the process by which government officials are selected (recruited). THEODORE LOWI, *At The Pleasure of the Mayor* (New York, 1964) and DEAN MANN, *The Assistant Secretaries: Problems and Processes of Appointment* (Washington, D.C., 1965) cover two important groups of officials. Local party officials are dealt with by LEWIS BOWMAN and G.R. BOYNTON, "Recruitment Patterns Among Local Party Officials: A Model and Some Preliminary Findings in Selected Locales," *APSR*, LX (1966), 667–676, and ROBERT SALISBURY, "The Urban Party Organization Member," *POQ*, XXIX (1965–66), 550–564.

Community Politics

The bibliography for Chapter 6 contains materials concerning community power structure.

JESSIE BERNARD, *American Community Behavior*, rev. ed. (New York, 1962) and ROLAND WARREN, *The Community in America* (Chicago, 1963) deal with community in a broad sociological sense. PAUL K. KATT and ALBERT J. REISS, JR., eds., *Cities and Society: The Revised Reader in Urban Society* (Glencoe, 1957) is a fine introduction to the demographic and social patterns which underlie community politics.

CHARLES ADRIAN and CHARLES PRESS, *Governing Urban America*, 3rd ed. (New York, 1968) is perhaps the best introductory urban government and politics text. OLIVER WILLIAMS and ADRIAN, in *Four Cities: A Study in Comparative Policy Making* (Philadelphia, 1963) indicate a new emphasis in the study of urban politics, also evident in the multi-community studies of community power structure. JAMES COLEMAN's important monograph, *Community Conflict* (Glencoe, 1957), provides a framework for analyzing some types of urban politics. MORRIS JANOWITZ has edited a collection of research articles on community politics, *Community Political Systems* (New York, 1960).

EDWARD BANFIELD has been a major political science contributor to the study of urban politics. His collection of readings, *Urban Government: A Reader in Administration and Politics* (New York, 1961), is a good source, as is the collection by OLIVER WILLIAMS and CHARLES PRESS, eds., *Democracy in Urban America* (Chicago, 1961). BANFIELD has provided a serious analysis of *City Politics* (Cambridge, Mass., 1963), co-authored by JAMES Q. WILSON, and a collection of case studies on Chicago, *Political Influence* (New York, 1961). Earlier, MARTIN MEYERSON and BANFIELD produced a study of the selection of public housing sites in Chicago, *Politics, Planning, and the Public Interest* (Glencoe, 1955). Recent studies of urban renewal continue this emphasis within community politics studies: see, for example, HAROLD KAPLAN, *Urban Renewal Politics* (New York, 1963), and PETER ROSSI and ROBERT DENTLER, *The Politics of Urban Renewal* (New York, 1961).

11 / POLITICAL PARTIES
AND INTEREST GROUPS

Definitions and Functions / Party Membership / Party:
Campaigns and Candidate Selection / Party Systems
and Organization / Party in Government / Interest
Groups: Origin and Organization / Interest Groups
and Government / A Note on Social Movements

DEFINITIONS AND FUNCTIONS

Political parties and interest groups are often studied together, in part
because of their occasional interlocking operation and perhaps more important similarity of functions. They may be distinguished by the *primary* functions each performs, although this results in a somewhat oversimplified formulation. A party is thus an organization primarily concerned with the
selection of candidates and their election to office, as well as with the running
of government after electing those candidates, and only secondarily with the
determination of the issues or programs on the basis of which the government
may be run. Interest groups, on the other hand, are primarily concerned with
achieving the programs they desire by having them adopted as the policies of
government, and secondarily with the selection of public officials. Political
parties *are* concerned with policies, but only as this helps them to achieve
electoral victories and to remain in office in the government; interest groups
are interested in candidate-selection, but largely in terms of achieving the
policy goals which are their primary aim. Confusing the distinction is the
recently-identified "electoral interest group," an interest group the primary
concern of which is to support candidates for office.

Political parties have been defined in terms of principles, Burke having
said that a party is a group of men united to achieve the principles on which
they are united, and there has been much discussion of "programmatic" or
"responsible" parties oriented around issues; however, it is now recognized
that this formulation neglects much which is relevant and meaningful about
parties. Thus, the questions of organization and continuity are neglected. A
recent definition which incorporates them is Chambers':

A political party in the modern sense may be thought of as a relatively durable
social formation which seeks offices of power in government, exhibits a structure

344

of organization which links leaders at the centers of government to a significant popular following in the political arena and its local enclaves, and generates in-group perspectives or at least symbols of identification of loyalty.[1]

On the basis of this definition, he challenges the earlier historical idea that America's two major parties existed continuously from the pre-Revolutionary period to the present. Chambers argues that the Federalists and anti-Federalists of the controversy over the ratification of the Constitution were "molecular" groupings (factions or cliques), and that "parties" did not de-velop until the mid-1790's; he also says they had to be re-invented in the 1830's after a "no-party" period. Thus, the definition adopted has clear impli-cations for the analysis one conducts.

Parties and interest groups perform a multiplicity of functions. Not only do parties choose candidates, they also assist in recruiting them, that is, they bring people into politics as well as help them choose between those already there. As we shall also see, parties not only winnow and present alternatives, but also stimulate those with views to exercise them through the vote, that is, they activate and mobilize. Another function is that of cue-giving and provid-ing an evaluating device; the political stimuli in a complex society are so many and so complex that the average individual, who does not devote much time or (psychological) energy to politics might find himself in a chaotic situ-ation if he had not some device whereby he could quickly label some ideas or candidates appealing, while rejecting others. The party label allows him to do this. Interest groups perform all these functions as well, although, because the scope of their concerns is normally much narrower than those of the parties, they are less helpful as evaluating devices for the individual, particu-larly if he belongs to several groups. Activation and mobilization they cer-tainly perform, although again perhaps on a more limited scale; recruitment is certainly of importance. While the relationship between interest groups and parties in terms of their shared functions has been noted above, more recent formulations of functions performed in political systems suggest an-other relationship. Almond wrote about interest articulation and interest ag-gregation, necessary if interests in the polity are to be "processed" by the system into outputs. (See pp. 107–108.) While in the American system parties are more concerned with aggregation and interest groups with articu-lation, each performs both. Before an interest group announces (articulates) an interest, it has usually aggregated the interests of the many individuals who are its members and adherents. Unless the group is one of pure homoge-neity, these individual views have to some extent been compromised in the process leading to the articulation, although this does not necessarily mean that a long, democratic decision-making process has taken place. Parties ar-ticulate interests, in some cases simply repeating those of interest groups (we find platforms often to be a record of interest groups important within a given

[1] William N. Chambers, "Party Development and the American Mainstream," *The American Party Systems: Stages of Political Development,* ed. William Nisbet Chambers and Walter Dean Burnham (New York, 1967), p. 5.

party) and in other cases stating new and independent ones. The prime function is of aggregating the requests of the many groups in the polity, a function also performed by legislative bodies.

PARTY MEMBERSHIP

We often talk of "party membership," although no one is exactly sure what it means. While we are fond of talking of the "card-carrying members" of the Communist Party, major parties in the United States do not have formal membership, with dues-paying and membership cards. In fact, in some jurisdictions, almost anyone can claim to be a "Democrat" or "Republican," frequently to the embarrassment of party leaders,[2] although, in other cases, certain minimal tests are applied. This is not to say that identification of the "party faithful" is impossible. One can point to candidates for office who have won the party's nomination and to those public officials elected under the party's banner, as well as to the official party leaders themselves (national committeemen and committeewomen, the state chairmen, district and ward leaders, and precinct captains). There are also the formal members of various party organs, such as Young Democrats or Republican Women. Of course, where registration exists, those registered under the party label could be considered "members" of the party. However, this does not exhaust the list of those who might be considered members of a party. There are, for example, those who contribute funds to the party or who contribute services such as passing out literature or getting out the vote—categories without which a party could not successfully function. There are also those who vote consistently for the candidates of a particular party. Some political scientists have pictured "party membership" as a set of concentric circles, each of which contains one of the categories of individuals mentioned here. The officials elected under the party label are at the center, in the smallest circle, with the party officials next, and so on out, in increasingly larger circles. This outward direction also indicates the origins of American parties, from within the government, that is, from the legislative caucuses, rather than from outside the

> **Caucus.   A meeting of party members at a certain level of government. A legislative caucus would be all members of a particular party serving in the legislature.**

government, as appears to have been the case with recently developed European "mass" parties.

Students of voting behavior have added another dimension, the psychological, through the concept of "political identification." Not only do they

[2] As an example, see the situation in the Ohio Democratic Party in 1962, when the nomination for Representative-at-Large was won by a man with the politically attractive name of Kennedy. He was extremely conservative on the issue of race relations; even though he ran as a Democrat in the general election, the party leaders ignored him, and he lost.

want to know for which party (or which party's candidates) a person voted, but of which party he considers himself a member, and with what strength. Respondents in surveys are asked to categorize themselves as "strong," "moderate," or "weak" Democrats or Republicans (with "independent" as an additional choice). Thus we have a subjective measure of party affiliation to supplement an objective one (For what party did you vote?). The party identification concept takes on even more significance when it is recognized that, for all the talk about "independents" (and a steady growth in the proportion who so identify), a majority of the American voting public place themselves in one or another of the partisan categories.

Another concept, the social-psychological one of "party image," recently has been used with some effect, and may be more useful than party identification in predicting the vote. Here we recognize that even if a number of individuals adhere to the same party, they are adhering to the party in the different ways *in which they perceive it*. Without this phenomenon, a party would be less likely to hold as adherents such diverse groups as are retained in the coalitions constituting the two major American parties. There are also differing orientations to party; for example, some relate to party at the national level, while others relate to it principally at the state or local level of government.

The "party image" concept suggests, contrary to Burke's view of party, that among those who are of a common party identification, there is not necessarily a common ideology or consensus on policy positions. Followers of the Democratic Party may not be very far from followers of the Republican Party on some matters, although position issues bring greater divisiveness between adherents of the two parties than do style issues. In fact, the views of the leaders of one party and the followers of the other party may not be far apart: "The views of the Republican rank-and-file are, on the whole, much closer to those of the Democratic leaders than to those of the Republican leaders." [3] What is significant is that leaders of the two parties are further apart than their followers; the higher the partisanship, the stronger the differences. Such differences, which are accentuated as party competition requires party activists to differentiate themselves in the public eye, help to explain why a party may choose a candidate who is not broadly appealing to the "center" of the electorate (e.g., the Republicans' choice of Goldwater in 1964). McClosky's findings suggest that agreement on views may bring party activists together, but such agreement is not what brings the rank-and-file together.

PARTY: CAMPAIGNS AND CANDIDATE SELECTION

A discussion of elections and all that leads up to them could perhaps take place under the heading of "Electoral Behavior," but no discussion of parties

[3] Herbert McClosky, Paul J. Hoffman, and Rosemary O'Hara, "Issue Conflict and Consensus Among Party Leaders and Followers," *American Political Science Review*, LV (1960), 422. The data of this study were collected in 1957–1958.

would be complete without consideration of elections because of the important role which parties play in campaigns and the candidate selection which is an integral part of them. While in many jurisdictions, elections, including party primaries, are now run largely by the government, elections were originally handled by the parties themselves. Party workers still play a large official part as poll watchers and election judges; and, while some candidates attempt to avoid the party label, partisan organization is the (or at least, *a*) main force in most campaigns except perhaps at the municipal level, often spelling the candidate's success or failure. This is not to say that party always predominates. Some would say that organization can exist apart from party, and clearly, the "packaged campaigns" that public relations firms have provided for some candidates in recent years suggest that parties clearly need many organizations (not the least of which are interest groups) to assist them. The reliance which many Presidential candidates place on public opinion polls, either those of commercial polling organizations or ones specifically conducted under contract for them, indicates the need to include another type of organization. Major campaigns cannot be run without money, but not all the financing comes from or through the parties, as recent writing on the subject of "money and politics" has shown us. Although parties do serve as fund-raisers, one could argue that they are simply collection agencies (or money-managers) rather than the prime instigators of political financing. And, as the political memoirs of candidates and their managers—see Stimson Bullitt's *To Be A Politician*, and *How To Win An Election*, by Barry Goldwater's campaign manager, Stephen Shadegg—have clearly shown us, there is often the "individual touch" which the candidate gives to his campaign, showing how not to be simply a captive of the party. There are also differences in style, such as that between "purists," who won't compromise and are more interested in maintaining their principles than in victory, and "professionals."

The role of party bulks largest in the selection of nominees to run for office in the general election. Even though we now take the direct primary for granted, for many years the general public had little or no say in who would run for office. After sufficient outcry was raised against "King Caucus," where candidates were chosen, the convention became the method for selecting candidates. In this procedure, intended to be more representative, delegates were elected to a convention, which was a meeting held only immediately before an election campaign for the purpose of choosing candidates and writing a party platform. Sometimes there was more than one layer of convention, each one selecting the delegates to the next higher level. In any case, although the convention is used to choose our Presidential candidates to this day, it was found that, instead of being representative, the convention was often easily subject to control by "party bosses"; a large group of people meeting infrequently had no continuing organization, no structure for developing choices separately from those suggested to them. In this situation, a leader could help bring about the selection of convention delegates predisposed to a particular candidate, thus making the action of the convention predetermined and anticlimactic. While conventions are often used to choose candidates at lower levels of government (such as the county), candidates for state-wide office now are chosen primarily through the direct primary. The voters, at least according to the rationale for the primary, pick from among candidates who offer themselves for the nomination, thus not being forced to take the choices of the party leaders. Of course, for the direct primary to be effective, more than one candidate must offer himself, and often this does not happen, or so many candidates appear that the voters' task in attempting to choose among them is extremely difficult. Sometimes not even a single candidate willingly offers himself, bringing about a situation where the party leaders must find someone to run, thus increasing their power. However, this is more likely to happen when a party is in a distinct minority situation, thus not necessarily increasing the power of the majority party leaders. Contrary to conventional belief, most candidates are not self-starters and their appearance on the ballot is at least in part the result of activities by individuals or groups unknown to the voter. Scholars also have examined the degree to which broad participation in candidate-selection actually exists. V.O. Key has reported in *American State Politics* that those who vote in primary elections are not representative of all the voters, much less of all those who vote for that party's candidates in the general elections. Those who vote in primaries (when turnout is usually small) tend to be the "hard-core" members of the party, the most partisan; those they select are not always the candidates who will make a sufficiently broad appeal to attract necessary votes from uncommitted voters, although the same result can occur when candidates are chosen in convention.

There has been recognition of the many variations of the primary. For example, in some states a person must swear an oath to support a party before being allowed to vote in its primary or prior registration as a member of that party may be demanded, while in other states voters have been allowed to vote in the primaries of any party. When voters may vote in *all* primaries at once, one has a "blanket primary." At its extreme, the voter could vote to nominate a candidate for one office in one party, then for another office in another party, and so on, but he could *not* nominate candidates for the same office in more than one party. The blanket primary has been largely discarded. The variations in the primary are often related to the characteristics of political development or competition in a particular area. Where party organizations are well developed, one is less likely to find open entrance to voting in a primary than one would where parties are not well developed or party is more a "state of mind" than an organizational phenomenon. The same is true with the former California practice of "cross-filing": when stronger parties developed, the procedure was eliminated.

> *Cross-filing.*   A candidate can run for the nomination of both parties; if successful, he would be opposing himself in the general election, thus assuring victory.

That the devices used to select candidates were and are effective is shown best by the efforts of party leaders to change them. Where a number of ethnic groups exist, all predisposed to vote for a party if represented on that party's "ticket," the direct primary may allow one ethnic group to capture all the nominations and thus drive off the other groups. In contrast, a convention might result in "balancing the ticket." In New York, "balancing the ticket" frequently results in a ticket composed of an Irishman, an Italian, and someone of Jewish extraction ("three-I" politics if one uses the word "Israelite"). In order to try to achieve balance without completely discarding "popular" participation in candidate selection, party officials have tried to combine the convention with the primary. Candidates are chosen in pre-primary conventions, then receive the party's backing in the primary, thus perhaps scaring away candidates without such backing. In Massachusetts, a person must receive a certain percentage of the convention votes before he can challenge the convention winner in the primary. In this "pre-primary convention" system, the convention winner is so indicated on the primary ballot.

Party leaders are not always correct in understanding the working of electoral forms. Although it is commonly argued that a bitter primary battle will hurt a party's chances at election time, Hacker has shown rather conclusively that a "divisive primary" makes little if any difference in general election outcomes.[4] Regardless of the effectiveness of the electoral forms, they are not all that is involved, and the systematic study of recruitment has shown the relevance and effect of other, less formal or structural factors. In addition, application of the structural-functional approach to the study of conventions has resulted in suggestions that conventions fulfill many functions beyond the manifest one of candidate-selection. They rally support, communicate enthusiasm to the party supporters attending the conventions, and may serve either to unify the party or to resolve conflicts between factions within the party without splitting the party irreparably. Application of this same approach to the election process itself indicates that, in addition to selecting governments, elections create solidarity, allow the release of aggression through legitimate channels, and provide incentives to citizens to inform themselves.

Presidential campaigns probably have received scholars' attention over the longest period of time. Much of the literature on the history of political parties is in effect a history of Presidential elections. This may be because our national parties are held together largely in terms of the every-fourth-year Presidential selection process, but also because the Presidential office, as the most important and visible one in American political life, has naturally attracted special attention by journalists, historians, and political scientists. Indicative is Theodore White's *The Making of the President 1960*, oft-used by political scientists for source material, which takes as its subject the campaign from its origins years before (no campaign has a history limited only to

[4] Andrew Hacker, "Does a 'Divisive' Primary Harm a Candidate's Election Chances?" *American Political Science Review*, LIX (1965), 105–110.

four years) to its conclusion. The White volume shows how candidates and the parties whose labels they bear have adapted to changing circumstance, particularly to the greater ease of travel (allowing Mr. Nixon to make the promise he would visit each of the fifty states) and the impact of national network television.

The greater role which Presidential primaries have played in achieving the nomination in recent years, shown particularly by their use by the late President Kennedy in 1960, has attracted attention. That these primaries have not replaced other selection devices totally is shown by their far smaller role in the Republican nomination of 1964, in which Senator Goldwater relied most heavily on the votes of delegates selected in state conventions. Although the Presidential primary is a form of direct primary, and although the national Presidential nominating convention is a convention, both are to a large extent *sui generis* and have received considerable treatment separately from general discussion of methods of candidate selection. The Presidential primaries vary noticeably from state to state, with some taking simply a "beauty contest" (or popularity poll) form, while others are handled through the election to the convention of delegates pledged to specific Presidential hopefuls. An increasing number of states have adopted the Oregon form of primary in which a state official determines who the genuine Presidential candidates are and enters them in the race (almost irrevocably), thus depriving them of their choice as to whether or not to enter a particular primary. The Presidential nominating convention has been the subject of one of the most massive of political science projects, that conducted by Professors David, Goldman, and Bain in 1952 (*The Politics of National Party Conventions*). The project provided not only a detailed state-by-state description of the procedure in each of the states but also the only full-scale and systematic treatment of a Presidential convention that we have.

Other aspects of a Presidential campaign to which attention most often has been given are characteristics a person needs in order to be nominated for the office, usually produced as a check-list of a person's "availability" for the job, or the methods by which he should be formally chosen. The continued debate over the Electoral College method versus direct election or some variation on the "unit rule" method now used in the Electoral College is typical of the latter concern.

Attention to campaigns and elections no longer is limited to the Presidential campaign and the role of the political party and its supporters in that campaign. Morality in politics—the "proper" uses of money and the conduct of "clean" campaigns—always has been of interest to the reformer, but it has been studied more systematically recently, so that we know much more about the sources of campaign funds for Congressional as well as Presidential elections, although we still do not know much about the process by which funds are distributed or the factors affecting the distribution. (This suggests the general problem of the difficulty of trying to study political parties, because of the fact that they keep their *modi operandi* so close to their chests.) The current controversy about reforms in campaign spending legislation has continued to focus interest on the subject of "political money." Political committees independent of the parties, e.g., the National Committee for an Effective Congress, discovered to be dispensers of money, have come under scholarly scrutiny. We now know that, as "Volunteers for Nixon," "Democrats for Eisenhower," or "Citizens for Johnson," voluntary groups can also play an important part in elections by attracting non-partisan voters.

Campaign rhetoric has always interested students of elections; some historians have studied party platforms to determine sources of particular planks, while others have exhibited them as examples of political compromise *par excellence*. More theoretically-oriented recent studies have dealt with the question of the contribution to rationality made by such rhetoric. Gerald Pomper, after an examination of campaign platforms, concluded that they probably contributed more to party-rationality (helping the party to victory) than they did to voter-rationality (helping the voter make a decision in his own best interest).[5] Another analyst concluded that the so-called "Great Debates," the television confrontations between Kennedy and Nixon in the 1960 campaign, did contribute to greater rationality by allowing a more direct confrontation of the issues.[6] In connection with that much-touted new campaign "gimmick," one might note that the viewing audience, while large, was largely captive, and that a substantial proportion of viewers did turn their sets off before the end of the debates. Although the debates, particularly the first one, are said to have contributed significantly to Kennedy's victory, it has also been suggested that at the end of a working day the American public is more interested in entertainment than in political edification.

Other discussion of campaigns has been in terms of strategy. We have had indications that candidates may have various goals in a campaign, for example, not just to win but to win big (to create a "mandate"), or to lose by only a small margin in order to cast doubt on the winner's program. Some political scientists have drawn on findings from voting behavior studies to suggest strategies. Thus Lewis Froman has said that a candidate should recognize different predispositions in the electorate (supporters, latent supporters, and opponents) and treat each differently. He says that rather than discussing issues with his supporters and making broad appeals to the opponents, the candidate should do the opposite in order to reassure his supporters and make his opponents think he is an exception to his own party.[7] Others, like Anthony Downs, in *An Economic Theory of Democracy*, have gone beyond candidate strategy to develop whole theories—based in part on game theory—of what parties need to do in order to obtain a majority. The clear

[5] Gerald Pomper, " 'If Elected, I Promise': American Party Platforms," *Midwest Journal of Political Science*, XI (1967), 318–352.

[6] John W. Ellsworth, "Rationality and Campaigning: A Content Analysis of the 1960 Presidential Campaign Debates," *Western Political Quarterly*, XVIII (1965), 794–802.

[7] Lewis A. Froman, Jr., "A Realistic Approach to Campaign Strategies and Tactics," *The Electoral Process*, ed. M. Kent Jennings and Harmon Zeigler (Englewood Cliffs, 1966), pp. 8–9.

direction of current writing on campaigns, as this may indicate, has been away from the descriptive and toward the behaviorally-oriented theoretical study or contribution to theory.

PARTY SYSTEMS AND ORGANIZATION

We tend to take it for granted that the United States has a two-party system. Political scientists long have been concerned with the operation of such a system, in comparison with the multi-party systems of countries such as France and the single-party systems of developing or totalitarian nations,[8] and explain the existence of two-party systems as a result of single-member legislative districts, the requirement of a plurality vote, and a single chief executive. The analysts have shown us that talk about a "two-party" or "one-party" system is loose unless we specify what we mean by party and its geographic scope. It is possible to talk about a two-party system in Presidential politics in America, because both parties have an opportunity to win the Presidency, although some analysts believe that the Republicans *as a party* cannot win the office unless they run a candidate with a non-partisan image, e.g., Dwight Eisenhower, although Richard Nixon's 1968 victory casts doubts on the suggestion. Although we have three major groupings (Democrats, Republicans, independents), this leaves us with two major parties.

There have been some elections in recent years involving more than two parties. In 1948, with the Progressive Party (Henry Wallace) and the Dixiecrats (J. Strom Thurmond), there were four and 1968 saw George Wallace's American Independent Party. These situations involve a national multi-party situation not repeated in the states. We also have had areas of the country held so dominantly by one party—most notably the Democrats in the South and the Republicans in northern New England and parts of the Midwest—that *de facto* one-party conditions have existed, at least for state-wide contests and many lower level (e.g., county) positions. Parties not represented on the national level have been visible in some of the states, for example, the Farmer-Labor parties of the upper Midwest.

These situations suggest the need to clarify the meaning of a "two-party" system for purposes of analysis. Such clarification usually requires some measure of party competition. A number of political scientists have categorized states by degrees of competition: "one-party Democrat," "two-party Democrat," "marginal" or "swing," "two-party Republican," and "one-party Republican" might be one; competitive, cyclically competitive, one-party cyclical, one-party predominant, and one-party as proposed by Joseph Schle-

[8] Ranney and Kendall would have five party systems: multiple-party, two-party, modified one-party, one-party, totalitarian one-party. Austin Ranney and Willmoore Kendall, "The American Party Systems," *American Political Science Review*, XLVIII (1954), 477–485.

singer is another.[9] Categorizations can be made on a number of bases: competition for Presidential office, for Senatorial and Congressional seats, for state-wide offices, and/or for county positions. In view of the fact that the division of the vote between the major parties is not the same at all levels of the party ticket, what items are used in the measure can make a difference in the categorization. Even when a state may be considered to have vigorous two-party competition for state-wide offices, there may be a number of state legislative positions and county offices which are not contested; in some states a majority of such positions are not contested in any single election. The period of time used in the measure can vary, although, to avoid categorizing on the basis of an atypical situation, the use of several elections is considered wise.[10] One can measure the percentage of elections won (the proportion of success), the duration of a party's holding office (the question of alternation in office), the percentage of the vote received in evaluating the degree of competition, or the percentage of legislative seats. It should be added that these measures also are used in connection with studies of legislative voting behavior and studies of policy outputs of the states, and they have also been related to population characteristics, including the size of particular communities, and socio-economic development. Thus significant differences between one-party and two-party states were found for such variables as percentage population urban, 1930 and 1950; percentage of the population Negro, 1950; total median income, 1949; and a coefficient of industrialization. Competition has been related both to socio-economic development and to the liberality of policy outputs. Formal models of party competition have been developed but they are a quite recent addition (and are still in preliminary stages).

Beyond developing such measures—and the development alone helps to clarify the meaning of party competition—scholars have devoted considerable attention to intensive analysis of specific types of party competition. Perhaps because it is felt to deviate from the American norm, one-party politics has drawn much attention, particularly in the so-called "Solid South" (the states which made up the Confederacy). Any move away from Southern one-partyism, whether it be the temporary defections of 1928 and 1948 or the seeming longer-run trends exhibited in 1964 Presidential and 1966 Congressional elections, receives much mention. Key and others have shown that "one-party politics" does not mean the absence of political competition, although it is competition of a different sort from that which exists where two well-developed parties battle each other. Instead of parties, we find "factions," loosely organized groupings of individuals which come and go, usually following a particular candidate rather than having a continuing existence independent of specific individuals. The factions create a fluid political

[9] "A Two-Dimensional Scheme for Classifying the States According to Degree of Inter-Party Competition," *American Political Science Review*, XLIX (1955), 1120–1128.
[10] This point is made by Robert T. Golembiewski, "A Taxonomic Approach to State Political Party Strength," *Western Political Quarterly*, XI (1958), 494–513.

situation, and thus seldom perform a party's cue-giving function. The vote for factional candidates tends to have a "friends-and-neighbors" flavor, with candidates achieving their highest votes in the areas in which they have lived or worked immediately before announcing their candidacies.

Pursuing political organization, some scholars have looked at another type of "one-party" situation, the operation of the political "machine," particularly in large cities. Although one can find tightly-controlled party organizations in rural areas, our image of machines defines them as urban phenomena, invariably corrupt and improper, with "honest" politics taking place only in the rural hinterland. Despite the inaccuracy of this "rural purity and urban sin" image, the machine has been of fascination to journalists and political scientists alike. Because the American citizen is supposed to cast his vote after independent consideration of the issues, a "controlled" vote given in exchange for favors—a job, keeping your son out of trouble with the police, a basket at Christmas—has offended middle-class political sensibilities. As Merton's article on the latent functions of the machine suggests, simple moral raillery at the machine (see pp. 99–107) and even the election of "fine and upstanding men" to municipal office did not change the foundation of the system on which the machine was built. On the contrary, it was the political and social environment which undermined the machine. A decline in immigration, a rise in literacy, dispersion of ethnic groups, the rise of unions, and the intervention of the federal government in the welfare function all played a role, although the direct primary was not without its effect as well. The decline in the number of existing powerful machines has lessened the interest of political scientists in them, but there is much we still need to know. Their effect on recruitment of candidates for offices and the general lack of independent campaigning by candidates, as well as the joint holding of political party office and public office, need further exploration.

If, as has been suggested, the formal organization of party at the local level is not strong and it is informal organizations that make the party effective, we need to go beyond exploration of formal organization in discussing party organization. The lack of full-time party functionaries suggests the need to explore further the role of volunteers in politics. At the national level, the role played by prestigious individuals who lend their names and efforts to advisory councils and other such efforts, important at least symbolically, might be further analyzed.

It should be noted that the organization of political parties, beyond a recitation of the many layers of party organization, has not received as much detailed examination as other aspects of the subject of political parties, at least not from American scholars. There is nothing equivalent to the work of Duverger or Michels.[11] Roberto Michels, by studying Socialist parties

[11] Maurice Duverger, *Political Parties: Their Organization and Activity in the Modern State*, trans. Barbara and Robert North (New York, 1959 [1951]); Roberto Michels, *Political Parties: A Sociological Study of the Oligarchical Tendencies of Modern Democracy*, trans. Eden and Cedar Paul (Glencoe, Ill., 1958 [1915]).

in Europe, developed the famed "iron law of oligarchy," that any organization's leaders will solidify their position in office ("Who says organization, says oligarchy"). While this may not seem startling, the deviation from democratic rhetoric of participation surprised Michels. There have been a number of case studies of local organization activity in America, in which the analysts have tried to treat the specific case as exemplary of broader phenomena, but these are still primarily case studies and, as such, limited in scope. This is at least in part a result of American scholars' emphasis on and interest in the issue-oriented aspect of political party activities. However, the distinction between patronage politics (organization politics) and issue politics is proving useful in the analysis of party activities, as when campaign-oriented and organization- (maintenance-) oriented party workers are contrasted. When party organization is studied, it tends to be examined one level at a time, leaving us without a comprehensive picture, even though parties on the national level are generally only tenuous entities, coalitions of state party organizations. The state party organizations and those at the county level are the more permanent, on-going organizations, although even they are to a large extent periodic and spasmodic in character, being fully "cranked up" only for elections.

The existence of National Committees for each of the major parties, with National Chairmen who make occasional statements about the excellent state of their party, and the fact that the parties have headquarters in Washington, have lulled many into thinking these organizations to be stronger than they are. They do indeed perform a variety of important functions, such as policy guidance and money distribution. The fact that the "opportunity structure" of political advancement tends to be national does make the parties national at least to some degree. Yet we also know that the National Chairman is usually an appointee of the party's Presidential candidate, and that the national party headquarters office is often only an extension of, or run from, the White House when the party is in power. National committeemen and committeewomen may play a larger role in the politics of their states than in national party councils, and Cornelius Cotter and Bernard Hennessy's recent book, *Politics Without Power: The National Committee*, suggests through its title the role played by those organizations. Yet even their work is only a beginning of a thorough exploration of this aspect of political parties. For example, we know almost nothing about the party in congressional districts, where it may be an artificial party jurisdiction. It may not even be organized, particularly in rural areas, where "there is little opportunity for the face-to-face contacts on which the intensely organized parties build a web of personal contact, loyalty, and obligation." [12] Recently, it has been claimed that we lack sufficient information to make a typology of parties in terms of their organizational characteristics,[13] although Frank Sorauf has

[12] Frank J. Sorauf, *Party and Representation* (New York, 1963), pp. 58–59.
[13] David Olson, "Perceptions by Congressmen of Their Party: The National and District Units of Party," paper presented to the Southern Political Science Association, New Orleans, 1967.

developed one based on articulation within organization, the regularity of activity, and the internal discipline and control of the party.[14] He then relates the party types to population density and legislative voting.

Parties are coalitions not only of state parties, but of major and minor interests in the society. It is for this reason that much of the historical concern with parties has been in terms of the history of which groups were allied with which party at which time. Historians of parties often identified parties in terms of what they saw as the dominant members of the coalition, thus leading to interpretations which pit a "business-" oriented party against a "people-" or "labor-" oriented party during most of our history. This interpretation gives rise to problems when dominant interests such as business are either favored by both parties, as appeared to be the case during the last quarter of the nineteenth century, or when the interests ignore the parties. Despite such difficulties, historical analysis can be quite helpful, as in reminding us that the Democratic Party's urban-labor coalition (which some analysts say is breaking up in the 1960's) did not antedate Roosevelt and the "New Deal." It also suggests that, while not ideologically divided, United States parties contain (and thus manage) many cleavages.

In addition to machines and other aspects of political organization, minor or "third" parties have fascinated students of politics, although treatments of them have been largely historical. Because they have not managed a Presidential victory, they are somehow discounted, leading some to ignore their possible effects, for example, attracting votes more from one major party than the other. The presence of major party platform planks "lifted" from the minor parties when the latter have become popular has been noted by political historians. This "borrowing" has served in part to make it difficult for the minor parties to continue their popularity, although it has been suggested that their failure to establish strong bases of organization at the state (and lower) level(s) has been a larger cause of their downfall.

The minor parties have espoused certain issues with a clarity possible because they have not been appealing to the broad spectrum of the public with which the two major parties must deal. This has met with the approval of political reformers who have long been attracted to the idea that our parties should be "responsible" or "programmatic" in nature. The seemingly greater emphasis of the British political parties on issues and the greater control which those parties have over a person's right to run as a candidate with that party's label have brought suggestions for the realignment of our two major parties into a "Liberal" Party and a "Conservative" Party. Often this is suggested by liberals in the Democratic Party who feel sorely burdened by the conservative Southern wing of the party. Political scientists for a long time were in the vanguard of those so arguing, as the 1950 APSA report, "Toward a More Responsible Two-Party System," indicates. The absence of party responsibility was "a basic weakness in the American two-party system. . . . The political foundation of appropriate governmental programs is very un-

[14] Sorauf, pp. 46–47.

stable when it is not supplied by responsible party action," it complained.[15] This voice is still heard, being shown clearly in James MacGregor Burns' *The Deadlock of Democracy*, in which he discusses the existence of two wings to each party, a Presidential one and a Congressional one, clearly indicating his preference for a "neater" arrangement. It is ironic to note that the differences between the British Labour and Conservative (Tory) Parties seem to be diminishing, thus bringing the British party system closer to ours while at the same time adoption of the British system is being urged here.

A number of attacks have been launched at the reformers' position. In one line of attack, it is suggested that the British system has been misunderstood. Thus, candidacies are not controlled solely by the national level of the party, but local constituency organizations have much to say about who shall run when there is a disagreement at party headquarters. Another problem is that the differences between the British and American polities have been ignored. Those attempting to import the British system are said to ignore the fact that we have a federal system of government and they, a unitary one. The

> **Unitary System of Government.**   One in which there is only one government ("local" governments excepted) dealing with the people; its scope is nation-wide. The country may be subdivided for administrative purposes, but major policy is made only in the national government. In a *federal system*, there is an intermediate level of government, known as states or provinces, between the people and the national government. The national government may still deal directly with the citizens, but the state governments have some independence of action. In a *confederation*, the central government may deal with the people only indirectly, through the state governments.

regional nature of some of our political issues is also said to be ignored; Julius Turner claims that state and local components of a national political party in this country could not be successful in some situations unless they could take a point of view different from that adopted by the national "wing" of the party.[16]

Our own party system has also not been perceived accurately. That parties, particularly at the local level, play a large role in the electoral process, thus to some extent making victorious candidates feel indebted to them, produces responsible party behavior. This is true even though each candidate may respond to a different "party," leaving a national structure lacking cohesiveness. In addition, close examination shows the relevance of party to actual political behavior. The effect of partisan identification has already been mentioned. Studies of legislators' votes reveal party to be the biggest single explanatory factor, far more important than constituency characteristics, which may, however, be reflected in the legislator's party. How-

---

[15] Committee on Political Parties, "Toward a More Responsible Two-Party System," *American Political Science Review*, XLIV (September, 1950, Supplement), v, 93.

[16] Julius Turner, "Responsible Parties: A Dissent from the Floor," *American Political Science Review*, XLV (1951), 143–152.

ever, others have noted a decline in the percentage of roll calls oriented around party, and Lowi has suggested that the fact that party voting is highest on procedural and distributive measures, while low on matters of regulatory policy, shows that the parties are not responsible.[17]

Before we can better evaluate plans for reforming the party system, we need to know at a minimum why our present one operates as it does. If, as it is alleged, our two national parties are like "Tweedledee and Tweedledum," that is, if their views converge, is it because our voters are clustered in the middle of the ideological spectrum, or because both parties try to appear in a favorable light? Are they the same because they both try to be brokers? Downs suggests that pressure to converge is greater on the lesser party when one party predominates, but this just begins a discussion of the subject. The idea that our two major parties do converge through appeals to the "vast middle" has not been unchallenged. Thus, Huntington, by examining the 1946 vote for Congress, showed that the closer the vote was in a Congressional district, the more liberal (i.e., the less moderate) was the Democrat.[18] While his study is suggestive, it is not conclusive, and others have indicated that the "traditional theory" of appeals to the political middle is irrelevant because American voters do not arrange themselves along an ideological spectrum.[19] A number of explanations for this lack of ideology have been offered in recent years. One is that the liberal tradition is almost as firmly entrenched as a folk religion would be, leaving no room for competition from another ideology. That there was no established (feudal) class with which the masses would have clashed removed an opportunity for the development of an ideology. In addition, economic prosperity (lessening clashes over material matters) and pragmatism (a result of coping with the frontier) are said to have produced the current situation.

The idea of bringing about responsible parties is not the only reform which has been proposed concerning political parties. Another, perhaps even more radical in its implications, has been to do away with party politics entirely, and to move to "nonpartisan politics." Coming from those who felt that party politics was inherently corrupt and immoral and that control of affairs should be returned to "the people," this idea was based on the implicit assumption (what Justice Holmes called the "inarticulate major premise") that, without parties, one would be without partisanship. That this equation of all political conflict with parties was inaccurate has become clear, as we are still left with conflict over political goals even where nonpartisan political systems have been most thoroughly installed. Nonpartisanship has taken the greatest hold at the municipal level, except in the largest cities where the

---

[17] "Distributive" measures include what are usually referred to as "pork-barrel" items, projects for individual districts. Here, the party is only acting as a "cumulator." Theodore J. Lowi, "Party, Policy, and Constitution in America," *The American Party Systems*, ed. Chambers and Burnham, pp. 270–273.

[18] Samuel Huntington, "A Revised Theory of American Party Politics," *American Political Science Review*, XLIV (1950), 669–677.

[19] Joseph Schlesinger, *Ambition and Politics*, pp. 122–123.

party machines have been able to resist it, and in special district governments. Only two states (Nebraska and Minnesota) have nonpartisan elections to the legislature, and in Minnesota, despite the technical nonpartisanship, the two legislative caucuses are based on the national party allegiances of the legislators. Many more states utilize nonpartisan methods of selection for the judiciary, possibly because of the belief that judicial matters should be divorced from partisan considerations and that judges should not have to campaign for election after rendering potentially unpopular decisions.

Nonpartisanship in name does not always mean nonpartisanship in fact. Beneath the nonpartisan label, political scientists are finding that a "rose is a rose is a rose," and that party organizations which operate openly in county politics (where nonpartisanship has not progressed far) and state and national politics reappear in the municipality in some other guise, either as local parties or as "citizens committees." Thus what appears on the surface as a nonpartisan arrangement may simply be a device for the dominant party to continue its control locally without doing so openly. Local parties have been of a wide variety; they are not all county or national parties organized with "different hats." Some are simply slate-making organizations or interest groups become endorsing organizations. In fact, one finds the entire range from completely fluid situations in which candidates are self-starters with their own personal groupings to help elect them to the other extreme, of the large-scale political machine with state and national ties. In the latter situation, exemplified by the Cook County (Illinois) Democratic organization, the local organization may effectively control the state party, thus decreasing the independence of any Governor of that party. At a minimum, the strength of the local political barons may be such that they are able to veto actions they do not like even if they cannot obtain all the programs they prefer.

Scholars concentrating on nonpartisan politics at the local level have given us a very thorough picture of the effects of removing the partisan label from the ballot. Adrian has shown, for example, that this rule, like most rules, is not neutral in its effect, although, because nonpartisan local elections frequently are held on an at-large basis, it is often difficult to sort out the effect of each element of the system. Thus, when we say that nonpartisan elections increase the chances for the downtown businessman to be elected at the expense of the workingman, we may be referring to the at-large rather than the nonpartisan aspect of the system. The latter makes identification of those responsible for decisions difficult, giving the voter less of a clear choice at election time. Some people can get elected in nonpartisan arrangements who would not be chosen if party labels had to accompany their names, and the removal of the party label increases the impact of ethnic voting in local elections. Nonpartisanship appears to work best in municipalities basically homogeneous in character, without cleavages which might provide the basis for continuing party organizations.

Local politics run on a nonpartisan basis also have an effect on the ties between local and county, state, and national politics. The existence of a separate set of local political organizations (when they are in fact not just the regular party organization masquerading under a different name) makes it difficult for the partisan organization to collect funds, while advancement from (nonpartisan) political office to higher (partisan) office is likely to be more difficult if not completely blocked. And certainly the "regular" political party is without patronage positions to award, thus decreasing its attractive-

> **Patronage.** Government jobs awarded primarily on a basis other than merit, most frequently on the basis of loyalty and service to a political party, or on the basis of friendship.

ness to some. Without pursuing this aspect of the problem further, we can say that we do know more about local nonpartisan politics than we do about local partisan politics, having been well served by those students of municipal politics with a behavioral orientation.

PARTY IN GOVERNMENT

Of all the area concerning political parties, probably the role of the party in government is the one about which we know least. This may be because of the tendency of American reformers to try to take the political party out of government, and this has led to a neglect of the part party activity really does play. Thus we know more about the provisions of legislation (the Hatch Act) which prohibits partisan political activity by civil service employees, and less about pressure brought to bear on government employees to work for their party. What information we do have has been provided more by Congressional hearings and through the work of journalists than by political scientists. We hear a great deal about our "bipartisan foreign policy," but until recently, it has been left to historians of diplomacy to record the outputs of such policy. Now we have studies, like Rieselbach's *The Roots of Isolationism*, which suggest that party is changing in importance as a variable in explaining Congressional voting on foreign policy matters. We do know something about the role party plays in the appointment of officials to high office by the President, particularly through the operation of the practice of Senatorial courtesy. Perhaps the reason we know as little about party-in-government as we do is that we have compartmentalized our study of party so neatly that it has generally dealt with only those pre-governmental aspects considered its primary functions (election of candidates) rather than its equally important but secondary functions (running the government). Thus party in the legislature is studied under the heading of "Legislative Behavior"; and the party leader role of the President is studied under the heading of the Chief Executive or Public Administration. Perhaps it has also been felt that because our government does not follow the British Parliamentary model, with votes of confidence for or against the majority party, therefore party is not operative at all. It needs to be recognized that party, although not the only thread holding government together today, is one of the most important. In any large government, the forces working for fragmentation—the "vice of departmentalism"—centrifugal rather than centripetal forces, are extremely powerful. Each government agency has its own clientele, whom it must keep generally satisfied; the workers in that agency have their own interests apart from that. The need for each agency to satisfy its clientele (and to look for support outside the executive branch) may stem from the lack of a strong, central party. One can argue that to have a government whose agencies are well controlled from the center, at least in the American political system, is the exception rather than the rule, and, as we shall see later (see pp. 432–433), it is only recently that the President has had administrative tools which assist him in this function. But party can assist in tieing together the various organs of the government. It does this to the extent it creates an organization, albeit formally "outside" the government, to which government officials can have a common allegiance, even if their selection may not depend solely or even, in some cases, largely on it. Common recruitment patterns for government positions, through the party, produce political "professionals" who understand the need for party discipline. To the extent it can provide both a platform of policies and, at a lesser level, a minimum frame of reference, party also integrates the various segments of government. Our studies of the municipal machine have shown us that an important function performed by the party organization was to hold together a government formally fragmented, particularly in the "weak mayor-council" version, where the mayor had no important appointment powers and the supervision of administration was in the hands of the council; although the mayor was not always the "boss" of the machine, through him the machine could work to provide government that worked with some degree of effectiveness. Despite having seen this at the municipal level, we have not pursued it adequately at the state and national levels.

Recently students of state legislation have become interested in what happens when the Governor is of one party and the legislature is of the other (or at least one house of the legislature is held by the other party). This "mixed government" appears to hinder the Governor's effectiveness with the legislature, but we still do not have systematic studies of the role of party when the Governor and the legislature are all of the *same* party, showing the gaps in our knowledge. It might be noted in this connection that it has been only recently that we have begun to develop studies like David Truman's *The Congressional Party*, which are a systematic examination of party *within* the legislature.[20] One can argue we must know about this first before we can talk about the effect of party *between* legislature and governor. It would appear that we have more systematic information about the role of interest

[20] But studies like Truman's tend to be roll-call studies rather than studies of the organization of the party in the legislature, which have been later in coming.

groups in the government than we do about political parties, and it is to the subject of interest groups that we now turn.

INTEREST GROUPS: ORIGIN AND ORGANIZATION

The term "interest group" [21] is one which is not value-neutral to all people, because the term "interest" often connotes self-interest, particularly economic self-interest, which is negatively valued by idealists, even if it is at the base of many actions people take. Yet "interest group" has been accepted by political scientists as a term which can be used without such connotations, and it is used, particularly in preference to the term "pressure group," because "pressure" has an even more negative connotation than "self-interest." If the individual in a democratic society is supposed to make his decisions rationally, on the basis of full information and a thorough canvassing of the alternatives available to him, then pressure is bad because it interferes with this process. As this brief discussion may have suggested, much of the writing about interest groups has had an evaluative and moralistic tinge. Interest groups have long been attacked as being anti-democratic. However, it is now recognized that, particularly in a large-scale society, collections of individuals can bring about desired changes in policy more effectively than (isolated) individuals, if in fact the latter can be effective at all. Thus what were denigrated as "factions" in the days in which the Constitution was being adopted,[22] as being opposed to our highly individualistic ways, now have been given grudging acceptance by the industrial society of the mid-twentieth century. There is even a group of political sociologists who have become enamored of the idea that, in a mass society, social institutions perform the extremely important function of serving as a "buffer" between the elite (the leaders of the society or polity) and the atomized individual in the "mass" below. Even if one does not accept the "mass theorist's" view of society as composed of a collection of isolated individuals, the "buffer theory" is plausible. In effect, it holds that the elites are less likely to be able to manipulate the members of the mass with such a layer of groups intervening, and that the groups also serve a function (of interest articulation) in the opposite direction, making it more possible for the individuals to communicate their views to the elite.

Until recently the attention of most political scientists dealing with interest groups has been focused on the large national groups with all the accoutrements which formal organization brings. The origins and develop-

[21] Before reading this section, it would be advisable to re-read the section on Group Theory in Chapter 4, in which the term interest group is defined and the philosophy of pluralism is discussed.

[22] *The Federalist Papers,* #10. James Madison's reference to "factions" may be to what we now know as political parties, but interest groups appear to be included in what he discusses.

ment of such groups have been relatively neglected. Most political scientists have simply studied a formal entity identifiable as an interest group, or more particularly, studied the behavior of its top-most officers and its staff. The membership of these political units is less often subject to scrutiny, at least by political scientists. However, the matter of membership is a less difficult one than it is with political parties, because most interest groups have some formal definition of membership. This is not to say that there are not many "followers" of the organizations, people who look to them for words of wisdom about important political issues without joining formally. Nor is it not to say that there are not varying levels of activity among the members, so that one could divide the members into "activists" and "passive members," but this is a different issue.

It has often been said, from deTocqueville to the present, that we are a "nation of joiners," thus leaving the impression that we all belong to many organizations. While some people do have a high rate of organizational membership, averages are deceiving because there are many citizens who belong to no groups. Organizational membership, like other forms of social and political activity, is in part a function of socio-economic status and such other variables as "political efficacy." In addition, the mere formality of membership does not necessarily mean high emotional involvement in a group. An individual's political activity can be more affected by a group for which he has high regard (an important "reference group") than by a group in which he has only nominal membership. Thus it could be argued that even "potential groups," which come into being to enforce the political "rules of

Potential Groups.   **Collections of individuals sharing a characteristic or attitude, but not (yet) interacting. The common characteristic or attitude provides the potential for interaction.**

the game" when they are broken, could serve as a source of cross-pressure.

Work on interest group membership has concentrated on the number of organizations to which people belong and on the resulting "cross-pressures" which may result from such multiple memberships. It has been alleged that multiple memberships create cross-pressures, competing stimuli which pull an individual in different directions, thus reducing his activity and moderating conflict. If individuals belonged only to organizations which reinforced one another, conflict between individuals would be increased, but it is argued that organizational memberships do not reinforce each other. However, Stanley Rothman has pointed out that, if one is talking about multiple memberships in formal interest groups, an individual is not likely to join organizations which take opposing stands on key issues, e.g., one is not going to belong to the National Association of Manufacturers *and* AFL-CIO.[23] Rothman's point is well taken, but we must recognize that informal groups and reference groups can create cross-pressures, and that some formal groups to

[23] Stanley Rothman, "Systematic Political Theory: Observations on the Group Approach," *American Political Science Review,* LIV (1960), 15–33.

which an individual belongs, not basically opposed on key issues, can take opposing positions on an item not central to them, thus putting the multiple member in a cross-pressured situation.

The work of sociologists studying community organization and related subjects has for some time suggested that single-minded attention to formally-organized groups does not provide a full picture of the group scene, either in politics or in any other sphere of activity. This is a point to which Arthur Bentley, to whose *The Process of Government* many political scientists pay homage, spoke directly. For him, an interest was defined in terms of activity, not in terms of organization. As David Truman pointed out years later, in *The Governmental Process,* probably the basic mid-twentieth century work on interest groups, organization is but one stage of interest group development. To use language of current-day social scientists, any patterned interaction between identifiable collections of individuals would constitute a group, and the activity would denote the interest. On this basis, even though there are many, many formally organized interest groups, we can add many, many more which should be examined to obtain a complete picture of their effect in and on the political process.

Not all groups, whether formal or informal, are directly involved in the polity, and, of those that are, not all are involved continuously. Truman developed the concept of "political interest group" to distinguish from other groups those which should be the subject of concern by the political scientist. The former are groups which make claims on others through the government (or, we can add, make claims directly upon the government). Studies of political behavior have shown this concept to be somewhat narrow, in that groups making claims on each other outside the political arena may have an effect felt in that arena, and other groups with no explicit political tasks may perform societal functions with strong political relevance. An example is the family's function of socializing children into the political norms of the system. "Work groups," that is, groups of individuals in frequent contact in a work situation, and "friendship groups," a more self-explanatory term, both perform important cue-giving functions with respect to voting choices in elections. A voter is more likely to vote if all the members of his work group have similar voting intentions than if they are divided, and an individual in the minority in such a situation may actually change his vote intention because of group discussion. This work shows the way in which the scholarly interests of the "small group" theorists (or at least some of them) in sociology have been carried over into the study of political science.

The family is, like the church, an example of a social grouping only intermittently involved in politics. While certainly there are groups formed with the specific intent of political involvement, other groups find themselves involved only when issues arise which their members consider important. Thus, a garden club may exist primarily for social reasons and garden beautification, but if the members feel strongly about a local anti-obscenity campaign, they may pass a resolution praising the local District Attorney for his action; this is an example where a group's political involvement is not even relevant to its manifest purpose. Even a trade association, formed to assist the members of an industry with their mutual problems, may not find itself involved with the government all the time, although a particular tariff or minimum wage bill may require the energy of its staff for a protracted period. As government regulations become more complex, it *is* likely that any interest group will become a "political interest group" at one time or another in its existence and that proportionately more of them will be frequently involved in political activity. However, the distance between the group and the political world on most matters has an impact on the degree to which the group is effective in politics when it does intervene there. As Campbell, *et al.*, have noted:

> As proximity between the group and the world of politics increases, the political distinctiveness of the group will increase. . . . As perception of proximity between the group and the world of politics becomes clearer, the susceptibility of the individual member to group influence in political affairs increases.[24]

Truman's concept of "political interest group" also appears to rest on a presumption that all interest group activity of the form we call lobbying runs from the group to the government. A number of studies of the government show that the agencies within the government are far from passive, and that they actively protect their own interests, both against other government agencies and also against thrusts from the outside, despite Congressional efforts to prevent expenditures for the purpose of agency public relations. Perhaps we can talk of a "governmental interest group" instead of a "political interest group," or, to use Almond's terminology, an "institutional interest." But the terminology chosen should not obscure the functions performed, which, in the long run, are the most important for the society.

The process by which individuals coalesce to become an interest group has not been extensively studied. One can imagine situations where a number of people, concerned about a particular problem, come together—for example, at a public meeting called by some irate citizen—to discuss a problem, and end up electing officers and drawing up bylaws on the spot. Americans' fondness for official positions and parliamentary procedure may predispose them toward formalizing their interest groups early. But one can imagine more gradual processes of group formation. Some neighbors who come together to protest the placement of a gasoline station in their residential neighborhood at first simply appoint one of their number as an informal spokesman. They then may move to another stage of organization by appointing a continuing chairman with responsibility for calling meetings to discuss similar attempts at intrusion into the neighborhood; later they may form an organization with dues and a treasury to deal with a wider range of neighborhood problems. If such a group were downtown merchants, it is easy to see how a Chamber of Commerce, with full-time paid staff, eventually could

---

[24] Angus Campbell, *et al., The American Voter*, p. 311; italics in original.

result. Organization serves to prolong the life of a group; so does the addition of functions, because they may require additional organization in order to be performed.

Most analysis, like the foregoing, has been based on the implicit assumption that a group forms either spontaneously or directly in response to some social or economic disruption of the status quo. While the power of leaders in existing organizations has been discussed, the role of individuals in establishing groups has been largely ignored. Robert Salisbury has recently suggested that groups often are initiated by "entrepreneurs," who try to sell their ideas to members of the public; if the entrepreneur is successful, a group is formed.[25] He also suggests that individuals do not join groups only to achieve the stated purposes of the group (or the "line" of the entrepreneur). In the "exchange" which exists between entrepreneur and group members, a number of types of benefits flow to the members. These may be characterized as material, e.g., economic; solidarity, e.g., friendship; or expressive, i.e., the assertion of values.[26] As long as a tolerable balance of benefits between entrepreneur and members is maintained, the members will stay in the group. Thus, if individuals receive material benefits from a group (as do members of labor unions, in terms of improved wages and working conditions), they may not care much what the group's leader (or entrepreneur) expresses by way of opinion on political matters. However, if they have joined the group for the friendship it provides, they may want to keep politics far from the group, and, if they have joined to express political principles, the entrepreneur's freedom of expression may be curtailed considerably.

This discussion should not lead the reader to the conclusion that all interests are organized interests. We can point to important interests in the society, ones which make themselves felt in the councils of government, which have little formal organizational apparatus. For example, in the case of intellectuals, of which scientists are an important subgrouping, "the pressure or interest group idea seems too rigid and confining to describe the complex processes by which scientific interests are professionally defined, generated, and articulated . . ." [27] While organizations of scientists exist, no one organization or group is overarching so that we can say "that group represents scientists." Even when formal organization has been carried further and has existed longer, as in the case of labor unions, we still cannot point to a single such organization; although the AFL-CIO appears to be the organization at the pinnacle, the very existence of the exiled Teamsters Union or the volun-

[25] Robert Salisbury, "An Exchange Theory of Interest Groups," *Midwest Journal of Political Science*, XIII (1969), 11.

[26] This is based on Peter Clark and James Wilson, "Incentive Systems: A Theory of Organization," *Administrative Science Quarterly*, VI (1961), 129–166. Salisbury has, however, modified their arrangement to substitute "expressive" for "purposive" benefits. He feels that, for many people, it is important to express values, even if the values are unachievable—and that they receive benefits even in the absence of goal-attainment.

[27] Avery Leiserson, "Science and the Public Life," *Journal of Politics*, XXIX (1967), 259.

tary withdrawal of the Automobile Workers suggests that not all labor interests are articulated through the AFL-CIO.

Once a group reaches a certain size, it is no longer possible for all the members to know each other, and there is a shift from a primary group (with face-to-face relations) to a secondary group (or "association"). In the latter, at least some of the communication between members is necessarily formal (memoranda, notices, and the like); with the development of this means of communication, an organization can expand in geographic space. This could mean a national organization, with perhaps a monthly publication and occasional newsletters on matters of importance, run by a paid staff operating under the direction of national officers who in turn are doing what the last national convention has bound them to pursue. We may find that, contrary to our ideal, the paid staff is making policy or helping to determine it (rather than simply carrying it out) because they are full-time while the elected officers are not; and we may also find that the size of the organization prevents any thorough-going system of representative government in the organization, with the most active members determining from year to year who shall succeed whom in office.

As noted at the beginning of this section, it is the large, formal organizations with staffs and Washington headquarters to which political scientists have paid attention: the American Medical Association (AMA), the National Association of Manufacturers (NAM), the American Farm Bureau Federation (AFBF), the American Federation of Labor-Congress of Industrial Organizations (AFL-CIO), and many others somewhat smaller and less well known. Often political scientists have classified these groups, not on the basis of what they have done or on the basis on which they are organized, but on the subject matter with which they deal: thus we have labor groups, business groups, farm groups, etc. One such category which has received much attention is the "cause group" or "principle group," the interest group devoted to a specific set of issues, whether it be the attainment of civil liberties (the American Civil Liberties Union [ACLU]) or the achievement of rights for Negroes (the National Association for the Advancement of Colored People [NAACP]), or some other cause, such as that espoused by the Committee of One Million, interested in the United States retaining recognition of the Nationalist Chinese government on Taiwan, or the Americans for Constitutional Action (ACA), who want a return to "constitutional" government. More recently the ends the groups pursue have been broken down into "welfare" and "status" goals. With respect to Negro civil rights, an example of the former would be the provision of more housing which meets standards of adequacy, while an example of the latter would be the desegregation of housing by passage of an "open occupancy" ordinance. Our focus on these groups has been largely on the policies they have pursued and the roles they have played in important legislative battles. The strategies they have used, and not just the policy content used in the strategy, have also been studied. Through such studies, we have seen that each interest group does not pursue its own interests totally independent of all other groups, although there are *ad hoc* organizations which develop for just one issue and then go out of existence. Often, however, such an *ad hoc* group is a combination or coalition of already existing groups operating as a "front" for groups not wishing to be directly identified. Coalitions also operate in other ways, as when groups decide to pursue a common course, but to operate through their own "regular" identities.

Scholars usually accept as given the positions taken by groups, without much attention to the process by which they have been generated inside the organizations. This leaves us seeing only the product at the end of the pipeline. However, the concern about the place of interest groups in a democracy, while usually discussed in terms of the groups' external relations, has led to an examination of their *internal* politics. A subject of both academic and legislative concern in recent years has been internal union democracy, with Congress aiming at the Teamsters Union in particular. Labor economists had known for some time that unions were not governed democratically, certainly not in the sense of contested elections between groups equivalent to political parties, in part because the union leaders had to face a determined (and not internally democratic) business organization in collective bargaining. What democracy there was existed in the responsibility of union leaders to the rank-and-file when the latter became unhappy about the terms of a collective bargaining agreement. In a now-famous study of the International Typographical Union (ITU), Lipset, Trow, and Coleman generated several hypotheses about factors which might produce or at least sustain internal union democracy (and perhaps internal democracy in other organizations as well). They showed, among other things, the role played by the "two-party" system in the ITU (the only union with such competition on a national basis), as well as by such factors as the relatively small distance in status between chapel (union local) leaders and the average member. The interest generated in internal union democracy has been weakly carried over to studies of a few other organizations, principally in terms of the question of how well group positions reflect members' views. For example, John Schmidhauser has discussed the lawyers within the American Bar Association (and state and local bar associations generally) who play a part in recommending lawyers as "fit" or "unfit" for judicial service, and he shows that they are older, better off financially, and more conservative politically than the average bar member.[28] But we do not have studies of the internal politics of business organizations, for example, to compare with the work of Lipset and his colleagues. If we recognize the role of the entrepreneur in generating and establishing organizations, we may be both less puzzled and less disturbed by what Michels thought was the inexorable development toward autocracy in organizations. If an entrepreneur started the group, the "autocracy" would have existed in the group *ab initio*. That members of the organization

[28] John Schmidhauser, *The Supreme Court: Its Politics, Personalities, and Procedures* (New York, 1961), pp. 6–29.

may not object to the control of power by group entrepreneurs (and may be either neutral to it or welcome it) is also more easily understood if one recognizes the variety of reasons for which individuals join groups and the variety of benefits they receive.

There has been a recent upshoot of interest in the staffs of these organizations, most particularly the "lobbyists" who deal with various branches of government. Part of this has come through the work of legislative behavior scholars on the way in which legislators perceive the efforts of lobbyists; they indicate rather convincingly that instead of applying pressure, lobbyists often simply supply information. Even when the lobbyist is attempting to be persuasive, if he is talking to someone already predisposed to his position, that individual may not perceive what he says as pressure. Eulau has recently claimed that the lobbyist has been a neglected individual, but the work of Lester Milbrath in discussing *The Washington Lobbyist* and of others in examining lobbying at the state legislative level has somewhat expanded our knowledge. Thus we can say that state lobbyists are more likely to use persuasion than simply to provide information and that they are less likely than their national counterparts to be full-time professionals in the lobbying field. We still do not know, however, as much about lobbyists as we know about laws regulating them, another effort of the political reformers. They have attempted to achieve full disclosure of sources of lobbyists' income and where it is spent, but more often have gained only a simple registration law for which little if any enforcement machinery is provided.

INTEREST GROUPS AND GOVERNMENT

Political scientists have given most attention to the external relations of interest groups. Interest groups as related to legislatures have received the most attention, although the interaction between interest groups and administration and interest groups and the courts has not gone unheeded. The earliest conception of such groups, as indicated in the label "pressure group," was that they exerted pressure on legislators, or at the minimum attempted to persuade them to vote for the position the interest group espoused, and that this was all the interest groups did, unless bribery or some other form of corruption was involved. The other functions which interest groups perform for legislators have been examined much more recently. We now recognize that legislators, particularly those at the state level who are without the assistance of staff, need information in the course of their work, and many interest groups are equipped and willing to provide the information. One might ask: "Won't this information be biased?" and the answer would have to be, "perhaps." But this casts light on another aspect of the situation in which the interest group finds itself. Any group which is not simply a one-shot *ad hoc* organization has to protect its interests over the long run in addition to attempting to gain its short-run goals. Providing biased material to a legislator who expected to receive "straight facts" would badly damage the position of the group with that legislator. The long-run goals of interest groups makes them vulnerable to the legislators. If interest groups begin to push legislators too hard, the latter have available the weapon of investigations of interest group practices and the possibility of more stringent group regulation. There are also legislators already persuaded to the interest group's point of view; they may be willing to perform favors for the group—and, in addition, they may not see the work of such groups as "pressure" at all. While most legislators are favorably disposed toward the approaches of some groups and not to those of others, recent studies have shown that one can classify legislators on the basis of their general attitude toward interest groups. Thus Wahlke and his associates have developed the typology of "resister," "neutral," and "facilitator," and have successfully related these categories to other aspects of a legislator's activity. The picture of individual legislators totally dependent on groups is frequently inaccurate; the relationship is bilateral, rather than one of invarying dominance of group over legislator. One can still find "pocket legislators," that is, legislators who are intimately connected with interest groups, either as officials or whose campaigns are largely financed by groups, although this practice appears to have decreased in recent decades. Because most legislators are "joiners," they are members of interest groups and probably predisposed to vote for the measures advocated by the groups of which they are members. While some moralists still take umbrage at this practice, it is as unrealistic to expect it to end as it would be to expect legislators to disavow all previous attitudes when they enter the legislature. Even if legislators vote the preferences of their membership groups, there are many issues to which these memberships are irrelevant; thus interest group affiliation is much less than a complete determinant of legislative behavior.

Interest groups generally have concentrated their efforts on the legislative branch of government. It is difficult, however, to measure the effect of the activity of such groups, in part because their most overt activity may be their least effective. Even if one disagrees with the cynical statement that if a group has to make a statement at a hearing, it has already lost a battle, it would not be difficult to recognize that interest groups have to, and do, accomplish some of their most effective work "behind the scenes." Off the public stage, compromise is easier and neither legislator nor lobbyist needs to feel as committed to a specific position. If a group has "access" to the subcommittee from which the legislation comes, and to whose recommendations considerable deference is given, the group's work is obviously less difficult than if it has to convince the majority of the legislative body to change legislation already proposed.

The legislative hearing, at which lobbyist after lobbyist troops to the witness stand to support or oppose legislation, does provide legislators with information on which to base decisions, and some legislators actually may be persuaded by what lobbyists say; however, the hearings perform other functions as well. They allow legislators to identify lines of opposition and support for legislation on which they may already have arrived at a conclusion; provide a "safety-valve" by allowing groups to have their say; legitimate the legislative process by making it possible for groups to get their views on the record; and may even serve more of a function for the interest group representative than the legislator, by allowing him to show the group which employs him that he is doing his job.

As legislatures became faced with more work and more complex problems, they began to delegate more and more work to the executive branch of the government, in part by prescribing the broad outlines of legislation, allowing the administrators to put the flesh on the skeleton of the legislation. As the work of administrators involved the making of policy as much as the implementing of what the legislature had done, interest groups affected by the administrators work had to turn their attention to that branch of government as well. This did not mean that they discarded the legislature; it meant that they had to work both the legislative and executive branches, to try to assure that battles won in one location were confirmed in the other, both by interpretation and by enforcement. If they lost, they had to soften the defeat by achieving a congenial interpretation of policy by administration. Perhaps political scientists ignored this aspect of groups' work because it was less obvious than the heroic acts performed in the legislative arena and, of course, without the legislation, there would be no administrative policy to fight over. Recognition that much legislation originates in the executive branch rather than in the legislature brought the realization that interest groups would want to help shape that legislation before it was formally proposed, instead of having to fight a rear-guard action against what they feel are harmful legislative proposals. This meant the establishment of regular working relationships with the executive branch agencies responsible for the programs in which they had interest. The particular aspect of administration-group relations which has probably received most attention is the alleged "capture" of the major federal regulatory commissions, e.g., the Interstate Commerce Commission, by the interests those commissions are supposed to regulate. The constellation of interests which provide the legislation establishing such agencies does not hold together, but the interests to be regulated have continuous relations with the agency. The agency cannot easily define the "public interest" because it has no tangible or organized representation of public views. It thus begins to develop an outlook which is sympathetic to the views of those regulated, resulting in a general lack of action, particularly where action might be harmful to the interests. Of course, if the interests propose something, the agency is usually more willing to respond with positive action.

There are some situations when, in effect, the interest group *becomes* the government, or has such a close relationship as to be indistinguishable. The members of boards established to license people to practice occupations may be the principal officers of the professional association in the regulated occupation. Less directly, the association may propose the individuals officially nominated by the chief executive. There are situations in which the interest group is not quite as powerful, but where it can still exercise an effective *veto* over nominations felt to be inimicable to the group's interests. It has been charged that this last-mentioned relationship has occurred with respect to positions on several of the large federal regulatory commissions. At the local level of government, another sort of relationship is exemplified by the Chamber of Commerce, which may handle much of the work relating to industrial planning and the location of new industry. The growth of local industrial development corporations with membership by both C of C officials and city executives illustrates the interlocking interest group-government relationship. Another area of overlap between interest group and government comes in the operation of any program which requires technical knowledge. When such a program is initiated, the government is not likely to have the trained manpower to run it properly; therefore, it must look for the manpower elsewhere and is likely to find it employed by the interests most directly relevant to the legislation. These new employees will bring to the government not only their technical expertise but also the point of view from their earlier positions, and thus the interest will be "represented" in the government.

To view the courts in the context of interest group theory has been difficult because of the norms that our judicial system should be impartial, "nonpolitical," and independent of the other branches of government. Yet judges do make decisions directly relevant to policy in our political system, and because the decisions affect interests, it would hardly be surprising if we found that interest groups did not in some way attempt to make their views known to the judges. That it is held improper for interest groups to "lobby" judges in the same manner that legislators or executive branch personnel are the objects of persuasion perhaps blinded political scientists to what interest groups do in the judicial process. We do know that such organizations are active in the bringing of test cases to challenge pieces of legislation or administrative rulings. They also make their point of view known to the courts, particularly at the appellate level, through the *amicus curiae* ("friend of the court") brief, in which they attempt to enlighten the judges on precedents and other legal points relevant to the case and favorable to their position. Another clear involvement of an interest group in the judicial process is the role of the American Bar Association in the selection of federal judges. While the A.B.A. claims it is interested in "competent" judges, it may be that the standards held by lawyers in the A.B.A. as to competence and "judicial temperament," being affected by their political ideology, are not the same held by either other lawyers or the general public.

Some group theorists have depicted the whole judicial process as a struggle between interests, classifying judges' decisions as "victories" or "defeats" for those interests. Even if interest groups (other than the A.B.A.) do not play a direct role in judicial selection, the group attachments of a judge are relevant to his decisions, suggesting we can talk of judicial selection as interest group representation. Interest groups affect what occurs after a judicial opinion is stated because compliance with legal decisions is not automatic. Here one can see the operation of interest groups directly in the political process again, but their relevance for a theory of what judges and courts do in our polity is obvious.

Perhaps to interpret all of the operation of government in interest group terms forces one to "fudge" one's data, but the pervasiveness of interest groups in the contemporary American political process is clear. That one *can* create a theory of political behavior based on interest groups, even if it contains some distortions, is witness to this. But one can easily go too far in this endeavor and must look at the relationship of interest groups to other factors affecting political outcomes to get a proper perspective on their operation.

That interest groups do not always deal immediately or directly with the government in attempting to seek their ends is becoming increasingly clear. Thus we find indirect pressure brought on legislators through the "grass-roots" work done to develop public opinion favorable to their cause; public relations work directly with the public has become a standard weapon in the interest group arsenal. Groups also urge individual constituents to discuss matters with their representatives, as when the American Medical Association contacted doctors in each congressional district to write their Congressmen about proposed Medicare legislation. The groups also work with political parties, although some pretense is usually taken to preserve a facade of neutrality, so that a group will not be denied access to decision-makers for allying itself solely with one party. Toward this end, groups establish separate political adjuncts, such as the AFL-CIO's COPE (Committee on Political Education) or the AMA's comparable AMPAC (American Medical Political Action Committee). Groups help recruit candidates or endorse the ones they prefer, contribute to their campaign chests, and even supply precinct workers to distribute literature. And interest groups also try to obtain planks in campaign platforms favorable to their point of view, particularly for their symbolic value. The scope of efforts by interest groups suggests again their pervasiveness in our political system.

A NOTE ON SOCIAL MOVEMENTS

In addition to political parties and interest groups, collective phenomena of considerable political importance are "social movements." Originally studied by sociologists under the title of "Collective Behavior," they have more recently attracted the attention of political scientists. They are usually far more amorphous and fluid than either parties or interest groups, although they may contain each. They sometimes serve as the prelude to such organizations. They are important from the perspective of the study of political parties and interest groups in that they often either underlie or provide the context for these more highly organized forms of political expression.

Among the social movements to which attention has been given by political scientists are Communism, the "labor movement," and the "Radical Right." While legal disputation rages as to whether the Communist Party-United States of America (CP-USA) is a "normal" political party or a foreign-dominated conspiracy (the latter view prevails in Congress, but not with all scholars), political scientists have turned their attention to the attraction which Communism has held for those who have joined the movement, particularly those who have later left it; to its involvement in the schools and churches; and to basic reasons why Communism (as well as Marxism and Socialism in less organized forms) generally has failed to receive a favorable reception in this country. The importation of social movements from Europe to the United States, or rather the failure of European-born highly ideological movements to take root in the pragmatic American political soil, has also been of some interest.

Because of its highly organized character, the "labor movement" has been studied largely through the interest groups in it. However, the unions' largely middle-class sympathizers have drawn attention, as has the matter of the intellectual leadership provided for the unions by those of middle-class background. Just as working men have been studied as the "labor movement," farmers have drawn attention in studies of agrarian radicalism and Populism, the latter in connection with the history of American political parties. Other occupational groupings have most frequently been examined in terms of their organized group expressions, but they can also be viewed as movements, quasi-movements or incipient movements—a perspective which provides a more complete picture than the solely group-oriented focus. Teachers can be studied this way, although their recent activity might best be viewed as part of a "protest movement" involving other occupational groupings and Negroes as well.

In recent years, the most thoroughly examined American social movement has been the "Radical Right," that is, organizations like the John Birch Society and the Christian Anti-Communist Crusade and their adherents. The explanations offered concerning the reasons for this behavior—and that of its purported predecessor, McCarthyism—have been variegated, but no overall theory has been developed. One of the earlier accepted explanations of McCarthyism was that it was the result of "social strains," that is, it resulted from displacement of and resulting insecurity among members of the lower middle class, those whose economic situation was marginal and who embodied in its purest form the traditional business values.[29] Perhaps because of McCarthy's Midwest political origins, this made sense. However, this explanation has been challenged by the suggestion that McCarthy was a Populist, a defender of the little folk against the big organization and those of privilege who inhabited that organization. The various views of McCarthyism were re-examined when the Radical Right (re)developed in the 1960's.[30]

[29] Talcott Parsons, "Social Strains in America," *Structure and Process in Modern Society* (New York, 1960), pp. 226–247.

[30] A good collection is Daniel Bell, ed., *The Radical Right* (Garden City, 1963), in which the Parsons article is updated.

A new version of the status dislocation hypothesis, for example, suggested that calling one's opponent a Communist increases the status of the name-caller at the same time it decreases the status of the person so labelled. The purported strength of the Radical Right among the lower middle class was asserted, but at least one study shows that the adherents of one important Radical Right group are actually of *higher,* not lower, status than the average member of the community in which they lived.[31] Still another study relates the rate of growth in a community to strength of the Radical Right; fast development produced dislocation, not only economically, but also (and more important) of values.[32] The differential strength of the Right ideology in certain occupations has also been shown, with greater strength among those with technical training than among those with some grounding in the liberal arts or humanities. However, psychological explanations have entered the arena to strike down the monopoly previously held by sociological explanations. One of the more fully developed of the former is that alienation from the political system, perhaps in part brought about by some of the above-mentioned social phenomena, provides the environment in which the Radical Right mode of thought can thrive.[33] Another challenge has come from an historically-oriented view, in which it is suggested that the Radical Right is simply a present-day (although virulent) variant of nativism or of the "paranoid style" which has existed for many decades in American politics.[34] Whichever explanation one finds most plausible and useful, the intensive examination to which the Radical Right has been put does suggest the utility for political scientists in going beyond the bounds of "political parties" and "interest groups" in their study of social collectivities in or relevant to politics.

BIBLIOGRAPHY

Political Parties: General

Texts. There are quite a few textbooks about political parties. For many years the definitive text on both parties and interest groups was V.O. KEY, JR., *Politics, Parties, and Pressure Groups,* 5th ed. (New York, 1964). Among standard parties texts have been IVAN HINDERAKER, *Party Politics* (New York, 1956); AVERY LEISERSON, *Parties and Politics: An Institutional and Behavioral Approach* (New York, 1958); and AUSTIN RANNEY and WILLMOORE KENDALL, *Democracy and the Ameri-*

[31] Raymond E. Wolfinger, Barbara Kaye Wolfinger, Kenneth Prewitt, and Sheilah Rosenhack, "America's Radical Right: Politics and Ideology," *Ideology and Discontent,* ed. David E. Apter (New York, 1964), pp. 262–293.

[32] Murray Clark Havens, "The Radical Right in the Southwest: Community Response to Shifting Socio-Economic Patterns," paper presented at American Political Science Association meetings, Chicago, 1964.

[33] Gilbert Abcarian and Sherman M. Stanage, "Alienation and the Radical Right," *Journal of Politics,* XXVII (1965), 776–796.

[34] Richard Hofstadter, "The Paranoid Style in American Politics," *The Paranoid Style in American Politics and Other Essays* (New York, 1955), pp. 3–40.

can Party System (New York, 1956). E. PENDLETON HERRING, *The Politics of Democracy: American Parties in Action* (New York, 1940), is an older volume of importance. A recent text of high quality is FRANK J. SORAUF, *Political Parties in the American System* (Boston, 1964). Volumes dealing with the Democratic and Republican Parties are CHARLES O. JONES, *The Republican Party in American Politics* (New York, 1965) and RALPH M. GOLDMAN, *The Democratic Party in American Politics* (New York, 1966).

Readers. A number of collections of readings deal with parties alone or with parties and either political behavior or interest groups. Among the better ones are:

WILLIAM J. CROTTY, DONALD M. FREEMAN, and DOUGLAS S. GATLIN, eds., *Political Parties and Political Behavior* (Boston, 1966);

DONALD G. HERZBERG and GERALD M. POMPER, eds., *American Party Politics: Essays and Readings* (New York, 1966);

FRANK MUNGER and DOUGLAS PRICE, eds., *Political Parties and Pressure Groups* (New York, 1964); and

JOHN R. OWENS and P.J. STADENRAUS, eds., *The American Party System: A Book of Readings* (New York, 1965).

History. A standard party history is WILFRED BINKLEY, *American Political Parties: Their Natural History,* 3rd ed. (New York, 1958). WILLIAM N. CHAMBERS, *Political Parties in a New Nation* (New York, 1964), and the articles in *The American Party Systems: Stages of Political Development,* ed. Chambers and Walter Dean Burnham (New York, 1967) employ a new look at party history and offer some new interpretations.

Parties: Systems and Organization

The texts mentioned here all deal with both one-party and two-party systems in American politics. V. O. KEY'S discussion of the differences between one- and two-party arrangements in the states, in *American State Politics: An Introduction* (New York, 1956), is very thorough. Also relevant are articles cited in the footnotes of this chapter concerning classification of parties. Specifically on one-party systems, Key —in *American State Politics* and in *Southern Politics in State and Nation* (New York, 1949)—is quite important. A more recent study is LEWIS BOWMAN and G. R. BOYNTON, "Coalition as Party in a One-Party Southern Area: A Theoretical and Case Analysis," *Midwest Journal of Political Science,* VIII (1964), 277–297.

RICHARD E. DAWSON, "Social Development, Party Competition, and Policy," *The American Party Systems,* ed. Chambers and Burnham, pp. 203–237, and RICHARD E. DAWSON and JAMES A. ROBINSON, "Interparty Competition, Economic Variables, and Welfare Politics in the American States," *JOP,* XXV (1963), 265–289, are examples of the use of classificatory schemes in testing the relationship between parties and public policy.

"Responsible Parties." Political scientists have often talked about "responsible parties." The initial statement in recent discussion was that of the American Political Science Association's Committee on Political Parties, "Toward a More Responsible Two-Party System," *APSR,* XLIV (September, 1950), Supplement. Two of the more important comments on that statement were AUSTIN RANNEY, "Toward a More Responsible Two-Party System: A Commentary," *APSR,* XLV (1951), 488–499, and JULIUS TURNER, "Responsible Parties: A Dissent from the Floor," *APSR,* XLV (1951), 143–152. A more recent statement of American politics from a party-

reforming perspective is JAMES MACGREGOR BURNS, *The Deadlock of Democracy: Four-Party Politics in America* (Englewood Cliffs, 1963).

Nonpartisanship.   The effects of nonpartisanship at the local level have been extensively explored. CHARLES ADRIAN, "Some General Characteristics of Nonpartisan Elections," *APSR*, XLVI (1952), 766–776, is a good introduction, to which OLIVER P. WILLIAMS and CHARLES R. ADRIAN, "The Insulation of Local Politics Under the Nonpartisan Ballot," *APSR*, LIII (1959), 1052–1063, is a valuable supplement. Other useful studies include:

ROBERTA S. SIGEL, "Partisanship and Non-Partisanship and Their Effect on the Perception of Political Candidates," *POQ*, XXVIII (1964), 483–496;

A. CLARKE HAGENSICK, "Influences of Partisanship and Incumbency on a Nonpartisan Election System," *Western Political Quarterly*, XVII (1964), 117–124;

GERALD POMPER, "Ethnic and Group Voting in Nonpartisan Municipal Elections," *POQ*, XXX (1966), 79–97; and

ROBERT H. SALISBURY and GORDON BLACK, "Class and Party in Partisan and Non-Partisan Elections: The Case of DesMoines," *APSR*, LVII (1963), 584–592.

Organization.   Party organization has been considered principally at the national level, although PAUL TILLETT, ed., *Cases on Party Organization* (New Brunswick, N.J., 1963), is more inclusive in its coverage. An older discussion of the national committee and related organizations is HUGH A. BONE, *Party Committees and National Politics* (Seattle, 1958), and the national committees are dealt with by CORNELIUS P. COTTER and BERNARD C. HENNESSY, *Politics Without Power: The National Party Committees* (New York, 1964). The staff of those organizations is explored by CHARLES E. SCHUTZ, "Bureaucratic Party Organization Through Professional Political Staffing," *Midwest Journal of Political Science*, VIII (1964), 127–142.

Parties: Functions and Activity

Functions.   The functions which parties perform are discussed by HOWARD A. SCARROW, "The Function of Political Parties: a Critique of the Literature and the Approach," *JOP*, XXIX (1967), 770–790. A relatively complete list of functions is to be found in FRANK J. SORAUF, "Political Parties and Political Analysis," *The American Party Systems*, ed. Chambers and Burnham, p. 50. Another useful discussion is E. E. SCHATTSCHNEIDER, "United States: The Functional Approach to Party Government," *Modern Political Parties: Approaches to Comparative Politics*, ed. Sigmund Neumann (Chicago, 1955), pp. 194–215.

Activity.   The activity of parties at the local level has been examined in a series of case studies. Examples are PETER H. ROSSI and PHILLIPS CUTRIGHT, "The Impact of Party Organization in an Industrial Setting," *Community Political Systems*, ed. Morris Janowitz, pp. 81–116; PHILLIP ALTHOFF and SAMUEL PATTERSON, "Political Activism in a Rural County," *Midwest Journal of Political Science*, X (1966), 39–51; and J. LEIPER FREEMAN, "Local Party Systems: Theoretical Considerations and a Case Analysis," *American Journal of Sociology*, LXIV (1958), 282–289. SAMUEL ELDERSVELD, *Political Parties: A Behavioral Analysis* (Chicago, 1964) is an extended community study of political parties.

Most descriptive studies of state politics are studies of political party activity. See, *inter alia*, JOHN FENTON, *Politics in the Border States* (New Orleans, 1957) and *Midwest Politics* (New York, 1961), and DUANE LOCKARD, *New England State Politics* (Princeton, 1959).

Elections and Campaigns

Presidential elections have received most attention. EUGENE ROSEBOOM, *A History of Presidential Elections,* 2nd ed. (New York, 1964), covers the full period of American history. Examples of volumes discussing recent elections and the election process are GERALD POMPER, *Nominating the President: The Politics of Convention Choice* (Evanston, 1963); DANIEL OGDEN and ARTHUR PETERSON, *Electing the President: 1964* (San Francisco, 1964); and NELSON W. POLSBY and AARON B. WILDAVSKY, *Presidential Elections: Strategies of American Electoral Politics,* 2nd ed. (New York, 1968). THEODORE WHITE'S reports, *The Making of the President 1960* (New York, 1961) and *The Making of the President 1964* (New York, 1965), have attained the status of classics. Detailed examination of elections in the Western states can be found regularly in *Western Political Quarterly,* for example, ROSS RICE, ed., "The 1964 Elections in the West," *Western Political Quarterly,* XVIII (1965), 431–526.

Presidential nominating conventions have been an object of specific study. PAUL T. DAVID, RALPH M. GOLDMAN, and RICHARD C. BAIN, *The Politics of National Party Conventions* (Washington, 1960), is the most complete such study. The platforms produced by those conventions are compiled by KIRK H. PORTER and DONALD BRUCE JOHNSON, *National Party Platforms, 1840–1960* (Urbana, 1961), and analyzed by GERALD POMPER, "'If Elected, I Promise': American Party Platforms," *Midwest Journal of Political Science,* XI (1967), 318–352. The debate stemming from the platforms and pervading the campaign is examined by JOHN W. ELLSWORTH, "Rationality and Campaigning: A Content Analysis of the 1960 Presidential Campaign Debates," *Western Political Quarterly,* XVIII (1965), 794–802. The 1960 Kennedy-Nixon debates were subjected to scrutiny by EARL MAZO, MALCOLM MOOS, HALLOCK HOFFMAN, and HARVEY WHEELER, *The Great Debates* (Santa Barbara, 1962).

JAMES W. DAVIS, *Presidential Primaries: Road to the White House* (New York, 1967), is an exploration of an important device leading up to the nomination. That primaries do not always hurt a party is suggested by ANDREW HACKER, "Does a 'Divisive' Primary Harm a Candidate's Election Chances?" *APSR,* LIX (1965), 105–110. The mounting expenses of election campaigns are discussed by ALEXANDER HEARD, *The Costs of Democracy: Financing American Political Campaigns* (Chapel Hill, 1962), and the collections of data by HERBERT ALEXANDER of the Citizens Research Foundation, for example, *Financing the 1964 Election* (Princeton, 1966). A good recent collection of analytical articles on campaigns is M. KENT JENNINGS and L. HARMON ZEIGLER, eds., *The Electoral Process* (Englewood Cliffs, 1966).

Interest Groups: General

The two most important books are clearly the older ARTHUR F. BENTLEY, *The Process of Government: A Study of Social Pressures* (Evanston, Ill., 1949 [1908]) and DAVID TRUMAN, *The Governmental Process: Political Interests and Public Opinion* (New York, 1951). A number of valuable theoretical analyses, drawing on Bentley, are PHILIP MONYPENNY, "Political Science and the Study of Groups," *Western Political Quarterly,* VI (1954), 183–201; EARL LATHAM, "The Group Basis of Politics: Notes for a Theory," *APSR,* XLVI (1952), 376–397; PETER ODEGARD, "A Group Basis of Politics: A New Name for an Ancient Myth," *Western Political Quarterly,* XI (1958), 689–702; CHARLES HAGAN, "The Group in a Political Science," *Life, Language, Law: Essays in Honor of Arthur F. Bentley,* ed. Richard W.

Taylor (Yellow Springs, Ohio, 1957), and a trilogy of articles: R. E. DOWLING, "Pressure Group Theory: Its Methodological Range," *APSR*, LIV (1960), 944–954; MYRON Q. HALE, "The Cosmology of Arthur F. Bentley," *APSR*, LIV (1960), 955–961; and ROBERT T. GOLEMBIEWSKI, " 'The Group Basis of Politics,' " *APSR*, LIV (1960), 962–971. HARMON ZEIGLER, *Interest Groups in American Society* (Englewood Cliffs, 1964) is a recent general treatment; ABRAHAM HOLTZMAN, *Interest Groups and Lobbying* (New York, 1966) is shorter and of a more introductory nature. In addition to the collections of readings mentioned at the beginning of this bibliography, H. R. MAHOOD, ed., *Pressure Groups in American Politics* (New York, 1967) is a good source. DONALD BLAISDELL, ed., "Unofficial Government: Pressure Groups and Lobbies," *Annals of the American Academy of Political and Social Science*, Vol. 319 (September, 1958), is a somewhat older collection of basic articles.

In addition to studies of formal groups, examination of the groupings which operate as interests without formal organization are found in the literature. Scientists are one such grouping, and their activities are analyzed in ROBERT GILPIN, *American Scientists and Nuclear Weapons Policy* (Princeton, 1962); WARNER R. SCHILLING, "Scientists, Foreign Policy, and Politics," *APSR*, LVI (1962), 287–300; and PAUL J. PICCARD, "Scientists and Public Policy: Los Alamos, August–November, 1945," *Western Political Quarterly*, XVIII (1965), 251–262. R. JOSEPH MONSEN, JR., and MARK W. CANNON, *The Makers of Public Policy: American Power Groups and Their Ideologies* (New York, 1965), examine other such groupings as well as more formal groups.

An early result of increasing interest in the comparative study of interest groups is HENRY W. EHRMANN, ed., *Interest Groups on Four Continents* (Pittsburgh, 1958), still a leading source of information.

Interest Groups and Government

Lobbying the Legislature. Classic studies are those by E. E. SCHATTSCHNEIDER, *Politics, Pressures and the Tariff* (New York, 1935); PETER ODEGARD, *Pressure Politics* (New York, 1928); and E. PENDLETON HERRING, *Group Representation Before Congress* (Baltimore, 1929). DONALD BLAISDELL, *American Democracy Under Pressure* (New York, 1957) and BERTRAM D. GROSS, *The Legislative Struggle* (New York, 1953) are more recent general works on the subject. LESTER MILBRATH, *The Washington Lobbyist* (Chicago, 1963), looks at those who do the lobbying as well as the process of group representation.

Interaction between lobbyist and legislator has been taken up at both the national level, in RAYMOND BAUER, LEWIS ANTHONY DEXTER, and ITHIEL DE SOLA POOL, *American Business and Public Policy* (New York, 1964), and the state level, most notably in JOHN WAHLKE, *et al.*, *The Legislative System* (New York, 1962), pp. 311–342. An earlier study of legislator-lobbyist interaction was OLIVER GARCEAU and CORINNE SILVERMAN, "A Pressure Group and the Pressured: A Case Report," *APSR*, XLVIII (1954), 672–691. Two recent valuable empirical studies are LEWIS A. FROMAN, JR., "Some Effects of Interest Group Strength in State Politics," *APSR*, LX (1966), 952–962, with a focus somewhat broader than only lobbying, and HARMON ZEIGLER, "The Effects of Lobbying: A Comparative Assessment," *Public Opinion and Public Policy: Models of Political Linkage*, ed. Norman Luttbeg (Homewood, Ill., 1968), pp. 184–205, a four-state study based on interviews with both legislators and lobbyists.

Administration. AVERY LEISERSON, *The Regulation of Administration* (Chicago, 1942), dealt with interaction between interest groups and administration. Little more was done until Truman's work. Treatment of the subject appears in SAMUEL KRISLOV and LLOYD D. MUSOLF, eds., *The Politics of Regulation: A Reader* (Boston, 1964). PHILIP SELZNICK, *TVA and the Grass Roots* (Berkeley, 1949), is an exploration of power relations between bureaucracy and interest groups affected by it in terms of the concept of "cooptation."

The Courts. Both JACK PELTASON, *Federal Courts in the Political Process* (New York, 1955) and VICTOR ROSENBLUM, *Law as a Political Instrument* (New York, 1955) deal with the effect of interests on the judicial process. CLEMENT VOSE, *Caucasians Only: The Supreme Court, The NAACP, and the Restrictive Covenant Cases* (Berkeley, 1959), deals with the role of interest groups in getting their cases before the courts. JOEL GROSSMAN, *Lawyers and Judges: The ABA and the Politics of Judicial Selection* (New York, 1965), deals with a group's attempt to influence judicial politics in another way.

12 / THE LEGISLATIVE PROCESS

Approach and Methods / Legislative-Executive Relations /

Representation / Legislative Organization and Operation /

Legislative Voting Behavior

APPROACH AND METHODS

The study of the legislative process in the United States has shifted rather radically over the years, from "arm-chair" analysis of Congress to intricate studies conducted "close-up" with the aid of voting records, interviews of legislators, and intensive observation of legislative activity. It has encompassed a wide variety of moods, from the historical-reportorial to the reformist-critical, and has emphasized a broad range of aspects of legislative behavior, from committees to party organization to legislative-executive relations.

One of the classics in the study of legislatures is Woodrow Wilson's *Congressional Government*, written in the late nineteenth century. This book, "must" reading for one attempting to gain perspective on studies of the legislative process, foreshadows a number of later developments. Writing in Baltimore, Wilson never ventured the forty miles to the Capitol to observe Congress. As "armchair" writing, *Congressional Government* may have encouraged other students of Congress to write only "at a distance." While Wilson did not check his impressions against accurate observations, he did not write "off the top of his head," relying instead quite heavily on Congressional documents, which can give a quite different portrait of Congress than can first-hand observation. Wilson also did not focus solely on Congress as a whole: he emphasized the role played by committees (the "little legislatures"). We tend to talk about "Congress," just as we talk about "the executive branch," although Congress (or the executive) is not a homogeneous, monolithic whole. It is a series of subsystems performing various functions and interacting with each other *within* the legislature as well as with bodies outside.

We also talk of the "legislative process" (rather than the "congressional process"), but the tendency of many writers has been to concentrate on either Congress *or* the state legislatures, more frequently the former. Few attempts have been made to see if findings for Congress and findings about state legislatures are similar or different. Even if we grant that Congress is large and complex and may require concentrated scholarly attention, such attention, without some comparable examination of state legislatures, emphasizes the unique character of Congress, rather than fitting it into a more general discussion of "legislative bodies." We also find attention to one house of the legislature rather than to both, particularly where Congress is concerned. While political scientists have been scrutinizing the House closely in recent years, the Senate appears to have received somewhat more attention from journalists, perhaps because writers want to determine whether it is the more conservative body (as the Founding Fathers alleged it would be),[1] perhaps because its members have been more exciting as individuals (in part a function of their greater visibility). In recent years, we note more attention given to state legislatures, because comparisons can be drawn between them. Other legislative bodies, such as city councils, school boards, and the like, have been quite largely neglected, although a major study of city councils in the San Francisco Bay Area is contributing immeasurably to our knowledge of the legislative process, particularly in groups not as large as the Congress or state legislatures. To expand our knowledge about legislative bodies we have also begun to consider institutions such as state constitutional conventions within the same theoretical framework as legislatures. While courts are usually considered under the title of Public Law, what we learn about decision-making in those bodies (not much different in size from city councils and county governing bodies) may help us to build theory concerning collegial decision-making groups.

Prior to the last ten to fifteen years, the principal concern of writers about Congress was where Congress fits in the total governmental structure; with its history; and with its structure, particularly procedure. The approach used has been formal and institutional; while behavioral studies of a quantitative variety can be found as early as the 1920's, they did not fall on fertile ground, and the seeds they provided did not germinate until the 1950's. Earlier scholars were interested more in Congress' place in our government than in Congress itself, and so tended to deal with it indirectly. Only when studies shifted from those "of the relative influence of the legislature in the total decision- or policy-making process in the United States" to "research on the patterns of influence *within* the legislature," the latter "characterized by perhaps more sophisticated conceptualization and greater use of quantitative data,"[2] did we get a more frontal approach to Congress (and the state legislatures).

Until the blossoming within the past decade, not many books on this subject stand out, although the work of former Congressman Robert Luce,[3] em-

---

[1] In large measure because of the broader constituencies which the Senators have by comparison with the Representatives, the Senate in many instances tends to be *less* conservative, not more, than the House.

[2] James A. Robinson, *Congress and Foreign Policy-Making*, rev. ed. (Homewood, 1967), pp. 1-2.

[3] Robert Luce's works, which Meller claims bridge the gap between old and new studies of the legislature, are *Legislative Procedure* (Boston, 1922); *Legislative Assemblies* (Boston, 1924); *Legislative Principles* (Boston, 1930); and *Legislative Problems* (Boston, 1935).

phasizing procedure, bears mention. Even much of the solid historical writing on Congress comes from the current period, in work such as George Galloway's *History of the House of Representatives*. Histories of specific earlier periods are now being written, making greater and more systematic use of the same sort of materials, such as voting records, used by political scientists in their studies of current sessions of Congress. Some of these historical studies contribute directly to our theory-building about Congress; an example is Dean Yarwood's study of persistence and continuity in the Senate, using the Senates of 1850 and 1860.[4] We now possess a considerable number of case studies about Congressional operation which have provided much of our specific knowledge, about both the process by which legislation is made and the substance of that legislation. These studies, perhaps the best known of which are Stephen Bailey's *Congress Makes a Law* (about the Employment Act of 1946) and Daniel Berman's *A Bill is Passed* (on the Civil Rights Act of 1960), deal with more than procedure, but the various steps by which a bill travels the Congressional route are made clear.

Reform Orientation.   Attention to "hot spots" or to perceived problems (like the lack of "party responsibility") has characterized much writing about Congress and the state legislatures. This writing has concentrated on reform of the institutions. However, the orientation is often such that proposals for reform do not stem from a prior systematic and objective examination of the institution; instead, the institutions are examined from the perspective of a preferred plan. Thus, the Anglophilia which characterized Wilson's *Congressional Government*, based on Wilson's admiration of what he believed the British Parliamentary system to be, has characterized much writing about reform of American legislatures. It has been only recently that we have examined possible consequences of reforms, what legislative attitudes toward reform have been, or how efforts at reform are handled (or, in the view of some observers, mishandled). Because there have been a number of reform orientations, we have had a number of views of Congress, none of which dealt accurately with the basic facts. "Party responsibility" advocates, including many political scientists, whose views are reflected in several APSA reports in the 1940's and early 1950's,[5] were so busy proposing reforms on the British model that they did not stop to consider the implication of the fact that party is the single most important variable explaining legislative voting. And others, who have thought that a neat, hierarchically-arranged structure is proper, have missed the actual patterns of behavior which do exist, because of what they perceive as "disorganization" and "chaos." As Robert Peabody has commented: "For those who like neat organizational charts, clear-cut lines of authority and strict party discipline, the House of Representatives is

[4] Dean Yarwood, "Legislative Persistence: A Comparison of the United States Senate in 1850 and 1860," *Midwest Journal of Political Science*, XI (1967), 193–211.
[5] Committee on Political Parties, "Toward a More Responsible Two-Party System;" Committee on American Legislatures, "American State Legislatures: Report," ed. Belle Zeller (New York, 1954).

bound to be a disappointment." [6] But patterns and order *do* exist, and can be found by those who do not presume models which fit best elsewhere.

Whatever the reform orientation, "reform" has generally been considered desirable by political scientists, particularly when it was thought to facilitate the passage of "liberal" legislation. They have been generous in offering proposals whenever Congress has undertaken to examine itself, as it did in the mid-1940's (resulting in the Legislative Reorganization Act of 1946, sometimes referred to as the LaFollette-Monroney Act) and in the mid-1960's (when a new Joint Committee on the Organization of the Congress held hearings). Political scientists have not been the only ones to contribute to this reform literature, although James MacGregor Burns' *Congress on Trial* and *The Deadlock of Democracy* (which introduces the idea of a legislative party as separate from the "Presidential party" [7]) stand out. Journalists have contributed much, as have a number of Representatives and Senators. Generally, if it was felt the changes would make passage of certain desired types of legislation easier, very little attention was devoted to the possible extended impact of the reforms. This willingness to reform Congress without first understanding it alienated many legislators. As Neil MacNeil recently stated, "the political scientist's understanding and description of Congress often are incomprehensible to the Members of Congress." [8]

The older, uncritical attitude toward reform has, to a considerable extent, changed. In the hearings in the 1960's, one heard not only (sometimes belligerent) pro-reform statements, but also different voices, questioning the validity of some proposed reforms because of their possible consequences. These voices came from younger men, trying to bring to bear a growing body of systematic, empirical and objective literature about Congress—much of it developed by those who had viewed Congress from positions as staff assistants. Although the "new" political scientists could not tell with certainty what the results would be, because no overall general theory of Congress had been developed, they could contribute useful suggestions, more useful because looking at Congress "close-up" from staff positions had focused their attention on the problems with which Congressmen were most immediately concerned. Other political scientists, not directly concerned with reform, have contributed studies which cast considerable light on topics which are the favorites of reformers. [9] Thus, Wolfinger and Heifitz's examination of seniority suggests that Southerners are not likely to continue to dominate committee chairmanships, certainly relevant to consideration of proposals to

---

[6] Robert Peabody, "Organization Theory and Legislative Behavior: Bargaining, Hierarchy and Change in the U.S. House of Representatives," paper presented to the American Political Science Association, 1963. Page 8.

[7] These do not, we now recognize, always pull in separate directions despite differences in constituencies.

[8] Neil MacNeil, "Congress and Its Critics," *New York Herald Tribune*, August 17, 1965. He added: "And theirs is frequently incomprehensible to the political scientist."

[9] For example, James Robinson, *The House Rules Committee* (Indianapolis, 1963).

eliminate the seniority method of chairmanship selection.[10] Despite these new voices, it is probably the case that the predominant tone of writings about the reform of Congress and the state legislatures is pro-reform and pre-scriptive, with relatively little empirical basis. A great deal of attention is paid, particularly by groups like the American Assembly, to matters of "house-keeping," such as salaries, new office buildings, staff assistance, and annual sessions. Such matters *are* important, but they receive a dispropor-tionate share of reformers' attention. We still do not have systematic non-normative literature on many of these formal-structural elements of the legis-lature.

New Approach. The new political science orientation manifests a sym-pathy, which is less a bias than a new perspective, for Congress itself. The political scientists now concentrating on Congress are not principally schol-ars in the field of public administration or political parties, as were many of those who earlier cast an eye on Congress. They have decided, as a matter of interest and division of labor, to concentrate on Congress. Some have adopted what has come to be called a "legislative-force model" [11] which em-phasizes the place of Congress as an independent branch of government. This involves both looking at Congress from Congress's viewpoint and rec-ognizing and giving due credit to Congress's contribution. It can mean, at an extreme, the view that Congress ought to be superior to the executive branch as the chief policy-maker (legislator) for the government, with the executive branch becoming subordinate to Congress. Absent this extreme position, the studies produced by those holding to the "legislative-force model" have con-tributed much to our knowledge of Congress. In any case, this theme, which is apparent in some of the work of Alfred DeGrazia,[12] is not realistic, for it fails to recognize the independent contributions which each branch of the government can make to the government's (and polity's) total functioning, and does not acknowledge certain advantages in policy-making which the executive branch possesses by way of massive information capabilities and day-to-day contact with problems. In short, one can embrace the legislative-force model and still recognize the crucial role of the Presidency for leader-ship, whether it be positive leadership in behalf of a program or simply nega-tive action in blocking what Congress (or anyone else) wants to do.

Most of the empirical behavioral studies of Congress have been carried out by individuals who, while they may not consciously have adopted the legislative-force model as a working basis, clearly have asked: "What can we

[10] Raymond E. Wolfinger and Joan Heifitz, "Safe Seats, Seniority and Power in Con-gress," *American Political Science Review*, LIX (1965), 337–349.

[11] The "legislative-force model" has historical roots in the normative view of legisla-tive supremacy, while the "executive-force model" has its roots in the executive suprem-acy concept.

[12] See his "Introduction," *Congress: The First Branch of Government*, ed. Alfred DeGrazia (Washington, 1966), and *Republic in Crisis: Congress Against the Executive Force* (New York, 1965).

find out by focusing on Congress as a principal governmental body?" Much more will be contributed to our knowledge, particularly of our national legislature, by people of this same persuasion in the near future. The Carnegie Foundation recently awarded the American Political Science Association a substantial grant to carry out an intensive study of Congress; this Study of Congress Project is resulting in a series of individual studies rather than one massive group effort. Among the topics being considered, which serve as an indication of areas about which we have needed to know more, are: the role of the minority party in policy-making, majority party leadership, seniority, legislative oversight of administration, minority party leadership, taxing and appropriations policy-making, committee staffing, the relation of urban-rural conflict to policy-making, relationships between House and Senate, the relation between the Congressman and his local party organization, and the President's relationships with Congressional party leadership.

Methods. A word about the methods used in studying Congress is necessary. Much work, beginning with Wilson, has been done on the basis of legislative documents. While documents are often scarce at the state legislative level except for a record of bills introduced and passed, at the national level there is almost an overabundance of material. At least one can say there is much material; whether it is the material appropriate for answering the questions the researcher wishes to ask is often another matter. While perhaps for the study of some subjects legislative documents are not most appropriate, there is no question that they have not been fully tapped. Not only can they serve as the basis for many more case studies whose cumulative impact on theory will be clearly felt, but they can also be systematically analyzed in the study of subjects not yet fully examined, such as committee member-witness interaction or patterns of floor debate and interaction.

With the growth of the behavioral approach, and the early concentration of the behavioralists on voting, attention was drawn to tools with which one could examine the voting of legislators. Often, at the state level, these were the only behavioral items which could be easily examined because of the absence of materials other than recorded roll-calls. And so we find ourselves with a large—and still growing—number of legislative roll-call studies. The multiplicity of factors affecting legislative behavior is clearly brought to the fore in these studies, many of which involve extremely sophisticated data manipulations. Usually, one Congress is the subject of voting studies, although some books show how data from several consecutive Congresses can be used to illustrate voting trends. However, even the data from one Congress provides much with which to work. And, while one obviously cannot go back and interview Senators and Representatives from the Nineteenth Century, one can apply present techniques based on roll-calls to those historical situations.

In connection with the carrying out of roll-call studies, there has developed what is almost a separate literature on the methodology involved in studying legislative voting. This literature, which has its roots in work by Stuart Rice and Herman Beyle almost forty years ago, deals with various indices to be used, with what constitutes a "party vote" and with methods for

> **Party Vote.**   To some, this means a vote in which a majority of one party votes against a majority of the other party. Others use some stricter standard, e.g., 75% of one party v. 75% of the other. The standard used is important in determining what percentage of roll-call votes fall into the "party-vote" category.

determining power in a legislative body. This is subject to the same problems as the determination of the meaning of "power" in political science generally. Among measures used are percentage of bills sponsored by a person which pass, frequency of voting on the winning side, and reputation among colleagues. One finds arguments about the relative advantages of various elaborate and sophisticated techniques, and one also discovers more basic arguments about what is shown by various measures. Even when articles are written principally to demonstrate a method, however, they contribute to our knowledge of the legislative process, because they are usually carried out using "real" data from a particular legislative session.

While roll-call data are easily available, access to that data only begins one's problems, even when the "proper" index to be used is determined. The principal question is: "What roll-calls will I use?" Selection of roll-calls for inclusion in a study can be carried out impressionistically, or on the basis of experience and informed knowledge about the legislature (as is true with *Congressional Quarterly's* measures), or one can use scaling to determine whether roll-calls fit properly into a set. While this last method involves more work, we can rely more completely on its results. Not only is more work involved when one uses scaling, but to have the use of a computer becomes imperative. While it would be inaccurate to say that paper-and-pencil studies of roll-call voting are "out," use of electronic data-processing equipment bulks larger and larger in the legislative research picture. The more sophisticated methodology provides "translation" problems for the non-mathematically oriented political scientist and the differences in methods used increase the difficulty of performing cumulative analysis of legislative voting studies; however, the new methods do make the studies more precise.

Two drawbacks of the heavy reliance on roll-call data in most studies are that they de-emphasize the legislative process prior to the vote, without which the vote would have little meaning, and they tend to de-emphasize the role of the individual, particularly where only one legislative session is studied and the legislators are looked at in terms of categories. This latter drawback has been attended to by several scholars who have examined the performance of different incumbents of the same legislative district.[13] Their

[13] Lee F. Anderson, "Individuality in Voting in Congress: A Research Note," *Midwest Journal of Political Science*, VIII (1964), 425–429; Lewis A. Froman, Jr., *Congressmen and Their Constituencies* (Chicago, 1963).

work shows that voting is by no means totally party- or constituency-determined. Use of other types of methods, not fully (or in some cases, not even partially) tested on legislative data, can provide different insights. One excellent example is James Barber's *Power in Committees,* a study of Connecticut town Boards of Finance, in which the real members of these boards dealt with a problem in a "game" situation. This study shows well what can be done with small-group analysis in the legislative field, and is an example of the broader point that, despite the answers roll-call analysis provides, we do not have to rely solely on this sort of research to develop our knowledge about the legislative process.

LEGISLATIVE-EXECUTIVE RELATIONS

The Executive Force Model. In looking at governmental structure as a whole, particularly at the "separation of powers," political scientists have emphasized relations between the executive and legislative branches. This was a concern of students of public administration long before it became important to scholars of the legislative process. In part because they were looking at the legislature from the perspective of the executive branch, and in part because they were often practitioners concerned with accomplishing a task, many writers on the subject adopted what has been called an "executive force model," which involves looking at Congress from the point of view of the President and the executive branch, for example, to see what happens to Presidential proposals once they are submitted to Congress. More important, it involves the implicit assumption that the President should be the chief policy-maker for the nation, in part because, given the complexity of domestic and international affairs, it is impossible for anyone other than the President to perform that task. With this perspective, the tendency is to emphasize the President's role in policy-making, to stress his monopoly or near-monopoly of information,[14] to view the proper role of Congress as one of facilitating the President's program, and thus to see any signs of Congressional initiative as obstacles (to the President). The legislature is expected to accept or ratify what the executive proposes, that is, to do no more than legitimate his suggestions.[15] At times, Congress is simply omitted from the equation completely. Thus, the budget is examined to see how it can be a more effective tool for the President without consideration of how it will affect Congress or with little concern for any displacement of Congress's power. Even when the apparent emphasis has been on Congressional functions, the perspective has been one of "What do they do to the executive?" not "What do they do for Congress?" One gets the impression from reading material about legislative oversight (review) of administration that Congressional requests

[14] Others suggest that the legislature has enough information, but doesn't know how to process it.

[15] "The executive proposes, the Congress disposes."

for information and committee directives on policy are resented and are improper. Perhaps each government executive would like to have a free hand in running his portion of the government, but this is not likely, if only because of the executive branch's internal friction, and in a democracy is not desirable because administrators are supposed to be the servants of the elected representatives of the people, not their masters. This is true even if it is granted that the President is the only "representative" of *all* the people (that is, the only one elected by a nation-wide constituency) and that he appoints many of the administrators.[16]

Those utilizing the "executive-force model" have produced much valuable literature about Congress, illuminating subjects about which we otherwise would know much less. The treatment which the Senate gives Presidential nominations has received much attention, particularly in those cases where confirmation has been delayed (in the hope the President would withdraw the nomination),[17] or in the very few instances in which it has been refused. The infrequency of refusal (and even of delay) has led to an examination of what occurs before a nomination is even offered to the Senate, particularly for positions (such as federal district judgeships) in which an individual will operate primarily within one state. The practice of "senatorial courtesy," which forces the President to consult with the Senators of his party from the state involved, and in which we see the Senators in effect controlling nominations, is perhaps a major difference between state and national governments.[18] The state legislatures have little power over appointments in most instances, although we do not know as much about the matter at the state level as we do at the national one.

In addition to the nomination-confirmation process, executive-oriented students of legislative-executive relations have cast most light on legislative control of finances and the budgetary process. Here the clear emphasis in recent years has been toward strengthening the chief executive's power over the budget, not only so that he may achieve his ends more successfully in his confrontation with the legislature but also so that he can control his own subordinates and keep his own program from disintegrating at the seams within the executive branch. Presidentially-oriented writers on budgeting have been frustrated by legislative treatment of the budget, particularly at the national level, because they would prefer a process by which the budget would be considered as one entire package at one time so that it could be examined comprehensively.[19] They tend to stress the procedures within the executive

---

[16] At the state level, the matter is more complicated because of the election of United States Senators and, in some instances, United States Representatives on a state-wide basis (although they are supposedly not elected to make *state* policy) and the election of a number of state-wide officials below the level of Governor, such as the Secretary of State and State Treasurer.

[17] Most recently in the case of some Negro appointees to federal judgeships.

[18] When there is no Senator of the President's party from that state, he will usually consult with House members or the party chairman from that state, although he is not required to do so—and, of course, these other individuals cannot vote in the Senate.

[19] At the state level, a well-developed executive budget device does not exist in all states.

branch for such overall review, and view unkindly the actions of administrative officials who build backfires against Presidential budget-cutting by developing allies for programs on Capitol Hill. And they tend to resist furiously suggestions that Congressional agents, such as the General Accounting Office, be allowed to participate in the sessions during which the budget is developed in the executive branch: this would be the end of the executive budget, they cry.[20] This is a good example of the difference in perspective produced by use of the executive-force model, on the one hand, and the legislative-force model, on the other. Men of the latter persuasion who view the budgetary process stress the incremental, segmental, and fragmented nature of the process; [21] this is quite different from the rational-calculating programmatic budgeting discussed by the executive-oriented writers. The former also advocate the incremental approach as a way of reducing the conflict which would allegedly occur if each program had to be totally reevaluated against each other program in each budget cycle.

Some writers have provided us with a perspective which allows us to understand why the legislature does not deal with the budget as executive experts would prefer. Perhaps approving the budget in line-item fashion instead of allocating funds to large object categories restrains the administrator, but the legislature (particularly in the states, where it often meets for only several months every two years) is searching for a device to control the executive branch. While the legislators cannot enter into the details of every administrative action, they can thoroughly structure how that action will occur by writing detail into the budget. This object can also be obtained through other, less formal, methods of control. Thus, the administrator had better not often violate the informal understanding reached at a meeting with legislators or ignore the language in the report accompanying an appropriations bill or he will find it difficult to obtain the funds he wants the next time around. And it is the continuing relationship between executive and legislature which makes the possibility of legislative control meaningful.

Students of executive-legislative relations not committed to viewing matters from the executive vantage point have begun to show us in detail what does happen to the executive budget when it goes to "the Hill." Richard Fenno's *The Power of the Purse*, although principally a study of the Appropriations Committees of Congress, clearly shows the way in which consideration of the budget "package" is parceled out to various subcommittees, with very little general "overview" by even the parent committee, much less the Houses of Congress, and with final action taken within conference committees. While it has often been suggested that legislators are frustrated by their relative lack of information and dependence on the executive for the data on which policy must be based, Fenno and others have shown that the balance is not as one-sided as some have pictured it—at least in the appropriations

[20] See the exchange between Robert Ash Wallace, "Congressional Control of the Budget," *Midwest Journal of Political Science*, III (1959), 151–167, and Frank Gibson, "A Bloody Tenet Washed and Made White: An Answer to the Proposal to Give Congress More Control over the Budget," *Midwest Journal of Political Science*, IV (1960), 76–82.

[21] Aaron Wildavsky, *The Politics of the Budgetary Process* (Boston, 1964).

area. Because of the seniority method of selecting chairmen, bureaucrats who come to defend their budget requests may find Congressmen who have been around much longer and are more expert than they. At the state level, the conventional wisdom is more likely to be accurate, which helps to explain attempts to develop legislative fiscal offices as a method for remedying the information imbalance.

That the legislature does not deal with all executive branch agencies in the same way is now clear. While legislators generally cut executive agency requests, in part from a suspicion that they have been "padded" to take the cut into account, they do look more favorably on some agencies than on others, and have even given some agencies more money than they have asked for—an action not possible in some states where the legislature may cut, but not add to, the Governor's budget figures. The agencies themselves do not deal with the legislature in the same way, some adopting more aggressive strategies than others. Students of the legislature have shown the impact of the executive budget in their recognition that it serves at least as an agenda from which the legislature works; clearly the setting of the agenda can be a crucial act in helping to determine a decision outcome.

Legislative-Executive Balance.   While the "power of the purse" is considered the most important of the legislature's methods of dealing with the executive branch, the general question of the balance between the two branches has received much attention, normative as well as empirical. Many figurative tears have been shed over what is believed to be Congress' loss of power to the executive. The recent establishment of a Subcommittee on Separation of Powers by the Senate (in the Committee on the Judiciary) is evidence of the concern the legislators themselves feel. Particular interest has been paid to foreign policy and national security policy, where the greatest erosion has occurred. The power of the House has increased in recent years as a result of the need for appropriations to carry out policies such as foreign aid; however, the frustrations of both Houses of Congress are still evident in debate over United States policy with respect to Vietnam, and in concern over the increasing use by the President of executive agreements, which do not require Senate ratification. The executive's argument that the Senate must accept a treaty as a whole package as it is offered to them, without amendment or reservation, also sticks in the craw of many legislators. The impact of Presidential leadership in this general area, despite the legislators' personal reservations, is shown by studies of shifts over time in voting on foreign policy items. When there was a change in administration, Representatives of the President's own party have followed his lead and shifted in the direction of being more "internationalist." [22] In the national security policy area, the dominance of the Defense Department is apparent, but Congress

[22] Mark Kesselman, "Presidential Leadership in Congress on Foreign Policy," *Midwest Journal of Political Science*, V (1961), 284–289, and "Presidential Leadership in Congress on Foreign Policy: Replication of a Hypothesis," *Midwest Journal of Political Science*, IX (1965), 401–406.

has insisted at times on the development of certain weapons and defense systems. The President has not hesitated to impound funds appropriated for such projects which he has not supported, thus increasing the temperature of the conflict. At the state level, the picture is mixed, with situations in which the Governor is limited both by the state constitution and a strong-willed legislature, but also situations in which the Governor's hand is a strong one and where he may even help pick legislative leaders.

In asking, "Where has the balance gone?" the question of where the *initiative* in policy-making rests has been a major one. If it is felt that predominance is measured by where policies are initiated, then there is little doubt that Congress has lost ground to the executive branch. But one must not confuse the formal point of origin with the actual one. Career civil servants, because of the expertise they develop from working full-time with the details of program administration, are crucial in the process of developing legislative proposals, but the basic ideas from which they work may have come from journalists, party groups, from legislators or social critics. (At the state level, uniform and model laws, proposed by the National Conference of Commissioners of Uniform State Laws, are another source.)

Before an executive branch agency submits a piece of legislation for action, that proposal may have been the subject of consultation between legislative and executive leaders, and may clearly bear the mark of the former. All compromise does not occur after legislation has been introduced, but often occurs before. The process of consultation between legislative leaders and the chief executive is a continuous one, although it may not always be highly visible, particularly when carried out through their assistants. Meetings of the "Big Four" or the "Big Six" with the President at the White House are not everyday occurrences, and the publicity they attract may be counterproductive to the accomplishment of compromise. (However, there is a question whether these meetings are really more than briefings, that is, whether they are in fact consultations with the legislators, whose views will make a difference in the policy ultimately adopted.) Particularly where the chief executive does not have a majority in control of both houses of the legislature, he must "bend" somewhere if he is to achieve his program in even small measure. This suggests that the development of legislation is often the result of interaction, of shared responsibility, rather than of executive dominance, and one can also clearly point to instances where legislation was initiated completely within the legislative branch without the executive branch serving even as midwife.

In assessing the relative roles of executive and legislative, we must recognize mid-twentieth-century facts of life. The complex and large number of problems which the government is called upon to handle have required not only longer (and more nearly continuous) legislative sessions, but also the delegation of more and more rule-making authority to the executive branch. The alleged loss of legislative power is not simply a result of Presidential "theft," but stems also from legislative "gift," delegations of authority which the legislators think imperative at the time. The problem is often one of "fast delegation and slow regrets," with concern over the impact of delegation coming at the point when it is difficult if not impossible to recover what has been given away, as in the case of the Gulf of Tonkin Resolution in the mid-1960's. The battle over the delegation (or "surrender," depending on one's point of view) of power is by no means over. There are times when the legislature wants the chief executive to assume responsibility for certain acts, perhaps ones the legislators find distasteful, such as the matter of taxation (particularly at the state level); there are other times when the legislature struggles manfully if not always successfully to regain power it has either given away or allowed to slip out of its hands.

As noted earlier, the appropriations process becomes a principal device for control. Other methods of legislative review have attracted much attention; for example, a question period for Cabinet officers before the entire Congress, modeled on the Parliamentary "question period," has been proposed as an innovation. But review does not allow sufficient control to satisfy many legislators. Constant demands must be made on the executive to supply information and constant effort must be made to keep administrators from hiding behind the doctrine of "executive privilege."

While legislative intervention in the administrative process is far-reaching and on a day-by-day basis, it is not necessarily systematic. Like much of the rest of the legislative process, it is often marginal and *ad hoc*: problems which come to a legislator's attention are dealt with. It is clear that many legislators consider it quite proper to intervene in administrative proceedings, even if they are quasi-judicial, as in the case of so-called independent regulatory commissions such as the Federal Communications Commission and Interstate Commerce Commission.[23] While these agencies may have been established in part because the legislature could no longer handle the load of decisions which needed to be made in a particular policy area, and while the agencies were made somewhat independent of the chief executive, many legislators (or their successors) never had any intention of making these units independent *of the legislature*.

There are some systematic methods by which legislative review of administrative action is obtained, in addition to the annual budget-appropriations cycle. One which has received recent attention is the committee veto device, in which the executive branch agency may take action in a given area but only after it has been submitted formally to the committee with the relevant jurisdiction for possible *dis*approval. This device places the burden for negative action on the legislators' shoulders, but gives them a final check before action is completed. The legislative veto, in which the entire legislature rather than one committee is given the chance to disapprove executive action, is also used, most notably with regard to administrative reorganization;

[23] See Seymour Scher, "Congressional Committee Members as Independent Agency Overseers: A Case Study," *American Political Science Review*, LIV (1960), 911–920, which is a case study of oversight of the National Labor Relations Board.

reorganization plans are effective unless either house (or both houses) disapproves the plan within sixty or ninety days. Such an arrangement is initially established by the legislature, which can always remove the power and require proposed administrative action to pass through the entire legislative gauntlet if it finds the legislative veto arrangement not to its satisfaction.

Oversight of administration is not the only area in which the question of legislative delegation of authority arises. At the state level, legislative control over municipalities (which are legally arms of the state) is a major issue, with much cry for "home rule" on the part of the reformers. Legislatures have moved from the day of issuing a separate charter for each new municipality to the enactment of general charter laws which provide one or several alternatives for local governments, and which can be handled administratively. And we have seen a further shift from legislative to administrative supervision of local governments, although the state executive agencies supervising local activities are themselves subject to scrutiny by the legislature. Home rule, the power of local governments to choose their own structure, is limited by state laws (as well as by state constitutions), and thus is ultimately dependent on legislative "good-will"; if the legislature chooses not to relinquish power, there is little that local governments can do about it. It is often the local state representative, who can obtain favors for the city he represents, who is most unwilling to see home rule granted. It is possible that, by delegating authority over matters which many observers consider trivial that legislatures would have more time to deal with "major" matters, by which is usually meant broad policy issues. But it is a fact of life that many of the "trivial" matters—in Congress, private bills, the appointment of postmasters, and nominations to military academies—bring more political mileage than major policy issues.

Legislative-Judicial Relations.   While most attention has been paid to the legislature's relationship to the executive branch, consideration has also been given to the interaction between legislature and court, almost solely at the national level. Students of public law, who usually are the ones considering this problem, have for many years been concerned with judicial review—the power to declare legislative acts invalid—and statutory interpretation by the courts. With the United States Supreme Court's shift in 1937 away from declaring Congress' economic legislation unconstitutional, greater emphasis has been placed on statutory interpretation and on "what the Court has done to the Congress." We have had both specific studies of judicial interpretation of statutes as well as more general discussion of how one finds a legislature's intent, if in fact one can talk about "legislative intent" at all. The Congressional unhappiness of the mid-1950's decisions of the United States Supreme Court in the internal security area, as well as more recent reaction to school prayer and reapportionment decisions, has given us greater insight into what legislatures do when faced with adverse court action: frequently they do little at all by way of specific legislation. Perhaps legislatures and courts come into conflict frequently, because courts have developed rules by which they limit the battles in advance. Such rules include the granting of a presumption of constitutionality to legislation unless it appears to restrict basic rights such as freedom of speech and the limiting to grounds as narrow as possible the issues considered for decision. Even when constitutional grounds are present, the Supreme Court may decide a case on some other basis. Whatever the motivation, conflict with the legislature is thus reduced. Friction is also reduced in the other direction. Generally, the courts are given considerable freedom to make their own procedural rules and great weight is often given to judges' recommendations about possible structural changes. Beyond this, many legislators feel that the courts should be the only ones to pass on important constitutional questions, although some feel that the legislature should first consider such matters. Donald Morgan has recently suggested that a "judicial monopoly" position on this question may lead to consideration of issues solely in policy terms when no court precedents exist or would place a burden of innovative policy-making on judges which they may not be able to handle.[24] The resultant absence of friction has meant that less attention has been paid to what legislatures do to structure of the judicial arena than, for example, with respect to rule-setting for the executive branch.

REPRESENTATION

Political philosophers have long concerned themselves with the proper relationship between rulers and ruled. With the development of representative government and permanent legislative bodies, the question became more immediate. Two basic views were developed: One held that the legislator reflected his constituents' wishes, while the other said he exercised his own best judgment. The first view required considerable contact with constituents so that the legislator could find what they wanted, leaving a problem when the constituents had mixed views or no views. The second view, most often associated with Edmund Burke,[25] usually involved the idea that the national, rather than specific or local, interests should predominate. While the philosophical argument about the proper form of representation continues, we now have some empirical studies of the roles which legislators take toward their constituents. Wahlke and his associates, in studying legislators in four states,[26] developed a three-fold typology of representational roles: some legislators consider themselves "delegates" (comparable to the first view stated above); others, "trustees" (the Burkean view); and still others, "politicos," who are a mixture of the trustee and delegate, often acting like a delegate at one time and a trustee at another. (That not all constit-

[24] Donald G. Morgan, *Congress and the Constitution: A Study of Responsibility* (Cambridge, Mass., 1966), pp. 25, 338.
[25] Because of his "Speech to the Electors at Bristol."
[26] John Wahlke, *et al.*, *The Legislative System* (New York, 1962).

uents expect their legislators to be delegates has been suggested.) Wahlke, *et al.*, also showed that legislators could be classified in terms of other representational roles: some concentrated on either state or district, some on a combination.

Legislators deal with their constituents on matters other than legislative issues. Many legislators receive a large volume of requests for action on various matters handled by executive branch agencies: delayed Social Security checks, alleged improper treatment by military authorities, inadequate consideration to a job application; political matters, such as postmaster appointments; and such trivial matters as requests for hotel reservations or tickets for plays. While reformers complain about the degree to which such matters reduce legislators to "errand-boys," most legislators take this "casework" seriously and some devote more effort to handling it than they do to legislating on major issues. Sometimes, this is justified as a way of "keeping tabs" on the way the executive branch operates, and corrective legislation does occasionally result from "casework" problems. At other times the only justification is that such work brings more votes than one's position on legislation. Other methods of handling such casework, particularly the Scandinavian-originated *Ombudsman* (an official who handles citizens' complaints against the bureaucracy), have received increasing attention by reformers both outside and inside the legislature.

Who communicates with the legislator is an important part of the question of representation. A legislator can represent (as a "delegate") his entire constituency only if he knows their views. Some legislators, particularly at the national level, make efforts to ascertain their constituents' views through public opinion polls, but, by the standards of social scientists, these are often not well constructed or are worded in such a way as to elicit support for the position the legislator already holds. In any case, the legislator's supporters are far more likely to answer and return them than are his opponents. Generally, the legislator hears from that part of his constituency favorably disposed toward him; many of those who disagree decide in advance that their views would not be taken into account. This is not to say that legislators never receive any criticism, but that their legislative mail is not an accurate sample of the total range of views in their constituency. "Inspired" communications stimulated by interest groups and often arriving in identical form further distort the representativeness of legislators' mail. Even if one concentrates not on the general constituency but on those most interested in a particular subject or most immediately affected (the "policy constituency"), those who communicate are not statistically representative. Selectivity, it should be noted, operates at both ends: in evaluating communications, the legislator may very well "screen out" or discount views which disagree with his, particularly if they seem to be "inspired." He also takes certain types of communications for granted, as when he does not view a contact by an interest group as "pressure."

Perhaps because of the above difficulties, election campaign results remain one of the principal devices by which legislators receive their constituents' views. This is true despite the difficulties of interpreting such results. The Senators' longer (six-year) term means that even where a clear mandate appears to exist immediately after the election, it will become outdated as issues shift during the term. For the veteran legislator, the campaign becomes a regular part of the legislative cycle; he plans his work to include increasing contact with his constituents as election time approaches, even if his opposition is not strenuous. Of course, some claim that any contact he has with his constituents is "campaigning" and that frequent visits to his district are part of this, but the *formal* campaign takes place over a much shorter period.

Recruitment. In discussing representation, political scientists have been interested in legislators' backgrounds, and the political and social characteristics of the constituencies from which the legislators come. These have been related to legislators' voting records, particularly their deviance from party-line voting. Matthews' concern with the former subject has already been mentioned. His work is typical of those who examine the income, education, and prior residence of our office-holders in comparison with those of the "normal" population. The "over-representation" of lawyers in legislative bodies has been considered by some. One explanation for this phenomenon is the "theory of convergence" offered by Eulau and Sprague,[27] who feel that lawyers inhabit politics because what lawyers do in the legal system and what politicians do in the political system are similar. But this is only one of a variety of explanations about lawyer-politicians, at whom we looked earlier.

The study of recruitment of legislative candidates has been broader than the examination of why lawyers decide to run. For example, *The Legislative System* contains material on the political socialization of legislators, including their recollections of their early exposure to politics through family and friends. Differential recruitment patterns in different situations of party competition have been shown, indicating that not all candidates are self-starters, and that some are in fact dragooned into being sacrificial lambs in hopeless situations. James Wilson's analysis of two Negro Congressmen, Adam Clayton Powell of New York and William Dawson of Chicago,[28] shows the impact of personal style on organization, and of organizational constraints on a legislator's behavior. Legislators' personal organizations do not simply spring up from the void after an election, but have their genesis during the campaign. The organization set up to bring about an election victory, even if shaped by him initially, shapes the legislator, and its impact continues past the election. Wilson's analysis also suggests the more general point that differing political situations in legislative districts produce different organizational responses.

A still different approach to recruitment is taken by James Barber, in *The*

[27] Heinz Eulau and John Sprague, *Lawyers in Politics: A Study in Professional Convergence* (Indianapolis, 1964).
[28] James Q. Wilson, "Two Negro Politicians: An Interpretation," *Midwest Journal of Political Science,* IV (1960), 345–369.

Lawmakers. Barber develops a typology of legislators, based on his studies of the Connecticut Legislature, dividing them into spectator, advertiser, reluctant, and lawmaker. His concern is with the relationship between their recruitment and their adaptation to the legislature, and he shows by his typology that not all legislators participate actively in the work of the legislature nor are happy with legislative life. Most elected public officials find themselves in a tense and ambiguous situation. While the electoral situation of some representatives is tenuous, others may stay around for many years, and this has given rise to interest in the factors which produce legislative continuity. Because of the use of seniority in legislative bodies, studies of "tenure and turnover" have always been of importance. Schlesinger's earlier-mentioned work on ambition's role in politics suggests that, not only will the possibility of promotion draw the legislator from the legislature, but it will condition his views, making him look to a broader constituency than do those intending to stay.

Reapportionment.   In the last half-dozen years, the subject of the apportionment of legislatures has been central to considerations of representation. After the Supreme Court decided in *Baker* v. *Carr*, 369 U.S. 186 (1962), to hear complaints about malapportionment, and particularly after the decision in *Reynolds* v. *Sims*, 377 U.S. 533 (1964), that both houses of state legislatures had to be apportioned on the basis of one man-one vote, the writing about reapportionment became voluminous. Public law scholars have examined the constitutional basis of the Court's *Baker* and subsequent decisions. Other political scientists became interested in ways of calculating the degree of malapportionment or the "value of the vote." Two measures used by the courts themselves were the ratio between the largest and smallest districts and the minimum percentage of the population necessary to elect a legislative majority.[29] The development of these and more sophisticated measures has proved very helpful in studies of the effect of malapportionment on policy outcomes in the states. The principal findings of these studies, which did not come until after the Court's reapportionment decisions, was that malapportionment was *not* significantly related to policy outcomes such as welfare expenditures.[30]

From examining the effect of malapportionment on policy outcomes, a number of scholars moved on to broader types of outcome studies. Generally, state expenditures were found to be more highly related to social and economic factors (level of education, per capita income, and the like), particu-

[29] At first, it appeared that a ratio of 1.5-1 (20% ± from the average) was acceptable, but the courts have been striking down apportionments with ratios smaller than 5% ± variance from the ideal. The latter measure mentioned in the text is the so-called Dauer-Kelsay index. Manning J. Dauer and Robert G. Kelsay, "Unrepresentative States," *National Municipal Review*, XLIV (1955), 515–575. All districts are arranged in order from smallest to largest; one then counts off a majority of the districts, starting with the smallest, adds up their population and ascertains the percentage of the state's population. Generally, this figure should be at least 48%. (In some states before reapportionment, it was as low as 20%.)

[30] Thomas R. Dye, "Malapportionment and Public Policy in the States," *Journal of Politics*, XXVII (1965), 586–601.

larly economic development levels, than to political factors such as partisan-ship.[31] A decreasing amount of variation in policy between the states, and therefore a lesser relationship between ecology and policy, has also been noted. However, at least one recent study suggests the increased importance of political factors (such as past expenditures) and explains earlier findings as a function of the inadequacy of the political variables considered.[32] Most of the outcome studies do not explicitly mention legislatures, although Dye does talk about legislative activity:

> Urbanization and industrialization among the fifty states does indeed result in significant increases in the number of bills introduced and enacted in state legis-latures. Urbanization appears to be the most influential determinant of legisla-tive activity.[33]

The relevance of these studies for the legislative process is nonetheless clear: the policy outcomes examined are primarily those enacted by the legislature, and if political factors are relatively unimportant, then legislatures possess far less discretion over policy-making than many people believe them to have. However, if, as Wayne Francis argues in *Legislative Issues in the Fifty States,* Dye's studies can be thought of as emphasizing the long-run effects of social and economic factors on the results of the legislative process, attention to more explicitly political short-run matters may show a clear relationship between such items and legislative outcomes, thus reinstating the impor-tance of legislative activity in particular and the political in general.

Had political scientists conducted outcome studies earlier, perhaps fewer people would have looked to reapportionment as the "salvation of the cities" and perhaps fewer people would have resisted it, although resistance from those likely to have their representation reduced would have occurred in any case. Political scientists' studies concerning the supposed cleavage between rural and urban legislators, showing that such a cleavage was often a myth, generally had little effect on people's expectations about reapportionment. People had expected that the "big cities," i.e., the central cities of metropoli-tan areas, would be the principal beneficiaries of reapportionment. This would have been true based on 1950 Census figures; however, the 1960 Cen-sus figures showed that most large cities except those in the South had begun to lose population and that the suburbs were as likely to be the major bene-ficiaries as were the cities. Of course, if the principal reason for eliminating malapportionment was to bring about adherence to a principle—of "equal representation"—then the impact of the decisions of the Court becomes less important, and the misestimations of political scientists are less significant.

Among other aspects of representation, the gerrymandering of districts to

---

[31] Thomas R. Dye, *Politics, Economics, and the Public: Policy Outcomes in the Ameri-can States* (Chicago, 1966), p. 142.

[32] Ira Sharkansky, "Economic and Political Correlates of State Government Expendi-tures: General Tendencies and Deviant Cases," *Midwest Journal of Political Science,* XI (1967), 173–192.

[33] Dye, *Politics, Economics, and the Public,* p. 216.

suit the majority party has been an irritant of long standing to political idealists. Sophisticated studies of apportionment have shown us the difficulty of
being sure a gerrymander has occurred.[34] Not all odd-shaped districts are
gerrymanders, for one thing, and other devices have been used to produce
the same effect, for example, using a multi-member district to dilute minority-
group representation. Because we have generally taken the single-member
district for granted, and because of its almost universal use (except for large
city legislative districts in the states), we have ignored other forms of representation except as *exotica*. Thus, despite the cry for greater rural representation by those opposed to one man-one vote reapportionment, we have not
paid much attention to functional representation, continuing to proceed on
our geographical representational base. Weighted (or fractional) voting has
provoked some interest as a device for making reapportionment more precise, but it is generally treated as an aberration, as are cumulative voting (in
effect only in Illinois, in elections for the lower house) and proportional representation (once used in several major American cities, most recently in
Cincinnati, but now no longer in use).

LEGISLATIVE ORGANIZATION AND OPERATION

Because of the importance of legislative organization and procedure to
the outcome of the legislative process, formal structure and rules have always
received much attention. It is only recently, however, that systematic attempts have been made to relate the organization and rules to outcomes
rather than simply to describe them. Consideration of the organizational aspects of the legislature has covered such matters as the formal leadership and
committee structure and the intricacies of parliamentary procedure, particularly at the national level where it has been developed into a fine art. At the
state level, where comparison is possible, we find attention to the relative
length and frequency of legislative sessions; to legislative size, with reformers calling for smaller and thus allegedly more manageable legislatures;
to legislative pay and expenses; and to (collective and individual) legislative
staff, including such bodies as legislative councils, bill-drafting services, and
legislative reference bureaus. Generally, the bicameral basis for legislatures
is taken for granted (although we find sporadic attention to Nebraska's uni-
cameralism), as is the partisan basis for election (with only Nebraska and
Minnesota the exceptions). Much of the reform attention paid to state legislatures has been with structural (or "housekeeping") aspects. In arguing that
state legislatures must do a better job if more power is not to drift to the federal level of government, methods for strengthening those legislatures are
proposed, and they often lean heavily toward providing more staff, salary,
and office-space, rather than dealing with the fundamental basis of legisla-

[34] Frank Sorauf, *Party and Representation*, pp. 21–31.

tive organization, such as the way in which legislators are elected and re-warded.[35]

Rules, Norms, and Roles.   With respect to Congress, there has now been some effort to show the impact of the rules, seldom neutral in their impact. This has generally taken the form of case studies of particular "problem areas" or "hot spots." One example is the impact of Senate Rule XXII (pro-viding for cloture on debate) on the development of civil rights legislation; another is the House Rules Committee, which is felt to block Presidential programs undemocratically. The first volume to result from the American Po-litical Science Association Study of Congress project, Lewis Froman's *The Congressional Process,* is a systematic study of the rules and their results. *The Job of a Congressman,* by Donald Tacheron and Rep. Morris Udall, put together for the newly-elected Congressman trying to adapt to his job, is an-other extremely detailed collection of rules and procedures. That legislative bodies are differentially dependent on rules has been recognized. Thus, we find the United States Senate generally functioning without them, and un-able to transact its business quickly if insistence on the rules is made (a useful parliamentary ploy in itself for the Senator wanting to extract something from the leadership), while the much larger House of Representatives needs to operate, and functions more effectively, with them. There are also rules of an informal, unwritten nature which are just as crucial to the operation of the legislature; these norms of legislative behavior derive from the internal social structure of the legislative body. Journalist William White, in *Citadel,* first espoused the theory that the Senate is the greatest club in the world. *Citadel,* which has been referred to as "an embarrassing love affair with the Senate," was followed up by political scientist Donald Matthews' *U.S. Senators and Their World,* a systematic treatment of the work norms of the Senate. Here we find description of these norms, for example, that freshman legislators should generally be seen and not heard, that hard work and silence are more often rewarded than frequent speeches to the press gallery, and that speciali-zation is the method by which to make one's way, as well as the recognition that the Senators most highly respected within the body are not always those best known outside it.

There are also norms for a member of one house of the legislature dealing with members of "the other body";[36] not only is there institutional jealousy of the executive, but the House and Senate are professionally jealous of each other, to the point where work can grind to a halt if the leaders of one House feel they are being slighted. Thus the House of Representatives resists intru-

---

[35] This point was brought to my attention in the persuasive argument by Richard Richman, dissenting to the report of the Illinois Commission on the Reorganization of the General Assembly, *Improving the State Legislature* (Springfield, 1967).

[36] This formalized language is an example of the way in which language forms are used to decrease conflict, as well as, in this instance, to denigrate a competing institution. Sup-posedly, if one is expected to call a colleague "The learned and distinguished member from California," one will not say what he really thinks. (One wag has suggested that the higher the flowery praise, the less one thinks of the object of the language.)

sions into its prerogatives in the fiscal area, insisting on originating appropriations as well as revenue legislation.

Norms for dealing with non-legislators are not as well developed, leaving the individual legislator much more on his own. However, regular patterns and orientations are present; Wahlke and his associates found legislators adopted roles in dealing, for example, with lobbyists (facilitators, resisters, and neutrals). That some legislators retain close ties with the interests which brought about their candidacies or elections is quite clear, particularly in the states where low salaries may make being on a group's payroll necessary for economic survival. People in this situation are referred to as "pocket legislators," while those in the legislature favorably disposed to a particular group (perhaps because of membership) are called "inside lobbyists."

As earlier discussion of the executive- versus legislative-force models may have implied, there are different roles which the legislators adopt vis-à-vis the chief executive: Some follow his lead, particularly if he is of the same political party; others give some extra weight to his pronouncements; still others resist his suggestions, because of an interest in asserting legislative independence and autonomy. Legislators also have roles vis-à-vis the so-called independent regulatory commissions, as is clear from the fact that some do not feel restrained by the stated norm that individual representations should not be made in quasi-judicial proceedings. Others feel they should respect (that is, keep hands off) such proceedings, and try to oversee the operation of administrative agencies in other ways. Studies of particular individuals can be fruitful in explaining norms. Ralph Huitt's study of Senator Proxmire, an "outsider" in the Senate, is an example which illustrates the existence of multiple roles among which legislators can choose.[37] While there may be one central role or set of roles, all non-compliers are not simply deviants unable to follow the common standards; some, like Proxmire, *choose* another role which they follow consistently, even if clashes with their colleagues result, perhaps because they feel it will help their re-election. Thus they are "marching to the tune of a different drummer."

One area involving a combination of rules and norms which has been in the spotlight lately is that of Congressional ethics. Norms enter the picture because the unstated norm that each legislator should *not* be his brother's keeper makes it difficult for any individual to propose formal rules to cover behavior the public thinks unethical. The norms of what is proper behavior (for example, concerning the use of campaign funds) are often not those shared by the public. The cases of Senator Thomas Dodd and Congressman Adam Clayton Powell in 1967 forced the Congress into action, both with respect to Dodd (censure) and Powell (exclusion), but also with respect to long-run action: establishment of Committees on Standards and Official Conduct.

Committees. Committees have drawn separate attention from legislative scholars. At the state legislative level, the number of committees in each

[37] Ralph Huitt, "The Outsider in the Senate: An Alternative Role," *American Political Science Review*, LV (1961), 566–575.

house and the number of committee assignments per legislator is an issue, particularly because of a large number of "paper" committees (ones which never meet) and the absenteeism caused by multiple committee assignments. Some "paper" committees serve as "vest-pocket" committees for the legislative leadership to bottle up legislation, but reformers would still decrease the number of committees. In the Congress, the Legislative Reorganization Act of 1946 reduced the number of committees (there are now sixteen in the Senate, twenty in the House) and realigned and clarified jurisdictions.[38] Not all committee jurisdictions are parallel, decreasing the number of situations where matching committees in the two houses, along with the relevant executive agencies, would act as continuing sub-systems in the policy-making process. The expectations within such sub-systems can be quite important, as in the case of appropriations, where the House Appropriations Committee is expected (both by outsiders and its own members) to cut funds, while the Senate Committee is seen as an appeals board of a more generous nature.

Devices used for selection to committees have been of interest and the procedures in the House have been fully described. The Republicans use a Committee on Committees with representation for every state with a Republican Congressman, although most decisions are made by an executive committee in which the largest delegations have greater weight; the Democrats use the Democratic members on the House Ways and Means Committee, with each man responsible for a zone. The importance of geographical distribution, the claim of some states to specific seats on committees, the factors such as seniority and past relations with leaders, which are looked at when an individual legislator is being considered for a committee have been discussed. Comparable material at the state level is lacking, as is true with many aspects of the subject.

Which committees are more important is another question that has been explored, in terms of the prestige rankings given to them by the legislators and in terms of legislators' movements from "lower" to "higher" committees. Whether membership on a committee is usually exclusive or is held in conjunction with other committee assignments has also been used as a measure of a committee's standing.[39] The method of selection of the subcommittees which proliferated after the 1946 reduction in the number of regular committees has not been fully explored, although the process in some of the committees has been exposed to examination. The growth of the subcommittees, which in effect undercut the reform of reducing the number of full standing committees, is an example of the way by which "complaints have been more

[38] When jurisdictional lines had been unclear, the Speaker of the House and the President Pro-Tem of the Senate had some flexibility in deciding to what committee to send a bill—and such decisions could be crucial. See Stephen Bailey, *Congress Makes a Law* (New York, 1950). With jurisdiction clarified, this discretion was decreased—a latent consequence of the 1946 Act. However, bills can occasionally be written by their sponsors in such a way as to determine where they will be referred.

[39] Louis Gawthrop, "Changing Membership Patterns in House Committees," *American Political Science Review*, LX (1966), 366–375.

effective in evoking reform action than the reforms have been in improving congressional action." [40]

The activities of committees, once their members are selected, have been examined mostly through case studies, even when the researcher was principally interested in developing theory. Committee members have been shown to be particularly concerned about their "policy constituencies," [41] as well as about committee integration, i.e., internal cohesion. A committee which maintains cohesion is much more likely to "get its way" when it reports a bill to the floor than one whose members are divided. Committee success is also a function of the norm of reciprocity, which reinforces that of specialization: you defer to the work of my committee, in which I am an expert, and I'll defer to the work of yours. Another internal committee norm in some committees is that of nonpartisanship; where it occurs, minority party members are actively involved in the committee's work by the majority, and the chairman and ranking minority member (who may become the chairman if party fortunes change) often work as a close-knit pair, a factor which often frustrates aggressive majority party members without much committee seniority.

Committee oversight of administration has been portrayed most thoroughly by Richard Fenno in his study of the House and Senate Appropriations Committees; however, because the appropriations process brings regular, annual contact between Congress and all agencies, the operation of that committee may not be representative of the others. Types of committee chairmen and the variations in their styles have been shown, for example, through a study of the Senate Banking and Currency Committee,[42] where we see the difference between a "service" chairman, interested in allowing subcommittee chairmen considerable discretion to pursue their own interests, and a "minority and restraining" chairman, who guides the work of the whole committee very closely and who does not allow subcommittees much flexibility. This suggests that committees differ considerably in terms of committee-subcommittee relations, with subcommittees possessing far more autonomy in some cases than in others.[43]

Special types of committees, such as joint committees (generally without power to recommend legislation), select committees, and conference committees, have also been studied. Finding out what happens in conference committees is most difficult, because they all operate totally in "executive session," that is, closed to all except the immediate participants (and usually without even the participants' personal staff). That many regular standing

[40] Charles O. Jones, *Party and Policy-Making: The House Republican Policy Committee* (New Brunswick, N.J., 1964), p. 4.

[41] Charles O. Jones, "Representation in Congress: The Case of the House Agriculture Committee," *American Political Science Review*, LV (1961), 358–367.

[42] John F. Bibby, "Committee Characteristics and Legislative Oversight of Administration," *Midwest Journal of Political Science*, X (1966), 78–98.

[43] One device by which the committee chairman *decreases* subcommittee autonomy is to keep subcommittees from having fixed jurisdictions, e.g., by simply numbering them rather than giving them subject-matter titles, or by giving them extremely broad (and overlapping) titles.

committees conduct their most important work in executive session has made knowledge of the committees' activity, except through indirect methods like the interview, quite difficult.[44] We thus can know more about legislative hearings, generally held in open session, than we can about "mark-up" of bills and the other areas where the compromise on which the legislative process depends is actually made.

Legislative investigations have been a subject of particular interest in recent years principally because of investigations in the internal security area, such as the work of the House Un-American Activities Committee (now the Committee on Internal Security). That all investigations conducted by legislators are not sensational, that all do not deal with the political beliefs of the witnesses, and that not all are televised needs to be stressed,[45] although, of course, the televised, sensational ones are those that have received the most attention. Regardless of the unhappiness which may have exhibited with the operation of HUAC, it is important to recognize the reasons for such investigations. The manifest purpose of all investigations is to see if there is a need for legislation, or to gather information on which legislation might be based. However, legislators may feel the need to gain publicity at the expense of the executive branch, to belabor executive officials who act superior to the legislators, or to try to lead public opinion or help manufacture it on particular subjects.

Legislative Party.   The role of the party in legislative operation is important, even without the existence of "responsible" parties. The extent to which our legislative parties are "responsible" has been discussed in the previous chapter; suffice it to say that some feel this ideal could be achieved by an act of will, utilizing existing structure. This view is felt by many to be overly optimistic and to be based on a lack of understanding of the foundation of the present role of party in the legislature. This role is largely organizational.

> There is considerable evidence to suggest that the primary function of congressional parties is organizational. . . . If the function of the legislative institution is to resolve conflict, then the political party functions to organize a conflict resolution process.[46]

The organization of legislative bodies is carried out in party terms: party committees assign legislators to committees, committee chairmen are members of the majority party, the Speaker of the House and the President Pro-Tem of the Senate are members of the majority party. It is true that there are some legislatures where the party's operative force does not extend beyond the first days in which the organizational structure is established, but in many other cases it does, even when it does not command or control all that occurs in the legislature.

[44] Executive sessions of Senate committees are open to the personal staffs of Senators; this is not true in the House.
[45] In fact, there is a House rule against televising committee hearings, established by the late Speaker Rayburn; the Senate leaves the decision about televising to individual committee chairmen.
[46] Jones, *Party and Policy-Making*, p. 5.

The party's involvement begins with assistance in a legislator's campaigns for re-election and with campaigns of non-incumbents for office. Each party has its own legislative campaign organization in each House of Congress, providing financial assistance and other services to candidates. This work is done as a supplement to, and to a large degree independently of, the work done by the campaign structure of the national party organization.

Generally speaking, one's legislative party label is dependent on his vote on organizational matters. If one votes for the Democratic candidate for Speaker, he is considered a Democrat, even if he never votes with a majority of his Democratic colleagues or with the party leaders again. Even this minimal identification with party did not come until the 1830's and after; the use of the caucus (a gathering of the members of the party in the legislature) as a tool for organizing the daily activity of the legislature did not come until after the Civil War. The caucus did become of considerable importance in the last years of the nineteenth century, before Congress rebelled against the powers of the Speaker. The caucus is not as important now in Congress as it was then, in part because of a reluctance to have it meet (particularly in the Democratic Party), because it might expose weaknesses rather than provide the basis for compromise. It falls far short of its ideal, which is to provide discipline when party members will not go along with binding decisions. However, the caucus or policy committees which the parties set up can still be useful even when binding agreement is not attempted, much less achieved. Thus, as Jones points out, such groups "can . . . provide a means for discovering the basis (or lack of it) for consensus by acting as a vehicle of communication" within the party; they can be "error-correction mechanism [s] . . . to reduce the element of surprise on the . . . floor," so that party members "have had a preview of what to expect from their own membership." [47] They can provide service and research to individual members and the leadership, of which they tend to be personal adjuncts, and can help with legislative scheduling. And party is still important as a reference group and as a source of friendship and expertise. There is still a "party line," which the legislator can ascertain and follow if he wants to, even though on major issues he may go his own way. David Olson pointed out recently that even when the legislator votes with the party, he may feel no *obligation* to vote with it; [48] the similarity of position may be more of coincidence than pressure or obligation, but the party position is still there.

Leadership. Because the leaders in the legislature are chosen by the parties, the discussion of legislative leadership is usually carried out in connection with discussions of party organization. Individual leaders, such as Lyndon Johnson as Democratic Majority Leader in the Senate, have been examined, as has the way in which leadership is passed from individual to individual.

[47] *Ibid.*, pp. 78, 143.
[48] David Olson, "Perceptions by Congressmen of Their Party: The National and District Units of Party," paper presented to the Southern Political Science Association, New Orleans, 1967.

Conditions for leadership change, such as frustration at not making expected gains at election time, have been suggested. The majority tends to be more satisfied with its leadership, but any party which recognizes the importance of recruiting "young talent" for future leadership positions will be more likely to have peaceful (as contrasted with contested) change. That some changes follow a firm pattern, while others are more fluid, has not been ignored. The whip system in the United States House of Representatives has been subject to scrutiny, so we know that whips perform important information-gathering functions in addition to collecting/corraling votes; they may provide accurate figures even when they intend to vote against their party's position. In addition to the formal leadership structure, we also find informal structures, of both large and small sizes. The Democratic Study Group is an example of the former; the group of men known as the "Board of Education," who met informally with the late Speaker Rayburn to exchange information and plan strategy, is an example of the second. State delegations, particularly of members of one party, play a leadership role on some issues in that they provide "cues" to members on voting, and are quite relevant to explanations of voting behavior, along with party and constituency. These studies of the formal and informal leadership have been supplemented by analysis of task leadership, often discussed in connection with specialization. We find that the formal leaders are not always the ones most effective in passing legislation, nor are they always the ones looked up to most by their colleagues as experts, although formal leadership usually gives a legislator high status with his colleagues. Francis has found that those with most influence (a key ingredient of leadership) had higher rates of interaction with their fellow legislators than did those with less influence, suggesting that, with few exceptions, leadership does not come to those who sit and wait.[49] Peabody, in examining the House Republicans, found the actual leadership and formal leadership closely congruent (as did Matthews for the Senate), but Peabody also found that some senior leaders "may have more to say about legislation in specific policy areas than the formal leaders themselves." [50] Where leaders stand with reference to other members of their own party has also been examined, some arguing that they epitomize the party's stand, while others claim that they are middle-of-the-road.

LEGISLATIVE VOTING BEHAVIOR

An important emphasis of legislative roll-call studies has been the role of party in legislative voting. The work of Julius Turner (*Party and Constituency: Pressures on Congress*), David Truman (*The Congressional Party*), and others has suggested that, at least since the New Deal, party has been the

---

[49] Wayne Francis, "Influence and Interaction in a State Legislative Body," *American Political Science Review*, LVI (1962), 953–960.

[50] Robert Peabody, "Organization Theory and Legislative Behavior," pp. 8–9.

single most important factor explaining legislative voting. Wilder Crane suggests that the existence of a "party vote" does not mean that party was actually an operative factor in producing the result.[51] He found party cohesion most easily maintained on trivial matters, ones about which legislators were least concerned, and "no necessary correlation between roll-calls alone and the degree of party pressure exerted upon or perceived by legislators." And Rothman argues that, in the period he studied,

> Statistics can tell only part of the story for the parties carried out vital duties even before a bill came to a vote. Roll calls do not reflect the significance of the power to staff working committees or to order the chamber's business.[52]

He thinks that students of roll-calls, by comparing American legislative party cohesion with that in the British Parliament, "have accordingly tended to dismiss American parties out of hand for not voting their members as a bloc in every instance." Others have found that party voting is highest on organizational matters (who will be Speaker; who will chair committees), less on "administration bills," and least on regional items and private bills.[53] Anderson has also noted that whether the party is in a majority or minority situation makes a difference in the proportion of roll-calls in which its members fall into a scale pattern.[54] Because use of party still leaves much voting unexplained, other factors must be found. A number of these are found within the legislature. Sectionalism is one. The South has received particular attention from a number of scholars, because of the cleavage it provides within the Democratic Party and because of interest in civil rights. Thus, the Southerners' changing attitudes on foreign policy (from an internationalist to a more isolationist stance) have been studied. Another is the state delegation. Truman's study of voting and state party delegations showed that issues which "divide the party as a whole do not split the state delegations in similar fashion," but instead increase delegation unity. He suggests that on highly controversial questions which divide a party, a Representative may look to other members of his delegation for advice and "cues" on how to vote. But Truman stresses that "the influence of the delegation is not completely consistent from state to state or from situation to situation," [55] depending in part on the party situation within the state. The existence of coalitions, particularly the "Conservative Coalition" (conservative Republicans and Southern Democrats), is another item of note, and one subject to explanation

[51] Wilder Crane, "A Caveat on Roll-Call Studies of Party Voting," *Midwest Journal of Political Science*, IV (1960), 237–249.

[52] David Rothman, *Politics and Power: The United States Senate, 1869–1901* (Cambridge, Mass., 1966), p. 74.

[53] Lewis A. Froman, Jr., and Randall Ripley, "Conditions for Party Leadership: The Case of the House Democrats," *American Political Science Review*, LIX (1965), 52–63.

[54] Lee F. Anderson, "Variability in the Unidimensionality of Legislative Voting," *Journal of Politics*, XXVII (1964), 568–585.

[55] David Truman, "The State Delegations and the Structure of Party Voting in the United States House of Representatives," *American Political Science Review*, L (1956), 1034, 1043.

through roll-call analysis, as is the phenomenon of bipartisanship in foreign policy.

Other factors are located outside the legislature. Characteristics of constituencies—particularly the demographic characteristics in census data—are frequently used, but party variables (competition) are also taken into account. And the relationship between the two is also explored, an important matter because constituency differences are often reflected in party differences. Not only is party competition examined, but the relationship between the Congressional candidate's vote and that received by the party's Presidential candidate is examined. Part of this study stems from an interest in the "coattail" problem, but scholars have now become interested in the effect the President's electoral percentage has on the Representative's voting in Congress. Because of the difficulty of finding census data gathered for geographic areas which "match" Congressional or legislative districts, usually only three or four demographic variables have been used in any one study. With the development of the Census Bureau's *Congressional District Data Book* (for the 88th Congress), more variables can be used.

MacRae's study of Massachusetts used such data as the basis for statements about deviation of certain legislators from party regularity. He found, among other things, that

> Those representatives with wide election margins . . . tend more to party regularity than those with close election margins. . . . Those representatives with close elections were more sensitive to district characteristics than were those with wide election margins.[56]

A similar relationship was found, for the Pennsylvania lower house, by Dye: "The greater the degree of political competition for House legislative office, the greater the tendency will be for representatives to cross party lines." [57] Froman, studying Congressmen rather than state legislators, found the highest party voting in the *most* competitive districts, as well as the most support for the President's program from these same districts.[58] A related finding by Thomas Flinn suggests that policy differences between the parties are not due to inter-party differences in constituencies, and that differing constituencies do not bring intra-party disagreement.[59] Looking at four types of Congressional districts (farm, city, worker, and Western), Mayhew found that Congressmen from districts most directly affected by an issue were more highly cohesive than those from "other" districts, with Democrats backing

[56] Duncan MacRae, Jr., "The Relation Between Roll Calls and Constituencies in the Massachusetts House of Representatives," *American Political Science Review*, XLVI (1952), 1051–1052.

[57] Thomas R. Dye, "A Comparison of Constituency Influences in the Upper and Lower Chambers of a State Legislature," *Western Political Quarterly*, XIV (1961), 478.

[58] Lewis Froman, Jr., *Congressmen and Their Constituencies*, p. 115.

[59] Thomas A. Flinn, "Party Responsibility in the States: Some Causal Factors," *American Political Science Review*, LVIII (1964), 60–71.

their brethren in the "interested" districts and Republicans drawing support toward the position in the "other" or "indifferent" districts.[60]

A variety of studies at the state legislative level have cast much light on the effect of party competition on legislative voting, although the findings are quite disparate. Thus, Jewell found that neither statewide competition nor legislative competition could explain party support voting in the legislature, although he found higher party loyalty in urban than in rural states.[61] Lockard found that close party competition produces party voting loyalty through party organizational strength.[62] Wahlke and his associates, in their four-state study, found party organizational strength related to competition between the parties, but thought it might also operate independently.[63] They also thought that the difference between Democrats and Republicans in basic ideology did not mean that such ideology is operative in the legislators' partisan roles, that is, it was not always reflected in voting, and varied with the particular legislative issue.

The studies involve the use of aggregate data, at least at the district end (e.g., % Democrat, or % urban, or per capita income). With the vast resources of the Survey Research Center, Miller and Stokes have presented findings which relate district opinion (survey data) to Congressmen's attitudes (also obtained through interviews) and to the legislators' votes (roll-call data).[64] They found the highest correlations between a legislator's perception of district opinion and his vote and between his attitude and his vote, with only slightly smaller relationships between district opinion and member's perception of district opinion or his vote. Cnudde and McCrone, refining the Miller-Stokes data, show no direct relationship between district attitude and member's attitude, and that the path from the district opinion to the member's perception to the vote accounted for the predominant amount of the direct relationship between district opinion and the legislator's vote.[65] As the use of attitudes by Miller and Stokes suggests, legislative voting studies have not ignored ideological matters, although there is a recognition, stemming from correlations between attitude and party or attitude and other items, that ideology may be a reflection of other matters in addition to being an independent variable affecting voting. The use of Guttman scaling and factor analysis in voting studies has allowed more complete examination of the question as to whether consistent attitudes or ideologies underlie the voting of legislators, and it does appear that this is the case with at least an important proportion of roll-calls.

[60] David Mayhew, *Party Loyalty Among Congressmen: The Difference Between Democrats and Republicans, 1947–1962* (Cambridge, 1966).
[61] Malcolm E. Jewell, "Party Voting in American State Legislatures," *American Political Science Review*, XLIX (1955), 773–791.
[62] Duane Lockard, *New England State Politics* (Princeton, 1958).
[63] Wahlke, *et al., The Legislative System*.
[64] Warren E. Miller and Donald E. Stokes, "Constituency Influence in Congress," *American Political Science Review*, LVII (1963), 45–56.
[65] Charles F. Cnudde and Donald J. McCrone, "The Linkage Between Constituency Attitudes and Congressional Voting Behavior: A Causal Model," *American Political Science Review*, LX (1966), 66–72.

BIBLIOGRAPHY

The Legislative Process

Reviews of the Field. Supplementing this chapter are HEINZ EULAU and KATHARINE HINCKLEY, "Legislative Institutions and Processes," *Political Science Annual,* ed. James Robinson (Indianapolis, 1966), Vol. 1, pp. 85–189, and two articles by NORMAN MELLER, "Legislative Behavior Research," *Western Political Quarterly,* XIII (1960), 131–153, and " 'Legislative Behavior Research' Revisited: A Review of Five Years' Publications," *Western Political Quarterly,* XVIII (1965), 776–793.

Overviews. These may be obtained from leading texts. Among the best are WILLIAM KEEFE and MORRIS OGUL, *The American Legislative Process: Congress and the States,* 2nd ed. (Englewood Cliffs, 1968), and MALCOLM JEWELL and SAMUEL PATTERSON, *The Legislative Process in the United States* (New York, 1966). There are a number of collections of readings which are also helpful. The oldest is *Legislative Behavior: A Reader in Theory and Research,* ed. JOHN WAHLKE and HEINZ EULAU (Glencoe, 1959). The best collection of new materials is *New Perspectives on the House of Representatives,* ed. ROBERT PEABODY and NELSON POLSBY (Chicago, 1963). Other general collections are *Legislative Politics U.S.A.,* 2nd ed., ed. THEODORE LOWI (Boston, 1965), and *Congress: Anvil of American Democracy,* ed. GEORGE GOODWIN, JR. (Glenview, Ill., 1967). Two collections of background papers prepared for the American Assembly are *The Congress and America's Future,* ed. DAVID S. TRUMAN (Englewood Cliffs, 1965), and *State Legislatures in American Politics,* ed. ALEXANDER HEARD (Englewood Cliffs, 1966). JOHN ROCHE and LEONARD LEVY have edited a series of documents, *Congress* (New York, 1964).

Congressional Activity

Summaries. A number of summaries of Congressional activity exist. *Congressional Quarterly,* in addition to its weekly reports, publishes an *Almanac* for each Congress, and its *Congress and the Nation, 1945–1964,* is a major reference compendium. *Western Political Quarterly* has for some years published a narrative account of each session of the Congress; see, for example, FLOYD M. RIDDICK and MURRAY SWEBEN, "The Eighty-Ninth Congress: First Session," *Western Political Quarterly,* XIX (1966), 353–374.

Case Studies. These abound, and usually revolve around particular bills. In addition to STEPHEN BAILEY, *Congress Makes a Law* (New York, 1950), on the Employment Act of 1946, also valuable are DON HADWIGER and ROSS TALBOT, *Pressures and Protests: The Kennedy Farm Program and the Wheat Referendum of 1963* (San Francisco, 1965); CLYDE JACOBS and JOHN GALLAGHER, *The Selective Service Act: A Case Study of the Governmental Process* (New York, 1967); and DANIEL BERMAN, *A Bill Is Passed* (New York, 1966), concerning civil rights legislation. A study emphasizing communications of affected individuals with legislators is RAYMOND BAUER, LEWIS ANTHONY DEXTER, and ITHIEL DE SOLA POOL, *American Business and Public Policy* (New York, 1963). The series of case studies, *On Capitol Hill,* by JOHN BIBBY and ROGER DAVIDSON (New York, 1967), is a series of vignettes rather than the story of one bill.

Rules and Practices. While portrayed in the case studies, these are examined more systematically in a number of places. LEWIS FROMAN, *The Congressional Process: Strategies, Rules, and Procedures* (Boston, 1967) is the best single systematic source. Aimed at new Congressmen but also useful for the student of political science is DONALD G. TACHERON and MORRIS K. UDALL, *The Job of the Congressman: An Introduction to Service in the U.S. House of Representatives* (Indianapolis, 1966). Less formal practices, or norms, resulting from the existence of legislative bodies as social institutions in their own right has been shown, both journalistically by WILLIAM S. WHITE, *Citadel* (New York, 1956), and more systematically by political scientist DONALD MATTHEWS, *U.S. Senators and Their World* (Chapel Hill, N.C., 1960), with respect to the Senate. The "view from inside" the House is provided by CHARLES CLAPP, *The Congressman: His World as He Sees It* (Washington, D.C., 1963), based on round-table discussions with a number of national legislators. Another good inside look is provided in CLEM MILLER, *Member of the House*, ed. John Baker (New York, 1962).

Reform. Demands are often made for reform of the formal practices. General writings on reform include ROBERT BENDINER, *Obstacle Course on Capitol Hill* (New York, 1964), and a number of works contributed by legislators, the most obvious being Representative RICHARD BOLLING, *House Out of Order* (New York, 1965), Senator JOSEPH CLARK, *The Senate Establishment* (New York, 1963) and *The Sapless Branch* (New York, 1964), and *We Propose: A Modern Congress*, ed. MARY MCINNIS (New York, 1966), proposals by the House Republican Task Force on Congressional Reform and Minority Staffing. *Congressional Reform: Problems and Prospects,* edited by Clark (New York, 1965), is somewhat more scholarly. Legislative attitudes toward reform are examined in ROGER DAVIDSON, DAVID KOVENOCK, and MICHAEL O'LEARY, *Congress in Crisis* (Belmont, Calif., 1966).

Methods

The method of roll-call analysis, used often by behaviorally-oriented political scientists in studying legislatures, is discussed by DUNCAN MAC RAE, JR., *Dimensions of Congressional Voting: A Statistical Study of the House of Representatives in the Eighty-First Congress* (Berkeley, 1958) and in LEE F. ANDERSON, *et al., Legislative Roll-Call Analysis* (Evanston, 1966). More sophisticated techniques are discussed in articles by MacRae, "A Method for Identifying Issues and Factions from Legislative Votes," *APSR*, LIX (1965), 909–926, and JOHN G. GRUMM, "A Factor Analysis of Legislative Behavior," *Midwest Journal of Political Science*, VII (1963), 336–356, and "The Systematic Analysis of Blocs in the Study of Legislative Behavior," *Western Political Quarterly*, XVIII (1965), 350–362, as well as by CHARLES D. FARRIS, "A Method of Determining Ideological Groupings in the Congress," *Journal of Politics*, XX (1958), 308–338. Warnings concerning roll-call studies are posed by WILDER CRANE, "A Caveat on Roll-Call Studies of Party Voting," *Midwest Journal of Political Science* [hereafter: *MJPS*], IV (1960), 237–249, but Crane is answered in part by FRED I. GREENSTEIN and ALTON F. JACKSON, "A Second Look at the Validity of Roll Call Analysis," *MJPS*, VII (1963), 156–166. Of specific studies using roll-call analysis, DAVID TRUMAN, *The Congressional Party* (New York, 1959) is, like MacRae's book, based on one Congress. Examples of work based on more than one Congress include LEROY RIESELBACH, *The Roots of Isolationism: Congressional Voting and Presidential Leadership in Foreign Policy* (Indianapolis, 1966), and DAVID MAYHEW, *Party Loyalty Among Congressmen: The Difference Between Democrats and Republicans, 1947–1962* (Cambridge, Mass., 1966).

Executive-Legislative Relations

Executive-legislative relations are covered most generally in JOSEPH HARRIS, *Congressional Control of Administration* (Washington, 1964); Harris had earlier looked at Senate confirmation of appointments in *The Advice and Consent of the Senate* (Berkeley, 1953). ROBERT ASH WALLACE, *Congressional Control of Federal Spending* (Detroit, 1960) examines the "power of the purse," as does RICHARD FENNO, *The Power of the Purse* (Boston, 1966), a study of the House and Senate Appropriations Committees. An earlier and important study of legislative review of administrative action is ARTHUR MACMAHON, "Congressional Oversight of Administration: The Power of the Purse," *Political Science Quarterly*, LVIII (1943), 161–190 and 380–414. Relations of executive branch agencies with the subcommittees having jurisdiction over their programs are shown in two articles by IRA SHARKANSKY: "An Appropriations Subcommittee and Its Client Agencies: A Comparative Study of Supervision and Control," *APSR*, LIX (1965), 622–628, and "Four Agencies and an Appropriations Subcommittee: A Comparative Study of Budget Strategies," *MJPS*, IX (1965), 254–281, as well as the earlier classic, J. LEIPER FREEMAN, *The Political Process: Executive-Legislative Committee Relations* (New York, 1955).

Other important aspects of executive-legislative relations are treated in RAYMOND H. DAWSON, "Congressional Innovation and Intervention in Defense Policy," *APSR*, LVI (1962), 42–57; FRANCIS E. ROURKE, "Administrative Secrecy: A Congressional Dilemma," *APSR*, LIV (1960), 683–694; a series of articles by CORNELIUS COTTER and J. MALCOLM SMITH, e.g., "Administrative Accountability: Reporting to Congress," *Western Political Quarterly*, X (1957), 405–415; and, at the state level, in SARAH P. MC CALLY, "The Governor and His Legislative Party," *APSR*, LX (1966), 923–942. Why legislators often react negatively to administrators is explored imaginatively in EDWARD SHILS, "The Legislator and His Environment," *University of Chicago Law Review*, XVIII (1950–1951), 571–584. WILLIAM C. MITCHELL also explores the tenuous position in which the legislator finds himself in "Occupational Role Strains: The American Elective Public Official," *Administrative Science Quarterly*, III (1958), 210–228.

Representation

Reapportionment. Basic treatments are to be found in GORDON E. BAKER, *The Reapportionment Revolution: Representation, Political Power, and the Supreme Court* (New York, 1966) and ROBERT DIXON, *Democratic Representation* (New York, 1968). An important early discussion of malapportionment was MAURICE KLAIN, "A New Look at the Constituencies: The Need for a Recount and a Reappraisal," *APSR*, XLIX (1955), 1105–1119. *Reapportionment*, ed. GLENDON SCHUBERT (New York, 1965), is a good research anthology of articles and other materials. *The Politics of Reapportionment*, ed. MALCOLM JEWELL (New York, 1963), a state-by-state treatment, and ANDREW HACKER, *Congressional Districting: The Issue of Equal Representation*, rev. ed. (Washington, D.C., 1964), deal with more specialized aspects of the problem. The question of whether rural-urban cleavage actually exists in state legislatures resulted in an important exchange: DAVID R. DERGE, "Metropolitan and Outstate Alignments in Illinois and Missouri Legislative Delegations,"

APSR, LII (1958), 1051–1065; RICHARD T. FROST, "On Derge's Metropolitan and Outstate Legislative Delegations," *APSR*, LIII (1959), 792–795; and Derge, "On the Use of Roll-Call Analysis: A Reply to R. T. Frost," *APSR*, LIII (1959), 1087–1099.

Methods of Selection. Proportional representation and cumulative voting are two special methods of choosing legislators which have been closely examined. The best discussion of the former is RALPH STRAETZ, *P.R. Politics in Cincinnati* (New York, 1958), which includes a clear technical appendix. The latter is described by GEORGE BLAIR, *Cumulative Voting: An Effective Electoral Device in Illinois Politics* (Urbana, 1960), and game theory has been applied to it by JACK SAWYER and DUNCAN MACRAE, JR., "Game Theory and Cumulative Voting in Illinois: 1902–1954," *APSR*, LVI (1962), 936–946.

Recruitment and Retention. The matter of who is selected for legislative positions, and who remains in the legislature, has been widely discussed. In important older articles, CHARLES HYNEMAN dealt with who serves, in "Who Makes Our Laws," *Political Science Quarterly*, LV (1940), 556–581, and who remains in the legislature, in "Tenure and Turnover of the Indiana General Assembly," *APSR*, XXXII (1938), 51–67 and 311–331. The dominant place of lawyers in the legislature has been taken up most recently by HEINZ EULAU and JOHN SPRAGUE, *Lawyers in Politics: A Study in Professional Convergence* (Indianapolis, 1964). Recruitment practices are dealt with by LEO SNOWISS, "Congressional Recruitment and Representation," *APSR*, LX (1966), 627–639, and, at the state level, by JAMES BARBER, *The Lawmakers* (New Haven, 1965). LEWIS FROMAN, *Congressmen and Their Constituencies* (Chicago, 1963) is a good single volume dealing with relationships between legislators and their districts and the effect of the latter on legislative voting behavior.

Legislative Structure

Committees. Committees have received much attention. Ways of selecting members of Congressional committees are dealt with in NICHOLAS A. MASTERS, "House Committee Assignments," *APSR*, LV (1961), 345–367, and the fascinating special problems caused by a legislator switching parties are noted in RALPH K. HUITT, "The Morse Committee Assignment Controversy: A Study in Senate Norms," *APSR*, LI (1957), 313–329. JAMES A. ROBINSON has examined *The House Rules Committee* (Indianapolis, 1963), often the subject of reform criticism. Subcommittees are treated in GEORGE GOODWIN, "Subcommittees: The Miniature Legislatures of Congress," *APSR*, LVI (1962), 597–604. Studies of special committees appear in a number of articles; an example is JOHN MANLEY, "The House Committee on Ways and Means: Conflict Management in a Congressional Committee," *APSR*, LIX (1965), 927–939. An historical treatment of a controversial committee is taken in ROBERT K. CARR, *The House Committee on Un-American Activities, 1945–1960* (Ithaca, 1952). Legislative investigations, for which HUAC is oft noted and criticized, have received a good general treatment in TELFORD TAYLOR, *Grand Inquest* (New York, 1955). One of the newest committees, the Joint Committee on Atomic Energy, is given thorough scrutiny in HOWARD P. GREEN and ALAN ROSENTHAL, *Government of the Atom: The Integration of Powers* (New York, 1963). A variety of matters dealing with committees, including their relationship to the whole body of which they are a part, is taken up in HOLBERT CARROLL, *The House of Representatives and Foreign Affairs*, rev. ed. (Boston, 1966)

Party.   The role of party in the legislature is discussed in terms of special party committees, as in CHARLES O. JONES, *Party and Policy-Making: The House Republican Policy Committee* (New Brunswick, N.J., 1964), and in terms of leadership, as in RALPH HUITT's study of Lyndon Johnson's reign as Senate Majority Leader, "Democratic Party Leadership in the Senate," *APSR*, LV (1961), 333–344, ROBERT PEABODY's study of leadership change: "Party Leadership Change in the United States House of Representatives," *APSR*, LXI (1967), 675–693, and RANDALL RIPLEY, *Party Leadership in the House of Representatives* (Washington, D.C., 1967). Less formal party groupings like state Congressional delegations and larger, broader groups have been examined. An example of the former is ALAN FIELLIN, "The Functions of Informal Groups in Legislative Institutions," *Journal of Politics*, XXIV (1962), 72–91, and a study of the administration-supporting Democratic Study Group (DSG), an example of the latter, is KENNETH KOFMEHL, "The Institutionalization of a Voting Bloc," *Western Political Quarterly*, XVII (1964), 256–272.

13 / PUBLIC ADMINISTRATION

Introduction / Administrative Organization and Reorganization /
Specialty "Tools" / The Chief Executive / Intergovernmental
Relations / Administrative and Organizational Behavior

INTRODUCTION

Public administration, more than any other subfield of political science, has tended toward a separate existence within the discipline. This relative isolation stemmed from its vocational purpose and from intellectual distinctions of its early years. Its "differentness" has been maintained, although in part for new reasons. One purpose of public administration specialists has always been to prepare individuals for the public service at national, state, and local levels, although there has not been agreement on what constituted proper training for the public service. Some have argued for a broad, "liberal" education; others, for a specific, job-oriented curriculum. The heavier the vocational (as opposed to educational) orientation, and the more specific the task for which students were being trained, the further from the rest of political science the field moved.

In public administration, the distinction between "policy" and "administration" was originally pursued as a hard-and-fast dichotomy. Policy was made, it was said, in the legislative branch, and carried out (executed) in the executive branch by administrators. Stress on this distinction was reinforced by belief in the doctrine of the separation of powers between legislative, executive, and judicial branches, as well as by the jointly-held ideas that politics was corrupt and that administration was neutral. This value-laden view led to attempts to take matters "out of politics," that is, to place control of government services in the hands of those not directly responsible to elected partisan political officials. While many have come to recognize that this distinction was much too simple, it did make executive branch structure the subject of special study. And the distinction was reinforced by the reform orientation of many of those interested in public administration in the earliest days; their preoccupation was with developing the best administrative arrangements for carrying out policy. The idea that there was "one best way" of doing things led to calling public administration a science, with "principles" of proper action. These "principles" were prescriptive in nature instead of being the descriptive generalizations we now associate with the word "science." They were also divorced from the ends or purposes of the organizations in which they were being used, although they did embody and imply certain values. The idea was generated that, if the ends were supplied, an administrative specialist could tell what should be done. Applied administration, which stressed economy, coherence and coordination, plus efficiency in operation, acquired a distinct management bias in its early years. This was not totally lost even when, in later years, the individual worker was taken into account, because the emphasis was often on how to satisfy the worker so he could produce more.

Perhaps because administration was considered something separate from policy, there has been much debate about how administration relates to democracy. Were administration simply considered an extension or part of the basic policy-making process, its compatibility with democracy might not be a matter of such controversy. Part of what gives rise to the issue is that administrative organization is most often structured hierarchically, particularly with orders flowing from the top down. (That power does in fact sometimes originate at the "bottom" of an organization, now recognized by many students of organization, does not change the basis of the argument.) Such "top-down" arrangements seem to conflict inherently with democracy, particularly when democracy is viewed in terms of mass citizen participation. A strong counterargument can be mustered that an efficient organization is necessary to implement what the legislators (the representatives of the people) have decided should be policy, just as there is little question that political and social movements could not succeed without the organizational apparatus they have developed and acquired. Administrators are also not untouched by public opinion, interest group representation, or even daily contact with the public. And bureaucrats, although chosen on the basis of merit, can be considered representative because of their linkages with interest groups and the legislative branch, or because of a similarity of characteristics with the total population from which they are drawn. If bureaucracy can be directed by the top leaders, it is at least compatible with democracy; the problem is to keep it from becoming an independent, monolithic force in the political system.

Because of its concern with the "best way" of organizing the government, public administration became largely structural and institutional in its approach. Some scholars found this way of examining organizations to be inadequate and sterile. They began to look at what individuals did within organizations. In their search for new materials with which to work, they developed the descriptive case-studies of the Inter-University Case Program (ICP). Studies of administrative history also helped in this effort. Later, to carry forward their analysis, they began to import concepts from sociology and psychology into the study of public administration, and for some years it looked as if we would have a behavioral study of public administration to supplement the earlier traditional study. However, those studying administration from a behavioral point of view have not limited themselves to the study of *public* administration, despite differences between public and private bureaucracies. Their emphasis on organizations in general has led to the development of an academic specialty at first known as "administrative behavior" and then as "organizational behavior" and "organization theory," examined by students of business administration and sociology as well as of political science. The field has become highly formalistic and mathematical, leading to a science of organization quite different from the earlier "science" of prescriptive "principles." The idea had remained while its contents had changed almost completely. Formal organization theory was more likely to be able to supply value-free principles than the earlier "science," although to supply them for the purpose of operating organizations was not its goal.

Scholars of administrative behavior concentrate on individuals in organizations, a result of human relations in applied administration. As a result, some have ignored the structural aspects of organization and what many political scientists feel is the crucial difference in contexts between public administration and administration in the private sector of the economy. This overemphasis on behavior without organization is no less incomplete than the earlier concentration of traditional public administration on organization without behavior. What probably has greatest appeal to scholars of administrative behavior who consider themselves political scientists is an approach which emphasizes behavior *within* formal public organization. Thus March and Simon suggest the general task of organization theory is "to analyze the interaction between the characteristics of humans and the social and task environments created by organizations." [1]

Particularly as it has become recognized that administration and policy are not completely disparate, and are intimately related to each other, students of public administration have become concerned about "policy development," with which we will not deal here at length. Their principal interest in this regard has been in the development of policy within the administrative organs of government, although it has extended to include the development of policy in the legislative and judicial branches of government. When this occurs, it is difficult to separate the study of public administration from the study of the entire governmental process. Studies of the "functions" of American government, that is, the specific policy areas in which the government has been involved, e.g., foreign affairs, agriculture, natural resources, and civil rights, have been derived from the "public administration and policy development" approach, with most attention being paid to "business and government." Most have become recitations of the specific policies adopted by the government, whether through executive/administrative, legislative, or judicial action. They are not as likely to be examinations of the process by which the policies were adopted or the role of administration in their working, although some light has been cast on important administrative problems. In work on national security policy, we have seen the problems of maintaining civilian control of the military and the effect of organizational forms on civilian supremacy. Recent attention to the subject of public higher education has contributed to our understanding of the administration of that field.

[1] James G. March and Herbert A. Simon, *Organizations* (New York, 1958), p. 12.

Concern about policy for the "Space Age" has cast light on the ways in which the work of science is organized in the government and the manner in which scientists work for and with the government. Yet, as Leiserson points out, we still know little about

> . . . *the controversial aspects* of recruiting, training, selecting and replacing leaders in the scientific community; organizing, financing, and directing scientific research; the articulation, representation, communication of the common and conflicting interests of scientific workers; and the active efforts of scientists to influence and modify the controls and requirements imposed by the political system upon the scientific enterprise itself.[2]

The examination of the relation between science and government has brought into focus the question of "government by contract," perhaps most visible in the area of defense procurement. If government is to have adequate specialized manpower skills and sophisticated hardware without producing the material itself, or without paying salaries to hire the individuals, then contracts with "private" industry or universities to provide the men and matériel are a logical means of operating.

ADMINISTRATIVE ORGANIZATION AND REORGANIZATION

In public administration's emphasis on the structural arrangements under which the government operates, the chief emphasis has been on the internal organization of the executive branch at national and state levels, with forms of local government (particularly municipalities) also drawing much attention. Thus organization charts with formal lines showing relations between parts of an organization have been heavily used, and much emphasis has been placed on the "charters" establishing units. Having established those structures, scholar-reformers have worked hard to reorganize them, trying to make them more efficient and economical. The impact of the "efficiency and economy" idea on administrative thought shows the influence which private business has had on those in the field of public administration. It also shows that the principal concern has been less on the degree to which goals are attained (which we might call "effectiveness") and more on the more limited question of how resources are allocated, or how much is accomplished *with a given amount of resources* ("efficiency"). Thinking about reorganization has been "faddish" in many of its practical applications. Thus, for many years, the emphasis of reorganizers of administration was on "taking administration out of politics." In more recent years, as it was recognized that the resulting "government by board and commission" weakened the position of the chief executive, the theme became to strengthen the executive's

[2] Avery Leiserson, "Science and the Public Life," 241.

power, so he can control the departments under his official supervision. In so doing, the reformers have been attempting to *re*construct that which they attempted to build for many years decades ago.

In addition to these enthusiasms of the moment, public administration was characterized by catch-words such as POSDCORB (planning, organizing, staffing, directing, coordinating, reporting, and budgeting), and by the above-mentioned "principles of public administration." One of the guidelines for administrative operation was that the "span of control" of an executive should not exceed nine or ten to allow him to manage all those reporting to him. While no one would deny that an individual's "span of control" is important, the rule of thumb was formulated (and applied) with little attention to either the administrator's capacities or functions or the type of task of those reporting to him. That one person could easily supervise twenty individuals if each worked well on his own in a small subject area was overlooked, as was the fact that five people might be too many to oversee if constant interaction with them was necessary or the task of each was crucial to the organization. Another principle was "an administrator's authority ought to be commensurate with his responsibility," that is, his recognized power ought to be that power necessary to perform the acts he was expected to carry out within the organization. A third was that an employee should serve only one master, with the implication being that only one master *could* be served. The reality in many organizations is one of contradictory directives or stimuli impinging on many workers; we often talk of the foreman as the "man in the middle" because of pressures from the workers he supposedly supervises and the management to whom he is responsible, or about the conflict between custodial and rehabilitative tasks in a prison. One may serve different masters for different purposes, and pressures may come laterally as well as vertically in the organization. Principles of this type have been labelled "proverbs" to indicate their lack of specificity and their grounding in the "oral tradition" of public administration.[3]

Because formal organization usually precedes organizational activity,[4] much attention has been given to how bureaus, departments, and sections are arranged in an organization. Among the most important early books were ones which dealt with federal departmentalization, and the early texts devoted much space to matters such as the proper placement of the various units in the organization chart of the agency. The different bases for establishing departments (area, clientele and expertise) were explored, and it was argued that the basis for departmentalization had to be consistent: one

[3] Herbert Simon, "The Proverbs of Administration," *Public Administration Review*, VI (1946), 53–67.

[4] Herbert Simon, Donald Smithburg, and Victor Thompson, *Public Administration* (New York, 1951) cite a situation where a federal government agency was established with only the barest of organizational structure. After the organization had functioned for six months, the formal structure was developed to reflect the informal patterns which had developed naturally. This is an exception to the usual procedure.

branch could not be set up on a clientele basis, while another was set up on an area basis. Bureaus were classified as either "line" (operating) units, taking direction from top managers; "staff," to give advice to the principal administrators; or "auxiliary," to provide services to "line" agencies. There has been much argument about whether the functions should be placed under separate multi-member commissions or single administrators responsible to the chief executive and as to what extent individual agencies should be allowed to participate in the work of the auxiliary units. For many years, personnel agencies tended to operate in isolation from the line agencies, simply providing them with the employees they asked for; the line agencies, as a result, felt that they were being provided what was convenient for the auxiliary agency rather than most appropriate for themselves. As a result, we have seen a shift toward greater cooperation between line and auxiliary units, with major auxiliary units having an individual within the line agency to work closely with them.

The relationship between the central office and "the field," a problem which has taken on an additional twist in a federal system because of the need to establish relationships between the national agency field offices and state or local agencies, was also fully explored. Various methods of supervising field offices have been examined, and there has been a great deal of debate about the amount of autonomy for those offices. What is desired is to grant them maximum adaptation to local problems and conditions while central control of policy is maintained, so that they do not adopt policies diametrically opposed to those of headquarters. We have also given attention to the interrelationship between field offices of different agencies and the coordination at the local level (generally unsuccessful in this country), coordination at the national level, and coordination through some intermediate (regional) arrangement have been examined. The French prefectural arrangement, whereby one national government official located at the local level serves as the person through whom all communications (from top to bottom, and bottom to top) for *all* agencies pass, has attracted the attention of some. So has the device of a Department of Local Affairs in which state policy toward local units is coordinated, both for the Governor and the local governments. The concern about headquarters-field relations is part of a greater concern about centralization and decentralization in government. This is more a matter of where important decisions should be made than simply one of organizational structure, because developed field services can exist in an organization although almost all important decisions are passed down "from the top." Solutions proposed for solving problems of headquarters-field relations, coordination, and centralization/decentralization have invariably involved new formal procedures and structures, which tend to draw attention away from the more informal alternative means. For example, it is normally assumed that coordination can come only through "directed rule," that is, a set of orders common to all units to be coordinated. But we do know that coordination can be achieved if all units possess a common purpose and, if not, it can be reached through bargaining and mutual adjustment.

The operation of the so-called "independent regulatory commissions" has

> **Independent Regulatory Commissions.** **Multi-member commissions, varying in size, established by a legislative body to make rules and decide cases with respect to a particular aspect of the economy it is wished to regulate. The terms of the members are staggered and long, to prevent the chief executive from naming a majority of the members quickly; only a bare majority may be from one political party; the members may not be removed by the chief executive if he disagrees with their decisions. Examples of such commissions at the national level are the Federal Communications Commission (FCC), the Interstate Commerce Commission (ICC), and the National Labor Relations Board (NLRB).**

consumed much attention, in part because of their crucial role in government regulation of the economy, although their placement in the allegedly tripartite structure of American government has been a source of confusion. They perform quasi-judicial and quasi-legislative functions, the former by deciding cases, the latter by issuing rules, and carry out work more narrowly defined as administrative, such as the routine issuing of licenses. This confusion has led to many demands for reform, including proposals that the judicial functions be placed in an administrative court and the rule-making and administrative tasks be assigned to regular cabinet-level "line" departments. These commissions, the "headless fourth branch of government," originally established to embody the "public interest," have been roundly criticized for ossification, for the increasing "judicialization" of their operation, and for being captives of the interests they were to regulate. That the last would occur is hardly surprising in view of the agency's day-to-day contact with those regulated and the lack of organization behind the public's (consumers') interest. This suggests the *symbolic* importance of the commissions and their actions. Their existence reassures the (unrepresented) public that their views are being taken into account, even when observers might suggest this is not in fact being done. There are some who go so far as to suggest that the establishment of the commissions was carried out with the view toward allowing private interests to achieve (with the sanction of government policy) what they might not have been allowed to do openly, but this view appears to be based on reading a purpose into the establishment of a unit on the basis of the results achieved. A variety of studies have shown that such agencies are not independent of the legislative branch, which establishes them, controls their structure and jurisdiction, and provides the funds with which they operate.

Receiving less attention but potentially important are government corporations, of which the Tennessee Valley Authority (TVA) is perhaps the best known. They are usually (but not always) established to handle certain revenue-producing functions of the government. They are relatively independent units, although they must rely on Congress for major financial support; once these corporations are in operation, their managers are free to run them as they see fit, although they must report periodically to the legislature on their activities and the General Accounting Office audits their books.

While bureaus, departments, and regulatory commissions are permanent parts of the government's structure, with an on-going identity, there are several types of units less formal, less permanent, more *ad hoc* in nature but nonetheless extremely important for the government's operation. These would include the "task forces" which often study a subject and produce proposals for legislative study or action; advisory groups through which a government department is able to tap the resources of individuals who do not want to work full-time for the government but who are not unwilling to have a working relationship with it, and interdepartmental committees established to work on problems which cut across jurisdictional lines. At the local level, the "civic committee" or "study group" on a specific problem not only brings free (i.e., unpaid) expertise within the government's reach, but serves functions such as identifying lines of opposition to executive proposals, drawing fire away from political officials, and legitimating proposals for which the chief executive might not win approval if he espoused them directly.

Administrative reorganization has received considerable attention in its own right. Suggestions for rearranging the federal government have been made almost constantly since 1937, when the President's Committee on Administrative Management (composed of three leading public administration specialists) was formed. Interest and effort reached their high points with the work of the two Commissions on the Reorganization of the Executive Branch, or Hoover Commissions (1947–1949 and 1953–1955). While we probably learned more about the operation of parts of the executive branch from the reports of the task forces and other staff of the two Hoover Commissions than was accomplished in terms of meaningful reforms enacted, the Commissions were extremely important, and have been granted the flattery of imitation: almost every such group at the state level is referred to as a "little Hoover Commission." Through the efforts of the Commission, and through continuing authority which Congress has placed in the President (subject to Congressional veto by resolution), much reorganization has taken place, and we have seen the addition of a number of Cabinet-level departments in recent years (Defense to replace War and Navy; Health, Education, and Welfare; Housing and Urban Development; Transportation).

At the state level, efforts to achieve reorganization to improve the Governor's powers have encountered stronger resistance, partly because state interests were well entrenched, and the Governor operated from a position of less initial strength than the President had. In addition, legislators have been more jealous of their prerogatives, and have felt they could oversee (and control) administration more effectively if the Governor did not acquire power through such reorganizations. Despite this resistance, and the centrifugal forces in the executive branch, reorganizations have occurred and their result *has* been greater power for the Governor, through tools such as better staffing, an executive budget, and elimination of some boards and commissions or their consolidation with regular executive departments.

The difficulty of reorganization at the state level has made even clearer what was evident at the national level—that the reorganizers, in concentrating on what has been called "bureau-shuffling" and "administrative aesthetics" (producing a "pretty" organization chart), had neglected the political aspects of the problem. This explains why at least some of their work went for naught when legislatures, where interest groups brought pressure, refused to enact reorganization proposals. Appeals to "economy and efficiency" did not attract enough support to offset the intense opposition of those who felt their interests would be negatively affected. This suggests, among other things, that where the various functions of government are placed administratively becomes quite crucial to their performance. That reorganizations can have major policy implications is shown by the formation of the Department of Defense from the former Departments of War and Navy; interservice rivalry, although it did not vanish, was affected, and the reorganization enhanced the ability of the civilians at the top of DOD to control the military. Location of a new program in an existing agency may mean its failure from the start because agency interests do not wish to see it thrive; at the same time, if given independence, the program may falter for lack of support from client groups, which an existing agency usually has. Despite the importance of such matters, relatively little attention has been given to the birth and death of organizations; almost all has been devoted to fully-functioning agencies.

SPECIALTY "TOOLS"

Among those aspects of the study of public administration which receive particular in-depth attention are administrative law, planning, O & M (organization and management),[5] budgeting and finance, and personnel. The last two are studied by those who intend to enter public administration as a vocation, and a considerable literature has grown up concerning each. Administrative law developed largely as law of procedure for administrative agencies, although it has other aspects, including the manner in which agency decisions are reviewed in the courts and doctrines the courts have developed to limit the executive's power. The subject has become extremely complex, and is now more often taught in the law schools than in Departments of Political Science. O & M is concerned with internal planning, with the running of the organization itself. Current interest in automation and the use of ADP

[5] Waldo has remarked: "Organization is the anatomy, management the physiology, of administration. Organization is the structure; management is functioning." Dwight Waldo, *The Study of Public Administration* (Garden City, 1955), p. 6.

and EDP (*a*utomatic and *e*lectronic data processing, respectively), for such matters as inventory control, controlling freeway traffic, or determining the most efficient bus routes, falls into the O & M category.

Personnel is generally taught as a technical specialty, revolving around such topics as position classification (how to categorize jobs and classify them in terms of levels of pay) and methods of recruitment and selection for the civil service. In-service training, as well as pre-induction training, has received increased emphasis by those who recognize the need for many employees to retool themselves or to acquaint themselves with new developments, and the United States Civil Service Commission has been doing much to develop mid-career training programs. Of broader importance is the question of *where* to find individuals to fill positions effectively. Indicative of concern with this problem has been research on recruitment and retention of "political executives," the top-ranking officials including under secretaries, assistant secretaries, and deputy administrators, who guide the work of major government departments. In securing these individuals, the President and his subordinates use methods outside party patronage channels, with varying recruitment patterns being used in and by different departments. "In and out" employees who move back and forth between government and private employment have been a valuable alternative to career employees. Concern over perceived inadequacies of those attracted to government service, at all levels, has led to work on the "image" of the federal service. Research in this area has shown that the image is not uniformly negative, being better at the lower levels, where the government has less difficulty in obtaining people, and worse at the higher levels, where the "problem" exists in severest form. There is also interest in the "representativeness" of the bureaucracy, the degree to which those holding government employment resemble the public in terms of social and economic characteristics.

Behind any work in personnel is some philosophy, often implicit rather than explicit, of the type of public administrator preferred. While there are a variety of alternatives, the three principal types appear to be administrative generalists, those trained in administration; professional specialists, trained in a specific subject-matter; and administrative specialists, trained in administering a particular subject-matter. The latter is the most recent, and is represented by such occupations as prison administrator, hospital administrator, research administrator or city manager. The latter field suggests quite well the trend toward professionalism in government, as does the Chief Administrative Officer (CAO) used in some strong mayor-council governments. The tendency in some cities with council-manager forms has been to turn most important matters over to the manager because he is a "professional administrator," without the recognition that biases inherent in his professional training will be reflected in his method of administration and that the council will be the ones ultimately held responsible if the manager should perform in ways the public doesn't appreciate.

In most formal programs of training for public administration positions, we have prepared administrative generalists, although it is often the subject-matter professional who receives the top administrative positions. Our administrative generalists are usually trained in programs the content of which is still heavily centered on personnel, budgeting, and O & M. They are clearly *administrative* generalists, not "amateur" generalists in the style of the British, whose administrators are drawn from the elite universities with "liberal arts" backgrounds; but they are also not trained with the passage of specific examinations in mind, as is done in still other countries. They are also not trained with any specific job in mind, and may be expected to perform either staff or line functions, just as the armed forces rotate their officers through both staff and line jobs, even though a person good at one may not necessarily be good at another. Their training as public administrators has not included much in the way of social science materials; this means that there is an over-emphasis on rational procedures and on "monocratic" organizations (where activity is carried out from the "top down"), at the expense of more pragmatic problem-solving methods borrowing on new theories about organizational behavior.[6]

Within the field of personnel, a number of topics with broad political ramifications exist. Among these is the possible formation of a career civil service among high-level government employees. Some claim this proposal, which conflicts with the Jacksonian idea that every man was as good as any other in performing government work and also with the current notion of a "representative bureaucracy," would establish an administrative elite. Other issues are whether the merit system should extend to include high-level administrative officials now selected through patronage; loyalty-security programs; implementation of codes of ethics for government employees, particularly to avoid "conflict-of-interest" situations; and restrictions on political participa-

> **Conflict of Interest.**   A situation in which a government official (whether elected or appointed), by taking an action in his official capacity, would affect individuals or, more particularly, businesses with whom he has some connection in his capacity as a private citizen. An official owning stock in a company requesting a contract from the government agency for which he works would be in such a situation.

tion of government employees. The federal Hatch Act, embodying such restrictions, resulted in part from a desire to protect government workers from the "lug" (compulsory contribution) exacted by political parties as a price of continuing employment, and in part from a desire to protect the public from overt political favoritism. Enforcement of restrictions in order to achieve these values appears to many to be an unfair limitation on government employees' rights. Similarly, the public's desire to have uninterrupted service from government agencies conflicts with the alleged right of government employees to organize, bargain collectively, and, where they feel it neces-

[6] Victor A. Thompson, "Bureaucracy and Innovation," paper presented at American Political Science Association meetings, New York, 1966; pp. 11–12.

sary, to strike to gain better pay and improved working conditions—and increasing attention is being paid to this important aspect of personnel. That state statutory limitations on the right to strike are often meaningless, particularly in the case of employees such as teachers who cannot be immediately or easily replaced, is now becoming clear.

Budgeting has immensely technical aspects. These include the proper way of preparing budget estimates so that a central budget agency can compare them and assist the chief executive in deciding budget policy, decisions about the form the budget should take so that it might be a planning tool, and various methods of presenting the budget or of collecting revenues, which shade over into the area of public finance, which is shared with economists. Thus we have had arguments about the time it takes from the beginning of the preparation of agency estimates to the time appropriations are enacted (at the present time a minimum of eighteen months at the national level). Whether budgets should be set up in the older line-item fashion, which severely restricts the individual administrator by decreasing the discretionary actions he can take, or in "performance" or "program" form, or whether operating and capital budgets (the latter for buildings) should be separated, are all oft-debated. They are not, it should be stressed, sterile "academic" questions. The form of the budget may magnify or decrease the apparent size of the budget, as occurred with President Johnson's budget for fiscal year 1969, or a budget deficit [7] (which, as we know, upsets many legislators) or may facilitate or make more difficult comparisons between various programs. Thus, with information presented in terms of numbers of secretaries or janitors to be hired and numbers of boxes of chalk to be purchased, it is difficult to visualize the end result, although it may be easier for an accountant to talk in these terms. To talk in terms of the number of patients cured, the number of children graduated, or the number of miles of streets paved, as one does with the performance budget, makes the end-product far easier to see, but may require a reorientation in thinking on the part of the preparer of the budget. Such a budget also requires prior setting up of major objectives by top executives, who often do not wish to make such difficult decisions. Thus, they tend to allow budgets to be developed, as they have been, from the "bottom up," that is, agglomerated from requests of individual agencies, rather than from the "top down." If goals are not stated prior to the process of collecting budget estimates, there will still be goals—the ones implicit in what is proposed in dollar figures by individual agencies.

The budget process, in which decisions are made over what programs to support, and in what amount, has generally been portrayed as a highly rational process in which the benefits and costs of each program are fully weighed, with ultimate decisions about their respective value being made. Recent studies suggest that this is not so, and that budgeting is marginal and

---

[7] The administrative budget (the one normally used) has shown a larger deficit than the national income accounts budget (which shows income and expenditures from the trust funds such as Social Security).

incremental rather than programmatic and comprehensive. Providing esti-mates for only a year at a time, instead of over a longer projection period, reinforces the incremental character of the process. Warnings have even been raised that attempts to justify the validity of each program at each bud-get period will only increase conflict, while decisions dealing only with in-creases or decreases from an understood amount or proportion of the budget are likely to decrease conflict. In this connection, the vast amount of what Victor Thompson calls the *dramaturgy* [8] of the budget process has been stressed, with each agency increasing its budget proposals because of antici-pated cuts and with the budget reviewer (and the legislature) cutting, both to eliminate the "padding" but to show relevant publics how effective a job is being done of saving money.

PPBS (Program-Planning-Budgeting System), initiated in the Depart-ment of Defense in the early 1960's and carried out by electronic data proc-essing equipment, is an example of a method supposed to provide more ra-tional judgments in the process of selecting programs to be carried out. Each agency is supposed to spell out its program goals clearly, examine possible alternatives for reaching those goals, and then apply cost-benefit analysis to

> **Cost-Benefit Analysis.   A procedure or procedures in which the costs of a program are weighed against the supposed benefits, resulting in a ratio, to help in ascertaining whether the project should be undertaken.** *Cost-effectiveness analysis* **determines whether a project, already undertaken, has achieved its purpose.**

the alternatives. It may have been successful in DOD because men-and-machine packages (the forces and those needed to operate them) are rela-tively easy to assemble. PPBS can't tell what range of forces (from conven-tional armies to nuclear bombers) to have available, although it can *help* in producing the "mix" by making comparisons easier. It also cannot tell whether or not to use the various forces in places like Vietnam. In other words, if cost-benefit figures are worked out, no system like PPBS can tell us whether to spend money on bombs or Head Start education because it can-not supply final values. It also may not be able to attach cost-benefit figures to all considerations involved in a program, such as an office-holder's losing of-fice or an organization's claim to existence. Some feel PPBS is no more than a fad or simply another name for the rational-comprehensive search and evalua-tion techniques which administrative specialists have been advocating by one name or another, for many years.

Not only have we seen the budget as something less than the rational comprehensive instrument it was thought to be, but more attention has been focused on it as a tool for the chief executive to use both in attempting to control executive departments under him and strengthening his position with the legislature. With respect to the former, the Budget Bureau helps control spending once money is appropriated by allocating funds to the

[8] See Victor Thompson, *Modern Organization* (New York, 1961).

agencies, to prevent their exhausting funds before the end of the year; it also assists the President in decisions concerning impounding of appropriated funds (funds the President chooses not to spend). Usually considered along with budgeting is the audit function. The General Accounting Office, although an arm of the Congress, has been scrutinized by scholars of public administration, who see auditing as an administrative task. They were particularly fascinated by the "settlement" function, by which GAO approved expenditures (after departmental finance officers had done so) for legality. Initially, such work was centralized and involved a staff of 14,000 people. GAO has moved in the direction of spot-checking, and has decentralized to the field and to working closely with individual agencies.

Planning, which to some involves major policy considerations and large doses of economics, has often been viewed by its principal adherents as a technical task. It is most often associated with land-use control at the municipal level, where it becomes a question of classifying parcels of land for residential, business, or commercial use, and providing for amenities such as parks, as well as locations for government buildings, such as city halls and schools. Planners, like those in the profession of city management, often lose sight of broader human aspects of problems with which they deal because of a concentration of numbers, figures, blocs of land and amounts of traffic to be moved. Planning decisions, like reorganization proposals, have political ramifications, for example, when middle-class suburbanites insist on zoning enforcement to keep businesses out of homes or gasoline stations from their neighborhoods, or when Negroes object to urban renewal as "Negro removal" because of inadequate provision for relocation of the dispossessed. Unless the political ramifications are taken into account, the work of the planners is likely not to be accepted in the community. Planning in the larger sense does exist, for example, in the work of the Council of Economic Advisers, the Office of Emergency Planning, and the National Security Council, but it does not receive as much direct attention as it did in the late 1930's and during World War II.

THE CHIEF EXECUTIVE

In large part because of their political importance, governmental units' chief executives—particularly the President and Governors—receive much attention from students of public administration. While some feel these officials are primarily "political" rather than "administrative," the study of their office and work is usually considered to be within the bailiwick of public administration, although proportionately more attention is given to the political aspects of their jobs than is true of many other aspects of the executive branch.

The President of the United States, considered by some to be the single most powerful government official in the world,[9] has been the focus of much research, which has resulted in some classic studies. How the President's powers have increased has attracted the interest of both historians and political scientists, who explain it largely in terms of the increasing functions of the federal government and continuing American involvement in world affairs, as well as the default of Congress in various spheres. The varying roles the President plays ("the many hats he wears") almost invariably draw comment; thus we know that he is not only chief executive but also commander-in-chief, head of his political party, principal diplomatic official, and originator of much legislation.

The way in which he uses his power has recently come under scrutiny. Richard Neustadt (advisor and staff assistant to President Kennedy) shows, in his book *Presidential Power*, that the President's power is neither automatic nor unlimited, and that he must both shepherd its use and augment what he has upon his election, when he may appear to have a "mandate" to carry out certain programs. If the President could control *when* he made decisions, he would be able to plan with some surety when he could use the reserve of "good will" and political power he had accumulated, but often he is not able to control the flow of crucial decisions, and they arrive for his decision when he would least like to have them appear. The pressure such crises present is what leads to the remark made about politicians in general, "If you can't stand the heat, get out of the kitchen." The President must act *as if he is President*, at least occasionally asserting himself, if he is to be effective. The example of President Eisenhower provides a picture of how a President should *not* act if he is to be authoritative. Whatever inherent strengths the position appears to have can be used or dissipated depending on the uses to which they are put. Among weapons which can be used in this effort are the President's press conference and his general relations with the mass media.

That there is a wide variety of Presidential styles, and that these styles are related to the President's programmatic desires, is also clear. Thus, "Silent Cal" Coolidge's mode of operation, however much decried by advocates of a strong Presidency, was ideal for his program. James MacGregor Burns has portrayed the variety of styles in terms of three basic models. These are the Madisonian, based on limited Presidential powers, bargaining among coalitions, and the idea of the separation of powers, thus implying deadlock; the Jeffersonian, utilizing strong leadership and responsible parties; and the one Burns says is used by most "strong" Presidents, the Hamiltonian, in which the President, in a highly personal way, works his will in the interstices of the Madisonian model.[10]

The official strengths of the President are often compared with those of

[9] Some consider Russian officials to be more powerful, particularly when a single dictator like Stalin is considered. However, to the extent that a "plural dictatorship" exists, based largely on positions in the Communist Party, the evaluation of the President presented here is often agreed upon.

[10] The models are spelled out in greater detail in James MacGregor Burns, *Presidential Government: The Crucible of Leadership* (Boston, 1965), pp. 108–115.

governors. The latter invariably come off weaker by comparison, with the exception of their "item veto," which the President does not possess. Governors find themselves elected on a long ballot, so that many officials on whom their program depends are responsible directly to the electorate rather than dependent on the Governor; they find powers distributed among many boards and commissions, which can be controlled only with great difficulty, if at all; they often serve short (two-year) terms, or cannot succeed themselves in office. Since the passage of the Twenty-Second Amendment to the United States Constitution, limiting the President to two full terms (or ten years), the Governors and the President are more nearly even in this respect. If comparisons are extended, mayors have even fewer powers. In all except "strong mayor" cities, the mayor, who may even have been chosen by his colleagues on the council rather than by direct election, may be no more than presiding officer for the city council, without powers to appoint administrators.

The most important executive official at the local level may be an appointed instead of an elected one. In the council-manager form of government, the city manager is a full-time employee with responsibility for directing all of a city's administration, although he is responsible to the council, at whose pleasure he serves. The superintendent of schools in a school district is in the same position with respect to the school board which has selected him. But both the manager and the superintendent are full-time while their "directing boards" are part-time, giving them a near-monopoly of information on which policy recommendations might be based; and both are considered to be professionals, who as a result may receive much deference from the laymen supposedly setting policy for them. Ideally, the council (or the school board) sets policy, while the manager (or superintendent) merely carries it out, but *in fact* the manager and superintendent may both recommend policy readily assented to by the council or school board, and implement such policy as well, making them far more important than their positions might look on paper.

Attention to the organizational framework in which the chief executive operates, called "the institutionalized chief executive," has been concentrated at the national level. We have seen the Bureau of the Budget grow from an agency which simply channeled financial requests to the Congress to one which assists in preparing the President's program, "clears" all legislative requests from executive agencies, and monitors the bills passed by Congress so that the President can intelligently consider them for approval or veto. Agencies similar to the Bureau of the Budget, often called Departments of Finance and Administration, have been developed in many states. The chief executive's problem in obtaining control over his own administration and his need to do something in competition with the legislature for control of individual departments is what gives rise to such agencies. Many pressures drive administrators in the direction of the legislature, among them the legislature's power of the purse and the assistance they receive from client groups through the legislature, but a recent study has suggested that state administrators prefer independence to control by either the Governor or the state legislature.[11] The executive branch is certainly not monolithic nor the chief executive's control that of a totalitarian despot, even if he wanted it to be that way. The executive may have to spend much time mediating and arbitrating within his own executive branch, limiting considerably his ability to *lead*, and he often is at the mercy of the "permanent government," the bureaucrats who continue from one administration to the next and whose vested interests serve as a constraint on any chief executive who would move in the direction of new programs. That he is the man at the top of the ladder is what brings so many decisions to the chief executive, because people want his approval or want to evade making difficult decisions, leading to the famous sign on President Harry Truman's desk: "The buck stops here."

Efforts to increase the staff available to the President, beginning with the report of the President's Committee on Administrative Management established by President Franklin Roosevelt in 1937 (and reporting in 1939), have been pushed forward by reform-oriented political scientists. The President's staff has expanded to the point where we must distinguish between the White House Office and the Executive Office of the President. The former is composed of the staff assistants to the President, allegiant to the man (the *President*), while the latter, in theory allegiant to the office (the *Presidency*), contains such agencies as the Bureau of the Budget, the National Security Council, the Office of Emergency Planning, the Council of Economic Advisers, the Office of Science and Technology, and the Office of Economic Opportunity. Some have indicated concern that the Presidency has become so institutionalized, so bureaucratized, that it will smother rather than assist the President. Those showing this concern also have shown an interest in the Cabinet, which Fenno calls a "secondary" institution, that is, one operating in the shadow and as a reflection of the President.[12] A President like Eisenhower who felt more at home with a well-defined staff arrangement provided the Cabinet with its own secretariat and some meaningful functions, while other Presidents, such as Franklin Roosevelt, Kennedy, and Lyndon Johnson, have preferred to operate with either fluid staff arrangements (FDR, Kennedy) or staff highly personally allegiant (Johnson). Also, each President tends to have a set of informal advisers, both in and out of government, whether called a "Brain Trust" or "kitchen cabinet." All this leaves the Cabinet with little important work to perform. The problems of using the Cabinet as a coordinating agency for the federal government suggest that it is "secondary" in another sense. Members of the Cabinet are at one and the same time members of the Cabinet as an institution and heads of departments, with their employees' interests and the interests of the agency to defend; in a conflict between the two, the latter is likely to be predominant, not the former.

The shifts in such matters from one chief executive to the next show the

[11] Deil S. Wright, "Executive Leadership in State Administration," *Midwest Journal of Political Science*, XI (1967), 1–26.

[12] Richard Fenno, *The President's Cabinet* (Cambridge, 1959).

importance of orderly transitions between administrations in a world where crises will often not wait until a new President is settled in office. Also of considerable importance has been the problem of succession in office in the case of Presidential death or disability, prompted most recently by President Kennedy's assassination and leading to the Twenty-Fifth Amendment, which allows the new President to nominate a Vice President in such a situation and provides more thoroughly for procedures to be followed in cases of Presidential disability. Because of crisis possibilities, a number of other reforms have been suggested, including the election of the President and *eleven* Vice Presidents to avoid emphasis on only one man.[13] This reform and others derive from the "lonely President" idea, that, in the end it is the President and *only* the President who makes decisions. This view encourages fear of one-man rule; from an analytical perspective, it also discourages generalizations about Presidents by stressing the unique way in which each operates.

Not only are executive-legislative relations treated in terms of matters like the budget, but they are also examined in broader perspective, as noted in Chapter 12. The relative strengths of the two institutions receive particular attention. The predominance of the executive branch (and the Presidency), clearest in foreign affairs and (more broadly) national security policy, has been shown not to extend to all other aspects of policy, especially domestic. It should be noted that the "enlargement of the Presidency" need not be at the expense of Congress, despite a continuing presumption to the contrary. Thus, the growth of the Presidency may come from an increase in government's responsibilities. In examining "mixed legislatures," with each house controlled by a different party, and the situation where both houses of the legislature are in the hands of the party opposite to that of the chief executive, scholars have cast much light on one of the important factors which affects the chief executive's power to achieve his ends, and have also shown that political party considerations cannot be divorced from the conduct of the chief executive's position.

INTERGOVERNMENTAL RELATIONS

The subject of intergovernmental relations (national-state, state-local, national-local, and intra-level) is not simply an administrative topic. For example, formal theories of federalism have been developed and the political issues involved in federalism, the "friction-points," have been examined. However, much of what attention has been paid to the subject has been to its administrative aspect. Earlier discussion of headquarters-field relationships and coordination of field activities may have already suggested this. Although the "politics of federalism" or the "politics of state-local relations"

[13] Herman Finer, *The Presidency: Crisis and Regeneration: An Essay in Possibilities* (Chicago, 1960).

receive attention in other areas, for example, public law because of the differing criminal procedure standards the Supreme Court has required of the states and the national government, the structural-administrative aspects bulk quite large.[14] This can be seen in discussions on conflict and cooperation between various governmental units: it is invariably the formal arrangements, such as the Governors' Conference (despite its considerable political ramifications) or the Council of State Governments, or the interstate compact, which come to the fore. It should also be noted that intergovernmental relations have been studied largely within the context of the American experience only. The variations on federalism in Canada, where the state governments have delegated powers and the central government the reserved powers, the reverse of the United States' arrangement, and in Germany, with its "administrative federalism," have been examined, but we still tend to concentrate on America.

The growth of the national government, particularly since the "New Deal" period of the 1930's, has directed much attention to the "proper" relationship between the national (usually called "federal" [15]) government and state governments, as well as to the increasing number of direct federal-local ties. One question is whether the national government's growth has been at the states' expense. Public finance studies of the relative expenditures made by the two levels of government, both overall and for specific objects, contribute to the answer. While findings vary depending on the period of time taken into account and the subjects of expenditure considered, they generally show a growth of state and local expenditures (and government activity) greater than that at the national level, particularly if federal defense spending is excluded. While much federal government growth can be attributed to state government unwillingness to undertake programs wanted by growing urban constituencies, as well as to inability of state and local governments to finance welfare expenditures during the Great Depression, it is not certain that all the federal government growth has been at the expense of these other levels.

Examination, particularly by the late Morton Grodzins and the Advisory Commission on Intergovernmental Relations (ACIR), established as a result of the work of the Kestnbaum Commission during President Eisenhower's administration, has shown that, instead of a "layer-cake" arrangement of clearly differentiated governmental levels, we have a "marble cake" of mixed functions. The levels clearly have become intermixed, and vertical integration in specific programs often exceeds horizontal integration at either na-

---

[14] They are also taken up here simply because this seems the most appropriate place. Some scholars consider intergovernmental relations a separate field, and there are separate courses taught in the subject. For the purposes of this volume, however, it has seemed best to treat the administrative aspects here, and other aspects usually considered to be within intergovernmental relations, such as local politics, elsewhere.

[15] Technically, we should talk of a "federal" *system,* including both national and state governments, rather than the "federal" *government,* but common usage is based on the latter.

tional or state level, because professionals working on subject-matter programs (such as public welfare) often prefer to work with other professionals
in their own field, at whatever level of government employed, than with individuals in other fields employed at the same governmental level. Often used
in the last few years is the concept of "creative federalism," a pragmatic attempt to place government programs at the governmental level where they
can be carried out most effectively coupled with efforts to strengthen the
state and local levels so that they can better carry out programs. Special
units, not falling neatly in the tri-level governmental arrangement with
which we are most familiar, have also been discussed in connection with the
question of which area is the best one to use for purposes of administration
and as remedies to perceived problems. Regional governments, of which the
Tennessee Valley Authority (TVA) is sometimes taken as a model, and interstate compacts for limited functions such as education (e.g., the Western
Interstate Compact for Higher Education [WICHE]) or transportation (e.g.,
the Port of New York Authority) have been suggested, although the political
obstacles to their implementation are almost insuperable because of the resistance of officials from existing units to any new entity to which loyalties
might be transferred.

While federal-state relations are at the heart of our federal system, scholars have devoted more attention to state-local relations, perhaps because
governmental reform efforts, such as merit employment, originated at the
state and local levels before being exported to the national level. While only
a few courses on Intergovernmental Relations exist, almost every political
science department has a State and Local Government course, usually part of
its introductory sequence. Until recently, these nuts-and-bolts courses have
dealt heavily with the legal framework and administrative structure of state-
local relations and local government.

Administrative relationships between state and local levels take place
within the legal boundaries established by state constitutions and judicial
interpretation of state and local powers, explored in the field of public law.
For example, the amount of flexibility allowed the local government in the
choice of structure is determined by the state constitution as implemented by
state legislative action. These local government forms, particularly in the
municipality, have been examined at great length by political scientists,
whose approach has been, as elsewhere, basically structural. The mayor-
council, council-manager, and commission forms of government—plus the
strong mayor, weak mayor, and strong mayor-with-chief administrative officer versions—have been examined at length, so that we know a great deal
about the basic ideal form each is supposed to take. (Forms for governing
other units of government, such as counties or special districts, have also
been examined, but less intensively, in part because there are fewer variations in each case.)

More recently, there has been added to this administrative examination a
more political one, which tells where each kind of government is more likely

to be found. Council-manager government (the current "fad and fashion") is more frequently found in newer, rapidly-growing, wealthier communities of under 500,000 in newer areas of the country (for example, far more in the West than in New England), particularly in the suburbs; while the mayor-council form still remains the most frequently used, with particular use in large cities with major political cleavages, and the commission form (the fad before council-manager) seems on the way out. "Political" analyses of the role of the city manager, who in theory is supposed to be a political neuter and who simply carries out the will of the city council, have also appeared. These recent studies show us that to be successful, a city manager must be finely attuned politically, that is, quite aware of the political ramifications of his and the council's acts. We also know he may become a political football in fights between factions of the council. The study of certain formal aspects of public administration has thus been supplemented in a valuable way, which has had an impact on the training of city managers. Originally engineers, now they are generally exposed to the social sciences in addition to more narrowly technical material, although some are still "local boys" without professional training instead of professional "outsiders."

These studies have shown that formal structures are seldom neutral in their impact and that various groups are likely to prefer certain forms to others. The city manager idea, like the commission form before it, appeals to those, like businessmen, who prefer "professionalism" and "efficiency and economy" in government. The at-large council elections which usually accompany the council-manager plan also seem to benefit the downtown merchant at the expense of groups either geographically concentrated or not well-organized on a city-wide basis, such as labor unions or minority ethnic groups. The separate school district, not responsible to the regular municipal government for either policy or revenue, appeals to the professional educator, who does not have to compete directly with other municipal functions for a share of the taxpayer's dollar and who can usually have a greater say in policy-making with respect to education than other forms would allow him to have. That formal structures, in addition to favoring some interests over others, may be insufficient to hold units together is shown by attention to the question, "Are cities governable?", raised particularly in connection with our very largest cities like New York. We know from our study of political parties that it was the party organization, the "machine," which provided the weak mayor-council form of government with its cohesion, not the structure itself.

Another area of state and local government which has received much attention from the structural specialists has been the problem of the metropolitan area. The analysts who have been called in to make major studies of these large conglomerations of many governmental units have often operated, like the big-city newspapers, on the assumption that the multiplicity of local governments was pathological and that what was needed was a rearrangement of local governments into a "super-government" encompassing the whole area or, at the least, some area-wide government administering some "area-wide" functions. Thus we were to move from one extreme, too much fragmentation, to the other, no autonomy for individual communities. The analysts failed to recognize that a variety of publics exist within a metropolitan area, and that not all (or even many) are metropolitan-area wide in their scope. They also neglected the political problem of convincing residents of small suburbs of the claim that such a big government would be more "efficient" and would provide better services than they were already receiving. This led to surprise and shock when, in city after city, plans for reorganization were voted down. Such plans have been accepted (in the United States) only in Dade County, Florida (Miami); Baton Rouge Parish, Louisiana; Nashville, Tennessee; and, most recently, the Jacksonville, Florida, area, with lesser consolidation in a few other locations.[16] We now have a number of case studies of what happened to the proposals in several of these communities, material describing the formalities in these places, and catalogs of the forces "pro" and the forces "con" such change, as well as much information about the metropolitan areas themselves. We can still probably say more about the specifics of what has happened in individual metropolitan areas than we can by way of generalization, although recent efforts to view central city-suburban and inter-suburban battles in terms of conflict theory or in the language of diplomatic relations have moved us in a more theoretical direction.

Other local problems discussed by those interested in administrative reorganization of local governments include methods for annexing land to cities, particularly in the unincorporated urban fringe; arranging contracts so that some governments can supply services to other units, as under California's "Lakewood Plan," where a county supplies services to its smaller municipalities; and limiting incorporation of new governments to prevent the birth of non-viable units. The formation of vast numbers of special districts, and the consolidation of many school districts, where the numerical reduction in the last twenty-five years has been quite impressive, have drawn particular attention in terms of such questions as why such units are formed and what problems are caused by their geographical overlapping. In all of these cases, the political and social ramifications of the problems have received less attention than the administrative formalities. This occurs despite findings that suburbs are more frequently annexed when the central city is of higher social status and that the "social differential" between central cities and suburbs is a more important factor affecting annexation than the relative permissiveness of the annexation law.[17] The formality is only a necessary, not a sufficient, condition for local government reorganization, because without political activity, the goal will not be achieved even where formally possible.

[16] In Canada, Toronto and Winnipeg have adopted federation-type municipalities for their metropolitan areas, and Toronto's has served as an ideal for many American metropolitan reformers.

[17] Thomas R. Dye, "Urban Political Integration: Conditions Associated with Annexation in American Cities," *Midwest Journal of Political Science*, VIII (1964), 430–446.

ADMINISTRATIVE AND ORGANIZATIONAL BEHAVIOR

The behavioral approach to political science did not pass public administration by, and it seems to have made off with at least part of the field, under the heading of "organization theory" or "organizational behavior," earlier called "administrative behavior." Organization theory, as its name suggests, is a highly theoretically-oriented subject, and in many respects is the most highly formalized of any of the fields related to political science. The emphasis is less on statistical presentation than on mathematical models of a highly sophisticated variety. Even when the models are not powerful, the stress is on theory-building. The development of "organizational behavior" stemmed not only from the general growth of the behavioral mood in political science, but also from the "human relations" approach to management. Prior to this, those seeking to improve organizational efficiency had concentrated on "scientific management" techniques, such as time-and-motion study, with which Frederick Taylor's name is associated. In "Taylorism," the worker was almost considered an inanimate object. It was presumed that if physical and mechanical conditions were properly adjusted and each job broken down into its basic components and effectively reassembled, production would rise. During studies at General Electric's Hawthorne plant, workers being studied not only increased their production when the lighting where they worked was improved, but *continued* their higher production later. The first finding had not been surprising, and followed from the researchers' assumptions; the latter finding was puzzling. Analysts finally decided that the workers were reacting less to the improved lighting conditions than to the attention paid to them. This finding touched off a whole new revolution in both private and public management as to means, although not ends: attention was to be paid to the needs of the workers, and productivity would thus rise.

While the "human relations" approach has been as badly overdone and as incompetently applied in some circumstances as was the scientific management approach before it, it did have an impact on the *study* of administration. Scholars became aware—in fact, they had found out at Hawthorne— that organizational structure and mechanics were insufficient to explain the output and action of organization. The behavior of individuals had to be taken into account, as well. The New Deal and World War II government participation of many political scientists interested in public administration heightened their awareness of the sterility of an approach which dealt only with organization charts and charters without an examination of what went on inside those organizations. Attention to behavior, or at least a less dogmatic and rigid approach restricting itself to organizational form and structure, thus came to characterize the field of public administration earlier than in other subfields of the discipline.

The new approach was not without its drawbacks. While it was applied to *public* administration at an early date, much of the writing was about organization in general, without regard to its public or private context. This was salutary to the extent that such a view emphasized similarities between public and private organizations, because it reduced the polarity between public administration and business administration, the field in which private organization had been discussed. However, to the extent context did affect organization, a major omission was being made:

> It is in its political character that public administration tends to differ most decisively from private administration, and to vary most notably from one country, or even one jurisdiction within a country, to another. . . . Public administrators as a group are far more deeply affected than private administrators in making decisions by large, complex, often vaguely defined, social objectives and by the need to adjust to a highly complex environment. . . .[18]

Among the particular topics which fall within the scope of administrative behavior is the role of the individual in the organization, explored from both sociological and psychological perspectives. The perspectives an individual brings to an organization (called "premises" by Simon, *et al.*) have an important impact on the way he views what occurs within that organization. In examination of these premises, particular emphasis is given to how individuals come to join specific organizations. From the organizational perspective, recruitment of those with values congruent with those of the organization [19] is important for goal-attainment, yet "costs" incurred must not become so high as to make the organization unprofitable, whether in financial terms or simply when measured against other types of gains in organizational performance. "Self-selection" helps solve the problem; individuals often gravitate toward organizations with which their personal views are compatible. While an organization may be simply a reflection of the (pre-organizational) personal goals of its members, many students of the subject feel that the values brought to an organization may in fact be altered by participation within the organization, or may simply prove irrelevant, in some cases producing an "organization man" who takes total direction from the organization. Many requirements made of an individual within an organization fall within his "zone of indifference," that is, compliance will not conflict with his personal values.[20] Other requirements may necessitate his removing himself from the organization, changing his values, or at least making some temporary alteration. To the extent an organization's members cannot control the stimuli

---

[18] Harold Stein, "On Public Administration and Public Administration Cases," *Essays on the Case Method in Public Administration,* ed. Edwin A. Bock (New York, 1961), p. 9.

[19] The problem of operationalizing "organizational values" is a difficult one, which has given rise to much discussion. To some, the organizational values are the sum of the values of the participant individuals; to others, the manifest purposes of the organization are what is crucial. Where there is a difference, the behavioralists opt for the former.

[20] The idea is that of Chester Barnard, whose best-known work is *Functions of the Executive* (Cambridge, 1938).

which come to the organization, conflict between personal values and organizational needs is more likely.

Which of the individual's values are operative in the organizational setting is affected to a large degree by personal relationships within the organization. The work-groups of which the individual is perforce a part; the friendship groups which develop, often around the work-group; the informal associations of fellow professionals—all have some bearing on how the individual worker will process the "fact premises" and "value premises" which come to him in the course of his work. The reinforcement of values initially instilled by professional training and anchored by prior experience can be particularly crucial, as we see in cases where professionals insist work be done *their* way rather than the way their organizational superiors wish it done. Because the professionals tend to be "cosmopolitans," with perspectives and experience covering a wide range, they are less likely to feel committed to the specific organization for which they are now working than the "local" who has come up through the organization and has had little exposure to the "outside world."

The importance of the individual in the organization is also shown by the amount of attention devoted to leadership, although this amount of attention is not matched by agreement on a definition of the concept. Most behavioralists feel that leadership is something different from formal position, although someone in a formal position *may* be a leader. The definition of a leader as "a person who is able to unite people in pursuit of a goal" [21] or of leadership as "a position within a group which is characterized by the ability of its incumbent to guide and structure the collective behavior patterns of group members in a direction dictated by his personal values" [22] suggest the basic elements on which there is some consensus. One is that leadership is not the same as domination; thus, an individual might be able to control the behavior of others without "leading" them. Those who undertake studies of leadership recognize its contextual basis—that one who leads in organization "A" may not lead in organization "B," although there may be a carryover of status from one leadership role to another which makes it easier for a person to become a leader in the latter situation. However, there are many studies in which "basic traits" of leaders, such as intelligence and height are examined without being related either to the organizational situation or to the leader's followers. One who makes a good subordinate (say, an "assistant to the President") may not become a good superior, particularly when the subordinate and his boss complement rather than duplicate each other. This suggests that leadership-succession is a problem which cannot always be solved simply by moving people "up the ladder" from one rung to the next; lateral entrance into positions of authority may prove more functional for the organization. Nor is it to deny that personal characteristics are important, but only to assert

[21] Simon, Smithburg, and Thompson, p. 103.
[22] Lewis J. Edinger, "Political Science and Political Biography: Reflections on the Study of Leadership," *Journal of Politics*, XXVI (1964), 652.

the need to consider them in relation to the setting in which they are found.

That "leaders are like their followers, only a little more so"—that is, they are slightly above the average for the group, without being exceptionally ahead of their peers—has been shown. Types of leadership functions have also been recognized, particularly by those who study small groups. Thus we find "social leadership" as well as "task leadership," with the same individual not necessarily performing both functions. The person adept at developing new ideas may not have the social skills necessary to effectuate them, and the person with the social skills may not be particularly original or may not have administrative abilities, and so on. Thus, an assembly line foreman with considerable knowledge about the mechanical processes under his supervision will not necessarily do well in a job involving much paperwork, even if it is a promotion.

Despite many attempts to compile lists of specific leadership traits, absence of agreement on those traits makes more difficult the task of those charged with selecting individuals for administrative/supervisory positions. Behavioral leadership studies have helped by identifying aspects of leadership which must be kept in mind in selecting an individual for such a position. Similarly, the existence of different bases for leadership has been often discussed. Max Weber, the famous German sociologist, distinguished between charismatic, traditional, and bureaucratic leadership, indicating that each had a different base—the former in personal magnetism, the second in the routine of what had always been done, and the last through formal structure in an organization. Other bases for leadership or authority, such as the prestige of the leader or the expertise he possesses, have also been recognized. A shift in the basis of authority from dominance to manipulation (from status to morale) has also been noted, showing that it is no longer thought to be sufficient in most situations to command that something be done, but that positive incentives must be used if potential followers are to become actual followers. It is from this feeling that we get the "participation hypothesis," that a worker will be more satisfied with his work if he is able to participate in the decision-making process, an hypothesis which is not always verified because some workers *want* to be told what to do and become uneasy when able (or forced) to determine their own work.

An organization is seldom completely at the mercy of the prior training/ experience of its employees; it can work to re-socialize them to the values of the organization, the prime purpose of orientation sessions or special in-service training near the induction stage. To the extent that the individuals are motivated to succeed within the organization, they are more easily subject to manipulation toward the organizational goals specified by superiors. Early statements about motivation and its relation to productivity were based on simplistic notions of "economic man," leading to the suggestion that higher salaries would bring about higher production. This idea often led to piece-rate incentives based on time-and-motion studies, to which workers were often hostile. Empirical studies have shown that, for many, once a salary is considered adequate, higher salaries do not motivate, but that other conditions (such as freedom to direct one's own work, compatible fellow-employees, pleasant working conditions) do. However, as March and Simon note, "high morale is not a sufficient condition for high productivity, and does not necessarily lead to higher productivity than low morale," [23] a finding which must frustrate company executives. That all are not motivated in the same way that they, the "upwardly mobiles," are motivated, and that there are "apathetics" not interested in higher position and higher pay, must be particularly galling to those trying to stimulate workers to produce more. Salary is still important, however, as shown by studies indicating that some treat their work not as central to their lives but as a basis for making money which they can utilize to pursue off-the-job interests they consider more important. Informal work groups often affect motivation, and certainly control productivity. These groups tend to set informal, socially-enforced work standards (both floors and ceilings), and the worker who is a "rate-buster" is likely to find himself ostracized. Different individuals are differently motivated, and various organizations appear to operate on the basis of different incentives, including material matters (salary), social rewards (group friendships), and ideas and principles.

The communication network within an organization, one of the principal informal "overlays" on the formal structure, has drawn considerable attention from students of administrative behavior. While much communication does proceed via formal channels, there is much where the communicators avoid or ignore the formal lines. This is particularly the case in communications between "staff" and "line" units. Requests for information from the former are supposed to run from subordinate line unit to superior to staff unit and back again. The top line unit is allegedly making the order on the advice of the staff, although, as a practical matter, the staff unit actually makes the decision. Informal communication, which occurs directly between subordinate line unit and staff unit, "short-circuits" formal channels and produces quicker results. Communication among members of the same profession, even if in different formal units, and between friends "off the job," already mentioned, are also of considerable importance. Although each agency tends to generate a great deal of necessary information internally, communication from those "outside" the organization can be crucial for its success. Mechanisms are not always adequately established for receiving and processing that information, and some organizations seem to shut themselves off from information counter to that desired, thus making the organization unaware of negative changing conditions.

Communication from outside the organization raises the question of organizational boundaries. While we usually define organizations in terms of their full-time employees, we can also define them behaviorally to include their clienteles, those in frequent contact, or those who, even in the absence of frequent contact, provide important stimuli which affect the organization's

[23] March and Simon, p. 48.

output. Students of public administration have long been concerned with the "ecology" of the organization (in John Gaus's terminology), but the number of studies of political context for organizations is few. Among the most important is one stressing the relationship between the organization and interest groups. Selznick suggests that "outside" groups which are not given a formal role in the organization but which have effective power to influence the organization's action have been informally coopted, and that groups given

> *Cooptation.* The process or act by which those in an organization involve those outside the group in its activities. Sometimes used to refer to leaders choosing others to succeed them.

formal power (such as membership on advisory committees) but without actual influence have been formally coopted.[24] Another useful study examines factors affecting relations between public administrators and the public they are supposed to serve.[25]

The subject of information-processing raises more general questions concerning organizational decision-making. According to one theory, before a decision is made, goals are clearly established, and ranked in order of priority; all the alternative means to those goals are canvassed; the costs of those means are determined; and then the alternative costs are weighed. The result is the single best possible alternative. This process suggests completely rational (in the sense of logical, unemotional) behavior, carried out in a fixed sequence.[26] Lasswell describes one such sequence as involving the following functions:

- intelligence
- promotion
- prescribing
- invoking

- application
- appraisal
- terminating.[27]

Many students of public administration now realize that decision-making in organizations is not rational-comprehensive-optimizing decision-making but is instead incremental, marginal, and satisficing in character. Decisions are

> *Satisfice.* A word brought to political science by Herbert Simon to indicate that decision-makers often stop with "adequate" or "satisfactory" results, instead of continuing to search for the optimum or "best" decision.

[24] Philip Selznick, *TVA and the Grass Roots* (Berkeley, 1949).

[25] Morris Janowitz, Deil Wright, and William Delany, *Public Administration and the Public* (Ann Arbor, 1958).

[26] That certain behavior may be rational for an individual or group although seemingly irrational on the surface may be difficult to understand, and requires a redefinition of "rational," but is important to grasp. If by rational behavior, we mean behavior contributing to the attainment of certain goals, then not all "rational" behavior is coldly logical. An example would be a woman's tears or other show of emotion which directs men's attention to her.

[27] Harold D. Lasswell, *The Decision Process: Seven Categories of Functional Analysis* (College Park, Maryland, 1956).

made as part of a process; each decision builds on what has gone before, but no single fixed sequence is automatically followed. Thus, Lasswell's "functions," which are related, it appears, to a chronological process, are all being carried out simultaneously to one degree or another—no organization is dealing with only one problem at a time—and thus these categories may not be the most appropriate for organizational analysis.

In any case, there appear to be different decision-making processes even within a single organization or unit of the organization. While a number of categories could be developed, an important one is that between programmed and non-programmed decisions, that is, between routine and non-routine matters. If most of the actions in any large, on-going organization are not made essentially by habit, the organization's activities would grind to a halt. A complete rational thought-process would take too long for "minor" or "trivial" actions and most workers carry out their work on the basis of what superiors say, that is, on the basis of authority, for *most* of what they do. When change is to take place, when an unusual situation develops, the decision-processes outlined by the older decision-theorists are much more likely to be followed. Some of the confusion about what actual decision-making processes are stems from the question of whether to call routine actions "decisions"; some reserve the word for innovative, non-routine, "non-programmed" actions, and thus get a rather different picture of the process than would the analyst who included habitual activities as well. Thus, Lundberg remarks:

> Many would have the term ["decision"] refer to decision as a product; that is, it is what comes of choice. Others believe decision to be the process of choice itself. For still others decision means a certain kind of choice. Some authors speak of decision as the processes leading up to the actual choice process, others combine in decision the processes leading up to and including choice, and still others go even further by including all processes leading up to, through and beyond choice (implying in most instances implementation).[28]

Most decision-makers find it easier to accept the past, modifying only by relatively small increments (at the margin), than to question the whole prior structure and to re-evaluate each part of a decision-problem each time it comes before them. In addition, they satisfice; to use an Army phrase, they do "the best job possible *under the circumstances*" rather than the "best job possible." Satisficing behavior occurs because, among other reasons, there are costs to finding out all the information; decisions must be made under pressures of time; and it may not be possible either to determine all the possible alternatives, much less to "cost" them, or to rank them in order of priorities.

Intra-organizational rivalry is another obstacle to rational-comprehensive decision-making. If each part of an organization could make decisions

[28] Craig C. Lundberg, "Administrative Decisions: A Scheme for Analysis," *The Making of Decisions: A Reader in Administrative Behavior*, ed. William J. Gore and J.W. Dyson (New York, 1964), p. 20.

without interference and interposition of any sort by other organizational units, and if some "invisible hand" would coordinate the decisions each unit reached independently, rational-calculating decision-making would be more likely to occur. But coordination does not occur automatically, and each organizational unit is usually looking out for its own interests. This means that decisions are often made by bargaining between units and by negotiation. As this suggests, organizations are not monolithic nor homogeneous, even if we do tend to talk about "the organization," to personify it for purposes of discussion. It is more appropriate to view organizations as coalitions of groups. This also suggests the importance of recognizing the place of power and power-seeking behavior in organizations, rather than over-emphasizing rationality, although we have tended to neglect power considerations in our work in public administration. At the same time we have neglected power, we have spent much time seeking for the Holy Grail of the "public interest," in terms of which administrators are supposed to administer, although the concept has been used more as a rationalization for action than as a stimulus toward certain acts.

That some decision-making is done by bargaining is not to deny that many decisions are made on high and passed down the "chain of command." This hierarchical arrangement is supposed to characterize the ideal-type organizational form known as *bureaucracy*, to which much attention has been paid ever since Max Weber developed the content of the concept. Weber suggested quite a number of characteristics for bureaucracy, in part to distinguish it from other forms of organization from earlier historical periods. A bureaucracy was hierarchical (and pyramidal) in form; communication was written and specific, and full records were kept; people were appointed to positions in a bureaucracy on the basis of merit, and they made careers of their positions; there was a sharp separation between one's personal goods and the material belonging to the organization; and the organization had a continuity beyond the life of any of its members.

According to Weber, a bureaucracy was the most advanced form of organization, as well as the most efficient, and was descriptive of large-scale organization in particular. Contemporary scholars have found much in Weber which is useful, and the characteristics of bureaucracy he suggests provide a valuable check-list by which to examine present organizations, but not all contemporary large-scale organizations operate as bureaucracies in Weber's sense. Universities, for example, have both a bureaucratic side and one operated at least partly under the collegial (collective) direction of the faculty; the former is that part concerned with such matters as providing meals, dormitory space, and supplies, while the latter is the part of the organization concerned with the unit's basic product, education. Other organizations, even business firms (which we might expect to be most "bureaucratic") diverge from the Weberian norm to one degree or another. Some scholars have suggested that the military is becoming more bureaucratic, largely because of the impact of technology, indicating that organizations can shift in the degree to which they approximate the bureaucratic model.

Studies of bureaucracy go beyond these elements to include the effect of such structure on the individual who works in that situation. While bureaucracy is thought by some to be the ideal form, those who examine its effect on personality often stress its dysfunctions, as when "bureaucratic personality," characterized by rigidity and over-attention to procedures, is the result. The individual often finds he can protect himself from reprimand by following the detailed procedures of the organization to the letter, even when this seems (to the observer) to conflict with carrying out the organization's goal. (Much of the seemingly endless paperwork the public bureaucrat performs is often more a result of his need to account to the public through the legislature than it is a result of his being part of a bureaucracy.) The "human relations" values of students of organizational behavior have led to their concern not only with the effects of bureaucratic organizations on personality, but with the effect of any organization. Their goal is that the individual's work situation help him to grow, to become more mature, and many organizational requirements, of which the assembly line is seen as the epitome, appear to these analysts to retard and stifle rather than develop personality. The impact of the humanitarian values of many social science researchers is perhaps no clearer anywhere than in this area of their work.

BIBLIOGRAPHY

Introduction

The relatively separate place of public administration within political science is discussed by ROSCOE C. MARTIN, "Political Science and Public Administration: A Note on the State of the Union," APSR, XLVI (1952), 660–676. A good introduction to public administration, covering many of the points dealt with in this chapter, is DWIGHT WALDO, The Study of Public Administration (Garden City, 1955).

Texts and Readers. Perhaps the best known of the early texts is LEONARD WHITE, An Introduction to the Study of Public Administration, 4th ed. (New York, 1965). Other texts include FRITZ MORSTEIN MARX, ed., Elements of Public Administration, 2nd ed. (Englewood Cliffs, 1959); JOHN PFIFFNER and FRANK SHERWOOD, Administrative Organization (Englewood Cliffs, 1960); FELIX NIGRO, Modern Public Administration (New York, 1965); JOHN PFIFFNER and ROBERT PRESTHUS, Public Administration, 5th ed. (New York, 1967); and the earliest of the behaviorally-inclined texts, HERBERT SIMON, DONALD SMITHBURG, and VICTOR THOMPSON, Public Administration (New York, 1951).

Collections of readings include ALAN ALTSHULER, ed., The Politics of the Federal Bureaucracy (New York, 1968); ROBERT T. GOLEMBIEWSKI, FRANK GIBSON, and GEOFFREY Y. CORNOG, eds., Public Administration: Readings in Institutions, Processes, Behavior (Chicago, 1966); and CLAUDE E. HAWLEY and RUTH G. WEINTRAUB, eds., Administrative Questions and Political Answers (Princeton, N.J., 1966), a collection of items from Public Administration Review. Two older collections of relevant items are DWIGHT WALDO, ed., Ideas and Issues in Public Administration (New York, 1953), and DONALD ROWAT, ed., Basic Issues in Public Administration (New York, 1961).

Case Studies. The background of the case studies so frequently used in teaching public administration is told in EGBERT S. WENGERT, "Case Studies in Public Administration: An Introductory Note," *Philippine Journal of Public Administration*, I (1957), 98–107, and the case method is further discussed in EDWIN A. BOCK, ed., *Essays on the Case Method in Public Administration* (New York, 1961). The first major collection of ICP studies was HAROLD STEIN, *Public Administration and Policy Development* (New York, 1952). More recent collections include EDWIN A. BOCK, ed., *Government Regulation of Business: A Casebook* (Englewood Cliffs, 1965); EDWIN A. BOCK and ALAN K. CAMPBELL, eds., *Case Studies in American Government* (Englewood Cliffs, 1962); and HAROLD STEIN, ed., *American Civil-Military Decisions* (University, Ala., 1963).

Administrative History.   Material for the present study of public administration can also be drawn from administrative history. In the writing of administrative history, a series by LEONARD WHITE is noteworthy: *The Federalists: A Study in Administrative History* (New York, 1948); *The Jeffersonians* (New York, 1951); *The Jacksonians* (New York, 1954); *The Republican Era* (New York, 1958). A more recent contribution concerning a single agency is DONALD WHITNAH, *A History of the United States Weather Bureau* (Urbana, 1961).

Bureaucracy and Democracy.   The relationship of administration and bureaucracy to democracy has been often debated. CHARLES HYNEMAN, *Bureaucracy and Democracy* (New York, 1950), is perhaps the single leading source. The topic is also discussed by DWIGHT WALDO, "Development of the Theory of Democratic Administration," *APSR*, XLVI (1952), 81–103; "Replies and Comments" appear at *APSR*, XLVI (1952), 494–503. The actual relationship between administrators and the citizenry, relevant to the bureaucracy-democracy problem, is explored in MORRIS JANOWITZ, DEIL WRIGHT, and WILLIAM DELANY, *Public Administration and the Public* (Ann Arbor, 1958). Other values involved in public administration are discussed by HERBERT KAUFMAN, "Emerging Conflicts in the Doctrines of Public Administration," *APSR*, L (1956), 1057–1073.

Public Policy.   General discussions are J. W. PELTASON and JAMES M. BURNS, *Functions and Policies of American Government*, 3rd ed. (Englewood Cliffs, 1967) and LEE S. GREENE and GEORGE S. PARTHEMOS, *American Government: Policies and Functions* (New York, 1967). Typical business and government texts are EMMETTE S. REDFORD, *American Government and the Economy* (New York, 1965), CORNELIUS P. COTTER, *Government and Private Enterprise* (New York, 1960), and MERLE FAINSOD, LINCOLN GORDON, and JOSEPH C. PALAMOUNTAIN, JR., *Government and the American Economy*, 3rd ed. (New York, 1959). Foreign policy is discussed in BURTON M. SAPIN, *The Making of United States Foreign Policy* (Washington, 1966), and RICHARD C. SNYDER and EDGAR S. FURNISS, JR., *American Foreign Policy: Formulation, Principles, and Programs* (New York, 1954), and agriculture in DALE E. HATHAWAY, *Government and Agriculture: Economic Policy in a Democratic Society* (New York, 1963).

SAMUEL HUNTINGTON, *The Soldier and the State* (Cambridge, 1957), and WALTER MILLIS, *Arms and the State* (New York, 1956), deal with civil-military relations, while DAVIS BOBROW has put together an excellent collection of readings, *Components of Defense Policy* (Chicago, 1965).

Administrative Organization and Reorganization

Organization.   One of the earlier works on organization of the federal administrative structure was SCHUYLER WALLACE, *Federal Departmentalization* (New York,

1941). It and DAVID B. TRUMAN, *Administrative Decentralization: A Study of the Chicago Field Offices of the United States Department of Agriculture* (Chicago, 1940), provide a good introduction to some structural problems, which may be followed up in almost every textbook. The problems of trying to find the most appropriate area for government units are dealt with in both ARTHUR MAASS, ed., *Area and Power: A Theory of Local Government* (Glencoe, 1959), and JAMES FESLER, *Area and Administration* (University, Ala., 1964). MARVER BERNSTEIN, *Regulating Business by Independent Commission* (Princeton, 1955) and SAMUEL KRISLOV and LLOYD D. MUSOLF, eds., *The Politics of Regulation* (Boston, 1964), deal thoroughly with the regulatory commissions. A good treatment of government corporations is V. O. KEY, JR., "Government Corporations," *Elements of Public Administration*, ed. Fritz Morstein Marx, 2nd ed. (Englewood Cliffs, 1959), pp. 219–245. The problem of coordination is touched upon by PAUL Y. HAMMOND, "The National Security Council as a Device for Interdepartmental Coordination," *APSR*, LIV (1960), 899–910.

Reorganization. The Reports and Staff Studies of the two Commissions on the Reorganization of the Executive Branch (the Hoover Commissions) provide invaluable material. Another useful source, despite its age, is LEWIS MERIAM and LAURENCE SCHMECKEBIER, *Reorganization of the National Government: What Does It Involve?* (Washington, D.C., 1939). HERBERT EMMERICH adds to our knowledge with his *Essays on Federal Reorganization* (University, Ala., 1950), as does MARSHALL E. DIMOCK, "The Objectives of Governmental Reorganization," *Public Administration Review*, XI (1951), 233–241.

The political difficulties of getting reorganization reforms approved is portrayed by KARL BOSWORTH, "The Politics of Management Improvement in the States," *APSR*, XLVII (1953), 84–99, and AVERY LEISERSON, "Political Limitations on Executive Reorganization," *APSR*, XLI (1947), 68–84. Attacks on some of the reorganization proposals and assumptions are made by CHARLES S. HYNEMAN, "Administrative Reorganization: An Adventure into Science and Theology," *JOP*, I (1939), 62–75, and JAMES FESLER, "Administrative Literature and the Second Hoover Report," *APSR*, LI (1957), 135–144.

Specialty Tools

Personnel. O. GLENN STAHL, *Public Personnel Administration*, 4th ed. (New York, 1956), is a standard text. STERLING SPERO, *Government as Employer* (New York, 1948), is also quite relevant. PAUL VAN RIPER, *A History of the United States Civil Service* (New York, 1958) provides necessary perspective. A large number of studies of federal officials have now been carried out. Among the most important are DEAN MANN, with JAMESON DOIG, *The Assistant Secretaries: Problems and Processes of Appointment* (Washington, D.C., 1965); W. LLOYD WARNER, PAUL VAN RIPER, NORMAN MARTIN, and ORVIS COLLINS, *The American Federal Executive* (New Haven, 1963); DAVID T. STANLEY, *The Higher Civil Service: An Evaluation of Federal Personnel Practices* (Washington, D.C., 1964); and the older but useful ARTHUR MACMAHON and JOHN MILLETT, *Federal Administrators* (New York, 1939). A different perspective is provided by FRANKLIN P. KILPATRICK, MILTON C. CUMMINGS, JR., and M. KENT JENNINGS, *The Image of the Federal Service* (Washington, D.C., 1964).

Budgeting. A basic treatment is provided by JESSE BURKHEAD, *Government Budgeting* (New York, 1956). A newer, less technical approach is taken by AARON WILDAVSKY, *The Politics of the Budgetary Process* (Boston, 1964). More formalized is OTTO A. DAVIS, M. A. H. DEMPSTER, and AARON WILDAVSKY, "A Theory of the Budgetary Process," *APSR*, LX (1966), 529–547. THOMAS J. ANTON, "Roles and Symbols in the Determinations of State Expenditures," *Midwest Journal of Political Science*, XI (1967), 27–43, deals with the interplay between actors in the budgetary process. Public finance, related to budgeting, is handled well in JAMES A. MAXWELL, *Financing State and Local Governments* (Washington, D.C., 1965), and FREDERICK C. MOSHER and ORVILLE POLAND, *The Costs of American Governments* (New York, 1964).

Chief Executive

HAROLD LASKI, *The American Presidency* (New York, 1940), CLINTON ROSSITER, *The American Presidency*, 2nd ed. (New York, 1960), and SIDNEY HYMAN, *The American President* (New York, 1954), are all standard works. Other important volumes on the Presidency include EDWARD S. CORWIN, *The President: Office and Powers, 1787–1957*, 4th rev. ed. (New York, 1957); LOUIS W. KOENIG, *The Chief Executive* (New York, 1964); and JOSEPH KALLENBACH, *The American Chief Executive* (New York, 1966). Two collections of readings are ELMER CORNWELL, ed., *The American Presidency: Vital Center* (Chicago, 1966), and DONALD BRUCE JOHNSON and JACK L. WALKER, eds., *The Dynamics of the American Presidency* (New York, 1964). RICHARD NEUSTADT, *Presidential Power* (New York, 1960), is an oft-quoted recent volume. ELMER E. CORNWELL, JR., *Presidential Leadership of Public Opinion* (Bloomington, Ind., 1965), deals with a particular aspect of Presidential power.

Governors are discussed in the Kallenbach volume and in COLEMAN B. RANSONE, *The Office of Governor in the United States* (University, Ala., 1956), and LESLIE LIPSON, *The American Governor: From Figurehead to Leader* (Chicago, 1939). A more recent treatment by Ransone is "Political Leadership in the Governor's Office," *JOP*, XXVI (1964), 197–220. DEIL S. WRIGHT, "Executive Leadership in State Administration," *MJPS*, XI (1967), 1–26, shows the lack of control the Governor has over the administrative structure.

The staff help the President receives is treated by RICHARD E. NEUSTADT, "Approaches to Staffing the Presidency: Notes on FDR and JFK," *APSR*, LVII (1963), 855–863. BARRY DEAN KARL, *Executive Reorganization and Reform in the New Deal* (Cambridge, Mass., 1953), covers the period during which the present Presidential staff arrangements were developed. Aspects of the work of this staff are treated by RICHARD NEUSTADT, "Presidency and Legislation: The Growth of Central Clearance," *APSR*, XLVIII (1954), 641–671, and LESTER G. SELIGMAN, "Presidential Leadership: The Inner Circle and Institutionalization," *JOP*, XXVIII (1956), 410–426, and more recently by JAMES DAVIS and RANDALL B. RIPLEY, "The Bureau of the Budget and Executive Branch Agencies: Notes on Their Interaction," *JOP*, XXIX (1967), 749–769. RICHARD FENNO's treatment of *The President's Cabinet: An Analysis in the Period from Wilson to Eisenhower* (Cambridge, Mass., 1959) gives us a thorough picture of that institution, and PAUL DAVID has added a useful discussion of "The Vice Presidency: Its Institutional Evolution and Contemporary Status," *JOP*, XXIX (1967), 721–748.

Administrative and Organizational Behavior

In addition to the material first presented in SIMON, SMITHBURG, and THOMPSON, *Public Administration*, HERBERT SIMON's *Administrative Behavior: A Study of Decision-Making Processes in Administrative Organization*, 2nd ed. (New York,

1958), was one of the first important contributions. Also relevant are HERBERT A. SIMON, "Recent Advances in Organization Theory," *Research Frontiers in Politics and Government*, ed. Stephen Bailey, pp. 23–44, and JAMES G. MARCH, "Some Recent Substantive and Methodological Developments in the Theory of Organizational Decision-Making," *Essays on the Behavioral Study of Politics*, ed. Austin Ranney, pp. 191–208. A major systematic collection of propositions related to organization theory is to be found in JAMES G. MARCH and HERBERT A. SIMON, *Organizations* (New York, 1958). One of several collections of readings on organization theory is ALBERT H. RUBENSTEIN and CHADWICK J. HABERSTROH, eds., *Some Theories of Organization*, rev. ed. (Homewood, Ill., 1966). More sociological is AMITAI ETZIONI, ed., *Complex Organizations* (New York, 1961). RICHARD M. CYERT and JAMES G. MARCH, *A Behavioral Theory of the Firm* (Englewood Cliffs, 1963) is a good example of more heavily formalized organization theory.

CHRIS ARGYRIS, *Personality and Organization* (New York, 1957), and Argyris's other work stresses the effect of organization on development of the individual personality. Orientation patterns which individuals have toward the organizations in which they work include the local/cosmopolitan distinction, first developed by ROBERT MERTON, "Patterns of Influence: Local and Cosmopolitan Influentials," *Social Theory and Social Structure*, pp. 387–420. An interesting application is ALVIN GOULDNER, "Cosmopolitans and Locals: Toward an Analysis of Latent Social Roles," *Administrative Science Quarterly*, II (1957–58), 281–306 and 444–480. The incentives which attract people to organizations and/or hold them there are discussed by PETER CLARK and JAMES WILSON, "Incentive Systems: A Theory of Organization," *Administrative Science Quarterly*, VI (1961), 129–166. The types of individuals-in-organization in terms of willingness to respond to incentives are among items covered by ROBERT PRESTHUS, *The Organizational Society* (New York, 1962).

Leadership. PHILIP SELZNICK, *Leadership in Administration: A Sociological Interpretation* (New York, 1957), and ALVIN GOULDNER, ed., *Studies in Leadership: Leadership and Democratic Action* (New York, 1965) are basic. One study of leader-follower relations in a public organization is ROBERT PEABODY, *Organizational Authority: Superior-Subordinate Relationships in Three Public Service Organizations* (New York, 1964). A collection of readings dealing with leadership in the more formal sense is JAMES DAVID BARBER, ed., *Political Leadership in American Government* (Boston, 1964).

Bureaucracy. The formal theory of bureaucracy is presented in *From Max Weber: Essays in Sociology*, ed. and trans. Hans Gerth and C. Wright Mills (New York, 1956). A collection of readings which is an excellent follow-up is ROBERT K. MERTON, AILSA P. GRAY, BARBARA HOCKEY, and HANAN C. SELVIN, eds., *Reader in Bureaucracy* (Glencoe, 1952). The work of PETER BLAU is indispensable in the study of bureaucracy. See his *Bureaucracy in Modern Society* (New York, 1956); *The Dynamics of Bureaucracy* (Chicago, 1955); and the more recent "Critical Remarks on Weber's Theory of Authority," *APSR*, LVII (1963), 305–316.

Decision-Making Theory. In recent years, several scholars have devoted much attention to decision-making in organizations under conditions of less than perfect information, and have challenged the older theory that a rational calculus underlay decision-making. CHARLES LINDBLOM, "The Science of Muddling Through," *Public Administration Review*, XIX (1958), 79–88, was one of the first to develop the idea, and Lindblom, Robert Dahl, and David Braybrooke have now written extended works about the subject. See ROBERT A. DAHL and CHARLES E. LINDBLOM, *Politics, Economics, and Welfare: Planning and Politico-Economic Systems Resolved into Basic Social Processes* (New York, 1953); CHARLES E. LINDBLOM, *The Intelligence of Democracy: Decision Making Through Mutual Adjustment* (New York, 1965); and DAVID BRAYBROOKE and CHARLES LINDBLOM, *The Strategy of Decision* (New York, 1963).

Intergovernmental Relations

There is only one major volume on the broad subject of intergovernmental relations; that is W. BROOKE GRAVES, *American Intergovernmental Relations* (New York, 1964). For this reason, the subject is usually handled through its component aspects.

Federalism. The theory of federalism is developed most fully in KENNETH C. WHEARE, *Federal Government*, 3rd ed. (London, 1953), and WILLIAM C. RIKER, *Federalism: Origin, Operation, Significance* (Boston, 1964). Other expositions of problems of federalism are ARTHUR W. MACMAHON, ed., *Federalism: Mature and Emergent* (New York, 1953) and WILLIAM ANDERSON, *The Nation and the States, Rivals or Partners?* (Minneapolis, 1955). The work of the late Morton Grodzins, probably the leading expert in the field, has been prepared for presentation by Daniel Elazar. See MORTON GRODZINS, *The American System: A New View of Government in the United States*, ed. Elazar (Chicago, 1966). DANIEL ELAZAR has also written material of his own, for example, *American Federalism: The View from the States* (New York, 1960).

State-Local Relations. Standard texts include CLYDE SNIDER, *American State and Local Government*, 2nd ed. (New York, 1965) and RUSSELL MADDOX and ROBERT FUQUAY, *State and Local Government*, 2nd ed. (Princeton, 1966). CHARLES ADRIAN, *State and Local Governments*, 2nd ed. (New York, 1967), is more oriented to the political process, as is DUANE LOCKARD, *The Politics of State and Local Government* (New York, 1963).

Types of government structure adopted under city charters obtained from the state are related to socio-economic characteristics in JOHN H. KESSEL, "Governmental Structure and Political Environment: A Statistical Note About American Cities," *APSR*, LVI (1962), 615–620, and LEO SCHNORE and ROBERT ALFORD, "Forms of Government and Socio-Economic Characteristics of Suburbs," *Administrative Science Quarterly*, VIII (1963), 1–17. A particular type of local government unit which has received much attention is analyzed by JOHN BOLLENS, *Special District Governments in the United States* (Berkeley, 1957).

Metropolitan Problems. A general textbook is JOHN BOLLENS and HENRY SCHMANDT, *The Metropolis: Its People, Politics, and Economic Life* (New York, 1965). There are many short volumes on the general subject, but they are too numerous to mention. JOHN BOLLENS, ed., *Exploring the Metropolitan Community* (Berkeley, 1961), concerning St. Louis, gives detailed data on one metropolitan area. WALLACE S. SAYRE and HERBERT KAUFMAN, *Governing New York City: Politics in the Metropolis* (New York, 1960), deals with the country's largest city and its environs. Case studies of attempts to reorganize metropolitan areas are many. Representative are EDWARD SOFEN, *The Miami Metropolitan Experiment: A Metropolitan Action Study*, 2nd ed. (Garden City, 1966) and HENRY SCHMANDT, PAUL STEINBICKER, and GEORGE WENDEL, *Metropolitan Reform in St. Louis: A Case Study* (New York, 1961).

Several excellent collections of articles on intergovernmental relations in the metropolitan area have appeared recently; they utilize conflict frameworks for the most part: PHILIP B. COULTER, ed., *Politics of Metropolitan Areas* (New York, 1967); MICHAEL N. DANIELSON, ed., *Metropolitan Politics: A Reader* (Boston, 1966); and THOMAS R. DYE and BRETT K. HAWKINS, *Politics in the Metropolis* (Columbus, 1967). Some of the more important articles on the subject include work by THOMAS R. DYE: "Urban Political Integration: Conditions Associated with Annexation in American Cities," *MJPS*, VIII (1964), 430–446, and (with HAROLD HERMAN, CHARLES S. LIEBMAN, and OLIVER P. WILLIAMS) "Differentiation and Cooperation in a Metropolitan Area," *MJPS*, VII (1963), 145–155. MATTHEW HOLDEN, "The Governance of the Metropolis as a Problem in Diplomacy," *JOP*, XXVI (1964), 627–647, provides a fresh perspective on metro area intergovernmental relations.

14 / PUBLIC LAW

Traditional Concerns / Political Approaches /

Judicial Behavioralism

Political scientists have tended to look at "public law" (or "constitutional law") as a separate field, to look at it in a narrowly legalistic fashion, to concentrate on the courts in so doing, and to emphasize the work of individual judges. They have tended to concentrate on the courts because, in America as in few other counties, the courts have the power of judicial review, that is, the power to declare acts of other branches of government unconstitutional. Because of this power, there has been an inclination to see the decisions of the courts as final, as "law," while other bodies' rulings are tentative until court-approved. In a country where the courts can at most interpret but cannot overturn the actions of the legislature, "law" is seen much more clearly as coming not from the courts alone.

The subfield designation "public law" is not only somewhat inaccurate because the subfield does not include all of law relative to governmental matters, for example, administrative law and international law, but it is also a misnomer because of the overly sharp distinction it encourages between "public" law and "private" law. This distinction implies that government is involved in the former, but not in the latter. Even in the field of "private" law, government is intimately involved, because courts are the forums in which private law cases are heard and because the rulings of judges help establish the framework of expectations in which "private" individuals operate. The concentration by public law scholars on the United States Supreme Court, which hears mostly cases involving governmental bodies and rulings they have promulgated, has led us to forget that state supreme courts and even the lower federal courts deal with a very large proportion of "private law" matters. The Supreme Court is, then, in a sense an unrepresentative court because of the high percentage of public policy questions it handles; however important it is in our system—and it is extremely important— study of it has led to a distorted view of what law is and how our legal process operates. As if the cases the Court actually dealt with were not sufficiently unrepresentative, scholars have dealt with only "leading cases," making the object of their study still more unrepresentative. Tradition is forceful and political science will undoubtedly continue with a "public law" subfield for quite some time to come, although recognition of the sort of matters discussed here has led to a change in the shape of, and emphases in, this subfield.

The impact of the legal profession has been greater on political science than vice versa. While political scientists do not study constitutional law with the cook-book or "how-to-do-it" orientation which has characterized Business Law in many Departments of Business Administration, until recently they also have not often studied law as social scientists. Usually by choice lawyers have not utilized social science except in limited instances, as when social science data was mustered in the "Brandeis brief" in attempts to

> **Brandeis Brief.** A brief submitted by a lawyer, composed principally of economic or sociological facts rather than legal argument. Named for Louis Brandeis, who used the device as a lawyer (before becoming a United States Supreme Court Justice). As originally developed, it was intended to show judges that legislatures could have had a reasonable basis for enacting certain types of welfare legislation.

uphold minimum-wage and maximum-hour legislation, and to show the negative effects of segregated school systems. Nor have judges drawn on it heavily. While they generally decide cases in terms of the categories into which individuals and facts fit rather than in terms of the individuals' idiosyncracies, they deal with those categories in the context of the specific constellation or pattern involved in the particular case—*not* in terms of the sorts of broad generalizations social science develops. Even though it is not often used even when available, social science information is not available in all instances where it might be used.

It was only recently that political scientists studying constitutional law began to use the methods of social science. Had political scientists earlier seen law as one of several outcomes of political activity, just as sociologists saw law as one of several methods of social control, the place of law (and public law) within political science might have been quite different, and the study of legal processes might have been much nearer the mainstream of social science. The differences in approach are explained by Maurice Duverger, talking about law and the sociology of law:

> For the lawyer, texts and institutions express the rules of positive law and the significance and scope of these rules must be established by a rigorous analysis based on fixed rules so that one can establish what the law is. The sociologist studies laws as an expression of a certain social condition, every society being reflected in its juridical system. He seeks to establish how far these rules are removed from reality. The lawyer studies the rules as rules, in their normative aspect: for the sociologist, the rules of law are objective social facts.[1]

In these terms, the scholar in the field of "public law" has operated in a fashion nearer to that of the lawyer than to that of the sociologist.

The field of public law can be divided, according to Glendon Schubert, into three domains—those of the traditionalist, the conventionalist, and the

[1] Maurice Duverger, *An Introduction to the Social Sciences,* trans. Malcolm Anderson (New York, 1964 [1961]), p. 50.

behavioralist.[2] Without necessarily totally accepting this division of Gaul with its titles of invidious distinction, we can recognize that a variety of approaches characterize the study of the judicial system and the cases that system produces, and we can perhaps use Schubert's division to organize our materials.

TRADITIONAL CONCERNS

Over the years, the principal concern of those who have studied public law has been with the content of decisions of the United States Supreme Court and with the document which has given rise to many of those decisions, the United States Constitution. Along with historians, political scientists have given much attention to the origins and growth of the Constitution. Not surprisingly, the inhabitants of any nation are particularly interested in the beginnings of their nation, and as we have operated since 1789 under one document, amended formally only a few times, that document has been the central focus of much of our attention to our origins. The flexibility of interpretation which has allowed us to retain that document has also received much attention. However, that we have treated the Constitution almost as a Bible has not helped objective examination of the document or its genesis. The force natural law philosophy has on our views of the Constitution is indicated in the title of Edward Corwin's volume, *The Higher Law Background of the Constitution*. The view of the law as fully developed for all time, remaining only to be discovered by judges, rather than made according to the processes of politics, has led to ever more emphasis on the original document, which is supposed to contain the seeds of all which has come after its adoption. It has also led to proportionately less emphasis on the process by which changing interpretations have developed in the intervening years. Stimulated by the major shift in constitutional interpretation of the mid-1930's, when the Supreme Court changed abruptly from attacking New Deal economic legislation to upholding it, this approach has begun to change. We now recognize, at least at the intellectual level, that our constitutional law is made and not found. Nonetheless, we still are drawn to what we see as the origins. Endless disputations about the Founding Fathers' intentions as to the meaning of the First Amendment give evidence of this, as does the amount of "law-office history" written by both lawyers *and* judges to prove a point. William Anderson's apt statement that we cannot talk about the *intention* of the fifty-five men at the Constitutional Convention, except perhaps to say that they *intended* to submit their draft document to the states for possible ratification, has not ended concern with what went into the document or reluctance to accept other than patriotic motives on the part of the men who gathered at Philadelphia.[3]

[2] Glendon Schubert, "Academic Ideology and the Study of Adjudication," *American Political Science Review*, LXI (1967), 106–129.

[3] William Anderson, "The Intention of the Framers: A Note on Constitutional Interpretation," *American Political Science Review*, XLIX (1955), 340–353.

The background of the Constitution has been ably treated. One can, for example, get a thorough view of the atmosphere of the time, the social environment, and particularly the environment of ideas, as well as a look at the Articles of Confederation, the system of government which, because it was thought to be ill-functioning, helped precipitate the movement toward adoption of a new frame of government for the former thirteen colonies. What went on at the Constitutional Convention can be found in many different versions; almost any basic American history text will provide the details of what occurred, the conflict between large states and small, the compromises made, the battle for ratification in the various states. One volume invariably studied in connection with the "original meaning" of the Constitution is *The Federalist* papers, written by Alexander Hamilton, John Jay, and James Madison. While much relevant political theory is included in the papers, originally published anonymously in New York, and while they do cast much light on what some supporters of the Constitution may have thought at the time, it must be remembered that they were written *after* the Constitutional Convention and in an effort to win ratification of the Constitution by New York.

Interpretation of what happened—and particularly why—has been a different matter. The best-known conflict has been over the part played by economic interests. Charles Beard's *An Economic Interpretation of the Constitution*, which emphasized the role played by holders of securities in bringing about the new Constitution and the relatively restricted access to the franchise at the time the delegates to the ratifying conventions were chosen, provided the chief shock to the nation's patriotic sensibilities. Beard's principal argument was that certain economic groups, particularly public creditors, "were adversely affected by the system of government under the Articles of Confederation"; that they tried first to amend the Articles to safeguard their rights; and that, having failed in that endeavor, they set out to have adopted "a revolutionary programme" outside the Articles, i.e., what became the Constitution, and then to obtain its ratification.[4] Revisionist historians have answered, claiming that Beard overemphasized the role of economic interests, treated the electorate as much more limited than it was in fact, and ignored differences among types of property-holders. Robert E. Brown has noted, "the conclusions which he drew were not justified even by the kind of evidence which he used. If we accepted his evidence strictly at face value, it would still not add up to the fact that the Constitution was put over undemocratically in an undemocratic society by personalty [personal property, i.e., securities]."[5] Perhaps Beard and others like him caused the shock they did because of the feeling that constitutions are "legal" and not "political." Certainly political scientists took a long time in moving away from this very view. But we must recognize that they are both legal *and* polit-

---

[4] Charles A. Beard, *An Economic Interpretation of the Constitution of the United States* (New York, 1941 [1913]), p. 63.

[5] *Charles Beard and the Constitution: A Critical Analysis of "An Economic Interpretation of the Constitution"* (Princeton, 1956), p. 195.

ical in character: the former because of the content and because their goals are to be achieved through law, the latter because of the goals themselves (for the polity) and the way they are agreed upon.

We have tended to concentrate our attention on the United States Constitution and have generally neglected state public law, although we have looked at state constitutions. When we do look at the latter, it is mostly in terms of their length (considered by many to be excessive), the frequency with which they have been amended, and the statute-type provisions included in them. Procedures for amendment have been discussed. In the last several years, constitutional conventions in several states have attracted interest, as attempts were made to "modernize" their constitutions. When we do look at the content of state public law, we tend to emphasize the restrictions which the state constitution places on legislative action or on the exercise of home rule by units of local government and the judicial interpretations of local government powers. The latter is important because, under "Dillon's Rule," the powers of local governments are narrowly construed and conflicts between state and local powers tend to be resolved in favor of the state. Thus, when a unit of local government wishes to carry out an action, that action is quite likely to be attacked in court. (This emphasis on legal authority means that the city attorney, or Corporation Counsel as he is called in some places, can have much influence through his advice to the City Council on the legality of proposed actions.) One other aspect of state and local law to which much attention has been paid is governmental tort liabil-

> **Tort Liability.** A *tort* is a wrong committed by one individual against another, forming the basis for legal action to recover a sum of money, called *damages*, for the injury. Because a government may generally not be sued without its consent, interesting legal questions arise when a government employee commits a tort against a citizen, for example, injures him with a city truck. The issue is whether or in what situations the government, rather than the employee individually, is liable for the tort, that is, can be ordered by the court to pay damages.

ity, containing many distinctions between "governmental" and "proprietary" functions of the government.

> **Governmental and Proprietary Functions.** An artificial legal distinction between those functions of local governments allegedly performed on behalf of the state ("governmental" functions) and those performed primarily for the benefit of the local inhabitants ("proprietary" functions). Different functions of local governments are classified differently in different states, and in some jurisdictions the distinction is being discarded.

Because our governmental system is a federal one, judicial review has meant that the Supreme Court has exercised the power to strike down acts of both the state legislature and the Congress, thus involving itself centrally in both the problems of federalism and of the "separation of powers" between legislative, executive, and judicial branches. The two are not the same problems, as shown by Justice Holmes' statement that he would not fear for the future of the republic if the Court lost its power to declare acts of Congress unconstitutional, but he would so fear if acts of the states could not be invalidated. The exercise of judicial review in particular subject-matter areas has been thoroughly examined and portrayed through collections of cases, although the Supreme Court's role in federalism has been less often studied. We also tend to ignore the federalism aspects of many cases, for example, the civil rights cases, thinking of them wholly in terms of their substantive law. This suggests that categorizing cases as "civil rights" or "commerce clause" or "federalism" cases may blind us to the multiple facets many of them have.

The origins of judicial review have been thoroughly scrutinized. It is perhaps somewhat startling to realize that this crucial aspect of our judicial process is not to be found explicitly in the Constitution. Certainly one can infer judicial review of state enactments from the "supreme law of the land" clause, which binds state judges to uphold the federal Constitution, or from a need for national uniformity. As to national legislation, judicial review can be implied from the very basis of what a Constitution is—a *fundamental* document superior to "ordinary" legislation. But it must be inferred. And to infer judicial review is not to solve finally the problem of the Supreme Court's power to review and reject acts of supposedly coordinate branches of the national government. For example, one could accept the Supreme Court's self-defined right to refuse to enforce decisions of other branches of the government the Justices thought were unconstitutional without saying that those decisions were unconstitutional, or one could define the Court's right to be final judge on matters relating to the judiciary, but not the legislative or executive branches. Of course, one can argue that, in 1968, the practice of judicial review has been so long accepted that it is "too late in the day" to argue otherwise, and that arguments are academic, moot, and futile, just as it is too late to argue what some Southerners continue to call the "alleged Fourteenth Amendment" was not properly adopted, because ratification was supposedly extracted by force. But such pragmatic arguments have not often satisfied constitutional scholars, who have insisted on "finding" some basis for the practice.

Judicial review is held to have started with the decision in *Marbury* v. *Madison*, 1 Cranch 137 (1803),[6] in which the Supreme Court, speaking through Chief Justice John Marshall, declared unconstitutional part of the Judiciary Act of 1789. In earlier decisions, the Court had reviewed acts of Congress and upheld them, and one can argue that they could not have up-

---

[6] Prior to the late 1800's, volumes of Supreme Court cases were cited in terms of the court reporter of the time, rather than in terms of the uniform consecutive United States (U.S.) series now in use. Thus, Cranch was the Supreme Court reporter at the time of *Marbury* v. *Madison*.

held them without the power to declare them invalid, but *Marbury* is still thought to be the first important instance of judicial review. In giving attention to it and other cases in which the Court has struck down legislation, we have to a corresponding degree ignored the Court's function of giving legitimacy to acts of other branches of the government when it upholds those acts.

What is interesting about *Marbury* is that it is a weak reed on which to base arguments for judicial review; it is a case more important for its *dicta*

> **Obiter Dictum.**   Statements made by a judge not immediately necessary for the decision in a case. In the plural, *obiter dicta*. These statements are distinguished from the *holding* in a case, the principle on which the decision rests, also called the *ratio decidendi* (rule of the decision).

and broad principles than its immediate impact. The case involved the claim by an appointee to a position as justice of the peace in the District of Columbia for his commission, which had been signed in the last hours of the Federalist administration (by Marshall himself, then Secretary of State), but not delivered. Justice Marshall first declared that Marbury was entitled to his commission, thus providing an opportunity to lecture the Jefferson administration. He then in effect reversed course by saying that for the Court to issue a writ of mandamus to Secretary of State Madison, as provided by the Judi-

> **Mandamus.**   A writ (court order) requiring a government official to perform a certain act.

ciary Act, would require the Court to act in Marbury's case in its original jurisdiction. Because Marbury was not in that class of officials whose cases

> **Original Jurisdiction.**   The power to hear a case in the first instance, rather than on appeal from another (lower) court. Most of the Supreme Court's cases come from its appellate rather than its original jurisdiction.

the Constitution placed in the Court's original jurisdiction, the Judiciary Act, claimed Marshall, was invalid for improperly bestowing additional jurisdiction on the Court. A number of problems exist here. For one thing, the normal procedure is for the Court to determine its jurisdiction (or right to hear a case) before deciding the case "on the merits"; Marshall reversed this order, but, had he not, he would not have been able to "lecture" the Jefferson administration. Secondly, he could have read the Constitution's grant of original jurisdiction as not being limited to the specified types of cases. He could also have adopted a canon of interpretation often since used by the Court—that of construing an act of Congress so as to hold it constitutional if at all possible; thus he could have held that the Judiciary Act only granted the power to issue mandamus writs when to do so would be consonant with constitutionally-bestowed jurisdiction. However much a *tour de force Marbury* v. *Madison* was, it began a practice to which political scientists have paid much attention, although the Supreme Court did not again declare an act of Congress invalid until the ill-starred case of *Dred Scott* v. *Sandford*, 19 Howard 393 (1857), a case which had clear political impact on the slavery-anti-slavery controversy leading to the Civil War.

Attention to judicial review has continued to the present day, even after some political scientists studying public law have begun to expand their focus and change their methods. The present-day discussion of public law, carried on by judges as well as professors of constitutional law, tends to be in terms of broad theories of judicial review—not only whether the Court should exercise it, but how and under what conditions. Thus we have Judge Learned Hand, who advocated, in *The Bill of Rights*, a limited position for the judiciary. Hand was answered by Professor Herbert Wechsler, who upheld the Court's right to judicial review but argued against "result-oriented" decisions and advocated that the Court only overturn legislative acts when it could do so under "neutral principles of constitutional adjudication"; he stressed the need for *reasoned* action, not just "naked power." [7] The difficulty of finding such neutral principles has led some critics of Wechsler to point out that, in effect, he is advocating an even more limited role for the Court than did Judge Hand, and to suggest that the search for standards "is little more than the lawyers' nostalgia for the legal view of the Court and the legal modes of discourse that prevailed before the advent of the political view of the Court." [8] If the standards could be found, they might create problems for the Court by restricting its freedom of action. For example, the statement in the school desegregation cases that the Constitution was "color-blind" made it difficult for the Court to recognize the validity, at a later date, of plans to remedy the effects of discrimination and desegregation by benefiting Negroes specifically.

Another approach to the problem of judicial review is to view its relation with democracy. Aside from the legitimacy of judicial review within the framework of our Constitution, many have been concerned about the power of individuals, not elected to office and removable only with extreme difficulty, to invalidate legislation passed by directly elected representatives. However much this may seem to clash with abstract majoritarian theories of democracy, the practice can be upheld as protecting the rights of minorities against a rampant majority, although this argument suffers from the fact the Supreme Court has not always so acted, and as enforcing the "basic" will of all the people (expressed in the Constitution) against the transient will of a limited majority. One difficulty with acceptance of this latter argument is that people may rely heavily on the Court to uphold and maintain the Constitution, rather than themselves fighting for the values embodied in the Constitution when they see those values threatened. In this connection, it is wise to remember Learned Hand's comment about the spirit underlying the Constitution: without the spirit, the Constitution is dead, and with it, judges are not needed to uphold it.[9]

[7] Herbert Wechsler, "Toward Neutral Principles of Constitutional Law," *Principles, Politics, and Fundamental Law: Selected Essays* (Cambridge, Mass., 1961), pp. 3–48.

[8] Martin Shapiro, *Law and Politics in the Supreme Court* (New York, 1964), p. 20.

[9] "The Spirit of Liberty," *The Spirit of Liberty: Papers and Addresses of Learned Hand*, ed. Irving Dilliard (New York, 1959), pp. 143–145.

Theories of judicial review deal with more than judicial review; they also are concerned with the larger place of the Court in our governmental structure. While generally written from a definite point of view, to spin a philosophy of where the Court should be rather than an empirical theory of where the Court is, and while still largely emphasizing structure and formal institutional factors, they show an increasing preoccupation of constitutional scholars with the political situation of the Court. In connection with viewing the place of the Court in our larger system of government, the "activism," "modesty," or "self-restraint" of the judges is often debated fiercely, and we have arguments about "judicial legislation." (In a sense, for a court to be called an "activist" body, it need only strike down something which someone feels is of benefit to him.) The supposed "intrusion" of the Court into civil rights areas in which the Congress had done nothing and the executive branch little, e.g., school desegregation, is actively attacked by the very people who had taken no action. The Supreme Court's willingness to entertain suits on the subject of malapportioned legislatures is perhaps the best recent example of an action provoking an extended debate over the Court's place in our political system. When the Court decided in 1962, in *Baker* v. *Carr*, that apportionment suits were justiciable (thus overturning *Colegrove* v. *Green*, 328 U.S. 549

> **Justiciability.**   Whether a court has the ability to deal with the case, because the case is in proper form for judicial decision or because courts can fashion a remedy if it is found that a right has been infringed upon. This differs from *jurisdiction*, which is the question of whether a court has the legal power (usually designated in the Constitution or in statutes) to hear a case. One class of cases the court has considered non-justiciable are those involving "political questions," that is, ones which it is felt other branches of the government should decide.

[1946], where some of the judges had said that reapportionment was a "political question" with which the Court could not concern itself), and especially since 1964, when the Court held, in *Reynolds* v. *Sims*, that both houses of state legislatures must be apportioned on the basis of population ("one man, one vote—one vote, one value"), the Court's jurisdiction was threatened, and constitutional amendments were introduced in Congress specifically to allow states to choose one house of their legislature on the basis of "some factor other than population." [10] It was charged that the Court had usurped the functions of the legislatures, and that the federal district courts (where complaints were initially to be brought) were acting non-judicially in drawing lines for legislative districts. In reply, Herman Pritchett has argued that the Supreme Court's decision, instead of stultifying state action, *stimulated* a number of states to reapportion themselves without having to be forced by court order to do so.[11]

[10] Constitutional amendments failed (receiving a majority, but not the necessary two-thirds, in the Senate), and nothing has come of the request to Congress by 32 states (of the necessary 34) for a constitutional convention to consider the subject.

[11] Herman Pritchett, "Political Questions and Judicial Answers," *Western Political Quarterly*, XVII (1964), Supplement, pp. 12–20.

There are still many political scientists, perhaps a majority, who continue to examine constitutional law from a "traditional" point of view. That is, they concentrate on doctrine and write on the basis of impressions—perhaps impressions guided by much reading, but not impressions tested systematically, and as a result often embodying implicit judgments (as Holmes put it, "inarticulate major premises"). The doctrine about which they write is often the doctrine of specific judges or of specific areas of the law. The part of the Constitution to which most attention has been paid has varied over time, tending to be that part concerning which the Supreme Court has made most of its rulings at any given time. Today, that is civil rights and civil liberties. But before 1937, and for a long period of time before that date, it was the government's relation to the economy, specifically the national government's use of the commerce clause as a basis for regulation and the Court's use of the "due process" clause of the Fourteenth Amendment as a device for invalidating state regulation of the economy. The Court's late nineteenth century unwillingness to uphold state legislation as "reasonable" under the Fourteenth Amendment caused interests wanting regulation to turn to the national government for action. When the national government proved responsive to these demands, the Court overturned the national legislation as an invalid exercise of Congress' power over interstate commerce. This was done in some instances by narrowly construing "commerce" to mean no more than transportation.[12] The travails of the labor unions at the hands of judges generally has received extended attention, even though the unions won recognition in the Wagner Act of 1935 and the courts earlier were restrained from using injunctions against the unions. The continuing involvement of the unions in cases appealed from the decisions of the National Labor Relations Board has kept the subject of labor law in the forefront of matter about which students of the Supreme Court write.

The area of civil rights and civil liberties has been particularly emphasized by the Court since the beginning of the "Warren Court," that is, the Court since Chief Justice Warren took office. Criminal procedure has received much attention, as the Supreme Court in the 1960's has taken giant steps to extend a variety of protections from the Bill of Rights, formerly enforced only against the federal government, to those involved in state prosecutions. Indigent state felony and misdemeanor defendants are entitled to appointed trial attorneys (*Gideon* v. *Wainwright,* 372 U.S. 335 [1963]) and to be represented during police interrogation (*Escobedo* v. *Illinois,* 378 U.S. 478 [1964]), as well as to be informed of their rights when taken into custody (*Miranda* v. *Arizona,* 384 U.S. 436 [1966]). Illegally seized material must be excluded from state trials (*Mapp* v. *Ohio,* 367 U.S. 643 [1961]) and the use of electronic eavesdropping to obtain evidence has been largely circumscribed (*Berger* v. *New York,* 388 U.S. 41 [1967]). Televised trials

---

[12] See, for example, *U.S.* v. *E.C. Knight Corp.,* 156 U.S. 1 (1895), in which the Court held that manufacturing preceded commerce but was not part of it, and *Carter* v. *Carter Coal Company,* 298 U.S. 238 (1936), in which mining was held not a part of commerce and to have only "indirect" effects on commerce.

have been struck down (*Estes* v. *Texas*, 381 U.S. 532 [1965]), as have convictions obtained when much prejudicial pre-trial publicity has existed (*Sheppard* v. *Maxwell*, 384 U.S. 433 [1966]). With most of these topics, concern of those writing (largely in the law reviews) has been with what the Supreme Court has said, not with what is actually done in police departments or with the degree to which compliance with such rulings might be expected. Some work dealing with criminal procedure *practices* in several states began to appear in the mid-1960's, but this resulted from research done in the 1950's, well prior to the Supreme Court's new decisions. While these and more recent studies all cast much light on the criminal law part of constitutional law, they are only minute particles in the total picture of what has been produced. And they illustrate the continuing division between the lawyers and sociologists interested in the *administration* of criminal justice, or in judicial administration, and political scientists.

Other areas examined by those studying doctrine include the church-state area and race relations. The decision of the Court in *Brown* v. *Board of Education*, 347 U.S. 483 (1954) and 349 U.S. 294 (1955), overturning the 1896 *Plessy* v. *Ferguson*, 163 U.S. 537, doctrine of "separate but equal" and ordering desegregation of the schools, directed political scientists' attention to this area. Work in the church-state area is perhaps of longer standing, and is represented by a number of major works. Freedom of speech and censorship has always attracted much attention, particularly concerning obscenity. Because the Supreme Court turned to consideration of the subject of obscenity only in 1957 (although a number of important lower court cases dated back several decades), writers have dealt with the subject in detail only recently. The conflict between a defendant's right to a fair trial and freedom of the press has been much at issue, as segments of the bar have moved to limit what lawyers can properly say concerning defendants in criminal trials, a move much criticized by the mass media. This issue involves a conflict between rights. Discussion of freedom of speech often revolves around the question of a ranking of rights, particularly whether First Amendment freedoms of speech and press should be given a "preferred position" or whether they should be treated on the same footing as other items in the Bill of Rights. To the extent one accepts the "preferred position" doctrine, it means that legislation dealing with freedom of speech and press does not receive the same presumption of constitutionality which legislation in other areas is often given by the courts.

All this examination of doctrine, whether by subject area or in terms of specific judges, contributes much. For one thing, it underlies the study undertaken by those with other approaches to the field. Without a knowledge of what the Supreme Court has decided, or the formal legal framework within which it operates, those who de-emphasize analysis of the content of doctrine would not be able to operate. Regardless of the factors which condition judges' decisions, what is said in courts' opinions is what has impact on other branches of the government, and so must be examined by those exploring the political setting in which judges operate. Just as Duverger has remarked, "the sociologist cannot ignore juridical analysis if he is to understand the meaning of the texts he is studying," [13] the political scientist cannot ignore the rules which determine which cases come to court in attempting to explain factors affecting judges' behavior. While political scientists, particularly the behavioralists, explicitly downgrade the importance of doctrine, they have to understand it in order to perform their analyses, and it can be argued that much of the best work they have done has been based on a thorough examination of the intricacies of the Court's opinions. The behavioralists have themselves been trained in the traditional approach to constitutional law; while it is possible to train students to perform the mathematical manipulations the behavioralists use, unless they are also trained in what the Supreme Court decisions *mean* from a doctrinal point of view or within the legal framework, they will not be able to contribute much to the development of a viable theory of the judicial process.

POLITICAL APPROACHES

Those who have devoted their attention to the political situation of the Court, to the "politics of the judiciary" or the judicial process, are called by Schubert "conventionalists." The origin of this label is unclear and, of the three Schubert categories, is the least suitable. Certainly, *political* analysis of the Court has not been conventional; it has not been the central mode of analysis in public law. If one has to attach a label, "politicists" (for all the difficulty of the word) would be the best one to use; Martin Shapiro uses the term "political jurisprudence" in writing of this approach. Those who, since the mid-1930's, have devoted their attention to the political aspects of what the Court does, have tried, for the most part, to examine that role systematically and objectively. They are "non-mathematical behavioralists," for their interest is in behavior, yet they have not generally utilized mathematical tools. Labels aside, they have contributed much to our knowledge of where the Court actually stands in the governmental and political arenas, although much remains to be learned.

Much of the veil of mystery and apoliticism which had surrounded the Supreme Court for many years was stripped away in the mid-1930's. This resulted from the controversy surrounding its striking down much New Deal legislation,[14] which led to President Roosevelt's unsuccessful attempt to "pack" the Court in the guise of reforming it (by placing an additional judge on the Court for every existing Justice over age 70 who did not retire). Explanations that the Supreme Court judges simply "found" the law were now

---

[13] Duverger, p. 50.
[14] See, for example, *U.S.* v. *Butler*, 297 U.S. 1 (1936), invalidating the first Agricultural Adjustment Act, and *Schecter Poultry Corporation* v. *U.S.*, 295 U.S. 495 (1935), eliminating the National Industrial Recovery Act.

considered simplistic, and it is recognized that, to the extent judges can show that they simply find the law made by predecessors or located in the Constitution, they are thereby relieved of the responsibility for the decisions they are currently making. However, there has been recognition that the myth that the judges only find the law (or the use of "neutral principles") is important in retaining the Court's legitimacy in the eyes of the public and in its achieving its goals. To the extent the Court is clearly seen as political, there may be greater resistance to acceptance of its decisions. Justice Roberts' statement that the job of the Court was simply to place a statute alongside the Constitution to see if they matched—now called the "slot-machine theory of judicial interpretation"—was understood to be mechanistic. As a corrective to taking the Court at its word and to viewing it as simply a law-making body supposed to follow precedent in the Anglo-American legal tradition, analysts began to view the Court as a political body. Some saw it as solely political, for example, as simply part of the process by which interests gained or lost ascendance in the political system, with the courts as rewarding or punishing, advancing or setting back, those interests. Such a view helped provide new insights, but was not without its drawbacks because of the overemphasis on the political and the underemphasis on legal forms and legal tradition. The Supreme Court, as the court of last resort in our governmental system, does not, by the admission of a number of its own members, feel as compelled to follow precedent as do members of the "lower" courts. However, *stare de-*

Stare Decisis.   Literally, "to stand on the decision"; precedent. To follow past decisions to the extent the situations in those cases are congruent with the situation in the case now before the court.

cisis does provide some outside limits to the speed with which the Justices might change their minds on a particular issue, and precedent is a powerful symbol to be invoked when one wants the Justices not to change the direction in which their decisions are moving. That judges are forced to use legal categories and a process of thought we have come to call "legal reasoning" is important, if only because it forces people to cast their arguments in special terminology; this gives advantages in the political process to some, those who are adept at the skill of translation. The existence of "legal" institutions apart from the "political" ones also means another arena in which battles will be contested, even if policy is made in both.

Through much of this, the attention of scholars was still devoted almost entirely to the United States Supreme Court, although the cases decided by the Supreme Court were only a minute fraction of all the cases initiated in the first-level courts. Of the cases which the Supreme Court is *asked* to hear (which have usually already survived several levels of courts), the high court accepts far less than 10%. This results from the discretion it has had, basically since 1925, to grant the writ of certiorari. This emphasis on the high court and

Certiorari.   An order directing a lower court to send the record of a case to a higher court for review. If certiorari is granted, that means that the

Supreme Court will review a case. The votes of four of the nine Justices are needed to grant certiorari.

other appellate courts has tended to reinforce, with respect to the lower courts, the view that courts are "legal" and not "political" bodies. While lower courts are not as openly policy makers as is the Supreme Court, the way in which they frame decisions helps determine the issues which the Supreme Court decides. The fact they are the last courts to hear most cases gives them considerable importance, as does their role as enforcers of Supreme Court rulings. If one views both trial and appellate courts as making policy, even though the latter may do so more obviously, and sees them as both part of the process by which policy is made *and* implemented, then the distinction between trial and appellate (or "lower" and "higher") courts becomes less useful for analysis.

It has taken considerable effort to view law as one of the many outputs of the political system, to see it as affected by some of the same considerations and pressures that condition more obviously political outcomes (like acts of legislators), and to see the Supreme Court as a policy-maker. To be sure, there is a special institutional framework within which "legal" decisions are made. Many of the participants within that framework have received special training (in law schools) which may affect their view of their task, and there are role expectations among people who work together (for example, on multi-member courts) which may also have their effect on the product of those bodies. Pressures which are expressed one way in the legislative arena may have to be expressed another way in the judicial arena. Thus, interest groups, although they would not hesitate to approach legislators or executive branch officials directly, are expected not to "lobby" or "pressure" judges openly. However, they can bring their points of view before the court in a variety of ways, including the initiation of test cases and the filing of *amicus curiae*

> **Test Case.** A case brought to test the validity of a new piece of legislation. Financial support is often provided by a group. The National Association for the Advancement of Colored People (NAACP) has used this as a major tactic to win much legal ground.

> **Amicus Curiae.** Literally, "friend of the court." A participant in a court case who argues legal points relevant to the case, on the basis that the decision will affect the interests which the group represents. The American Civil Liberties Union (ACLU) often participates in cases on this basis.

briefs. Others have suggested that many articles in the law reviews, published by almost all of the nation's law schools, are meant to be read by judges and are intended to convince them of the virtues of a certain point of view. The manner of expression may be different, but the politics is nonetheless there. And courts, as only one participant in a multi-participant political arena, may themselves take actions to protect themselves against incursions of other participants seeking to increase *their* power or to forward their collective goals or the goals of their individual members; it should be noted that an increase in power within the Supreme Court for a judge may work against power for the Court in its external relations. Such actions, whatever the language in which they may be cast or the special form they may take, are clearly "political."

Much of the analysis of the politics in which the Court has been involved has been devoted to the interaction between Court and Congress and between Court and the President. The interaction between Court and Congress has been viewed more frequently, partly because the Court has more frequently dealt with legislative action (even if after an executive branch agency has begun to enforce the legislation) than with administrative action, although in the area of internal security and freedom to travel, administrative action has been the core of Court decisions. The reaction of the legislature has also been more vocal than that of the executive, with threats being made to restrict the Court's jurisdiction. A period of such threats occurred in the 1950's, after a series of decisions concerning internal security. In 1956 and 1957, the Court limited government action in this field but then, in 1958 and thereafter, backed off from its initial position. Congressional action against the Court, aimed at limiting the Court's appellate jurisdiction of internal security cases, did not pass, although whether because of the Court's "backtracking" or not is unclear.

The reaction of legislative bodies to judicial decisions is not the only way in which legislative and judicial branches interact; the relationship is bilateral. While the dialogue between judges and legislators is not as open as the confrontation between legislators and administrators, the dialogue nonetheless exists. Some of the ambiguity in statutes is purposeful—not only to assist in passing bills in the legislature, but to shift to the courts the responsibility for making more "final" decisions, in short, buck-passing. There are times when the Court strikes down a law as being "void for vagueness"; in so doing, it is telling the legislature not that it may not pass a law on that subject, but that it should rethink what it has done and enact something more precise. The courts are also frequently called upon to determine "legislative intent," in the course of interpreting statutes. Doing so is difficult, and if the courts reach a conclusion at variance with what the legislators feel they intended, they can (and will) pass "corrective" legislation, thus continuing the dialogue. In looking at court-legislature relations, we should also note that the legislature participates with the court in the process of considering the constitutionality of statutes. There are some legislators who adopt what Morgan calls the "judicial monopoly" theory—that only judges should determine constitutionality, and that legislators need not think in terms of constitutionality in the absence of judicial precedents to guide them. Others, however, feel that each branch should exercise a responsibility in such matters and that, for example, the legislature should not enact legislation which the legislators feel to be clearly unconstitutional or of doubtful validity. Thus some legislators attempt to anticipate what the courts would decide if a law were challenged, indicating that the courts' power of judicial review is not measured solely by the number of times it is exercised: its very existence has an effect which reduces the number of times the judges actually have to strike down laws.

In addition to looking at the interaction between the court and the other branches of government at the national level, and at the political situation which may give rise to cases, political scientists have begun to turn, in the last decade, to the study of the impact of Supreme Court decisions. The lack of compliance with the school desegregation decisions may have served to attune political scientists to this phenomenon. In addition, there is a concern that law will be brought into disrespect if not complied with, directing our attention to those situations in which compliance does not occur. The first work in this area was largely descriptive, telling what various communities did or did not do in response to desegregation orders. Then, we began to see studies of local compliance with the decisions in the church-state "released time" cases. Desegregation, church-state relations, and other civil liberties topics have been the ones on which the students of the Court's impact have concentrated, both because of the Court's predominant concern with civil liberties matters and because these decisions have been the most controversial ones in recent years. While no general theory to explain reasons for the Court's impact has yet to be developed, political scientists working in this area have begun to move away from simple narrative description to comparative studies and the generation of hypotheses explaining why Supreme Court decisions do not promptly end controversies or why the decisions help to bring about changes in long-standing local situations. Sociologist Melvin Tumin, in *Desegregation: Resistance and Readiness,* has pointed out that the Supreme Court has served as a convenient scapegoat for Southern community leaders who may have wanted to desegregate schools but found themselves in a political situation which prevented their initiative in the matter. Such factors as the pre-existence of relevant state court rulings and the ambiguity or precision of the Supreme Court's opinions have been suggested as affecting the impact of that Court's decisions. The situation in which judges operate has an effect on them, conditioning their decisions before they are reached. We have seen this to be the case in the behavior of federal district judges charged with handling school district desegregation plans in the wake of *Brown* v. *Board of Education.* Federal judges in the South, natives of the area, were placed in a difficult personal situation by what was officially expected of them, and many of them followed local *mores* rather than enforcing the guidelines established by their judicial superiors on the Supreme Court, despite the trial court judge's usual dislike of being overruled on appeal. However, not all judges acted the same way, as we can see from Charles Hamilton's typology of judges as judicial aggressors, resisters, and gradualists.[15]

While most impact studies have been carried out concerning particular

[15] Charles V. Hamilton, "Southern Judges and Negro Voting Rights: The Judicial Approach to the Solution of Controversial Social Problems," *Wisconsin Law Review*, 1965, 72–102.

cases, some analysts have been interested in a more generalized impact: what the public thinks of the Supreme Court as a result of its decisions. The specifics of what the Court has done have not been well communicated to affected or interested publics, because of such matters as deficiencies in newspaper reporting and the complexity of the Court's decisions. But people have impressions of and opinions about the Court even when they have no information on which to base them, as is often true of other areas of public opinion as well. Kessel found that the strong supporters and strong critics of the Supreme Court were more likely to have gone to college than the average member of the population. He found an overall distribution of attitudes favorable to the Court, but found a highly-motivated minority opposing what the Court had done. He concluded that "the decisions of the Supreme Court have had more effect on the reputation of the Court than [have] the activities of its antagonists." [16]

An area crucial to the political setting of the Court is judicial selection. At the national level, the President nominates and the Senate (usually) gives its "advice and consent." Only once in this century has a Supreme Court nominee (John Parker) been rejected, although delay has been applied by the Senate in the hope that the nomination would be withdrawn; perhaps the most notable cases of this involved Louis Brandeis, ultimately confirmed, and Abe Fortas, whose nomination to be Chief Justice was withdrawn. (The same tactic has been used with Negro appointees to the lower federal judiciary, but confirmation has usually come ultimately.) Appointments to the federal district courts are affected by "Senatorial courtesy," a practice whereby a nominee must be cleared with the Senator(s) of the President's party from the state in which the nominee is to serve. Not only Senators and party leaders but also American Bar Association officials are involved in the judicial selection process. The bar's attempt to get judges of proper "judicial temperament" is not without its ideological overtones, because "judicial temperament" is not always the same thing to all people, particularly where "liberal" nominees are involved, and the approval of nominees may be made largely by an unrepresentative portion of the bar, those who are older, better established, and more conservative.

One of the characteristics sought by the bar in a nominee to a high court position has often been prior judicial experience, on the grounds that such a person will be more willing to uphold past decisions. However, it has been demonstrated that Supreme Court judges with prior judicial experience are *less* likely to uphold precedent. There are other notable examples of new judges who do not vote as expected by those who appoint them. The story is told of President Theodore Roosevelt's search for a person to appoint to the Supreme Court who would vote "the right way" on anti-trust cases. After protracted correspondence, Roosevelt felt that Oliver Wendell Holmes, then on the Massachusetts Supreme Court, would be the man. In the first anti-

[16] John H. Kessel, "Public Perceptions of the Supreme Court," *Midwest Journal of Political Science*, X (1966), 191.

trust case to come before the Supreme Court after Holmes' appointment, he voted the "wrong" way. Said "Teddy": "I could make a man with a stronger backbone out of a banana!" More recent examples have been Justice Frankfurter, a member of President Franklin Roosevelt's "Brain Trust" while a Harvard Law professor, but conservative in his votes as a Justice, and Justice Warren, as a judge a leading upholder of civil liberties, who started his career as a police prosecutor. As the Holmes example suggests, ideology is probably the single element at which the appointing official looks most closely in choosing judges for the Supreme Court, although it is less important at lower levels. The judge's religion and the area of the country from which he comes may also be important. While members of the political party opposite that of the chief executive have been appointed, it is not common. Descriptions of background characteristics have been presented so that we may see how "representative" the judges are with respect to the general population. Just as the effect of prior judicial experience on judicial behavior has been examined, so has the effect of prior political party affiliation and ethnic background. Differences in voting on cases have been found between Democrats and Republicans, although this probably is more a result of their ideology than their party preference *per se*.

Judicial selection at the state and local level has attracted much attention, in part because of the variety of devices used and the reliance in the majority of states on the election of judges, in comparison with the federal process of appointment for life ("during good behavior"). Reformers have long debated the advantages and disadvantages of electing or appointing judges and, when they are to be elected, the virtues and defects of nonpartisan versus partisan elections. It has become clear that what appear on the surface to be elective arrangements often turn into *de facto* appointive ones, because Governors fill unexpired terms by appointment and the norm that one does not usually challenge a sitting judge works to protect most judges from serious election challenge. Plans combining aspects of both appointment and election have been put forth, of which the most notable is the so-called "Missouri Plan." In this arrangement, the Governor must appoint a judge from a list of three names given him by a selection commission (half laymen, half lawyers appointed by the bar). After the judge has served at least one year on the bench, he runs for a full term without opposition, the electorate being asked simply, "Shall John Doe be retained in office?" Experience in Missouri seems to suggest that this plan becomes the equivalent of lifetime appointment; whether it provides better judges than a straight partisan elective plan, as it is alleged to do, remains a more open question. That state judges are often selected by more openly "political" methods than are federal judges means that we are perhaps more aware of the political context in which state courts operate than we are at the national level, and of the effect of judges' decisions on local officials, as when a judge's favorable action on a prosecutor's request increases his chances of winning re-election, or when judicial patronage has an effect on political party structure.

Just as we have pictures of the politics of judicial selection and of the interaction between Court and Congress and Court and President, we also have portrayals of interaction within the Court. At first, this consisted of descriptions of the formal procedures by which the Court accepted cases, heard argument, discussed the cases and voted in conference, and the procedure by which opinions were assigned for writing, although generally less attention was paid to this structure and procedure than was paid to the judges themselves. Because no one besides the Justices is admitted to conference, the most junior Justice in terms of service acting as "messenger" and "doorman," we had no way of knowing what went on "behind the purple curtain." Through thorough examination of off-the-bench statements, reminiscences and the private papers of deceased judges, we now have a more thorough picture, although polemicists still hint darkly that the law clerks who assist the Justices have the judges in their power and insert "revolutionary" ideas into their opinions, a statement difficult to disprove without hard-and-fast knowledge of the procedures by which the judges do operate. For example, Alexander Bickel, in *The Unpublished Opinions of Mr. Justice Brandeis,* has shown that opinions are altered in the process of circulation to other judges for comment, and some, once written, are withdrawn once they have had their effect on other judges. His work also suggests that judges might withhold dissents because they are new to the Court, do not want to emphasize a "bad" point in the majority opinion by objecting to it, or want to limit the number of times they dissent so as to make each more effective. With respect to opinion assignment, we have seen that the procedure is far from random, and that the assigning judge (the Chief Justice if he is in the majority) may assign the opinion-writing to a "moderate" rather than a more extreme judge, both possibly to attract other judges within the Court or at least maintain the majority, or to have more persuasive effect outside the Court. For example, having Justice Tom Clark write the majority opinion in *Mapp* v. *Ohio,* in which illegally seized material was excluded from state trials, was more effective—because Clark was a former Attorney-General—than having Justices Douglas or Black, known as liberals and whose views were more predictable, write the Court's opinion. Norms within courts, such as that operating to restrain dissent, have also been discussed, and pressures leading to their being modified or discarded have been examined; for example, that controversial or "harder" cases make up a proportionately larger segment of the Supreme Court's cases is offered as a reason for higher rates of dissent.

JUDICIAL BEHAVIORALISM

The empirical study of judicial behavior is part of what has come to be called "jurimetrics," or "the scientific investigation of legal problems." [17] Jurimetrics, which can be contrasted with the normatively-oriented *juris-*

[17] Hans Baade, "Foreword," *Jurimetrics,* ed. Baade (New York, 1963), p. 1.

prudence, has concentrated on problems of storage and retrieval of law data and on the use of symbols in law, in addition to behavioral analysis of judicial decisions. The behavioralists have devoted the most systematic effort to attempting to determine what factors explain judges' decisions, although they have been (rightly) criticized for emphasizing attitudes (as determined by their methods) and ignoring other factors. They are searching for patterns, rather than presuming that each judge's behavior is random and idiosyncratic. We have known for some time that judges' personal views inserted themselves in cases, as when the majority justices in *Plessy* v. *Ferguson* asserted that separateness was only a "badge of inferiority" if the Negro insisted on seeing it that way, or in the series of cases in which a majority of the Supreme Court struck down state regulation of wages and hours as an abridgement of "freedom of contract," provoking Justice Holmes' famous dissent, in *Lochner* v. *New York,* 198 U.S. 45 (1905), that the Fourteenth Amendment does not enact Herbert Spencer's *Social Statics.* The question is whether we would look at them in terms of individual examples or more systematically. In trying to find the reasons behind judges' voting, the behavioralists are carrying on from an earlier tradition, that of the legal realists, although it has been suggested that legal realism has had less influence than the empiricism of other areas of political science. The legal realists insisted in looking behind the law as stated to law in action. This is perhaps best indicated by Holmes' statement that the life of the law is not logic, it is experience, and by his "bad man theory of the law," in which he held that the law was no more and no less than what a "bad man" would want to know of his lawyer in asking if he would be convicted for a certain act. At its most elementary, legal realism attempted to explain judges' actions partly in terms of the judges' hunches or what they had for breakfast (an "alimentary theory of judicial behavior"). While they did not seek the broader generalizations of the more theoretically oriented behavioralists, they were interested in judges' actions, not simply in what the judges said, which they recognized as largely rationalization for positions already arrived at. As Dorothy James points out in distinguishing traditionalist, realist, and behavioralist:

> The traditionalist firmly maintains that the Emperor is majestically apparelled. The realist indignantly asserts that he is stark naked, and hints at infantile dependence problems for those who require him clothed. The behavioralist wishes to ascertain why he is not clothed, and constructs indices by which one may determine on any given occasion, the degree of his exposure. Little of the inquiry is ever appreciated by the Emperor.[18]

Except for an early study by the psychologists Thurstone and Degan involving factor analysis of Supreme Court voting patterns,[19] the earliest work

[18] Dorothy B. James, "Role Theory and the Supreme Court," *Journal of Politics,* XXX (1968), 160.

[19] L.I. Thurstone and J.W. Degan, *A Factorial Study of the Supreme Court* (Chicago, 1951).

involving sophisticated empirical tools was that of Herman Pritchett.[20] His principal interest was in finding out who on the Supreme Court had voted with whom, and he concentrated on patterns of interagreement between the judges. When more political scientists undertook to examine judicial voting behavior on a large scale, they at first took up where Pritchett had left off. Thus Glendon Schubert applied "bloc analysis" to the voting of the judges. He expanded the indices used by Pritchett, looking at such matters as agreement in dissent and agreement in the majority, and worked from the resulting "blocs" to locate judges in terms of their relative liberalism or conservatism. Schubert, particularly in *Quantitative Analysis of Judicial Behavior*, used for analysis not only the United States Supreme Court, but also the Michigan Supreme Court, with its somewhat different procedures for opinion-assignment. As this indicates, the behavioralists have, to some extent, begun to reinvolve us in examination of the state courts, although without the backlog of traditional studies we have concerning the federal high tribunal. The advantage of the use of state courts for analysis is the possibility of comparative work. For example, one may want to know whether a scale which holds for the United States Supreme Court or the Michigan Supreme Court is specific to that court or characterizes the pattern of decisions in other judicial bodies.

In addition to bloc analysis, or rather building from it, Schubert utilized game theory in examining the Court, attempting to see whether coalitions of judges voted in such a way as to increase their power. His principal applications were with the New Deal Court, where he saw Justices Hughes and Roberts as a two-man team ("Hughberts"), and with the granting of certiorari in Federal Employers Liability Act cases. In the latter, he dealt with the problem created because the certiorari grant requires only four votes while five votes are usually necessary for a majority. He found that certain definite strategies appeared to be followed by justices on the court, although his work did not relate the power of an individual judge within the Court to the power of the Court externally. More recently, using "cue theory," other political scientists have begun to identify factors (cues) which affect when judges will vote to grant certiorari and the combination of those factors which must occur for the grant to be given. Sociologist Eloise Snyder explored the Supreme Court as a small group, paying special attention to the movements in voting behavior of Justices over time in relation to each other; she found that Justices assumed a middle-of-the-road position when first on the Court, only later moving toward one or the other extreme (liberal or conservative).[21] It is relevant here to remember that labelling a judge as "liberal" or "conservative" in terms of scaling or bloc analysis is relative; the range of opinions on the Court at one time helps determine where a particular judge is located on

[20] Herman Pritchett, *The Roosevelt Court: A Study in Judicial Politics and Values, 1937–1947* (New York, 1948).
[21] Eloise Snyder, "The Supreme Court as a Small Group," *Social Forces*, XXXVI (1958), 232–238.

a scale; changes from one term of Court to another may not be shifts in a judge's ideology so much as a result of personnel changes on the Court. Similarly, those at the extremes of a scale are not necessarily more intense in their positions than those at the "center."

Schubert, while perhaps the most prolific and best known of the judicial behavioralists, was not alone; a host of others began to write at the same time, of whom the most notable are perhaps Harold Spaeth, Sidney Ulmer, Fred Kort, and Samuel Krislov. With the exception of Kort, they (including Schubert) were primarily concerned with the attitudes which they felt underlay judges' decisions. In essence, their argument was that if the votes of Supreme Court justices in a number of cases formed a Guttman scale, then the judges' position on a common underlying attitude explained their votes. This directed their attention to "split decisions" of the Court, because unanimous decisions did not distinguish between judges, and to this extent what they examined was not representative of all the Court did. In a sense, they were interested in the same problem (explaining why judges voted as they did) as more traditionally inclined political scientists, but they refused to rely on impressionistic doctrinal analysis for their conclusions. As a result, they often arrived at different conclusions concerning particular problems with which the "traditionalists" had dealt. Most of the latter had, for example, viewed Justice Frankfurter not as a conservative—in fact, this view was strongly rejected—but as simply an advocate of judicial restraint, as a "judge's judge." Yet Harold Spaeth's analysis of Frankfurter's votes seems to show conclusively that Frankfurter was in fact conservative rather than simply restraint-oriented.[22] Glendon Schubert produces evidence concerning Justice Roberts' voting behavior which shows that both Hughes and Roberts switched from the conservative to the liberal bloc when the Court was threatened by Roosevelt's court-packing plan. This conflicts with an explanation Justice Frankfurter later offered for Justice Roberts, that Roberts had made up his mind to change his position on minimum-wage cases before Roosevelt's proposal, but that the case embodying his "switch" was not handed down until after FDR had made his attack on the Court, with the decision announcement being delayed by the illness of one of the Justices.[23]

Schubert shows that cases which seem to deal with the same semantic content often do not scale, and that cases which do scale often manifest different semantic content. While the first scaling work on judges' attitudes—what Schubert calls "psychometric analysis"—seemed to show linear dimensions, that is, simple liberal-conservative continua, Schubert has gone on in his most recent work to suggest the multi-dimensional nature of judges'

[22] Harold Spaeth, "The Judicial Restraint of Mr. Justice Frankfurter—Myth or Reality," *Midwest Journal of Political Science,* VIII (1964), 22–38. See also Joel B. Grossman, "Role-Playing and the Analysis of Judicial Behavior: The Case of Justice Frankfurter," *Journal of Public Law,* XI (1963), 285–309.

[23] Glendon A. Schubert, *Constitutional Politics* (New York, 1960), pp. 165–168. Felix Frankfurter, "Mr. Justice Roberts," *University of Pennsylvania Law Review,* CIV (1955), 313–316, reprinted in Schubert, pp. 168–171.

attitudes operative in cases. Thus we find economic liberalism and civil liberties liberalism as separate scales rather than part of a common dimension, as well as finding different judicial ideologies which are combinations of liberalism and conservatism on economic and civil liberties matters. Coupled with views of the judicial role as part of a judge's ideology, there are many possible combinations of outlooks with which judges respond to the stimulus of the case before them.

The work of the behavioralists did not go unchallenged; in fact, fireworks of a typical "traditionalist-behavioralist" variety broke out. One thus found the usual reaction to behavioralists—that they were counting instead of thinking—as when John Roche remarked that "the spell of numerology . . . seems to have fallen over the study of politics" and suggested that Schubert and Kort "seem to have confused the scientist with the book-maker." [24] They were also challenged in more serious ways. For example, it was suggested that cases were classified on the basis of the judges' statements of the facts, that is, as filtered by the judges' perceptions and reported after the decision, rather than on the basis of the way the case came to the courts, and that the scales depended largely on the analyst's initial classification of a case in terms of major content—important where several issues might be included—although this can be overcome by dealing with "issues" rather than "cases," where more than one of the former appears. It was also charged that attitudes used to explain consistency in voting patterns were inferred from the patterns themselves, thus providing circular analysis; no independent measure of attitudes, such as from off-the-court statements or survey analysis, was related to opinions, although Nagel and Westin have suggested that off-the-bench attitudes do not relate to court decisions.[25] In addition, Theodore Becker, a behavioralist who has perhaps carried on the most systematic running battle with the "Schubertians," has said, in *Political Behavioralism and Modern Jurisprudence*, that the more extreme behavioralists, in concentrating on attitudes, ignore the importance of the "judicial role" as a possible explanatory factor, a factor which might produce the same result as the inferred attitude. In essence, he says that the question is whether the legal system and legal roles affect judicial behavior or whether judicial behavior is unrestrained and simply a reflection of personal values little different from decision-making in other arenas. Thus, if the law says all are to be treated equally, and a judge is consistent in his rulings, is it because of what the law says (the "law variable"), or the consistency of his personal attitudes (the "non-law variable"), or both? The behavioralists reply with the certitude of those who use Guttmann scaling: if a set of cases scales, it scales; there is an underlying consistency, by definition. They presume that the

<hr />

[24] John P. Roche, "Political Science and Science Fiction," *American Political Science Review*, LII (1958), 1028–1029.

[25] Alan Westin, "Out-of-Court Commentary by United States Supreme Court Justices, 1789–1962: Of Free Speech and Judicial Lockjaw," *An Autobiography of the Supreme Court* (New York, 1963), p. 28. Stuart Nagel, "Off-the-Bench Judicial Attitudes," *Judicial Decision-Making*, ed. Glendon Schubert (New York, 1963), pp. 29–53.

judges were "result-oriented"; in classifying judges' votes, the behavioralists use categories such as "pro-government" and "anti-defendant," rather than categories derived from law or doctrine. They adamantly refuse to accept the manifest content of an opinion in preference to the underlying factors their analysis shows, as when Schubert says that the consistency of response shown by scaling

> . . . appears to provide a much better general explanation of how and why the Court makes its policy choices than does the alternative traditional theory of *stare decisis*, that consistency in the manipulation of precedential legal rules and principles is a function of legal craftsmanship.[26]

Yet Schubert and Becker are not as far apart as perhaps Becker (or both) would believe, for Schubert's recent work does deal with judges' dogmatism and pragmatism vis-à-vis previous decisions of the Court, and Schubert has conceded that the rational framework in which judges operate does have a great effect on them, as when he notes that "the roles of Supreme Court justices are defined in such a way as to give maximal emphasis to the importance of rational factors." [27]

Scaling is not all that the behavioralists do. Survey analysis has been used, for example, in a questionnaire study of legislators and judges to determine which group was more conservative. Judges were found to be more conservative than legislators and administrators on economic and free speech issues, but not on internationalism and restricting the electorate, with different patterns on still other issues.[28] This work by Nagel and other interviewing by Becker and others suggests that we may not be as hindered in exploring the judicial world as was earlier thought to be the case. Judges have been thought to live in a world apart, to be super-human once they don the robes, and it was thought unseemly to approach them with questions. That they are not so removed is shown not only by the extra-court roles some have played, as when Chief Justice Warren chaired the Commission to Investigate the Assassination of the President and Justice Jackson was the United States government's chief advocate at the Nuremberg war crimes trials, but also by their more frequent contacts with lawyers in the activities of the bar. The limited successes of Nagel, Becker, and others should not, however, let us forget that we cannot study the judicial process as openly as we can the legislative process; the decided displeasure, including the enactment of prohibitory federal legislation, at social scientists' "listening in" to juries in order to learn more about them should make us wary, and even those judges who consented to be interviewed will not comment on cases before the courts of which they are members. Fred Kort's work has been directed to attempting to predict the results in cases. Using content analysis he proceeds by isolating fac-

[26] Glendon Schubert, "From Public Law to Judicial Behavior," *Judicial Decision-Making*, ed. Schubert, p. 3.
[27] Glendon Schubert, *The Judicial Mind: The Attitudes and Ideologies of Supreme Court Justices, 1946–1963* (Evanston, 1965), p. 13.
[28] Nagel, "Off-the-Bench Judicial Attitudes."

tors in a set of cases on a common subject (and here he, like the scalers, must use traditional training to sort out cases), and then determines whether a given combination of factors is seen by the judges (in terms of their vote in a case) as crucial, so that, if the same set of factors comes up again, the same result will occur. Kort's methods have been challenged by mathematicians, but he claims his work is only exploratory, and admits that his tests of prediction cannot be applied to a case when a fact not previously encountered appears, or when judges decide to change the rules and adopt new doctrine.[29] One can criticize Kort's work also by likening it to the old idea that the law is simply to be found, not made: for the predictor, the law is "all there," in the attitudes of the judges, and simply needs to be uncovered. Schubert himself has gone beyond the use of scaling to factor analysis, and to what he calls "psychometrics," in which larger patterns of judicial attitudes, for example, ideologies, are extracted from voting records by extremely sophisticated methods possible only with the aid of computers. Schubert, as the pioneer among the behavioralists, has "lost" many political scientists because of the complexity of his work, and his own optimistic estimates to the contrary, has not succeeded in displacing older approaches to the study of constitutional law.

Conclusion.   Some other portions of the field, perhaps less central than the ones already discussed, need to be mentioned. These are areas either shared with other sub-fields in the discipline or ones which those interested in public law also deal with. In the first category are administrative law and judicial administration, both of which, but particularly the former, have been concerns primarily of those in the public administration field. While administrative law courses have been taught in the law schools for some time, it was the public administration specialists who were the primary political science custodians of the subject, because of their interest in the so-called independent regulatory commissions, organizationally part of neither the executive branch nor the court system. Constitutional law scholars have been interested in the degree of judicial review accorded the decisions of these agencies, and those involved in study of legal doctrine in the field of government relations with business cannot avoid dealing with them. As it is recognized that regulatory commissions are, like courts, collegial (i.e., multi-member) bodies with many recorded votes, some of the same analysis applied to the courts by the behavioralists might very well be applied to them, although this has not been done. Judicial administration, a minor aspect of public administration, has become more important as court structures have become more highly institutionalized, with formal administrative bodies to assist with such matters as the gathering of data about docket loads and assignment of judges to help reduce those loads where they are heaviest. The supervisory power of the United States Supreme Court over lower federal courts (the basis for some of the Supreme Court's decisions in the criminal procedure field) has

[29] Fred Kort, "Simultaneous Equations and Boolean Algebra in the Analysis of Judicial Decisions," *Jurimetrics*, ed. Baade, p. 161.

drawn further attention to this topic, as have the various proposals for reform of such matters as the post of United States Commissioner (now replaced by magistrates) and jury selection, stimulated by the work of Senator Joseph Tydings' Senate Subcommittee on Improvements in Judicial Machinery. Attention has also been directed to this area by the work of the President's two crime commissions, that on crime in the District of Columbia and the larger and more crucial Commission on Crime and Law Enforcement, as well as by the products of the important University of Chicago jury project of the last decade, in which such matters as the reasons for court delay and differences between judges and juries in evaluation of cases have been examined.

Criminology, a field which has, until recently, been almost totally the province of the sociologists, has come under the scrutiny of political scientists as the Supreme Court focused upon the area of fair trial in criminal cases. The political situation affecting the administration of justice at the state and local levels has particularly attracted the attention of political scientists, concerned with the "allocation of justice" (or the "rationing of justice")—with why different members of the community are treated differentially by law enforcement officials. This topic is one which comes within the purview of public law mainly because those who have shown interest in it have been previously doing work in the public law field. The same is true with respect to the activities of the legal profession. While it is sociologists who have undertaken work on what can be called the "ecology of the legal profession," that is, the organization and pattern of legal practice, political scientists have not been far behind, particularly in relating this structure to participation in politics. The question of the lawyer in politics has been of interest to the student of legislative politics for some time, because of the predominance of lawyers among legislators, but the interest in this subject is now one clearly shared with public law experts, showing how artificial some of the subdisciplinary boundaries in fact are, or how easily specific subject-matter concerns cut across such boundaries. The earlier-mentioned interest of public law scholars in the bar's concern about judicial selection has reinforced the stimulus to continue to explore what lawyers do and the relevance of that work for the political-legal system.

BIBLIOGRAPHY

Constitutional History

The history of the early period of the United States, prior to the writing of the Constitution, is treated well in CLINTON ROSSITER, *The Seedtime of the Republic* (New York, 1953), and MERRILL JENSEN, *The Articles of Confederation* (Madison, Wisc., 1953). The Constitutional Convention itself has received much attention, most recently in CLINTON ROSSITER, *1787: The Grand Convention* (New York, 1966). Original documents are available, both in JAMES MADISON, *Notes of Debates in the Federal Convention of 1787 Reported by James Madison* (Athens, Ohio,

1960) and in MAX FARRAND, *The Framing of the Constitution of the United States* (New Haven, 1931), as well as in SAUL K. PADOVER, *To Secure These Blessings: The Great Debates of the Constitutional Convention of 1787, Arranged According to Topics* (New York, 1962).

The best available material on this period is to be found in ALFRED KELLY and WINIFRED HARBISON, *The American Constitution: Its Origins and Development*, 3rd ed. (New York, 1963). The Kelly and Harbison volume is also probably the best available text covering the constitutional history of the entire American experience. Other volumes dealing with the same material include ARTHUR N. HOLCOMBE, *Our More Perfect Union: From Eighteenth-Century Principles to Twentieth-Century Practice* (Cambridge, Mass., 1950); LEO PFEFFER, *This Honorable Court: A History of the United States Supreme Court* (Boston, 1965); and CARL BRENT SWISHER, *The Growth of Constitutional Power in the United States* (Chicago, 1946). More detailed treatment of an early period of our constitutional development is C. PETER MAGRATH, *Yazoo: Law and Politics in the New Republic: The Case of FLETCHER v. PECK* (Providence, R.I., 1966). A particular type of history, manufactured for arguments in particular cases, known as "law-office history," is discussed by ALFRED H. KELLY, "Clio and the Court: An Illicit Love Affair," *The Supreme Court Review 1965*, ed. Philip B. Kurland (Chicago, 1965), pp. 119–158.

Also useful in understanding the history of constitutional development, and of the Supreme Court in particular, are biographies of judges. Among the leading biographies are ALPHEUS THOMAS MASON, *Brandeis: A Free Man's Life* (New York, 1956), and CAROLYN DRINKER BOWEN, *Yankee From Olympus* (Boston, 1944), about Justice Oliver Wendell Holmes. Among the less well known about whom volumes have been written are Justices William Johnson and Morrison R. Waite. See, respectively, DONALD G. MORGAN, *Justice William Johnson: The First Dissenter: The Career and Constitutional Philosophy of a Jeffersonian Judge* (Columbia, S.C., 1954), and C. PETER MAGRATH, *Morrison R. Waite: The Triumph of Character* (New York, 1963).

The Work of the Court

Casebooks and Summaries.   The primary text for the study of constitutional law is the casebook. Some examples are ALPHEUS THOMAS MASON and WILLIAM BEANEY, *American Constitutional Law*, 4th ed. (Englewood Cliffs, 1968); ROCCO TRESOLINI, *American Constitutional Law*, 2nd ed. (New York, 1965); and ROBERT E. CUSHMAN and ROBERT F. CUSHMAN, *Cases in Constitutional Law*, 2nd ed. (New York, 1965.) A massive casebook is PAUL A. FREUND, ARTHUR E. SUTHERLAND, MARK DE WOLFE HOWE, and ERNEST J. BROWN, *Constitutional Law: Cases and Other Problems*, 2nd ed. (Boston, 1961), two volumes. One dealing with only civil rights cases is MILTON R. KONVITZ, *The Bill of Rights Reader: Leading Constitutional Cases*, 3rd rev. ed. (Ithaca, N.Y., 1965).

Annual reviews of what the Court has decided are a common feature of the scene. DAVID FELLMAN wrote such articles for the *APSR* for many years, although they have been discontinued; see "Constitutional Law in 1958–1959," *APSR*, LIV (1960), 167–199 and 474–493, or, for 1959–1960, *APSR*, LV (1961), 112–135. PAUL BARTHOLOMEW writes summaries for *Western Political Quarterly*; see, for example, "The Supreme Court of the United States, 1963–1964," *Western Political Quarterly*, XVII (1964), 595–607. At times, authors concentrate on developments in a particular area of the law during a term of Court, e.g., ROBERT G. MC CLOSKEY,

"Deeds Without Doctrines: Civil Rights in the 1960 Term of the Supreme Court," *APSR*, LVI (1962), 71–89, and WALTER F. MURPHY, "Deeds Under a Doctrine: Civil Liberties in the 1963 Term," *APSR*, LIX (1965), 64–79.

In addition to casebooks and summaries, we have an occasional treatise—an attempt to discuss what the Court has done, topic-by-topic, so as to provide a complete description of the Court's doctrine at a given time. *The Constitution of the United States of America, Analysis and Interpretation*, ed. Edward Corwin (Washington, D.C., 1952) is one such. BERNARD SCHWARTZ's effort is more recent: *A Commentary on the Constitution of the United States*, 2 vols. (New York, 1963). A treatise embodying a definite point of view is WILLIAM WINSLOW CROSSKEY, *Politics and the Constitution in the History of the United States* (Chicago, 1953), 2 vols.

Case Studies.   How the Court arrives at its decisions, and how cases come to the Court, as well as what happens to them after they are decided, are elements all portrayed well in case studies of particular cases. One of the more important is ALAN WESTIN, *The Anatomy of a Constitutional Law Case* (New York, 1958), which examined the way in which the Steel Seizure Case, *Youngstown Sheet and Tube* v. *Sawyer*, 343 U.S. 579 (1952), was brought to Court. A number of the studies collected in *The Third Branch of Government*, ed. C. Herman Pritchett and Alan Westin (New York, 1963) and prepared by LUCIUS and TWILEY BARKER, *Freedoms, Courts, and Politics: Studies in Civil Liberties* (Englewood Cliffs, 1965), help illustrate further the context in which Supreme Court cases arise. Two civil rights cases given excellent book-length treatment are *Gideon* v. *Wainwright*, 372 U.S. 355 (1963), extending the right to counsel, in ANTHONY LEWIS, *Gideon's Trumpet* (New York, 1964), and *Gomillion* v. *Lightfoot*, 364 U.S. 339 (1960), an Alabama gerrymandering case, in BERNARD TAPER, *Gomillion Versus Lightfoot: Apartheid in Alabama* (New York, 1965).

Doctrinal Analysis.   In addition to the summaries of the Supreme Court's activity, which usually involve at least brief analysis of the cases described, there is much literature concerned with the Court's decisions in particular areas of the law. One collection of materials analyzing Court doctrine is ROBERT C. MC CLOSKEY, ed., *Essays in Constitutional Law* (New York, 1967). Treatment of the doctrine developed by particular judges is frequent. Thus we have WALLACE MENDELSON, *Justices Black and Frankfurter: Conflict in the Court*, 2nd ed. (Chicago, 1966), and SAMUEL KONEFSKY, *The Legacy of Holmes and Brandeis* (New York, 1956), as well as collections of the decisions of individual Justices, such as MAX LERNER, ed., *The Mind and Faith of Mr. Justice Holmes*, and VERN COUNTRYMAN, ed., *Douglas of the Supreme Court: A Selection of His Opinions* (Garden City, 1959).

Because the Supreme Court has been particularly concerned with civil rights cases in recent years, the flow of material on that subject has been particularly heavy. A good collection of the law review materials on civil rights is MARTIN SHAPIRO, ed., *The Supreme Court and Constitutional Rights: Readings in Constitutional Law* (Glenview, Ill., 1967). A recent useful attempt to develop a comprehensive position on free speech matters is THOMAS I. EMERSON, *Toward a General Theory of the First Amendment* (New York, 1963), and SAMUEL KRISLOV, *The Supreme Court and Political Freedom* (New York, 1968), has made another such effort. Many of the articles in PHILIP KURLAND, ed., *The Supreme Court Review* (Chicago, each year), are devoted to analysis of specific important civil rights decisions.

In addition to untold pages in legal periodicals, ALBERT P. BLAUSTEIN and CLARENCE CLYDE FERGUSON, JR., *Desegregation and the Law* (New Brunswick, N.J.,

1957) and the work of NAACP attorney JACK GREENBERG, *Race Relations and the Law* (New York, 1959) clearly indicate the state of the law in that area up to the present decade. The collection edited by (then Senator) HUBERT HUMPHREY, *Segregation: Cases and Commentary* (New York, 1964) places the leading court decisions (which are included) in the larger social context, and includes material by psychologist Robert Coles, who has closely followed the children who first entered previously all-white schools in cities like New Orleans and Atlanta; see ROBERT COLES, *Children of Crisis: A Study of Courage and Fear* (Boston, 1967).

In addition to desegregation, two other important areas covered in the literature are church-state relations and censorship. Important works on the former include WILLIAM VAN ALSTYNE, "Constitutional Separation of Church and State: The Quest for a Coherent Position," *APSR*, LVII (1963), 865–882; LEO PFEFFER, *Church, State, and Freedom*, rev. ed. (Boston, 1967); and ANSON PHELPS STOKES and LEO PFEFFER, *Church and State in the United States*, rev. one-volume ed. (New York, 1964). A recent discussion is WILLIAM A. CARROLL, "The Constitution, the Supreme Court, and Religion," *APSR*, LXI (1967), 657–674. MORRIS ERNST and ALAN SCHWARTZ, *Censorship: The Search for the Obscene* (New York, 1964), provide a general introduction to censorship. Thorough works, dealing with government relations as well as the constitutional law on the subject, are JAMES C. N. PAUL and MURRAY SCHWARTZ, *Federal Censorship: Obscenity in the Mail* (New York, 1961), concerned principally with literature; IRA CARMEN, *Movies, Censorship, and the Law* (Ann Arbor, 1966), and RICHARD RANDALL, *Censorship of the Movies: The Social and Political Control of a Mass Medium* (Madison, 1968).

Political scientists interested in civil rights matters have begun to deal with aspects of their subject which extend beyond Supreme Court rulings. WAYNE LA FAVE, *Arrest: The Decision to Bring a Suspect Into Custody* (Boston, 1965) and DONALD J. NEWMAN, *Conviction* (Boston, 1966), are examples of studies of the actual working of the criminal law. JEROME SKOLNICK, *Justice Without Trial* (New York, 1966) and ARNOLD TREBACH, *The Rationing of Justice* (New Brunswick, N.J., 1964) are similar valuable studies.

Courts in the Political Process

Readers.   Four collections of readings provide a fine introduction to this aspect of public law. They are:

ROBERT SCIGLIANO, ed., *The Courts: A Reader in the Judicial Process* (Boston, 1962);

WALTER F. MURPHY and C. HERMAN PRITCHETT, eds., *Courts, Judges, and Politics: An Introduction to the Judicial Process* (New York, 1961);

JOHN SCHMIDHAUSER, ed., *Constitutional Law in the Political Process* (Chicago, 1963); and

THOMAS P. JAHNIGE and SHELDON GOLDMAN, eds., *The Federal Judicial System: Readings in Process and Behavior* (New York, 1968).

General.   There are a number of general treatments of the Supreme Court's place in the American governmental and political system, and a few of the position of lower federal courts or of state courts. Examples include the work of the late Justice ROBERT JACKSON, *The Supreme Court in the American System of Government* (Cambridge, Mass., 1955); JOHN P. FRANK, *Marble Palace: The Supreme Court in American Life* (New York, 1958); and ALEXANDER BICKEL, *The Least Dangerous Branch* (Indianapolis, 1962). See also the collection of articles, "Policy-Making in a

Democracy: The Role of the United States Supreme Court—A Symposium," *Journal of Public Law*, VI (1957), 257–508, particularly ROBERT A. DAHL, "Decision-Making in a Democracy: The Supreme Court as a National Policy-Maker," 279–295. More narrowly focused on judicial review are HOWARD DEAN, *Judicial Review and Democracy* (New York, 1966) and CHARLES L. BLACK, JR., *The People and the Court: Judicial Review in a Democracy* (Englewood Cliffs, 1960); Black presents a more involved argument than Dean. A leading study of the "law-making" function of the Court is FRED V. CAHILL, *Judicial Legislation* (New York, 1952). What a "policy-oriented" judge might do in order to achieve his goals is hypothesized by WALTER MURPHY, *Elements of Judicial Strategy* (Chicago, 1964). Two collections of statements by the judges themselves, which provide a useful base for comparison with observers' analyses are ALAN WESTIN, ed., *An Autobiography of the Supreme Court: Off-the-Bench Commentary by the Justices* (New York, 1963), and ALAN WESTIN, ed., *Views From Inside* (New York, 1961).

Supreme Court interaction with the Congress is considered in WALTER MURPHY, *Congress and the Court* (Chicago, 1962), a study of the Congressional reaction to the internal security cases of the 1950's; DONALD G. MORGAN, *Congress and the Constitution: A Study of Responsibility* (Cambridge, Mass., 1966); and HARRY P. STUMPF, "The Political Efficacy of Judicial Symbolism," *Western Political Quarterly*, XIX (1966), 293–303. GLENDON SCHUBERT, *The Presidency in the Courts* (Minneapolis, 1957), is the standard treatment of Court-President interaction. MARTIN SHAPIRO, *The Supreme Court and Administrative Agencies* (New York, 1968) is an exploration of the Court's relationship with the increasingly important part of the executive branch. This matter is also dealt with in ARTHUR S. MILLER, *The Supreme Court and American Capitalism* (New York, 1968), almost more an essay in the theory of the corporation than a public law disquisition. The Supreme Court's role in relation to our federal system is seen through the treatment by JOHN SCHMIDHAUSER, *The Supreme Court as Final Arbiter in Federal-State Relations, 1789–1957* (Chapel Hill, 1958).

Other courts than the Supreme Court are discussed by WALTER MURPHY, "Lower Court Checks on Supreme Court Power," *APSR*, LIII (1959), 1017–1031, and by KENNETH N. VINES, "Political Functions of a State Supreme Court," *Studies in Judicial Politics*, ed. Vines and Herbert Jacob [Tulane Studies in Political Science, Vol. VIII] (New Orleans, 1963), pp. 51–75; and VINES, "The Role of Circuit Courts of Appeal in the Federal Judicial Process: A Case Study," *MJPS*, VII (1963), 305–319.

Interests. Two volumes which discuss the Supreme Court in terms of the representation of interests are JACK W. PELTASON, *Federal Courts in the Political Process* (New York, 1955) and VICTOR ROSENBLUM, *Law as a Political Instrument* (New York, 1955), both of which helped open up the "political" study of the Supreme Court. Clement Vose has been the leading scholar on the role played by interest groups; see VOSE, "The National Consumers' League and the Brandeis Brief," *MJPS*, I (1957), 267–290; *Caucasians Only: The Supreme Court, The NAACP, and the Restrictive Covenant Cases* (Berkeley, 1959); and "Interest Groups, Judicial Review, and Local Government," *Western Political Quarterly*, XIX (1966), 85–100; plus LUCIUS BARKER, "Third Parties in Litigation: A Systematic View of the Judicial Function," *JOP*, XXIX (1967), 41–69.

Impact. Illustrative of the recent emphasis on the impact of Supreme Court decisions are a series of studies concerning church-state cases. Two now often-cited articles are GORDON PATRIC, "The Impact of a Court Decision: Aftermath of the McCollum Case," *Journal of Public Law*, VI (1957), 455–463, and FRANK J. SORAUF, "*Zorach* v. *Clauson:* The Impact of a Supreme Court Decision," *APSR*, LIII (1959), 777–791. More recent books are RICHARD M. JOHNSON, *The Dynamics of Compliance: Supreme Court Decision-Making from a New Perspective* (Evanston, 1967), and WILLIAM K. MUIR, *Prayer in the Public Schools: Law and Attitude Change* (Chicago, 1967).

Judicial Selection.   Those dealing with the courts' political role have been interested in the process by which judges are selected. In addition to the studies of the characteristics of those judges, for example, JOHN SCHMIDHAUSER, "The Justices of the Supreme Court: A Collective Portrait," *MJPS*, III (1959), 1–57, and SHELDON GOLDMAN, "Characteristics of Eisenhower and Kennedy Appointees to the Lower Federal Courts," *Western Political Quarterly*, XVIII (1965), 755–762, we have studies relating background characteristics to judicial behavior. Among the leading articles is JOHN SCHMIDHAUSER and DAVID GOLD, "Stare Decisis, Dissent, and the Background of the Justices of the Supreme Court of the United States," *University of Toronto Law Journal*, XIV (1962), 194–212. Another examination of the relation between background and behavior is STUART S. NAGEL, "Testing Relations Between Judicial Characteristics and Judicial Decision-Making," *Western Political Quarterly*, XV (1962), 425–437. Other Nagel articles include "Political Party Affiliation and Judges' Decisions," *APSR*, LV (1961), 843–850, and "Ethnic Affiliations and Judicial Propensities," *JOP*, XXIV (1962), 92–110. JACK W. PELTASON, *Fifty-Eight Lonely Men: Southern Federal Judges and Desegregation* (New York, 1961), deals with the problem Southern-born and raised judges have in enforcing desegregation decisions.

JOEL GROSSMAN has portrayed an important aspect of the selection process in *Lawyers and Judges: The ABA and the Politics of Judicial Selection* (New York, 1965). The selection process in one state is analyzed in RICHARD A. WATSON, RONDAL G. DOWNING, and FREDERICK C. SPIEGEL, "Bar Politics, Judicial Selection and the Representation of Social Interests," *APSR*, LXI (1967), 54–71.

Behavioral Studies

Leading Scholars.   In any consideration of judicial behavior studies, the work of GLENDON SCHUBERT is foremost. He has provided two important summaries of the work of the behavioralists, "The Study of Judicial Decision-Making as an Aspect of Political Behavior," *APSR*, LII (1958), 1007–1025, and "Behavioral Research in Public Law," *APSR*, LVII (1963), 433–445; edited two collections of articles, *Judicial Behavior: A Reader in Theory and Research* (Chicago, 1964), and *Judicial Decision-Making* (New York, 1963); and provided a full-length treatment of judicial psychology, *The Judicial Mind: The Attitudes and Ideologies of Supreme Court Justices, 1946–1963* (Evanston, 1965). "The 1960 Term: A Psychological Analysis," *APSR*, LVI (1962), 90–107, is another example of his work. Other leading behavioralists include HAROLD SPAETH and S. SIDNEY ULMER. Spaeth's work is exemplified by "Judicial Power as a Variable Motivating Supreme Court Behavior," *MJPS*, VI (1962), 54–82, and "The Judicial Restraint of Mr. Justice Frankfurter—Myth or Reality," *MJPS*, VIII (1964), 22–38. (On the points raised in the latter article, see also JOEL B. GROSSMAN, "Role-Playing and the Analysis of Judicial Behavior: The Case of Justice Frankfurter," *Journal of Public Law*, XI (1963), 285–309.) Among Ulmer's many articles are "The Analysis of Behavior Patterns of the

United States Supreme Court," *JOP*, XXII (1960), 647–652, and "Supreme Court Behavior and Civil Rights," *Western Political Quarterly*, XIII (1960), 294–311.

The behavioralist most interested in predicting decisions has been FRED KORT. His original article was "Predicting Supreme Court Decisions Mathematically: A Quantitative Analysis of the 'Right to Counsel' Cases," *APSR*, LI (1957), 1–12. Mathematical criticism was made by FRANKLIN M. FISHER, "The Mathematical Analysis of Supreme Court Decisions: The Use and Abuse of Quantitative Methods," *APSR*, LII (1958), 321–338; Kort responded, 339–348.

Criticism.   Attacks on the work of the behavioralists have come from a variety of sources. WALLACE MENDELSON is perhaps representative of those criticizing from an essentially traditional point of view. One exchange is that between Mendelson, "The Untroubled World of Jurimetrics," *JOP*, XXVI (1964), 914–922, and FRED KORT, "Comment," 922–926; Mendelson's response is at 927–928. He also attacks in "The Neo-Behavioral Approach to the Judicial Process: A Critique," *APSR*, LVII (1963), 593–603, to which "Replies and Comments" appeared at 948–951.

A critique from a position which recognizes the political setting of court activity is JAMES L. and MARILYN J. BLAWIE, "The Judicial Decision: A Second Look at Certain Assumptions of Behavioral Research," *Western Political Quarterly*, XVIII (1965), 579–593. Another constant critic is THEODORE BECKER, who considers himself a behavioralist although he does not use Schubertian analytical techniques. See "Inquiry into a School of Thought in the Judicial Behavior Movement," *MJPS*, VII (1963), 254–266, as well as his expositions of the importance of survey research on judges: "Surveys and Judiciaries, or Who's Afraid of the Purple Curtain," *Law & Society Review*, I (1966), 133–143, and "A Survey Study of Hawaiian Judges: The Effect on Decisions of Judicial Role Variations," *APSR*, LX (1966), 677–680. Becker develops his thoughts most fully in *Political Behavioralism and Modern Jurisprudence* (Chicago, 1964).

15 / COMPARATIVE GOVERNMENT AND POLITICS

by David M. Wood

The Transformation of the Field / The Comparative Method / General Conceptual Frameworks and Theories / Sub-Fields of Comparative Government and Politics

THE TRANSFORMATION OF THE FIELD

The boundaries which divide the field of comparative government and politics from other fields of political science are probably as hard to delineate as any which are identified in this volume. Perhaps the most serious problem is the fact that the conception which political scientists have had of the field has been radically transformed within just the past decade. This transformation has proceeded to the point where a generational cleavage exists, a cleavage based upon the divergent views of the field which predominated during the eras in which various political scientists were first introduced to the discipline. As a consequence an historical introduction, tracing the evolution of the field, is in order.

In broad terms the transformation which has taken place has been from a field which would most appropriately be labelled "foreign governments" to one which might most adequately be called "comparative political systems." To understand what has taken place it will be best to divide these two terms into their component parts and to show how the field has changed: (a) from the study of "foreign" political phenomena to the study of political phenomena "comparatively," and (b) from the study of "governments" to the study of "political systems." The author's bias should be made clear from the outset: he will attempt to make the case for the latter perspective. It should be kept in mind, however, that the end result is not yet agreed upon, and that there are respectable arguments that can be made in opposition to further travel along the present road.

From Foreign to Comparative. The term "comparative government" has a classical, time-honored history. Certainly an important feature of early political science curricula, dating back several decades into the nineteenth century, was inquiry into the similarities and differences between forms of government, as a means of getting at answers to a more fundamental and

486

even more classical problem: Which forms of government are the best? Comparative government at this time was essentially one branch of political theory. At its best, it proceeded from classical assumptions as to the nature of man as a political animal and deduced ideal forms of political organization against which the existing systems of government were compared.[1] Governmental systems and specific forms were classified and compared, a process essential not only for the purpose of evaluation, but also for that of systematic description.

Professor Harry V. Eckstein has pointed to the late decades of the nineteenth century as a period in which American political science, influenced by a "primitive positivism," effected a divorce between its normative and its descriptive concerns.[2] In the realm of "comparative government," scholars turned from a concern for the evaluation of governmental forms to a pure description. By and large they retained the analytical categories developed by their predecessors, but began to shape their meanings to fit descriptive rather than normative purposes. Thus, for example, a pure ideal-type democracy, while it continued to be a tool employed in normative political theory, no longer had utility for specialists in comparative government, and the definition of democracy was loosened to permit inclusion of a congeries of actual governmental forms and socio-political conditions.

Having deprived themselves of one kind of theoretical concern, American specialists in comparative government failed to seek new avenues of theoretical inquiry. Instead they immersed themselves in the data of political institutions, stressing accuracy of description above all else.[3] The quest for exact knowledge inevitably moved them to become specialists in increasingly narrow ranges of political phenomena; they confined themselves to the governmental systems of particular regions or countries and even to the na-

[1] E.g., John Stuart Mill, *Considerations on Representative Government* (London, 1861).

[2] Harry Eckstein, "A Perspective on Comparative Politics, Past and Present," *Comparative Politics: A Reader*, ed. Eckstein and David E. Apter (New York, 1963), pp. 9–11.

[3] For example, the account by James K. Pollock of Nazi Germany at the height of Hitler's power, *The Government of Greater Germany* (New York, 1938), is almost a straight descriptive account of institutions preceded by a rapid survey of the events (not their underlying causes) leading up to Hitler's assumption of power. The Nazi-dominated agencies of government are described more in terms of legally defined functions than in terms of their place within the Nazi design for a totalitarian system. Description of administrative structure follows the standard descriptive techniques used to analyze the bureaucracies of democratic systems. Most basically, no effort is made to locate Nazi Germany on a spectrum of political systems showing its similarities to and differences from other dictatorships and the crucial ways it could be contrasted with constitutional democracies. No evidence is shown that the author felt this regime was worth studying *as a particular kind of regime* rather than, as he evidently regarded it, as the regime that Germany (worth studying for its own sake) had at that time. Similar narrow-focused studies of democratic systems make less peculiar reading today only because we are more inclined to take their unspoken assumptions for granted. Contrast Pollock's approach with those of Carl J. Friedrich and Zbigniew Brzezinski, *Totalitarian Dictatorship and Autocracy* (Cambridge, Mass., 1956), and Hannah Arendt, *The Origins of Totalitarianism* (New York, 1958).

ture of particular institutions within particular countries. The tendency was for scholars to be trained as experts especially in the governmental systems of particular countries or areas, usually in Western Europe or the British Dominions. Those scholars who concentrated their efforts upon countries other than the United States continued to label the general field within which they worked "comparative government," but the comparative aspect of their efforts had to a large extent become lost. The term "foreign governments" was more appropriate for the "field" as it was treated in American political science. Comparative government textbooks generally were organized on a "country-by-country" basis, with each of the governmental systems covered separately and a minimum of comparative material included which linked the individual country sections to one another.[4] A few exceptions appeared, including ambitious projects such as the classic works of Herman Finer and Carl J. Friedrich, but courses in comparative government tended to adhere to the "country-by-country" pattern, with only the major powers of Europe ordinarily covered.

By World War II, however, newer concerns were beginning to press in upon the students of "foreign governments." An underlying assumption of the narrow descriptive focus had been that the more advanced states of the world had either achieved, or were in the process of achieving, democracy. Countries which had not yet reached a sufficient state of maturity to merit democracy or which, though sufficiently advanced by the then standards of modernity, were still undergoing the throes of institutional democratization were not quite considered fit subjects for study, since they were at best temporary or pre-political phenomena, of interest today essentially to the anthropologist and tomorrow to the historian. Furthermore, given a confidence

[4] An early comparative government textbook, Frederick Austin Ogg, *The Governments of Europe* (New York, 1918), contained the following nine sections: Great Britain, Germany, France, Italy, Switzerland, Austria-Hungary, the Low Countries, Scandinavia, and the Iberian States. The section on Great Britain was divided into the following eight chapters: the Foundations of the Constitution; the Constitution since the Seventeenth Century; the Crown and the Ministry; Parliament: the House of Commons; Parliament: the House of Lords; Parliament: Organization, Functions, Procedure; Political Parties; Justice and Local Government. Probably the leading comparative government textbook of the post-World War II period was John C. Ranney and Gwendolen M. Carter, *Major Foreign Powers* (New York, 1949). It contained four sections: the Government of the United Kingdom, the Government of France, the Government of the Soviet Union, and the Government of Germany. The British section contained brief units on the politically relevant aspects of British society and called constitutional history "political heritage," but otherwise the topic breakdown was virtually the same as Ogg's. In both texts the emphasis is upon accurate description of the functions and powers of institutions of government in each of the countries studied. This is not to suggest that comparative statements were never made. (E.g., Ogg: "On paper France has to-day a parliamentary system of government substantially like that which prevails in Great Britain. . . . Parliamentary government in France means, however, in practice something very different from what it means across the Channel. The principal reason why this is so is to be found in the totally different status of political parties in the two countries." Pages 312–313.) Numerous *ad hoc* comparisons of this nature are to be found, but the emphasis is upon what makes country X different from country Y, not upon what makes one *class* of countries different from another. (See the section on "The Comparative Method" for a discussion of the importance of classification in comparison.)

in the future as well as in the merits of democratic forms of government, the motivation to ask searching questions about the consequences of various governmental forms or about the forces that produce one type of political outcome rather than another simply did not exist. Without the motivation to formulate theory, the motivation to test theory was absent, and without that motivation real comparison across countries was deprived of its essential purpose.

The events between 1914 and 1945 brought such complacency to an end. American political science was perhaps slower than European political science to ask fundamental questions about the abrupt breaks in the expected march of progress which occurred most spectacularly in Russia, Italy, Germany and Japan, as well as in a host of smaller countries in Latin America and Central Europe. But by the end of World War II no student of foreign governments could avoid asking himself why events like the two World Wars and the Great Depression had brought about the reversal of democratic trends in some countries while accelerating such trends in others. One could not help being aware of the fact that there existed in the recent political experiences of dozens of countries a veritable laboratory in which to test propositions about the way governmental systems behave under stress and the factors which bring about changes in political forms. What was more, there were appearing on the scene or waiting close by in the wings dozens more of the formerly colonial countries of Asia and Africa, for which political institutions were being carved out with or without concern for the well-catalogued experiences of their older brethren. Political scientists were worried about the preservation of democracy as the dominant form of government in the world or simply about the best way of assuring that the fragile systems newly emerging would have the best opportunity for stable development. They found ample reason to build theory to help find answers to the problems immediately at hand, because they found themselves woefully bereft of a body of theory upon which to draw for adequate leverage over the question of how to provide new nations with stable democracy.

By the 1950's the field of "comparative government" was ready to reclaim the first half of its traditional label. There appeared in short succession a series of sharp criticisms of the existing state of theory and knowledge, stimulated undoubtedly by the 1953 critique of the discipline of political science by David Easton [5] and led by Roy C. Macridis' pungent attack in 1955 upon traditionalism in the field of comparative government.[6] In essence the field was reprimanded for its failure to take the opportunities afforded it to contribute to empirical theory. This contribution would come through forming concepts and conceptual frameworks, generating theory from the juxtaposition of concepts and empirical fact, and testing and refining theory and concepts through continual application to experience in other cultural and institutional settings. A new generation of political scientists was exhorted to

[5] David Easton, *The Political System* (New York, 1953).
[6] Roy C. Macridis, *The Study of Comparative Government* (Garden City, N.Y., 1955).

engage in the quest for theory building at various levels of generality. Foremost among the points made was that theory could be generated from the study of a single governmental system only by the use of a conceptual framework permitting it to be treated as one instance typical of others sharing certain characteristics, and that theory could be built and established only by testing it in all or most of the governmental systems of the type setting the theory's boundaries. Comparative government, in short, required the comparative method.

From Governments to Political Systems.   The second aspect of the recent transformation that has produced the field of "comparative political systems" results from the world events referred to earlier as well as from developments indigenous to the discipline of political science as it has evolved in the United States. The crisis of democracy which has visited the twentieth century has brought into question the adequacy of the traditional emphasis in political science upon the formal institutions of government to account for or even to anticipate the rapid and staggering political changes that have taken place in all but a few sheltered havens of political stability. Political scientists all over the world have been forced to look at institutions outside but impinging upon the formal organizations of government, such as political parties, pressure groups, and the mass media. Already common in the United States by World War II, such avenues of inquiry have become widespread in European political science only since 1950.[7] Europeans have also lagged behind their American counterparts somewhat in the examination of the more inchoate phenomena of politics, such as political culture, public opinion and voting behavior, although leading European political scientists are catching up to their American counterparts very rapidly in these areas and are beginning to provide real leadership in some realms.

One of the results of the quest to move beyond the study of formal institutions has been the problem of settling upon a new label to characterize the emerging "comparative field." In the early 1960's an effort was made to refer to the field as that of "comparative politics," a device designed to change the focus from institutions, as had been suggested by the term "comparative government," to process. The new term, however, was vulnerable to attack on two opposing grounds. On the one hand, those taking a narrow view of the term "politics" could say that this would be to confine the field to the study of the "inputs" into the political system and the roles played by institutions such as pressure groups, political parties, legislative bodies, and executive leadership units, to the detriment of concern for "output" processes such as administration and adjudication. On the other hand, it could be argued that this broadened the term to permit the study of politics in almost any conceivable setting, including the extra-governmental. In the absence of an overarching conceptual framework permitting politics surrounding government

[7] See Maurice Duverger, *Political Parties,* 2nd English ed., rev. (London, 1959); Jean Meynand, *Les Groupes de Pression en France* (Paris, 1958); and S.E. Finer, *Anonymous Empire: A Study of the Lobby in Great Britain* (London, 1958).

of a nation-state to be compared with politics, say, in a private corporation, the extension of the field beyond the traditional realm of legal government and the interactions directly relevant to it would be impossible, however desirable it might be in pure theory. Furthermore, the use of the term seemed to make it difficult to draw the boundaries between what belonged in the field of comparative politics and what has traditionally been placed within other fields of the discipline of political science. Thus a field of "politics" has traditionally been singled out for study by methods and assumptions peculiar to it. To a large extent it has been "uncomparative" in the past, having developed in this country as the study of American political phenomena. However, recent trends in the study of American politics have shown an increasing interest in the comparison of American political parties, legislative bodies, voting behavior, etc., with their counterparts in other advanced Western countries. To the extent that this is happening, a tendency toward the blending of previously separate fields is occurring, one which augurs well for future prospects of greater unity in the discipline.

However, if we assume that it is still possible to speak of a separate comparative field, we must ask what, if anything, can be the contribution of a field which until quite recently has been largely the study of discrete aspects of foreign governments to a discipline which is searching increasingly for general laws of political behavior and is asking political scientists to develop their knowledge of political phenomena independent of national idiosyncracies and unrestrained by cultural biases. What is the unique characteristic of this field which equips it to contribute what other fields cannot? The answer would seem to be that, of the various empirical fields of the discipline, only the comparative field offers an overview of political phenomena in general within a given country, an overview which can be taken prior to any subdivision of the various aspects of a country's government and politics, such as is implicit in the delimiting of fields such as politics, public administration, and judicial behavior. Furthermore, whereas the latter fields have, until very recently within American political science, been conditioned to a large extent by the properties of American government and politics, the effort to make the comparative field really comparative has forced specialists in particular countries or areas to re-examine their assumptions as to the proper categories for analysis and to search for conceptual models of general applicability. Accordingly, it has been widely recognized that structural categories such as courts, legislative bodies, and cabinets, however adequate for an understanding of the realities of certain countries, are hopelessly unrealistic as guides to the essence of the political realms of other countries. Instead, political scientists have searched for abstract processes and functions which are performed by some structures in all countries, but not necessarily by structures which appear the same or even bear the same labels from one country to another.

The search for categories has led to the search for broad-gauged conceptual frameworks which will relate the abstract categories to one another.

While a variety of these have been offered by seminal theorists such as Easton, Almond, and Deutsch, most writers who have either offered them or borrowed from and adapted them would say that what has been sought has been a mental picture of something called a "political system," i.e., a set of interrelated variables conceived to be politically relevant and treated as if they could be separated from other variables not immediately relevant to politics. A set of concepts considered to make up a political system is advanced not to help one to understand the government and politics of any single country, but to aid in understanding government and politics anywhere. The study of particular countries or of particular kinds of structures or processes (sub-systems) can be related to this broader conceptual scheme with the hope that work done in one realm will be compatible with work done in another realm, to the extent that similar definitions are employed and concepts are given similar content by different users.

Criticisms. This attempt to develop a common framework to add real comparability to comparative study has not escaped heavy and arresting criticism. Some has been focused upon the attempt to move outward from the central core of political study, formal government, to encompass areas of human life studied within other disciplines, such as social psychology or anthropology. This criticism is by no means confined to the field of comparative political systems. If the central concern is to preserve the identity of political science by concentrating upon a realm which only political scientists are equipped to handle, we would be circumscribing ourselves so narrowly as to make our own utility to other disciplines virtually nil. Knowing as we do the human weaknesses to which institutions are subject, there can be no really persuasive argument for confining ourselves to the formal aspects alone. Yet once we proceed beyond this realm, the possibility of defining boundaries which political scientists on the one hand and other types of social scientists on the other would agree to honor seems quite remote. Nor does it seem useful to worry ourselves greatly about the problem. Different political scientists will find themselves constrained to borrow from the sister disciplines, and even to become second-hand sociologists or psychologists to different degrees, depending upon their interests and their backgrounds.

A more impressive challenge has been mounted from the opposite direction. The effort on the part of specialists in comparative political systems to develop models of supposed universality which are intended to neatly encompass all of the variables considered relevant to politics has encountered heavy opposition from the area specialists who adhere to the so-called "configurative" position.[8] The configurative argument is a two-fold one: (1) The attempt to separate the political from other social and cultural realms is deemed artificial, and an interdisciplinary approach to the study of exotic countries is advocated. (2) The quest for universal models is considered fruitless, inasmuch as historico-cultural differences are so great as to render cross-

[8] See Gunnar Heckscher, *The Study of Comparative Government and Politics* (London, 1957).

cultural generalizations meaningless. At best comparison of countries within an area of the world whose political units share common experiences and traditions is possible, although hazardous. Cross-cultural generalizations of a global nature would distort reality to too great an extent. The "configurativist" is impressed by the variety of cultural settings and their impacts upon the political realm. To carve out a political system and hold it separate from indigenous cultures is to do violence to the richness of human experience, or so the proponents of configurativism would argue.

An analogy can be drawn between the tension which the political scientist feels in moving beyond his familiar Western setting and that experienced, perhaps in more acute form, by the economist. The economist who seeks to specialize in the economies of, say, the Latin American countries finds himself in a difficult position. On the one hand, he is sensitive to the need for disciplinary rigor in attacking analytical problems in economics of whatever nature. On the other, he is faced with the admonitions of the Latin American area specialists to pay strict attention to the aspects of Latin American culture which differentiate economies in that area of the world from those he would encounter elsewhere. As an economist he would be moved to regard Latin American economies as falling into a class or classes of economic systems as defined in the typologies of general economic theory, rather than as entities having unique cultural patterns determined by geographic conditions and religious beliefs. The Latin American specialist may feel that he can predict economic events in Latin America and prescribe ways of adjusting to them better than can a much more thoroughly specialized economist because he knows the cultural limits which produce certain kinds of behavior an economist might judge "irrational" on the basis of his formal models.

Yet this would be to ignore the indispensability of economic theory for any systematic approach to economic problems, wherever they are found. The Latin American specialist must balance what he knows about economics with what he knows about geography, social structure, village culture, and political behavior. The point is that he needs each of these disciplines to be usable *tools*. Each discipline must refine a body of central concepts which can be adjusted to meet the specifications of particular contexts, but without which there can be no way of systematically taking into account the influence of variables which must be weighed in the problem-solving equation. The problem which the area specialist faces as he tries to deal with political phenomena in areas of the world which Western political scientists have only lately begun to study in depth is that the tools which political science affords him are ill-suited for the less inviting environs in which he is trying to employ them. Rather than shrug their shoulders and conclude that political science has few, if any, insights to bring to the problem because it is too parochial and culture-bound, political scientists have recognized the necessity to universalize their conceptual framework and, as a later section will indicate, not negligible steps have been taken in this direction.

THE COMPARATIVE METHOD

Up to this point in the discussion the term "comparative" has been left vague and ill-defined. What we have tried to convey is the idea that the field under discussion is differentiable from other areas of inquiry within political science principally in its focus upon whole political systems, not in its use of the comparative method, which is an aspect of all phases of political science insofar as it is scientific. The only reason for including the term comparative in the designation of the field is to emphasize that the responsibility which the field has to the discipline of political science is to treat the political systems existing in the world as units for comparison in the general quest of theory-building and testing in political science. The student of comparative political systems, in other words, is doing at the "macro" level what all other political scientists are doing when they are attempting to advance the science of politics: he is taking a number of instances of a particular type of political unit (in this case the nation-state as a political system), formulating propositions pertaining to all of the instances he is examining, testing the validity of the propositions for each of the instances (national political systems), and refining or abandoning his propositions on the basis of the results. Other political scientists deal with other units of analysis, such as individual voters, legislators, pressure groups, administrative agencies, or units of local government. To the extent that they are attempting to expand the body of political science knowledge, they too are being comparative. The student of a legislative body, for example, will be testing propositions pertaining to the behavior of individual legislators. He will be in essence *comparing* these individual units in determining which of them conform to his expectations, under what circumstances they do and do not, and for what types of legislators the propositions are confirmed. The term "comparison" is less frequently employed for the method used in studying units at the micro level, but the essential method that is used in scientific inquiry at this level is the same as that employed at the macro level when scholarship is truly comparative.

The pervasive quality of the comparative method becomes evident when we attempt to identify the various operations involved in systematic comparison. The following discussion separates processes that are not necessarily followed in order in any comparative endeavor, but all are involved whenever one is trying to compare in a thoroughly systematic manner. The processes are: definition of conceptual units; classification; formulation of hypotheses; and testing of hypotheses.[9]

Definition of Conceptual Units. One only compares those things which one conceives to be *comparable*. This means that any two items being com-

[9] The following discussion has been heavily influenced by Arthur L. Kalleberg, "The Logic of Comparison: A Methodological Note on the Comparative Study of Political Systems," *World Politics*, XIX (1966), 69–82.

pared must have attributed to them by the comparer some characteristic in common. A tree may be compared with a man only if the comparer has in mind a general element of similarity, such as the necessity for each to receive life-sustaining nourishment from its environment. The two could then be compared in terms of the different ways in which life-giving nourishment is obtained by them. Thus, the focus of attention in comparison may be upon differences and contrasts; but the comparison itself is possible because some element of similarity, however lonely, is postulated as existing. Similarly, two systems of government as widely divergent as those of the Soviet Union and Switzerland may be compared if it is posited that all systems of government have a certain characteristic in common—e.g., authoritatively allocating values for a society. The Soviet and Swiss systems can then be examined with the object of ascertaining by what processes values are authoritatively allocated in each, or, perhaps, what are the mechanisms by which government receives information as to what groups or categories of citizens value and by what means this information is converted into authoritative decisions. The answers to these questions would differ greatly between the two systems, but it would at least be possible to pose the same questions for each because of an initial conception of governmental systems as mechanisms for authoritatively allocating values.

The units which we compare are *conceptual* units in the sense that they are the objects of *definitions* to which the real phenomena we say we are comparing more or less conform. In comparing the Soviet and Swiss governmental systems we really are comparing two things we are calling governmental systems, with whatever we choose to include within that abstract definition, plus whatever else we draw from our observations of the real Soviet and Swiss systems that appear to make them conform to our definition of governmental systems. Elements which we have observed that are irrelevant to what goes into the definition of a governmental system we simply leave out of the two packages we are comparing. We may decide, for example, that the electoral process in the Soviet Union, however crucial its counterpart in Switzerland, is irrelevant to the authoritative allocation of values for Soviet society. So we simply leave it out of our scheme of concerns. But the electoral system in Switzerland may play a crucial role in (a) determining who will hold authoritative positions and (b) providing an alternate means of giving the authorities clues as to the strength of support for particular authoritative allocations. For an understanding of the way these functions are performed in the Soviet Union, one would have to start with the Communist Party, since it has been crucial both as a recruitment channel to leadership positions and as a means of filtering information upward as to people's wants and needs. Thus we are comparing processes or functions, not structures that look alike in the formal sense. Our definition of the concept of a governmental system has told us what we should be interested in and what we should ignore.

In the field of comparative political systems we are comparing *macro*

units: entire political systems which perform functions for large complex societies. As noted earlier, political scientists in other fields compare units of
lesser scale, such as individual voters, legislators, pressure groups, political
parties or municipalities. This does not mean that the student of comparative
political systems does not study units of lesser scope than the national polity.
It does mean that he studies them as elements within the context of a national
political system and that he is interested in them only in so far as they help
him to characterize the system as a whole. A student of public administration
might examine the structures of the central bureaucracies in Britain and
France and compare them in terms of a general theory of organizational behavior. A student of comparative political systems would be more apt to ask
of the same structures how they perform the function of recruiting people to
leadership positions in the system as a whole. The conceptual frameworks
employed will differ as will the general theory tested in the two separate
fields. This can be traced to the fact that the basic unit of study is administrative organization in the one field and national political systems in the other.

Classification.   In speaking of the comparative method we are apt to
point to classification as a necessary accompaniment, without realizing that
classification is a type of a more general aspect of the scientific method: measurement. Whenever we compare units which are deemed similar, we do so
in terms of variation among them with regard to certain criteria. Thus we
may compare short men with tall men by assigning heights to each of the men
we are studying in terms of feet and inches and see if there is a tendency, for
example, for weight to increase as height increases. Alternatively we may set
dividing lines between tall, medium-sized, and short men at, say, six feet and
five-feet-six-inches, and see whether the average weight for men in each of
the three categories grows as we move upward in height. The latter procedure, strictly speaking, is an example of classification. It would also be a
blunter tool than the former, since there are precise measures which can be
assigned to very slight gradations in height. In most measurement problems
in political science, however, such precision is impossible. Even where we
can talk in terms of different quantities of some characteristic, as, for example, the strength of an individual's attachment to a particular political party,
the quantities themselves will not admit of specific numerical designations.
Hence we are forced to fall back upon general categories, like strong Democrats, weak Democrats, and strong Republicans, and most of the time the
element of human judgment in assigning particular instances to particular
categories is very strong.

When we have defined precisely the conceptual unit with which we are
dealing, we have only begun the process of determining the specific elements
which will be manipulated in the eventual process of hypothesis testing. The
hypotheses we will be testing will specify that given characteristics of the
units in question will be accompanied by other characteristics. In order to
test the hypotheses, it will be necessary to classify the units in terms of the
characteristics to be considered. Thus, if we hypothesize that, among Euro-

pean countries, those with higher standards of living will have a greater tendency to be democratic and stable, we will be required to classify countries in terms of four criteria: (1) geographical location; (2) whether or not they are democracies; (3) whether or not they are stable; and (4) the level of their living standards. Seymour M. Lipset has attempted a similar feat and has found that there is a tendency for European countries which are democratic and stable to have higher living standards than those which are dictatorships and/or unstable.[10] Note here that he has first qualified the unit of analysis from an initial universe of European political systems to include only democracies and to exclude those national political systems which he does not judge to be democratic. From here he makes further judgments as to what constitutes stability and instability and as to what are relatively high and low standards of living. The judgments he makes will not receive the overwhelming acquiescence of all students of comparative political systems, but the best he can do, under the circumstances, is to be quite explicit as to the criteria he has chosen and his reasons for choosing them.

Classification, like the comparative method itself, has perhaps been more readily identified with the field of comparative government and politics because of the necessity to make broad general judgments as to the characteristics of very complex phenomena. Students of whole political systems have found it inescapable to attempt judgments as to whether particular systems are democracies or dictatorships, totalitarian or constitutional systems, parliamentary or presidential systems, federal or unitary systems. Adding to the complexity has been the problem of distinguishing between the formal characteristics of political systems and their realities, which may depart from the formalities in fundamental respects. Political scientists in other fields have either avoided the comparative method until quite recently (as is true, for example, in the field of state and local government, despite the seemingly rich resources for comparative study in this area) or they have sought measures which are more precise than the kind of judgmental classification which has been the staple of the field of comparative government and politics. In the field of political behavior, major strides have been taken in utilizing the comparative method to analyze the political behavior of individual human beings. Attitude scales have been devised of the type designed to range individual respondents along continua between polar attitudes. Yet, given the essentially ordinal nature of the data employed, human judgment in classifying the respondents is employed: either the judgment of the observer directly as in coding of open-ended responses, or the combined judgment of the observer and the respondent—that of the former in devising categories from which the latter must choose, and that of the latter in making his restricted choices.

Hypothesis Formulation and Testing. Hypotheses are, or ought to be, related to a general body of theory, the further refinement of which the scholar seeks to advance. The conceptual tools of the field of comparative

[10] Seymour M. Lipset, *Political Man* (Garden City, 1960), pp. 27–45.

politics may be utilized to make it possible to develop theory ordinarily the property of some other field of political science. Thus a student of legislative behavior may ask himself whether it makes any difference in the roles which individual legislators perform whether or not a political system is of the Presidential or the Parliamentary variety. A student of administrative organization might inquire as to whether the problems of maintaining equilibrium in its relationships with its environment are greater for central government agencies operating in a federal system than for those in a unitary situation. The specific hypotheses to be tested derive from fields of political science other than comparative political systems, but, in order to test their applicability in more than one national political setting, it is necessary to borrow some of the conceptual apparatus of the field of comparative political systems.

The question remains: Is there a general body of theory that is the exclusive property of the field of comparative politics and which makes the problems that specialists in that field attack different from the problems dealt with in other fields? Most of the other fields of political science involve the study of some particular segment of politics and government which can be held separate from the others and about which the question can be asked: What conditions its behavior? A student of voting behavior will ask about the determinants of who votes and how people vote. A student of legislatures may want to know what determines the nature of the outputs (enactments) of the legislative process, or he may ask what determines the way individual legislators will vote, or the roles they will assume in the legislative arena. A student of pressure groups may be interested in what determines the strategies which different groups use in pursuing their objectives. For each of these concerns there exists a body of more or less integrated theory, which could be reduced to a number of general statements and a larger number of specific hypotheses susceptible of being tested empirically. In the field of comparative political systems, since the basic unit of analysis is the entire political system, the questions posed tend to be of the variety: What determines the behavior of entire political systems? This gives rise to the question: In what ways do political systems "behave" or what questions does one ask of them? Among the questions which specialists in the field have asked are: (1) What determines the degree to which political systems will be responsive to popular demands? (2) What determines the degree to which outputs of the system will be sufficient to meet the threats of external pressure or domestic crisis? (3) What determines the degree of support which the system will receive and extract from the populace, whether in the form of voting, tax-paying, or personal service in times of crisis? (4) What determines the degree of institutional stability within the system? (5) What determines the level or internal violence which the system must withstand? (6) What determines the capacity of the system to produce effective leadership to meet the needs of the times?

It is at the point that we begin to ask questions of this fundamental variety that we become aware of the traditional ties between the fields of normative political theory and comparative political systems. Eckstein has pointed out that the latter field has only very recently begun to live up to the promise that was contained in the work of Montesquieu.[11] Empirically oriented scholars in the field desperately need the guidance of theorists attuned to thinking in terms of the fundamental objectives of man as a political animal. Within the field of normative political theory, there exists a wide array of propositions concerning the questions posed in the preceding paragraph. The propositions ordinarily beg to be tested empirically, and many which find their way into the lore to the point of being standard textbook assumptions have not really been given adequate tests. There are two basic strategies which could be employed, and students of comparative politics are tending to go one or the other of these routes depending upon their own tastes, probably a fortunate development. Either we could comb the literature and our old classroom notes for untested propositions, then find ways of operationalizing them and testing them piecemeal, or we could begin by working out a general theory of comparative political systems and proceed to the task of hypothesis formulation and testing only after we have an overall blueprint which tells us which propositions are worth pursuing further. Either of these strategies, especially the latter, by itself would probably bear a minimum of fruit. Were we to confine ourselves to the piecemeal approach we would be unable to draw our knowledge together in systematic fashion. To draw upon the analogy of legal systems, our body of knowledge would look much like English common law: a body of uneven, uncodified, isolated principles upon which one could draw for help in dealing with particular problems, so long, that is, as one knew where to look. On the other hand, were we to develop the theory before concerning ourselves with the more specific hypotheses we would be essentially in the position of the Medieval scholars engaged in the updating of Roman Law. We would be involved in endless disputation over the truth or falsity of abstract, untested principles. In fact, like the discipline of political science in general, the field of comparative political systems contains the analogues of both the common law judges and the Medieval legal scholars. What is to be hoped is that the interchange between them will produce as a synthesis the eventual codifiers who will bring general theory and tested generalizations together into a self-contained, internally consistent, but empirically sound body of knowledge.

GENERAL CONCEPTUAL FRAMEWORKS AND THEORIES

In the rest of this chapter, we will consider approaches to the study of comparative government and politics which lean rather far in the direction of general conceptual frameworks and general theory, rather than in that of specific, narrow-gauged hypothesis formulation and testing. This will, admittedly, put an overemphasis upon one particular "school" of writers in the

[11] Eckstein, "A Perspective on Comparative Politics," p. 23.

field and will focus upon what are more promises of future realization than stores of already gathered riches. The justification would seem to be that, so long as we are regarding the field of comparative government and politics as distinct and separable from the rest of the discipline of political science, while at the same time borrowing from and contributing to other fields in the discipline, we ought to concentrate upon developments which take to heart the assumptions underlying the field's distinctiveness and promise and attempt to bring to it conceptual coherence and clarity, plus a degree of theoretical potency hitherto unattained. Three such efforts are discussed below: (1) the effort by David Easton to draw together a number of definitions into a conceptual framework known as *the political system;* (2) the *structural-functional* approach of Gabriel Almond, also an attempt at a conceptual framework, with, however, some suggestions for classification which portend a way of arriving at theory; and (3) a wide array of writing which puts forth a variety of theories, some partial, some general, about what has been termed *political development.*

Easton's Political System.   The term "political system," as should be apparent from what has preceded this section, is fashionable in contemporary political science. In the present context, however, the term transcends the common social science fetish for jargon, because its potential conceptual utility for the field of comparative government and politics is great. Given the fact that the field is all about whole nation-states viewed as conglomerations of *political* interactions, some conception is needed of a set of interactions related to the production of political outcomes for the society which the nation-state encompasses. A variety of ways of conceiving of a political system are possible, but at the present time, that advanced by Easton enjoys the widest currency and is, indeed, the most comprehensive and sharply defined of any systemic model extant in the discipline.[12]

Easton quite clearly states that he does not conceive of his analytical scheme as being itself a general theory. Rather he regards it as a possible first step in the direction of general theory. His strategy is to establish a network of general definitions on which political scientists can agree which can, in turn, serve as the basis for a general theory. He hopes that the concepts he advances will be of sufficient generality that they would be applicable whatever the cultural context and whatever the level of analysis. Thus his model should be relevant (i.e., capable of generating theory of relevance) to politics in any country of the world and to any decision-making unit within any country. One ought to be able to conceive of government and politics in the Soviet Union or in Uganda in terms of his model, just as one can the government and politics of a Western democracy. And the model ought to be applicable to what goes on politically at the state level in the United States, or in the municipal arena in Belgium, or in an African tribal setting, or even in an administrative agency, a legislative body, a business firm or anywhere decisions are made that are binding upon someone.

[12] Easton's basic model is outlined earlier in this volume. Pages 108–11.

In the first instance Easton's contribution is to focus the attention of political scientists upon a question of great potential interest to the field of comparative political systems in particular as well as to political science in general. He insists that the question has not been posed explicitly by political scientists and that it would have to compete with questions which political scientists had been more inclined to ask themselves, especially those regarding the locus and distribution of power. His question is: How do political systems persist in a world of stability and change? He would like at least some political scientists to be inquiring into the factors which determine the viability of political systems and the mechanisms by which they are able to maintain themselves in the face of challenges. In the simplest sense his way of approaching the problem is to conceive of political systems as organisms responding to stimuli. Under normal circumstances such organisms will receive ordinary stimuli to which their response mechanisms are presumably adapted. Under conditions of stress, however, the organism may be forced to resort to extraordinary adaptive action in order to maintain itself. A political system, being a social mechanism whose role in society is to provide it with authoritative value allocations in order for conflict over values among society's members to be contained, will receive stimuli continuously that have at least the potential of presenting it with severe stress. To the extent that the political system is incapable of containing conflict in society with its authoritative value allocations, then the conflict may, in some form or another, turn in upon the political system itself and threaten one of its vital elements or even its very existence.

A situation of stress for a political system develops when the interaction between its "essential variables" threatens to break down. Easton identifies three such variables: demands, supports, and outputs. Demands and supports, the input variables, must be coming into the system in order that it may not cease to function due to lack of use or attention. However, they are potential sources of stress and must be maintained at manageable levels. An excess of demand relative to the system's capacity to produce appropriate outputs (i.e., value allocations) will mean an overloading of the system and potential immobility. A high level of support for the system is desirable, but, either because of its incapacity to satisfy demands or for extraneous reasons, support may be withdrawn and the system may not be able to sustain itself any longer.

Easton has received criticism for the abstract nature of his concepts.[13] It is true that they do not take the observer of politics in a given cultural context very far in his search for understanding of what he observes. What they do contribute, however, is a drawing of attention toward questions of real importance for *comparative* study. To the extent that political scientists confine themselves to questions of the locus and distribution of power, their capacity

[13] See, for a balanced critique, the review by Philip E. Converse of David Easton, *A Framework for Political Analysis, American Political Science Review,* LIX (1965), 1001–1002.

to deal with a wide variety of politics will be severely limited. The very meaning of power takes a wide array of different forms in different cultural and institutional contexts. Moreover, in highly unstable countries it is difficult even to find it. Easton's question is of broader applicability, although not perhaps of universal interest. To ask what are the bases of political system persistence may not make a great deal of sense when we are examining stable countries like those in North America or parts of Western Europe. But when we go outside of this context it becomes apparent that relatively few countries exist wherein there is not a more than remote danger of revolution, civil war or at least *coup d'etat*. Many countries in fact owe their continued existence in the face of external threats to the ability to keep internal conflict within bounds. Persistence of a separate political system for such countries is far from being an arid academic question. In fact, consideration of the factors making for political stability or instability in non-Western countries can lead us indirectly to raise questions about Western countries that we have long since forgotten about. If stable modern Western political systems are used as models we may be able to ascertain what are the crucial differences between them and the developing countries of the non-Western world which are now pushing the latter in certain developmental directions different from those experienced in the West. To the extent that we are aware of the element of a need for self-preservation which operates in the process of political change we are providing ourselves with a tool of potential value for analyzing situations and understanding their roots in cultural settings far removed from our own. We are given a means of transcending our own assumptions by asking questions that do not require commitments to democracy, freedom, constitutionalism, or any of the difficult-to-export Western values. We suspend our judgments as to the degree to which the conditions we observe are faithful to these values and we ask simply: How well did this political system respond to this particular stress? Was a particular political change made in accordance with the system's need to persist or was it dysfunctional from that standpoint? Perhaps we can even turn to the Western historical experience with this more neutral perspective and ask what were the factors producing a fairly smooth transition to modernity (where this occurred) and whether or not the values we hold uppermost and our institutional expressions of them are dependent upon the unique pattern of stimuli and responses which we experienced, which, given the more complex world of the late twentieth century, could not be expected to be reproduced. More will be said of the applicability of the Easton approach to the contemporary concern of political scientists for the study of political development. For the moment, suffice it to say that his greatest potential contribution to the study of comparative politics is to focus our attention on a problem which has a breadth of conception equal to the scope of the field.

Almond's Structural-Functionalism. Like Easton, Gabriel Almond attempts to fashion a useful conceptual apparatus.[14] However, unlike Easton,

---

[14] See the earlier treatment (pp. 107–108) of Almond's structural-functionalism.

he goes further to suggest certain hypotheses regarding characteristics that are likely to be found in juxtaposition with one another in given political systems. Since the hypotheses relate to the general area of political development theory, they will be dealt with in the next section, while the conceptual framework will be discussed in the present one.

Almond also presents a model of a political system, but one in which the basic elements are conceived of in a more static sense, albeit the overall model is presented as a more dynamic one than Easton's. To Almond both the inputs and the outputs of the political system should be analyzed in terms of functions which are performed somewhere in the system. His question is: Who performs what functions (i.e., what structures perform them) and what is the style of performance? The analysis here is more akin to the time-honored institutional approach to political science than is Easton's. Almond is less concerned with the analysis of on-going processes than he is with determining the role which persistent structures play within a political system. And he does not ask what contribution the structures make to the continued functioning of the system. Rather, he assumes an operative system and inquires as to the attributes of the system much as one would ask about the overt physical features of an individual human being. Easton, to extend the analogy, would be more interested in the life-sustaining processes of the individual. Functions to Easton would be the requisite operations that would have to be performed by the organism in order that it may maintain itself. Functions to Almond are simply subdivisions of the principal activities of the unit being studied. Given the principal role which political systems play, that of exercising a legitimate monopoly of the means of coercion over society, certain subroles are played by different component parts of the system. But interest articulation, interest aggregation, political communication, rule making, rule application, and rule adjudication are seen not as functions whose performance is crucial for the persistence of the system, but rather as functions which are normal parts of any on-going system whose continued persistence is not really in question.

In his most recent work, *Comparative Politics: A Developmental Approach,* Almond has made an effort to come to grips with the problem of instability and structural impermanence by identifying two functions which contribute to the maintenance of the system—political socialization and political recruitment—and four "capabilities" of political systems—the regulative, extractive, distributive and responsive. The former are elements which Easton does not take directly into account in his focus upon categories capable of grouping discrete political events. Both are gradual, almost imperceptible processes, the cumulative effect of which upon a political system may be very important. The capabilities are ways of classifying the substance of what Easton calls outputs. By the inclusion of these units in his model, Almond is probably in a better position than Easton to account for long-term trends in the fortunes of political systems, even though his focus upon the more static elements of politics leaves him less able to identify more immediate and specific sources of strain.

Approaches to Political Development. The frameworks which Easton
and Almond have developed show considerable promise as possible means
by which broad theories of political development which have enjoyed currency of late may be reconciled with the more static analytic schemes which
have been the traditional characteristic of political science—comparative
government and politics being no exception. If the principal units of analysis
in the field are whole political systems, then whatever theory may be developed will necessarily focus upon the question of how whole political systems
change. Theory directed toward the political behavior of individuals concerns itself with what motivates that behavior, what influences the political
choices which individuals make. Similarly, complex collectivities of human
beings are interesting to political scientists for the "choices" which they
make. These can take the form simply of policy outputs or more fundamentally of alterations in the nature of the system itself, whether by sweeping
revolution or by piecemeal decisions and imperceptible adjustments in the
behavior of large numbers of individual actors. The choices which a political
system makes may, of course, result from events external to the society in
which the system is imbedded. However, in large part, conditions within the
social environment of the system can be looked to for explanations, especially
of systemic changes of a long-term and irreversible nature. It has been in a
search for societal explanatory factors for the changes, both revolutionary
and evolutionary, that have taken place on such a breathtaking scale in the
twentieth century that specialists in comparative government and politics
have turned to theories of development, political, social, economic, and psychological.

Most commonly political scientists studying the phenomenon of modernization have treated what they call political development as a dependent
variable, using other facets of modernization as independent variables. Accordingly, broad-gauged changes occurring in the political realm are usually
regarded as subordinate to the general processes of (1) industrialization, (2)
urbanization, (3) the spread of education and literacy, (4) increasing exposure to the mass media, and (5) the expansion of a secular culture. These independent factors are said to account for a variety of more strictly political
developments such as (1) the growth of modern bureaucracies, (2) the development of a sense of nationhood, (3) the advent of political parties, (4) the
expansion of popular political participation, (5) the increased capacity of the
political system to mobilize resources for the accomplishment of its ends, and
in the most modern polities, (6) the decline in the missionary fervor of political movements.

Roughly speaking, two broad types of schema have been advanced for
dealing with the tremendous wealth of political and extra-political phenomena which the study of political development conjures up. Both may be regarded as conceptual models upon the basis of which general theories of political development, as well as more specific hypotheses, may be erected.
They are what we shall label (a) the continuum model and (b) the stages

model. Each has seen a variety of manifestations. The examples discussed here should be regarded as illustrations only.

Continuum models of political development tend to view the developmental process in terms of a series of discrete variables, each identified by a range of possible states that national entities may be in at various times with respect to some specific criterion. Thus nations may be ranged according to level of Gross National Product per capita, percentage of the adult population that is literate, number of hospital beds per thousand population, or according to more strictly political criteria such as percentage of the working population employed by the central government, or percentage of the adult population participating in national elections. Less quantifiable, more judgmental criteria may be employed, such as the degree of bargaining which takes place between autonomous political groups, or the extent to which merit criteria are employed in the recruitment and promotion of government employees, or the extent to which charismatic leaders tend to prevail at the national level. Variables of both quantitative and judgmental nature can, for example, be subjected to multi-variate analysis or factor analysis, with the object of testing hypotheses as to the relationships between variables. Particularly, theorists who posit a common movement along a broad array of fronts from less modern to more modern conditions, and who see a functional relationship between social, economic, psychological and political indicators of modernization, find this type of conceptual model an economical and highly systematic way to portray the phenomena which interest them. Its drawback is the danger of fragmentation of concern, especially in the absence of any over-arching theory. Social scientists who have utilized this approach have been more likely to succeed when they have posited a relatively small number of variables thought to be tightly interconnected. More elaborate schema have tended to be overwhelmed by a richness of potential relationships.

The second model, which posits stages of development, is often intellectually more stimulating, although not often satisfying the most exacting standards of precision. Here there is either a Marxian-like confinement to one explanatory factor as the key to the transition from one stage to another, or an attempt to bring together a configuration of interrelated factors which are expected to alter in unison from forms appropriate to a given stage of development to those appropriate to the succeeding stage. While it is hazardous to generalize from a wide array of different offerings, it is safe to say that at least three stages are usually postulated whenever an attempt is made to develop a stages model for application to countries the world over: (1) the traditional stage, characterized by an overwhelmingly rural society and agrarian economy, with appropriate political forms; (2) the transitional stage, still with a rural society, but characterized by an economy embarking on the early stages of industrialization and a political system which is accordingly undergoing transformation; and (3) the modern stage, characterized by a largely urban society and a mature industrial economy, with the appropriate political forms. In a general sense, the political system moves from (1) the traditional focus upon local concentrations of power with little articulation between the center and the periphery to (2) the transitional stage in which structures are emerging to involve the increasingly available masses in the political system while improving upon the technical means of expanding the power of the center into the periphery, and from there to (3) the modern state with its centrally engineered economy and its perfected institutional means of involving all of society in the daily affairs of the individual at the same time the individual becomes involved in the national endeavor through whatever official means of participation are available to him. More specifically, sub-systems of the political system, notably the administrative sub-system and the political culture, similarly undergo this process of development by stages. Needless to say, the stages models have been criticized by more rigorous methodologists for their tendency to oversimplify highly complex phenomena and for forcing the experiences of particular countries into a mold perhaps more appropriate for some countries than for others.

In any event, both types of models are based upon an image of a largely dependent political realm and a largely independent extra-political realm, with movement in the economic, social, psychological and political realms highly intercorrelated. Only the more extreme stages models assign pre-eminent importance to any one factor, usually the economic one of industrialization. All tend to look to the same general factors to explain why different countries have political institutions with different capabilities and why the capabilities of political institutions in a given country change over time. Particular writers have stressed the explanatory power of particular types of variables without by any means insisting upon their transcendent importance. Some writers have even sought to hold the political factor independent, showing its impact upon factors within the other realms. This has been particularly prevalent in studies of nations in the transitional stage, when political impetus is seen as necessary to other forms of development.

What the general theories of political development have often suffered from is the absence of any coherent *political* model of the developmental process. The analysis is often left at the point where extra-political factors have set the stage for political change. Political change itself has tended to be dealt with more with the time-honored tools of the historian than with the sharper analytical tools of the political scientist. This may be due to the fact that political science has traditionally had a static concept of the political realm. Perhaps out of deference, perhaps out of antipathy, or both, the political scientist has left to the historian the task of accounting for and dealing with change. Accordingly he comes ill-equipped to the recent concern for rapid political change. Until recently he has been forced to rely upon other social scientists to help him account for it, and his own efforts at dealing with the phenomenon of political change itself have been confined to generalities; he has floundered in abstractions of limited utility or has been content to rely upon the surer ground of historical description.

Partial approaches to political development, stressing particular aspects and dealing with them systematically, abound. Well-integrated and comprehensive models of political, as opposed to other kinds of, development are harder to come by. In fact, we find ourselves forced back upon the Almond and Easton models which, although they do not purport to be exclusively developmental models, may in fact be called into service for the purpose of systematic political developmental analysis. Almond's model has been more explicitly set forth for this purpose recently in *Comparative Politics: A Developmental Approach*. Its functional categories can be viewed as political variables which are dependent upon changes in the socio-economic context of the political system. As the society undergoes modernization, political structure becomes more functionally specialized as well as more highly centralized, while political culture undergoes secularization and, beyond a certain point, develops pragmatic, bargaining strains. As power is centralized in the structures of the system performing the functions of rule-making, rule application, and rule adjudication (the output functions), specialized national structures are developed for the channeling of inputs into the system (associational interest groups, aggregative political parties and the mass media). Structures of both the input and output varieties develop considerable autonomy vis-à-vis one another, a process which is even seen occurring in advanced totalitarian systems.

Insofar as political culture is concerned, Almond sees the structural developments accompanied by attitudes congruent to them. Thus, at a late stage of development, people are conditioned to see limits to the power which the various structures may exercise and to tolerate limitations upon their own objectives. Restraint upon the part of competing groups, and, hence bargaining on behalf of the attainment of proximate, partial objectives comes to be seen as a virtue as the interdependence of elements within the system gains better appreciation. Earlier in the train of development people find it difficult to conceive of their objectives as being reconciled with those of groups in society perceived as enemies. Conflict tends, under such circumstances, to be uncompromising and unproductive of mutually satisfactory results. Still earlier, a largely parochial culture confined conflict to a community-against-community basis, with attitudes within the walled-off communities being relatively harmonious. Industrialization and urbanization brought about the break-down of community in the traditional sense and threw man up against his fellow man in an impersonal and frightening fashion. As a consequence he sought community in class, religious, or ethnic groupings which transcended the local community and brought him to war with his fellow man in competing groupings over broad, poorly understood abstractions. In the most modern cultures man may be learning to live with the broader perspective while at the same time seeking meaning in the concrete and the proximately realizable.

While the Almond perspective is rich in potential for analysis of the general trends of political development, it is deficient in categories for an examination of the dynamics of the process of change itself. One imagines that, as a society modernizes, its corresponding political system will go through the phases of structural and cultural modernization which Almond indicates. Yet just how, specifically, this happens is left to the imagination. Will it be a slow, evolutionary process, or will it proceed by convulsive jerks? The Easton model permits us to approach this question directly.

If we follow the Easton perspective, changes which occur in the structural components of the political system occur in the form of adjustments made by members of the system to stress upon the system. The insistence by Easton upon the necessity to conceive of boundaries which separate the political from the extra-political enables us to conceive of the impact of modernization upon politics as a series of environmental stresses which force the political system to react. As the economy becomes more highly complex and its elements interdependent, as people find themselves pressed together and no longer autonomous, and as the political system finds itself challenged by other political systems beyond its territorial boundaries with superior, or at least threatening, technological capacity to do it military, economic, or political damage, changes must take place within the political system to enable it to cope with the challenges. The penalty for failing to meet them may not be non-persistence of the system, although external military threat could pose this possibility. But the anxieties and tensions which an overloading of demands and/or a withdrawal of support will place upon elites and non-elites alike will require an eventual adjustment designed more or less consciously to restore some degree of certainty in the future. Such an adjustment might be simply a change in leadership, with some attendant change in the outputs of the system. Or it might mean a restructuring of the political institutions, including perhaps the input as well as the output structures. It might even mean a change in the territorial definition of the community, an acquisition designed to strengthen the nation in the face of an external challenge, or a purifying bloodletting to restore the integrity of the essential community (as, for example, in the French granting of independence to Algeria in 1962). In any event, while Easton does not regard them explicitly as such, the changes which will take place in response to stress will add up in the long run to political development. Easton, in other words, provides the means of dealing analytically with the linkages that must be made between Almond's t_1 and t_2. The later period differs from the earlier period in certain respects. Almond compares the two and seeks an explanation for the difference in the general modernization of society which has occurred. Easton prepares the way for a more detailed study of the events which took place between the two periods, showing more specifically how the environmental events that together make up "modernization" put stress upon the political system, evoking a series of specific political responses which together add up to "political development." Both frameworks are useful for sticking political meat on the bones of the general theories of political development. And the two approaches are complementary; neither need be regarded as excluding the other.

SUB-FIELDS OF COMPARATIVE GOVERNMENT
AND POLITICS

From the more general models of political systems and theories of political development, let us move to the sub-fields within the field of comparative government and politics. In so doing we move to the comparative study of sub-systems of the political system and of the patterns of political development which are peculiar to them. Again, we will be talking about areas of inquiry that are now in the stage of becoming, in the sense that the mode of thinking about them displayed here has only recently gained currency among political scientists and is by no means universally shared.

In the past political scientists studying the political parties of country X or the office of the chief executive of country Y have proceeded from a general body of assumptions and definitions developed rather pragmatically to fit the needs as they saw them of their particular objects of study. To the very limited extent that comparative studies of parts of the political whole were undertaken, students were forced to develop models of greater generality, appropriate for all of the cultural settings considered but not necessarily reaching beyond the particular aspect of political systems studied to lodge it within the total political fabric. Thus political parties were studied, whether comparatively or not, as separate entities, and the categories used were derived from the particular concerns of the student about political parties. They did not derive from an overall conception of political systems and the place of political parties within them. By the same token developmental models of sub-systemic aspects related the environmental events directly to the changes taking place within the sub-system, often without considering the role played by the sub-system within the total political system and the intervening variables of a political nature which conditioned the impact which environmental events have had upon particular sub-systems. To the extent that concern for the intra-systemic relationships was shown, there was usually no attempt to fit them together within an overall systemic model.

One can go further and say that the study of political sub-systems among American political scientists has been dominated by the perspectives that have emerged from the study of sub-systems of the American political system. Categories which seem appropriate for the study of American politics have been carried over to the study of politics in other countries. For example, the study of pressure groups as elements playing an important role in determining the decisions made by government has been one very potent theme in the study of American politics because of the exceptionally active role which pressure groups play in American politics. The "pressure group" approach to the study of governmental decision-making sub-systems seems to American political scientists to be a natural route to take and one which ought to be fruitful for the study of political systems abroad. To a considerable extent American political scientists have been successful in moving their European counterparts to a sensitivity to the value of looking at pressure group influence in European political systems. The partial nature of such an approach becomes immediately evident in the alien context, however; perhaps it should have been more evident in the American. Had American political scientists been operating from a general systemic model of their own political system, they would have been concerned in the first instance not with the power or influence exercised by pressure groups, but with the question of how effectively the desires of people in society for political action of certain kinds are communicated to those making authoritative decisions. Such a question would force one to deal with pressure groups within a larger framework which includes an understanding of the content of the political culture, of the roles performed by the mass media, by the political parties, by revolutionary movements, by political leaders, by administrative agencies, and by opinion leaders at the small group level, to name only a few. The actions of each of these structures can be viewed as constituting a sub-system, or the interaction between any two or more of them can be considered a sub-system.

If the relationship between pressure groups and a legislative body were to be viewed as a sub-system, they would be studied from the perspective of their interdependence in the performance of the function of interchanging information as to the nature of demands for systemic outputs and the nature of the outputs themselves. Instead of this, the preoccupation of American political scientists with the power which pressure groups exercise has narrowed the focus primarily to the consideration of only one side of the interaction, the actions which pressure groups engage in as they seek to influence governmental decision-makers, and it has yielded a relatively static kind of analysis. The study of pressure group-legislature interaction could be undertaken profitably in systems wherein pressure groups exercise little power but have a function to perform as a means of giving expression to discontent among disadvantaged groups and of serving by their very existence to provide symbolic satisfaction to them.[15] Meaningful questions could be raised about the degree of skill exercised by the authorities in making use of the groups to maintain an adequate level of support even in the absence of an ability to satisfy demands. Furthermore it would be possible to assess the systemic changes which would have to come about before the pressure groups could perform a more influential role. By starting with the group approach assumption that pressure group influence must be there if the study of pressure groups is to be fruitful, interesting avenues for comparative inquiry are automatically shut off.

The comparative study of various sub-systems of the political system has experienced an uneven development. In some areas the perspective domi-

---

[15] See Easton's comments on the "stress-reducing function of representation" and "symbolic gratification from outputs." *A Systems Analysis of Political Life* (New York, 1965), pp. 252–253, 390–391.

nant in the study of American government and politics continues to prevail; in others a broader comparative perspective has begun to emerge, based upon a systemic model. Three such areas are described briefly in the remainder of this section.

The Comparative Study of Political Cultures.   The study of political attitudes has been especially dominated by an American-centered perspective because of the fact that the techniques for the measurement of public opinion have been developed to a large extent in this country and have been exported to Europe and elsewhere for widespread application only very recently. As a consequence the content of our knowledge about political attitudes can be largely characterized as a knowledge of American political attitudes. The influence of the United States in this field has given rise to the danger that questions developed in the United States for application to American samples may be posed with insufficient alteration to samples of the populations of countries with substantially different cultures.[16] However, in the past decade, substantial sophistication has been gained in this realm, and a growing pool of indigenous expertise in some European countries is rapidly supplying us with a wealth of variable attitudinal data. Quite obviously, to study political attitudes comparatively, it will be necessary to take great care in framing the questions that are to be asked in ways such that they will be interpreted as meaning essentially the same things in all of the countries studied. For this purpose concepts are needed which transcend the cultural limits of any single country, and, for this, systemic concepts must be employed.

The term "political culture" as it is employed here was originated by Almond, and refers to the pattern of psychological orientations which people in a given society have toward objects within their political system. One would study the political culture of a country by asking a representative sample of its population questions about the knowledge they have about political objects (cognition), their intellectual estimates of the worth of political objects (evaluation), and the direction of their emotions concerning political objects (affect). Presumably an array of dimensions would be constructed along which respondents could be arrayed regarding such matters as the level of their political information and the extent of their support for systemic objects such as political leaders, various political roles, other members of the system, and themselves as political actors. The configuration of all such dimensions would then constitute what is known about the political culture. By asking similar questions of respondents in other countries, it would be possible to develop country profiles and to compare countries with one another.

In the late 1950's Gabriel Almond collaborated with Sidney Verba in writing *The Civic Culture*, a now-famous study of the political cultures of five nations: the United States, the United Kingdom, West Germany, Italy, and Mexico. In reporting their findings they explicated a typology of political cul-

---

[16] See the discussion by Gabriel Almond and Sidney Verba of the problem of standardizing the interview situation in *The Civic Culture* (Princeton, 1963), pp. 57–61.

tures which may have considerable value for the study of comparative government and politics in so far as it relates to the concern for systemic analysis. Political cultures will, according to Almond and Verba, be classifiable into three broad categories, if it is kept in mind that no culture will fit one of these categories exclusively, since there will be elements of all three types in any political culture. The *parochial* culture is one in which low cognition of political objects is evidenced and, as a consequence, questions as to evaluation or affect are meaningless. The *subject* culture is one in which cognition, evaluation and affect are relatively high in so far as the outputs of the system and output structures are concerned, but wherein cognition or at least affect and evaluation of inputs and input structures are low. This contrasts with the *participant* culture, wherein, whatever the case of orientations toward outputs and output structures, cognition, evaluation, and affect are high as regards input and input structures.

The implications of such a typology for comparative study are two-fold. In the first place, we may assume that the political culture is a sub-system of the political system, and that its functional relevance for the system can be seen in the necessity, for systemic persistence, that the political culture contain orientations that are congruent with the actual conditions of the system's operative elements. Thus a parochial culture would be congruent with a system in which people lived in isolated communities having little if any contact with the central authorities, with the effective membership of the system being confined to a relatively small elite involved in governing the country. A subject or participant culture, while difficult to conceive of under such circumstances, would be incongruent with a system of this type, since members of the system would be aware of the existence of a central government and desirous of obtaining its outputs, but dissatisfied with the absence of effective output structures reaching out to the periphery. The characterization of a political culture as falling essentially into one of the categories of the Almond-Verba typology, or as containing two or more sub-cultures of different types, enables us to see the functional interrelationship between political attitudes and political structures and to identify an important source of systemic imbalance wherever it exists.

A second value of the typology is that it can be used to specify in operational terms the psychological aspects of political development. Thus the expectation that political change accompanies social and economic change can be tested in the psychological realm. Will parochial attitudes give way to subject or participant attitudes as people are brought into contact with others in a larger political system and are made aware of the existence and character of central political structures? Will subject attitudes yield in time to participant attitudes with increasing sophistication, or will an opposite development occur, i.e., will government grow more distant in a mass society and people come to have a sense of powerlessness? To be sure, the Almond-Verba types are gross and superficial. Their effort, after all, was of a pioneering nature. But the ground has been laid for further refinement accompanying more potent research designs and questionnaire items which tap dimensions of still greater relevance to the study of systemic change and persistence.

There are means by which political culture, even when viewed in the Almond sense, may be studied other than by conducting attitude surveys. Evidence as to the content of political culture may be gained by content analysis of the mass media or by depth study of particular individuals deemed representative of certain cultural types, whether the individuals be members of the political elite or of the mass. In any event, we are, at best, able only to obtain indications of the nature of a phenomenon so vast and complex that it has defied careful analysis until quite recently. Yet specialists in comparative government and politics have always sensed the importance of political culture for comparative study. Differences between countries have traditionally been explained in psychological, as well as historical, geographic, and economic terms. When pushed to give an adequate explanation for the different attitudes of the Germans and the French toward their political institutions, political scientists frequently have thrown up their hands and conceded that it is due to differences in the "national characters" of the two peoples. But this has not taken us very far. The circularity in such explanations is almost too evident. In the first place one says, "the Germans and the French behave differently because of differences in national character." Then, when asked how one knows that their national characters are different, one replies: "Why, look at the different ways in which they behave." Certainly the literature of comparative government and politics contains efforts to uncover systematically indicators of political culture which are independent of the behavior we would like to use political culture in part to explain. However, the recent steps taken in the direction of giving political culture a usable definition and placing it within a broader conceptual framework where it is given separate identity but at the same time is functionally related with the other elements of the framework make it much more likely that it will be filled in with appropriate content and used effectively in the process of theory building and hypothesis testing.

The Comparative Study of Political Parties and Party Systems.   The systemic perspective has not as yet really caught hold in the sub-field of political parties and party systems. Comparison has been confined to the development of typologies, an endeavor dominated by Maurice Duverger's *Political Parties*. Political scientists have only recently moved beyond the standard classification of party systems in terms of the number of parties (one-party, two-party, multi-party) to attempts to develop types of party systems which have more meaning in terms of their consequences for the larger political system. However, little attempt has been made to push the inquiry to the extent of seeking the functional relevance which the political party sub-system has for the political system as a whole. Duverger's typology of political party structures has the virtue of being related to a general theory of political development, although his tendency to view political development as a continuous movement in a left-ward direction has retained little meaning in the context of recent European trends, as Duverger himself today recognizes.[17] However, his distinction, now classic, between cadre and mass parties has been of great usefulness in identifying party types in systems at fairly early stages of development. More recently Otto Kirchheimer has suggested a new party type, the "catch-all" party which combines the pragmatic, election-winning orientation of the cadre party with the centralization and mass membership of the mass party, a combination which seems to fit the characteristics of a number of the larger parties in Western Europe, especially those in the United Kingdom and West Germany.

If the sub-field of comparative parties and party systems is to experience the same renaissance as that of political cultures, there will have to be an effort made to come to grips with the problem of defining the systemic role which parties perform. Can the political party system be viewed as a sub-system performing a function which is vital to the maintenance of political stability? If so, what is it? Here again, we see the influence of the American political scientist's view of the American political system restraining his ability to proceed from broad systemic concepts in dealing with sub-systems comparatively. Because of the difficulty we have in regarding the political parties in the United States as anything more than broad coalitions joined together for the purpose of effectively waging periodic electoral battles, our tendency has been to identify the function which parties primarily perform as that of trying to get candidates elected, with whatever else they do being considered secondary and even derivative.[18] European political scientists, on the other hand, have been particularly impressed by the role parties have played as conveyors of ideology and as spokesmen of the interests of major classes or religious groups within society. Thus, they have seen the parties as being oriented toward the achievement of certain goals which transcend the gaining of office. American parties have been seen by Europeans as not really political parties in the modern sense since they lack coherent doctrine and structure. Americans, for their part, tend to be suspicious of the more ideologically oriented European parties because those parties seem unconcerned (in the short-run, at least) with what Americans assume all true parties seek: the gaining of public office.

What both perspectives have lacked is a notion of political party that is broad enough at least to enable us to study parties and party systems comparatively without being seriously limited in the range of countries we may examine. Recent efforts to consider the developmental patterns which political parties in the West have experienced promise to lead the way to a more satisfactory concept, at least one capable of making comparison possible as among party systems in Western countries. Seymour M. Lipset and Stein Rokkan have recently found it possible to suggest that party systems (and, by

[17] Maurice Duverger, *La Democratie sans le Peuple* (Paris, 1967), pp. 85–125.
[18] See Leon D. Epstein, *Political Parties in Western Democracies* (New York, 1967), p. 9.

implication, most of the party units within them), whatever their individual peculiarities, have generally shared a common characteristic with respect to the systems in which they are imbedded: they direct conflict which otherwise might be disruptive of authority into normalized channels.[19] Even though certain parties seek to recall incumbents from office, their opposition to the incumbents takes a form which permits frustration, bitterness, or anxiety which members of the system feel toward the incumbents to be vented through means congruent with orderly politics. One might go a step further and suggest in Easton's terms that parties are valuable to the system insofar as they serve as devices at election time to register the amount of support for the authorities, the regime and the political community. In this way they not only give a controlled expression to conflict, thus potentially sublimating tendencies to give more violent and illegal vent to discontent, but they also act as a thermometer registering the degree of support coming into the system and alerting the members of the system to dangers when they occur.

It is the author's belief that great potential for advances toward a systematic comparative study of parties and party systems is now in the offing, at least in so far as the study of open, competitive party systems is concerned. Whether or not a functional definition of a political party sub-system such as that suggested above can be carried over to non-competitive, largely one-party systems would be a difficult question to answer. Does the Communist Party of the Soviet Union, for example, register levels of support existing among members of the political system, in addition to its more obvious function of seeking to mobilize support for the system? If it does register support levels accurately, it is certainly not through the medium of free elections, but rather through a more difficult to perceive process of feeding back into the system information about reactions of people to the system's outputs. Political scientists have argued for years the issue of whether a "political party" in a "one-party system" is really a party and if the "system" is really a system. Until we can establish a conception of political parties which transcends cultural bounds better than most of those advanced thus far, the debate would seem to be a sterile one.

The Comparative Study of Public Administration.[20]   The American study of public administration has perhaps gone further than any other field of American political science in the direction of developing a culture-free conceptual framework for approaching its objects of inquiry. The heavy influence since World War II of the theory of bureaucracy developed in Europe has insured that, at the very least, the dominant model for the study of Amer-

---

[19] Seymour M. Lipset and Stein Rokkan, "Cleavage Structures, Party Systems and Voter Alignments: An Introduction," *Party Systems and Voter Alignments,* ed. Lipset and Rokkan (New York, 1967), pp. 1–64. Myron Weiner's recent study of the Indian Congress Party can be read as a study in the process by which a political party functions to channel conflict into the political system in such a way as to lessen its disruptive potentiality. *Party Building in a New Nation: The Indian National Congress* (Chicago, 1967).

[20] The author has relied heavily for the general discussion which follows upon Ferrel Heady, *Public Administration: A Comparative Perspective* (Englewood Cliffs, 1966).

ican administrative forms has not relied upon categories appropriate only for American institutions. It is possible to assert, of course, that of the various structures common to advanced Western countries, administrative organization is the one which is most likely to have developed an integrity relatively uninfluenced by particular cultural givens of the nations within which it is found and therefore to contain properties that are common to it no matter what its cultural context.

The bureaucratic model has been enthusiastically adopted by students of public administration in developed countries as a means of measuring the actual administrative institutions observed against an "ideal-type" model of rational administrative organization, i.e., organization perfectly developed to fulfill some set programmatic objective. Involved in the conception are such principles as hierarchy, role specialization, achievement criteria, and the establishment of rules to guide administrative performance. Quite obviously such a structure would have to rest upon a cultural base conducive to its adequate functioning. Thus, for example, the criterion of achievement as a basis for evaluating the performance of administrative personnel and for assessing the credentials of candidates for administrative positions would have to rest upon a cultural base which places a premium upon individual achievement and which has internalized criteria for recognizing it. Political scientists have generally assumed, with Max Weber, that only an advanced society with a culture featuring legal-rational concepts of authority would be capable of sustaining administrative structures approximating the bureaucratic model. However, it has only been fairly recently that they have turned their attention to the question of what one might expect administrative structures to look like in a pre-modern or developing political system.

Despite their relatively non-American-centered perspective, American students of public administration have had a tendency to resist the abandonment or serious modification of the bureaucratic model as they have moved from the realm of advanced, complex nations to that of the nations still undergoing modernization. Here they have been beset by the malady afflicting comparative study in general: the tendency to put the structure first and to assume that the function performed by a given structure in one context will carry over to a similar structure in another context. This accounts for the frustration of American specialists in public administration as they have attempted to apply their expertise in the role of technical advisers to the governments of Asian and African countries. Invariably they have found that the structure set up along the rough lines of classical principles has failed to behave as expected or even to display standard aberrations familiar in Western settings. Most perplexing has been the difficulty of maintaining stable boundaries between the administrative organization and its political environment. On the one hand, achievement criteria have been violated, often in wholesale fashion, as political considerations of personal loyalty, ideological purity, or both have become predominant in personnel policy. On the other hand, administrative agencies have shown a tendency to step beyond the bounds of their assigned functions and to seek a role, sometimes in the absence of clear political initiative, in charting the direction and pace of the modernization of their countries.

Two approaches have cropped up in the comparative study of public administration to deal with these perplexing phenomena. The first has proceeded from the assumption that the admixture of politics and administration will of necessity be relatively great in a developing country and has attempted to set forth a new applied field of public administration, that of "development administration." In line with the pragmatic traditions of the field of public administration, advocates of this approach have sought to lay down guidelines for the use of the newly developed instruments of power which administrative agencies, however far they depart from the bureaucratic norm, exercise in the emerging nations as modernizing forces. Granted that the new structures are imperfect by Western standards, they often are the closest thing to a modern element (in terms of the training and value structures of their personnel) existing in the developing country, with the frequent exception of the Army, nevertheless itself a structure modeled after the bureaucratic ideal. Thus, from the perspective of developmental administration, the key question is not whether or not the administrative structures will become innovative modernizing forces within their countries, but how they will do so.

The second approach is less pragmatic and applied in nature, being more academic and concerned first and foremost with acquiring an intellectual grasp of a relatively unfamiliar phenomenon. This approach is to ask whether the bureaucratic model, with modification, can be used to understand administration in developing countries, or whether a new model must be developed to gain a more adequate understanding and to advance scientific concerns. The students of modern organization, whether public or private, in modern societies had already gone a considerable way toward modifying the bureaucratic model almost beyond recognition in seeking to take into account the informal features which, while derogating from the bureaucratic norms, were seen as necessary adjustments to the realities of human frailties and the political uncertainties of the organization's environment. Still, the bureaucratic model had been useful as a starting point, as a base against which to measure and then to account for the deviations. Are the deviations from the ideal type seen in developing countries so great as to render such measurement meaningless?

The problem of finding a model appropriate for the study of administrative structures in developing countries has been the subject of very systematic treatment by Fred Riggs, who is decidedly of the opinion that the use of the formal bureaucratic model will only result in inaccurate assessments of the nature of administration in what he calls "transitional societies." He considers it especially misleading to assume that administrative structures in transitional societies can acquire the same degree of autonomy with respect to other structures as can their counterparts in fully modern societies. Adopting a structural-functional approach, he points to the likelihood that administrative structures in transitional societies will not be able to confine themselves to the functions legally assigned to them. Rather they will be performing a series of non-legal functions accounted for by the fact that they will be unable to maintain their separateness from other social structures. A government bureau may be found performing a role in the maintenance of a kinship system, or it may be called upon to serve as a medium of communication between the elites and the masses or become a mechanism for the reinforcement of the authority of village elites. Thus its manifest function is lost from sight, and it becomes impossible to study it even as a departure from the strict bureaucratic norms. On the other hand, Riggs rejects the idea of abandoning the formal model entirely and adopting the assumption of the anthropologist that one is dealing with an undifferentiated social whole. The transitional society, after all, contains elements of both the modern and the traditional. Riggs advocates an approach which combines the insights of the anthropologist into primitive, undifferentiated society with those of the more functionally specific social sciences into the complexities of modern, industrialized society. His "prismatic" model supposedly represents the mid-way point between the "fused," undifferentiated society and the "diffracted," functionally differentiated society, the terminology being drawn by analogy from optics—the prism performs the function of diffracting undifferentiated, fused white light into a rainbow spectrum of distinct colors. What is noteworthy in Riggs' provocative suggestions is that he is attempting to place the administrative sub-system into a larger system and to show both its functional relationship thereto and its conceptual consequences. Hence, his effort can clearly be placed within the field of comparative political systems. To the extent that Riggs and others sharing his assumptions have provided a framework for further undertakings in the field, the study of comparative public administration has moved further to date than have the other sub-fields of comparative political systems.

The study of public administration in *modern* settings has not escaped the effort to infuse it with a more comparative perspective. A noteworthy example of such an effort is Michel Crozier's *The Bureaucratic Phenomenon*. It is an effort by a Frenchman to come to grips with the American science of public administration and to show its limitations when applied to a cultural setting different from the American, even though not lacking in the principal attributes of modernity. Crozier's work can be expected to have a substantial impact upon the field of public administration in the United States precisely because it makes use of the bureaucratic model and shows that in many ways the model approximates the reality in France to a greater extent than it does in most modern countries, given certain crucial aspects of the French political culture. Furthermore, he shows that extensions of bureaucracy to its self-consistent extreme, involving a high degree of impersonality and rigorous barriers to favoritism, were at once dysfunctional from the standpoint of organizational efficiency and positively functional from the standpoint of individual, *intra*-personal equilibrium. Unlike the American organization man, the Frenchman was disinclined to seek close personal relations with his associates and preferred to maintain his distance from superiors, peers and subordinates alike, while insisting upon equality of treatment at each level. The "human relations" approach, so prominent in the American science of administration, appears to have an uphill battle in France because the Frenchman does not see the bureaucratic setting as an appropriate one for the development of close personal ties and because the Frenchman sees authority relations as threatening, preferring to keep his distance from those who have authority over him, even if this means less humane treatment at their hands.

By examining bureaucratic behavior in the French context, Crozier has presented the American student of public administration with a paradox: if bureaucratization is an element of modernization, then the French political culture's greater capacity to tolerate rigid bureaucratic situations would seem to suggest that France, in this respect at least, is more modern than the United States. Yet Crozier is the first to argue that this is not the case. Indeed he insists that the aspects of the French mentality which are conducive to rigid bureaucracy are pre-modern elements which will disappear as France becomes more generally "bureaucratized." What French bureaucratic structures have hitherto evidenced is a dysfunctional form of bureaucracy no longer prevalent in most Western countries. Modern organizational concepts stress the importance of integrating the individual into the life of the organization, and the modern organizational man is one who can readily adapt himself to a variety of organizational situations, without suffering the trauma seemingly experienced by the Frenchman when thrown up against new and unfamiliar authority relationships. Whether Crozier is right in expecting Frenchmen to adapt to the demands of modernity (and many writers have attested to the fact that they are not doing so at breakneck speed [21]), his book is further evidence of the potentiality for broadening our understanding of political phenomena by testing our generalizations in unfamiliar contexts.

Conclusion.   The preceding discussion will undoubtedly have evoked the objection with many readers that the author has overreached himself. It is artificial, it may be argued, to separate a "comparative" field from the rest of political science and say that only that political science which adopts a certain perspective (i.e., some combination of the systems approach and structural-functionalism) can be considered truly comparative. However, the reader must be reminded that the "comparative method" is not the exclusive property of one branch of political science, but is common to all scientific inquiry. However, the conscientious use of the comparative method in comparative government and politics can supply a badly needed corrective to American political science, the various fields of which have developed primarily as the study of American political phenomena and employ conceptualizations which are not generalizable to politics wherever found. It is only

[21] See Stanley Hoffmann, "Paradoxes of the French Political Community," *In Search of France*, ed. Hoffmann (Cambridge, Mass., 1963), pp. 1–117.

by adopting a general conceptual scheme that is not culture-bound that we will be able to taste the full fruits of using the comparative method. No single conceptual framework has yet proven its relative utility for comparative purposes, let alone its absolute freedom from cultural restraints. Nevertheless, the effort to find a workable general framework that will relate politics to its environment, that will fit the various aspects of politics into a coherent framework of universal applicability, and that will make it possible to deal meaningfully with the problem of political change, is one distinguishable avenue of approaching the task of developing a science of politics and one which seeks to meet head-on an imposing impediment to the attainment of that science: the problem of transcending cultural differences.

BIBLIOGRAPHY

The following bibliography contains, for the most part, works of a *cross-national* nature. Those which focus upon a single country are listed because of some aspect of potential utility for cross-national study.

General References

Classics. The comparative approach to political study is at least as old as Herodotus (Fifth Century B.C.). A few of the most celebrated classic examples dealing with the age-old problems of nation- and state-building are ARISTOTLE, *Politics;* MACHIAVELLI, *The Prince* and *Discourses;* and MONTESQUIEU, *The Spirit of the Laws.* Noted modern works which anticipated or reflected the concern for the proper ordering of the polity in the age of mass society include JOHN STUART MILL, *On Representative Government;* JAMES BRYCE, *Modern Democracies,* 2 vols. (New York, 1921); HERMAN FINER, *The Theory and Practice of Modern Government* (New York, 1932); and CARL J. FRIEDRICH, *Constitutional Government and Democracy* (Boston, 1941).

Textbooks. Most textbooks in the field of comparative government and politics are presented as descriptive analyses of government and politics in a few major countries other than the United States. The most common collection of countries for introductory courses is probably the United Kingdom, France, Germany, and the Soviet Union. Textbooks featuring the major Asian countries have become more prominent in the last decade; those listed here are among the best. Recently, several paperback series of single-country studies have been published; a number of small countries ignored by the "major powers" textbooks have been given adequate textbook coverage in this way.

CARTER, GWENDOLEN M., and JOHN H. HERZ. *Major Foreign Powers.* 5th ed. New York, 1967.

BEER, SAMUEL H., and ADAM B. ULAM, eds. *Patterns of Government: The Major Political Systems of Europe.* 2nd ed. New York, 1962.

MACRIDIS, ROY C., and ROBERT E. WARD, eds. *Modern Political Systems.* Volume I: *Europe,* 2nd ed.; Volume II: *Asia.* Englewood Cliffs, 1968 and 1963.

Readers and Collections of Essays. The two most comprehensive readers are those by Macridis and Brown and Eckstein and Apter, the latter being an especially rich collection. The remaining selections are more specialized.

MACRIDIS, ROY C., and BERNARD E. BROWN, eds. *Comparative Politics: Notes and Readings*. Rev. ed. Homewood, Illinois, 1964.

ECKSTEIN, HARRY, and DAVID E. APTER, eds. *Comparative Politics: A Reader.* New York, 1963.

GEERTZ, CLIFFORD, ed. *Old Societies and New States: The Quest for Modernity in Asia and Africa*. New York, 1963.

ECKSTEIN, HARRY, ed. *Internal War*. New York, 1963.

FINKLE, JASON, and RICHARD W. GABLE, eds. *Political Development and Social Change*. New York, 1966.

Methodology

Critiques of the Field. The methodological revolution in the field of comparative politics has developed concurrently with the broader trends in the discipline of political science. Accordingly, the leading early statements challenging traditional approaches (the *APSR* article; Macridis) coincided with Easton's wide-ranging critical review of the discipline. Heckscher's statement is a balanced and challenging rebuttal of those who would attempt to make comparative government and politics a universal science, ignoring the irreducible historico-cultural realities of separate nations and areas of the world. Support for this viewpoint is presented by Pye, who lists the fundamental differences between Western and non-Western countries which require separate conceptual formulations appropriate to the non-Western context. In a more narrowly focused and tightly reasoned article, Kalleberg takes the newer school to task for having paid insufficient attention to the logical requirements of the comparative method.

EASTON, DAVID. *The Political System*. New York, 1953.

"Research in Comparative Politics." *APSR*, XLVII (1953), 641–675.

MACRIDIS, ROY C. *The Study of Comparative Government*. Garden City, 1955.

HECKSCHER, GUNNAR. *The Study of Comparative Government and Politics*. London, 1957.

PYE, LUCIAN W. "The Non-Western Political Process." *JOP*, XX (1958), 468–486.

KALLEBERG, ARTHUR L. "The Logic of Comparison: A Methodological Note on the Comparative Study of Political Systems." *World Politics*, XIX (1966), 69–82.

Blueprints for Research. Various outlines for the future development of the field have been presented. They include those listed below, as well as some of the items listed immediately above. The volume edited by Ward also serves as a guide to the student contemplating field research abroad, outlining the problems he might confront and the skills he should acquire.

KAHIN, GEORGE MC T., GUY J. PAUKER, and LUCIAN PYE. "Comparative Politics of Non-Western Countries." *APSR*, XLIX (1955), 1022–1041.

ALMOND, GABRIEL A., TAYLOR COLE, and ROY C. MACRIDIS. "A Suggested Research Strategy in Western European Government and Politics." *APSR*, XLIX (1955), 1042–1049.

RUSTOW, DANKWART A. "New Horizons for Comparative Politics." *World Politics*, IX (1957), 530–549.

WARD, ROBERT E., ed. *Studying Politics Abroad*. Boston, 1964.

General Conceptual Schemes. The principal statements of the respective conceptual frameworks of David Easton and Gabriel A. Almond are listed below. The entries by Deutsch, Spiro, and Etzioni should alert the student to the fact that the question of whether any one particular scheme will be of general utility remains wide open.

EASTON, DAVID. "An Approach to the Analysis of Political Systems." *World Politics*, X (1957), 383–400.

———. *A Framework for Political Analysis*. Englewood Cliffs, 1965.

———. *A Systems Analysis of Political Life*. New York, 1965.

ALMOND, GABRIEL A. "Comparative Political Systems." *JOP*, XVIII (1956), 391–409.

———. "Introduction: A Functional Approach to Comparative Politics." *The Politics of the Developing Areas*, ed. Almond and James S. Coleman. Princeton, 1960. Pages 3–64.

——— and G. BINGHAM POWELL, JR. *Comparative Politics: A Developmental Approach*. Boston, 1966.

DEUTSCH, KARL W. *The Nerves of Government: Models of Political Communication and Control*. New York, 1963.

SPIRO, HERBERT J. "Comparative Politics: A Comprehensive Approach." *APSR*, LVI (1962), 577–595.

ETZIONI, AMITAI. *The Active Society*. New York, 1968.

Quantitative Applications. Efforts to use quantitative techniques of data analysis, such as multiple correlation and factor analysis, to nation-state attributes treated as variables have begun to produce interesting results. Deutsch, Fitzgibbon and Johnson, Cutright, and Tanter seek to gauge the interrelations between attributes such as urbanization, mass media exposure, economic development and inter-party competition. Banks and Textor have produced a volume in which the nations of the world for which information could be obtained are ranked according to nearly 200 discrete quantitative and qualitative criteria. The inter-correlations between the rankings have been factor-analyzed by Gregg and Banks. The remaining volumes in the list are products of the very promising Yale Political Data Program. Russett, *et al.*, rank the nations of the world according to a variety of "hard" indicators of economic, social and political characteristics. The volume edited by Merritt and Rokkan includes essays on the state of political data collections and the uses to which they have been and can potentially be put.

DEUTSCH, KARL W. "Social Mobilization and Political Development." *APSR*, LV (1961), 493–514.

FITZGIBBON, RUSSELL H., and KENNETH F. JOHNSON. "Measurement of Latin American Political Change." *APSR*, LV (1961), 516–526.

CUTRIGHT, PHILLIPS. "National Political Development: Measurement and Analysis." *American Sociological Review*, XXVIII (1963), 253–264.

TANTER, RAYMOND. "Toward a Theory of Political Development." *MJPS*, XI (1967), 145–172.

BANKS, ARTHUR S., and ROBERT B. TEXTOR. *A Cross-Polity Survey*. Cambridge, Mass., 1963.

GREGG, PHILLIP M., and ARTHUR S. BANKS. "Dimensions of Political Systems: A Factor Analysis of *A Cross-Polity Survey*." *APSR*, LIX (1965), 602–614.

RUSSETT, BRUCE, *et al. World Handbook of Political and Social Indicators*. New Haven, 1964.

MERRITT, RICHARD L., and STEIN ROKKAN, eds. *Comparing Nations: The Use of Quantitative Data in Cross-National Research*. New Haven, 1966.

Developing and Developed Countries

Concepts of Political Development.   There has been a massive recent outpouring of works which attempt to come to grips with the elusive problem of intellectualizing rapid political change in the context of the process of modernization. Packenham and Weiner classify the theories and concepts available in the literature; the former catalogs theories of "political development," while the latter concentrates on definitions of the less inclusive concept of "political integration." Willner and Huntington challenge students of political development to sharpen their analytical tools and to be open to alternative developmental paths, including "political decay." Among broad overviews of the development process, Arendt and Organski are especially provocative for students interested in the earlier political developments of European nations, including Russia, while Emerson and Apter focus upon contemporary political development in Asia and Africa. Nettl and Johnson seek to bridge the gap between Europe and the "Third World."

PACKENHAM, ROBERT A. "Political Development Doctrines in the American Foreign Aid Program." *World Politics*, XVIII (1966), 194–235.

WEINER, MYRON. "Political Integration and Political Development." *The Annals*, Volume 358 (1965), 52–64.

WILLNER, ANN RUTH. "The Underdeveloped Study of Political Development." *World Politics*, XVI (1964), 468–482.

HUNTINGTON, SAMUEL. "Political Development and Political Decay." *World Politics*, XVII (1965), 386–430.

ARENDT, HANNAH. *The Origins of Totalitarianism*. New York, 1958.

EMERSON, RUPERT. *From Empire to Nation: The Rise to Self-Assertion of Asian and African Peoples*. Cambridge, Mass., 1960.

ORGANSKI, A.F.K. *The Stages of Political Development*. New York, 1965.

APTER, DAVID E. *The Politics of Modernization*. Chicago, 1965.

NETTL, J.P. *Political Mobilization*. New York, 1967.

JOHNSON, CHALMERS. *Revolutionary Change*. Boston, 1966.

Studies of the Development Process.   The following are among the most frequently cited works which seek to distill from the study of particular modernizing countries the fundamental sociological and psychological factors impeding or promoting political development. Lerner compares six Middle Eastern countries, focussing on the ability of individuals to *empathize* with other members of their nation as a key property in the nation-building process. Banfield is concerned with factors *inhibiting* the integrative process in Southern Italy. Pye's study of Burmese political culture viewed primarily at the elite level yields pessimistic conclusions regarding the readiness of today's "developing nations" for the onslaught of modernity. By contrast, Lipset's study of the United States as a new nation brings into sharp relief the elements which left the American nation free to lead the rest of the world into modern political life.

LERNER, DANIEL. *The Passing of Traditional Society*. Glencoe, 1958.

BANFIELD, EDWARD C. *The Moral Basis of a Backward Society*. New York, 1958.

PYE, LUCIAN. *Politics, Personality and Nation-Building: Burma's Search for Identity*. New Haven, 1962.

LIPSET, SEYMOUR M. *The First New Nation: The United States in Historical and Comparative Perspective*. New York, 1963.

Developed Political Systems.   Most writers have found it difficult, if not impossible, to discover enough common elements of *political* similarity between modern democracies and modern dictatorships to permit systematic comparison. The model presented by Friedrich and Brzezinski for totalitarian dictatorships and that by Eckstein for stable democracies provide few, if any, parallels. However, the recent emphasis upon a "de-ideologization" of political movements in Western Europe, noted by Lipset, seems to be finding echoes among writers on the Soviet Union. Meyer attempts the application of some concepts developed for the study of more open systems in his textbook on the Soviet system. That the barriers between the study of open and closed systems are indeed breaking down is further evidenced by the effort of Brzezinski and Huntington to show similarities as well as contrasts between the Soviet Union and the United States and by Dahrendorf's treatment of the Nazi regime as a step in Germany's political development rather than as a break in continuity.

FRIEDRICH, CARL J., and ZBIGNIEW BRZEZINSKI. *Totalitarian Dictatorship and Autocracy*. Cambridge, Mass., 1956.

ECKSTEIN, HARRY. "A Theory of Stable Democracy." *Division and Cohesion in Democracy: A Study of Norway*. Princeton, 1966. Appendix B.

LIPSET, SEYMOUR M. "The Changing Class Structure and Contemporary European Politics." *Daedalus*, XCIII (1964), 271–303.

MEYER, ALFRED G. *The Soviet Political System: An Interpretation*. New York, 1965.

BRZEZINSKI, ZBIGNIEW, and SAMUEL P. HUNTINGTON. *Political Power: USA/ USSR*. New York, 1965.

DAHRENDORF, RALF. *Society and Democracy in Germany*. Garden City, 1967.

Sub-Systems of the Political System

Political Culture. Stein Rokkan's call for "comparative micro-analysis" is being answered by the development of what may now be considered a new subfield of political science, the study of political culture. Important refinements in the concept of political culture are to be found in the essays of Kim, Verba, and Christoph. Recent studies have benefited greatly from the work of McClelland in analyzing the personality structure that is congruent with modern political culture. Among the most influential studies to date have been those by Converse and Dupeux and Almond and Verba, the latter having an introductory blueprint of breathtakingly ambitious quality.

ROKKAN, STEIN. "The Comparative Study of Political Participation: Notes Toward a Perspective in Current Research." *Essays on the Behavioral Study of Politics*, ed. Austin Ranney. Urbana, 1962. Pages 47–90.

KIM, Y.C. "The Concept of Political Culture in Comparative Politics." *JOP*, XXVI (1964), 313–336.

VERBA, SIDNEY. "Comparative Political Culture." *Political Culture and Political Development*, ed. Lucian W. Pye and Sidney Verba. Princeton, 1965. Pages 512–560.

CHRISTOPH, JAMES B. "Consensus and Cleavage in British Political Ideology." *APSR*, LIX (1965), 629–642.

MCCLELLAND, DAVID C. *The Achieving Society*. Princeton, 1961.

CONVERSE, PHILIP E., and GEORGES DUPEUX. "Politicization of the Electorate in France and the United States." *POQ*, XXVI (1962), 1–23.

ALMOND, GABRIEL A., and SIDNEY VERBA. *The Civic Culture*. Princeton, 1963.

The Comparative Study of Parties and Party Systems.   The works of Ostrogorski (1902), Michels (1915), and Duverger (1951) can be said to constitute a classic triumvirate, to which Lipset's variegated compendium of hypothesis testing and theory construction should be added, before one dips into recent materials on contemporary and historical parties and party systems. The four collections of essays survey the field adequately and present new findings and insights.

OSTROGORSKI, M. *Democracy and the Organization of Political Parties.* 2 vols. Garden City, 1964.

MICHELS, ROBERT. *Political Parties.* New York, 1959.

DUVERGER, MAURICE. *Political Parties.* 2nd English ed., rev. London, 1959.

LIPSET, SEYMOUR M. *Political Man.* Garden City, 1960.

ALLARDT, ERIK, and YRJÖ LITTUNEN, eds. *Cleavages, Ideologies, and Party Systems.* Turku, 1964.

LA PALOMBARA, JOSEPH, and MYRON WEINER, eds. *Political Parties and Political Development.* Princeton, 1966.

DAHL, ROBERT A., ed. *Political Oppositions in Western Democracies.* New Haven, 1966.

LIPSET, SEYMOUR M., and STEIN ROKKAN, eds. *Party Systems and Voter Alignments: Cross-National Perspectives.* New York, 1967.

Comparative Public Administration.   Any survey of the literature in this area must start with Weber's classic statement of the concept of bureaucracy. Of contemporary developments, the works by Riggs and Crozier are among the currently more influential. Heady surveys the literature cogently in his brief essay; further insights into the direction in which comparative public administration has been moving can be gained from the volumes edited by Siffin, Heady and Stokes, and LaPalombara.

WEBER, MAX. "Bureaucracy." *From Max Weber: Essays In Sociology,* ed. and trans. H.H. Gerth and C. Wright Mills. New York, 1958. Pages 196–244.

RIGGS, FRED W. *Administration in Developing Countries: The Theory of Prismatic Society.* Boston, 1964.

CROZIER, MICHEL. *The Bureaucratic Phenomenon.* Chicago, 1964.

HEADY, FERREL. *Public Administration: A Comparative Perspective.* Englewood Cliffs, 1966.

SIFFIN, WILLIAM J., ed. *Toward the Comparative Study of Public Administration.* Bloomington, 1957.

HEADY, FERREL, and SYBIL L. STOKES, eds. *Papers in Comparative Public Administration.* Ann Arbor, 1962.

LA PALOMBARA, JOSEPH, ed. *Bureaucracy and Political Development.* Princeton, 1963.

16 / INTERNATIONAL RELATIONS

by John Houston

The study of international relations has become an important academic concern in the twentieth century for fairly obvious reasons. Two world wars of unprecedented and catastrophic magnitude, a considerably larger number of more limited conflicts, and the continuing threat of a final and ultimate holocaust have been the dominant political events of the period. Those have sufficed to create an awareness that only through a sustained and serious effort to comprehend the forces at work within the international political system is man likely to create some possibility of continuity for the civilization he has thus far produced.

Such a study of necessity deals primarily with the inter-action of the members of the international community of nation-states or, to put the matter another way, with the behavior of the international political system. The term international relations suggests a vast and variegated panorama, composed of international conferences, the comings and goings of diplomats, the signing of treaties, the deployment of military forces, and the flow of international trade. It also includes the more subtle but nonetheless profoundly significant dissemination of ideas and ideologies among multitudes of men, shaping their perceptions of reality and influencing their allegiances and loyalties.

This is obviously an extremely complex field of study, which helps to explain the fact that so many other academic disciplines—sociology, psychology, economics, anthropology, and history, to name only a few—have become involved with the subject. But while these other disciplines have made many valuable contributions toward better comprehension and understanding of international relations, the position taken here is that the political dimension of the international system is the most significant dimension, and that consequently political science must be the core discipline for the student of this subject.

The international political system, the environment within which international relations exist and develop, embodies an enormous range of conflicts of interest, based in part on incompatibilities of values and in part on disagreement over the best way to implement accepted values. Because of the considerably greater size and complexity of the international system, the number and kinds of conflicts are much greater than at the national level. The key point is, however, that these conflicts of interest are reflected and resolved in one way or another through the actions of nation-states, referred to by some writers as the actors within the international system. Nation-states are, by definition, pre-eminently political phenomena, having evolved to serve the function of protecting their citizens against external threats and of authoritatively allocating values within the state. States are most visible because of the existence of their political institutions or governments. Although no one would argue that states have objective existence beyond that of the human beings who comprise them, one must acknowledge that these human beings can for the most part reach many of their most highly-esteemed goals only through the functioning of such political institutions. Thus, although the range of private contacts across national boundaries is increasingly extensive in an age when the technology of transportation and communication is evolving at such a rapid rate, it remains true that the most significant contacts at the international level are those which develop through the formal and informal machinery involved in inter-governmental relations. This being the case, the role of the political scientist in the study of international relations must of necessity be a primary one, even though he may gain greatly from the contributions of his fellow social scientists in other disciplines.

In his study of the international system, the political scientist must be very much concerned with the problem of identifying the real actors whose decisions determine the behavior of that system. Reference has already been made to nation-states in this regard, but obviously it is not states *per se* which make and implement decisions toward the realization of objectives. Rather it is such human decision-makers as foreign ministers, ambassadors, presidents, prime ministers, and chiefs of staff who are involved. Actually, in terms of significant influence on foreign policy decisions, the listing must go much further to include such figures as key legislative leaders, especially chairmen of foreign affairs and armed services committees. In national political systems where decisions are sensitive to currents of public opinion, the role of editors, political leaders, columnists, and teachers may also be significant. It must be apparent from all this that the identification of specific actors whose influence is important in a given setting may be a very difficult problem. It must also be apparent that within a given national system the possibility exists of conflicts arising between or among the foreign policy objectives of various groups or interests. For example, there may be a demand from powerful economic interests for tariff protection, as opposed to the desire on the part of the foreign ministry to strengthen political relations with another country through increased trade. In most such instances the inter-action within the national political system will produce a final resolution of the conflict and a resultant decision which will thereafter be implemented internationally through formal and official governmental channels. The possibility also exists for informal interest group contacts across national boundaries. Groups of various types—economic, humanitarian, or ideological—may make efforts to coordinate pressure on several governments in the direction of a desired common policy. In the great majority of cases, however, the international system being what it is, final meaningful action requires or involves formal governmental decisions. At the same time, while it may be a convenience to refer to states as the protagonists in the political drama of contemporary international relations, one must never mistake the appearance for the reality and must keep in mind that national decision-making systems as a whole are involved.

Since the international political system is the principal focus of the discipline of international relations, a review of its origins and subsequent development is relevant. The generally accepted starting point is the Peace of Westphalia in 1648, which finally resolved the long-drawn-out struggle of political and religious forces known as the Thirty Years' War through the definition and recognition of the sovereignty of the nation-states of Western Europe. For several centuries, the system thus established was essentially confined to this area. Because of the fact that the states involved were relatively homogenous culturally, the conflicts among them tended to be relatively limited and did not threaten the basic stability of the system itself. As these states extended their influence into other continents, however, inevitably these other areas were drawn into the framework of international relations. By the end of the nineteenth century, the entire world was thus involved, as European powers established their control or influence over vast areas of Asia and Africa, and as such non-European powers as Japan and the United States attained great power status.

As a result of the two great world wars of this century, which some have described as European civil wars, the influence of Europe on world affairs began to wane. This was reflected especially in the disintegration of the former great colonial empires and their conversion into a large number of new states. The viability of many of these new units appeared to be questionable, but all were accorded legal recognition as sovereign members of the international community and thus as actors of whatever degree of influence within the international system. Another great change in this century has stemmed from the Russian Revolution, itself to some degree a consequence of World War I, as a result of which profoundly disturbing ideological conflicts were introduced into the system. Thus, what for three centuries was a system dominated by a few great European powers, all of whom shared generally comparable value systems, was transformed into a global structure composed of a great number of states of varying capabilities and of extremely diverse cultures. In place of relative ideological homogeneity, the system came under the influence of a profound and enduring conflict among value systems of great heterogeneity and incompatibility. At the same time, a technology evolving at a bewildering rate of speed was largely changing the physical environment within which international relations take place. Small wonder, then, that the dominant traits of the contemporary international system were instability and uncertainty.

A key point which must be made at the outset, especially from the perspective of the political scientist, concerns the important structural difference between the international political system and the political systems of the separate nation-states. Within each of the latter states, there is a monopoly of decisive force, normally recognized as legitimate, which is available to prevent the use of violence in protest against decisions which are made in the resolution of conflicts of interest within the national system. Also typically within a nation-state, especially a relatively mature one, is an accepted value system, which tends to minimize the development of severe conflicts in any case. By comparison, the international political system has no centralized locus of supreme power capable of suppressing resort to violence by major actors within the system. Beyond this, it is characterized by the co-existence, sometimes peaceful and sometimes not, of competing value systems and ideologies which frequently generate conflicts of interest that would be difficult to resolve in any instance and are especially so because of the absence of effective peace-keeping machinery and procedures. For all these reasons, it is hardly surprising that the history of international relations has been so characterized by instability and violence.

In attempting to understand the behavior of the international political system, one might logically begin with an examination of the objectives which states attempt to achieve and then proceed to a consideration of the so-called capability factors employed toward such achievement. One might then consider some of the typical patterns of inter-action which develop as a result of the efforts to implement policy on the part of nation-states. Finally, one should have some regard for the possible approaches to the non-violent resolution of conflicts of interest generated by such inter-action.

OBJECTIVES OF STATE POLICY

All behavior of states is goal-oriented. Argument is often possible with respect to the wisdom or rationality of the choice of goals but not with regard to the existence of goals *per se*. An important point in this connection which needs to be made at the outset is that simultaneous pursuit of multiple goals by a state is possible and, in fact, not uncommon. This creates the possibility, of course, of conflict among goals, which is also not uncommon. For purposes of analysis, however, each of the principal objectives which states typically seek to achieve will be considered separately.

By general agreement among most students of international relations, the highest priority objective of all states is survival. This might seem to be axiomatic, yet survival for nation-states has special meaning because of the fact, already noted, that the international system itself provides no guarantees in this regard. Thus, each state must of necessity be constantly mindful of possible threats to its continued existence. Survival as such, however, while a necessary end, is not a sufficient one for most states. Ideally, a sense of security is a highly desirable condition. No one, whether an individual or a society, likes to live in the belief that his existence is suspended by a thread which may be snapped at any moment. Consequently, states, like individuals, follow courses of action which in their belief are likely to maximize the probability of survival.

In addition to security, prosperity or a high standard of living is virtually always an objective of state policy. This is notably observable at the present moment in the case of a large number of less-developed states which have recently become a part of the international system, but it is hardly less so with respect to the highly industrialized states in the northern hemisphere, all of which pursue foreign policies designed to improve the conditions of life for their citizens. One of the most common conflicts among objectives is that between security and prosperity, particularly in time of international crisis. Then, as the Nazis put it in the 1930's, the choice may be between "guns and butter." Such a conflict illustrates very well the relationship between foreign and domestic policy. If the demand of the citizenry for affluence is very strong and if their political influence within the national political system is very considerable, the resources available for the achievement of foreign policy objectives may be limited to the point that security is threatened. Conversely, skillful political leadership may be able to exploit real or alleged external threats to security in such a way as to distract public opinion from an unsatisfactory domestic situation and thereby strengthen the political position of that leadership.

Survival, security, and prosperity are all self-evident goals of policy, not difficult to demonstrate. Some of the more subtle, less tangible, and more complex objectives which are nonetheless significant relate to the value systems and ideologies of the actors involved. All states profess to be concerned with justice and with the attainment of liberty, usually allegedly both for themselves and for others as well. The problems involved here in reaching agreement in specific instances on the meaning of such terms are among the most common and most difficult within the area of international politics, especially in an age in which ideological conflict is such a prominent part of the landscape. Some states are clearly much more highly motivated in this regard than others, especially those in which revolutionary fervor is burning at peak intensity as compared to those which have attained relative complacency and tolerance of diversity.

One objective which has not yet been mentioned but which must be considered basic to international politics is power. Power is one of the most controversial concepts in the entire literature of international relations, both from the point of view of its nature and of its moral connotations. Power here is considered to be the ability of one actor to induce, by whatever means, specified behavior by another. Furthermore, power thus defined is in and of itself amoral. The question of morality attaches to the ends with respect to which power is employed. One possible exception might arise when power is regarded as an ultimate end in itself, which, from a strictly rational point of view, seems hardly to be a tenable position. Nevertheless, because of the previously mentioned self-dependence of states for survival, and because of the tremendous uncertainties and imponderables of international relations, statesmen traditionally have sought power seemingly for its own sake, without reference to any immediate ulterior objective but rather as an increment to a fund against which to draw in the event of unexpected contingencies. Ultimately, of course, even in this type of situation, power is actually a means rather than an end.

Because of the fact that power is always relative to a relationship, one state can gain power only at the expense of another, where an adversary or conflict-of-interest situation exists, whereas with respect to such clearly ultimate objectives as security or prosperity, two or more states may all benefit, as in the case of a disarmament or trade agreement. This suggests that much effort should be made by foreign policy decision-makers to discover or identify those with common interests in minimizing power competition.

Prestige is closely and functionally related to power and power as an objective of state policy. Prestige is normally the consequence of the possession of power of whatever dimension, political, economic, or military, and its presence is very likely to enhance the influence of the state possessing it. On occasion, there may be a lack of correlation, however, in that a state which in objective fact has lost some degree of the basis of its power may continue to enjoy prestige, and thus influence, for some time thereafter, before its image in the eyes of other states adjusts to reality. Of course, the reverse sequence is also possible.

THE DIMENSIONS OF POWER

As a result of the nature of the international political system, which lacks any effective centralized machinery for the authoritative allocation of values among the members of the system, the rewards which each state is able to achieve depend to a large extent on the power which it can bring to bear as a means of influencing the behavior of other states. Of course, power is a key component of the political process at any level, national or international, but for reasons already noted, the kinds of power utilized and the manner of utilization differ significantly as between the two levels. Within the international system, the ability to employ the threat or the actual use of force is of central importance, whereas at the national level, this capability normally has much less significance as compared to economic power and power to influence opinion.

Broadly speaking, the dimensions of power which states employ in international relations may be grouped under three headings: military, economic, and political. Obviously these are closely inter-related in practice, but for purposes of analysis may be considered separately. Military power is the dimension which has special and distinctive association with international, as compared to national, politics. Itself dependent on economic and political factors, once created and possessed it becomes the decisive type of power which can be employed, as Machiavelli noted long ago, to gain control of other means of influence, both economic and political. In a conflict of wills between actors which can be resolved in no other way, force becomes the *ultima ratio*. Although the use of force is presently legally circumscribed and restricted to situations presumably involving the necessity for self-defense, in actual practice the decisions taken with respect to the employment of force continue to be essentially autonomous.

A complete analysis of the nature of military power is far too broad a subject to be attempted here, but certain salient aspects may be identified. The complexity and the scope of military power have expanded in recent decades almost beyond the power of the imagination to comprehend. The kinds of weapons and the possibilities for their use exist in great number. Only a relatively few states, however, have the means to exploit this situation significantly, and only two, the United States and the Soviet Union, have the capability to develop the full panoply.

Military capabilities are classified broadly under nuclear and conventional headings, with each of these including numerous sub-categories. A vital component of nuclear power is the delivery system, presently involving the use of ballistic missiles, both land and sea-based. The range of capabilities of a great power must be enormously extended, however, from the thermonuclear to the smallest type of conventional weaponry. Because of the obviously catastrophic implications of nuclear weapons, the atomic age (with the signal exceptions of Hiroshima and Nagasaki) has seen military conflict deliberately restricted to non-nuclear dimensions. Even here, however, existing destructive capacity vastly exceeds anything known hitherto.

A great power by definition must possess the means of responding adequately to any challenge to its vital interests at whatever level of weaponry. This has tended to limit the extent to which conventional ground armies can be reduced. The great nuclear powers must also develop and maintain a symmetrical nuclear relationship with one another, however, to maintain a relationship of mutual deterrence. Symmetry in this context is a highly complex concept, requiring not so much mathematical equivalence as the mutual possession of invulnerable retaliatory capability which can inflict destruction unacceptable to the other party. Even in these terms, however, because of the uncertainties attaching to the measurement of such symmetry and because of the awesome consequences of a failure to attain such a position, the temptation is very great for a state to work toward actual preponderance. Such action naturally stimulates a comparable response from other powers, and the escalation of an arms race is under way. The same problem exists in principle with respect to other categories of weapons, although with slightly less terrifying implications. The basic fact is that a military power which can develop the most varied types of weapons systems in the largest quantities and deploy them geographically to the broadest extent will clearly enjoy the greatest advantage in this dimension of international relations. Put thus simply, the formula perhaps seems not too complex. Combined, however, with the immensely rapid rate of technological change in the military field and with the accompanying immense increase in costs, it produces a situation where only the most affluent states can afford to compete at this level.

At a lower level, however, non-nuclear states, sometimes of very limited capabilities, have been able to employ infiltration, subversion, and various types of guerilla activity very effectively in waging so-called "wars of na-

Guerilla Activity.   **The actions of irregular forces, usually lightly armed but highly mobile, who mount attacks on government units from bases scattered throughout the territory nominally under the control of the government they aim to overthrow. They seek and often enjoy the support of the civilian population among whom they operate.**

Wars of National Liberation.   **A term often employed by Communist and other leftist theoreticians, which refers to armed struggles waged by revolutionary forces in the developing areas of Asia, Africa, and Latin America. The objective is to overthrow colonial regimes, of which there are very few remaining, or, more commonly, national governments allegedly submissive to the interests of industrialized capitalist states, usually designated as "imperialist."**

tional liberation." Although such strategy is often dominated more by political than by military means, the latter is usually an essential component. Given the conditions of instability obtaining throughout much of the formerly colonial and less-industrialized areas of the world, it seems fair to assume that this kind of military action will continue to be prominent in international relations.

Although the military instrument is often the most visible and dramatic means of bringing influence to bear by members of the international system, the economic and political instruments are nonetheless of great importance. In fact, in the absence of critical confrontations of power, the latter are normally the means most commonly employed to implement the respective foreign policies of the member states. Economic policy can be used both positively and negatively, as reward and as punishment in relation to other states. Under the former heading might come such practices as foreign aid in the form of both grants and credits from industrialized to developing states, extended principally in the hope of winning some degree of support from the recipient. Conversely, the withholding or the cutting off of such aid might be used as a sanction against actions or the possibility of actions deemed injurious to the interests of the industrialized state. The United States Congress, for example, has often enacted legislation which has required the withholding of various kinds of assistance from countries trading in various ways with the Communist bloc, especially at times when the United States has been engaged in military conflict with a Communist state. The Soviet Union has tended to concentrate its foreign aid programs within a relatively few key states, whose strategic significance for Soviet interests has been regarded as considerable. In recent years, as a result of Congressional restrictions, the United States has tended to follow the same policy.

There is the further possibility of measures which are mutually advantageous to all participants, classically illustrated by reciprocal trade agreements involving reduction of trade barriers on both sides toward stimulation of greater exchange of goods and services. One key point to note in this regard is that employment of the economic instruments of policy is today far more deliberate and calculated, and more politically controlled, than was formerly the case, especially during the pre-World War I era. In the earlier time, purely economic factors were allowed to govern developments to a great degree (this, of course, had the effect of benefitting those countries with the strongest economies). Beginning in the 1920's, however, an ever-increasing list of political controls was imposed on international trade and investment for both economic and political considerations. Exchange controls and manipulation of exchange rates, the establishment of quotas and tariff increases were only some of the devices employed. The economic policy of Nazi Germany provided probably the extreme example during the 1930's of the extent to which economic policy could be used to obtain political objectives, especially with reference to the establishing of political dominance by Germany over the lower Danubian basin. Since World War II, the United States has been the principal protagonist working toward a restoration of some reasonable facsimile of the old liberal international order through such devices as GATT (General Agreement on Trade and Tariffs), including the "Kennedy Round" of multilateral tariff negotiations embodying the most-favored-nation principle, and through strengthening the machinery of inter-

> **Most-Favored-Nation Principle.** Often included in trade agreements among states, obligating each signatory to extend to the others any relevant benefits or concessions granted to any other state.

national trade and investment, including the International Monetary Fund and the International Bank for Reconstruction and Development. It must be acknowledged, however, that like virtually all states, the United States has been mindful primarily of its own interests. In the belief that these would be advanced most by unilateral rather than multilateral programs of foreign aid, it has depended primarily on the former type.

In a certain sense, the most fundamental approach to power would seem to involve the effort to influence opinion, beliefs, and attitudes, since these are directly related to human behavior. Both military and economic policies obviously have great significance in this context, but beyond these there is the possibility of utilizing instruments and techniques which are purely and immediately manipulative and influential with respect to opinion. In an age of mass politics, when great numbers of people are, at least in times of crisis, sensitized to international political issues and thus, even in authoritarian societies, have some degree of significance for decision-making, and in an age when the technology of communications has evolved so rapidly, the utilization of propaganda (defined simply as an effort to influence opinion) or psychological techniques in foreign policy is inevitable. The efforts of both sides during World War I to influence mass opinion represented the beginning of a new era in international relations in this respect. At the end of the war, the appearance of the new Soviet government, relatively weak militarily but possessed of a revolutionary ideology, and of a passionate belief in the validity and also the persuasiveness of that doctrine, placed its principal reliance on the use of propaganda as an instrument of policy. The fascist states followed suit shortly thereafter. Ultimately the more liberal and open societies had no alternative but to enter the competition on a permanent basis (although, as noted above, they had been among the pioneers in this regard during World War I). Thus, although the Communist states today devote the largest amount of resources to the waging of "psychological warfare," all major

> *Psychological Warfare.* **The strategy of employing various forms of propaganda through various communication channels to influence the population of another state in a way favorable to the position of the originating state in a conflict of interest situation.**

powers maintain massive and continuing programs for this purpose, utilizing all media of communication for this purpose. The Voice of America, Radio Moscow, and the British Broadcasting Corporation are only a few, if among the best known, operations in this area.

Realistically speaking, one must include those activities generally referred to as "subversion" under this general heading. Here, human agents,

> *Subversion.* **The undermining by various means, normally clandestine, of the loyalty of part or all of a population toward either the betrayal or the overthrow of its government. Subversion usually relies heavily on interpersonal contact.**

fully committed and highly motivated, are the medium through which the message is passed. In many situations, such inter-personal contact is the most effective means of all of influencing the opinions of the target audience. One may expect that increasing utilization of this approach will be made by all the major actors within the international system.

For purposes simply of communicating with other powers in a manner which seeks to minimize the possibility of misinterpretation and which concentrates efforts on relatively rational persuasion of the formal decision-makers of other powers, each state maintains a diplomatic service, composed of ambassadors, ministers, and lesser-ranking foreign service officers, which represents its government in foreign capitals, transmitting the instructions received from its own foreign office and reporting back on developments within the host countries. Although some skeptics have asserted that modern communication technology has converted diplomats into "the telephone girls of history," it is obvious that very great importance will continue to attach to the analysis and evaluation of events by skilled professional diplomats. In point of fact, diplomacy is undoubtedly the single most important instrument available working toward the stabilization of the international system through the accommodation of conflicts of interest among the member states. In the day-to-day functioning of the system, countless diplomatic interchanges take place, many of which are little noted publicly, but all of which are essential to the maintenance of peaceful relations among states. In the absence of any authoritative source of decision-making, diplomatic bargaining is the most promising alternative non-violent approach to an allocation of values within the system.

COMPONENTS OF POWER

Any analysis of the international political system requires of necessity an examination of the components of power, or capability factors, available to the actors within the system. Such an examination can help in making an assessment of the capabilities of the various actors and thus, to some extent at least, enable one to discern which states are likely to be important in their influence on developments within the system.

There are many elements which contribute to the power of a state. Some of these are relatively fixed or permanent, and some may undergo considerable change. An example of the former would be geographical size and location, while an example of the latter might be the stage of industrial development of a state.

In the past, some writers have argued that geography is the single most important factor for international relations, that the size of a state, its location relative to other states, its climate and its topography are all basic in determining both the foreign policy interests of and the alternative choices open to decision-makers. One of the most famous modern political geographers was Sir Halford Mackinder, who argued at the end of World War I that international politics were likely to be dominated by developments in what he called the "Heartland," that part of eastern Europe and western Asia which drains into the Arctic Ocean or land-bounded lakes and marshes and is thus protected from the threat of the seapower of the great maritime states (Mackinder later modified his original theory to include the eastern United States within the critical zone).[1] Nicholas Spykman, a Dutch scholar who in his last years taught and wrote in the United States, challenged Mackinder's

[1] Sir Halford J. Mackinder, *Democratic Ideals and Reality* (New York, 1942).

position by arguing during World War II that it was control of the so-called "Rimlands," those coastal areas lying along the great oceans of the world, that would be strategically decisive.[2] Clearly, such technological developments as the inter-continental ballistic missile have greatly altered the significance of geography for international relations. However, they have not changed the fact that a state large in terms of area is less vulnerable to nuclear attack than a small one, or that in a conventional, as opposed to a nuclear war, space can be traded for time. The latter was done by the Russians during World War II, when the Red Army was able to retreat over great distances, fighting delaying actions to slow the German advance and thus allowing additional Russian strength to be mobilized. This type of strategy was not possible for France, a much smaller state. For a country separated by a great distance from its principal allies, as in the case of the United States, geography is important in determining the significance of seapower and of the maintenance of an overseas base structure.

Another of the basic elements which affects national power is population. As in the case of territory, size is a necessary but not a sufficient condition for great power status. A huge population in an economically under-developed country is more likely to be a handicap than an asset. The combination of high rates of population growth with under-developed economies produces one of the major problems of the contemporary international political system. The feeding of a rapidly-expanding population makes much more difficult the accumulation of savings necessary for economic development.

Nuclear weaponry greatly reduces the significance of military manpower. However, if one should assume that conventional, limited war is the most probable kind of war (given the continuance of a nuclear stalemate), the number of divisions maintained by a state is by no means unimportant. Beyond this, it seems probable that, notwithstanding the introduction of automation, large, industrialized economies, which are the prerequisite for a significant military establishment, will for a long time to come require a labor force which only a large population can provide.

Economic power requires more than a labor force, however. A broad resource base is virtually a necessity, including such energy sources as coal, petroleum, hydroelectric installations, and, increasingly in the future, nuclear power facilities, together with a broad range of critical metals such as iron, copper, chrome, manganese, aluminum, nickel and lead. Large areas of fertile, productive farm land represent an advantage in assuring self-sufficiency in food production. It is true that the development of synthetics may reduce the importance of some items, and it is also true that international trade may provide access to items not naturally within the national domain. In time of crisis or actual conflict, however, it is of great importance to have maximum self-sufficiency and assured access.

Complementing the resource base is the efficiency of the economic sys-

[2] Nicholas J. Spykman, *America's Strategy in World Politics: The United States and the Balance of Power* (New York, 1942).

tem. For decades, argument has continued between the supporters of relatively decentralized capitalist economies and those favoring socialist or planned models. On the basis of the empirical evidence available, it would appear that either capitalist or socialist economies are under optimum conditions capable of rapid growth. At the same time, there are examples of both types which have proved to be notably inefficient. The critical factors would seem to center principally on the energy and rationality of the decision-makers in the allocation of resources in accordance with a well-considered system of priorities. Rapid and balanced economic growth is essential if a state is to play a significant role in international relations, given the increasing scale of demands placed on economic systems, including foreign aid, armament, and domestic consumer satisfaction. There is no doubt that a prosperous economy is also a source of prestige, and thus of influence.

From many points of view, and especially in an age when politics and economics are so inter-dependent, the government or political system may be the most critical element of all in determining the capabilities of a state. No matter what geographic and resource advantages a country may have, no matter how large, vigorous, and well-educated a population, nor how productive an economy, if the political system produces decision-making that is irrational, stupid, or ineffective, all else is likely to go for naught. Modern government is at the very center of the nervous system of society and in most instances is the most important variable in the social equation. Without an adequate performance by those in governmental roles, a society cannot function, whether domestically or in relationship to other members of the international system. Here, again, much has been written about the relative merits of democratic as compared to authoritarian systems in responding to the challenges of international politics. The latter obviously have some advantages with respect to making swift changes of policy, unimpeded by the inertia of popular opinion, as in the classic case of the Nazi-Soviet Non-Aggression Pact of 1939. Such tactical flexibility has undoubted advantages, especially in the short run. Authoritarian systems may also find it easier to impose austerity on the populace, toward mobilization of maximum resources for the achievement of foreign policy objectives. On the other hand, when there is no opportunity for dissenting opinion to challenge erroneous judgment, the cost may be high, as it was with respect to Hitler's conduct of strategy during World War II, or in the case of Stalin's politically motivated decimation of the Soviet military command immediately prior to that war. Whatever political system a state may have, it should be able to produce decisions on the basis of rational assessment of the problem and non-doctrinaire selection among alternatives.

PATTERNS OF POWER

Any analysis of objectives, instruments, and capability factors is in itself quite inadequate for a full understanding of the dynamics of the international system. These items must be regarded as merely the components. The key question has to do with the forces which determine their particular arrangement at any given time. What, historically, have been the great issues or problems that have created the conflict relationships which have been such a permanent and dominant element of international politics?

To begin with the broadest kind of generalization, one can say that at any given time there are a number of states which for a great variety of reasons are relatively satisfied with the status quo, and a number of states which, for a similar variety of reasons, are notably dissatisfied—a condition which normally obtains, obviously, in virtually all human affairs. At any given moment, there will be a certain distribution of values among the members of the international community, determined to a considerable degree by the pre-existing power relationships. The sources of discontent with such a status quo may derive from any of a number of causes. One state may feel that the existing distribution of wealth within the system is inequitable. In the late nineteenth century, for example, imperial Germany, a late starter in the race, felt entitled to acquire a colonial empire and related seapower that would be, to some extent at least, comparable to what was already possessed by Britain and France. Some theorists of international politics have posited a differential in the growth rate of states as a fundamental factor leading to conflict. One country's economy will develop more rapidly as a result of greater mastery of technology or a national value system which produces a relatively more disciplined work force, either voluntarily or through coercion, which is able to exploit such mastery more efficiently than other states. On the basis of greater population and greater economic productivity, a state, if it chooses, can increase its military power and thus be in a position to bargain more effectively for a larger share of the benefits available. In practice, as a state gains in power from a growth rate differential, it is very likely to become increasingly dissatisfied with the existing distribution of values and to seek in a variety of ways to alter the distribution in its favor.

Again, a state may be motivated by ideological factors. During the nineteenth and twentieth centuries, one of the most powerful dynamic forces affecting international relations has been that complex and in some ways mysterious phenomenon called nationalism. As the nation-state has come

Nationalism. A feeling on the part of a number of people living in a specific area that they constitute a unique and valuable group, with a necessity and indeed a right to enjoy the means necessary to achieve fulfillment through the realization of certain commonly cherished goals. Historically, these goals have originally been of a cultural nature, but almost always eventually have become political.

increasingly to be the indispensable instrument for the achievement of not only cultural but also economic and security values, nationalism has become increasingly politically oriented. Perhaps the extreme form of nationalism in the twentieth century has been found in Fascist totalitarianism. Theoretically, at least, Communist totalitarianism has stressed class rather than national allegiance, although developments within the international Communist movement in recent years suggest that national rather than class interests are dominant in influencing political behavior here as elsewhere.

From the time of the French Revolution on, one of the relatively unchallenged assumptions affecting international relations has been that people possessing cultural (which usually also means ethnic) unity should be entitled to political independence in order to give the fullest possible expression to their cultural values. Given the fact that there was a great disparity between political and cultural boundaries, this belief was bound to constitute a profoundly unsettling influence in international affairs.

Although nationalism has been referred to as the secularized religion of our time and the decisively controlling factor affecting men's social values, one can still note some influence deriving from conventional religion in international affairs. To be sure, the Thirty Years' War is far in the past, but there is little question but that the conflict between Communist and non-Communist systems has been aggravated by the anti-religious position of the former. On the other hand, many observers believe that progress toward building a Western European community was aided during the 1950's by the fact that the leading statesmen and political parties of the three key countries involved, France, Italy, and West Germany, were all Christian Democratic, or Catholic-oriented politically. Other examples of the influence of religion may be found in the tension between Moslem Pakistan and Hindu India, or between the Arab states and Israel. It seems most unlikely, however, that traditional religion will ever again have its former political importance.

Seemingly of considerably greater importance than religion in the contemporary international system is race. Racial characteristics are usually sufficiently conspicuous to reinforce strongly feelings of identity or separateness and thus to complement those forces contributing to the development of nationalism. Related to this is the historical fact that the European world which was globally dominant during the nineteenth and first part of the twentieth centuries was ethnically different from that of the subject peoples. The anti-colonialist movement has been strengthened immensely because of this. A legacy of the age of colonialism is the potential thus established for making race a key issue in international politics. Certain states have already sought to exploit the possibilities inherent in this situation. Should lines of conflict be established on such a basis, reinforcing political and ideological differences, the danger of race war could be very considerable indeed. It is for this reason that some observers have hoped that such multi-racial political groupings as the British Commonwealth might provide an example of inter-racial cooperation rather than conflict.

What might be called ideological messianism (Professor Morgenthau's

Ideological Messianism.   **The belief that a given society's value system is so superior to any other that it should be imposed on other societies to the maximum extent possible by whatever means are required, including the use of force.**

term is "nationalistic universalism")[3] has been a dominant force in twentieth century international politics. This has been most conspicuously exemplified in the efforts of Communist states to extend their political values to other areas in the belief that the implementation of these values will result in greater justice and/or freedom for all concerned. Non-Communist states, somewhat defensively to be sure, respond in kind, attempting primarily to prevent the extension of Communism and wherever possible to reinforce the strength of non-Communist value systems. In practice, of course, there is often a close relationship between or among nationalism, racism, religion, and political ideology, resulting in an extremely complex blend, which makes the task of the political analyst very difficult as he seeks to comprehend the real operative forces behind international political behavior.

Whatever the cause of dissatisfaction with the status quo may be, the so-called revisionist states employ various combinations of means, depending

> **Revisionist State.**   **A state which is dissatisfied with the existing situation within the international political system with reference to one or more categories, such as territorial boundaries, distribution of wealth, or existence of value systems, and which consequently seeks to achieve a relevant adjustment or alteration.**

on their resources and on their concepts of political and military strategy, to alter the existing arrangement. Such action is resisted by those states who believe that their interests are identified with or best supported by the prevailing situation. To present the picture in this way, of course, produces a great over-simplification. At a time such as the present, when unprecedented revolutionary change is taking place throughout so many dimensions of human affairs, there are very few political leaders who are unable to grasp the fact that massive change is inevitable. The problem becomes one of attempting to guide or channel change in directions that will best serve one's interests and values. At this point, ideology may become significant; however, as always, the observer must remain alert to the possibility that it may serve merely to justify decisions taken for more materialistic reasons, such as additions to power, prestige, or wealth of states. Insofar as ideology operates authentically in such a context, it will reinforce efforts by states to influence change so as to secure, preserve, or strengthen existing values esteemed by those states, such as individual freedom, greater social and economic equality, or cultural autonomy.

States may perceive that certain processes of change are likely to be more compatible with the preservation of values than others. This question is symbolized by the frequent reference on the part of Western leaders to the necessity for peaceful change. There tends in practice to be a correlation between the advocates of peaceful change and supporters of the status quo or those who desire change to take place only gradually. Those who seek more far-reaching change or wish it to come more swiftly are more likely to accept the

[3] Hans Morgenthau, *Politics Among Nations*, 4th ed. (New York, 1967).

use of non-peaceful methods. They may argue that the rules governing peaceful change have themselves been shaped by the status quo powers to minimize the possibility of change adverse to the interests of these powers, and thus they may assert that the procedural as well as the substantive status quo is in need of alteration.

The development of nuclear technology has had vast implications in this regard, leading most statesmen to acknowledge the necessity for the renunciation of most kinds of war as instruments of policy. As noted earlier, guerrilla action, linked to so-called "wars of national liberation," presently would seem to be one of the principal choices of those states unwilling to limit themselves to peaceful change.

In the effort to exercise influence on events, of course, the utilization of power is indispensable. Since power is relative, all states engaged in the struggle seek, of necessity, to maximize their power. There are various policies possible here. A state may attempt to increase its power through unilateral action, such as shifting resources internally toward a build-up of military power. The rate of economic growth may be increased so as to provide for an increase in economic aid to other states for the purpose of influencing their alignment. Mobilization of domestic opinion may be regarded as essential to the support of such policies.

Beyond unilateral efforts lies the possibility of acting in concert with other states who have similar interests. Typically this involves the negotiation of treaties of alliance with other states, such as the Franco-Soviet Treaty or the Rome-Berlin Axis before World War II, or NATO or the Warsaw Pact of the post-war period. Such treaties obligate the signatories to assist one another in specified ways, often by providing military support in the event that one signatory should be attacked by a third power.

This competition among states for allies often results in, or more probably may be specifically intended to achieve, what is referred to as the balance of power. A vast literature in the field of international relations exists on this subject. Some of this is primarily descriptive, purporting to demonstrate how the principle of the balance of power has been perhaps the single most impor-

> **Balance of Power.** Usually, an equilibrium relationship among the capabilities of several states or groups of states inter-acting with one another. Occasionally, however, the term is used to describe an actual preponderance or "favorable" balance between one state or group of states and another.

tant determinant of the policies of states, and some has been prescriptive, arguing that in a multi-state system, no better guide exists for statesmen interested in securing their countries' interests. Comparisons have been made of the situation which existed for some centuries prior to World War II and of the post-war period. During the former time, a number of states of roughly equal power constituted a so-called "multi-polar" system, within which each state enjoyed considerable freedom of choice in selecting its alliance partners, with consequent flexibility for the system as a whole. Since World War II the two super-powers, the Soviet Union and the United States, have dominated the functioning of a bi-polar international system, within which the

Multi-Polar and Bi-Polar Systems.   **A multi-polar system includes a number of major states, typically at least five, of roughly equal power or capability. A bi-polar system on the other hand is characterized by the existence of only two major powers, whose capabilities, generally comparable, are far beyond those of any other states within the system.**

freedom of the smaller states to determine their alliance partners is much more limited, with a consequently greater rigidity for the system as a whole.[4] It can be argued that the stability of the bi-polar model is less than that of the multi-polar, on the grounds that a change in the weight of an important or dominant state has a much more upsetting effect than where the equilibrium is the result of a relationship of a much larger number of elements.

With respect to the prescriptive approach to the balance of power, it is asserted that in the absence of a reliable central authority with a decisive preponderance of power over that of any single state or likely group of states, a country can best defend its position by seeing to it that its own power, together with that of its allies, is sufficient to deter any would-be aggressor. Critics of this position argue, however, that because of a number of imponderables, such as national morale, it is impossible to measure power with sufficient precision to prevent an erroneous calculation by a given set of decision-makers, on the basis of which an assumed superiority may lead to an attack. It is further argued that because of this uncertainty, states, in an effort to achieve a margin of safety, set off competitive arms races which have a destabilizing effect. It is further argued by some that an actual preponderance of power in the hands of the relatively status-quo states is a better protection of stability, and that the greatest danger of conflict is likely to arise when a previously inferior state or group of states begins to close the gap which previously separated it from the more powerful opposing elements. For better or worse, however, it would seem that for the foreseeable future the balance of power will be an empirically operative principle in an international system composed, as it is, of a number of independent actors.

Treatment of the subject of the balance of power would be incomplete without some mention of those states which consciously attempt to remain outside the power contest, in the belief that their interests can best be advanced by such a policy. Some of them go further to argue that the interests of the entire international system are served by their non-alignment, which serves to reduce the stakes of the game. They assert that they are thus enabled to devote their full energies to internal development, so badly needed in the case of the so-called "emerging" nations which have been the principal advocates of this position. At the same time, this bloc of states could well

[4] For a comparison of the multi-polar and bi-polar systems, see Morton A. Kaplan, *System and Process in International Politics* (New York, 1957).

provide the decisive increment of power to one side or the other in the existing bi-polar balance, and for this reason, members of the bloc have been the
object of much attention from both sides. They are not unmindful of the advantages they enjoy from this double courtship, which provides an additional
incentive to remain unaligned.

LIMITATIONS ON THE ACTORS

No treatment of the international system would be complete without reference to international law and international organization. Although the
foregoing discussion has emphasized the significance of power as a dominant influence in international relations, one should be conscious of the fact
that a body of legal norms has long existed, setting forth the legal rights and
duties of states and also specifying remedies, including sanctions, to be utilized in the event of any violation or non-observance thereof. Although it is
obvious that power has been far more influential in international politics
than has law, especially as a restraint against unacceptable behavior, law
nonetheless has had a part to play. One hopes, moreover, that the time will
come when law will be much more important in regulating international relations than it has been hitherto. Such a hope can be better sustained if the
role of law within the international system is viewed from a perspective
which highlights its past development and suggests the most significant possibilities for the future.

The evolution of international law has progressed over a long period of
time. Some writers trace certain principles at least as far back as to Roman
law, especially the codes of Justinian. Formal treatises on the subject began
to appear in the late medieval period and more especially as the modern state
system began to take form. Hugo Grotius, whose classic work, *de Jure Belli ac
Pacis,* was published in 1625, is sometimes referred to as the "father of international law." Emerich de Vattel produced a highly influential work, *The
Law of Nations,* in 1758. Grotius and Vattel, along with more recent writers,
are sometimes cited in United Nations debate today. These early scholars
attempted both to codify or organize the existing body of rules of behavior
which states appeared to acknowledge as to some extent binding, and to prescribe norms of ideal models, in many cases deriving from natural law, to
which they believed states should conform. Beginning in the nineteenth century, as the number of treaties creating legal obligations multiplied rapidly,
the so-called "positivist" school of international law became increasingly important, holding that the only true law was that which was explicitly recognized as such by states in the form of treaties or conventions. In the twentieth
century, the signing of treaties has proliferated far beyond anything known
in the past, and it is probably fair to say that the positivist position is dominant. However, the general principles of law, which derive from or which at
least were identified in the great treatises of the past, are acknowledged as

sources of rules in such authoritative documents as the Statute of the International Court of Justice.

One problem for some theorists of international law, notably the Austinians who hold that law must be a command from a superior to an inferior supported by adequate power, is that the "subjects" of international law, that is, the entities in whom legal rights and duties are vested, are states, which under international law itself are on a plane of legal equality. This problem is simply part of a larger theoretical question, having to do with the source of obligation. If one does not accept the concept of natural law, inherent in the order of the universe and thus necessarily governing the relationships of states, a position to which few authorities today subscribe, it is most difficult to develop an explanation of the binding force of international law. There is no superior authority with power sufficient to coerce any single state into observance, as the Austinian theory would require. If one cites the recognized principle that states are bound by those rules of law to which they have consented, the question may still be asked whether they may not withdraw their consent as freely as they originally gave it. The most reasonable explanation of the fact that states do in practice observe international law to a degree that is quantitatively impressive is probably to be found in their realization that without such observance the kind of minimal international order which is normally recognized to be in the general interest would simply not exist.

It has been often noted that international law is a comparatively primitive system of law in that there is no authentic international legislative process to produce it, that the authority of international courts to interpret it is severely limited, and that there is no reliable executive agency to enforce it. Because of the above-mentioned rule that no state can be bound by a rule of law to which it has not fairly explicitly consented, normally through accession to a treaty, the formulation of new rules of general applicability is usually a tedious and cumbersome practice. Diplomatic conferences are convened, prolonged negotiation follows, and then each signatory must secure the approval of the requisite national authority, normally the legislature, before the rule becomes effective.

Consent is also a key factor in determining the jurisdiction of the International Court of Justice, the judicial organ of the United Nations. No state may be forced before the court involuntarily. This means that when a dispute with significant issues exists between states, the decision-makers usually prefer to retain as much influence over the settlement as possible, using negotiation or some other procedure which limits the influence of third parties. This largely explains the relatively small number of disputes, most of these being of marginal significance politically, which have been submitted to the Court since it was established. It is true that under Article 36 of the Statute of the International Court of Justice, states may obligate themselves in advance to accept the compulsory jurisdiction of the court in certain categories of disputes with other states making the same commitment, but the importance of this article has been minimal in practice.

If the Court should hand down an important decision, the possibility still exists that the party whose interests were affected adversely might still refuse to comply, in which case the other party could appeal to the United Nations Security Council. The Council would be under no legal compulsion to heed the call, and it might well be precluded from doing so by a veto from one of the permanent members. This would leave the aggrieved party with not much else beyond self-help, and even here the threat or the use of force would be prohibited by the United Nations Charter. This problem has not been significant in practice, however. Virtually all decisions of the court have been accepted by the parties, probably because, as noted, the cases have not concerned critical issues.

The substantive principles of international law essentially determine the rights and duties of states. The basic concept underlying many of the fundamental rights (and the correlative duties) is that of sovereignty. Implicit in or

Sovereignty.   A legal attribute of a state which entitles it to make decisions with respect to matters within its jurisdiction free of external restraint or coercion. Political reality often conflicts with legal fiction, however.

deducible from this basic concept are many of the other substantive rights of states, such as the right to juridical equality, the right of self-defense when the national existence is threatened (this is one of the most difficult and complex rights to define in practice), or the right to exclusive jurisdiction (with certain exceptions) over persons and property within the national boundaries. In order to assure the observance of these rights, international law imposes corresponding obligations, for example, to refrain from the threat or use of force against any state, to recognize certain privileges and immunities of diplomatic representatives of other states, to provide a certain level of protection to aliens generally, and to refrain from attempts to intervene with respect to matters which are within the so-called domestic jurisdiction of other states. The obligation to refrain from the use of force, set forth most clearly in the United Nations Charter, in effect rules out the legality of aggressive war, although a legal definition of aggression has thus far been impossible to achieve.

It should be noted that in relatively routine areas, such as those relating to diplomatic immunities or to conformity to the stipulations of commercial treaties, the performance of states is very good insofar as adherence to the requirements of legal norms is concerned. There is a vast network of legal obligations which is on the whole recognized and implemented in the daily routine of international relations. Where international law breaks down most frequently is in those extremely critical areas where power relationships among states are pivotal. Ironically, it is here that the observance of international law is most important, insofar as the maintenance of international peace and security is concerned.

The basic problem is one which affects any legal system, that of adapting to change, of adjusting norms which evolved in one historical circumstance to a new and different one. At no time has this problem been more acute than at the present, when the rate of change is so much greater than ever before. At such a time, international law may seem to offer no solution to conflicts of interest among states. One party to a dispute may be unwilling to submit the case to the International Court, not because of a difference of opinion as to what the relevant rule of law may be, but precisely because the acknowledged rule is held to be unjust. This, in the opinion of some writers, is the essential distinction between so-called "justiciable" disputes, namely, those to which the Court can find a legal solution, and "political" disputes, where the validity of the existing law is rejected by one of the parties. The revisionist states are among those most likely to challenge the existing body of international norms. For example, many of the newly-established states, created from the former colonial empires of Western Europe, feel that traditional international law reflects too much the values of the imperial period during which it developed. Another challenge, more in terms of juridical theory than in practice, comes from the Communist states, which maintain that all legal norms are simply the rationalization of power relationships, and that traditional international law is simply the product of the power struggle among the ruling elites of the capitalist societies during the past several centuries. This being the case, in the Communist view such law is increasingly inappropriate in an age when socialist societies are becoming so much more significant. It must be noted, however, that in practice the Communist states invoke as readily as anyone the rules of existing international law which support their position. In this connection, some academic political scientists have argued that there is a direct relationship between the configuration of the international political system and the norms of international law. The norms that are operative under a bi-polar system differ from those associated with a multi-polar situation, an example being the recent decreasing effectiveness of the prohibition against intervention, given the frequent situations in which intervention may be of decisive importance for the maintenance of a bi-polar balance.

Notwithstanding the different perspectives and interpretations regarding the validity of existing international law, under the auspices of the United Nations a definite pattern has been established of creating new international law or of modernizing traditional international law through the drafting of important multi-lateral treaties with regard to such important matters as genocide, human rights, the nuclear test-ban, the non-military use of outer space, the law of the high seas, and the political neutralization of Antarctica. Implicit in this process is the recognition on the part of all members that the essential existing structure of international law, whatever its ideological or philosophical origins, is realistically the starting point from which future developments must take off.

Closely related to international law but also clearly reflecting the influence of international politics has been the development of international organization, which has proliferated so rapidly during the middle part of the twentieth century, represented most significantly by the creation of the United Nations. International organization is clearly a response to widely-felt needs within the international political system. Without question, the greatest need of all in a thermonuclear age is of peace and security, and the United Nations, the principal intended function of which relates to the satisfaction of this need, is thus the dominant international organization of our time. Surrounding it are a considerable number of other international organizations, operating in functional and regional fields, where the multiplication of such agencies has been most impressive. The explanation of this multiplication lies in the fact that the world is becoming ever more interdependent technologically and economically, as a result of great changes in such fields as transportation and communication. In such a situation, some kind of organization of the infinitely complex relationships thus created is mandatory, if the international community is not to founder in confusion and disarray.

The roots of contemporary international organization go back to the nineteenth century and beyond. Political theorists and philosophers have dreamed of a world order that would provide peace and justice since the state system first began to emerge from the medieval period. Many imaginative blueprints and models have been drafted and constructed by such eminent figures as Kant, Bentham, Penn, and others, whose ideas were to have demonstrable influence when the time came to move from theory to the world of reality. In the nineteenth century two developments reinforced this trend. One took the form of a slowly growing international peace movement, of which the most important consequence for international organization was perhaps the sensitizing of public opinion to an awareness of the problem of peace at a time when the means of destruction were growing rapidly more formidable. At the same time, an ever-increasing number of technical or functional organizations were created to deal with such important questions as the orderly and efficient international movement of the mails, the regulation of international communications (first telegraph and telephone, later radio as well), the standardization of railroad equipment, and the establishment of uniform weights and measures. All these matters were essential to the further development of the international economic system and more efficient trade and investment. The organizations concerned were called public international unions. They were based on treaties and had rudimentary organization in the form of periodic conferences, smaller executive councils, and permanent secretariats.

During this same nineteenth century, a slow but significant movement took place in the political dimension that was to have great influence on the shape of twentieth century international organization. This had to do with the increasing practice of the great European powers of consulting periodically toward the solution of political problems primarily affecting smaller states but with potential importance for the large countries, especially should an outbreak of violence occur. Those powers came to be known collectively as the Concert of Europe, and their consultations did much to stabilize the international political system during the half-century preceding World War I. They also furnished a precedent which influenced the structure of both the League of Nations and the United Nations, whereby the great powers assumed primary responsibility, commensurate with their capabilities, for the maintenance of international peace and security.

The League of Nations was by far the most significant international organization to have been established by the end of World War I. It was the first formal organization whose primary function was not technical but political, having to do with the preservation of peace. Largely a consequence of the tragedy of World War I, it was intended to replace the balance of power, discredited in the eyes of many at that time as a cynical and treacherous arrangement largely responsible for that war, by a new system of collective security. Aggression would presumably be deterred by the anticipated support of all other member states for the victim which would result in hopeless odds for any would-be aggressor. Beyond this, the member states assumed certain legal obligations not to resort to the use of force until an impressive array of pacific methods of settlement had been exhausted. The basic premise was, of course, that the great powers would react appropriately even in instances where their own immediate interests were not threatened, to uphold the inviolability of the principle of collective security. When this premise proved to be notably unfounded during the 1930's, the League rapidly declined into impotence.

The creation of the United Nations at the end of World War II as a successor to the League would seem to constitute recognition of the indispensability of such an organization for the kind of international system which now exists. There is considerable structural continuity between the League and the United Nations, although the latter goes beyond the former with respect to the inclusiveness of the legal obligation to abstain from the use of force (except in self-defense) and also with respect to the powers of the principal organ responsible for the maintenance of peace and security, the Security Council. Once again, however, as in the case of the League, the principal premise on which the organization was established, in this instance the unanimity of the great powers who are the permanent members of the Council, proved to be completely unfounded. Consequently, the effectiveness of the United Nations as a peace-keeping instrument has been considerably less than was hoped for at the time of its organization. In those rare instances where there has been congruence of great power interests, however, the United Nations has often performed with considerable effectiveness, as, for example, in the Palestine crisis of 1948 or in the Indian-Pakistani war of 1965. Some of the leading scholars in this area believe that, lacking such congruence, the greatest contribution the United Nations can make during the present era is to prevent peripheral conflicts among smaller states from expanding to the point where the important interests of the major powers are affected.[5] According to some interpretations, this was exemplified by United Nations action in the Congo crisis.

The structure of the United Nations reflects a compromise between the principle of juridical equality and political reality, the former being represented in the General Assembly, where all members have equal voting power, and the latter in the Security Council, where the principle of unanimity (the "veto") assures the permanent members, and more especially the two super-powers, influence more proportionate to their actual capabilities. When the Council, intended to have the primary responsibility for the maintenance of international peace and security, became paralyzed as a result of the conflict between the Soviet Union and the United States, an effort was made through the "Uniting for Peace" resolution, adopted in 1950 at the time of the Korean War, to shift the center of decision-making to the Assembly. For a time, this alternative seemed to offer some promise. After the mid-1950's, however, United Nations membership increased so rapidly that the resulting complexity of bloc representation made it difficult to achieve the necessary two-thirds majority required for any position on any important vote, as at the time of the Lebanese crisis of 1958. Thereafter, as during the Congo crisis of the early 1960's, it seemed possible that the assumption of an imaginative and creative role by the Secretary General in implementing broadly-drafted directives from the Council or the Assembly might somehow preserve the effectiveness of the United Nations as a peace-keeping agency. Once again, however, Cold War factors intervened, so that as of now it seems unlikely that any organ of the United Nations can take action unacceptable to either of the super-powers, especially since it has proved impossible to require the payment of assessments necessary to finance peace-keeping operations unacceptable to any of the major contributors to the United Nations budget. Only in those relatively rare situations where there is some perceived commonalty of interest is action possible.

For these reasons, many observers at the present time feel that the United Nations and its related agencies (such as the United Nations Educational, Scientific, and Cultural Organization [UNESCO], the Food and Agricultural Organization [FAO], the World Health Organization [WHO], and the International Bank for Reconstruction and Development) can make their principal contribution to the strengthening of peace through the so-called functional approach. This falls generally within the area of economic development and involves a multi-lateral effort to raise the standard of living in the developing countries through technical aid (including the training of engineers, scientists, agronomists, and other specialists who are essential to the modernizing of an economy) and through grants and loans to finance the purchase of capital goods necessary for more rapid industrialization. One school of thought has held that the habits of cooperation developed through

[5] On this, see Inis L. Claude, Jr., "The United Nations and the Use of Force," *International Conciliation*, No. 532 (March, 1961).

common effort to resolve such relatively non-political problems may eventually carry over into the political area and make more feasible an approach to the solution of presently intractable political questions. Other observers are more dubious about these possibilities, however.

Unquestionably the relationship between the developed and the developing countries (as some have put it, the "North-South question") will be one of the dominant issues in international relations over the next several decades. Ideally, this would seem to be an area where the United Nations system could make a maximum contribution through a series of multi-lateral programs which would enlist the support of many states, each of which would have some component to add. In the process, the prestige of the United Nations should be enhanced toward greater effectiveness in the political field.

In addition to those agencies which are of special relevance to this question are a number of others whose activities are valuable and in many cases essential to the satisfactory functioning of the international economic system, such as the International Monetary Fund (stabilization of exchange rates, with consequent influence on national fiscal and monetary policy), the International Civil Aeronautics Organization (coordination of international air transport), and the International Labor Organization (improvement of working conditions, elimination of unfair competition dependent on exploitation of workers). Altogether, there are more than a score of such important agencies, whose work is indispensable to the international flow of goods and services, and to economic development generally.

Another approach to the subject of international organization places great stress on the potentialities of regionalism. The arguments for a principal reliance on regional rather than general organization include assumptions that countries within a region are likely to have both a greater knowledge of and an interest in the problems peculiar to that region, and that they will have both a stronger sense of group identity and a greater homogeneity of values systems, all of which strengthen the possibilities of effective joint action. Opponents of a primary reliance on regionalism point out that historically there have been frequent intra-regional conflicts (Western Europe providing a prime example of this), and that a series of regional organizations, unchecked by any higher authority, might easily evolve into a standard balance-of-power arrangement. This question was faced during the planning for the United Nations. Winston Churchill tended to side with the regionalists, but when President Roosevelt became convinced of the superior advantages of the global or universal approach, his views prevailed. The United Nations Charter nonetheless allows considerable scope to regional arrangements, the most highly developed of which is the Organization of American States (OAS). Since World War II, there has been a considerable multiplication of regional agencies (many of which are also functional), including the European Coal and Steel Community, the European Economic Community, the Council of Mutual Economic Assistance, the Arab League, and the Organization of African Unity. It seems fair to say, however, that the most important future development in international organization, at least with respect to peace-keeping, will probably be at the global level, even though such regional organizations as the Organization of American States have made and will continue to make valuable contributions to the solution of intra-regional problems.

DEVELOPMENTS IN THE STUDY OF INTERNATIONAL RELATIONS

One should not conclude a review of the basic subject matter of international relations without an effort to examine the various approaches that have been taken toward the study of this material. Such an examination may indicate and to some extent explain the manner in which the field of study has developed and also suggest possibilities for further progress toward greater understanding of the complex forces at work within the international system.

The academic study of international relations in its modern form first emerged significantly during the period immediately after World War I. The reason for this is fairly clear. There was a great incentive to explore the factors which contributed to the onset of that appalling conflict, and there was a closely related desire to strengthen the institutional framework, primarily the League of Nations, that had been erected to prevent any repetition thereof. During the 1920's, the very existence of the League and the apparent progress made under its auspices toward peaceful relations among states created great optimism generally, and led scholars and teachers to give central importance to international law and organization in their approach to the field of international relations.

With the decline of the League in the face of fascist aggression in the 1930's, a mood of disillusionment set in. Teaching and writing gave increasing attention to the role of power and minimized the significance of law. This trend continued through World War II and culminated in the appearance of a celebrated treatise which had great influence for a considerable time thereafter, Professor Hans Morgenthau's *Politics Among Nations,* the first edition of which appeared in 1947. In addition to its emphasis on power, the book represented one of the first efforts to develop a comprehensive theory of international politics, as compared to much earlier writing which had been primarily narrative and descriptive. Because of its emphasis on political realism, the book touched off a debate for several years centering on the proper role of power as compared to the place of idealism or more conventional and traditional moral values as a guide to policy.

From this time on, the quantity and methodological sophistication of research and writing in the field increased at an accelerating rate, until today a single scholar can hardly hope to stay abreast of developments within the entire field. Basically, the trend has been away from the descriptive and legalistically-oriented approach of the inter-war years toward an effort to develop a body of theory which would identify and explain the significant forces and principles operating within the international political system. Most research and writing in the field in recent years has been empirical and quantitative, concerned with observing and measuring various categories of data relating to the behavior of the international system in an effort to discover trends and probabilities that will make prediction more feasible. Relevant materials from the disciplines of sociology, anthropology, and psychology have been incorporated in this writing, on the premise that the behavior of the system is ultimately determined by the behavior of individuals, operating in specific political contexts, to be sure, but nonetheless directly and significantly affecting the inter-action of the major units within the system.

The concept of power continues to be central for many scholars, although, as previously noted, the concept has been subjected to increasingly rigorous scrutiny by a number of critics. Many of the latter challenge both the validity and utility of the concept for analytical purposes, arguing that it is far too imprecise for the elucidation of the complex inter-relationships which determine the configuration of the international system. Basically, however, with whatever qualifications and reservations, it seems evident that the behavior of the international system can hardly be comprehended without reference to the idea of influence exercised by one state upon another, whether this be defined as power or in whatever other terms.

Most scholars are in agreement at this point that the field is so extensive and so variegated that the development of any single general theory to explain the system is far in the future, if, indeed, it is ever to be achieved. In this regard it should be noted that some studies have attempted to set forth descriptions of the possible models of the system, both historical and hypothetical, and to specify in considerable and precise detail the requirements in terms of state behavior both for internal stability of any given model and for transformation of one model into another. Although these studies do not profess to represent final or fully developed theoretical positions, they have been extremely useful in providing perspectives from which fresh insights into the dynamics of the international system may be derived.

Most writing in the field, however, has involved attempts to investigate specific sectors of the field toward construction of so-called "middle-range" theories. Thus, one such study has employed a wide range of data tending to focus on the flow of communications and the existence of comparable value systems and expectations in an effort to discover the conditions favoring or making probable the political integration of previously separate units.[6] The conclusion here seems to be that such data can provide significant indicators of the likelihood of such integration but that this phenomenon has been less frequent in recent decades. A related study has investigated the antecedents

[6] Karl W. Deutsch, *Nationalism and Social Communication* (Cambridge, Mass., 1953).

and consequences of such functionally-integrated systems as the "supra-national" organizations of Western Europe in the 1950's, such as the Coal and

> **Supra-National.** According to many writers, supra-national organiza-tions are to be distinguished from international organizations on the grounds that in the former category a significantly greater degree of sover-eignty or decision-making authority is transferred from the member states to the institutions of the organization.

Steel Community,[7] while another has been concerned with the important question of the "spill-over" in such relationships from the functional to the political level.[8] Still another approach which has had considerable influence at the policy-making level has involved the application of bargaining theory to inter-state relations, especially with reference to the important problem of achieving effective deterrence of aggression in a nuclear age.[9] Because the variables involved here are so complex, plausible or "common sense" conclu-sions may be dangerously misleading in terms of policy formulation, and a rigorous analysis may be of very great value.

A pioneering examination of the process of decision-making focused sharply on the manner in which stimuli received from the international sys-tem in the form of perceived threats, challenges, or opportunities may pro-duce specific responses from the complex bureaucratic and political apparatus of the modern state.[10] This obviously is a very critical area for an understanding of the functioning of the international system, as demon-strated by the subsequent appearance of a series of comparative analyses of the foreign policy-making processes of a number of states, which have helped to illuminate some of the strengths and weaknesses of the various political and administrative arrangements in this context. Since decisions of national political systems with respect to foreign policy can be regarded as critical in-puts of the international system, an assessment of the relationship between the two levels has come to be regarded as important. A related question of much contemporary significance concerns the impact of civil war in a revolu-tionary age on the structure and balance of the international system. The above listing is intended to be suggestive only of the many kinds of ap-proaches recently undertaken toward the study of international relations.

Given the dynamic nature of the international system and the revolution-ary changes taking place therein, and given further the high stakes attaching to the achievement of a more orderly and reliable regulation and stabiliza-tion of relations among the actors within the system, one can only hope that this proliferation of studies will continue at an accelerated rate. Whether or not one believes, as some have suggested, that the study of international rela-

[7] Ernest B. Haas, *The Uniting of Europe: Political, Social, and Economic Forces, 1950–1957* (Stanford, 1958).

[8] Amitai Etzioni, *Political Unification* (New York, 1965).

[9] Thomas Schelling, *The Strategy of Conflict* (Cambridge, 1960).

[10] Richard Snyder, H. W. Bruck, and Burton Sapin, *Decision-Making as an Approach to the Study of International Politics* (Princeton, 1954).

tions is the most promising route to the development of a grand theory of politics in general, in that the political behavior of any single state can hardly be understood except within the context of the international political system, it seems difficult if not impossible to deny that such a study is certain to continue to be of central importance to our time.

New Perspectives in International Prestige Theory: The Chaco Dispute °

With the collapse of the Spanish colonial empire in the Western hemisphere, the question of national boundaries posed problems for all the new Latin American states, and the Chaco War (1928–1938) exemplifies the struggle for definitive boundaries which extended well into the twentieth century for several of these nations. The long period of diplomatic bickering between the governments at Asunción and La Paz which preceded the military hostilities would doubtless have been prolonged indefinitely had it not been for the alleged discovery of petroleum deposits in the Chaco wasteland combined with other historical developments in these the only landlocked states in Latin America. The outbreak of armed conflict in December, 1928, ushered in a ten-year period in the national life of both Bolivia and Paraguay characterized by the death of more than 100,000 of their men and a further debilitation of their governments and economies in comparative relation to their previously weak position in international society.

But the actual military contest between the two South American nations provided opportunity for a second, and in many ways more significant, type of international conflict: that between the United States and the Argentine Republic for what I have termed "subjective" prestige dominance within the hemisphere. The *objective* warfare—that for military and economic goals—between the two military belligerents appeared to thrive independently of the peacemaking efforts of the two diplomatic protagonists. The *subjective* conflict—directed toward the achievement of reputation for moral prowess—could not have been conducted, on the other hand, unless ostensibly for the purpose of settling the military struggle. Thus, both the Argentine foreign office and the United States State Department apparatus seized the opportunity presented by the historical and the material setting and the way which it spawned as means for more legitimately pursuing prestige rivalry in the hemisphere. The Chaco War represents a prime example of the intervention of international actors in which would have otherwise remained a narrow, isolated and provincial conflict between two relatively insignificant national actors. The Washington-led Pan American machinery, the Argentine-dominated ABCP power group, and the League of Nations all sought entry into the conflict, professedly in the role of peacemaker, and the localized boundary controversy expanded until it ultimately

° SOURCE: William C. Garner, "New Perspectives in International Prestige Theory: The Chaco Dispute." This article is published for the first time in this volume. It has been included to give the student a greater acquaintance with two aspects of the field of international relations. One is a further exposition of the writing of some of the more theoretically-oriented contemporary writers in the field. The second is an application of a model developed by one of those writers to a specific example of behavior in the world of international relations. We thus have here, in a short compass, theoretical development, a case study, and an example of the application of theory to a specific case.

encompassed every major peacemaking mechanism that existed during the interwar period.

The Theoretical Dichotomy: "Common-Sense" versus "Symmetrical" Theory. It has been said that most of the problems arising within the professional student corps of international politics relate to the issue of methodology *qua* methodology. While no one seriously questions the necessity of providing an empirical orientation for study, contemporary scholarship evidences a growing alarm at the internal fragmentation which pursuit of transcendent theories has produced. Knorr and Verba have submitted recently that "progress will be made in theories of the international system only if [the] various approaches begin to converge and move in the same direction." [1] One is tempted to treat the theoretical dilemma with what might appear to be the cynicism of Charles McClelland's observations. "Common-sense" and "symmetrical" approaches to international politics are characterized in these terms:

> Common sense theory is generally a descriptive and generalized explanation of something anybody should be able to discern in the phenomena of international relations.
>
> Symmetrical theory is more difficult to comprehend because . . . it will seek to account for all possible courses, alternatives, and outcomes in a hypothecated state of affairs. Further, the state of affairs may be entirely "theoretical" so that the theorist may take pains to indicate that his structure of related propositions does not have a reference to anything that has happened in history, or perhaps ever will. In fact, the theorist makes his way into all the nooks and crannies of a conceptual structure built in his "imagination" until he gets all the essential parts in the right places and in the right relationships. The result may be a symmetrical theory such as Morton A. Kaplan's *System and Process in International Politics* (1957).[2]

It is not the purpose of this study to consider the relative merits of the two trends, if indeed one chooses to accept the dualism, but to use the described dichotomy as a convenient departure for more pertinent considerations of the role of international prestige theory. The following discussion focuses on Hans Morgenthau and Morton Kaplan, both of the University of Chicago, as prototypes of the two positions described by McClelland.

Although various professional students of international politics have criticized the theoretical stance of Hans J. Morgenthau,[3] neither the behaviorally-oriented nor the more intuitive theorists who cry for further refinements in the theory would doubt the importance of the so-called "realist" school. The approach aids in the clarification of traditional beliefs often held implicitly by other scholars, i.e., those

---

[1] The International System: Theoretical Essays, ed. *Klaus Knorr and Sidney Verba* (*Princeton, 1961*), pp. 1–2. For the most recent critiques of contemporary international theory, see Charles A. McClelland, Theory and the International System (*New York, 1966*); Horace V. Harrison, The Role of Theory in International Relations (*Princeton, 1964*); Human Behavior and International Politics, ed. J. David Singer (*Chicago, 1965*).

[2] McClelland, "The Function of Theory in International Relations," The Journal of Conflict Resolution, IV (1960) 314–315. See also McClelland, Theory and the International System, pp. 1–32.

[3] Hans J. Morgenthau, Politics Among Nations: The Struggle for Power and Peace, 4th ed. (*New York, 1967*).

things, which McClelland believes that "anybody should be able to discern." [4] The Morgenthau analysis has made explicit concepts which are invaluable as hypotheses for those investigating the dynamics of history. The approach reemphasizes the actors in the international system, the nation-states. It sets forth clearly the differences between the domestic and the international spheres of political interest. Most importantly, I think, it focuses attention on the concepts of power and national interest, however vague the discussion, as the prime motivational factors of politics among nations. In sum, Morgenthau is saying that an adequate appraisal of the international system must include recognition of the *sovereign* entities which compose that system and hammer home to the student and practitioner alike the locus of *real* power motives as opposed to those which would seem to be desirable for the international arena. Morgenthau's now famous statement that "International politics, like all politics, is a struggle for power" epitomizes the position. Traditionally characterized by dream world abstractions, the "moralistic-legalistic" approach to international analysis received its decisive denouement in the Morgenthau-Niebuhr era.[5]

The concept of national interest being the explicit key, Morgenthau's trilogy of "status quo," "imperialist," and "prestige" strategies has become the transcending tool for a realist analysis of international behavior. The idea of "keeping," "increasing," or "giving the appearance of" power has not been novel for American political science, however.[6] One witnesses it in the earliest domestic political studies of Harold Lasswell in that the latter's "safety," "deference," and "income" correspond to the three-fold classifications of Morgenthau.[7] Others have likewise accepted the relevancy of the classification to their analyses of international affairs. Ernst Haas, for example, speaks of the goals of "self-preservation," "self-extension," and "self-abnegation." [8] Liska advances "security," "prestige," and "welfare" as goals, the fulfillment of which are "determined by [the nations'] relative power." [9] The three goal classifications are subsumed within the proposition that politics is the study of the pursuance of "interest defined in terms of power," whether it be in the purely intellectual emphasis of empirical research in psychological behavior or the controversial religious ethic of writers such as Reinhold Niebuhr or Nicolas Berdyaev.[10] The "power" or "realist" school, of which Morgenthau is chief expositor, is to be commended for the precise differentiation of those goals which have been tacitly or explicitly assumed by a large number of political scientists and students of international politics.

[4] McClelland, "The Function of Theory in International Relations," 314–315.

[5] In addition to Morgenthau's Politics Among Nations, see the earlier and, at the time, more controversial statements of his position: In Defense of the National Interest (New York, 1951); "Another 'Great Debate': The National Interest of the United States," APSR, LXVI (1952), 961–998. Note also two important works by Reinhold Niebuhr, Moral Man and Immoral Society (New York, 1932) and Christian Realism and Political Problems (New York, 1953).

[6] Morgenthau, Politics Among Nations, pp. 36–37.

[7] Harold D. Laswell, Politics: Who Gets What, When, How (New York, 1936), pp. 13–41.

[8] Ernst B. Haas and Allen S. Whiting, Dynamics of International Relations (New York, 1956), Chapter IV.

[9] George Liska, International Equilibrium (Cambridge, 1957), p. 15.

[10] For a significant psycho-philosophical treatment of the term "subjective," see Nicholas Berdyaev, Slavery and Freedom (London, 1950); see also Niebuhr, Moral Man and Immoral Society, pp. 114–115.

More refinement and systematic theorization is indicated, however, with respect to the third factor in the Morgenthau trilogy—prestige. What of governmental actions which are not "normally obvious attempts to gain control over other nations?" [11] It is necessary to ask if "interest defined in terms of power" may include those national goals which are much more subjectively and morally oriented than is typically the case. Morgenthau defines the prestige goal as the desire "to impress other nations with the power one's own nation actually possesses, or with the power it believes, or wants other nations to believe, it possesses." [12] Schwarzenberger, with the same general reference to reputation for objective forms of power—e.g., military, economic, and technological—observes:

> It is easy to make light of prestige, but within a system of power politics, a state's prestige is its first line of defense. Prestige is the recognition of status, and loss of face may be the first stage on the road which leads to more than the loss of merely imponderable assets.[13]

Whether or not scholars have been adequately concerned with the concept of prestige is open to conjecture. It is my opinion that they have not. Empirical inquiry into the area remains insufficient to explore more deeply and realistically the moralistic-legalistic approach mentioned above. It would appear that the areas of conciliation, arbitration, and general peacemaking in some instances may be conceived in still further subjective and intangible terms than the simple "hint" of armed force. Both common-sense and symmetrical theory have neglected this important area.

It is apparent, then, that the "realist" concepts of Morgenthau, however revolutionary for the subdiscipline, need further clarification to meet the pertinent objections of the would-be more precise theorists.[14] The need for a deeper probing into the motives of international actors is indicated, that is, a more precise definition of the national interest concept to meet the requirements of an empirical science of international politics, specifically when that science is directed to such phenomena as the diplomatic conflict revolving around the boundary war between Bolivia and Paraguay.

The Symmetrical Approach: Kaplan.   In contrast to Morgenthau's sole reliance upon a rather hazily-defined balance of power mechanism, Morton A. Kaplan provides a series of six models which purports to give opportunity for more refined and explicit description of international events. Kaplan's purposes include (1) the discovery of regularities in patterns of international behavior, (2) the establishment of a science based on predictability, and (3) the definition of terms and axioms from which "timeless propositions" may be derived.[15] While only two of the six constructs have been validated historically—the balance of power and the loose bipolar systems—the balance of power is not considered by Kaplan to be relevant for the post-World War I period and the loose bipolar model seems only to apply to

[11] *Note Stanley Hoffman's rather severe critique of Morgenthau in* Contemporary Theory in International Relations (*Englewood Cliffs, 1960*), *pp. 30–38 at p. 35.*

[12] *Morgenthau,* Politics Among Nations, *p. 70.*

[13] *Georg Schwarzenberger,* Power Politics (*New York, 1951*), *p. 164.*

[14] *One of the more ambitious attempts to categorize the criticisms of contemporary prestige theory is found in Charles O. Lerche and Abdul A. Said,* Concepts of International Politics (*Englewood Cliffs, 1963*); *note pp. 232–233.*

[15] *Morton A. Kaplan,* System and Process in International Politics (*New York, 1957*), *p. 3.*

the Cold War struggle between the Communist bloc and the United States with its allies. It is this latter model which I have found to be interestingly applicable to the analysis of the Chaco diplomatic warfare between the United States and Argentina.

International theorists—both "common-sense" and symmetrical—assume relevance of the prestige factor only within the material context. This paper seeks, however, to demonstrate that subjective prestige can be both "realistic," associated with the power or influence of nations and, in various situations, a legitimate goal for national actors choosing from a broad gamut of interest alternatives. Moral goals, realistically defined within the framework of the national interest and conspicuously devoid of objective implications, appear to have been the primary bases for the diplomatic struggle between the blocs led by the governments at Washington and Buenos Aires. This type of conflict, in turn, affected their respective relations with the universal actor, the League of Nations, in a pattern adhering to the rules of loose bipolar behavior set forth by Kaplan. In the following analysis comment will be made on the relationship of the Kaplan model to the facts of the Chaco diplomatic dispute.[16] The twelve rules of the system will be given in the order used by Kaplan, followed by references to the diplomatic data.[17]

1. "All blocs subscribing to directive hierarchical or mixed hierarchical integrating principles for the international system are to eliminate the rival bloc."

The blocs led by the United States and the Argentine Republic have been classified as mixed hierarchical systems [18] since the foreign policy mechanisms of both bloc actors were largely decentralized. That is, while the Argentine and United States governments were able from time to time to exercise directive power within their respective bloc structures, they were not consistently capable of doing so in contravention of the growing hemispheric ideal of inviolable national sovereignty. None of the subsystems within the two bloc conglomerations could be considered to be a permanent satellite of either of the two governments.

The rivalry between the two blocs was based on a mutual desire to maintain or to achieve, through the use of "status quo" policies (the United States) and "imperialist" policies (Argentina) dominance of the peacemaking apparatus of the region. Such purposes formed the basis for the diplomatic competition between them, the Chaco War merely providing opportunity for pursuance of a veiled, then overtly hostile, prestige rivalry. It should be recognized that without the War, it would have been impossible to carry out this type of struggle.

2. "All blocs subscribing to directive hierarchical or mixed hierarchical integrating principles for the international system are to negotiate rather than to fight, to fight minor wars rather than major wars, and to fight major wars—under given risk and cost factors—rather than to fail to eliminate the rival bloc."

The significance of such terms as "fighting," "minor war," and "major war" are understood in this study only within the context of diplomacy. The use of prestige as

[16] *A more detailed account is William R. Garner*, The Chaco Dispute: A Study of Prestige Diplomacy (*Washington, 1966*).

[17] *The loose bipolar "rules" appear in Kaplan, pp. 38–39. The fourth rule is not relevant and is omitted here.*

[18] *Kaplan, pp. 54–56, 75–76.*

the orienting concept is vital at this point to an understanding of the theory. If the substitution of the moral for the material is made, then references to fighting are explained always within the framework of diplomatic warfare. While no precise criteria have been devised for this study, "minor" rather than "major" diplomatic warfare takes precedence because of the extremely sensitive nature of the conflict. The United States and the Argentine Republic did on occasion engage in what would appear to be "major" diplomatic warfare—e.g., the White-Espil conversations in Washington during 1933—but only within the assumed risk of destroying the public image which was crucial in the competition. In the traditional sense, the action is still considered to be a "limited" type—i.e., diplomatic as opposed to military— but the gamut of alternatives mentioned in the above rule are all found within the limits of the subjective conflict.

   3. "All bloc actors are to increase their capabilities in relation to those of the opposing bloc."

   In the Chaco diplomatic struggle the capabilities [19] are of a moral nature. They include the ability to embarrass, to attack the opposing nation without appearing to be ideologically dishonest, and to gain strategic moral goals within the system as exemplified by the August 3, 1932 Non-Recognition Declaration of the Pan American neutrals and the ability of the Argentine Republic to use the League so effectively in the 1933–1935 period. Occasionally, this strategic use of moral capabilities may be recognized in the relations between the peacemakers and the Bolivian and Paraguayan governments, as in Paraguayan President Ayala's statements aimed at the United States in September, 1932, and Bolivia's pressures on both conciliators to allow League entry. Primarily, however, this use of moral capabilities is the tool of the diplomatic belligerents explained exclusively in moral and propagandistic terms within the framework of prestige rivalry.

   5. "All bloc actors are to engage in major war rather than to permit the rival bloc to attain a position of preponderant strength."

   The applicability of this rule is seen in the degree of hostility generated in the competition between the two diplomatic protagonists. The White-Espil conversations in the fall of 1932 and the messages from Francis White and Secretary Stimson to Washington's Geneva representative during 1934 and 1935 evidence the use of "major" diplomatic warfare in the face of the Argentine threat to usurp the traditional hemispheric position of the United States. Likewise, Argentina, under the Foreign Ministry of Carlos Saavedra Lamas, was willing to use rather daring diplomatic tactics to prevent the continuation of that traditional role by the United States. Given the limitations imposed upon Washington by acceptance of the Good Neighbor Policy and the espousal of absolute non-intervention in 1933, it is evident that the United States could pursue no other course than that of bitter, if somewhat futile, diplomatic combat with her rival at Buenos Aires.

   6. "All bloc members are to subordinate objectives of universal actors to the objectives of their bloc but to subordinate the objectives of the rival bloc to those of the universal actor."

   [19] *Moral capabilities are substituted since Kaplan stipulates that, "The capability variables specify the physical capability of an actor to carry out given classes of actions in specified settings." Page 11 (emphasis mine).*

The succession of overtures and rebuffs given the League of Nations by the United States and Argentina during the course of the Chaco War indicates their use of the universal actor as a pawn in the bilateral diplomatic struggle. Throughout the military conflict the denial of League entry by Washington was based on its ideological position of opposing intervention on the part of European powers in the affairs of the hemisphere. And, the United States could concede such intervention by Geneva only through a realistic, though painful, recognition of both its own and Argentina's failure to settle the boundary dispute. On the other hand, the Argentine Republic was relatively unhindered by its traditional ideological position; for, even though that government had remained somewhat aloof from the international organization, it had long exercised leadership among those South American republics which looked to Europe for many of their material [20] and ideological values. It was therefore far less difficult for Argentina to press openly for League intervention in the Chaco conflict. After it became evident to the government at Buenos Aires, as well as to the League and to the United States, that ABCP efforts had been largely ineffectual, Argentina was able to champion League intervention with far more ease than was the United States. This cooperation with the universal actor during the latter stages of the war was "functional" in that it won for Argentina a prestigious reentry into the international organization, chairmanship of the Chaco Peace Conference at Buenos Aires for Saavedra Lamas, plus generally acknowledged reputation, shared to a limited extent with the League, for being the primary force in the settlement of the boundary war. One cannot but be reminded of the axiom given by Machiavelli: "Nothing makes a prince so much esteemed as great enterprises and setting a fine example." [21] However desperate her actions to forestall such an unprecedented entry, the United States was forced finally to accept League intervention and was able to glean relatively less prestige in spite of a reluctant and rather feeble avowal of the principles of the universal actor during the latter months of the conflict.[22]

> 7. "All non-bloc member national actors are to coordinate their national objectives with those of the universal actor and to subordinate the objectives of bloc actors to those of the universal actor."

Regardless of the presence of any objective interest in the Chaco dispute—such as the European trade in arms with the military belligerents—or the absence of such an interest, non-hemispheric nations throughout the dispute either tacitly or openly inferred that the League was the only body legally or morally qualified to deal with the military situation. In either case, European members of the Geneva organization were reinforced in this conviction by the fact that both Bolivia and Paraguay were League members and thus entitled to and bound by Geneva's jurisdiction.

[20] *Cole has observed this tendency of the ABCP nations in the realm of economic alignment. G. D. H. Cole,* Introduction to Economic History, 1750–1950 *(London, 1960), p. 90.*

[21] The Prince, *trans. W. K. Marriott, Chapter XXI, paragraph 1.*

[22] *The behavior of the Argentine Foreign Minister won him the Nobel Peace Prize in 1938, a graphic demonstration of the "functionality" of his actions within the rules of the loose bipolar model. The fact that Lamas accepted the award only on the condition that it be accounted an honor to the Argentine nation indicates the worthiness of a recent observation by A. F. K. Organski: "Most diplomatic protocol is based on the fiction that diplomats are nations . . . A diplomat is, in short, a symbol and must be treated as if he were what he represents."* World Politics *(New York, 1959), pp. 37–38.*

8. "Bloc actors are to attempt to extend the membership of their bloc but to tolerate the non-member position of a given national actor if non-tolerance would force that national actor to support the objectives of the rival bloc or to join the rival bloc."

While there appears to have been little effort on the part of either of the two diplomatic disputants to increase permanently the size of their blocs, Argentina made some attempts in this direction through implicit appeal to the hemisphere for strengthening her position vis-à-vis the United States. The ability of the United States to expand her influence as seen in the unanimous support of all non-ABCP Power hemispheric nations of the Non-Recognition Declaration of August 3, 1932, is a definite example of the applicability of the rule in a temporary increase in the size of the blocs. Likewise, the relative ease of Argentine cooperation with the League demonstrates this rule. It should be pointed out, however, that the ABCP bloc was not increased in size by this association with Geneva since the European organization entered not for the purpose of defeating the Washington-led neutrals, but for conciliation of the military conflict and only coincidentally the ABCP-Neutral prestige dispute. Likewise, the ability of both the United States and the Argentine Republic to mobilize their respective blocs for action specifically fitted to the Chaco situation shows applicability here.

9. "Non-bloc member national actors are to act to reduce danger of war between the bloc actors."

The rule is evidenced in the constant emphasis of the European powers on the necessity for the military belligerents to settle their conflict through the use of League machinery. Moreover, if the military question were formally submitted to the League and a successful settlement effected, the diplomatic conflict would lack the stage upon which it was being pursued. Specifically, if the ABCP and Pan American blocs relinquished all diplomatic responsibility for the dispute, the League of Nations would have eradicated the occasion for the prestige battle being waged between the United States and Argentina. Explicitly, therefore, League machinery seemed to be the logical and necessary organ for settling the military conflict and, implicitly, for terminating the diplomatic rivalry.

10. "Non-bloc members are to refuse to support the policies of one bloc against the other except in their capacity as a member of a universal actor."

This rule is closely aligned with number nine. The opinions of all interested non-bloc-member national actors were institutionalized in League machinery. These included some Latin American states which cooperated from time to time with the universal actor; for example, Guatemala's inclusion in the League Committee of Three to investigate the dispute. The League-sponsored embargo on arms was another example of non-bloc-member support, as were the concerted sanctions taken against Paraguay in 1935 under the provisions of the Covenant regarding disciplinary action against member states.

11. "Universal actors are to reduce the incompatability between the blocs."

The League of Nations sought entry into the boundary dispute to settle the conflict between Bolivia and Paraguay, to gain for itself a measure of prestige for making that novel move into the hemisphere, and, tacitly, to assuage the diplomatic conflict between the two opposing hemispheric blocs. Although relative emphasis must be placed upon the first two objectives, the settlement of the diplomatic conflict was both inherently assumed and logically included in the successful achievement of entry and conciliation.

12. "Universal actors are to mobilize non-bloc member national actors against cases of gross deviancy, for example, resort to force, by a bloc actor. This rule, unless counteracted by the other rules, would enable the universal actor to become the prototype of an international political system."

Without referring to the declining strength of the League of Nations during the 1930's, the possibility of Geneva's forming an international political system was remote. Unquestionably, the United States wielded the greater authority within the hemisphere, an area not heretofore included within the League's sphere of de facto jurisdiction. There are two cases of "gross deviancy" apparent in the behavior of the peacemakers during this period. The first was the conflict of jurisdiction between the United States and the Argentine Republic, defined as "deviant" behavior because it frustrated the primary role of the League in preventing or settling conflicts between member states.[23] Secondly, the flow of arms from one mediating nation (the United States) through the territory of the other hemispheric peacemaker (Argentina) was likewise dysfunctional because it too frustrated the League's responsibilities in the dispute. The marshalling of the forces of European and other nations against the arms traffic substantiates this rule for the diplomatic conflict. In spite of the relative weakness of the League, the importance of the contribution of Geneva to the final settlement of the dispute is seen in the acquiescence to the League embargo by the United States. While the United States' ban on arms sales to Bolivia and Paraguay did not immediately result, Washington did institute an embargo of its own, either as a result of the pressures of world public opinion emanating from Geneva or from the vagaries of foreign policy prevailing in Washington at that time. Whereas Washington followed the universal actor from a distance, the European nations whole-heartedly accepted the provisions of the embargo through League institutions. Argentina approved, although she refrained from instituting the ban on Paraguay ostensibly on the grounds of the internationalization of the Paraguay River based on the 1953 bilateral treaty between the two nations. In regard to the rule's application to the diplomatic rivalry between Argentina and the United States, the continuation of the competition between the two and what seemed to be the resulting prolongation of the Bolivian-Paraguayan hostilities would constitute such a "deviant" situation as to demand non-bloc-member mobilization through Geneva.

Stability [24] within the Kaplan model is attained when six conditions are met. Numbers one, four and six, the most applicable of these from the standpoint of the present study, are discussed in the following section.

First, some mechanism within the system must communicate to the various actors within the system the "oughtness" of the rules applying both to their re-

---

[23] Morton A. Kaplan, "*The International System as a Source of Dysfunctional Tension*," World Politics, VI (1954), 501.
[24] *Kaplan*, System and Process, pp. 6–8.

spective role functions within the system and to the general rules of that system. That is, the actors must internalize the rules applying to the other actors.[25]

The communication channels of the Pan American movement, represented in the United States Department of State and the various financial interests engaged in operations in the Latin American area, have traditionally transmitted the "ought-ness" of the rules put forth by the United States for the Latin American area. With the evolution of a loose bipolar situation and the threat of the universal actor, the same channels communicated the "oughtness" of continued United States leader-ship, the importance of the Monroe Doctrine as the basis for that attitude on the part of the Washington government, and the "insidious" nature of the European threat posed by the League and those Latin American nations which were aligned with it. Likewise, the United States was able to "internalize" those rules guiding its recip-rocal conduct—i.e., the "status quo" nature of Washington's policy vis-à-vis both Argentina and the League of Nations, and the "imperialist" strategy of Buenos Aires in opposition to the United States. Moreover, the historical ties of the Argentine Republic with Chile, Brazil, and Peru—not only in terms of their common distrust of the Northern "Colossus" but also in their economic and ideological preferences, communicated the "oughtness" of the South American counter-alliance.

> Fourth, either the blocs must remain within a similar capability range, or some other method of internal or external inhibition must act to prevent one bloc from taking advantage of its preponderant capabilities.[26]

Ideological restrictions within the Washington-led bloc have already been dis-cussed in an earlier section of this paper. Quite obviously the objective capabilities of the two leading bloc actors were vastly unequal. There had never been any indi-cation that Buenos Aires felt that it was capable of presenting a meaningful eco-nomic or military challenge to the United States.[27] During the era of the Good Neighbor Policy and the Montevideo Conference of 1933, however, there became evident a relative parity in subjective power between the two with their respective blocs. And, coincidentally, the then current ideological stance of the United States made conflict other than that for dominant moral influence impossible. The requi-site bipolar stability was attained during this period by the rise of Argentine prestige capabilities under the leadership of Carlos Saavedra Lamas. That the prestige po-tential of the two nations was equal or approaching equality was indicated by the unprecedented alarm generated in Washington with the recognition of Argentine capabilities.

> Sixth, the blocs must attempt to increase their capabilities. If either bloc is not able to defend itself, non-member actors and universal actors will prove ineffec-tive in this respect.[28]

[25] Kaplan, p. 39.
[26] Kaplan, p. 40.
[27] "When the coercive component of state capability diminishes in its effect to achieve state purposes . . . the relative role of non-coercive influence cannot help but increase in importance and scope." Lerche and Said, p. 231. It is interesting to note that the authors of the above statement feel that non-coercive (i.e., non-objective) elements in prestige rivalry result in "a self-defeating international enterprise [since] no rewards formulated in the classic framework of world politics can be derived from such a contest." P. 233.
[28] Kaplan, p. 40.

In spite of the approximately equal power of the opposing hemispheric blocs, Argentina used the League of Nations to tip the prestige scales in its favor. Still, League entry was only indirectly utilized for the purpose of terminating traditional United States hegemony. While it is obvious that Geneva hoped to set a precedent in entering the hemisphere and that the major obstacle to that purpose was the United States, the League's purpose throughout was settlement of the Chaco conflict. It must be assumed, however, that the League recognized that achievement of this primary goal would likewise effect a termination of the diplomatic warfare which thrived in the environment of the military conflict.

   Conclusion.   The foibles of the peacemakers vis-à-vis the military situation most probably prevented an efficient and rapid settlement of the Chaco conflict, for not until Bolivia and Paraguay were nationally exhausted was the war terminated. The League, as universal actor, could then provide the institutional setting within which Argentina, with the reluctant cooperation of the United States, could lead in the final settlement of the conflict and gain the lion's share of prestige at the Buenos Aires peace negotiations. In terms of a "realist" interpretation, it appears that the mixture of the two distinct types of international conflict was not conducive to settlement of either of them.

   In this case study, there appears to have been no direct correlation between objective—i.e., economic, military, and technological—power and the capability of Argentina and the United States to pursue, in parity, their struggle on the plane of prestige rivalry. While it is obvious that the United States had great military and economic power, aside from its diplomatic and moral influence in the hemisphere, and that Argentina was probably the major economic and military power on the South American continent, neither of the diplomatic protagonists could afford to utilize their respective objective capabilities. Such would have, in the case of both nations, irrevocably jeopardized their primary prestige goals. Further, such activity would have been useless in this, a conflict for hemispheric subjective ascendancy. Moreover, on several occasions the economic and military capabilities of the two nations actually provided deterrents to their primary objectives. With respect to the arms embargo, for example, Argentina's loss of face with the League through the publicity afforded her smuggling activities and secretive economic and military aid to Paraguay threatened Buenos Aires' goals. The government at Washington was likewise embarrassed by the actions of private firms in the United States and the tardy enactment of the Chaco arms embargo by the United States Congress in the face of mounting pressure from the League. Moral goals, realistically defined within the framework of the national interest and conspicuously devoid of traditionally assumed objective implications, appear to have been the primary bases for the diplomatic struggle between the blocs and each of the League of Nations.

   It appears that the jurisdictional conflict which characterized the Chaco conciliation efforts most probably contributed to the difficulties involved in obtaining a final settlement. Goals and purposes toward which conciliation of the Chaco belligerents was *only a means* seem to explain the successive diplomatic interventions of the Washington Commission of Neutrals, the ABCP Power bloc, and the League of Nations. Rivalry between Buenos Aires and Washington for the recognition which conciliation of the dispute would bring them, the complex motives of the universal actor, and the intransigence of Bolivian and Paraguayan military and governmental elites—all contributed to the ten-year diplomatic fiasco. In the final search for a realistic peace, altruistic declarations were discarded and the moral pretenses of the conciliators appreared somewhat tarnished.[29]

BIBLIOGRAPHY

ARON, RAYMOND. *Peace and War: A Theory of International Relations* (Garden City, 1966). The *magnum opus* of one of the ablest contemporary scholars in the field. The author approaches the subject from a number of perspectives before integrating these into a final impressive framework of analysis. An important book.

BLOOMFIELD, LINCOLN P. *Evolution or Revolution? The United Nations and the Problem of Peaceful Territorial Change* (Cambridge, 1957). An examination of the contribution of the United Nations to the resolution of a basic dilemma of the international system: the balancing of stability with peaceful progress toward territorial adjustment.

———. *The United Nations and United States Foreign Policy*, rev. ed. (Boston, 1967). A cool-headed appraisal of the political realities underlying the institutional facade of the United Nations and of the problems and potential these offer with respect to the implementation of United States foreign policy.

BRIERLY, J. L. *The Law of Nations*, 6th ed. (Oxford, 1963). Unquestionably the most useful introduction to the study of international law. Informal, concisely comprehensive, and gracefully written, it is an admirable work.

CARR, E. H. *The Twenty Years' Crisis, 1919–1939* (London, 1942). An early but still significant treatise on international relations, with important influence on subsequent writing, arguing essentially the realist case at a time when this was far from fashionable.

CLAUDE, INIS L., JR. *Power and International Relations* (New York, 1962). A lucid, carefully written, and well-argued analysis which sees the rational use of the balance of power (with the help of the United Nations) as the most promising approach to the management of conflict.

———. *Swords Into Plowshares*, 3rd ed. (New York, 1964). By all odds, the best general introduction to the subject of international organization, combining perceptive evaluation with stylish presentation.

COOK, THOMAS I. and MALCOLM MOOS. *Power Through Purpose: the Realism of Idealism as a Basis for Foreign Policy* (Baltimore, 1954). Argues that the United States can be most effective in foreign policy through clarifying and strengthening its own moral principles, with emphasis on the value of creative freedom.

COPLIN, WILLIAM D. *The Functions of International Law: an Introduction to the Role of International Law in the Contemporary World* (Chicago, 1966). An interesting effort to place international law within a theoretical framework deriving largely from recent developments in social science concepts, including game theory, political socialization, and political culture.

CRAIG, GORDON A. and FELIX GILBERT, eds. *The Diplomats, 1919–1939* (Princeton, 1953). A very useful collection of essays assessing the performance of a number

---

[29] *In spite of the historic importance of the application of Secretary Stimson's nonrecognition doctrine to the Chaco dispute in the Declaration of August 3, 1932, it is evident that by granting Paraguay her military conquests in the final boundary award, the principle was clearly flouted. Ann Van Wynen Thomas and A. J. Thomas, Jr.,* Non-Intervention: The Law and its Import for the Americas *(Dallas, 1957), p. 246.*

of prominent diplomats of the inter-war years during various critical phases of that period. Often absorbing and always enlightening.

DEUTSCH, KARL W. *Political Community at the International Level: Problems of Definition and Measurement* (Princeton, 1953). An examination of the critical prerequisites to political integration, with emphasis on communications and value systems. An influential work.

HAAS, ERNST B. *The Uniting of Europe* (Stanford, 1958). A scholarly analysis of the conditions and consequences of the establishment of the functional, "supranational" organizations of western Europe in the 1950's. The author is not entirely optimistic about the implications for the achievement of broader objectives.

HAYES, CARLTON J. H. *The Historical Evolution of Modern Nationalism* (New York, 1931). A pioneering but still rewarding examination of the process through which the cultural nationalism of the eighteenth century evolved into the dominant political force of our time.

HERZ, JOHN. *International Politics in the Nuclear Age* (New York, 1959). A consideration of the impact of nuclear weapons on traditional statecraft. The author suggests that major revisions are urgently required in the assumptions and premises of the past several centuries, and specifies those which he considers to be most urgently needed.

HINSLEY, F. H. *Power and the Pursuit of Peace: Theory and Practice in the History of Relations Between States* (Cambridge, 1963). An excellent account of the development over several centuries of the more significant and influential theories of international organization, complemented by a scholarly analysis of contemporary practice.

HOFFMAN, STANLEY, ed. *Contemporary Theory in International Relations* (Englewood Cliffs, 1960). An able and highly critical assessment of many of the recent theoretical approaches to the study of international relations (with representative passages from the works considered), supplemented by an argument for the merging of the empirical and normative positions.

——. *The State of War: Essays on the Theory and Practice of International Politics* (New York, 1965). A series of essays focusing on the implications of the competitive relationships among states which tend to dominate the functioning of the international system. Emphasis on the historical and philosophical approach.

KAHN, HERMAN. *On Thermonuclear War* (Princeton, 1960). The famous and influential (at one time, at least) argument for the "thinkability" of nuclear war and for the strategy that should consequently be developed by the United States.

KAPLAN, MORTON A. *System and Process in International Politics* (New York, 1957). An original and influential application of systems theory to international relations, involving a rigorous analysis of relationships among key variables, as well as a development of possible models of the international system, both historical and theoretical, deriving from different relationships.

——, and NICHOLAS DE B. KATZENBACH. *The Political Foundation of International Law* (New York, 1961). An informal analysis of the important relationship between political power and legal norms. Kaplan's well-known systems approach is utilized extensively, to good effect.

KELSEN, HANS. *The Law of the United Nations* (New York, 1950). An immensely erudite, if legalistic, critique of the United Nations Charter, often critical of what the author considers to have been unfortunate lapses in both substantive content and draftsmanship.

KISSINGER, HENRY. *The Necessity for Choice: Prospects of American Foreign Policy* (New York, 1961). A broad review of many of the problems of United States foreign policy in the 1960's, including deterrence, arms control, diplomatc bargaining, and the role of the new nations. Closely reasoned and insightful.

KNORR, KLAUS. *The War Potential of Nations* (Princeton, 1956). An able analysis of the significance of the economic factors for military capabilities in international politics.

KOHN, HANS. *The Idea of Nationalism* (New York, 1944). A study of the development of modern nationalism, especially of the prophets and movements which contributed to it. A very useful survey.

LAUTERPACHT, HERSCH. *The Function of Law in the International Community* (Oxford, 1933). A very important essay examining many of the major problems, issues, and potentialities, by one of the foremost scholars in the field of the modern period.

LISKA, GEORGE. *International Equilibrium: A Theoretical Essay on the Politics and Organization of Security* (Cambridge, 1957). An argument for the central importance of equilibrium as an objective of state policy. Provocative but not wholly persuasive.

MACKINDER, SIR HALFORD J. *Democratic Ideals and Reality* (New York, 1942). The famous argument, originally addressed to the victors of World War I, stressing the significance of geography for international relations, and underlining especially the strategic importance of the "Heartland" of the Eurasian land-mass.

MACRIDIS, ROY, ed. *Foreign Policy in World Politics*, 3rd ed. (Englewood Cliffs, 1967). A valuable collection of studies of the foreign policy decision-making processes, and also of the related substantive foreign policies, of a number of the major powers. Excellent coverage of an important area.

MORGENTHAU, HANS J. *In Defense of the National Interest* (New York, 1951). A somewhat controversial work which argues for the reality and primacy of the national interest (the author is concerned primarily with the United States) based on geography, history, and relationships to other states, which should provide a guide to foreign policy.

———. *Politics Among Nations*, 4th ed. (New York, 1967). Probably the most famous and influential international relations text of the modern (post-World War II) period. One of the first attempts to develop a theory of international politics, in this case emphasizing the role of power and arguing for stress on "realism" rather than on legal or moral aspects of policy.

NICOLSON, HAROLD G. *Diplomacy* (London, 1939). One of the wisest and most informed essays available on the general practice of diplomacy, by a long-time British professional.

OSGOOD, ROBERT E. *Limited War: The Challenge to American Strategy* (Chicago, 1957). An attempt to deal with a crucial problem of policy in a nuclear age: the application of power for moral ends under self-imposed conditions of restraint, for the achievement of goals less than total.

RIKER, WILLIAM H. *The Theory of Political Coalitions* (New Haven, 1962). An important application of game theory to the problem of forming political coalitions. Contains some specific and significant recommendations for United States policy.

ROSECRANCE, RICHARD. *Action and Reaction in World Politics: International Systems in Perspective* (Boston, 1963). An interesting analysis and comparison of the variations in the structure of the international political system over a period of several centuries.

ROSENAU, JAMES N., ed. *International Aspects of Civil Strife* (Princeton, 1964). A useful collection of essays dealing with an important problem, pointing up the changing relationship between civil war and the international political system resulting from ideological conflict, guerrilla warfare, subversion, etc.

——, ed. *International Politics and Foreign Policy: A Reader in Research and Theory* (New York, 1961). A useful collection of essays bearing on the functional relationships between the international and national political systems.

ROSENNE, SHABTAI. *The World Court: What It Is and How It Works* (New York, 1963). A very useful and comprehensive description of the origins, structure, and procedure of the International Court of Justice, together with summaries of many of the cases which have come before the Court.

SCHELLING, THOMAS. *The Strategy of Conflict* (Cambridge, 1960). A skillful application of bargaining theory to the complexities of international politics, especially in the area of military capabilities. An important work.

SINGER, J. DAVID. *Deterrence, Arms Control, and Disarmament: Toward a Synthesis on National Security Policy* (Columbus, 1962). A clearly written and cogently argued study of a highly complex subject. The author makes an eloquent plea for a progression from stabilization of military capabilities to ultimate mutual disarmament.

SNYDER, RICHARD C., H. W. BRUCK, and BURTON SAPIN. *Decision-Making as an Approach to the Study of International Politics* (Princeton, 1954). Detailed and rigorous analysis of the structure and process of foreign policy decision-making in relationship to environmental setting. An influential book.

SPROUT, HAROLD and MARGARET. *The Ecological Perspective in Human Affairs, with Special Reference to International Politics* (Princeton, 1965). An important essay dealing with the manner in which the motivations of human decision-makers in relation to their perceptions of environment condition the foreign policy of states, and with the effects on policy produced by the objective reality of the environment.

SPYKMAN, NICHOLAS. *America's Strategy in World Politics: The United States and the Balance of Power* (New York, 1942). An eloquent plea to the United States at the time of World War II to acknowledge the necessity for balance of power politics. Also an influential rebuttal to Mackinder's Heartland thesis, emphasizing the strategically decisive consequences of control of the coastal areas of Eurasia.

THOMPSON, KENNETH. *Political Realism and the Crises of World Politics* (Princeton, 1960). Traces the sources of political realism, as the author defines the concept (in comparison with legalism and moralism, which he tends to deprecate), and then applies the doctrine to the problems of United States foreign policy. In the Niebuhr-Morgenthau tradition.

DE VISSCHER, CHARLES. *Theory and Reality in Public International Law* (Princeton, 1957). Regarded by some as something of a modern classic, this wise and perceptive study contains some penetrating and broadly philosophic commentary on the place of law in the international system.

WALTERS, F. P. *A History of the League of Nations* (New York, 1952). A thoroughly detailed and scholarly review of the record of the League, comprehensive and very well done. The standard general work.

WOLFERS, ARNOLD. *Discord and Collaboration: Essays on International Politics* (Baltimore, 1962). An important collection of essays on some salient issues of international relations by one of the best-known scholars in the field. Both philosophic and analytical, the writing does much to stimulate reflection on the subject.

WRIGHT, QUINCY. *A Study of War*, 2nd ed. (Chicago, 1965). An encyclopedic examination of the institution of war, its causes, its functions, and its relationship to various civilizations and cultures. An impressive work.

——. *The Study of International Relations* (New York, 1955). An important attempt to integrate the field of international relations, indicating the significant contributions of and inter-relationships among the academic disciplines concerned, and suggesting a method for the organization of relevant data within a comprehensive field matrix.

YALEM, RONALD. *Regionalism and World Order* (Washington, D. C., 1965). A comprehensive assessment of the significance of regionalism. The conclusion is that the possibilities for a reconciliation of regionalism and universalism in a time of conflict are limited.

INDEX

Note: The bold-face numbers indicate a definition. Most of the definitions are those set off in bold-face type within the text, but some will be found in the discussion in the text

A

academic freedom, 211, 247–248, 251–252

activists, 58, 333–336, 347, 364

administration, *see* public administration

administrative behavior, 419, 421, 427, 439–447, 496, 498; communication, 443; Hawthorne studies, 439; individual's relation to organization, 419, 440–442; and interest groups, 114; motivation, 441–442; role of informal groups, 441; *see also* bureaucracy, leadership, public administration

administrative history, *see* public administration

administrative law, *see* public administration

aesthetics, 73; role in science, 21, 22

aggregate data, *see* data

alienation, **56,** 67, 313, 320

allocation of values, authoritative, 10–13, 495, 501, 531

Almond, Gabriel, 107–108, 333, 345, 366, 492, 500, 502–504, 507–508, 511

American Association of University Professors (AAUP), 211

American Political Science Association (APSA), 4, 166, 203, 210–212, 228, 252–253, 301, 357, 385; *American Political Science Review,* 210; committees, 211, 253; Committee on Professional Standards and Responsibilities, 211; constitution of, 212; functions, 210–211; meetings, 210; membership, 203; studies by, 211

American political thought, *see* political theory

amicus curiae brief, 373, **467**

analogies, use in theory, 72–73

anonymity, *see* survey research

anthropology, 7, 15–16, 45, 87–88, 180–181, 242, 257, 326, 492, 526, 553

approaches to political science, 35–48, 205–206, 454–456; anthropological, 87–88; behavioral, 35, 43–47, 229, 383, 418, 439; categorizations of, 35; comparative, 42, 205, 486–499, 501–502; conflict between behavioral and traditional, 47, 229–242, 251, 322–323, 476; discipline-based, 35, 87; empirical, 35–38, 206, 300; geographical, 88–89; group theory, 113–116, 363–374, 509–510; historical, 35, 39, 41, 205, 384; ideological, 40; institutional, 40–43, 230, 383, 418, 490, 503; legal, 35, 41, 215, 553; macro v. micro, 63, 109, 494; normative, 35–38, 41, 279, 300, 303–304, 487; philosophical, 38–40, 203–205, 230, 277–304, 326, 397; psychological, 87, 89–90, 205, 312–313; relations between, 229–242; relative use in subfields, 47–48; relative emphases, 46–48; scientific, 35; sociological, 95–97, 309; structural, 40, 418; structural-functional, 95, 98–99, 350, 500, 502–504, 507, 517–518; traditional, 35, 418; *see also* behavioral approach

Aquinas, St. Thomas, 280, 288

Aristotle, 27, 41–42, 203, 213, 279, 284–290, 301; causation in, 285

Arrow's Paradox, 136

associations, *see* groups

Articles of Confederation (U.S.), 457